* BACHELOR BESS

THE AMERICAN LAND

AND LIFE SERIES

Edited by Wayne Franklin

BACHELOR BESS ✳ *The Homesteading Letters of*

Elizabeth Corey, 1909–1919 ✳ *Edited by Philip L. Gerber*

Foreword by Paul Corey ✳ *Afterword by Wayne Franklin*

University of Iowa Press ✳ *Iowa City*

University of Iowa Press, Iowa City 52242
Printed in the United States of America
First edition, 1990

Design by Richard Hendel

Printed on acid-free paper

Library of Congress Cataloging-in-Publication Data
Corey, Elizabeth.
  Bachelor Bess: the homesteading letters of Elizabeth Corey, 1909–
1919/edited by Philip L. Gerber; foreword by Paul Corey; afterword by
Wayne Franklin.—1st ed.
    p.   cm.—(The American land and life series)
  Includes index.
  ISBN 0-87745-302-0 (cloth), ISBN 0-87745-303-9 (paper)
    1. Corey, Elizabeth—Correspondence. 2. Pioneers—South Dakota—
Correspondence. 3. Women pioneers—South Dakota—
Correspondence. 4. Farm life—South Dakota—History—20th
century. 5. South Dakota—Social life and customs. 6. Frontier and
pioneer life—South Dakota. I. Gerber, Philip L. II. Title. III. Series.
F656.c67   1990   90-36047
978.3'031'092—dc20   CIP
[B]

To Bess, who wrote these letters,

To Paul, who saved them,

and

To Gene, who found them.

At last [my brother Fuller] told someone

that he thought it a wonder that I,

a girl alone among strangers, had done

so well—better than most of the men

had done.

—Elizabeth Corey, 1911

✳ CONTENTS

Seeing this collection of my sister Bess's letters after so many years, the first image that fills my mind is that of a discarded wagon wheel. I can see it clearly through the mists of eighty years. Its axle is buried in the ground, allowing the wheel to revolve on the horizontal plane. Boxes are attached at regular intervals, and our rural mail carrier has only to give the wheel a spin as he slips mail into separate boxes for the farms in the area.

On this mail-wheel Bess's many letters, each in its turn, rested in the box marked *E. O. Corey* while it waited to be picked up by a family member, usually myself.

This wheel stood at the northeast corner of an intersection of north-south and east-west roads near Marne, Iowa. Into the southwest corner of that intersection fitted the one-room school I attended. At the southeast corner, behind a windbreak of trees, were the farm buildings of our nearest neighbor. And at the northwest corner stood the buildings of our family farm.

How my family managed to squeeze into the four-room house my father had built on our Iowa farm has always baffled me. I never knew when that house was completed and moved into. Sometime in the 1890s I would guess.

A great day for my mother, apparently. The original house on the land had been infested with bedbugs, a condition common to frontier homes. Sometime later I learned about the extreme care taken that no bugs be carried into the new home.

When I was born in 1903, my father, Edwin O. Corey, was forty-seven. My mother, Margaret Morgan Brown Corey, was forty. My oldest brother, J. Olney, was seventeen; my oldest sister, Elizabeth F.

Elizabeth F. Corey, ca. 1927. Photo courtesy Marie Harmon.

The Corey farm near Marne, Iowa, as it appeared during Elizabeth Corey's girlhood. Photo courtesy Margaret Nelson.

("Bess"), was then sixteen. My brother H. Fuller came next at fourteen, followed by Robert L. ("Rob"), nine. My second sister, Ethel G., was seven, and finally came Challenge R. ("Chall"), five. Then around eight o'clock on the evening of July 8, 1903, almost five and a half years and several miscarriages later, I joined the family.

Many years after, in a moment of self-revelation, my mother told me that I had been a "promise." She didn't elaborate. My own conclusion was that the promise came from my father and meant no more sex between them.

Bess told me of my birth-evening. As she remembered it, "We had to wait supper on you."

Psychologists say that two things frighten babies: loud noises and a sensation of falling. No one ever said whether there was a thunderstorm that evening in 1903 or any time shortly thereafter. A middlewestern thunderstorm can produce some very loud noises. And up to the age of fourteen I was hysterically fearful of thunder.

That hot July night I became the ninth person to live in the 840 square feet (or approximately that) making up that four-room house. I am not positive of that square footage. But if I have erred, it has been on the liberal side.

I was probably born in the "big" bedroom, which was half of a square that measured twenty-four by twenty feet, or twelve by twenty feet. It was large enough to accommodate two double beds. I don't remember any closet, but there may have been a curtained-off area which hid clothing. Those double beds would take care of four adults. A cradle set between them would take care of me.

A door from this room opened into a sitting room—not a parlor or a living room, but a sitting room—which was approximately the same size as the bedroom. A wood- or coal-burning stove stood against the partition wall. On the east wall the front door opened onto a porch. Next came a window. Beneath it stood a lounge, a homemade bunk with board slats supporting a four-inch pad. I remember the pad as brown, but I haven't the faintest idea what the composition of the padding was. Someone could and did sleep on it when circumstances required. Above it and on either side of the window hung enlarged photographic portraits of my father's parents, Grandfather and Grandmother Corey.

On the opposite side of this room stood a floor-to-ceiling walnut bookcase and desk. Glass doors closed over the family's best books: a set of *Chamber's Encyclopaedia*, the five volumes of Gibbon's *The Decline and Fall of the Roman Empire*, *Napoleon and His Marshalls*, *Washington and His Generals*, Mark Twain's *Roughing It*, Charles Kingsley's *Westward Ho*, and a large paperback edition of Cooper's *Leatherstocking Tales*.

A drop-leaf desk across the center of this piece of furniture hid pigeonholes for business papers and shelves for stationery. The desk leaf was supported by wooden rods that could be pulled out beneath each end. Below the desk was a wide drawer, and the bottom section had two hinged doors which shut away more storage. At night the room was lighted by a hanging kerosene lamp that could be pulled down or run up to the ceiling out of the way.

From the desk end of the sitting room a door led into the long, narrow, twelve-by-twenty-foot dining room and kitchen. Directly across from the door stood the huge black kitchen range, fueled by wood or coal. On the wall beside that door was a shelf on which rested the clock my parents got as a wedding present January 1, 1885.

I grew up learning to count the strokes of that clock as it struck the hour and half hour when I lay awake at night. I still have it today. When I'm awake at night I still count the strokes to know the time.

Our dining table stood beneath this clock. It was a walnut extension table, and when we weren't eating it was pushed back against three chairs along the wall. A window at the south end of the room looked down the path to the barns and other farm buildings. Beside it on the left stood another floor-to-ceiling desk made of some soft wood and painted. The upper bookshelves were glassed in. The shelf of the drop-leaf desk was held by folding metal supports. This desk had knee-hole space beneath the drop leaf, and on each side were drawers. As I remember, each of us boys had a drawer to keep our personal items. Mine was the lowest on the right side.

From the desk across that end of the room, a large chest covered the space to the corner. Outdoor clothes such as coats, jackets, and caps were hung in that corner. Between the garments and the window hung our party-line telephone. An outside door swung back from the west wall and, when open, it hid most of the hanging coats. The door opened into a summer kitchen. Most farmhouses in Iowa had such a summer kitchen where the cooking was done in hot weather.

At the other end of this long kitchen–dining room was a floor-to-ceiling cupboard made of wainscoting. Beside it was a door into the "little" bedroom with its double bed and single bed. In 1903 our house had beds for seven and a cradle for me, but there were nine in the family. Someone had to sleep on the homemade padded couch in the sitting room. I don't know who that was.

However, in the summer my brothers and perhaps even my father slept out in the barn. That wouldn't have been too bad after a crop of soft, aromatic new hay had been brought in. When September 1904 came along, Olney and Bess were in school in Walnut, eight miles away. Except on weekends, they boarded with a town family, which took some pressure off our home.

Then, in February 1905, unexpectedly, my father died of pneumonia.

That must have been a traumatic time for my mother. She was left with seven children and a 160-acre farm, unpaid for. Counting the cradle for me, there were then beds for the entire family.

As I pieced things together, slowly, over the rest of my life, my father's death had been the culmination of a series of devastating blows to the family which began in the late 1890s or the early part of the twentieth century.

I didn't know until many years later that my father had been a promising young politician. He had been a supervisor in Shelby County and also acted as the county treasurer. In 1935, while I visited Bess in South Dakota, she showed me a very much worn newspaper clipping. It concerned the accountant who checked the books of the ninety-nine county treasurers in Iowa. He reported that my father's books were the only ones that balanced. Bess showed me that clipping proudly.

But then my father's younger brother had been caught forging some checks. That ended my father's political career and involved the entire family in raising money to keep the brother out of jail.

About that time, our oldest brother, Olney, developed epilepsy. The Victorian explanation of the cause for that malady was a stigma upon the family, especially when the ignorance of the medical profession of the time went along with the myth.

A reader of Bess's characteristically outspoken letters will also notice the many linguistic evasions. In using them she was in tune with her time, for those were the days of euphemisms. Of course the new house my father had built was equipped with no indoor plumbing. There was an outhouse, a privy, but it was never so called. A board walk led to it north of the house by the orchard fence. To use it, we always went "out north." Indoors, chamberpots rested beneath the beds. Generally in our house they were called vessels, but specifically they were referred to as the little owl or the yellow owl and the white owl. It was a long time before I discovered the figure of an owl printed beneath the handles.

Our house was small, even if new and substantial. It was surrounded on the north by an acre of apple orchard in full production. A lawn which stretched from the front door to the north-south road was filled with a variety of large trees: maples, elms, catalpas, a linden, a cedar, and a pine. From the south side to a white picket fence lay the vegetable garden. Directly up a bank to the west our small fruit garden contained every good thing that would grow in western Iowa: blackberries, raspberries both red and black, currants red and black, strawberries, grapes, and special trees such as pear, peach, and cherry. Everything was protected by a dense windbreak of maples, willows, and boxelder. All this must have been a proud dream to my father and to the rest of the family.

It is hard for me to imagine the emotional pressures my father and the whole Corey family had been enduring. For some reason, father was considering moving the family to Arkansas and had made a trip down there accompanied by my mother and me, not yet two years old. That must have been an act of desperation.

Sometime while I was growing up, I learned that my mother and father had considered separation. Apparently, a split of allegiance shook the family. I believe that Olney and my younger siblings sided with my mother, but Bess and Fuller took my father's side. As I grew up I remembered a miniature yacht that my father had carved for Fuller. It was very elaborate, with tiny pulleys and fittings. It fascinated me where it stood on a workshop shelf.

And there was the newspaper clipping that Bess had treasured all those years. Once she told me an anecdote about my father. She had been baking cookies. He came into the kitchen and asked if he might taste one. She offered him his choice of the cooling cookies. He took one, hesitated, then took a second. With a grin, he took a third and put it between the other two, saying, "Guess I'll make a sandwich." It was obvious that this memory was a very happy one to Bess. But it left a guilty feeling that shows in her letters.

My father's sudden death ended any family dissension but confronted one and all with a farm to run. I believe that Olney may already have quit high school, gone to normal school, and taken a teaching job, but he had to give that up because of his health. Most of the heavy farm work settled on Fuller and Rob. Neighbors helped. I remember stories that even Bess wore a pair of her brother's overalls and helped with the haying.

Somehow the farm work got done, but my mother was too busy managing and doing to pay much attention to me, so I was turned over to my sisters. Later I was told that Bess used to put me to sleep by humming a Strauss tune and waltzing me around the kitchen–dining room in her arms.

The farmhouse was still crowded, so Bess quit high school, took a summer session at normal school, and began her career as a teacher. For several years she taught schools within a twenty-mile radius of the home place. That reduced some of the pressure in our tiny house.

But Iowa winters were tough, and in those days before antibiotics sickness was rife. I can remember Olney being very sick. He may have had pneumonia, which would have added to my mother's fears, pneumonia having taken her husband. My brother's bed had been set up in the sitting room and he had around-the-clock care. Neighbor women came in to help.

Clothing had to be washed. A hand-operated washing machine was pulled into the summer kitchen, and the wet laundry was hung out on a line next to the garden. In the freezing weather the clothes froze hard as boards.

I remember my mother bringing in an armload of frozen clothes.

It must have been a crisis day. Olney lay critically sick in the sitting room. My older brothers were out doing chores. I don't know what Ethel was doing. But my mother stood by the dining table with frozen garments hugged in her arms. Her scarf-bound face was white with frost, melting only a little. Then she began to cry. That was the first time I remember seeing her cry. Perhaps that's why it's still vivid in my memory.

But Olney recovered that time, and spring finally came. I was very sick myself with something or other the winter I was three. But I never remember Bess being sick with anything more than a cold. In those days of dirt roads and horse-and-buggy travel, it was difficult for her to get home over weekends. But from wherever she was teaching she wrote letters, and those letters became the high point of our midday meal.

As soon as I was old enough to walk out to the intersection of our roads, it was one of my daily chores, when school wasn't in session, to fetch our mail. From the road side of the wheel of boxes, I couldn't reach our own. But by climbing the bank on the opposite side and revolving the wheel, I could bring our box within my reach. And of course I could recognize Bess's handwriting on a letter.

When I was in school, Olney got the mail. Because of his seizures, he didn't do much farm work. The doctors had advised my mother to encourage him to take up some hobby. I can remember him undertaking taxidermy. He was given a corner in the workshop where he stuffed and mounted wild ducks. And after he tired of that he took up photography. His first camera was a large black box. I don't remember that the folding camera had come on the market yet. If it had, it was too new to have reached western Iowa.

But the arrival of one of Bess's letters became a high point in relieving the monotony of farm life. The envelope was always addressed to "Mrs. M. M. Corey." Mother never opened it immediately. It lay on the table where she sat at mealtime and was opened and read only after all the family was present and had finished eating the midday meal (dinner) or the evening meal (supper).

The seating arrangement around our long extension dining table varied only with the absence of a family member. Olney occupied the head of the table. That was where my father had sat when he was alive. The table was pulled out from the wall to give room for my other brothers to get into their chairs: Fuller first, then Rob, then Chall. On Olney's right, if Bess had been home, that would have been her place, then Ethel, then mother next to the breadboard and the loaf of home-made bread. And I was pushed up to the table in the family highchair wherever there was a spot it would fit.

All of my siblings had used that highchair. Unlike later chairs with a table that swung up and over the youngster's head, or a table that slid into grooves or clipped onto the arms, the table of this one was hinged to the arm on the left side and swung across the front and latched onto the right arm. The finish was yellowish, scratched and dented by the spoons of six previous exuberant or irritated youngsters.

But long after I had outgrown that chair, I used it. First, its swinging table ceased to function properly and was removed. Then the right arm broke off. Finally the left arm went, so that the chair resembled a modern barstool with a back. And when it was not in use at the table it sat against the wall to the sitting room between the hinged side of the door and a piece of dining-room furniture we called a safe. This was a homemade cupboard with four shelves, doors covering the front, and screen-covered openings at each end. It was probably as cool a place as any in the room in those days before refrigeration. Food from butter to cake was stored here between meals. And while my highchair stood in its corner by the safe, it was a favorite place for me to retire to if I had been scolded or was irked by something. And there I cringed during booming, lightning-filled Iowa thunderstorms, while none of the others in the family seemed to notice.

As long as I lived on the farm, that was my chair. All the others in the family had fixed places at the table, but that highchair and I were always pushed up wherever we would fit.

Whenever a letter from Bess came in the mail, it lay on the usual red-or blue-checked tablecloth a little to the left of my mother's place until the meal was finished. Then, very deliberately, she opened it and began to read: "Dear ma and all."

From wherever she was teaching, Bess wrote long, chatty, gossipy, informative, and always amusing reports of her experiences. She usually boarded with a farm family a half mile or closer to the school she taught. She described the kids she taught and the family where she stayed. Because of the road and traveling conditions, she seldom got home except for holidays even when her school was within twenty miles of home.

Perhaps a most vivid early set of letters came while Bess was teaching in a Danish community to the northeast of our farm. That year we learned a lot of Danish words and phrases: *Dansker*, Dane (my spelling is phonetic, the way the words sounded to me); and *fumf* of *Yuni*, the Danish Independence Day, Fifth of June; and *Gott ein Hemmel*, a phrase which scandalized my mother and I was never allowed to use.

Then, in June 1909, just before my sixth birthday, Bess set out for South Dakota.

Her intention was to stake out a claim, homestead the land, and teach school. She was twenty-one and on her own. Beginning with the train trip to Dakota, her letters started coming with full details.

Our family entertainment in the evenings had always been reading aloud from books available at the school library. I lived from day to day for the coming events in *Tom Sawyer, Ivanhoe*, and *Twenty Thousand Leagues under the Sea*. But that summer of 1909 began our own family serial. The motion picture industry had hardly started. Radio was never even dreamed of in farm-state Iowa. And no one would have entertained the remotest belief in the possibility of TV "soaps." But on the Corey farm we had our own continuing adventure story. And when my mother began to read one of Bess's letters she got complete and rapt attention from around our long dining table.

From time to time, Mother would start reading a sentence, hesitate, stop, and then go on, obviously skipping a passage. No one in the family ever dared ask what had been left out. It wasn't until many years later, when I read those letters myself and came upon parts I knew had been omitted in the family reading, that I realized the reason. Those passages concerned things that Victorian custom said only women should hear about.

When Bess's Dakota letters first started coming home to Marne she signed them "Lovingly, Bess." But after one detailed account of a flirtation, she signed her letter "Lovingly, Bachelor Bess." All of us around the table laughed over that. But I'm not sure that it didn't shock my mother a little. Later Bess shortened the signing to just "B. B."

Sonoma, California
May 1988

✳ ACKNOWLEDGMENTS

Ever since that blistering August day in Pierre when the letters of Elizabeth Corey were first brought to my attention, the list of those who have been generous in helping to get them into print has been swelling. It was John Borst, curator of manuscripts, who first set down in front of me and my wife a pair of gray museum-board boxes with a laconic, "You may find these interesting."

The boxes were innocent enough in appearance. We had been busy for two days already, rummaging through old clipping files and dusty directories and yellowing manuscript memoirs, knowing only that, presuming it existed, we were interested in "something special, something unique" concerning the homesteading days in South Dakota. I had been born and bred there but, of course, like so many native sons I had defected decades ago. Now I seemed to have engaged myself in a somewhat unfocused search for roots.

I paid those glossy gray boxes scant attention, being rather dutifully engrossed in the not overly exciting account of yesteryears composed by a settler none too strong in the memory department. The mercury in local thermometers was pushing well above 100 degrees and I was really not in the mood for beginning something new just now. I gestured to Gene; she was welcome to start on those formidable boxes if she wished. Five minutes—or ten—later, her eye caught mine. "I think this is IT," she whispered. "Is what?" "Is that Special Something you've been hoping for."

Those boxes, of course, contained the letters of Elizabeth Corey, ten years' worth of them, complete with their original envelopes. I skimmed the letter my wife handed to me. Then another. By the time I had tasted a third, selected somewhat at random, I was hooked. This was a *writer*, no question about it. On her pages events of 1909 and 1910 suddenly took on life, drew one in. This was a writer! I spoke the word. Gene nodded her agreement. Since that time, Gene's role has bordered closely on collaboration, and she prepared the drawings for this volume, based on Bess's sketches.

That autumn I was on exchange at the University of Delaware, but while in Newark I attempted to reach—if he lived—the man who had deposited his sister's correspondence in the archives at Pierre. I found him at last: a continent away, on a hilltop in Sonoma County, California. Even though he had already turned eighty-three, Paul Corey proved to be an indefatigable gentleman, loaded with enthusiasm for my notion of editing the letters of this unusual woman, his sister, who liked to dub herself "Bachelor Bess."

More important than mere approbation, as I found during the next April while visiting with him on his oak-wooded tract, wherever it concerned Bess and the family they had belonged to, Paul was a treasure house of information—as by rights he should be, having himself employed his family and their Iowa-farm background for the notable trilogy *Three Miles Square* (1939), *The Road Returns* (1940), and *County Seat* (1941) which established his reputation as a novelist.

It is Paul who has performed the third miracle connected with Elizabeth's letters (the first being that they were written at all, the second being their preservation). As his sister's only remaining sibling, Paul is the last to possess firsthand memory of life at Corey farm, and that memory is clear. His illuminating, precise replies to dozens upon dozens of queries concerning arcane (to me) references in Bess's letters have been invaluable.

Paul also led me to Margaret Erickson Nelson, his and Bess's niece, daughter of their sister, Ethel. And to Margaret I owe a debt nearly as great but different in kind, for it was she who located further letters both from and concerning "Aunt Bess" as well as memorabilia and family photographs, which lent a sharp physicality to many who until then (even though they may have played continuing roles in the letters) had been dim and shadowy—mere names. In these regards Margaret's sister, Marie Harmon, has helped as well. Margaret was instrumental in establishing contact with Lilah Morris, widow of Rob Corey, who was with Bess in her last hours. Lilah provided an eyewitness account of those final days in Pierre and of Bess's funeral.

To my own sister, Pauline G. Davies, I am grateful for constant support and encouragement. Something of a genealogist and local historian in her own right, Pauline has been unstinting in locating books that explore early times in Stanley County and in forwarding clippings of all sorts gleaned from her research into early newspapers, including the accounts of the Johanna Gadski concert which so impressed Elizabeth Corey in Aberdeen during the SDEA teachers convention of 1915. Further, Pauline has upon occasion taken the initiative in exploring potential contacts with persons who knew Elizabeth Corey, and the ultimate results of those explorations have enriched this volume.

Besides John Borst, several at the South Dakota Historical Society in Pierre have been of help. Dayton Canaday, now retired, has been succeeded as state historian by Ann B. Jenks, and she has proven to be equally cordial and just as helpful in placing resources at our disposal. Bonnie Gardner gave us the unimaginable privilege of rummaging somewhat at will through her extensive files of vintage photographs, professional and amateur, with their fascinating visual account of early times. Ila Wiedemeyer located essential volumes of South Dakota lore, besides leading us toward former pupils of Elizabeth Corey. Laura Glum was helpful as well. Harold Schuler, busily researching his new volume on Fort Pierre and the fur trade, took time out to answer questions and to help us locate valuable early records concerning old-time rural schools and teachers. Schuler's history of Pierre and Fort Pierre, *A Bridge Apart*, saved us many hours of laborious digging.

In Fort Pierre we were invited to the home of Flora Huston Zieman, who spoke with us about old times and Elizabeth Corey. Daughter of the George Hustons who ran the Huston House hotel, Flora was a mere infant when Elizabeth sought employment there during the summer of 1909. Of greater importance (until she withdrew from school to marry a rancher out Hayes way), Flora had been a member of Elizabeth's senior class in the local high school. Most of the surviving members of that small class of '27 are scattered over the nation now, but several have done their utmost to delve sixty years into the past and come up with their impressions of this woman (to a teenager she must have appeared to be so *very* much older) who came out of the Bad River wilds to occupy a desk in classrooms with them and thereby earn the high school diploma that would allow her to continue teaching. Among these are Edna Farrell Brzica, Cecilia Callahan Ellis, and Vera Callahan Ritzo. I think here especially of William P. Hart, who generously supplied the photograph of the Fort Pierre High

School class of '27, and Clara Leap Graham, who at her home poised high above Santa Cruz, California, required no more than a glance at Bess's graduation photo to exclaim: "That's our girl! And her graduation dress—it was lavender purple."

Clarence Berdewald of the Verendrye Museum of Fort Pierre has been generous in allowing use of photographs from its unique collection. In Fort Pierre also we were aided by Kathy Klemann (married to a descendant of Oscar Klemann) at the Stanley County Register of Deeds office. And Marie Carlisle assisted with materials concerning her brother-in-law, Bess's friend Flagg Carlisle; she was joined in this effort by Flagg's daughter-in-law, Donna Carlisle of Rapid City. The Hall of Fame supplied further Carlisle material.

A highlight of our Fort Pierre experience was our conversation with Bud Gould and Louis Bruce at the latter's home along Bad River. As children both had known "Miss Corey." They took us by car into the lands where their families and Bess had homesteaded, a drive which at times involved riding through bare fields and over hogbacks, there being (if possible!) even fewer roads through that territory in 1988 than when Bess staked her claim in 1909. Both these gentlemen have offered rare family photographs for use in this volume.

In Pierre itself we were assisted at the headquarters of the South Dakota Educational Association (in which Bess Corey was a faithful member); at the office of the state superintendent of public instruction, where some of the scarce records concerning early teaching careers are preserved; and at the Hughes County Register of Deeds office.

In Midland we are grateful to the Midland Pioneer Museum and to Ervin Sheeley, who unlocked the museum for us on a closed day. Our discovery that Ann Ahboltin Sheeley had gone to school to Elizabeth Corey at Lance Creek in the 1920s was a bonus we had not anticipated.

In Sioux Falls, Robert Kolbe was generous in allowing examination and use of his comprehensive collection of postcard photographs from the era of homesteading. At the University of Iowa, Robert McCown, curator of Special Collections, generously helped me to search the Paul Corey Papers for references to Bess. Also in Iowa City, the collections of the Iowa State Historical Society were put at my disposal, the same at the society's headquarters in Des Moines. And in Harlan, where Bess Corey began her Dakota adventure, Lorna Tinsley of the Shelby County Historical Society provided a tour of the local museum.

In Dayton, Ohio, Mildred Adcock has been helpful with information concerning her father, Fuller Corey, who homesteaded on land adjoining Bess's in 1910; she supplied the photograph of Fuller and his bride, Teresa, that appears in this volume.

On my local campus of the State University of New York, Jim Dusen has made his photographic services available; and in the Document Preparation Center, where Vicky Willis has cooperated wholeheartedly with this project, Terry Collins has been tireless and uncomplaining during the extended period while Bess Corey's letters and the rest of the manuscript have been compiled, corrected, and placed on computer; her work has been ably continued and brought to a conclusion by Lauren Nicholson. In a moment of need, Barbara Guhde was generous with her assistance.

Finally, from the first moment I proposed this volume of letters to the University of Iowa Press, my editor, Holly Carver, has been enthusiastically supportive in ways that have eased my long task considerably. More recently, copy editor Mary Hill has worked valiantly to save me from myself, succeeding more often than not; whatever blunders remain are mine alone.

✳ INTRODUCTION

The Dakota land boom which brought Bess Corey west of the Missouri to Stanley County was part of a larger effort aimed at finally closing the frontier by populating those mid-continent lands which had been bypassed in the general westward movement of population. Homesteaders traveled to these new territories, not in covered wagons or by mule train, but by railroad, and once having arrived at their destinations they were likely as not to find that the automobile had preceded them, never mind the near absence of roads. Living conditions on the barren plains were primitive at best, but many of these latter-day pioneers saw their experience as being temporary. They came with the expectation of remaining only long enough to "prove up" on a homestead; the idea was to gain title, sell out at a profit, and return home with the booty.

The land boom was promoted heavily by ever-expanding railroad systems which had passenger tickets and acreages to peddle and which anticipated future profits to be made in hauling farm produce from the Dakotas to the world. So motivated, they promoted the new territories with a hype that would put a contemporary huckster to shame. In 1893, for instance, the Chicago, Milwaukee & St. Paul invited easterners to settle in South Dakota's "Next big City, Sisseton," the "Gateway to a Rich Agricultural County." The prospects of mineral-rich medicinal springs and "Artesian Water at 500 Feet" were but tempting portions of the great opportunity which included assurance that a lot purchased for $50.00 would "TREBLE and even QUADRUPLE within one to three years."[1]

Nearer to Stanley County lay the Rosebud Indian Reservation, and when it was opened to settlement soon after the turn of the century, its lands—among the most arid in the state—were described by promoters as "good average farming country" having the same potential as other farm lands along a line drawn straight east to Chicago and possessing a "water supply as good as any country on earth. . . . sufficient to insure abundant harvests."[2] By 1902 railroads were busily penetrating that region. An early settler in Lyman County, Myrtle Yeoman Holm, writing in 1905, speaks of the rapid progress of the tracks "coming through this country from Chamberlain to the Black Hills." Holm, who apparently was widowed, was typical of one kind of settler, family members who traveled together and settled close to one another but alone on individual homesteads. Employing her father's homestead as a central point of reference, Holm locates her grandmother on a claim two miles north, her aunt two miles east, and her own land one mile south. Her experience underscores one of the unique qualities of the land boom: the relatively sizable number of single women who participated, so many, writes Holm, that one "must wonder where they all come from." While reiterating the general news that "land here is on the boom," she nevertheless sounds an ominous note with the news that her friend John Smith has given up his claim: "He said this country was too dry for him."[3]

When Stanley County itself was opened for settlement, the West Land Company of Pierre issued pamphlets touting the "Free Homesteads" of central South Dakota as constituting "ten thousand quarter sections [of] fine land" in a locality where a single dollar would go as far as five in the "older" states, an area blessed with "good water, fine climate, and sure success for the man of industry and frugal habits."[4] Such publicity could be highly persuasive. Surely it worked its magic upon Elizabeth Corey, who in 1905 at the age of seventeen had begun a career as a rural schoolteacher near her home in western Iowa. To qualify for the free-land bonanza offered by the U.S. government, however, one must have reached one's majority. Like many young women of her time and station, Bess Corey yearned for greater career options. For her, the social changes which legitimized a single woman's choice to "go west" lent that option an immense appeal. It was adventure. It might be profitable. And it promised to deliver her from a family situation which left much to be desired. While she bided her time, watching as other Iowans took advantage of the opportunity to claim land in South Dakota, Bess's own dream took shape. By 1909 she was twenty-one, the Dakota bubble had not yet burst, and she was determined to change her life.

Paul Corey has described the family that his sister Bess left behind when she decided to change her life, casting her lot with the homesteaders settling South Dakota in 1909.[5] Family and friends could not be transported any more than could her flourishing career as an Iowa schoolteacher. But the profession itself, being portable, came with her, furnishing a potential means of support while Bess located and "proved up" on a homestead. In fact, she traveled west quite relying upon her ability to get a teaching job which would bring in those dollars so essential for hiring the heavy work to be done in making her claim habitable: building a shack, breaking the sod, dredging a dam, fencing a garden.

That means of livelihood, besides her suitcase and a parasol, was all that Bess had with her when the Northwestern Railway deposited her on its brick depot platform at the edge of boomtown Midland during the wee hours of the morning of June 3, 1909. It would still be dark at that hour, and no transportation would run even the short distance into Midland until five in the morning. But in June the sun dawns early, and the breaking light would give Bess a chance to look around her at this strange new universe she had entered. South of the railroad tracks she might spy a scraggly line of willows and cottonwoods edging the bank of Bad River, the only trees of any consequence in the vicinity except for clumps of brush in the draws and breaks leading down to the water's edge. Beside her, before she moved indoors to occupy a pewlike bench away from the night chill, stood a new, red-painted frame depot, double-storied, tall, and angular. Its board sign announced MIDLAND. To the north lay the clustering frame buildings of Midland itself, a town created by and for the railroad. Between 1906 and 1909 this "jumping off place" for emigrants had grown from a bare spot on the valley floor to a town of nearly four hundred population.

Charged with excitement, surely, and perhaps experiencing a good deal of apprehension as well (had she, after all, done the prudent thing?), Bess Corey to pass the time struck up a conversation with the night agent at the depot. As coincidence would have it, he too, like her and so many others, had come west from Iowa; and from his lips she had her first direct account of the territory lying beyond Bad River and past Midland as far as the eye could reach: Old Stanley County. Like it or not, this was what she had come to and where she would spend the remainder of her days.

Old Stanley County (Bess soon enough would begin referring to

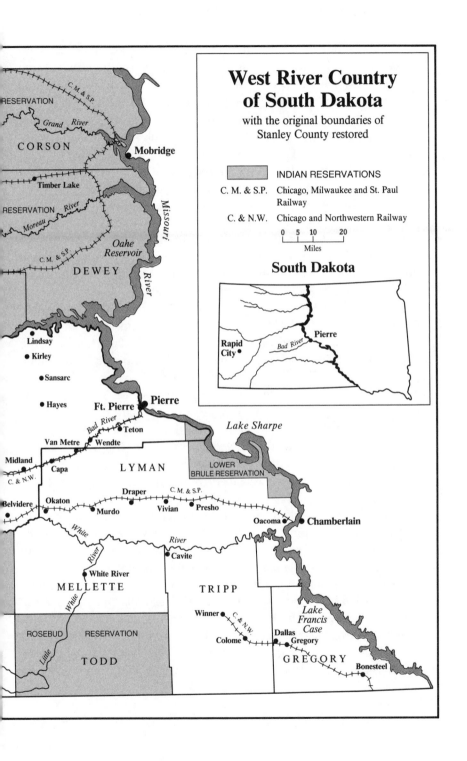

West River Country of South Dakota

with the original boundaries of Stanley County restored

INDIAN RESERVATIONS

C. M. & S.P.   Chicago, Milwaukee and St. Paul Railway

C. & N.W.   Chicago and Northwestern Railway

0   5   10   20
Miles

South Dakota

Rapid City

Pierre

Bad River

RESERVATION

C.M. & S.P.

Grand   River

CORSON

Mobridge

Timber Lake

RESERVATION   River

Moreau

C.M. & S.P.

DEWEY

Oahe Reservoir

Missouri River

Lindsay

Kirley

Sansarc

Hayes

Ft. Pierre   Pierre

Bad River

Teton

Lake Sharpe

Van Metre   Wendte

Midland

Capa

LYMAN

LOWER BRULE RESERVATION

C. & N.W.

Draper   C. M. & S.P.

Belvidere   Okaton

Murdo   Vivian   Presho

Oacoma   Chamberlain

White   River

River

Cavite

White River

MELLETTE

TRIPP

White

Winner   Lake Francis Case

ROSEBUD   RESERVATION

Dallas

Colome   Gregory

Little

TODD

GREGORY   Bonesteel

it as "this homely man's country") had a history both brand new and impressively old. The dominant feature of that entire high plains area was, as it always had been, the Missouri River. For untold millennia the river had meandered its wide and muddy track through Dakota Territory, swelling as the Cheyenne and Bad emptied into it, sometimes rolling along at a rate approaching ten miles an hour. Until some time after Lewis and Clark passed through and were greeted by Indians at the mouth of Bad River in 1804, little exploration had taken place. The Missouri valley was then the domain of the Arickaras, who cultivated the fertile bottomlands and lived peacefully in their willow-pole lodges over which earthen insulation was heaped for protection from the elements—until the more warlike Sioux drove them out. The Sioux lived more like nomads, camping in portable tepees and depending for food upon the immense herds of buffalo and other wild game then inhabiting the vast mid-continent grasslands.

Lucrative trading in furs, especially buffalo robes, led to the establishment of a stockaded trading post: Fort Tecumseh, built by the French Fur Company and located where the Teton (later known as the Bad) met the Missouri. Tens of thousands of buffalo pelts were floated downriver on shallow bull boats, until the flat-bottomed steamboat *Yellowstone* traveled successfully upstream from St. Louis in 1831, proving the river navigable in both directions. Aboard the *Yellowstone* was fur trader Pierre Choteau, Jr., who decreed a new trading post three miles north of the Teton. Named Fort Pierre Choteau, this outpost evolved into the settlement of Fort Pierre.[6] Much later, between 1909 and 1919, whenever Elizabeth Corey speaks of going to town, this is likely to be the town she is referring to.

Fort Pierre has had a long seesaw history of boom and bust. But by 1880 it was an important way station on the western trails. A year-round population of some three hundred souls might be expected to swell at any time with a secondary population of as many as five hundred transients: dock workers, freighters, bull whackers, and homesteaders. Gold had been discovered in the Black Hills and although the Hills were sacred to the Indians, nothing could keep the whites out. Soon the railroad laid track as far as Pierre, but there it stopped, halted in its swift advance by the river's breadth. Ferryboats hauled people, wagons, stock, and supplies across the Missouri, and from Fort Pierre the long, slow trains of heavy wagons pulled by oxen headed out for the west.

The town was a true storybook place, a wild West frontier settle-

South Dakota cowboys on the streets of Fort Pierre, ca. 1909. Photo
courtesy Verendrye Museum.

ment, in 1880 snidely ruled out of polite society by the territorial governor, who dubbed it the "delectable paradise of mule skinners and
bull whackers." The governor pointed out, lest he be misunderstood,
that he meant not the city of Pierre, quietly expanding on the eastern
bank of the Missouri, but that other "disreputable place now standing
on the western shore, without law and order."[7] Fort Pierre changed
much for the better as the years went on. In 1910 it boasted a population of twelve hundred and had at hand most accoutrements of civili-
zation, including a city government (mayor and board of aldermen), a
courthouse befitting the town's status as county seat, two banks, three
hotels, a high school, city gas plant and waterworks, an opera house,
grain elevator, brickyard, hospital, churches accommodating Catholic,
Congregational, and Episcopal worshippers, and two weekly newspapers.[8] Yet Elizabeth Corey, working there as a cook in the Shannon
House to support herself while searching for land to file claim to, un-
blinkingly scorns Fort Pierre as "this rotten town," specifying chapter
and verse to document its offensiveness.

Until 1889 the citizens and merchants of Fort Pierre lived with
the Damocles sword of eviction dangling over their heads, for the very
ground on which they stood was in technical violation of the Great
Sioux Reservation. The reservation, its origins linked to the Yankton
Treaty of 1859, called upon the Indians to relinquish eastern lands in

Dakota lying between the Big Sioux River and the Missouri, a step that led at once to the establishment of Dakota Territory but also to bloody skirmishes between the military and the tribes, who sensed themselves being pushed inexorably westward. In the Laramie Treaty, negotiated with Chief Red Cloud and signed in 1868, the Sioux gave up claim to practically all of their lands lying east of the Missouri in return for continuing title to all lands lying west of the river. This vast region, to be known as the Great Sioux Reservation, supposedly was to remain Indian property forever; but after the discovery of gold in the Black Hills and establishment of the right to passage through Indian lands, the rush was on.[9]

Fort Pierre became the easterly terminus of the most convenient route overland to the Hills, a trail leading oxen trains west to Willow Creek, then on to Lance and Frozenman creeks near Hayes (where Elizabeth Corey searched unsuccessfully for a claim in 1909), onward to the forks of Bad River, and thence to Deadwood—in all, 170 miles distant. Overland freighting kept the hamlet of Fort Pierre alive, as services like banks and bars, transient hotels and boarding houses, wagon shops and livery stables, and docks and freight warehouses sprang up in response to needs of the clientele passing through. This economic boom endured until the rug was pulled out from under it by the establishment in 1886 of a railroad from Nebraska into the Hills—a considerable shortcut. For a time, Fort Pierre assumed the aspect of a ghost town.[10]

The boom revived in 1890 after President Benjamin Harrison officially proclaimed the Great Sioux Reservation to be open and available, the decimated Indian tribes being sequestered on smaller portions of land near the Rosebud and above the Cheyenne. The more than 14,000 quarter-sections of potential homestead land lying between the Cheyenne and White rivers, an immense tract running some hundred miles east to west and as much as sixty miles north to south, had long been viewed with covetous eyes by settlers across the river in Hughes County, where most of the attractive acreages had already been claimed. A huge portion of these west-river tracts became Stanley County, and its boundaries were extended further in 1897 to become what now is remembered as "Old" Stanley County, encompassing more than twenty-six hundred square miles totaling in excess of two million acres.[11]

Fort Pierre, despite its placement on the extreme eastern border of the county—the Missouri River—received a boost by being named county seat. Always unwieldy in a political sense, Old Stanley County in 1914 was broken into three: Stanley, Haakon, and Jackson counties. But when Elizabeth Corey detrained at Midland depot, the county was at its largest dimensions, and she stood at its east-west midpoint (hence the name Midland).

The town across the Missouri, meanwhile, was rapidly evolving as a big sister city to Fort Pierre. Largely because of its central geographical position within the new (1889) state of South Dakota, Pierre won a spirited battle to become the state capital. Quite automatically, this victory sparked a building boom in which one of the chief monuments was the Locke Hotel, where in 1909 Elizabeth Corey worked briefly as a chambermaid and assistant cook.

The 120-room Locke, four stories tall and of solid brick, was called the most elegant hostelry of its day, with footed bathtubs and doors fitted with solid brass hardware. It boasted its own electric light plant and was the only hotel west of Chicago to be warmed by the clean heat of natural gas. A commodious ballroom occupied its second-floor "court," ringed by third- and fourth-floor balconies, and there the first gubernatorial inaugural ball was staged. A dinner for two hundred guests, prepared by the Locke's French chef for the opening of the hotel in 1890, included a menu listing roast turkey, ham, and quail, broiled trout, and "Ballottine" of duck, with a range of pastries, fruits, and ice creams for dessert. Male guests came attired in swallow-tail coats and white ties, and after dinner the Sewall and Robinson Orchestra played music for dancing. The Locke boasted a large swimming pool that actually was a spa, fed by natural hot springs, and, in fact, the hotel was officially called the Locke Sanitarium Company, advertising far and wide that "Rheumatism and Diseases of the Skin, Liver, Kidneys and Urinary Organs can be Cured by Drinking and Bathing in Water from Pierre's Mineral Spring."[12]

When Elizabeth Corey labored in its kitchen, the Locke was in its heyday, but its existence was only one sign of Pierre's ascendancy. By 1910 the population had burgeoned to 3,656.[13] Within five years any number of imposing business blocks had gone up (chiefly of brick, for the city now had its own brickyard), as well as a brand new railroad depot, city auditorium, high school, federal building, National Guard armory, and Carnegie Library. The downtown streets had been raised, a complete sewage system had been installed, and throughout the city installation of new sidewalks and graveled streets was under way. In 1910 at a cost of $78,000, the Pierre Methodist congregation completed their new church, which at once became a local showplace.[14] This was the church where Elizabeth Corey heard the pipe organ which was the congregation's pride and joy and commented, "My! Its a fine one—seventy one pipes!" Teachers arriving in Pierre from the western counties for the annual meeting of SDEA could now reach the city by train, for between 1905 and 1907 the Missouri was spanned by its first and greatly needed railroad bridge. Elizabeth Corey, stopping in Fort Pierre, crossed en route to the convention by the "dinkey" interurban, which rattled back and forth throughout the day.

The centerpiece of the Pierre building boom, by all odds, was the newly built state capitol. The rotunda beneath its towering neoclassical dome was opened to the teachers on the first evening of their convention for a reception. The guest of honor was Gen. William H. H. Beadle. It was through Beadle's unflagging efforts as territorial superintendent of public instruction that the government had been pressured into assuring that two sections of land in every township would be set aside to be rented or sold purely for the financial benefit of the state's schools. Even then, General Beadle was known as "The Man Who Saved Our School Lands," and the immediate occasion of the Pierre reception was the unveiling of his full-length sculpture, carved from Tennessee Bond marble, a life-size statue paid for solely by pennies saved and contributed by pupils in schoolhouses just such as those in which Bess Corey presided.[15] Along with two thousand others, Bess stood in line to give the general's hand an appreciative shake.

Such was the life that was beginning to thrive on the two banks of the Missouri River and that Elizabeth Corey observed during that summer of 1909 prior to filing claim to land ten miles southwest, along Bad River. She found that a universe of social (as well as geographic) distance lay between the graveled streets of Pierre and the outlands of Stanley County where the homesteaders broke sod on their claims. One must realize that Bess Corey, once launched on her career as schoolteacher and homesteader, saw the city of Pierre only seldom and on very special occasions. She did come to Fort Pierre, her place of business, whenever she could (or must), usually catching a ride in a neighbor's buggy or hayrack (before acquiring a team of her own) or hailing one of the passenger or freight trains that snaked their way eastward along the valley of Bad River. But the overwhelming balance of Bess's time was spent in close-knit, totally rural neighborhoods which never extended much more than five or six miles in radius from

The semicompleted South Dakota state capitol as it stood when Elizabeth Corey arrived in Pierre in 1909. Robert Kolbe Dakota Collection.

her schoolhouses and her homestead. She began, and she remained, a country girl.

✳ Supposing that every shred of record concerning Old Stanley County were somehow, catastrophically, to vanish, the sole exception being Bess Corey's letters, we still would possess, through them, access to an accurate, firsthand, and rather astoundingly complete account of the homesteading experience west of the river in South Dakota between 1909 and 1919. The Corey letters are far from being restricted to things personal. They are that, surely; few letters contain more intimate revelations of a young woman's aspirations or emotional turmoil than these. But the letters strike far beyond that bare circumference to treat of every important dimension of the life immediately surrounding her at that time and in that place.

That Bess should be able to turn herself into an all-around commentator will come as no surprise when one considers her own gregarious personality, her experience with farm life, and her brief but intensive career as an Iowa schoolma'am. Bess was a natural communicator and, having an ideal audience for her letters, she was motivated to the fullest extent possible. Although only twenty-one, she had been on her own since she was seventeen, had taught school since she was eighteen. She had busily scribbled long, newsy letters home for nearly five years already; her cub reporting days were over, her apprenticeship served. Landing at Midland depot, she was ready at once to begin her accounts of this new adventure and in fact used her few hours of Midland layover time to write the first of her letters home to the Iowa family who waited expectantly on the farm near Marne. Her family wished to know more than the mere generalities of how everything was going in her life; they wanted to hear precisely what this new world of homesteading—and the West—was all about. Bess proceeded to tell them.

There was, to begin with, the land itself.

Always marginal, at times blessed with abundant rain, but more often its naturally semiarid self, the region for decades had been known to cartographers as the Great American Desert. The high plains had made an ideal summer habitat for millions upon millions of buffalo, who thrived on the native grasses and rolled in the deep wallows that dotted the region. But now the buffalo were all but gone, eradicated, except for a few strays—and Scotty Philip's herd in the Buffalo Pasture upriver from Fort Pierre.[16]

Dakota's west-of-the-river territory was not in any sense Iowa farmland, all roly-poly Grant Woodishly rounded, the green fuzz of trees softening every crease of hill. Nor was it the flat-as-a-table fields of eastern Dakota, where furrows ran straight and were limited in length only by a plowman's imagination. Elizabeth Corey was struck by the difference at once; the land here was, as her sister, Ethel, would express it in 1915, "hills and the level country all mixed up together." And their brother Fuller, joining sister Bess in a homesteading venture of his own in 1910, had seen it in the same way, telling his mother that the hills in Stanley County were like her big hill in Iowa "only about fifteen or twenty times as high" and some were "straight up."

Despite impressions that might be cast by Fuller's sense of awe, the land was not truly mountainous. Hilly and rough, yes, and full of bluffs and draws. Such uneven terrain naturally engendered creeks and rivers, but every water system except the Missouri itself was prone to going bone dry, and even the Big Muddy earned its nickname, being very shallow-muddy and often falling to a depth too low for navigation.

This was not farmland of the traditional kind and never would be, even though the government was handing out patents to 160-acre parcels as if they would make functioning farms patterned on the eastern model. All too often the ground out here was baked hard as adobe brick; and when wet weather finally did arrive, that crusty soil melted into a thick gelatinous clay called gumbo which clung as tenaciously as tar to boots, wagon wheels, and hooves. It could be "almost death to a team," said Elizabeth Corey in 1914 as she estimated the depth of the spring gumbo to be eight to ten inches deep. In 1916, when her buggy broke down during rainy weather, Bess was obliged to head for home on foot; by the time she reached her shack, her "feet were like tubs," weighing her down with sticky gumbo.

High plains weather was a force to be reckoned with, even by one as dauntless as Bess Corey, whose upbringing on a western Iowa farm might be supposed to have provided her with an excellent preview of what she could expect to find in Dakota. A settler had to brace herself for the wildest of extremes. Within three weeks of Bess's arrival, for instance, the thermometers in Fort Pierre were registering temperatures in excess of 100 degrees; July was "beastly hot," and during August Bess noted that only one place in the nation—Arizona—could compete with Dakota for blast-furnace heat. By January, however, Bess was singing a different tune altogether, describing the snow as being different from Iowa snow and more terrifying, a result of strong winds and a lack of trees. When the sun flashed out upon that blank expanse of white, no sign of color relieving it, the experience could be eerie. All of this Bess records in her letters, following it with accounts of the spring floods that sent Bad River howling, flooding homesteads and stranding settlers on their roofs. During summer months a sudden cloudburst could produce similarly drastic results, and there were other, equally dangerous summer storms to contend with. Hail with stones as big as walnuts could spell instant death for a grainfield, and cyclones regularly wreaked havoc in early summer as the high plains tornado season opened. The sighting of a funnel cloud sent settlers scurrying for the caves that doubled as fruit and vegetable cellars.

Add to this a brand-new threat—to Bess Corey as to most other emigrants: the rattlesnake. Among Bess's first real shocks was the discovery that her 160 acres were so infested by venomous serpents that it amounted to little more than a rattlesnake den and that she should not be surprised at having a chance to kill half a dozen just in crossing her claim. Following her neighbors' lead, Bess at once adopted the habit of taking a "snake stick" with her on every trip outside her shack. She made plans to screen her door to keep the unwelcome "buzzers" out, and she sharply curtailed her after-dark hikes. Most frightening

Bad River where it joins the Missouri at Fort Pierre, ca. 1909. Robert Kolbe Dakota Collection.

of all was the clear danger to children, particularly to those toddlers too young to comprehend their hazard, and the tales Bess passes along of snake-bitten children strike at the heart.

Bess Corey's upbringing on the farm went a long way toward preparing her to live in such an environment. For one thing, she was able at once to view a tract of land with a practiced eye, alert to its realistic potential for grazing or for a crop of grain. She understood elementary necessities such as the need for settling near a water source (which a surprising number of homesteaders failed to grasp at once)[17] and, since she comprehended that the land in Stanley County was better suited to horse and cattle ranching—and then made a determination to build a horse ranch for herself, she was less vulnerable than those who came west expecting to raise rich fields of corn or wheat or oats, come rain or come drought.

To Bess's advantage, her farm childhood meant that a thousand questions scarcely need be posed concerning the minutiae of soil texture and hillside slope, tools and their uses, fencing needs and costs, or care of stock. This was, after all, a young woman who had successfully managed a family farm during the summer of 1908 while her mother had been hospitalized. Bess had achieved a high level of versatility in tasks that ran the gamut from nursing the sick to burying the dead. She could sew a fine seam or whip up a hearty meal from scratch, and she was already accustomed to the improvising that might be required in any and all situations.

To Bess, raised among horses and cattle, pigs, sheep, and poultry (let alone being the older sister to a large family of boys), the process of mating and resultant birth was a practical matter of everyday routine. The facts of sex posed no real question (although very real dilemmas concerning love and romance surely made up for that). And Iowa farm girls, if they knew anything at all, understood how to dress for a wintry blast—in good, solid wool and plenty of layers. Considerable portions of the Corey letters are occupied with accounts of Bess's garments, from "neither tackle" (her euphemism for lingerie) to boots. She needed no reminder that the Stanley County hinterlands was not the spot for high fashion and so was ready at the drop of a hat to don men's heavy union suits or woolen shirts, if that was what it took to survive. She knew what boots were for and was surprised at the number of girls who wore out pair upon pair of shoes before adopting "Dakota style" footwear. It pleased her no end to discover that her own solid work shoes had caused favorable comments among the men living along Bad River.

Accustomed all her life to being around animals, Bess Corey knew about as much as there was to know about horses. She loved them, was an expert rider (wearing a split skirt and riding jacket), and soon became known up and down Bad River for her fine team of black mares and the buggy in which she traveled everywhere, uphill and down, fording streams, climbing bluffs, and cruising the hogbacks into town, unconcerned whether roads existed or not. Her mares, Kate and Nell, were far, far more than mere horses; they became the symbol of Bess's independence, bringing an end to the day when she must depend upon the uncertain kindliness of neighbors or acquaintances for transportation and ushering in an era when she felt free to pick up and go, on a momentary whim, if she chose, no matter the time or the weather. Those steeds were her wings.

Dwelling places in settler territory left much to be desired. But the overcrowded and semiprimitive living conditions prevailing on Corey farm did much to prepare Bess for the Spartan life required of a Dakota homesteader. She expresses little shock, for instance, when first she views the "home" available to her during her first teaching assignment. Instead of recoiling, she rather matter-of-factly describes the place for what it is, employing the farm analogies that come to mind:

a vacant shack reminiscent of an Iowa corn crib, a chicken coop of a place whose jerry-built walls allowed the prairie wind to howl through at will. That shanty was not too much different from what the usual homesteader called home all year round. On the plains, the absence of trees pretty well ruled out log cabins, leaving the homesteaders dependent upon lumber hauled in by train as far as the railroad tracks might reach, then carried by wagon overland to the claim site. Most often the claim shack was a flimsy contrivance built on a balloon frame of two-by-four lumber sawed into studs and nailed together to form the four walls. With luck there might be a wooden floor. A roof, of course, was essential; often it sloped from front to back (that chicken-coop effect!) and was constructed of planks nailed atop the framing of the walls, then layered with rough black tarpaper. Outer walls were planked also and the tarpaper nailed down with lathing strips to hold against the furious winds that could be expected to blow interminably, summer or winter. A door, a window (perhaps two), and the dwelling might be thought complete, the inner sides of its walls left unfinished, bare studs and planking.[18]

The various descriptions offered in Bess's letters confirm this generalized description, present an effective picture of the primitive conditions prevailing in most lives along Bad River, and emphasize the comparative grandiloquence of Bess's plans for her own shack: a *two-room* house (with a dividing wall rather than a blanket strung between the areas for privacy) that avoided the chicken-coop style with an A-shaped roof (providing a tiny storage attic) and even a minuscule cellar dug in desperate hope of placing canned goods and winter vegetables out of reach of the pervading frost. She had come, not to "camp out," but to stay!

✻   The schoolma'am who got off the train at Midland station in 1909 was no shrinking violet or clinging vine in any sense of those words. She was a large woman. Standing five foot seven, Bess rather proudly placed herself among the tallest women in the entire Corey clan. And she was heavy. Despite shedding ten pounds during the summer of 1908, she still had weighed in at more than 180 pounds. She had weighed that much for years, and apparently she always would. Come what may, she would forever fluctuate between ten pounds this side—or that—of two hundred. Once in awhile, visiting Fort Pierre, she might "waste a nickel" checking her weight on a public scale;

but while Bess often appears to have accepted her size as being her fate, her continuous references to it tell us that it remained a concern.

At the same time, Bess Corey was very much a people person. She could no more have thrived in a country devoid of people than she could have breathed on Mars. It helped that she was not bashful. She had a special need always to place herself within a circle of human companionship, whether that circle be her rural-school pupils, a nearby homesteading family, or an organization of teaching colleagues. Here and there Bess's letters strike an uncharacteristically plaintive note which will cause the reader to understand, with something of a start, that this jolly, indefatigable, and forever gregarious woman may possibly be a Stanley County version of the sad clown, always needing to appear so full of mirth and forever exceeding the other members of her circle with her devil-may-care attitude. But whether it be natural or feigned, Bess Corey's flair for getting on with people pops out from every page of her letters and very clearly is a trait that helped her to overcome the social hazards of her chosen time and place.

For all its big-sky grandeur, western South Dakota is lonely country, capable of inspiring in many as much fear as awe; to be isolated on the barren plains can breed a deranging homesickness. During the homesteading era that type of homesickness was endemic; in a settler lacking strong motivation and easy adaptability, isolation could bring the symptoms on rapidly. The distinction separating personality types is nowhere more clearly perceived than in the psychological distance between Bess Corey's first letters home and those of her brother Fuller. Bess's pages are laden with observed detail. They quite obviously spring from a gush of adrenalin inspired by encountering the new and the novel, and they easily convince a reader that Bess is motivated by a genetic enthusiasm for future prospects. By contrast, the very first sentence which Fuller writes—"I am now alone in Besses house and feeling rather blue"—prophesies the doom of his homesteading adventure. There was plenty along Bad River to keep Fuller occupied, had he been so disposed, but nothing quite worked for him, and as soon as he fulfilled the minimum legal requirements for gaining title to his land, he backtracked for good to country and people he knew better and could handle more easily.

Bess, who stuck it out, spends much time dwelling upon activities that fill time creatively and so fight the blues. For men, there was forever much hard work to be done: sod breaking, plowing, sowing, and reaping, erecting buildings and barns, dredging dams, digging basements and cisterns. Livestock required continual care, and there were endless trips to town for fetching supplies, picking up mail (one's own and the neighbors'), and locating workmen prepared to build or repair what the homesteader himself could not. Of necessity there was much sharing of this work between the sexes, but women were equally busy with their gardening, sewing, mending, scrubbing, cooking, and canning. The washing of clothes itself was a major undertaking, not to be completed within the span of a single day. And there usually was the supervision of children, so many homesteaders being young and raising sizable families. But even an unmarried person had more than enough to do and was easily kept busy. In a single letter Bess (officially engrossed in her role as schoolma'am) speaks of completing at home a heavy round of washing, scrubbing, ironing, baking, churning, and fruit preserving; all of this was accomplished, one understands, without benefit of electricity or machine.

Bess writes often of activities on a more exclusively social plane, "doings" that might ward off the ever-lurking specter of loneliness. Much visiting, of course, with a visit often leading to an invitation to spend the night piled two or three together in one bed. Having no family to return to and only a dark and cold claim shack waiting at the end of her trail, Bess readily accepted most such offers. Conversation was endemic, a sharing of one's little triumphs and tragedies, empathically responded to on both sides. The homesteaders on Bad River discovered soon enough that their schoolma'am could hold up her end of a good "jawing" session without any help at all. Besides that, she could tell a good joke and take one, too, even at her own expense if she had to. Visiting—it was less a luxury than a necessity—extended into a myriad of group activities: quilt tying, rag-rug socials, taffy pulls, popcorn feasts, picnics engaged in on any pretext, surprise parties the same, Christmas tree celebrations, Eastertime egg roasts, excursions by wagon to gather wild plums, chokecherries, and buffalo berries in a bend of Bad River. And there were games: croquet or checkers or card games such as Pitch, Old Maid, or Five Hundred. There was more than enough such entertainment to fill any idle hour.

Groups of men might band together for sport hunting. The buffalo might be gone, most of the antelope as well, but they could shoot jackrabbits and coyotes. Sometimes they took potshots at prairie dogs (after killing his first of those clever little creatures, Fuller Corey swears never again to repeat such a dastardly act). The women formed more formal groups. They had their Pollyanna Clubs and Kill Kare Klubs, whose names tell all, and lodges such as the Royal Neighbors, which Bess Corey joined in Fort Pierre even though she could attend only on rare occasions. She found something compatible with her own positive-thinking philosophy in the message printed across the red silk ribbons worn by Royal Neighbors during meetings: "Smile, Darn You, Smile!"

Universally popular, apparently, was the box social for which the women (not necessarily only the unmarried) packed individual suppers into boxes trimmed with crepe paper and varicolored ribbons from the drygoods store in town. When the boxes were auctioned off, a purchaser won the privilege of dining with the woman whose name lay on a card inside. The unmarried Bess Corey unashamedly promoted box socials, expressing a keener than ordinary interest in the Leap Year Box Social held on Bad River in 1916. In fact, she was its chief organizer. Although hoping that this gentleman or that might be high bidder on her boxes, she was ready to hazard a chance, be a good sport, and possibly receive in return a pleasant surprise: nothing ventured, nothing gained.

A box social might be combined with dancing, Bess Corey's odds-on favorite entertainment. Despite her size, Bess loved to dance and apparently was light on her feet, for invitations were always forthcoming and she never failed to have an escort. Readers will note that Bess is not in Stanley County for a full week before she is escorted to the settlers' ball in Hayes by the handsomest man in the area, Clarence E. Coyne, deputy county sheriff and later mayor of Fort Pierre as well as South Dakota's secretary of state.[19] A dance combined with a box social provided a complete evening's entertainment, beginning with supper and ending—whenever the spirit moved. "I danced the sole about off my shoes," she confided to her family after one of the neighborhood dances. "Got home in time for two or three little hours sleep this morning." For these dances, musicians were in great and constant demand. This fact explains much of the anticipatory curiosity surrounding Fuller Corey's arrival in South Dakota in 1910; he was good with a fiddle, and Bess had broadcast that news in advance.

At times, even a buoyant person such as Bess might cave in to the blues, and then her homesickness spilled over onto the pages of her letters in spasms of nostalgia for the old life, the farm, the family, the remembered pleasures of the turning year, and the group holidays it brought as the seasons changed. At times Bess admits more than she intends, perhaps, as in this remark, which begins in denial before easing over into open admission: "I don't get homesick—not when I'm awake anyway, though they say I sometimes cry in my sleep and talk to [my mother] but—oh, how I wish sometimes that [Fuller] and his violin were here—I get so lonesome for music!" Such spells of morbidity were most likely to be triggered as the winter wore on, perhaps on a gloomy afternoon by sighting a pack of hungry wolves from a schoolroom window or on a night when the stillness was broken by an eerie chorus "as if every coyote in Stanley County was howling for its ma." The sight of fresh cut flowers in a Fort Pierre confectioner's window during winter months was sure to make a sudden and heart-wrenching impact, but the greatest and most unflagging inducers of loneliness and nostalgia for everything and everybody left behind in Iowa were special family occasions such as her birthday (November 15, just as the world outside grew dark) and, of course, the family holiday supreme, Christmas. There are moments in the letters when Bess's pen appears to have taken on a life of its own, crying out in an anguished wail of yearning and desperation: "*I'm so homesick!*"

Bess had her own personal means of combatting loneliness when stranded, solitary, in her shack or schoolhouse. At one time she took up the zither as a hobby, and she did a good deal of reading, in 1911 subscribing to six magazines of current events and educational matters as well as the more general appeal *McCall's*. When her brother Olney died in 1913 and Bess inherited his box camera, she brought it back to South Dakota with her and whipped up a makeshift darkroom in her claim shack, sending off by mail for the proper chemicals as she learned to develop and print her own snapshots. Other hours could be filled pleasantly by attending to that great craze of the age—pictorial post cards. Bess mailed such cards by the fistful and received batches by return mail. Cards worth saving were clipped into one of the special albums manufactured for the hobbyist. By the Christmas season of 1910 she reports her first album already stuffed full, with more cards lying around loose and, as it were, demanding a new album so insistently that she very nearly regrets spending her spare dollar on a new hair ribbon.

Clearly, though, above all other diversions, Bess Corey treasured her letter writing. The scores upon scores of letters mailed to her family over the years became a running conversation continued via the U.S. mails. A single letter by itself might extend by postscripts

from day to day prior to being mailed. Her account at times is calculated, employing set pieces such as her magnificent explanation of the
procedure for filing a claim in which she explains how and why she
has purchased a "relinquishment," a tract being abandoned by its
original claimant, that will locate her along Bad River about ten miles
southwest of Fort Pierre. But at most other moments she is the soul of
spontaneity ("Oh! I almost forgot to tell you I retrimmed my blue plush
waist this afternoon—will enclose a scrap of the trimming"). She
wrote at any and all times, whatever the occasion or the distraction,
and employed whatever paper and pen or pencil lay at hand. She cor-
responded on a more-or-less regular basis with dozens of people, and
she is fond of mentioning in letters to her family the number of envelopes she is putting in the mail or the list of friends she has heard from
recently. Best of all for Bess's emotional well-being, letters received
from "back east" could be taken out again and again for a renewed
savoring of their contents. "Say, I've read those letters over several
times but would like to read them several times more," wrote Bess of
some Corey family correspondence that had been shared with her; "is
they any hurry about [returning] them?" Bess's letters were a lifeline
connecting her to places and people who mattered crucially.

✳ A mainstay of Bess Corey's life in South Dakota (because thereby
she earned her daily bread) was her work as a schoolteacher in the
one-room rural schoolhouses of that day. Being a woman and alone,
Bess simply could not accomplish by herself all that was required to
establish a homestead. But she brought with her to the lands lying
alongside Bad River a means of livelihood that served her well in hiring
done what she could not do by herself.

The emigrants flooding into South Dakota after 1900 brought
with them, in very many cases, families of young children desperately
in need of tutoring. Educational regulations then being rather lax,
schoolhouses had a tendency to spring up in the unlikeliest of places,
wherever a cluster of families wanted a school of their own. For a
teacher who could qualify, jobs were readily available, and Bess Corey
brought with her not only four years of Iowa experience but a cur-
rently valid Iowa certificate as well. She managed to land a school
almost as soon as she was able to determine the area in which her
homestead claim would be made—she wanted home and job to be as
close to each other as possible, naturally. Her rounded portrait of conditions operative in those all-too-often-makeshift schools of home-

Lance Creek School near Hayes, S.D., where Elizabeth Corey taught ca. 1920. Photo courtesy Ann Ahboltin Sheeley.

steading days on the high plains surely belongs among the unique and authentic records of that curious corner of American life, now virtually vanished: the rural one-room school.

The Stanley County schools in 1909 fell under the jurisdiction of the county superintendent, then Grace Reed, who in 1906 had emigrated, like Bess, from Iowa.[20] Grace Reed, who rapidly became a heroine to Bess, checked out her fellow Iowan's credentials and looked over her record of experience; and then, contingent upon the newcomer's passing requisite state examinations in certain fields of study (drawing, civics, South Dakota history), she issued her a first-grade certificate. This type of license authorized Bess Corey to teach on the grammar-school level for a two-year term.[21]

Bess's first job, at Speer School, was handily close to her claim. Happily, this meant that she could superintend the building of her claim shack during the fall of 1909. That was no easy task, even granting the proximity of claim to school, when one considers that she was preparing simultaneously for her three examinations and (not passing) then immediately needing to prepare, under stress, for a retake—and, being Bess Corey, desperately hating the very prospect of failing at anything.

By itself alone, a day spent in one of these rural schools could be long and hard. And after occupying her claim shack, Bess found herself arising at five-thirty in the morning in order to wash, comb her hair, get dressed, prepare breakfast, and set off (on foot) for school by seven, determined to have her schoolhouse stove heating by eight o'clock. Bess often taught settlers' sons who had passed their nineteenth or even their twentieth birthdays, and these older pupils could sometimes be counted on to help out. During that first year Bess had good-natured help from sixteen-year-old Howard Speer, who hauled fuel in for the King Cole stove, sharpened pencils, and carried the schoolma'am's dinner pail from home for her. Pupils such as Howard could be welcome company for a young teacher far from home and carrying heavy responsibilities. A reader senses Bess's great relief on that chill afternoon when a pack of wolves is sighted near the schoolhouse and Howard snaps tension with his quick-thinking announcement that it can't be the little children the predators are after because wolves are known to relish schoolma'am suppers above any dish in the whole wide world.

Even though a school board technically carried responsibility for keeping its school building clean and in repair, much of the actual work fell by default upon the schoolma'am, and on a day in February during the winter break (her school came to a halt during the worst weather months), readers discover Bess at work. She has undertaken the cleaning of Speer School all by herself, sweeping walls and ceiling free of dust and stove-soot, washing begrimed windows, desks, seats, and blackboards, cleaning the wash stand with its basin and ewer where pupils tidy up prior to eating the lunches they bring with them from home, even scrubbing the floor and entry porch, first with a broom, then on her knees. It is a rough task, but one well done and to complete it is gratifying. "My shoulder hardly ached a bit," is Bess's only comment.

No shirker, she. Nor could any rural teacher neglect the absolute necessities, if she (and most were women) hoped to survive. No one expected a convenience such as running water in a rural school (any more than running water was to be had in a homestead, for that matter), but each school came furnished with flimsy wooden privies, one for boys, another for girls, stationed over pits dug in the soil back of the schoolhouse (and for this reason sometimes called "backhouses"). While teaching at Klemann School, Bess provides an account of the efforts that must be made in order to coerce her reluctant school board into repairing these outbuildings. When she moves to Mathews School, Bess spots an outright danger. The carpenter who cut the holes in the "two seater" apparently having had no eye for size, Bess's smaller pupils are in mortal danger of plummeting six or eight feet down into the vault itself, with what dire results one can easily imagine. The tension in the schoolhouse whenever one of the little girls asks to "go out back" is not relieved until the ingenious Bess rigs up an emergency device comprised of a rope attached to tomato cans with pebbles in them, a mechanism that the victim can rattle loudly in case of catastrophe.

Questions of safety were one thing, questions of security another. The schoolma'am occasionally elected, perhaps for reasons of weather, to stay overnight in her schoolhouse. The building invariably was isolated, the surrounding population sparse and scattered, and if help were ever to be needed it might be a long time coming. It sometimes happened that travelers, strayed or lost on the plains, might stumble upon an empty schoolhouse and spend the night. They were welcome to the shelter. One of the standing rules among the settlers was that doors must never be locked against a neighbor's need—and every homesteader was your neighbor. Conversely, travelers felt free to enter whatever shelter they came upon, by force if necessary, should it be unoccupied and they in dire straits. But other prowlers were another thing entirely, and occasionally there were such, even in distant Stanley County. The discovery on more than one occasion that someone unnamed has been in the schoolhouse overnight without leaving the customary explanatory note gives Bess pause, particularly when she reflects that her nearest neighbor is at least half a mile away.

Schoolteachers on the high plains frontier moved often, sometimes every year, and for a variety of reasons. Bess Corey was no exception. What these nearly annual relocations do for the readers of Bess's letters is serendipitous, for her moves introduce them regularly to a new corner of the county, a new cast of homesteading families, a new raft of problems. From Speer School to Klemann School to Mathews School to Thomas School is not so far in miles (although Bess did tend to measure all distances by the radius from her claim), but Stanley County had organized itself into neighborhoods and each neighborhood was a world unto itself. Each September the reader is launched with Bess into the first page of a wholly new chapter whose discrete plot lines Bess is not too long in discerning and passing along. In the meanwhile, the reader becomes aware of family upon family of settlers. A veritable rollcall of Stanley County ensues, name after name, clan upon clan, people who made an impact upon the history of the area and whose descendants, in more cases than not, reside there still: Bahr, Bucholz, Carlisle, Clow, Dean, Donahue, Ericksen, Foutts, Gordon, Gould, Hoisington, Huston, Jennings, Klemann, Leggett, Mathews, Mcpherson, Murphy, Newlin, Nordin, Obele, Porter (one of them married County Superintendent Grace Reed), Reese, Robar, Rovang, Rowe, Scarborough, Scripter, Seieroe, Sonnenschein, Speer, Stone, Strunk, Thomas, Vessey, Walsh, Walton, Whalen, Ziggler. The list goes on.[22]

In this cast of thousands some play bit parts while others star. Any number of characters make repeated entrances and exits, as, for example, Clarence Coyne, the deputy sheriff, who, long after squiring Bess at the Hayes settlers' ball, shows up one day at the schoolhouse. Having maneuvered his automobile across the hills, he has come to enlist Bess's help in locating a fugitive. And Flagg Carlisle, like Bess a rural teacher but also an incipient lawyer, turns up again and again: as a member of the young social crowd with whom Bess runs, as a fellow attendee at Fort Pierre summer teacher institutes, as the wiped-out victim of cloudburst and fire in Cottonwood, where he has been filling out a term as superintendent of schools and preparing simultaneously to open his first law practice.

The spotlight glares as well on those families with whom Bess Corey boards while teaching her various schools. These were the people whom she came to know the most about, sometimes to her delight and sometimes not. We meet first the Stones, Grant and Mae, and their quartet of youngsters, whom the pun-loving Bess at once dubs "the pebbles." It is these active youngsters who are bribed with pennies on a cold winter's eve to play at the far end of the Stones' one-room claim shanty so that they will not shake the table at which Bess writes her letters to the family at Corey farm. Mae Stone, at twenty-six, was very close in age to Bess (they seemed destined to become close friends), and Grant was not much older. We read of his employment in building Bess's claim shack, of his expertise at ripping open her tough buffalo sod with his breaking plow, and of his many occasional kindnesses—trips into Fort Pierre on his wagon, letters fetched in from town—until the sad day when it dawns upon Bess that a wife's jealousy of her husband's attentions has roused Mae's ire and turned her into a foe.

We meet next the Klemanns, ex-Wisconsonians, with whom Bess at first is delighted to board at the promise of a bargain price of $10.00 a month (and the prospect of a room all to herself), only to discover, once installed, that board has gone up to fifty cents a day and she is sleeping two to a bed like everyone else. Whenever a schoolma'am went out to board with a family whose children attended the district school, potential conflict lurked around every corner. It was precarious to be a child's supervisor all day and then to become a mere spectator as the child interacted with parents and siblings during the evening; in worst cases, this duality of roles brought out a Jekyll and Hyde quality that could be disconcerting, even dangerous. It is problems with school behavior and attendance that lead in Bess's instance to strife between the elder Klemanns and the schoolma'am, precipitating her departure from both home and school.

We enter next the home of Roy and Perle Newlin, the poverty-stricken and desperately in love young couple in whose primitive shack Bess begins her tenure at Mathews School. On this new homestead the total absence of outbuildings—including a privy—shocks Bess, who notes in her usual direct and pragmatic manner that not a tree or a shrub exists within half a mile to shield a person who goes outside to perform her necessities. Toward the Newlins, who are considerably younger than she, Bess feels protective in a maternal manner, and it is with them that she experiences some of her happiest times and most poignant moments. One of the most affecting emotional peaks in her entire story concerns the sudden death of the Newlins' newborn infant and Bess's attempt to console the distraught father and grief-stricken mother by dressing the tiny corpse for a memorial photograph to be taken with the box camera once owned by the dead Olney Corey—only to have the shutter-spring snap into fragments at the critical moment. Few scenes in Bess's letters can match this for its ability to depict the sledgehammer blows that life on the frontier could deliver to a homesteader.

And then there come the red-headed Donahue clan, children everywhere and another on the way, providing one more highlight as Bess depicts that strenuous day early in 1914 when Mrs. Donahue appears at the schoolhouse, unannounced and in labor, younger offspring in tow, requesting that Bess hitch up her team of black mares and go in search—right now!—of her husband, Mike, and the local midwife. The rest of that day, which sees the arrival of "another red-headed Irishman," who at once begins "complaining about the hard times in this country," and concludes with the schoolma'am's offer to shut down her school for two weeks while she stays with the Donahues, cooking and cleaning, as a surrogate mother—this is Bess Corey at her storytelling best. The Donahues would remain friends for life, and one of the daughters, Mary, would follow Bess's lead and become a rural schoolteacher.

As with any teacher, some of Bess Corey's academic seasons were happy ones, some not. One spring she might leave a district with relief on both sides, but depart the next year sharing regrets all around. One thing that never varied was her dedication to her chosen profession. Her pupils came first always, and the reader is not excluded from accounts of the sweat expended in prepping them for the annual statewide examinations that determined whether they would pass to the next level or repeat a grade. Most satisfying of all appears to have been the steady accretion of respect for the schoolma'am, first as a young woman with pluck, grit, drive, and determination, later as a true professional. Bess's unquenchable thirst for compliments is never hidden; each line of praise that comes her way is passed along to the family in Marne.

The most welcome compliments were those that arose from within the ranks of her profession. We watch as one of these rewarding moments comes from the county superintendent most admired by Bess, Grace Reed, on the day when Bess calls at her office in Fort Pierre to inquire how it can happen that, following Reed's recent surprise visit to Speer School, there have been nothing but positive comments. Where is the other side of the coin? Hasn't every teacher some faults? Doesn't everyone need correction? What happens to Bess after placing her neck on the block in this manner might cause any young teacher to float on air, as Reed leans forward in her kindly way to tell Bess straightforwardly that she has made no adverse criticism for the simple reason that there is none to be made; further, she stands ready to use the influence of her office in helping Bess to obtain whatever school in Stanley County she may fancy. No wonder that Bess Corey leaves that office feeling, for once in her life, truly valued; no wonder she speaks of gaining a feather a yard long in her hat!

From that day onward, feeling that she has been labeled "one of the best" by someone she respects so highly, Bess has a reputation to uphold. And uphold it she does. A reader travels with her to the regular teachers meetings, called institutes, held throughout the year in various little towns along Bad River. At one of these, in 1912, Bess has the thrill of becoming the first rural teacher invited to chair such a meeting, a signal honor. The reader goes to Pierre with Bess late in 1911 to attend her first annual convention of the South Dakota Educational Association (SDEA), and from there to later such conventions held in

Grace Aimee Reed (Porter), superintendent of schools in Stanley County, ca. 1910. Photo courtesy Verendrye Museum.

larger eastern centers such as Aberdeen and Watertown, gatherings of two thousand and more teachers in group meetings led by university professors and other celebrities of the educational world. It is at such SDEA conventions that Bess is introduced to music which strikes as far as possible beyond the group-sings and Sunday school choirs that have heretofore marked the boundaries of her cultural universe. In Aberdeen she attends a recital by Johanna Gadski, Wagnerian star of the Metropolitan Opera;[23] in Watertown she enjoys an evening of song by David Bispham, baritone of the same opera company.

It is in the annual county institutes held in Fort Pierre, attendance mandatory, that Bess Corey's Stanley County reputation crests, in particular during the institute of summer 1914. Bess is confounded when a prestigious visiting instructor, Professor W. F. Jones of the state university in Vermillion, singles her out from among the large assemblage of county teachers. Jones explains to the gathering that there is a thing known as "teaching ability" of which they are all aware, but that teaching ability is not quite the equal of another quality, which he calls "*wonderful teaching genius.*" As he speaks, the entire room realizes, along with Bess Corey, that he is referring specifically to her. Like it or not, Bess has been visited by instant celebrity, and a reader feels her cringe and preen at the same moment. She hears another instructor comment as he approaches a knotty problem in pedagogy: "Where's Miss Corey? She's a good authority on this." And others begin to remark, "Let's ask Miss Corey" or "Miss Corey said ———."

At once everyone attending the institute not only knows Bess but is eager to be called a close acquaintance. Her fame appears to have spread beyond institute walls to the city streets, where townspeople greet her by name. And at a private party for institute instructors, Dr. Jones continues his praise by declaring flatly: "Miss Corey is the best thing we have in the Institute." Meanwhile, "Miss Corey," proud as a peacock to have won friendship and respect not only from her peers but from the "visiting firemen" who stand so much "higher up" in her profession, confides to her mother that she is nonplussed by being hauled out of the anonymity of the crowd and made so extremely conspicuous: "I'm so darned big anyway!"

It is not long, of course, until a sense of responsibility "as big as a house" settles on Bess, diluting her euphoria. But nothing can entirely quell Bess's deep gratification at having such sudden and unaccustomed popularity thrust upon her. She glows with fulfillment, and the reader savors her moment of triumph along with her.

✱ For a modern, psychologically oriented reader there seems little doubt that the most engrossing of Bess's many ongoing stories will be that which concerns her intricate relationships with the family at home—"Ma, and the rest," as she so typically heads her letters. In particular, her relationship to her mother will fascinate as it gradually emerges from out of the gray and undisclosing vapor into the light of day.

Bess Corey may have arrived in Midland with but a single suitcase, but she rode west freighted with immense emotional baggage. This was, a reader should bear in mind, a girl who had lost her most beloved parent, her father, and who felt rejected and dismissed by her mother. Familial problems that had been simmering for a long while were threatening to boil over, and one observes with keen interest, safely and from a distance, as this human process (which is not without its morbid aspects) unfolds, surely and inexorably. It bubbles to the surface of the letters only occasionally, however.

Margaret Morgan Corey invariably is the addressee of Bess's letters to Marne, Iowa, and clearly it is her mother whom Bess feels most compelled to inform, entertain, challenge, and placate. Tugged desperately in one direction by the necessity for pleasing herself and in an opposite direction by her felt obligation to make a friend of her reluctant mother, Bess found herself more often than not in emotional turmoil and often felt terribly put down. Much of what intruded between mother and daughter may be forever secret now (although Paul Corey suggests, perhaps with good reason, that their undying strife was born of parental discord). Wherever the full truth lies, one thing never alters as the letters proceed; again and again Bess despite every rejection attempts to make her mother happy with what she is accomplishing in the West. Margaret Corey appears to remain forever apprehensive and unsatisfied, angry and belittling, no matter what the achievement.

That Margaret Corey wrote fully as many letters to Stanley County as Bess mailed home to Marne seems clear. (What became of them remains a mystery. The Coreys were savers, but, as with most letters, after Bess's death they probably were junked or destroyed.) However, what Mrs. Corey said in those lost letters often can be reconstructed satisfactorily by way of her daughter's replies. Also, Margaret was in the habit of using the versos of Bess's envelopes as scratch pads. The dozens of topics and events she listed on these to jog her mind as she wrote to Stanley County with Clay Township news would indicate that her own epistolary style made a good match for her daughter's: newsy, anecdotal, and gossipy; loaded with people, places, and events. A glance at one such prompt-list—this from the verso of Bess's letter of September 5, 1911—will indicate something about the range:

Petes corn	Earl's business
School house	Johnnies f—— m——
The clothes	Roy's auto
Christian [Science?]	His longest trip
Mrs P——	Laura's school
Dam & plowing	Theater show
Cider	Uncle Sherman
Frost	Cousin Sue
Henry S——	Fishing
Ball game	Chautauqua
Rob's letter to Fuller	Sunday S[chool]

It seems evident that Margaret Morgan Corey's letters were loaded not only with the minutiae of life on the farm and within the family but with polemic as well. Whatever may have been said outright or strongly suggested, Bess responds continually to being "roasted" by her mother. At times she flares up like a struck match, ignited into a fury by an especially gratuitous attitude or outrageous claim, throwing up her hands in despair of ever being either understood or appreciated by her intractable family (meaning, 99 percent of the time, her mother).

At the same time, Bess's exasperation-at-long-distance is countered by frequent professions of filial affection whose sincerity we have no reason to doubt. Bess's words strike well beyond the perfunctory or the merely dutiful in expressing concern for her mother's health and general well-being, burdened as Margaret was with the heavy obligations of running a family farm without a husband. For special occasions, when the impulse strikes and the pocketbook provides, Bess wires flowers from Fort Pierre to Marne. She declares on her mother's birthday that she wishes she could send a rose for every year and would do so except for the exorbitant cost. She restrains herself also, it would seem, for fear of adding to the charges of extravagance which emanate regularly from Marne.

There is no question but that Bess Corey felt she had been pushed precipitously and with a rather rude shove from the familial nest. Her

mother not too long after the death of Edwin Corey, husband and father, made it clear to her that there was not room at home for all the
children. Bess, being older than the rest and thus better able to survive
on her own, would have to do just that. A good deal of truth resides in
that pronouncement, rude shock as it must have been, and it left Bess
with a deep sense of disfranchisement, a feeling of having been disowned, stranded, and abandoned, suffering no end of psychic damage
while still in her formative years. Bess interprets her dispossession as
the cruel act of a mother who, although admittedly under her own
shock of recent bereavement, seems all too willing and even eager to
sacrifice her daughter in favor of her sons. On the other hand, if one
of the Coreys must leave, Bess was a logical candidate. The eldest son
and child, Olney, had never been strong, and he would perish in 1913
of the epilepsy that afflicted him. The next in line after Bess was
Fuller, a strapping sixteen when the father died and the tallest and
strongest of the clan, but Fuller was needed at home. His help was
essential if the farm were to support and feed the group.

Bess's running debate with her mother persists from beginning to
end of her letter-writing years, easing and intensifying according to
circumstances. A reader will sense a determination on Bess's part
somehow to regain and hold within the family membership a solid
position of, if it could not be love, then at least respect. That note is
struck as soon as Bess reaches Stanley County and speaks out sharply
in reply to her mother's denigrating comment to the effect that if Bess
has gone to Dakota only to wind up as a lowly chambermaid, she might
as well have stayed in Iowa. This curt dismissal of Bess's effort to keep
her head above water financially inspires her manifesto: "Heaven
knows I've seen trouble enough and know what it is to be out in the
world among entire strangers, without friends or home, but I'll never
give up till I drop."

Probably with no more than the dimmest recognition of what she
was doing, Bess appears to have selected the wild west-of-the-river
plains not only as her unique opportunity for biting off a personal
chunk of the vaunted American Dream (160 acres of land nearly
free for the taking) but also as a kind of battlefield upon which she
might prove herself. By assuming the prerogatives usually reserved for
males, and frontier Dakota was nothing if not a male preserve, Bess
was driven by a determination finally, somehow, to compel her mulish
family to recognize her achievement and even, with good luck, to ac-
knowledge her superiority.

In this struggle to establish an identity, the brothers Corey would play adversarial roles. The impulse to migrate westward in search of one's fortune was strong and widespread, and Bess encouraged its growth in the boys by inviting them, by enticing them, or even by daring them to compete with her for familial admiration on the wind-swept, grass-covered plains of South Dakota. This combative side of Bess Corey's personality, this readiness and even eagerness to "slug it out" with her adversaries, breaks through the otherwise calm surface of many of her anecdotes. One of the most clear-cut instances is that in which she tells of a visit to the home of Peter Seieroe, her pupil at Mathews School. Peter's big brother Harry is older than she as well. Bess makes a point of telling her brothers that Harry Seieroe, who stands taller than Fuller and is meatier, has been teasing her. When she has taken all she intends to take, she explodes in a fury: "I just went for him and slapped him clear up to a peak. I'd make a feint and he'd throw up his arm to protect one side of his face and I give him three on the other side before he could move." The assembled crowd can scarcely believe their eyes, and Mr. Mathews, "who is quite a boxer himself," has a question for Bess: couldn't the two of them spar around a bit "with mits" just to see how good a pugilist she really is?

Except for Olney, none of the Corey boys was of legal age when their sister emigrated. This time lapse provided her plan with an op-portunity to ripen. Beneath that irresistible surface of her letters with their exotic wealth of frontier anecdotes and the cumulative minutiae of daily living, one can discern something else taking shape. It is a rather well-defined, though of course never stated, subtext, a tripartite message, subliminal and highly persuasive. It declares (1) that the unimaginable terrors to be encountered in the Bad River country de-mand exceptional courage and fortitude; (2) that Bess Corey possesses that requisite toughness and personal force and so can surmount these daily hazards; and (3) that her brothers probably are not quite up to meeting the demands met morning, noon, and night by their big sister, who, "only a girl," is somehow, inexplicably and against terrible odds, making it.

This strategy emerges at last from a thousand reminders of close calls with illness and injury and violence, a drumming on the notion that her family in Marne, so safe and sound, can have little realization of how terribly close they have come to not having a daughter and sister at all after this or that or the other recent brush with disaster. Another portion of the submerged message arises out of continual negative prompting, in dire warnings to the boys *not* to attempt the homesteading route to success, in pleas to the mother not to let them risk it. Always the directive to Margaret Corey is the same: "*keep your boys in Iowa till they are twenty one years of age or past.*" Don't let them come to Dakota where they might be bitten by a buzzer or dragged by a wild horse or frozen in a snowdrift; make them stay at home where they will be safe and protected. Bess will kill the snakes and send them the trophies; let the boys be content. Bess was willing to go further, to taunt her brothers outright: "Don't let Olney get a notion of coming out here for if he persisted in staying he wouldn't last six months" and "Rob must be crazy [to think of coming to] S.D. If he had a chance to try it he would be back in a week with all the starch taken out of him." How could any red-blooded American farm boy in 1909 risk the certain ignominy involved in backing off from such a dare? One can visualize young Rob Corey glancing up as his mother reads that sentence, flushing probably, retorting with a growl: "That's what *she* thinks!" In 1915 Rob took up the dare.

Bess's melange of mixed messages couples her disparagement of her brothers' abilities with a strong peppering of accounts that speak of her own increasing prowess with those traditionally male power implements, shotgun and revolver. On a plum-gathering expedition in 1909, young John Porter guesses that he will enjoy some entertainment with the new schoolma'am from Iowa. He dares her to shoot his "five magazine windchester," using as a target the plum pail belonging to neighbor Adolph Buchholz. "John showed me exactly how to hold the gun and I listened 'shust so meek as Mosses,'" wrote Bess as she regaled her family with the story. "I only shot once—that was enough to convert Adolphs plum pail into a first class culander. John said 'By Gosh you hit it!'" Her stock soared. She does not fail to include regular reports of her rising status among the locals, who insist on making "such a toot about [her] nerve, pluck, push, grit and so on" that it warms her feet merely to think about it. "I was never so popular before," she writes, "and it makes me feel queer." While warning her brothers away, Bess declares simultaneously that she cannot wait until they are able to join in her adventure. She writes Fuller in particular about how very fine it would be if he were to come along to Dakota as soon as he turns twenty-one. He can file on land she has already scouted out near her own claim. She promises that "the two of us together will have plow land enough to balance up the pasture land and we'd have a fine stock farm."

It is Fuller, in fact, who appears to be the ultimate target of all of Bess's come-or-don't-come news flashes. Fuller was the right age, he was the picture of health, and his departure from Iowa would leave his mother without the one son she relied upon the most. Bess offers Fuller every inducement, sending him, for example, those detailed descriptions of the process for claiming a homestead, telling him (who has no money) how very cheaply it can all be accomplished, and assuring him, should he have qualms, that if he does not wish to settle permanently in Stanley County that after proving up he can sell out at a nice profit and leave. She dangles a carrot before his eyes: how nice it would be "to have a piece of land of your own." She has broken a path to ease the way, can tell him just how to go about the whole thing; her friends will be his friends, and everything, to use her own favorite term for it, will be absolutely "hunkey-dory." And if he prefers to do it all his way, rather than hers, then that is what he may do. She describes a no-lose proposal.

It is small wonder, then, that Fuller Corey, his appetite whetted, should leave for Stanley County the moment he reaches his majority, and no surprise, either, that his arrival on Bad River leads immediately (as Bess must have known it would) to friction, unhappiness, and dissension. As unsuited temperamentally for the isolation of homesteading as his sister is able to adapt to it, Fuller is morose. It becomes rather clear that he has been conditioned in advance to do a bit of watchful reporting on Bess to his mother, and he begins a series of letters critical of his sister, providing details which confirm Margaret Corey's strong suspicions concerning her daughter's spendthrift ways. Getting wind of this defection, Bess retaliates with tales of her brother's own extravagances, his loutish behavior, his sloth, and his pernicious resistance to adapting to conditions. The fight is on. As happens so often with siblings, both feel wholly justified in taking their stands and both at the same time are badly mistaken. The truth is that, for a tangled heap of reasons which are very real but which neither brother nor sister understands, the two are incompatible, and Fuller's adventure ends as it must, badly.

It is remarkable (or, on the other hand, perhaps no surprise at all considering the intricate and Byzantine ways of family feuds) that it should be from Fuller that Bess Corey at last wrings the ultimate accolade. As the months drag along and Fuller has an opportunity to investigate a number of other settlers and their claims and to hear their tales of woe, he comes upon many a quarter-section of land that he considers to be worth less than any ten acres of his own claim next door to Bess, the land she had picked out for him (and that she will "inherit" when he leaves for good). Now and then he is startled to hear that settlers have paid out rather sizable amounts of money to be located on what he considers to be very unattractive land indeed, and the more such experiences are repeated, reports his sister, the more Fuller realizes just how well he has done by following her advice. "At last," she declares on a note of triumph, "he told someone that he thought it a wonder that I, a girl alone among strangers, had done so well—better than most of the men had done."

An unequivocal admission of this sort appears to be what Bess had been aiming for all along. But it by no means concludes the involvement of Fuller and other members of the Corey family with Bess's Dakota adventure. Fuller was succeeded by brother Challenge (what an ideal name for one taking up the Dakota gauntlet!), but Chall Corey's visit was even less auspicious than Fuller's, a good portion of his time in Stanley County being spent laid up in bed with a crushed leg suffered during a summer storm. Then came Rob, who did little more than pass through the territory and return home, eventually to purchase the home place from his mother. After much urging, Margaret Corey herself appeared in Stanley County, and while her visit seems to have transpired without bloodshed, we have no first-hand account of it for, apparently, she did not write letters home as the children did and so there were none to be saved. Bess had hoped that young Paul Corey might accompany his mother to visit her homestead, but he never did, probably because he was too young to be interested in such a trip; and after 1918 he was off to Atlantic to live and attend high school, the first of his family to advance so far in education.

Of all Bess's family visitors, only Ethel, her lone sister, appears to have had a truly good time. Probably this is because Ethel traveled in the most favorable season of the year and, more so, because she had no intention ever of becoming a homesteader but instead was bent on having a pure holiday for herself. As a result, she stayed on and on, delaying her departure date, remaining continually on the move, draining the most from the experience and loving every exciting moment of it.

As for Fuller, after Bess had handled the rental of his acreage for a time, acting as his "agent" (an unsatisfactory process for her to manage while teaching hither and yon), she purchased his claim outright from him. As seen in the sketch, that gave her 320 acres with an over-

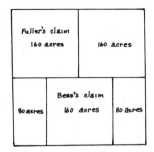

lapping boundary which in a sense made it all a single tract. Brother and sister never lost track of each other, but one of the final salvos in their continuing skirmish comes when she hears from her mother in 1915 that he is having a rough time finding himself. "Poor old [Fuller]," she responds. "I should like to see him settle some where where he would not be much exposed to the elements or have heavy physical labor exacted of him. I'm afraid he was not born to lead." The final twist of the knife.

❋ Ralph Waldo Emerson described the communicative process as bringing together one person who burns to tell the new fact and another who burns to hear it. He could have had Elizabeth Corey in mind because in her letters the ideal writer was joined with the ideal readers. Prior to her western emigration she had put in at least four years of apprenticeship as a letter writer to her family, but the subject matter for which she was born and that would set her epistolary talent ablaze did not appear until she stepped down onto the soil of Stanley County, South Dakota, in 1909.

At that moment, the perfect writer—this irrepressible, inexhaustibly enthusiastic farm girl off on her first great adventure in the wide, wide world beyond the borders of her home parish—was joined with her audience nonpareil, the folks back home: "Ma, and the rest." Bess could not wait to express the land and the life she had found waiting for her at the end of the railroad track. For their part, the family at supper time cast furtive glances at the waiting envelope but stifled their natural curiosity until the meal was done; then they hung on their sister's every sentence as her most recent letter was read aloud by their mother.

Once off the train and immersed in this radically new and raw society of homesteaders, Bess Corey wrote home compulsively, a driven woman striving against all odds to cram into her pages every outrageous fact, every grotesque incident, every colorful locution. And still her family cried for more, leading her to protest that not *every* moment of her life could be spent pencil in hand. The sheer impossibility of her task was self-evident, of course. But are not all writers who face a subject that looms larger than life doomed from the start? A pair of expressions from Bess's early letters from Dakota say it all, in that regard: "I dont know where to begin" and "If I had been where I could get letters mailed I would have written one this size about three times a week but now I've forgotten dozens of things I meant to tell you."

The personality glowing through Bess's letters is one with the liveliest of interests in the English tongue, especially in the living, breathing quality of the vernacular. In her very first reports from west of the river (I have said that Bess utilized even her hour or so "between trains" in Midland to rush a letter into the mail) she bombarded the family with the lingo of the region, newly encountered. The Coreys are reminded that what they know at home to be a parasol is called out West a "sunstick," while a country inn becomes a "road ranch." As her pages flow on, she tells of "wranglers" and "claims" and "relinquishments." The distinction between "break" (as in "breaking sod") and "brake" (as in "Cheyenne River brakes") is pointed out. The family in Marne soon know what is meant by "proving up" on a claim, what a "soddy" might be, and that a reference to "gumbo snatchers" leans not only on the homesteaders who have encroached upon the open range but refers also to the tenacious clay soil beneath their boots.

The language of the letters is refreshingly colloquial, while jaunts into local slang become not embarrassments so much as pleasure trips. A reader soon becomes accustomed to—even begins to anticipate—contemporaneous phrases such as "hunkey dory" (okay) and "going to roost" or "hit the perch" (retiring for the night). If a compliment is intended, the word of the moment is "gimsizzer," sometimes twisted into "gimsnuffer" ("a gimsnuffer of a good time"). Many a knowing smile must have passed from face to face around the Corey supper table as passages were read aloud by a mother who could scarcely guess what her exuberant daughter might write next: "Wages is so dratted scarce, in this homely man's country you have to work like sixty for your board [to] say nothing of wages. I am Queen of the kitchen or chief cook and bottle washer or what ever you wish to call it. She wanted me for a year but I didn't say much for she has the name of being the worst crank in the two cities and seldom keeps a girl long—they mostly leave. Caroline says the Mrs is a little afraid of me for she has actually begged my pardon after giving me a roasting." Here, each of Bess Corey's siblings must have recognized their absent sister's inimitable and uninhibited voice in the act of *speaking* to each of them, separately as well as collectively. A monologue such as that quoted above would bring Bess directly into the kitchen to join the circle around the table; the family, for the moment, would be complete once again. For this was the big sister they all knew so well, and her written words must have borne the very accent and timbre of her voice across the distance separating her from them. To hear Bess announcing that Rob Corey, should he dare to come out to Stanley County, would be back home "in a week with all the starch taken out of him" and compound the damage by predicting that "he would look worse than a much chewed dishrag by the time he got back" must have made brother Chall, for instance, giggle as he gave his tablemate Olney a dig in the ribs with an elbow. Aside from her intuitive awareness that the minutiae of everyday living do not merely record life but actually constitute it, one great secret of Bess's letters is that her language retains every earmark of the spoken tongue. Even when calculated, it never smells of the lamp. Were she living in a later era and mailing tape recordings to Marne, one cannot imagine her voice altering by a single iota.

To be out West, far away, alone and altogether on her own, had its scary aspects, no doubt about it. Bess battled these as did the boy who whistled while passing the graveyard; she kept extremely busy and she maintained her saving sense of humor. That ability to discern the comic spills over into every report from Stanley County. The Locke Hotel, where Bess worked prior to filing her claim, may have been the newest and grandest establishment in all the northwest (*it* surely thought itself to be), but Bess rapidly deflates its ego by disclosing that it has no immunity from that ubiquitous scourge, the bedbug. She had met these pests all along her route. At the grand Hotel Dakota in Sioux Falls, the "big bugs" of the town appeared ready to contest her "claim to the room," she says, but these bugs at the Locke could be called—well, the only suitable word for them was "fierce," the term which was rapidly becoming Bess's cliché of the moment to describe anything truly outrageous. At the Locke, it seemed to Bess that every "big bug" in Pierre had congregated in her room, and her mock account of their onslaught becomes the reader's introduction to her capacity for full-throated laughter that must have had a literary birth in books such as the copy of Mark Twain's *Roughing It* which was kept in the family bookcase in Marne: "They have tossed all the pillows in the middle of my bed and are roosting about on them singing songs. At present they are singing 'There'll be a Hot Time in The Old Town Tonight.'"

The tradition of the tall tale must also lie behind Bess's description of a "greenhorn" backtracking from Stanley County after being repulsed by heat and desert, thorn and rattler: "The last I saw of him he was headed southeast and going over the hills in a way that had snapped the last button of[f] his coat tail and the tears of homesickness and discouragement he shed have caused the Missouri to rise to such a highth that the inhabitants of several small towns have taken to the hills." Bess's fondness for the tall tale (which we remember as emerging from the oral tradition) is exceeded only by her adoration of the pun. She truly loved a good pun—or a "bad" one. Moving in as a boarder with the Stone family and dubbing their brood the "little pebbles" provided her with endless opportunities for spinoff jokes, as when she explains why she has moved for privacy into the abandoned shack on the Stone claim. It is because "the four little pebbles bump together a good deal and that makes quite a noise." She could be totally shameless in her punning. How does a Dakota cowboy propose marriage? He rides up to the door of the young lovely he fancies, yanks out his six-shooter, and declares, "Wilt thou?" Then he watches as she wilts! Bess knew that her family of growing brothers would happily split their sides over such hilarious plays on words, and every evidence we have of the Corey boys—who differ not at all from boys in general—would indicate that her aim was directly on target.

The first decade of the twentieth century was not a time when any well-bred young lady used "cuss words" lightly, but to pun on them apparently was permissible, and Bess Corey found the current surrogates for "damn" to hold a particular thrill. She is daring enough on one occasion to fabricate (or repeat) the tale of a land-seeker who is told he cannot get a drink to slake his mounting thirst during an extended scouting expedition "till we get to Millers dam." After arduous travel the party reach the dam—on a smelly bank of clay and manure and brush, inhabited by a flock of ducks. By this time the poor land-seeker is desperate enough to gulp down half a pailful of swill and to pronounce it "the darndest dam water he ever drank."

Even on the free-and-easy frontier it was considered outside the pale to speak candidly in polite society of a host of intimate matters.

Paul Corey has called attention to the multitude of euphemisms current among his family members, and his sister's letters, as one might expect, are sprinkled generously with them. An example is the term "little mansion," which sooner or later a reader recognizes as a genteel substitute for privy or backhouse or—a term Bess employs elsewhere—outbuilding. Menstruation being as taboo as defecation, so far as language is concerned, Bess substitutes the verb "to celebrate," variously rendered, as in its nominative form, "my July celebration" (not to be confused, surely, with her Fourth of July celebration). A lady's more intimate garments, whether considered as fancy lingerie or plain underpants, came under the same censure. The new term "bloomer" might be an allowable exception to the interdiction, but Bess uses the locution "neither tackle" (sometimes rendered as "nether tackle") apparently to designate everything from nightgown to panty. To "commit sideways" (suicide) and to "offer up" (vomit) provide softened linguistic approaches to other painful topics.

"Am studying Art very diligently," writes Bess in 1910, and "the lessons are few and far between but well studied. Took another lesson Friday evening." It helped her family to know that "Art" in this instance was Art Scripter, a bachelor neighbor. The pun on her beau's name is a typical example of Bess's use of her various suitors (who at times could be pretty mind-boggling) as the butt of her jokes. Possibly this tendency owes something to her mother's inordinate interest in Bess's love life, a prying sort of curiosity which potentially could be diminished by her daughter's surface tendency to make light of the men in her life. Whatever the explanation, humor more often than not is tied in with courtship, as in the jest concerning one of her first beaus, Adolph Buchholz (a jest via which Bess also takes cognizance of her presence in Sioux territory): "Adolph is Bohemian and if any one ever says any thing against my Bohemian lad they'll find 'Big Squaw heap fight.'"

To mingle humor with ethnicity reflects the reality of the South Dakota homesteading population, where ethnic groups like the Bohemians mingled with the general crowd to a greater degree than was happening in the settled and comparatively homogeneous farm population of western Iowa. Bess was ever conscious of ethnic strains, even when they were British Isle in origin, as when she presupposes that her English heritage is destined to tangle wickedly with the Irish background of her neighbor Oscar Walton. She regularly refers to Oscar as the "goosekicked Irishman" and relishes parodying his Irish locutions, as in his tribute to the fine taste of her green-tomato dish cooked with mustard and vinegar: "Lickin' good—go fine with praties."

To the high plains came many Danes, as well as Swedes and other Scandinavians ("Scandihooligans" Bess calls them, using the lingo of the time), and even more numerous were immigrant Germans (whom she invariably refers to as "dutchmen"). To banter such terms places Bess comfortably within the social context of her time—the age, for instance, of the coon song and an era when ethnic humor ran riot on the vaudeville stage. Jokes at the expense of ethnic groups were by no means confined to the theater, of course, and Bess Corey loses few opportunities for passing nuggets on to her family where that type of humor must have been as popular as it was elsewhere in the land. She loved the Dutch dialect postcards of the day; one which described a skinflint as "long mit luf un short mit money" made her think of Fuller.

Because so many of Bess Corey's suitors emerged from ethnic backgrounds and because humor had become a hallmark of her reports on the courtship aspect of her personal life, the reader regularly comes upon imitations of first-generation English speech. More often than not, a result of the makeup of the population, these parodies concern Germans, in her words "Dose By Yinks Dutchmen." One such Dutchman, Daddy Krug, drives his private automobile all the way from Fulton, S.D., just in order to visit Bess and press his case. Following his brief stay, Bess, who has deliberately been less than her usual hospitable self, guesses the fellow will not return, confessing to her family in Marne that she *hopes* he will not come again, because "if troubles neffer come single for why should I get married?"

A rather important question can evolve quite naturally from such a remark: Why *did* Bess Corey remain single? There is no easy answer here; certainly there is none that stands out with any clarity in her letters. Invariably, she suggests, the eligible men who courted her were considerably older than she and/or were widowers in search of a stepmother for their brood of youngsters. She wanted none of this, possessing a sufficient brood already in her annual replenishment of pupils at school. But why she never married when on every hand the members of her crowd of young single people were succumbing to matrimony must remain a puzzle for the reader to determine. It is as much a puzzle as is the reason why, so early on, she elected to close her letters with the distinctive signature *Bachelor Bess*.

✱ A NOTE ON THE EDITING

To come upon this cache of letters, cold, in their original form at the South Dakota Historical Society, and there to turn the newfound pages one by one, never anticipating or being able even to guess at what might be said—or how it might be expressed—has been a unique and often a thrilling experience. To ease an original Bess Corey letter from an envelope where it may have lain undisturbed for seventy years (because not all of her letters proved to be in the safekeeping of the archivists in Pierre) provoked even more intense excitement.

One could never predict what might tumble out from between these brittling pages as they unfolded. Bess was fond of making enclosures: snapshots of Dakota taken with her dead brother Olney's box camera and contact-printed under the glaring sun of her homestead yard; newspaper clippings that her brothers might enjoy or profit from; a scrap scissored from a length of gingham that will give her family a better sense of the dress she is sewing; a silk ribbon she has worn pinned to her "waist" (that era's term for a woman's blouse) at a professional event; or ribbons that she has presented to her pupils—blue for boys, pink for girls—to mark their mutual farewells as a successful school year draws to a close.

To duplicate that inimitable appeal connected with a hands-on examination of the original documents is an impossible dream, admittedly. Nevertheless, it has remained my guiding principle in editing Bess's letters, and it has governed my attempt to translate them into print in a manner that might suggest as highly as possible the excitement inherent in touching, fingering, turning the manuscripts themselves. That ideal has been kept in mind even while striving for that close-as-possible approximation to the act of reading the holograph letters, those hundreds of pages of handwriting which, one understands, can represent no more than a fraction of the immense number of letters Bess actually mailed from South Dakota to acquaintances, friends, and family in states to the east.

In making this attempt, foredoomed as it must be, I have found it helpful to keep in mind certain facts concerning the letters and their author. For one thing, the sequence was initiated by an individual of twenty-one years who was raised on an Iowa farm remote from centers of population and quite unaware (through any type of firsthand experience) of the broad geographical world whose bewildering diversity spread in every direction beyond the formal boundaries of Clay Township. Elizabeth Corey's first years of formal education were restricted to attendance at a rural grammar school at the crossroads opposite her family farm, a schoolhouse not so very different from those in which she herself later presided as schoolma'am. On top of this frugal schooling was spread a layer of "frosting," a ninth-grade year in the public school at Walnut, a small town about seven miles from Corey farm. That extra year was mandatory for a teacher, in order that one holding a teaching permit might be said to possess more education than the pupils one taught.

Elizabeth thirsted for education. She remained acutely aware of her inadequacies, although her apprehensions were calmed to a degree when she was told by two of her "higher up" friends in the world of education, Minnie Ashton and Grace Reed, that, paltry as her background might appear to her, what truly mattered was not the schooling that she didn't possess but rather the ingenious, inventive manner in which she was able to make use of the training that she did have. Elizabeth's teaching in Iowa country schools from 1905 to 1909 inevitably contributed its bit to her learning process, but nine years was the sum total of her schooling when she came to Stanley County. Despite her mother's having been a schoolteacher before her marriage to Edwin Corey, the farm was not a spot where schooling was pushed with great effort, and this makes all the more remarkable Bess's control of vocabulary (really quite sophisticated) and expression (highly varied).

I like to remember also that fully one-half of Bess Corey's homesteading letters were composed within her first three years of residence in South Dakota. Those were the years of greatest discovery and highest motivation. Although the great majority of her envelopes are postmarked Fort Pierre, that is happenstance. The letters were com-

Main Street in Fort Pierre, ca. 1902, showing Fischer Brothers supply store (center) and the Range Mercantile Co. (left). The first automobile (lower right) had been brought to town, and the basement for the city's most imposing structure, the Stock Growers Bank, was being excavated at the corner of Main and Deadwood streets (lower left). Photo courtesy Bud Gould.

posed in the various localities where Bess happened to be living or visiting or teaching, in hamlets such as Lindsay and Hayes, in hope-to-be towns up and down Bad River such as Wendte and Teton and Van Metre. She scribbled in her claim shack, at a neighbor's homestead, in her schoolhouse of the moment. Then her letters were carried by a friend or a Northwestern Railway train into Fort Pierre for official stamping.

Elizabeth wrote her letters to Marne not only from scores of localities but also under a wide variety of circumstances, some propitious, some not, and each writing situation tended to affect her manuscript in its own way. There came peaceful moments when Bess gained the luxury of writing at comparative leisure, using pen and ink and (when a perceptive friend might send her a box for Christmas) a fine linenized stationery. She relished suitable equipment and high-quality supplies. Letters produced in this context tend to be at wide variance with others: the handwriting is more controlled, spelling and punctuation conform more rigorously to standard modes, the entire aspect of the page is more orderly, neater all around.

At other moments, perhaps the majority, Bess wrote under the constraints placed upon her by a daily life already jampacked with activity; she continually regrets the necessity for having too many irons in the fire, and then she adds another. Sometimes she began—or completed—a letter while propped in bed (perhaps to keep warm) and wielding a pencil. Her stationery was whatever might lie conveniently at hand and it rested on her knees. In such a position, it was next to impossible to write well, or even as legibly as one might wish. Good-naturedly but with tongue deep in cheek, she commented in 1910: "This is great writing but I'm on the bed."

Bess's concern is indicated in numerous such references to the handicaps under which she was compelled to write. As an example, while boarding with the Stones and "busy most every minute," she still would not neglect her precious correspondence even though, in a tiny, crowded claim shack, conditions could be very far south of perfect indeed. One day she baby-sat the pebbles, who played actively around the table where she attempted to write, causing it to "fairly dance" beneath her page. They became such an annoyance that Bess was driven to promising each pebble a penny if only the group would play in the other end of the shack. Even then, she reported, impatient Ruth would jostle her elbow every other minute "and want to know *when* I was going to give her that nickel." When Mae Stone came home and asked what little Ruth was doing with money in her fist, the child was quick to exculpate herself by exclaiming that she had earned it "for jogging the table when Miss Corey was writing."

Moments arrived when letter writing was so compulsive that to keep up with it Bess stole time from the job. She records a morning in March 1910 when her pupil Myrtle Stone arrives with a handful of mail, school director Oscar Walton having ridden into Fort Pierre to fetch it. Bess pitches in at once, not only reading but composing replies as well, and she has already completed two letters when out of the blue, unannounced, her county superintendent appears on a surprise school-evaluation visit.

To Bess, letter writing was less a hobby and more a secondary occupation, and both the arrival and departure of the mail were likely to be events of magnitude. On February 27, 1910, the winter doldrums were relieved for her by receipt of a packet, her first mail delivery in ten days; it contained nine letters and four postcards. Birthdays, far from home and friends, were always emotional times for her, especially during her first years on Bad River. Following her first birthday as a homesteader, Bess was delighted to receive ten birthday cards as well as a pair of good letters. However, mail could be a fine surprise whatever the time of year, and in July, a year after Bess's arrival in Midland, Grant Stone, just back from Fort Pierre, dropped by to deliver a note from her institute roommate, Miss Kempton, a letter from her grandmother, and cards from her mother and Mary Lanigan, her schoolteacher friend in Marne. "How I did laugh over Mary's card!" Bess wrote home. "It is a picture of a scrawny dog with corkscrew curls and a big bow of ribbon and says 'I guess I'll be a darned old maid.'"

The reception of such bundles of mail implies the reciprocal expenditure of much time and effort and attention, and Bess was "kept hopping" composing timely replies to the goodly number of people with whom she was determined to maintain contact. In this context it is understandable that she might face bewilderment deep enough to declare: "I just get so mixed [up] on who I owe letters and who I don't owe letters [that] I hardly know where I'm at." The process also meant a continuing expense; it was a drain on her meager resources but one which she considered to be indispensable. By the end of her ninth month on Bad River she had spent nearly five dollars on stamps alone. Considering that it then cost two cents to mail a letter (*any* letter, evidently, for some of Bess's envelopes were stuffed rather heavily), that cost could mean that perhaps 250 letters may have left Fort Pierre carrying her return address. And since Bess was inordinately fond of sending penny postcards, her total pieces of outgoing mail might well have exceeded that number.

As any proud worker might do, Bess gave considerable thought to the tools of her trade. She liked good paper, and plenty of it. This was known to her friends, who found her an easy person to shop for. "Tell [brother] Paul that old Santa remembered me out here too," she told the folks at home after her 1912 Christmas. "Received a box of linen stationery. He said he would rather have given me a ribbon but thot there was more chance of my using the stationery." Bess also was more than willing to exert herself for the sake of her paper. Following the end-of-school picnic held for pupils, parents, neighbors, and friends in 1912, she had something to boast of: "By the way, have you noticed my new stationery? Look at it close now for it is the prize I won. On the bottom of the box it says 'Winner of 100 yard dash' and I wish to state that I won it fairly and squarely."

When the only available stationery was unsuitable, Bess wrote nonetheless—but apologized. "This paper is dreadful," she confessed to her mother from the Newlins' shack in 1915, "but it's all I have here." "A couple of pounds" of good stationery were waiting in a box of freight in Van Metre, but with Bad River then going into spring flood stage, Bess had no idea when she might be able to drive in to the railroad depot and fetch it home. If she were scribbling a fast note as she waited in the morning for her pupils to congregate at the schoolhouse, Bess might have to set down her words on a sheet yanked out of a ruled tablet of pulp: pure scratch paper.

Understandably, in these letters the informality of her approach rises dramatically. The handwriting itself has a greater tendency to sprawl and less attention is paid to the niceties of epistolary form. Many a letter was completed, or had to be broken off abruptly, while a neighbor paused at her door in his trek to the post office in Fort Pierre. Then the irrepressible flow of recent events gushed so furiously that she could not keep up with it, so she might remark that she had four hundred items to tell about, and no time, and leave it at that. Bess's hurried letters, her odd-moment letters, far outnumber letters composed at leisure, and in them the pressure of time is evident in her lack of attention paid to details of spelling, sentence structure, and punctuation. Her use of the dash, for instance, seems to expand geometrically in such notes. However, in their original forms, all Elizabeth Corey's letters are perfectly readable and present remarkably few problems so far as communication is concerned. Whatever difficulties exist are occasional.

Those occasional difficulties are, of course, the target of what editing I have done in order to enhance the presentation of the letters in this edition. In attempting to preserve as much as possible the overall flavor of the letters, I have resisted most temptations to regularize the prose: one might better attempt to contain Old Faithful in a standpipe! Where I have deviated from the holograph text, I have compelled myself to come up with a very good reason indeed, one that I could accept even while playing devil's advocate. Here I have kept before me another principle emerging from the letters themselves: it is the knowledge that, whenever (even on the subconscious level—perhaps chiefly there) communication was pitted against correctness, Bess invariably went for the former. To state it another way: arriving at a point of decision between matter and manner, Elizabeth automatically swung toward a concentration on matter, leaving her method to grope its own way home as best it could.

In most every case, then, my "acceptable" reason for tampering has concerned the issue of clarity. When trapped between the choice of presenting Bess Corey's language precisely as laid down and making an alteration in order to present it in a manner that will not mislead, confuse, or puzzle the reader, I have sometimes opted for that alteration. But in so doing, I have made every effort to keep my emendations to a minimum.

In a relatively small number of cases, I have added words (always penned securely into restraining brackets). This has occurred only when I felt, as on occasion I convinced myself I did, that their omission would create doubt as to Bess's intended message. Ambiguity is the enemy here.

No writer is without her unique problems, and one problem here is that the Corey vocabulary is away out in front and running ahead of Bess's ability to keep up with it in the technical sense. Considered aside from spelling, the vocabulary is actually rather sophisticated, as demonstrated by a few of the less-than-commonplace terms whose spelling Bess has mastered: *appendicitis, accusation, assertion, Chautauqua, embroidery, extravagant, prejudice, relinquishment, separate, solemn, souvenir,* and *succeeded.* She refers often to her writing paper, as we know, and invariably distinguishes *stationery* from *stationary,* not the mark of a neophyte orthographer.

On the other hand, in reading Bess's letters one encounters all too many misspellings that suggest ingrained habit and remain consistently at variance with standard practice, private demons such as these: *buisness, broght, cloke, complement* (intending *compliment*), *culander, desided, desireable, differance, discription, excursionests, gasolene, haveing, highth, inhabitents, lariet, milage, patchs, poney, turpentin, warrent.*

The greater share of Bess Corey's spelling difficulties combine into rather simple categories. She has problems in adding suffixes to words ending in vowels (*oweing, nerveous*); with the doubling of consonants (*atic, bussy*); with past tenses (*payed*); with homonyms (*to, too*); with two-word compounds (*hence forth, some where*); and with consistency (water may *freeze* or *frieze*). Bess learned as she went along. As she begins her South Dakota adventure she writes of visiting *Souix Falls,* but soon she adopts the accepted *Sioux Falls.* Similarly,

Hayse evolves into the proper *Hayes, Kleman* into *Klemann.* She was by no means intractable. In spelling as in other areas, life was a learning process.

Because of her considerable number of inconsistencies (*I've ate* and *I've eaten* can appear almost side by side in a letter), I have concluded that Bess, when faced with an empty page of stationery, focused her attention 100 percent on her message. She speaks onto her page, and this is one of the charming aspects of her prose. But she is apt to speak with an utter disregard for ordinary formalities such as the periods which traditionally follow the abbreviations *Mr.* and *Mrs.* At other moments the apostrophe and the question mark would appear to be undiscovered territory for her.

What should be the editorial approach to these idiosyncracies of style, these "differences" which both characterize Bess Corey's prose and, too often, impede it? I have adopted the practice, in most instances, of ignoring the discrepancy, of *not* making silent corrections. I have done this in order to preserve, so far as possible, the unique quality of the prose. On the other hand, the omission of the period that ordinarily closes an abbreviation is a simpler matter to overlook than is the omission of the period that marks the close of a sentence. When this omission occurs, and when the felony is compounded by a failure to provide the capital letter that usually alerts a reader to a new thought or a change of subject, then confusion is predictable. It is in such instances that I have found myself to be most willing to adjust the Corey prose in order to forestall misunderstanding and reduce ambiguity. To achieve division between sentences and to punctuate analogous situations, I have added (always within brackets) commas, semicolons, and periods whenever I felt them to be indispensable to an unimpeded reading of the letters.

For similar purposes, I have used bracketed additions and notations in other instances as well: to correct obvious omission of letters or words; to call attention to errors of fact or intention; to clarify misspellings that will create problems for the reader if not dealt with; to complete pairs of dashes; to make further identification of persons for whom only initials are provided; and to regularize certain lapses in punctuation that raise questions of intent.

If the reading of Bess Corey's letters is facilitated and not impeded by such editorial intrusions, then my objective will have been achieved.

✱ BACHELOR BESS

✳ ELIZABETH COREY'S

HOMESTEADING LETTERS

WRITTEN FROM

STANLEY COUNTY,

SOUTH DAKOTA

Feeling somewhat superfluous in her own family and wishing to broaden her horizons, Elizabeth Corey made plans to leave Iowa and lay claim to free government lands in west-central South Dakota. She and Lida Smith, a friend and fellow schoolteacher from Harlan, Iowa, plotted a trip which would take them to South Dakota via the newly installed Northwestern Railway. At the time they set out, their ultimate goal was Scarborough Ranch, northwest of Fort Pierre and beyond Sansarc, in the former Indian lands recently opened for settlement. Lida was related to the Scarboroughs, who assured the girls of help in locating land to claim under the Homestead Act.

✳ 5:30 A. M. / JUNE 1, 1909 / HARLAN, IOWA
TO MRS. M. M. COREY

Dear Ma,—We reached here on the 1:08 Saturday afternoon and while resting before our trip up town we planned o[u]r longer trip. Lida's [1] mother was to have written to her sister a week ago telling when we would be at Sansarc [2] but she didn't. She gave no reason[,] only laughed and said she made up her mind she wouldnt. I didn't say anything—in fact Lida didn't leave any thing for me to say if I had wanted to. If the letter had been sent as had been arranged we could have left on the 9:07 train Sunday and caught the Tuesday stage but as it was they wrote at once and we had to wait till this (Tuesday) morning. We will take the 9:07 to Manning[,] change for Manila[,] change again—go from there to Souix City then to Huron S. D. then to Pierre then to Midland then by stage to Hayes they [sic] by Mail to Sansarc then Uncle [sic] Nora will meet us and take us the rest of the way. We wont get there till Thursday evening. If for any reason you wish to write befor you hear from me again *address at Lindsay,*[3] *S. D. c/o Nora Scarborough.*[4]

Have been very busy while here[,] have mended my cravanet, put shields in my coat and various other little things. It has rained several times quite hard but I attended the Memorial Sermon Sunday evening[5] and the Bacalaurate Sermon[6] Sunday evening. I was up town yestering [sic] afternoon—just caught a glimpse of George[7] as we were driving pretty fast[.] Lida talked to him last evening over the phone. Lida had a date with Art for the evening & G[eorge] said to come up town and have ice cream with him but I declined. He said he would be at the train to see us off.

Must close
Bess

*** JUNE 3, 1909 / MIDLAND, S.D.[1]
TO MRS. M. M. COREY**

Dear Ma and the rest,—Will try and give you the history of the trip so far, as we have to wait here for the stage. Say but the connection between Harlan and Midland are bum!! I told you before, I believe, how Mrs Smith failed to send the message agreed upon so we had to start Tuesday morning. We were at the depot befor 8:30 and the train didn't leave till 9:07. We hadnt been there long befor George [Stewart] came, then Arthur, then Louie Wilcox. Louie brought us a dainty but substantial lunch and the boys talked till train time then they took our baggage aboard[,] bid us good bye and urged us to write so we got a pretty good start.

At Manning we purchased tickets through to Souix Falls then went up town to spend the rest of the time between 9:55 and 12:42.

*The Chicago & Northwestern Railway depot at Midland, S.D., where
Elizabeth Corey ended her rail journey from Iowa in June 1909. Photo
courtesy Midland Pioneer Museum.*

We got back in time to eat our lunch befor starting. It rained quite
hard between Manning and Manilla and a good deal after we changed
cars at Manilla. We got through to Souix Falls at 8:25 and took the
hack to the Hotel Dakotah where we took a room for the night. Swell
place that!! Touch the button once for an errand boy, twice for ice
water, three times for hot water and so on. We retired at once but I
soon found that some of the "big bugs" of Souix Falls were ready to
contest our claim to the room. Lida seemed to get along with them
pretty well but they tried to put me out and war ensued in which I
received many wounds and committed one murder in self defense—I
got off easy as those fellows are personal enemies of the judge. I only
got about two hours good sleep that night. Yesterday morning we went
up town to see the city and purchase a few cards then went down to
the river to watch the falls a while. We took the 11:15 a.m. train to
Salem where we waited till 5:30 p.m. then to Huron where we waited
from 8 something till 9:20 p.m. then through to Midland and got here
at 3:25 a.m. and had to wait at the depot till 5:30 a.m. when we came

up to the hotel,[2] from here we take the stage at 1 or 1:30 p.m. for a 28 mile trip to Hayse.

The night agent here has a claim[3] up that way which he has proved up[4] and he kindly told us a great deal about the country. He came here from Iowa three years ago. While he has been here Midland has grown from one store and three or four houses to a town of three or four hundred inhabitents[.] Lida took possession of the sofa [in the lobby] and has slept all forenoon. I thought I would take a room and sleep this forenoon as I've had scarcely two hours sleep either of the last two nights but when I found it was 75¢ for a bed I decided to write a letter and keep awake the best I could. Its quite a hard trip and as I can hardly afford postcards and it isnt very comfortable writing guess I'll wait till I get some where[.]

Good bye for now[.]

Elizabeth F Corey

The rains have been heavy about here[,] the Missouri was high and the Cheyenne nearly took her R R bridge out last evening settling the middle pilings several inches[.]

* JUNE 6, 1909 / LINDSAY, S.D.
  TO MRS. MARGARET COREY

Dear Ma,—Well this is Sunday evening and the rest are talking politics (?) so I thought I'd try and write a bit—don't know where to begin—am afraid I may tell you the same thing over five times before I get through with it.

We reached here late yesterday P.M. after a hard trip and the worst connections that were ever made I believe.

You see where the mistake was made[—]we should have taken the Northwestern straight through from Harlan to Midland but I thought Lida knew best so went to Manning then to Manilla then to Souix Falls where we staid all night then to Salem S.D. where we spent the afternoon then through to Huron then to Midland[.] We got there a little after three in the morning and left there by stage at about twenty minutes of two. The stage proved to be a lumber wagon drawn by a team of bronchos. There was the stage driver, a young Jew and we two girls beside about half a ton of mail and freight etc. It was twenty eight miles and we reached Hayes[1] at a quarter of eight. Oh! what a trip that was! Fortunately we could hold a parasol or "sunstick" as they call it here. It is generally too windy for that. One of us had to carry the sunstick and the other had to hold the lunch basket but Lida bumped my hat so much I carried the sunstick, and the basket too some of the time while Lida made a mash on the driver and when I objected to the basket Lida told what a crank I was till I couldn't have stood it if the "Wandering Jew" hadn't carried the sunstick for a few miles. and when we stopped at Phebe, the little store and Post office half way between Midland and Hayes [and] Lida and the driver got out to get fruit and pop and such the Jew looked disgusted and said something about anyone who would stop at a place like that. Oh Lida and I haven't disagreed more than about twenty seven or thirty times. You see Lida took a suitcase and a *great big* telescope beside sunstick and lunch basket. I didn't mind taking the two suitcases but I did hate to carry my suitcase and the telescope for they were the two heaviest of the whole push. But I had to some times. The Hayes Hotel is a one dollar a day house. We took a bath and went to bed. Our room was rather inhabited—we fastened a few up with pins on the wall [and] then we had more room. There was a big Hop at the hall in Hayes on Friday evening. The claim holders both men and women for miles around rode in and they had a fine time. People in a new country get acquainted rather quickly you know and in twenty four hours I found myself somewhat acquainted in Hayes even if I can't talk up to every man I see like Lida can. Yes I'll have to 'fess up I went to the dance. Mr C E Coyne[2] ask to take us and I wanted to be excused but Lida was crazy to go and the landlady said if she went I must go to[o] so we went. Mr Coyne is Irish. He is a Deputy sherif of this county[,] a real estate man[,] a notary public and is considered the finest young man in the county. He is medium height, well built, very handsome, I never saw a nicer appearing gentleman or received more polite attention. At twelve we returned to the hotel for supper and as midnight supper does not agree with Lida she asked to be excused and Mr Coyne excused her. Lida said as soon as we were out of sight "Darn him I believe he was glad to excuse me." We had a very dainty supper—sandwiches, pickles, coffee, icecream and cake. We talked about half an hour or so and then he wanted to go back to the [dance] hall and I asked to be excused. Well of course it was rather late when I turned in and the next morning Lida tried to kick me out at twenty minutes to five and I never succeeded in getting her out befor seven before.

We rode with the mailman from Hayes to Sansarc and started

Hayes, S.D., where Elizabeth Corey attended her first settlers' dance in June 1909. Photo courtesy Verendrye Museum.

out with the mailman to Kirley[3] but we were too much for his rig[—] it broke down before he could get out of town. We caught a ride with a couple of Danes and reached Kirley Tuesday about 12:30[.] I believe there was only one person there who had any idea where Scarboroughs lived and that was young Adams. He said if we would wait till he drove out home and got a different rig and team he would take us out to Scarboroughs. We told him we'd wait. We reached here about 5:30 I believe. That was Saturday and yesterday they rec'd the letter saying we were coming. They get their mail twice a week from Lindsay but sometimes it is possible to get letters mailed oftener.

Saturday evening I rode Russels brown poney a little while. There are three Scarborough children[—]Will who is about Fullers age, Russel who is Challs age and Ruth who is about four I guess.[4]

Sunday forenoon we spent in riding over the prairie. It is very high here with level patches which run off into brakes or rows of gullies[;] we are about four or five miles from Cheyenne River. The river is very high at present so we can't go fishing for a while yet. There are a few claims here but most are "covered." Guess we will uncover a few[.] And may soon be reckoned among the "soddies" or "Johnnie come latelys." Down at Hayes they call claim holders "Gumbo snatchers."[5] Sunday evening I rode Russels poney again. The stirups had been let out and when I got on my feet were about six inches above them and the first next thing I knew I was going over the prairie just a hooping. I pulled and pulled on the reins but might as well try to hold a cyclone. It seems that the poney is what they call a wrangler—one used to round up horses[—]and as soon as I hit the saddle the poney put out for an old gray horse over on the prairie and of course I went along. I didn't realize what was the matter till late in the evening. Fortunately the old gray ran up by the house after a time and Will caught the poney. He shortened the stirups and got me a whip. He said the pony needed a more severe bit but the folks would probably never hear to it till Russel had been ditched a few times or half killed or something. The rest of course all knew what ailed the pony and they laughed till they cried[.] Lida will have to tell every one she sees for a month o' Sundays. All Will said was "Darn my soul but you can stick on good." And in spite of all Lida says she hasn't the nerve to ride him herself if there is another horse in sight.

Yesterday we drove during the forenoon—didn't get back till about two o'clock. I burnt my face almost to a cinder. In the afternoon we hauled water from the spring and I cut Mr Scarborough's hair. It is raining today and we are all in the house. The house is a one room affair.

Will close for now. Perhaps I will get this mailed sometime soon[.]

Address.

Elizabeth F. Corey

Lindsay, S. D.

c/o T N Scarborough

Let Mary L——[6] read all of this and Jan and Valerie[7] all but a little—there's a little of it wouldn't interest them any way.

✳ JUNE 22, 1909 / PIERRE S.D.[1]
TO MRS. M. M. COREY

Dear Mamma,—It has been two weeks since I wrote you[.] I hope you have not worried about me. I will begin where I left off two weeks ago today[.]

The next day (Wed) Lida and Will rode over to look over the claim Lida had decided to take and I washed dishes, made beds and then started to make an apron Mrs Scarborough wanted made. When Lida came home I was sewing and Mrs S was in the garden. Lida took a notion to roast me and she kept it up untill I couldn't stand it any longer so I ran off across the prairie out of sight of the house way off down in the sage creek brakes. After a while Russel came down and tried to talk an arm off of me. He gave it up after a time and went back to the house and I went back to my fence corner. After a bit Will came down on horse back and told me it was dangerous to be on foot in the bull pasture which covers several thousand acres and sometimes contains several dozen wild range bulls and he said I must not go down sage creek[,] that a man who knew the country might get lost in the sage creek brakes[,] and he said I should not go any where without a snake stick or something to protect myself with as a "buzzer" might appear any minute[.] He talked, scolded, threatened and coaxed. He declared that he knew Lida had been up to something and he was bound to know what it was. He found out nothing except that she had called me "lazy." He said not to pay any attention to Lida[;] she was to darned old and set in her ways for any one to mind[;] he said when she got too much for me to tell her to go to the devil and then do as I pleased in spite of her. He said the storm was going to break soon and wanted me to ride back and let him walk. I wouldn't so he rode back one way and I walked back the other.

It rained in the afternoon so we played games—Russel and Ruth made us an awful time. The next day will killed a rattle snake out where I had been. There were four or five rattles and a button[.] I'm going to send them to Olney. A few days after that someone killed a small one up by the house. I've seen a good many but never heard one rattle or never saw one alive[,] am always just a little too late.

Will and Lida have an awful time all the time. Will is such a torment and it didn't take him long to find out that no matter how Lida treated me I would help her as soon as any one began to torment her and no matter how well I stood by her if any one would tease me she would help them[;] that disgusted Will and he has spent all his spare time since a teasing Lida and he knows how to too I'm here to tell you. He made her bawl once. As he says "Darn my soul if you can't get Sally Annie Waddles on her ear in no time[.]"

I uncovered a claim and the following Saturday Will took us to Hayes to file. Lida filed but when I came to file on the second choice I found that one of those long legged evil eyed monsters called men had beat me to the land office and got my claim so I was up against it. Lida was on a rampage all the way there and most the way back. She nearly drove us both crazy and she said thing[s] I wouldn't repeat to my own mother and Will who was raised in town could keep pace with her[.] He told me afterward he knew he had said thing[s] he wouldn't want anyone to say to his sister but Lida got to showing off with her plain talk and be —— if he'd be out done by her. He was so disgusted[,] once he said if she wasn't his own cousin he'd slap her old face good and he would yet if she didn't shut up and another time when she was acting so horrid he told her he bet she had lead mor[e] than one man astray. She kept it up till at last he got to teasing her and kept at it till he made her just bawl and then he kept it up till I jawed him a bit and told him he aught to be ashamed of him self.

Well after Lida got her claim Mr Scarborough shut up like a clam and I couldn't get a word out of him about a single claim and if it hadn't been for Will I don't know what I'd have done. He took me across the country t[w]o afternoons[;] once we drove ten or twelve miles one afternoon and about twenty another. I have two or three claims spotted but I have to look them up some though.

Yesterday (Monday) I came to Fort Pierre with some neighbors of Scarboroughs[;] they drove the whole distance (about sixty miles) in the one day. We reached Ft Pierre[2] about supper time. I took a room and this morning I looked about a bit[,] was offered a place at five dollars a week and board but couldn't begin till next week. So I came over to Pierre and found a place here at the Locke Hotel.[3] I don't know how I will like it. There is a Bankers Convention going on here and they are crowded. The regular chamber maids get twenty dollars per month but they take me as an extra for a few days at a dollar and a quarter a day then the manager's wife[4] spoke of wanting help for a few days at making up a batch of table linnen and then she said she thought she would want me as assistant cook at thirty a month. That is as good as fifty any where else as I get my board and time and place to do my own washing and ironing[.] This is a big house. Usually they keep three chamber maids busy from 7:30 A.M till 5 PM but now during the rush they have six. If I had been where I could get letters mailed I would have written one this size about three times a week but now I've forgotten dozens of things I meant to tell you.

Well I must close[,] address me at present

Elizabeth F Corey
Locke Hotel
Pierre,
S.D.

❋ JUNE 23, 1909 / LOCKE HOTEL / PIERRE, S.D.
TO MRS. M. M. COREY

Dear Ma,—Will start you another letter and write a little at a time just as I get a chance. I haven't a very good chance tonight as all the big bugs in town have gathered in my room it seems. They have tossed all the pillows in the middle of my bed and are roosting about on them singing songs. At present they are singing "There'll be a Hot Time In The Old Town Tonight." Guess they are blank right about it as Lida says[.] I didn't sleep much last night but fell into a sound sleep this morning and woke to hear the rain upon the roof and a boy screaming "Strawberries and cream for breakfast" through the key-hole. Oh goodness no! *We* don't have strawberries. Strawberries are for bankers[.] *We* go to the kitchen and get a plate and the cook gives us a spoonful of warmed over potatoes and a piece of meat then we go get a few slices of bread and some thing to drink, then we go to the servants hall and sit down to a table made of long pine boards and eat our breakfast with a tin spoon or fork which ever we prefer.

Breakfast over at seven then we go to work. I helped Anna Skudal, the first floor chamber maid[,] till three o'clock this afternoon then Mrs Twiss[1] sent me down to help the pastery cook. I helped in the kitchen from half after four till a quarter till eight.

This new work makes me feel stiff in the joints as Paul tells about so will close for now and go to roost—

Bess

JUNE 27, SUNDAY.

Well now look at me will you. I'm not where I was[,] I'm where I went to. Friday evening after supper the bell boy brought us five extra girls our wages and told us that Mrs Twiss said the rush was over and we were no longer needed. Oh the Locke works all kinds of schemes to get help during a rush and when the rush is over, good bye to you.

Well I packed my suitcase and put [out] for the boat house—one of the girls went clear down with me and I took the next boat for Ft Pierre—the river was very high and the wind was strong—the waves were several feet high and looked like soapsuds on top[.] the boats used here are run by gasoline engines and will carry thirty or fourty people. When the waves are high the boat moves like a horse on an easy gallop. Every one wore coats and the spray would hit my face every once in a while with force enough to startle one. Well I got accross alright—thats the fourth time. I went right to the Huston house.[2] Mrs Huston had no place for me so I phoned to Shannon House[3] and the Mrs said for me to come at once so I did[;] she gave me a room 7x7 ft. which fortunately contained but a single bed a commode and a

The Locke Hotel in Pierre, S.D., where Elizabeth Corey worked as a cook's helper while seeking a homestead in 1909. Robert Kolbe Dakota Collection.

chair so there is room for my suitcase and the door will open far enough to let me in easily so I'm all right though I have but one window and there is a wall about four feet from it so it lets in very little air or light. I was sick as de deuce the first nigh[t] I was here but am alright now and they don't have bugs[!] "Wages is so drated scarce," in this homely man's country you have to work like sixty for your board [to] say nothing of wages. I am Queen of the kitchen or chief cook and bottle washer or what ever you wish to call it. She wanted me for a year but I didn't say much for she has the name of being the worst crank in the two cities and seldom keeps a girl long—they mostly leave. Caroline [Hore] says the Mrs is a little afraid of me for she has actually begged my pardon after giving me a roasting[.]

Good Night.

Bess

JUNE 29, TUESDAY.

Well here we come again[,] some body head us off. Say[,] I have the worse luck. I'm not at the Shannon House now I'm at Mr Gordon's[.][4] Monday morning the Mrs put Caroline to work up

The Huston House, Fort Pierre, S.D., where Elizabeth Corey sought employment in 1909. Robert Kolbe Dakota Collection.

stairs and left the kitchen entirely to me. The blasted stove was all stuffed up so it wouldn't work so I had to get breakfast on the gass. [O]f course the orders came in fast. I had soft boiled eggs, eggs fried, steak and pancakes all at once but was getting on fine till the Mrs came in and *stood* there and jawed and threatened to turn off the gass entirely and said I should have been down at four o clock and cleaned the stove out. I told her to get out so I could work. [S]he said she would just stay right where she was[,] that I wasn't much if I got nervous that easy. After breakfast she was going to show me how to make pies her way. She was only going to have me use a ornery little teacup not full of grease for four large pies. Fortunately one of the girls came in just then and asked her something and as she turned I slid in a great big spoonfull of butter and she never knew the differance. After dinner she admitted to the girls that the dinner was fine "even the pies."

Caroline Hore[,] a middle aged woman who has been working there[,] said that I should not try to do alone what the Mrs would try to put on to me for she said no woman on earth could stand it and she said I would ruin my health and break down under such a strain. So after dinner Monday when the Mrs began to roast me about something

I hadn't done yet I told her that there was too much for one girl and she said "Well when you think there is more here than you can do just let me know. There was a girl in my office just now who could do all the work here quicker than scat so whenever you think there is more here than you can do just let me know and I'll get another girl." I turned on her and said, "There's more here than I can do and do well so get your other girl and get her quick.["] I thought for a minute she would faint. She started to tell me that it was a hard day, the first days always were the hardest[,] but I just reminded her of what she had said and repeated what I had said. She got angry and I pretty soon thought Avoca[5] had come to the surface in the middle of Ft Pierre. She came out soon afterward and said I might be dismissed. I packed up at once. She wouldn't pay me a cent[.] Well I went to the Huston House. Mrs Huston said she had seen Mrs Gordon's hired girl go by with her suit case and I better go down at once and see about the place. Mrs Gordon has been poorly for some time and was to have an operation preformed but was taken very ill so the operation had to be put off. She is better now but is waiting to get her strength up. her sister Mrs Nelson and the two Nelson children are here to stay till after Mrs Gordon return's from the hospital so she didn't need a hired girl but she said if I cared to come and help a bit for my board I was welcome to come and then after her sister was gone I could do all the work and she would pay me wages. I didn't know of any other place so I came down this morning. It will keep me from spending my money for board. I had an hour off this forenoon and nothing to do this afternoon.

It has been desperately warm these days 101° and 102° in the shade so they say. It is the coolest here of any place I've struck about here. The house is on the bank of the Missouri. When the water comes up good and high they just move out. The fence on the east side is quite close to the house—there is a buggy track just out side the fence and the river is high enough now so it comes almost to the track[.] I think I could eat cherries out under the trees here and spit the stones into the river. There are ever so many gasolene launches and large row boats tied up along here. I noticed one pretty launch when I went to throw a pail of slop into the river[;] it had the name "Johnny Welter"[6] painted on the side. I'm interested in Johnny these days *see*? There were two large steamboats on the river here last week that would hold several hundred people. They said that between four and five hundred people went from Pierre up to the islands picnicing one day last week while the other [steamboat] took a load out to the Buffalo Pasture[.][7] I would like to go out to the Buffalo Pasture some day[;] it must be great to see a hundred or more buffaloes feeding at once[.]

Will close for now[;] write me everything. at Ft Pierre

[Unsigned]

＊ JULY 5, 1909 / FT. PIERRE, S.D.
TO MRS. M. M. COREY

Dear Mamma,—Yours of the 3rd received just before dinner, was glad to hear from you—it is the first in several weeks—in fact the first since befor I left Scarboroughs.

You didn't say you were all well or how you were getting along but suppose as you didn't say any thing you must be *"fair to middlin'*[.]"

Yes I suppose I did have a chance to work for my board at home but you said you could get along better without me than with me and there wasn't room for us all to home and that I could make out better than the rest could so under the circumstances I think it behoves me better to stick it out here even if I do skip a few meals and work for my board sometimes than to be a burden on some one else. I think it kind of mean to kick a fellow when he's down, for Heaven knows I've seen trouble enough and know what it is to be out in the world among entire strangers without friends or home but I'll never give up till I drop. That last check I cashed for convenience when at Hayes and placed the money in the Ft Pierre Bank and now use a check book as that is the safest. I still have more than half the money I left home with and mean to keep enough ahead to go back to Iowa with if I'm ever sent for.

Mrs Gordon said Saturday evening she was going to start to pay me wages Monday (today)[.] I didn't ask how much but the work doesn't seem to be very hard—after Mrs Nelson and the children go, there will be just Mr & Mrs Gordon and myself to do for and there is no water to carry and the washing machine is run by water power.

Mrs Nelson says that though the fates seem against me now that "Its a long road that has no turning" and I'll have a run of luck some day to make up for it. I sure did hate to give up the Carlson place.[1] It

was in an ell shape like this 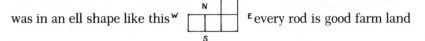 every rod is good farm land

Fort Pierre, S.D., in 1909. Robert Kolbe Dakota Collection.

and it beats your place all hollow in lots of ways and there was lumber enough on the place (except roofing) for a 10x12 house but $175 was too steep for me.

I got my coats back[.] Nieter was damaged in the least.[2] Mrs Nelson and I went to the Majestic Saturday night again and are going tomorrow evening. I have orders to buy no tickets.[3]

This morning we watched the steamboat, Rosebud,[4] start on her way from Pierre to Sioux Falls with a load of excursionest[s]. They went up bad River[5] a little way to get some who were staying at the Huston House so they passed within a stones throw of the house. The Missouri was the highest last evening it has been this season—in fact it was nearly to the fence. I was out to measure it. I put one foot at the bottom of the fence and swung the other out to see how far it would go over the water. Alice screamed till I had a notion to fall in but thought better of it.

You must tell Paul what happened to Ted E Bear.[6] A short time ago he got out and went up town. Some ornery cuss must have been waiting for him for he was back in less than twenty minutes and Mrs Gordon didn't know him and what's worse the poor little scamp didn't know himself. The head third of him was painted coal black the middle third was bright yellow and the tail third was of the brightest red. Ted

E would look around at him self and of all the shying and running you ever saw Ted E had reached the limit. They soaked him in turpentin and washed him through two or th[re]e waters. He looked pretty good then except his eyes but about that time the dope began to affect his skin and then he was a streak of double geared howl going about the place for most of a night and day. So tell Paul not to let Twigs[7] stray off to the neighbors any more.

As Ever—Bess

**✳ JULY 18, 1909 / FT. PIERRE, SO. DAK.
TO ROBERT L. COREY**

Dear Rob,—I was sure glad to hear from you—there see where Ted E. landed—he has been running out where they were watering the lawn and the silly little fool ran himself almost to death and when they tried to stop him he gave one jump and landed in the middle—see? Well to begin with where I went on from—I didnt expect to hear from any of you boys as mamma said you boys enjoyed my being so far away you couldnt hear me jaw and I didnt suppose you would risk a "jaw" letter. But you and your Uncle Dunlavy[1] are a credit to the family—I had a splendid letter from your uncle a few days ago. And by the way I've had two or three postals from a Harlan gentleman[;] the first one has, "Happy Recolections and Fair Greetings" in gilt letters and the last one has—

> "I hear th' swate smile of me darlin
> Win th' wind whispers soft thro th' vine;
> 'Tis a frame of grane leaves
> Filled wid memories sheaves
> Win I drame by that windy of mine.["]

He wrote almost a letter on each card.

I've lost a bunch of letters a few days ago. I can't find any trace of them so I dont know how in the world to answer them.

It has been beastly hot the past few days and Alice Nelson, Mrs Gordon's niece who is visiting here[,] has been having the rheumatism and I have to rub *Capsolin*[2] on her limbs and my right hand is almost blistered with it so it isn't very comfortable writing or anything else.

So you want to know about the land buisness do you[?] Well that will take a week, but here goes—When a man comes here to home-

Homesteaders and landmen in Stanley County, S.D., ca. 1900. Robert Kolbe Dakota Collection.

stead he picks out a piece of open land[,] goes to the government land office[,] describes the land[,] swear[s] he's taking it for a home and pays fourteen dollars filing fees, then within six months he builds a habitable house, digs a well, remains for fourteen months from the time he goes on, then he gets two neighbors to come to town with him and swear that he has been living on his place and improving it and he pays fifty cents an acre and then as soon as the patent[3] comes from Washington, D.C. the land is his. or if he stays five years from the time he first went on he can prove up without the fifty cents per acre. Now suppose a fellow named Tarbox comes up here and takes up a homestead and after he has been here six months his feet begin to get cold and suppose a fellow named Corey came through there to look at land and took a fancy to the piece that Tarbox has and you get Neighbor Gasspipe to take you over to see Tarbox and you say "Tarbox what'll you take for your relinquishment?"[4] and if Tarbox feet are awful cold he may say "You can have the whole works for seventy five dollars" and you say "Alright come on" and then Gasspipe will bring you and Tarbox to town and Tarbox will go to the Land Office and say the land wasnt what he thought it was and he would like to through it back to the government so he will be at liberty to file on another piece if he should want to at any time so he signs a paper to that effect and as Tarbox goes out one door you go in the other and file on the piece that

A U.S. Land Office, where homestead claims could be filed, need not be more substantial than the claim shacks of the settlers. Robert Kolbe Dakota Collection.

Tarbox relinquished, then Gaspipe will tell Jones that "Corey bought the Tarbox relinquishment[.]" Well now suppose that the day befor you saw Tarbox he sold twenty five bu. of early potatoes at two dollars per bu. and that warmed his feet a bit and when you asked him what he'd take he said a thousand dollars and you say "Thats too darn high," and come back to town and you meet a man and if he is a land man you wont know it and he says "Looking at land?" and you say "Yes" and he says, "what'd you see?["] and Gaspipe say[s] "Why Tarbox offers his relinquishment for a thousand but Corey thinks its too darn high." Well Mr Landman "contests" Tarbox claim. Tarbox testifies in court that he has been living on his place and improving it but Mr. Landman proves that Tarbox was speculating on his claim instead of keeping it for a home so Tarbox is beat. Now the man who contests has the first right to file on the place but Mr Landman already has more than a quarter section of land so he has no filing right so all he can do is hold it till the three months are up and then its open land again but in about a week Johnnie Clabermilk comes along and says

[to] Mr Landman "I want land what can you do for me?" and Mr Landman says "Why Johnnie I'll file you on the best claim on the Frozen Man [Creek] for seventy five dollars" and Johnnie files on the old Tarbox place and steps in Tarbox shoes and Tarbox ties what is left of the potatoe money up in his sock and starts back to Kansas[.]

Now while all this was going on Corey took the next train west but the heat of the sun is so intense that every rod of road must be inspected for fear of the rails being spread and the train ditched so its slow work. That evening he came to the roads end and went to the road ranch[5] for the night. In the morning he found that the bugs had gone off with his shoe strings. They left a note saying that he might use cord but they couldn't—that the strings were better than Dakota shoestrings and they needed them in their business. He started across the country and by nine o'clock was so thirsty he didn't know where he was at. He asked the driver where he could get a drink and the driver said "Not till we get to Millers dam" and he[,] Corey[,] says "Where's that[?]" The driver said, "bout five miles up the road." Well when they got to Millers dam Corey was *awful* thirsty. As they came down a little draw Corey saw a bank of clay and manure and brush and stuff and above this bank was a pool of water. On the water a flock of ducks were swimming. If they had reached the dam five miles sooner Corey would not have "cared for any" when it came to drinking but as it was he drank half a pail of it and pronounced it the darndest dam water he ever drank. As he started back to the wagon he heard a "buzzer"—it was the first he had ever heard but he knew what it was and jumped back—when he jumped back he landed in a large bunch of cacti [and] one or two of the thorns went though his shoe; in great misery he sat down on a large stone to draw out the thorns but as the stone had been out in the sun several days, he didn't sit long. The driver killed the snake and gave Corey the rattles. Corey said "What'll you take to drive straight through to Ft Pierre[?]" The driver said twenty five dollars and Corey said "go it." At Ft Pierre he paid the driver and after counting what money he had left he put it in his shoe and hit the pike for Iowa. The last I saw of him he was headed southeast and going over the hills in a way that had snapped the last button of[f] his coat tail and the tears of homesickness and discouragement he shed have caused the Missouri to rise to such a highth that the inhabitants of several small towns have taken to the hills.

Well I must close[;] hoping to hear all the news from home soon—

Sister Bess

✳ POSTCARD / AUGUST 10, 1909 / FORT PIERRE, S. D.
TO MRS. M. M. COREY

Dear Ma,—Don't bother about me—am getting along pretty well
and will write you a long letter when I find out for sure where I am at
if you want me to[.] Am glad you are doing so well with the work but
you don't say how *you* are feeling. I had five cards and three letters
last week. Had a card from G[eorge]. E. S[tewart]. just before he
started on his trip and one since[.] That makes two in less than a
week—going some? Aug 2nd was out in the country about fifteen
miles with a gentleman from Pierre[.][1] More later—hope to hear from
you soon—E. F. C.

✳ AUG. 14, 1909 / FORT PIERRE, S. DAK.
TO MRS. M. M. COREY

Dear Ma,—I guess I haven't written you much since befor I fell
in and I didn't want to write you till I got over the effects of it for fear
you would worry. It was this way—I have been in hard luck or at least
it seemed so and about the time I'd get about as blue as I could get
then I'd get a letter from you giving me a dig or two then I'd get reck-
less and there are chances to loose more than life in this rotten town
any way. Well three weeks ago Sunday evening Minnie Nelson and I
started to run drift logs on a bet. It went pretty good at the start and I
was out quite a little ways and went to jump to the next log and my
ankle turned and I went in. It was more mud than water but I got
out—which is a wonder perhaps—as a girl went in up about here a
while back and they never recovered her body and never expect to. It
had the same effect as the hailstorm last spring but I'm all hunkey
dory now and will be real good now if you write as good letters as the
last one and now for fear you will object to my calling this a rotten
town let me tell you a few. What would you think of a full length photograph of a naked woman falling out of a man's pocket? And what do
you think of girls like Ethel and Gracie[1] with babies[?] and it isn't safe
for an unprotected woman out side the house hardly at night and one
night I heard a man coming t'word my door and as there was no door
there I says "don't you come here[.]" he said "Why not[?]" I said "because I've gone to roost" and he came right on in saying "Well I wont
hurt you[.]" He never came back and *he never will.*

Now keep your boys in Iowa till they are twenty one years of age or past.

Now I suppose you are anxious to know about the land part of it. After receiving Robs letter I took a half a day of[f] and went over to Pierre and talked to a land man.[2] he thought he could find something that would beat the Carlson claim. I had a letter from him at the end of the next week saying he was called by business to the farther side of Minnesota but would be back in a few days. He was detained a week longer than he expected. I phoned to him when he got back just to jog his memory. He said he would be in Ft Pierre that afternoon but he never showed up so I phoned again and he asked when he might come to talk things over and Mrs Gordon couldn't let me off till eight in the evening. So he came in the evening. He said there was a claim out south west of Ft Pierre about twelve miles that a fellow filed on a year ago but having never lived on it had been contested and as neither of us had seen the land he thought we better go out and look at it. Mrs Gordon said I might have a day off the next Sunday or Monday (Aug 1st or 2nd) so we desided to settle the day over the phone later on. The following Saturday he phoned wanting to go on Sun. so we desided to start out at nine o clock. I was ready by a little after nine and at half after ten here came Mr Hastings[3] on foot and the cheapest looking creature I ever saw—one evening befor that, when he was down he got to talking and forgot an appointment he had made to meet a man up town and one other time he was late and I told him I thought that was one of his failings and he said "I'll be here Sunday morning at nine and *be on time*[.]" So no wonder he looked cheap at half past ten. He said he had been having "The *dickens* of a time" and couldnt get a team either side the river but O'Riley expected his auto back at half past eleven and he had engaged that for the afternoon and we could make the trip in half a day in that. He was to phone me as soon as the auto got in but as it didn't "get in["] he came down about 3 P.M. saying he had hired a team for the next day and we would start at nine the next morning. Well we left town about a quarter of eleven the next morning and got back close to nine in the evening. And oh the fun of that trip!! Talk about teasing! Mr Hastings could make the whole bunch of Corey boys ashamed of them selves. He is a young batchlor who professes to be so "old he don't remember things like he used to." We found the claim better than represented. being a relinquishment there is quite a little cost but have that fixed up with Mr Hastings so its alright and I filed this afternoon—holler all you want to but don't tell anyone for a few wks. till I get my receipt please. There is a school about two miles from there where they say they have eight months school in the year and get forty five a month. The director was looking for a teacher this last week so I'm going to apply at once. Miss Reed[4] the Co[unty]. Sup[erin]t[endent of Schools] said she would honor my certificate but I must write exams in the other three branches[,] *S Dak History, drawing* and *Civics*[,] so I've got the books and am ready for work. I forgot to tell you that I left Gordons Friday forenoon after giving her two week[s] warning. Have a room at the Huston House at present but mean to have my house put up as soon as possible so as to get things straight before school begins. If you and the boys will pack all my belongings and send them I'll make it square with you[.]

Please pack my things in good strong boxes that I can use[.] Ethel may have my trunk. The sooner my things are packed the better but *please don't ship till I send you word.*

When you get my trunk and dresser drawer emptied and all my shoes and clothes out of the way you'll have lots of room won't you?

I would like to have my things put in boxes about the size of the window seat in your room with covers to them and instead of nailing them so awful tight just rope them like a trunk couldn't you?

Grandma[5] asked me once if I could use any flour sacks and I said "When I start out for myself I can use a few dozen" and she said alright. Now I could name twenty five good uses for flour sacks and would gladly pay freight on a hundred even if freight is high and money scarce. Say if there should be thirteen cents over on any account in my favor and it won't pinch you in any way I'd like to have it. Every one pays 10% interest up here you know and I'll be a little tight at first you know. But don't pinch yourself cause I can make a go of this any way.

Please don't forget my odds and ends of dishes but don't get in *anything* that isn't *mine*. Oh say I received a card from Gracie Haynes a few days ago saying they expected me back to teach their school[6] next year[;] will you please phone up and see? Thank them and tell them I am going to teach here next year and didn't know they were depending on me till a few days ago.

I received Olneys letter.—I spose Uncle Jim[7] thought my wish bone was where my back bone auto be. They grow at the same rate up here. When you first get in town you'll see some fellow out at the knees and elbows singing

"Get a bottle of Johnathan's soothing dope,
And get yourself used to bein' broke[.]"

In about a week you'll look like him and sing like him[.]
    Will send Fuller a smile pretty soon if I don't hear from him[.]
                Write soon
                As Ever E. F. C.

✴ AUGUST 18, 1909 / THE HUSTON HOUSE /
   FORT PIERRE, S. D.
   TO H. FULLER COREY

Dear Fuller,—Come here a minute—I want to tell you something.
I suppose ma received my letter saying I had filed on a piece of land.
Today I received my receipt from the Land Office so its all hun-
key dory. Now what I want to tell you is this—my land is the E2
SW4 & W2 Se4 of Sec 2 Twp 3N 30 E.—B.H.M.[1] so it lays like

this——and there is about a hundred acres to the south that

is level but the north sixty is not so smooth—it is quite rolling but has
no ditches so but what it can all be plowed but north of that the land
is quite hilly but is open land. Mr Hastings says it isn't apt to be taken
for two or three years yet because it is rough. He thinks it would be
fine if you come up as soon as you are twenty one and file on some of
the rough land and the two of us together will have plow land enough
to balance up the pasture land and we'd have a fine stock farm. I
bought a relinquishment instead of taking the open land because the
rough land can be got cheap for years yet. There are some folks out six
or eight miles farther than I who have three quarters and would give
some one a good price to prove up on the other quarter and sell it to
them. There isn't as much level or—you know what I mean—fairly
even land on there whole section as I have on my quarter. They are
going to have a horse ranch so they say. Now you see its this way[,]
you wouldn't want to live on your quarter all your life but if you want
to you can prove up in fourteen months and be through with it or
not—its just as you wish and what ever you go at its nice to have a

piece of land of your own. I can tell you just what the expense would be or nearly so any way. It would cost you $15 to come out here, $14 to file, $50 to build your shack and if you prove up in fourteen months it will cost you .50 cents per acre or $80 and you have to break ten acres they say and at $4 per a[cre] that would be $40. and all together that would be about $200. But of course you don't need to go at it that way.

I am thinking of proving up on the five year plan. Then I won't have to pay the $80 when I prove up so you wont see me in Iowa again for six years perhaps. Now I think it would be fine if you would come out when you are twenty one and kind of go in with me and we could both prove up on the five year plan and at the end of that time we would be pretty well off as crops sell very well here and by that time Rob would be ready to start out and we could give him a real good start and turn the buisness over to him and we could go away to school or do something else and not have to worry about where the next dollar is to come from.

I got my relinquishment cheap because the fellow was in a pinch[.]

Don't let ma crowd herself in any way to send me money for I guess I can make out.

I haven't heard from that School Director[2] yet but if I dont get that school there are plenty of others so its alright anyway. Now I have my Land Office receipt I don't care if you tell every one you see that I have a claim and I think its a cracking good one.

Tell all the girls to write to me and tell the boys to write too for I get awful lonesome and I can't take time to write many letters as I am studying S. D. History[,] drawing and Civics and I haven't very much time left.

Don't let Olney get a notion of coming out here for if he persisted in staying he wouldn't live six months.

Bed bugs, fleas, mosquetos and flies are so very very thick here[—]why you can go to any lumber yard and lift up a new board and the bed bugs will just run right and left.

For the past thirty days there has only been one place in the U.S. as hot as Pierre and that is a place in Arizona. So you see we have had it hot. Yes I'm telling you the truth for that is acording [to] the government register. But it has never been so hot here before so it may not be so bad next summer. George Stewart sent me a post card a while back that said "Be cheerful[.] We'll have a blizzard next winter[.]" That card fit the place fine.

Tell Valerie [Harris] to answer my letter or I'll come and see her about six years from now.

I've a notion to try the plan Mr Hastings used when he was at college in the east. He wrote to a couple of girls back here—they were sisters—there names were Ina and Iza and after he had had two or three letters from each of them he would write to Iza and say something like this[:] "What ails Ina I haven't heard from her for the dickens of a while"[;] of course Iza told her sister and her sister would write two or three more letters [and] then he would write to Ina and say "What ails Iza I haven't heard from her for the dickens of a while" and then he would get another letter or two from Iza. So he managed to get about three letters from each girl for ever one he wrote them.

I'd like to try that on Iowa folks but I'm afraid it wouldn't work.

Gee I wish you were out here to drive away the men—darn 'em. The wemon say "You'll have to let 'em love you up a little or you'll never get along in Dakota" but I can't bring myself to it. There is one old fool here who is gone on me and was telling Mrs Reese[3] about it. She told me and I dont know how I'll ever shake him off.

The wemon all swear here till it makes the chills run down my back. must close soon[,] your sister

Bess.

P.S. I notice that my spelling is fierce but if you can make it out[, then it's] alright.

E. F. C.

* AUGUST 20, 1909 / FT. PIERRE S. DAK.
  TO MRS. M. M. COREY

Dear Ma,—I don't know where I left off at. I have the school out near my claim and am to board with a family named Stone[1] for a few months till I get a little money ahead and they get my shack built so dont plan to ship my stuff till the last of Stept. I have met Mr Stone and I think I will like him but as I told Rose[2] when I wrote her I don't know about Mrs Stone and the little pebbles. I will be about a mile from school till I get my shack built then I'll be two miles. I'm going out with Mr Stone this afternoon.

Please keep track of all the little things I speak of so as to get every thing in when you do ship. Every thing seems to be going all hunkey-dory now.

I have to write exam[s] in those three branches Sept 17th but teachers are allowed two days in the year here to write exams[.] They draw their wages just the same and dont have to make up the time. I get $40 per month and it don't cost but a $1 to write exams here.

Mr Hastings phoned here yesterday to engage my company for a ride in the evening. I told him he would have to excuse me. He wanted the reason and I wouldn't give it. He asked if I would give it when next we met and I wouldn't promise. I have a sneaking idea we would meet pretty soon if I staid in town so am glad I'm going out this afternoon. He has always appeared to be a perfect gentleman but one girl here says he is rather swift. Mrs Reese says I'm foolish to turn him down for that so long as he seems so nice for she thinks the other girl is jealous. Mr H is pretty well off and his new auto will be here in a couple of weeks so may be I've missed a lot of fun. I went up town with one of the Birkbeck twins after that phone call and Mr Stine treated us to ice cream. The cream was fine and so is Mr Stine [even] if he is married.

It is almost dinner time so I had better close. My money is holding out alright so dont worry. And I'm "bein' good" just *awful good* and the people from out my way say I have a fine piece of land. Am going to prove up on the five year plan so wont get back to Iowa inside of six years. Take care of yourself and write

Yours with love
Bess

* AUGUST 21, 1909 / FT. PIERRE, S. DAK.
  TO MRS. M. M. COREY

Dear Mamma,—Here we are again. I suppose that before you get through reading this you will be mad at me again.

Yesterday we left town about half after four and reached Mr. Stones about eight o clock[;] it is eleven miles out and my school house is a mile farther down the trail. I dont know yet how I will like the Stones but the four little pebbles[1] bump together a good deal and that makes quite a noise. It won't bother me much as I expect to see very

little of them. I take my meals with them but have moved my belongings into the vacant shack of Miss Faith Hunt the former teacher who
is a sister of Mrs Stones. She has proved up and gone away. I have the
whole shack to myself and am far enough from Stones so I have all my
time to study, read, write, mend and sleep and as I have a fine bed and
no bugs I sleep well and I certainly enjoy being alone after a spell of
hotel life.

I don't expect to move into my own house till perhaps the last of
October but as I have the shack to myself here Mr Stone says there is
nothing to hinder your shiping my goods right away and it would give
me more time to get ready for winter. I am planning my winter living
already[.] Fruit here is rather scarce and I can't afford to pay *eighty
cent*[s] *a peck* for apples to put up but if you could spare a barrel of
apples just get them ready and ship them as soon as you can. I could
dry some and they say there is a great many wild plums on the river
which are to strong alone but would go fine with apples and I do like
plums *so* well. Mrs Stone said she would pay half the freight on the
apples if you would send them and she would get a way for us to go to
the river for the plums. Of course though I don't want you to run your
selves short. Mrs. S[tone] said she would let me have two or three
citron to preserve as she has a good many and she will also have more
cucumbers than she can use so I think I'll put a 3 gal jar of them down
in salt as we used to at home then I can make them up as I want them.
The Stones are wretchedly poor. You cant buy things on time here and
Mrs S admitted today that she couldn't send for what she needed
yesterday because they were at the end of their rope. When folks here
get land broke and raise their living they live fat but poor people
who haven't much breaking done have to scratch. I'm a lucky dog
though—I have an eight months school instead of six and may get $45
instead of $40 so you don't need to bother about me at all at all. I'll not
have to suffer as lots of people do in this new country.

My school will begin Sept 6th and close Dec 26th for eight weeks
vacation during the bad part of the winter. It begins again Feb 21st
and closes June 10th[.]

I will have fifteen or twenty pupils several of whom are young
men of Fullers age[2] or nearly that—hence the ninth grade[.]

I am to have a two room house 8x16 which make[s] two small
square rooms. which I find will be an advantage over one large square
room. Mr Stone has built every shack in sight of here and many others

and he said he would haul the stuff and build the house for $8⁰⁰ which will make the cost of the house $50 or a little more. Then I must have a dam put in as soon as possible in order to catch the fall rains. And that will cost me $4 per day for a man and team and it *may* take several days. One side of my quarter is fenced and I would like to fence the other three sides as soon as possible. The posts and wire will cost me $33 or about that and I'll have to pay a man $2 per day to put it up.

Oh say there is a little dandy of a stove here that they say bakes fine and Mrs S[tone] said she thought her sister would sell it for four or five dollars as she is through with it.

Would Ethel or one of the boys grind coffee enough to fill a fruit jar and send it with my things? That would last me a year perhaps for company and the like of that and it would hold its strength if it was air tight I guess. I'll pay you for all those odds and ends and your bother too if you'll put a price on it and wait a while for the pay and don't plan on sending me a cent of money for I can get along fine and you'll need every cent.

Don't let any of the boys get a notion of coming out on a visit for living is so high and the round trip alone would cost one thirty dollars. If any of them want to come let me know and when I see a chance I'll send for them.

Potatoes were $2 per bu. but are going down some now and I hope will go down more befor I have to get my winters suply. Meat is a fright and eggs $.25 per doz but it wont pay me to get chickens till next year as I would have to buy feed for them and thats fierce. Eggs are fifty and sixty cents here in the winter time.

I'll have no fall breaking[3] done as people who have tried it say it doesn't pay. I will have at least ten acres broke next spring.

My board here is $3 per week and Rob would starve on what I've had to eat so far. If I can get time to do a little sewing for Mrs S it will help out on the board though.

If I get this finished I can take it to Sunday School tomorrow down at the school house and am to meet a young man there who is going to town Monday and he'll mail it for me, see?

Well Mamma I did jaw a good deal last Spring but folks dont always have fractured collar bones and perhaps when I come home for my next visit six years from next Xmas you will have forgiven and forgotten and we'll have a good visit and no jawing anywhere.

Please dont forget a ball of cord and all the rolls of pieces like my duds—I guess there are a good many rolls of mine in that long box in the sitting room and all the dishes that belong to me[—]perhaps there will be enough so I wont have to buy any more for a while.[4]

I wonder if the children would have bid me good bye[5] if they had known I wasn't coming back.

Well I must close as I want to write a few cards [.] I hope I'll hear from you soon and please ship my stuff as soon as possible.

With love to all I remain
As Ever—Bess

✳ AUGUST 29, 1909 / FT. PIERRE S. DAK.
TO J. OLNEY COREY

Dear Olney,—I received your letter a long while ago and ma's just a few days ago—Have had several letters—one from Mr Hastings and one from Uncle J. D.[1]—nothing like having relatives who know your business. Uncle feels badly about your failing in the exams,[2] only 45% in arithmetic!! how did you manage it kid? You must have got bothered. I am awful sorry you didn't make it—I wish you had done as I wanted you to—take the common branches one time and the higher ones next and combine exams[.] I'm sure you would have made it that way. I'm sweating at present over S. D. History and Drawing[—]every one says the exams are fierce here. Lots of Iowa teachers are down and out *here*.

I'm trying to have fun enough to make up for the hardship and cares. I come pretty near it too. When in Ft Pierre I had a little fun with Byron Clow[3] the Co[unty] Treasurer—he's just a young fellow and a regular Gimsizzer too. One day he turned everything in the hotel sitting room upside down looking for something and as he frequently looses his hat I asked him which one it was—that time he happened to be looking for a needle but couldn't find one so I loaned him a great big one I had in my pocket book[.] Shortly after, I came through the office where he was sewing the buttons on his bathing suit and I said "Why, you *can* sew can't you[?]" He replied with a big grin "Oh yes I'm a regular son-of-a-gun to sew[.]" I told him one of my brothers could sew on buttons and mend quite well and he made a slight motion toward his feet and said "Oh yes I often sew up things with the base ball stitch[.]" Now I want to know if its the base-ball-stitch that *you* use.

Rob must be crazy about S. D. If he had a chance to try it he would be back in a week with all the starch taken out of him. Why, he would look worse than a much chewed dishrag by the time he got back[.]

I was to Sunday School last Sunday, out driving Tuesday evening, to a party last evening and to Sunday School today[.]

Yes Im getting *quite* particular—if I can't go out with the best fellow in a community I wont go with any. I went to the party with Adolph—geemanie—gosh I can't tell you what his last name is[4]—*I* never use it any way.

Adolph was here helping Mr Stone put up hay. One day at dinner he asked if I was going to the party—of course I looked wishfull and said "I'd *like* to go." Adolph said "Well you get ready and I'll come along and we'll go to the party" and thats just what we did. Folks here think they have a big joke on us but the joke isn't on us[,] its on the wagon.

Adolph is Bohemian and if any one ever says any thing against my Bohemian lad they'll find "Big Squaw heap fight."

Tell Fuller that Adolph has a machine with which to make rope—he can make about six dollars worth of good rope out of a dollars worth of twine.

You asked if I knew Hazel Groat, Nellie Irwin[5] and the rest of that crowd—yes I've met them—know a little of them—have heard a lot of them from reliable sources—they are the girls who laid down in some mens laps at Chautauqua last year—Look out or they'll get the best of you—they're what Will [Speer?] calls "Regular blue girls" and I might imagine from what I hear that your main study this summer was *Civildevilment* or something in that line—Oh well! go it again!—"Tis from our failures we learn most[.]"

Tell ma she don't need to bother about bed clothes for *me* as I will have no use for them but to send my pillows please as they add to the comfort of most any seat after a ride of twenty miles or such a matter in a lumber wagon over *these* roads behind a team of bronchos or Indian ponies.

The bed mamma suggested wouldn't do at all—just think of the valuable room it would take up—every one who saw it would yell "Loco" and run.

Say! my quarter is a regular rattle snake den—its *nothing* to kill half a dozen in crossing it. You wouldn't catch me any where near there with out a snake stick. I'll have a screen door on my house so the snakes can't get in so all I hate about it is I wont dare go outside the door after dark as that is when every one around here, who has been bit, got bit.

Tell ma I'll see about the pillow cases but I do wish some of you would find out what ails Grandma[.] I've sent her cards but she dont answer and it bothers me. Once Grandma showed me a great big grain sack full of sugar and flour sacks and asked me if I could use any of them[.] I told her that I couldn't then but when I started out for myself I could make use of several dozen—now I'm ready for them but don't like to write about it as I dont hear from them.

Don't let ma settle up my account—she needs the money worse than I do and we dont use money much to speak of up here—we are kind of above money here[.] *I dont want a cent of money from home but please ship my stuff right away quick.*

I'm trying the real estate business a clip—just one clip you know—not much risk. I might loose seventy five dollars I haven't got but I'm just as apt to make thirteen cent[s]—anyway I'll have the experience.

When ma sends me her figures so I know how she stands financially I'll send her mine *perhaps* and not before.

Paul wouldn't say good bye to me[;] now I'll never come to see him or ask him to come to see me till he straightens things up[.]

Ma dont need to worry about *me* "not haveing the heart to explain" and her suggestion that Mr H[astings] was of the "Geo[rge] Welsh stripe" is enough to make a person raise Ft Pierre and light the gass under it[.] How the deuce should *I* know how old M B Hastings is? He looks to be the sunny side of fifty *any how*. He is tall—well built—smooth shaven—neither gray nor bald headed and would be pretty good looking if it wasn't for his face[,] especially his nose which might have been put on a trifle warm or more likely got a little cold befor it was finished[.]

I haven't been extra well all the time out here. I guess its the damn water—this time of the year the damn weeds[6] are so bad you know. Mrs Stone says she is going to boil the water I drink after this for not being used to it[;] she was afraid I would have a run of typhoid[.]

I made a worse break here the other evening than I did at Hayes. They were telling mo[s]queto stories and I said the mosquetoes around my shack were big as cats. Mr Stone wanted to know what I'd been drinking and I said "Nothing but this *dam* water[.]" Mr S has been worrying ever since—he says he knows now they ought not to let me drink it but they have nothing else[.] See where I squoshed that bed bug at the top of this sheet[?][7]

I have a pretty good team in view—will write more of them after seeing them.

Was wondering what ailed the fit of some of *my* clothes and now I know its because they aint pegged topped[.]

The nearest station to my claim is Teton[8] but my address and shipping point is Ft Pierre as the roads are so much better and the seven miles difference in distance dont amount to any thing here. Am about sixty five miles from Lida and as far I guess from Louie W. and when I write I shall say "The roads are impassible between me and thee[.]"[9]

Well I guess I better close and do up dinner work and get supper for the pebbles as the Stones are not here.

MONDAY AUG 30
We had company from Pierre last evening. I forgot to tell you I was up to see Adolphs mamma one afternoon.
Love to all
Sister Bess
Please let ma read *this* E F C

✳ SEPT 12, 1909 / FT. PIERRE S. DAK.
TO MRS. M. M. COREY

Dear Ma,—Barrel of apples not yet heard from and if you dont send me some duds pretty soon I dont know what I'll do—I hardly dare go to town for fear I'll get run in. I suppose you read the letter I wrote Olney. I didn't get to go to the river that Wednesday because it rained and I didn't get to town that Friday because I had been so sick Mrs Stone wouldn't let me risk it. Ella Van Hise an Indian girl came out that evening with Mr Stone and staid with me till Monday evening. She isn't a thoroughbred but she is a "pretty good grade." She is from Pierre. She said she was not personaly acquainted with M B Hastings but that he kept mighty good company in Pierre any way.

A week ago today the whole neighborhood or rather the people in it went to the river for the day—there were several wagon loads of us. Adolph Bucholz and John Porter[1] rode horse back. John rode beside Ella and talked to her all the way and Adolph rode beside me but as I

The bridge over Bad River at Midland, S.D., ca. 1910. Photo courtesy Midland Pioneer Museum.

happened to be in a cranky mood I would neither see nor speak to him so every once in a while he would ride back and talk to the boys in the next wagon a while. But when we got to the Porter ranch house and stopped for dinner Adolph rode up dismounted and assisted me from the wagon—of course I had to thank him and that broke the ice. After dinner we all went to gather plums. Howard Speer[2] and Adolph asked us girls to pick with them. We wouldn't at first but as we didnt have any luck we finally told the boys to show us some good plums. They took us across Bad River—the boys were both helping Ella so I attempted to cross alone and went in but I was pretty well dried off befor we got to the plum thicket a mile or so farther on. We sure had a picnic. We picked three bu[shels] or more *and* had them in two two bu. grain sacks then we had to get them to the road—a distance of about a mile. Howard took one sack, Ella and Adolph took the other sack and I took the four pails. The trials and tribulations of that trip are beyond discription. Howard did fine but the other two dropped their sack on the average of about once every rod I believe—if I had had but one pail I'd have carried it beneath the sack and caught a pail of plum cider. Befor we got to the "Little Pork-you-pine"[3] they started to run and when I reached the bank there was Ella, Adolph and plums in wild confusion at the bottom[.] We got them started again—then when the boys were helping us through the fence John Porter stopped and shot at a stubble duck. He missed it but Ella screamed so she scared it to death so it made no differance. John and we girls staid with the plums while the boys went to start the crowd home—in crossing the bad river Adolph went in so I'm not the only one. After the boys were gone Ella talked dogs, guns and horses in a way [that] created great admiration on Johns part. I kept rather still at first but after a while I said I'd like to try his gun which is a five magazine windchester. The idea of an Iowa Schoolmaam shooting a gun when the little squaw screamed at the sound of one was most to much for John. First he dared me to shoot the gun then he dared me to shoot at Adolphs plum pail. After he dared me I had to didn't I? He placed the pail upside down in the road and all went back quite a long ways. John showed me exactly how to hold the gun and I listened "shust so meek as Mosses" while Ella stood with clasp hands and open mouth ready to let off all kinds of a warwhoop at the first bang. I only shot once—that was enough to convert Adolphs plum pail into a first class culander. John said "By Gosh you hit it" and ran for the pail.

There was some misunderstanding about the plums so all I have to remember the occasion by is the pail I used as a target and the remains of the handkerchief I loaned Adolph to tie up the plum sack with.

Monday being Labor Day I began my school with a days vacation for which I will receive two dollars. Monday Mr Stone was going to the saw mill for a load of saw dust so we girls went along and picked plums. I finished putting up what was left of mine yesterday—had twenty nine quarts which I consider good after all that were eaten during the week. Monday evening Ella went to Speers where she has been the rest of the week. My what a week this has been—Oscar Walton[4] was here three evenings[,] Adolph two and Howard and Ella[5] two. I began my September celebration[6] Monday, which, with it being the first week of school, so much company and the dam water was almost too much for me. I was sick last nigh[t]. Am much better now but rather weak. I didn't try to go to Sunday School this morning,

I have nine pupils and there are several more to start later. They are much in love with me as yet.

Several men about here have quite an admiration for the schoolmaam on account of her heavy shoes—it seems that most girls wear out several pair of fine shoes before they swallow their pride and come down to Dakota style. Shortage of money saved me that time.

Some one suggested that I'd get homesick after while and hit the grit[7]—One man exclamed "Her get homesick?!! Yes I see her goin across those hills toward Iowa so fast you could play checkers on her shirt tail[.]"

Folks say the new schoolma'am has plenty of grit or "she's a mighty plucky girl." I hope they'll never have occasion to change their minds.

There has been several large rattle snakes killed near the school house lately—Mr Stone killed a little one between here and there yesterday. Does Fuller know how to use dynamite? They dynamited the den on my claim three times—the first time they killed 148 and by that time the odor was so frightfull they had to clear out—they got 300 all together and they say they believe three thousand got away. Why after the explosion Mr Stone looked into the pit and he said they lay as close together as the fingers of your hand—they were stunned but of course no one cared to go in after them. If I can get a couple of nice large ones alive I'll have their fangs extracted and send them down to the children. They make nice pets but of course it wouldn't be wise to let them get away.

I'll never wish my hair was black any more[—]it shows the gray hairs enough as it is. Mrs Stone remarked on it yesterday when I washed my head—I don't see what started it to turn so soon but perhaps it will stop now I'm getting a little bit settled. It doesnt show any, I don't think, except when my hair is down.

Mr Stones mother used to be a Miss Scramlin of near Momence Ill.[8] and he has a picture of his grand mother that looks exactly like a picture of an old lady you have. Now what do you know about that? The letter you forwarded is a what do you call em—it has no name signed—just "From a Friend." Its a mans writing—says if you do you'll meet with great happiness and if you dont you'll come to grief. What did you want to know for? Shall I send you the letter? Have you got a mouse?[9] If you have just cough it up.

Say ma we are allowed two days of every year for exams and our wages go on just the same and we get two dollars a day and milage for attending teachers meetings—I hope they have one every Saturday this term.

Will you please give that drawing book of black Board Designs[10] to Mary Lanigan as there is one like it here.

I have four gallons of cucumbers down in salt—can you beat that?

What ails Olney[;] has he been sick? Where is he teaching?

Have you heard from Grandmas lately? Ive ate something every day at school except Friday I forgot to and I've eaten something for breakfast every morning since I came out here except one or two so you see I'm "bein awful good" even if I am a long ways off.

SEPT 13TH[,] MONDAY MORNING
Was Olney sick last night? I dreamed of him all night again. Will finish this as Friejouff[11] may go to town today[.] Please write and ship good[s] soon as possible or I'll frieze to death.

Love to all
Elizabeth F Corey

* SEPT 26, 1909 / FORT PIERRE, SO. DAK.
  TO MRS. M. M. COREY

Dear Ma,—I received yours of the 17th this week and letter of the 6th and 7th last week. As I've not written you since two weeks ago today I'm starting in on an all days job.

Your letter which I rec'd two weeks ago tomorrow was much the worse for wear as it had been carried some three days in various coat pockets. The one end was worn through and the letter and check were partly out when I got it. The check was not fastened to the rest so its a wonder it wasn't lost.

Sept 14 I attended the surprise party on Ella Bucholz and such fun as I had. There were but ten unmarried young people there and they were Ella and I and eight young men. Most of the folks around here had thought I was one of the starched up kind at first but Oscar Walton the youngest school director has gone to living on his claim and his shack is just down the road here a little piece and when he gets lonesome of an evening he comes up to Stones. The first evening he was there I just talked a few minutes then came over to my shack. After I was gone he said "My I didn't suppose Miss Corey could talk that much." He spent three evenings there that week and two each week since so by the evening of the party we were quite well acquainted and as he is Irish we scrap all the time.[1] He began to torment as soon as he got to the party. I stood it as long as I could then warned him that I would get even—of course no one thought I could. I turned to Mrs Bucholz and asked if she would do me a favor—she said she would gladly do me any number of favors. I warned her that it was a big one and she promised faithfully to grant it then I asked if when she moved to town next week she would take Mr Walton along and leave Adolph out here instead. Oscar had been paying Ellas[2] lots of attention the past few months and the way they've been bothering him since isn't slow[. A]fter they found I could talk too we just all pitched in and had a regular time: When it came supper time they were short of dishes so Howard Speer, young [John] Porter and I drank our coffee out of soup dishes and Jhelmer Blumgreen[3] ate so much we gave him a dose of castor oil to prevent his getting sick. Gee but he squirmed even tho we dished it up in water melon.

Friday the 17th I went to Ft Pierre with Mr & Mrs Stone and two of the pebbles. I wrote the exam—haven't heard from it yet but they can several first grade teachers from Iowa at every exam so I don't expect much. I suppose I'll have to write over in November but it don't make such a great sight of differance anyway only it would hurt my pride to begin to fail now. The directors said they guessed nothing serious would happen if I did fail. We brought my barrel of apples out that evening. If I had been real smart and had had a few things less in my head I would have sold three or four dozen in town at Ft Pierre rates (.50 per doz.) and paid the freight out of it. The freight was a dollar thirty seven.

The next day I worked at the fruit all day. Ella Erickson[4] came over about supper time—Oscar Walton came over after supper. We had a high old time till Oscar ran against the table and upset the milk. Mrs Stone said we had to clean it up so Oscar carried the water and I scrubbed. Then we all agreed the next number was 23[5] so we all cleared out. Ella staid all night with me and we talked till most morning.

Sunday morning Ella and I went to Sunday School—there were very few there and they were of the dis[h]water stripe[6] so *we were it.* Ella was organist and "chief squaker" as she expressed it and I was Supt.[,] Bible Class teacher, Sec. & Treas. and Librarian and today I didn't attend S. S. at all at all.

When we got back from Sunday School young Porter was here. He helped me tie down my jars of preserves and said the sample tasted like more. We had a lot of fun but he told Mrs Stone things when I wasn't around that spoiled all my fun for the rest of the week. He told her that Ella Bucholz was awful jealous of me because Oscar spent more time here than he did up there. I dont believe it but I'm not going to run any risks—I've heard to much about Bohemian Blood to do that. So the next time Oscar came over for the evening I saw him coming and streaked off over here. But the next time I was working with my fruit so I couldn't get away. I didn't talk to him any and he didn't stay long. Mr Stone says if I dont cut it out he is going to explain things. I don't know what to do—guess I'll just wait and see what will happen.

I made my sweet apple pickles yesterday and that finished the apples. I took out the plums I had canned and made them up with apples. Some of the plums were in Mrs Stones jars. I now have two two gallon jars of cucumbers down in salt, two one gallon jars of plum preserves[,] two one gallon jars of plum butter and two one gal jars of plum jell beside two two quart cans of plums and two two quart cans of sweet apple pickles and some dried apples—have eight more two qt cans to fill but am going to have some beet pickles, citron preserves and sich.

Mr Stone says if you are not getting more than sixty cents per bu. for your apples and have any to spare you might ship up a few barrels as a speculation and he will see to them for you. And if you are going to ship me winter apples you aught to start them by the last of October.

When you write I wish you could send me your receipt for [1]plumpudding, [2]salad dressing [3]chillisauce [4]catsup and the [5]mustard dope for onion and tomato pickles[.]

Am to have an 8×10 ft cellar boarded up so the snakes can't get in.

It was a mistake[—]*that* snake den isn't on *my claim*[.]

They are thinking of only having two weeks vacation at Xmas time which will close the Spring term the last of April making it possib[l]e to raise a big garden next year—which will be a big help to me.

My school is sure a great one. I have some pupils that keep me guessing *some* of the time and some that keep me guessing *all* of the time and *one* that keeps me guessing *all the time and then some*. He's just a little pill but he's a caution. I told them they *must* stop throwing paper out the window and shortly after I caught the little scamp in the act. I sent him out after it and By jing! if he didn't start out that window so fast I hardly had time to get him by the heels[.]

I'm going to copy a song or two for the boys when I get time. One is "On My South Dakota Claim" to the tune of "In The Good Old Summer Time[.]" I only remember that "Id rather eat bacon till my stomach is achin on my South Dakota claim." I can just hear Rob sing it now.

My small pupils made strenuous objections to number work so I changed my desk into Ft Pierre, cut out paper money and with marbles[,] dominoes and pasteboard shacks I started each to holding down a claim on his desk top. One day I heard angry whispers and went to investigate—one youngster said the other was "too high" and the other said "I aint either. One dollar's enough for the pigs but he aught to give me two dollars for the old sow."

We have a fine croquet set at school and they have some lively games some times[.]

Who is teaching the home school this fall? "Our Little Irisha Rosa [Gillette]"? I wonder where My Dear Gasspipe is—he could have had the north school for the asking I guess—he was a good teacher in arithmetic if he didn't get all the problems. Just befor I came up here a gentleman was talking to me about his teaching and I told how he said he "shook 'em all up together and stood 'em out in rows" and the other party says "Yes he plants 'em in rows but some how they come up in *hills*[.]" That made me think of the classes that were in five separate places in the book. Well I'm glad to be in Stanley Co[unty] where the teachers all seem to be gentlemen excepting whats ladies.

Say Holger and Freddie or George Sorensen[7] failed to get their rulers the last day of school if they haven't gotten them yet I wish Rob would get them to them.

I've met the Shares several times this last week—Ben says he is coming up and would I please to let him know at once if ever I was to get another barrel of apples.

I'm certainly much obliged for those apples and so are all the neighbors.

Keep cool? Golley Moses I should say I do! Everyone else has on their winter underwear and I dress just the same as I did last July.

I received your card Monday 20th[.] I've had letters from Gracie [Haynes], Mary [Lanigan], Lida [Smith], Ida Wever Lay,[8] Anna Stewart[9] and one or two others beside several cards since I wrote last. Anna sent me a lovely postal from Denver but I never rec'd it, and the last one G[eorge].E. S[tewart]. sent several weeks getting here. It says "I just love moutaining—it's so embracing" I've had some beauties of post cards of late[.] I sent George a card this last week—I hadn't answered his last three and some of them were so very pretty. Every one who looks at my cards knows him as the "Irishman" and Mrs Stone remarked the other day "I think that Irishman is getting no better fast[.]" Lida told me a lot about him in her letter and I suppose she knows(?)

I'm almost starved so I guess I better close and go over and see how dinner is comming for its half after one. I'll not seal this so I may write more later.

Yours truly

Elizabeth F Corey

Rec'd word this evening that the Post Master "wished to goodness that schoolma'am would hurry up and send an order for that package[.]"[10] Will know tomorrow by this time what it is[.]

✳ OCT 10, 1909 / FORT PIERRE, SO. DAK.
   TO MRS. M. M. COREY

Dear Ma,—I havent written since a week ago today—no two weeks ago I guess it is. I didn't intend to write you again till after I rec[']d those boxes but I guess I better.

I'm in no mood to write tonight either, have been soreheading it around here all day.

I finished my first month of school Friday Oct 1st. The next day I went over in the field and talked to Oscar about my warrent[1] and he said he would make it out and bring it over that evening and he did. I tell you it just beats the billy deuce the times I'm having. Did I tell you that Oscar used to pay attention to Ella Buchholz and he's done quit and its most broke her up in buisness. She thinks if I had staid in Iowa she would have had a clean sweep. Well when Oscar got here he found the Bucholz boys here to spend the evening and they were bound not to go till O—— went and O—— was bound not to go till *after* they had gone and it wasn't an overly pleasant evening. Of course the Irish beat the Dutch. The next day (last Sunday) Stones took me down to Browns[2] to get my warrent signed. We also stopped at Nielsons[3] and drove over my claim some—found a dandy place for a dam not very far from where I shall have my house built. It is a very favorable place—I don't think it—the dam—will cost me over $20. They usually charge .50 per hour but I'll only have to pay .40 per hour for mine. The lumber for my house comes to $83 or more and the hauling is $8 and the building .20 per hour. I suppose I could get a chicken coop like the one I've been living in for less than that but be plagued if I want to stand on end, sleep on edge and walk in and back out for the rest of my days. It is 10 ft one way and 8 ft tother, the roof slopes one way and it is built just like a corn crib only the boards are closer together, the studdings are three and four ft apart and it has a little square window in each end. It was papered inside and out but these winds make the paper tired and it has broken down in spots so the weather howls through. It might be alright for one who spent the "cold nights" with a married sister or Dutch Uncle or some such. One girl tried to winter in the like and her neighbors found her froze to death in bed so I wont try that.[4] The house I'm *going to have perhaps* is to be 12 × 16 ft with an A roof, two 12 × 8 rooms and a boarded over ceiling to form an atic. Will have one window up above so it will make a good store room so when you come up I can store away the whole blank family you see.

This last week O—— was over Monday evening with a letter to be mailed and Tuesday evening after the mail and last evening to bring the mail down. Tuesday eve I rec'd your note and the freight bill—much obliged—last evening I rec'd a card saying the freight arrived the 6th[.] I cant get it till next Wednesday. After the first day they charge storage—twenty five cents the first day and twenty cents every day after that so with the .32 excess freight charges it will amount to something especially if I have to pay the regular .50 cent per cwt. for hauling.

I have to attend a Teachers meeting in Ft Pierre Oct 23[.] My school gives an entertainment Oct 30, Write exam the second week in Nov attend another meeting Dec 4th and get up some kind of Xmas doings. They told me if I got *over* 80% in *everything* in *exam*, my Iowa certificate would hold so 74 put me down and out so I have to write the whole buisness. Have to read or rather study thirteen chapters of "Civics and Health" before this first teachers meeting and twenty three more befor the next meeting.

Had a little time in school one day—as Mr Speer would tell you "One of 'em got gay and she kind of checked his motions[.]" I didn't get to go to the party Friday evening—it was [so] frightfully dark that most all who did go got off the road and into the fence[;] one crowd got lost—kept going till they broght up where they started so perhaps its just as well I didn't go especially as Ella [Buchholz] wasnt there. Its a desperate game we are playing—we three—Ella is evidently playing for *keeps*, guess I'm playing for *excitement*, and getting it, and I don't know what the other party [Oscar Walton] is playing for.

Wish you could let me know something of the Scramlins you know—the names please. I think Mr Stone and I are some relation—guess our great great great grandmothers swopped cats[.] I rec'd a card last evening that beats every thing yet. Tis a picture of a kid about Pauls size holding by the belt a pair of ladies much betrimmed neither tackle and underneath it says "A pair of lace curtains for sisters sitting room"—was glad I didn't get here till after Oscar and Mr Stone had finished their remarks.

Well I may write more befor this goes to mail. Am getting along very well but am rushed to death almost, most of the time[.] Hope this finds you well[.] Please write me a *long* letter when you can and let me know how you are financialy and physicaly.

WEDNESDAY OCT 13,

Here I go for another dive[.] Monday morning I awoke to find it growing colder every minute. [B]y night it was awful cold and I was sick or almost—another postponement you know—got my feet hot just befor noon and wasn't prepared for the consequences—got chilled coming home—am feeling fine now.

Mrs Nielsen brought my boxes out Monday evening and I got into some warmer duds and got my blankets on my bed so after unpacking some I got a good warm nap and felt as good as new.

I had heard them tell how things froze in this shack but didn't think much of it till I went to wash my face yesterday morning and found I was up against the "cold hard facts" of the case. froze up! well I should say! even the tank froze up and the Speer kids[5] have been sliding on the dam.

The boxes were alright—am much more obliged than I can tell in one short letter. How did Jennie [Noon] and her ma[6] know I was so desperately fond of blue dishes? And with Valeries cake plate, Orlas[7] toothpick holder, Mrs Harrises cup and saucer and my Xmas cup I can serve coffee and cake when Oscar and Ella(?)[8] come to see(?) me and be blessed if I don't drink cocoa out of the cup Terrence sent, cool it in the saucer Johnie sent and pour in imaginary cream from the pitcher Mary sent[.][9] But by darn why didn't you send the cow and the milking machine?

It was so good of them all to send the dishes. Please thank them for me—I haven't time have been working night and day and will till Nov 15th. It was good of you to send so much stuff—dozens of things I didn't expect—the vegetable torpedoes and $2.00 worth of salt pork will help me out fine. The lids on two of the cans got dislocated and the pebbles they have eat the dope and licked the dishes clean. Oh say[,] the what you call him only charged me the .32 for the freight—being good after calling me "Mrs Gordon" I guess.

I see several dozen things here that I had given Ethel—am much obliged just the same and I see the boys all did their share. What were the gourds and the gray cloke for? Where is that gray skirt I shortened last spring for a knock about? did I give it to some of you? I wish I had my dictionary[;] twould save me buying a new one. Have read Uncle Walter's [10] letter. Must close now with love to all—Bess.

* OCT. 17, 1909 / FORT PIERRE, SO. DAK.
  TO MRS. MARGARET COREY

Dear Ma,—Yours of the 13th at hand. I *did* appreciate that registered package—its contents kept me from freezing to death for several weeks. I wish you would quit digging it into me all the time—I dont expect you to write two or three times a week when you're so busy and have so much to think about and if I've got to write a whole chapter on every separate thing I might as well give it up to begin with.

Mr. Stone rec'd your card and will get the apples in a day or two I presume.

'Twill be nice if your potatoes turn out well—I only know of one man out here who has any to spare and people have been paying .75 per bu[.] and digging them themselves. Mr. Reese doesn't want to sell any more—he is going to bury them and sell them at $3 or $4 next Spring. "Rosa" [Gillette] must be the same uncertain little piece she has always been. Well I suppose "Its the water etc."—as Glen[1] says.

Am sorry that Olney is out of school—does he expect to go back or what is he going to do?

You must have a heep to contend with, and Ethel too, she has as hard a time as I did when I was her age. Wish I could do something to help you but have all I can handle here. Wanted to make another payment on the Lana note but dont see how I can for a while yet.

Will write a little note to M. C.—can get it all straight the quickest that way and save you the bother.

Mr Reese told Mr Stone if he wanted to come over and harrow the potatoe patchs today he might have what potatoes he got so he decided to do it. Mrs Stone has to stay at home so close and has been wanting to go down to see Mrs Speer so bad I told her I would do up the work and bake the bread, so she went down that far to spend the day. So the whole blank family are gone. I wont undertake to work all day Sunday again for a day or two though.

Mary Lanigan writes me better letters than any other girl I correspond with but she does get so blue—she says she knows she'll never see me again and the things she says about "That darned Irishman" as she calls him, for letting me stay up here, are just a few.[2]

I spent last Thursday night with Mrs Speers and Friday she sent one of the girls up with a little pail of green tomatoes and a package of mustard—she said she had no vinegar and was afraid the tomatoes would spoil. I had no vinegar but borrowed some of Grandma Foutts[.][3] I had a two qt can full and a few beside—would have mixed them with onions and made a gal or two if I had had vinegar enough. I put the few I had over into a qt jar—had it about half full[—]had Oscar take them over to Grandma Foutts as she had never tasted any made this way. O—— says possession is nine points in law and that he would have nine for every one Grandma got—would count them three times to make sure. He said they are "Lickin' good—go fine with praties."[4]

Have the boys seen anything in the papers about the "Polecat King" of Missouri? A fellow by the name of John Jones I believe it is is starting a skunk ranch[;] he expects to make it pay big so they say. How is that for a business? In some ways I wouldn't mind trying it—skunks are kind of pretty little animals but I dont like their stinking disposition.

If you send me another box of stuff could or rather would you send my dictionary and a few such, please?

Must close for now perhaps will write more later.

With Love—Bess

P. S. Have cut out sending post cards its too expensive.[5] If you are going to send any thing cold weather will hurt it needs to be *quick*— E. F C.

---

* POSTCARD / NOV 3RD 1909 / 11:45 P. M.
TO MRS. M. M. COREY

Dear Ma,—Have a letter started but dont know when will get it finished[.] Teachers meeting fine—social a success—

House nearing completion   Party Nov 5th—

Examinations 12th   Moving 13th

Birthday 16th

Thanksgiving 25th

Teachers meeting Dec 27th

Your letter recd last Friday—Much obliged for what aint got here yet. Getting along fine.

Oct 31st Hallow-e'en
Too bright for the old boy
Best regards to everybody—tell them to write
Had a nice letter from Gracie.

With Love E F C

✳ NOV. 6, 1909 / FORT PIERRE, SO. DAK.
TO MRS. MARGARET COREY

Dear Ma,—I started you a letter a week ago but its no good now. Guess I haven't written you a letter for most a month.

I attended that teachers meeting in Ft Pierre October 23rd—It was fine and Mr Stone wouldn't take a cent for the trouble he was to on my account so it was clear gain. I rec'd two dollars for attending and one-ten milage making \$3 [10] for the day. While in town I *managed* a lumberman and Mr Stone brought a jag of my lumber that evening—The material for my cellar, house and "The little mansion"[1] will I believe amount to about \$90.

Last week Mr Stone hauled out the lumber and dug the cellar which was an awful job—it is only 8x10x5 but you see it was genuine prairie, unbroke sod, land that has never been worked and has had little rain since last spring. Mr. Stone did very well—it took him about three days or a little better—that's at .20 per hour you know. And while all of that was going on I was working most day and night on the entertainment. Only had five pupils to help me and two of those were little tads—Oh the work of getting up an entertainment in this homely man's country—why the contrivances the makeshifts and substitutes are enough to make one laugh and cry at once. Fancy work? I tell you when we get orders from the School Board we just hop to it. I guess perhaps I didn't tell you that I hurt my left shoulder twice since I came to Dakota—They say I used it too much befor it got st[r]ong and am to make up for it. But don't worry I'm taking good care of it and have never had to have it in splints. Well they sent me word that if I had to have help with the curtains that Glen Speer was a good hand and would help me *Sunday* the day after the teachers meeting. So I went down in the afternoon. Glen put up three small shelves on each side of the school house for the jack o'lanterns. Then we strung up a lariet rope till it looked like a Chinese puzzle and the curtain, a couple of bed blankets sewed together, with string sewed along like this 〰〰 we strung on the rope—it worked quite well[.] We worked by candle light long after dark[.] Then I came home alone— didn't mind the dark but that morning I stepped on a board with a nail in it and run the nail into my foot about there ⬭×. Had to step on the board with the other foot to pull it out. It bothered then but is O K now. Among other little(?) things that week I had to trim six boxes[2]— five beside my own[.] You can't draw a line and say "Thus far and no farther"[—]out here you've got to be ready to do it all if you make a success of any thing. Had good luck with the baskets or boxes—they all sold well.

I went down Saturday morning and worked all forenoon finishing every thing up. When I got back Miss Foulon the teacher from eight miles south was here—had come up horse back after her warrent—We went over to Oscar's right after dinner and got our warrents then as Miss Foulon desided to stay all night I had to make and trim a box for her as she had never trimmed one and didn't dare try. Got through just in time to help pack the boxes. Didn't take time to eat any supper myself. Miss F[oulon] rigged out in my best white waist and muffler[.] I wore my old white waist with the big holes under the arms and my jumper suit. We each wore one of those black hand painted wristlets—(They lap over as far on my wrist as they used to gap)[.] We reached the school house at 7 P.M. as I had to prepare the fishpond and black my little King Cole.[3] Oscar came early and helped with the fishpond.[4] I read the program, drew the curtains and did all the dressing room work. Had every thing where I could put my hand on it and got along fine—they didn't have to wait on a single number hardly—We had twenty numbers on our program about half were tableaux—every thing took fine—every number was well clapped. Had a lovely evening, a good crowd and took in $15.35 which was considered fine for out here (They had two socials last year and only got about $12 altogether). The jack o' lanterns were the only light except back of the curtains. They said Oscar wanted my box but Adolph beat his time. The fishpond took well[.] Mr Stone auctioned the boxes and took charge of the fish line and money. Adolph helped me put on the fish back of [the] curtain. We had lots of fun. When they had to wait and got impatient Adolph would sing out "Line broke" and then we would just take our time to fix it.

I wish you could have all been here. It must have been alright for

I received complements and congratulations till if I could have found a hole big enough I'd have crawled in even at the risk of meeting a rattle snake. Miss Foulon left quite early the next morning and was hardly out of sight when Oscar came over. Adolph came a little later and both were here to dinner. Mrs Stone made me sit between them at table. I had plenty of room at first but they got nearer and nearer till I couldn't move my elbows enough to eat so I had to say "I've plenty, thanks" and quit. Mr Stone cant forget about it.

I was at a large party about five or six miles from here last evening. Stones didn't go and I rode in a *buggy*. Now what do you know about *that*? I just had the time of my life. During the evening I was trying to get a good one on Oscar and he exclamed "Oh quit, you threw me over-board once[,] isn't that enough" or some thing of that kind—which brought a big laugh but it wasn't ten minutes befor he gave me a good chance to hand him a bunch.

Mr Stone has been working over at my place five days this week. Glen Speer has been helping him. I expect to move a week from today if nothing happens.

You want to know how I am financialy so here goes—Relinquishment $60[,] Hasting[s'] fee $15[,] release $1[,] filing fee $14—Total $90—$30 paid leaves note for $60 at 10% int held by Mr Hastings. Then the lumber—Ive paid nearly $40 and there's a note for $50 at 10% int[.] Then I'm behind five weeks board or $15 and I expect I owe Mr Stone $25 for hauling and work and there's the dam to put in yet and I'll have to get a ton of coal which will be $10 and the hauling of it $4 more. I have about $18 in the bank and $4 in my pocket book and will draw another months wages in three week's and have most of what is absolutely necessay for my new home—thanks to your thoughtfulness. So I can make out. I don't want you to pinch yourself to send me money—guess a little hardship wont hurt me as you've seen a great deal of it though not quite like this.

Am going in next Friday to write exams again[;] thats $1.

I am writing this letter in bed. It is now about 12:30 and as I did not get home last night till this morning I will close for now and add a P S later.

With Love—Bess

P. S. Nov 7th—Mrs Stone and I were over to my house today. Its a dandy little home I'll be having soon. Please tell Mary and ask her why she don't write. Have I offended her?

I told you before that I "managed" a lumberman but I didn't know how well till today. When Mr Stone took my lumber bill in to get it figured on he told Mr. Keyser[5] he wanted his lowest possible figures. When he got the figures he asked Mr Keyser if he couldn't let him have it cheaper. Mr Keyser swore at him to beat the band and said he *could give* it to him. Mr Stone asked about terms of payment and Mr Keyser said like all the other lumbermen he must have the cash before the lumber left the yard so I thought I was up against it but went to see what I could do. I succeeded in making very desireable terms in a few minutes. Mr Stone jumped him about it and he said I was a mighty plucky girl and if he wasn't married already I could put my shoes in his old trunk any day. Mrs Stone was telling me about it today and said Mr Stone wondered how I worked that fellow so slick.

When I get moved Ill send you a plan that will show where all the chairs sit.

Well I must close—say you sent me Robs dictionary instead of mine did you know it? Mine is larger and more compled with black binding. Wish you would send me my crochet hook next time and penholders please[.]

                                        With Love—Bess

❋ NOV. 16, 1909 / FORT PIERRE, SO. DAK.
   TO MRS. MARGARET COREY
   7:30 P.M. AND SNOW TWO FEET DEEP

Dear Ma,—I wonder if any of you are thinking of me on this my twenty second birthday. I have certainly thought of you all today. Thought I'd have to write you a little befor my light burns out.

A week ago last night Oscar was over to Stones and befor he had been there very long I excused myself and put out for the shack across the road and I guess he thought I was prepairing for the exams for he was over real early the next evening with newspaper clippings about the presidents cabinet and outher things beside a question book— said he hoped I could use them 'twould save such a lot of work. Wasn't he good?

Last Thursday for the first time in my life, I saw oxen at work. There were four of them hitched to a big wood wagon—say but they go fine and are the proper thing for out here and are so much cheaper than horses.

The Speer boys started in school last week—Glen about like Rob and Howard about like Fuller and Howard seems to like to talk to the school ma'am. Friday Howard took me down to write the exams. I say that trip was worth a four dollar dog. I had a jolly good time.

Howard is a splendid talker so our conversation never lagged. When we were almost to town I dug out a silver dollar and handed him. He looked as if he hated to take it and after he had put it away he told me what a time he had had that morning. He said "When any of us kids have any change we generaly put it in one of those little cups on the clock shelf and every morning when dad builds the fire he goes along and tips those cups and if he finds any change it goes into his pocket and we never see it come out again[.]" Well it seems Howard had saved up a little money from helping some one and had it hid in a bureau drawer. He intended [to] drive the ponies—one is his and one is Glens—but Glen is always afraid Howard is going to get ahead of him a little some where and so made such a roar that he had to drive his pony with one of his fathers big horses. When he was all ready to start he went for his money to find that his father had got it all and wouldnt give him a cent which left him with nothing to pay for his dinner or team shelter unless I happened to give him something before we got to town. Howard was so angry I guess from what he said he cussed every thing in sight. He declared he wouldn't go one step—that he didn't care if I didn't write the exam or if I quit the school—that people who would do such things didnt deserve to have a school or any thing else. But his mother felt so bad about it he gave in and went. I was remarking that I had so much shopping to do I didn't know how I'd ever get through and he said if I'd give him a list he would help me—that he was used to getting things for folks when he went to town. He is a mighty good hand at it and we were all through by half after eleven so I went down to Gordons a few minutes while he went to feed the team. I got back first and was waiting for him at Fishers store[.][1] I was rather amused when he sang out clear across that department store "Ready to go to dinner yet?" Every one smiled and so did I for it sounded so much like Rob.

The exam was dead easy beside the other one but of course I dont know how I will come out.

Adolph Bucholz came and held the team and talked while Howard loaded up—I had told him at the social that I intended to write on that day so he had been down and looked through the register to see if I was in town and then he almost missed me after all. He's a great lad—Oh yes[,] and I got to talk to Rudolph [Klemann][2] and Fridtjoph too. I received a letter from Jennie Noon—please tell her I was very glad to hear from her and will try to write her soon.

Befor bed time Friday night it was snowing and kept at it almost all the time till last night or this morning rather. Three days of it and there is more snow on the ground now than there has been on at one time for two or three years they say[.] I moved into my new house Saturday in spite of the weather.

Good night—more later—Bess

NOV. 21ST.

Will try to write another chapter. I have put in the week of my life I believe—a week ago yesterday I packed up and moved—had had no time to come over to clean out my house so we had to put everything in right on top of the sawdust, shavings and bits of boards. Mr Stone put up the stove and built a fire then went on home. Some of the dirt from the cellar is thrown east of the house in front of the door and with no step a plenty of it was brought in. I worked like a slave till nine o clock then after a supper of sardines and crackers I went to roost. Seldom has a meal tasted better to me than that first one in the new house. I worked as hard as I could all day last Sunday and didn't have things half straight then. The next five mornings I was up at half past five or before and it keeps me bussy then to wash, dress, comb my hair, get my breakfast and be ready for school at seven. I like to have my school fire built by eight. When it is stormy I have to start for school in the dark. I faced the storm Monday morning and went in knee deep a good bit of the way then the wind shifted and I had to face it going home that night. Speers thought sure I would come home with the children and when they got home without me they sent one of the boys after me—he cut cross lots and after going half a mile the storm lifted a little and he saw me going up Cornels hill so he went back. It has been better since Monday. Tues. it was clear and cold and blew the snow off a little and Wednesday they broke a road part way. Monday eve Mr Stone left a pound of butter at the school house and Tuesday eve a gallon pail most full of milk and Wednesday they butchered and he brought me a big chunk of beef which he put in a sling so I could carry it easy.

Tuesday Howard asked me if that wasn't the darnedest longest two miles I ever tried to walk. I wanted to tell him yes but instead I said "Why it isn't *two* miles is it?" You aught to have seen his face for a minute[.]

"It's a dandy little home." Elizabeth Corey's claim shack with the builder's daughter, the "littlest pebble," Weltha Stone, on the front stoop. Photo by Elizabeth Corey, ca. 1913.

Several from this part of the country went to town Thursday[.] Mr Speer brought my barrel out to his house. Haven't found out yet who paid the freight. Every one "Don't know any thing about it." I got the mail too—ten birthday cards and two letters—how glad I was to get them—Tell Paul I had my birthday bird on Friday[.]

Friday evening I started home and had gone about half a mile when I saw several hundred range cattle approaching from the north and Speers Bull from the south—one fence between and I on the side where the range cattle were. There was no use going back so I kept on going but I wondered mighty fast on which side of the fence the walking was the best—desided to stay where I was as Speers bull will even attact a man on horseback if he hasn't a rope. The herd, or part of it rather, reached the fence ahead of me a ways—the huge range bull roared and Speers bull roared and the rest watched me. Just then Glen Speer hove in sight—coming across the quarter at a rate that made the snow fly and swinging a long rope—the only thing on earth that range cattle are afraid of I guess. He separated them and watched till I was past and I'll tell you right now I never was as glad to see my grandmother as I was to see Glen Speer that time.

I haven't had to carry water—just melt snow you know—have had my tub full of snow water by the stove all the time and more than once I've gone to bed at nine thirty with a good fire and when I got up at five thirty have had to strike quite hard with my fist to break the ice on the tub while smaller things freeze up solid. My house is one of the warmest and best built houses in the country so you see we are having a spell of weather. I dont mind it like some folks do and every one is good to me—I have lots of invitations to stay over night or over Saturday & Sunday.

I started bread Friday evening. I suppose you wonder how I kept my yeast from freezing. I did like every one else out here—put it in a tight can, wrapped it up good and took it to bed with me and if holding that darned thing all night isn't enough to give any old maid bad dreams I don't know—I don't think I ever had better luck with bread though.

Yesterday forenoon Howard, Mrs Speer and three of the girls came over and brought the barrel—every thing in it was all right—the day we were in town Howard went down and had them put it in where it wouldn't freeze. We opened it—took everything out then Howard put the barrel down cellar and the apples back in it. I kept the spotted ones. Then he put the box with the potatoes down also: he put the box on top the barrel just leaving a little room to get the apples out—said he was afraid I'd fall in head first some time when I was alone and couldn't get out again. I made as if to shut the door on him and he turned back to the apple barrel saying that would be alright as long as the apples lasted so I let him out—had him bring up some and told him to fill his pockets—he slapped his pockets saying "Gosh they're as full as they can hold now" and so they were.

Beside the barrel they brought me a two quart pail of milk—said I should keep the pail—and a table about as wide as the one you have by the cupboard and half again as long—'twas up in their attic and they had no use for it at present so I no longer use a store box. And they brought me four little pie pumpkins and a grain sack full of vegetables—three squash beside beats, carrots, onions and turnips. Mrs Stone gave me a pail of beets and four citrons. I bought a dimes worth of onions in town now I guess I have a peck all together and a good half bushel of beets. And in one corner I have half a ton of coal and in another all the shavings and bits left over from building [the house] so I'm all right in all kinds of weather.

My house is this shape:

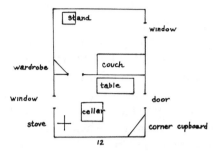

Cellar 8 × 10, attic large and roomy the ladder going up to it is just south of the cellar door—have only been up high enough to look in as I cannot pull my self higher with one hand[.] I have no chairs. Mr Stone says they have some extras stored away and he will bring over one some time. at present I'm sitting on a nail keg. The couch is one like Mrs Harris has but not so wide—I bought it for a dollar and a half from a family moving out and I make my bed on it the way I learned how at home. Mrs Speer has a cot bed stored away that she says I can have the use of if I want it. I told her I wouldnt need it unless I should have company for a week or two some time. She also has almost enough half worn rag carpet to cover my sittingroom floor which she says she never expects to use again and if I want to put it down I'm welcome to it.

Everybody makes such a toot about my nerve, pluck, push, grit and so on till it most makes my feet warm for so far it hasn't been half as hard as they seem to think it is still they'd most break their necks to do something for "Miss Corey." I was never so popular before and it makes me feel queer.

Did I tell you that when Mr Stone went for the lumber that Mr Keyser said he was out of four inch soft flooring and gave him two in. hard at the same figures and he also said he was out of the little windows with eight by ten inch panes at eighty cents so gave him at the same price $1.25 windows with 10 × 20 in panes. It looks queer but I hope I know enough to keep my mouth shut.

Oh yes[,] I must tell you about some of my neighbors. Two dutchmen, one a widower the other an old maid, their name is Bahr.[3] One has crooked eyes and can see trouble farther off than any mortal I ever heard of before. He is always getting mad at some of his neighbors and then he goes over to Speers much excited and tells them all about it in

Dutch of which they can't understand a word and he always end it up with "By yinks, I hit him in the eye" so Howard speaks of them as "Dose By Yinks Dutchmen[.]"

Once they were so mad at Billy Niece they were going to take the gun and shoot his hide so full of holes it wouldn't hold pumpkins so when the boys come out here they must plan on "Bein good[.]"

It has been storming since Speers left yesterday and its almost bedtime. You don't need to worry about me though for I'm all right while Im here and I wont start out when I cant see the trail and Mrs Speer made me promise I wouldn't start home another night when it was so stormy.

Mr Stone got the barrel of apples alright. You have no idea how much I appreciate yours and Grandma's letter and those post cards—would like to write each one s[e]paratly but just can't get time. Made a batch of pickles and my first cake in the new home today.

Yours With Love
Bess

* POSTCARD / NOV 28TH / FT. PIERRE, SO. DAK.
  NINETEEN HUNDRED AND THAWING A LITTLE [1909]
  TO MRS. M. M. COREY

Dear Ma—Howard left your note on the way over to Ericksens and if I get this written before he gets back will get it mailed tomorrow. My letter must have reached you ere this, telling you of our spell of weather—just getting ready for another spell. No I haven't bough[t] a trunk and when I do it will be a bureau.

Am real well thank you but have been soreheading it around here all day—one of those "By Yinks" was here this morning. I could kill a dozen cats if they were Dutch. Please make your next note thirteen chapters and send me two or three penholders. With love to all I am

Your Little Girl E. F. C.

* POSTCARD / 7 DEC 1909 / FT. PIERRE, SO. DAK.
  TO MRS. M. M. COREY

Say Ma if you have any hot weather down there just send us a few bits will you. Last week was a fright. Two storms—staid two nights at Speers—Wed & Fri—one rainstorm—changed into snow like the one you had last Jan and one just the kind you read about. wish you would send me a gun—have a batch of rusks for ammunition which would last a while.

Tell Ethel the organ I was going to get her for helping her ma is in the milk pitcher.

What is Toad[1] in such a rush to get through by Jan 1st for[?]

Guess who wrote this and please ans[.]

Am O K   Dec 6 1909

✱ DEC. 8, 1909 / FORT PIERRE, SO. DAK.

TO MRS. M. M. COREY

Dear Ma,—It is a quarter of nine but I must write you a few lines any way.

Last week was a caution—it started to rain Tuesday evening and Wednesday morning I went to school in the rain then it turned cold and stormed to beat the band so I went home with the Speer Children. Thursday it was a little better and I came home then Friday it stormed so that Mr Speer came after the children and insisted that I go home with them again—I didn't want to but he said it was no use for me to start out as I'd never make it in such a storm[—]he said he *would try* it in a case of absolute nescessity but not other wise so I thought I better not try what a man wouldnt risk so I staid with Speers again and went home about noon Saturday.

Saturday afternoon I sorted the apples and washed them all—canned up the ones with spots in them—had about six qts and then as it seemed to be getting colder every minute I dyed some flour sacks and got them ready to cover a comfort it was about eleven that night when I went to bed. Sun[day] I baked bread, pumpkin pies and rusks—the bread and pies are fine but the rusks are what I suppose Mr Speer would call "Cranky like de devil[.]" They are surely fierce.

You folks *think* you know something about cold weather but you dont. I had got used to having my hair, eyebrows and eyewinkers covered with frost and ice till I looked like Santa Clause when I got to school but Sun. night beat that all hollow. I went to bed with the covers over my head and just a little air hole over my right eye and when I woke up in the night I found when I put up my hand to turn down the covers that my hair and the blanket were covered with hoar frost[.]

Monday morning it was blazing cold—I put that heavy gray wool skirt on for an under neath skirt—and wrapped as warm as I could. I got to school at five minutes till eight but the stove is in such a bad condition it took me fifteen minutes to clean out the ashes and start the fire. About that time my feet began to feel queer and by the time I was through sweeping I was ready to dance the "Highland Fling." I saw Mr Stone coming with Myrtle[1] and when he got there I had a note written to Mrs Stone asking if she had any thing in the house of which I could make bloomers as I got so cold about the branches and if she would send to town for some woolen stockings for me first time she got a chance. Plague take Mr Stone he read the note and it tickled him so he had to tell Speers about it. Mrs Speer said the wording of the note most killed him off. Mrs Stone sent me a pair of her woolen stockings and Miss Hunts bloomers that night when Mr. Stone came after Myrtle.

Howard wanted me to go home with them Monday evening—he said it was far colder than in the morning and I'd frieze to death—he talked till he was red in the face and then gave it up. When he got to the door he turned back and said "Well if you do start home you'll find how cold it is by the time you get to the dam and you better turn of[f] there and cut a crossed to our place[.]" When Mr Stone came for Myrtle he said I was to go home with him or down to Speers but he thought I better go down to Speers and I got there just as Mrs Speer finished: "Well if Miss Corey tries to go home such a night as this she needs a right good thumping[.]"

I guess my heels were pretty well nipped and should have been thawed with snow Mr Stone said. I walked the floor most of the forenoon and sometimes I could hardly keep my voice steady but when it began to shake all the other voices began to shake too—even Howards so I *had* to keep a stiff upper lip.

My but Howard is good to me! He brings my dinner to school and takes the pail home, gets in coal, sharpens my pencils and all sorts of such things[.]

Tuesday Mr Speer went to town and I sent for some heavy union suits, some woolen stockings and heavy dark brown outing flannel for bloomers. I staid all night there again last night and got into some warmer duds.

The chill Monday morning caused a postponement and the warm clothes acted the other way. I was "took" before noon today.

I came home tonight to find every thing froze up tight as a brick both up stairs and down cellar—apples potatoes and all—they rattle around like stones.

By the time I got my fire started I felt rather tipsy and jarred up against the oven and the stove pipe came unjointed. I would have sat down and cried for my maw but I knew it wouldn't do any good so I just worked till I got it fixed and whistled "Good Old Summer Time" while I was at it. Yes[,] honestly[,] I've whistled most all the evening.

A pack of wolves passed the school house yesterday afternoon. Howard says its school ma'am they're after. He says they like school ma'ams better than anything else and can scent them a long ways off. He said if they ever attact me to pursuade them to let me off for a week or two till I faten up a little better then perhaps I can get a gun befor I meet them again.

I realy must beg, borrow or steal money enough to get me a gun and a licence for there isn't a tree or telaphone pole to climb here[.]

Did I tell you about my dinner pail? Just as big around as a pint cup and twice as high. One day it didn't seem to hold enough and I remarked that I guessed I'd have to put sideboards on it. That tickled the children and they took it home. Now *that* is going the rounds and is applied to all sorts of things. Its always "We'll have to put sideboards on it like Miss Corey said about her dinner pail."

Say Mr. Stone woke up Monday night and found one of his ears friezing. He says this is colder than he ever saw since he came out here.

When I got home last Saturday I saw about the first thing that my ink bottle had been having a swell time so will have to use a pencil in real Soddie style here after.

I have twelve flour sacks the color of the piece enclosed[.]

Mr Stone went to town today so will not seal this till I see what mail I get. When some of you are feeling rich I wish you would get that jewelry of mine at Nielsons[2] and pay the bill[.] I'll make it square with you.

Did you ever settle up our accounts to see how much I owe you? And did you give Toad that ten spot I owe him?

If you have any means of finding out anything of L. Wilkins of Guthrie Center and his daughter Leana who married a fellow named Share I wish you would—find out if she is at home at present—it might save a heap of trouble if it could be learned quietly[.][3] Do you suppose Uncle John[4] would know any thing of them[?]

Your card rec'd Monday eve. Must close and retire it is almost eleven so

Good Night—Bess

SATURDAY EVENING DEC 11

Last Thursday morning was clear but bitter cold. I reached the school house just as Mr Speer did on his road to town so I sent by him for a sweater—It is a boys sweater of heaviest dark gray with a band of navy blue about the neck and down the front and buttons with six very pretty large pearl buttons.

I staid all night at Speers Thurs. night[—]was about all in—almost shook my teeth out—Howard said I seemed to have quite a chilliness and if I had gone home I'd have sure knocked the stove pipe down. Mrs Speer put me to bed after an early supper—said I was coming down with a cold—put a hot flat iron at my feet—brought me quinine tablets and a cup of water and when I didn't stop shaking put Mr Speer's fur coat on top all the rest of the covers so by morning I felt as good as new.

Have been working like a good fellow all day today and am gong on with my kinckerbockers after supper.

I tell you pioneer life didn't end in the long ago—its a fright the way some poor wretches have to live. I am very fortionate and can live up to my motto "Do all the good you can to all the folks you can in all the ways you can and smile, darn you, smile." and the worse my luck the more fun I make of it and folks who come with long faces to sympathize go home laughing and saying "What fer a schoolma'am we got this year anyway[?]"

I owe most of my popularity though to my being such an honest and cheerful liar. I try to be neighborly too but I'm about disgusted. You know that pail of salt pork you sent me? Such things usually last a good while out here where they are well taken care of and I thought I could make it last the whole six years but it wont last long at the rate the last piece went. I had a piece—oh, about as big as the salt shaker, I guess[—]that I had cooked with beans three times and it was as good as ever when that Dutch neighbor borrowed it to cook with beans when he had company[.] the old dunce left it on the plate and when the dog washed the plate he ate it up so when I wanted Irish stew for supper tonight I had to get out another piece of pork. Well as Lida [Smith] would say "Such is life in the far west."

Is Mary L. still teaching the rusty headed Andersens? Why dont she answer my letter? Tell her to drop me a card a week befor she starts so some of us can meet her in Ft Pierre.

Must close and get to work—

Lovingly—Bess

✳ DEC. 21, 1909 / FORT PIERRE, SO. DAK.
TO MRS. M. M. COREY

Hello here[,—]ink once more[,] what do you know about that? I'm at Speers again—cant stay away long. Its good weather too—came down to use the sewing machine—didn't know there was so much sewing about just one pair of neither-tackle till I tried it. sewed 'em right here with every one looking on—say but the weather is fine[, and] so was last week. I came to school a week ago Monday morning and got home Friday eve, staid one night at Stones and the rest of the nights at Speers. Ruthie [Speer] says she hopes I will spend Xmas here and that I'll be awful homesick cause she says she would just like to see me squall. I guess she will-nit[not].

Only three more days of school this term—exams, term reports, and everything topped off by a "Hard Times Candy Pull" Friday afternoon. Am getting along fine but I'll bet a four dollar dog that someone will get slapped clean up to a peak before Xmas. This letter will be rather mixed as there is "somethin doin" here. Am coming down here Thursday eve to help make candy.

Was very glad to get your letter and Pauls and Mary L's also[.] have got my Dakota Certificate [and] am proud(?) of it[.] I [have to] tell you it is just good for one year.

Wasn't that awful about Elsie Long[1]—thats another that I bid good bye so thoughtlessly expecting to meet again and now she's gone. There were at least a dozen young people of my acquaintance who went suddenly when no one expected such a thing[.] I begin to wonder when my turn is coming. Oh well it doesn't make much diff anyway only I kind of wish the boys had said good bye to me when I left but of course they never stop to think that I'm not the only one that was ever cranky. Sunday some of the folks got together and compared notes and as none had seen a smoke at my house they began to fear I had perished on the road home Friday evening. The drifts were fierce but I made it.

It will soon be Xmas—My! I wish that box was here—dont suppose I've money enough for the freight but will make it some how. I tell you if you invite me to eat Xmas dinner with you Dec 25, 1915 I'll be Johnnie on the spot when the bell rings. But don't expect [me] to make Iowa sooner than that[.]

I wrote Jennie some time ago and will mail Grandma a long letter tomorrow.[2]

I wrote that last letter to you a week ago Saturday evening and the next day Mr Speer and Howard stopped at my house and left me a chair, half worn rag carpet enough to cover my sitting room floor, a two qt pail of milk, a big piece of fresh pork, some head cheese (like mother used to make) and a good sized bunch of twine. Thats the way it goes all the time.

My but I wish Fuller was here with his violin[3] for a while only I'm afraid he would freeze up[;] but then its warmer now. Yesterday it was 22° in Ft Pierre.

You might run over a while Xmas day—I'll be half a mile south of the school house. well I must close and go to roost.—Have nothing to give this Xmas but my best wishes and you know you have that[.] Well Merry Xmas to you all[.]

Goodnight
Bess.

✱ DEC. 28, 1909 / FORT PIERRE, SO. DAK.
TO MRS. M. M. COREY

Dear Mamma,—It is half after nine and I should not be writing so I'm going to. That last letter I wrote at Speers and was feeling like the monkey that got the first dip in the rense water.

Last Thursday evening—no it was Wednesday evening I came home after school and made candy till half after eleven—am getting to be a gimsnuffer at making candy—can make four kinds—Howard says he likes them all best. Took a syrup pail of candy to school Thursday—it didn't take the youngsters long to make it look tired. Thurs. evening I went down to Speers [and] we made candy—that is Mrs Speer and I did—the rest ate it so fast we like to never got through— just had the dickens of a time with the boys.

Friday was "*Last Day.*" We had our "Hard Times Candy Pull."

Howard and I made the candy and every one pulled. I had nothing to give the children so made them cards shaped like the one enclosed tied two together with Xmas ribbon, their name on the top one and Xmas greetings on the bottom one. Friday evening I helped Mrs Speer make crackerjack—genuine article with peanuts in.

I have three Xmas presents. Mrs Stone gave me a beauty of a button box, Myrtle gave me a pretty Xmas card and Speers gave me an enameled quart cup. We had some fun about the cup. Some time back when I was at Speers Mr Speer brought one home from town and was asking us what we thought of it—Mr Stone was there and said it would be "just the thing to drink milk out of" and I said "one like that would be just the thing to bile taters in" and we each got one for Xmas. They are shaped like a pint cup only a little more flat.

Xmas day there was lots of company and lots to do so I never had time to get homesick. Just before supper Howard hitched to the bob-sleigh and we went to take Ben Share[1] some Xmas goodies. We found him feeling better and longing for a breath of air so we took him over to Speers for supper and the evening then Howard took him home again.

I almost forgot to tell you I rec'd two very pretty Xmas post cards and Mr Keyser sent me one of the most beautiful calanders I ever saw—a large one—18 × 20 inches[.] I came home yesterday (Monday) forenoon. Mrs Speer wanted to borrow some things so Howard brought me over [to my claim]. He staid till half after eleven and helped me quite a bit—passing remarks on every thing he touched just like Rob. He cut shavings to start the fire and jawed about the butcher knife till I had to remind him that he bought it him self. When he put the coal in he said "Say you have to chew it up fine for this little stove don't you[?]" Asked if the package in the window was fastners for the cupboard doors and then put the top ones on for me—said he put 'em a little crooked to match the door—dropped a screw—found it behind the slop pail—remarked that he was afraid he'd dropped it in the spittoon.—asked something about my not washing the dishes befor I went to school—rattled the dishes around till he found what was left of two kinds of fudge and of course he didn't do anything to it after he found it. Next he went in the sitting room—said "Why! you take time to make your bed befor you go to school!" then he saw my mitten—you remember that little red knit mitten of mine? so small you couldn't get you[r] little finger into it. Well I took a piece of white

drawing paper and at the top wrote, "Single still["] under that wrote
"Why?" and under that fastened the mitten and pined it on the wall.
Howard said "Well who the deuce ever gave *you* the mitten I'd like to
know." I sent him down cellar after apples and jell and he declared
that a can of plums were working, that the cans of apples had froze
and burst, that snow had drifted in on the coal, that the jars of jell
were labled preserves and oh such a time as he had. If the Corey boys
and their cousin Howard[2] ever get together, my! but wont the natives
suffer!

The Speer boys and I have a high old time because their mother's
mother's brother's daughter married my mother's brother and Mrs
Speer says that makes us cousins so Mrs. Grundy cant talk if we do
have a little fun.

The roads are rather fierce yet I guess and its storming some
more. Mr Speer was talking a while back of going to town and Howard
asked if the sled wouldn't be like the Chinamans auto[,] "Goee like
hellee[,] no pushee[,] no pullee" and his father said it would be different in one respect—there would be plenty of "pullee[.]"

Since I came home I've melted snow, done a big washing, finished
my comfort around the edge and covered the partition between the
sittingroom and kitchen with heavey building paper. Was to have gone
back to Speers tonight for the rest of the week but there's so much to
do here. I want to iron and scrub, sew my carpet and put it down, take
a bath, scrub my hair, make out my reports and do some mending.
Would like to go to town one day this week if possible.

We are going to have plum pudding and ice-cream New Years Day
perhaps[.]

Have not heard from the chest yet but my! it will seem good to
have some thing that a cow boy hasn't a key to. These darn cow boys
go through every thing you've got and if you dont like it you can lump
it. One night shortly after I moved, one of them roped the "little mansion" out north here and pulled it up by the roots—left it on one corner—Who ever did it must be on to the buisness as the anchor posts
were a foot and a half in the ground. The worst of it is they carry
skeleton keys[.] I told you didn't I about comming home one night
after dark and finding my door unlocked? Gee I wish I had had some
kind of gun that wasn't to heavy to carry, they wouldn't bother me then
as they've been convinced that I'm a good marksman or soon would
be. There were two six inch boards nailed accrossed the lower part of

my east window to keep the range horses out and yesterday when we got here we could see the tracks in the snow where one had come up to the window and attached his rope to one of the board[s] and rode east. The board, which was nailed with large nails[,] snapped square in t[w]o[—]one half was a rod or so from the window[,] the other half hung by one badly bent nail.

Well my stove don't burn good tonight and its bitter cold so will close and go to roost as my teeth are rattling[.] May add a P.S.

with love Bess

DEC 31, 1909 FRIDAY — NEW YEARS EVE — Am at Speers again—stove smoked me out.

Got up yesterday morning pulled on my stockings and shoes and ran out and started my fire—it began to smoke—I worked with it as quickly as possibly but was soon almost over come with smoke—just grabbed my big coat and rushed out doors—thanked my lucky stars I had no near neighbors as I perched there on a snow drift coughing and choking and trying to lace my shoes—was also thankful it was some what warmer—when the smoke thinned I went in and dressed then tried it again with no better result so packed my suit case straightened up a bit and started for Speers. Was kind of chilly around the edges when I started but soon warmed up to it as a great deal of new snow had fallen and had drifted the track full. Befor I was half way here I was ready to drop the suit case and myself in the snow and shuffle off this mortal coil—it surely was fierce. Howard had started for a jag of hay and saw me comming and came after me—took me around by the hay stack—made me tramp hay. Was about all in when I got here.

Yesterday afternoon I made three pillow slips and today I made another pair of bloomers—have one of the mittens knit for Ruthies doll—beat Glen all ter smash playing checkers this evening. Last evening I got beat playing another game.

Darn that goose kicked Irishman[3] he done gone went off without seeing about my warrent and I'm treed by my shortage of dingbats.[4] I have it on Mr Keysers account as he will have that note to pay I suppose—Guess he wont be so stuck on me now as they told about—will make it up to him when I can.

Glen is going up to Stones bright and early in the morning if he wakes up and if Mr Stone is going to town will get him to mail some letters so thought [I] would finish this.

Have been laughing at Fannie[5]—she said she would watch the old year out but would not set up to watch the new year in.

You must not worry about any thing I write—the cowboys are mostly a pretty good sort—all except a few like Sunshine[6]—the way they propose to a girl—they ride up to her door—draw a six shooter and say "Wilt thou[?]" and she wilts. One girl was engaged to a man back east so she didn't wilt and he shot her—her folks were rich and went after him and he got to be manager in the shirt factory for two years—he won't get out for a year yet and Sunshine has eloped with another man's wife so guess I'll get along alright.

Much obliged for the box, hope I get it soon—Please write Your Little Girl Bess

✱ JAN. 5, 1910 / FORT PIERRE, SO. DAK.
TO MRS. M. M. COREY

Dear Ma,—I dont suppose that last letter I wrote is on the road to you yet but will start another. The letters missed connections with Mr Stone but he brought the mail—had several Xmas postals and the package you sent—the box was cracked accross the bottom—the handkerchiefs were very pretty—thanks to the givers and senders. What were those two dodingeses in the bottom of the box—no one knows—Howard says "The Lord only knows and he wont tell"—begin to think he is right about it.

Went to school from Speers Monday—Howard brought me home Monday eve to see what ailed the stove—fire started fine—not a bit of smoke—guess the smokestack isn't high enough and it only smokes when the wind is in one direction. He staid an hour or so and almost teased the life out of me—said he'd rather see me cry than look so sober. It was snowing befor bedtime Monday and kept it up most of yesterday—was so bad I couldn't make it—started for school but came back—first day I've missed on account of weather[.] This is wednesday morning—two or three minutes to seven but far to dark to start out—am going to try in a little while—got to do something—coal most gone—might as well cool off one place as another.

If you can possibly spare me some money please send it and send it quick—what ever you can spare. The school board is so scattered and some of them gone am having trouble getting warrents—owe some thing like a hundred and fourty and am in suffering need of some things. I believe you folks can stand the racket better down there than I can alone on a South Dakota claim[.] Its pretty hard to see folks out at the elbows this kind of weather when I owe them money. Have not heard from box or registered letter yet but hope to soon—In Haste

Bess

P S—Reached school this morning with about life enough left to build the fire—feel pretty bum—am at Speers again—will stay here till I get money and coal—am pretty near all in—drifts are fierce. Please come on with the mon[ey] if possible—with love   E. F. C.

**✱ JAN. 13, 1910 / FORT PIERRE, SO. DAK.
TO MRS. M. M. COREY**

Dear Ma,—Chest and registered letter received Tuesday evening—was never so glad to get anything before in my life as I was to get that letter—much obliged for the check—it will help me out fine. Am going down tomorrow with Mr. Blumgreen and Mr. Ovank(?)[1] if nothing happens and teach on Saturday—thought I could write a few lines in spite of the racket[.]

Guess you have the note—its either with other papers at German Bank[2] or the north pile of papers in the little drawer in the south side of the Sitting room book case.

Box was O.K. but the lower pieces fell off the ends when Howard unroped it. Yes you did fine[—] have most of my "belongings" now except "Little brown jug" a little glass & cup that Miss Conners[3] gave me—a few pen holders—one Ethel gave me and one Will Copley[4] gave me but they can come on later with other things and I'll pay the freight next time and tell Fuller to never pay more than 10¢ *per cwt* bridge toll. Walnuts were fine we cracked a six quart pail full last eve and even Howard said he got his suficiency full for once. The rest are put away.

Yes the pork was alright but a little goes a long way and as it has a long way to go I hate to see folks so wasteful and careless—By the way his dog came over to my house one day and ate some of my pancakes and passed in his checks before he could get home—the old boy thought he was poisoned I guess.

Camp stool is fine for many things—will tell you what I use it for later.

Olney fixed those needles and hook[s] proper—the boys fixed things up fine.

Will send Uncle Walters letter back. The carpet rags will make my rug a little larger. I don't remember giving anyone that sterescope but if I did its alright only it would have been a help in school and Sunday School—the set of views would. Am glad you sent nuts instead of post toasties as I have a suply of the la[t]ter—Expect to use the foot warmer tomorrow if I go. Am wearing my new back comb—she's a peach and the side combs are a pair.

The boards that came off can be nailed on again so its all right.

Yes[,] please pay Fuller that ten spot as I owe it to him—what I promised him if he would finish eighth grade and I expect he needs it.

Your hogs must be doing pretty good—hope you will write me how every thing is rounding up for March 1st[.]

Tell Rob not to bother his head about finishing [school] this year—perhaps 'tis all for the best—make the most of every minute and he'll get through all the better some other time. You folks don't want to take it any harder than you have to[—]just remember that "*The evil a person does rebounds upon themselves*" so when others play you a trick just remember that they get their own for their meanness and dont do any thing you dont want to come back to you or yours—and often things explain them selves later or turn out for the best—Please dont get provoked at my preaching as I really practice it.

Ask Rob if he dont want to join my lodge[5] and wear a red ribon badge with the words Smile, Darn You Smile.

Was much grieved to hear that one of the few people who ever appreciated what a fine woman my mother is had passed in his checks—am afraid I wont know old Clay T'w'p[6] when I get back[.]

Used to think I knew something about work being piled up but I never did realy till I got into this homely mans country.

Was so glad to hear from Olney—tell him I will write him soon.

Dont know if I would know how to use a rocker—am used to "sitting on the floor with my feet hanging down" as they tell about.

Most of my fruit is up in sugar so stood the cold alrigh[t] and frozen grub is alright when its hot.

Have so many letters to write it almost makes me daffy[.] It still storms nine days in the week—was over home last Sunday—dont expect to go again till Spring if I can help it—They say four horses couldn't get a load of coal over there and I cant wade snow four feet deep four miles a day and set all day with wet duds—stuck to it till I got so stiff I could hardly navigate—am boarding at Speers for now[.]

Have just made up my mind not to go town tomorrow[.]

Would like to write you about fourteen more chapters but must close[.]

You will doubtless be proud of the way I fixed that check when you get it back—just lay it on to "circumstances" and forget about it.

Must close—I thoroughly appreciate all the trouble and expense you folks were to on my account and hope to some day make it up to you—love to all[.]

Bess

❋ JAN. 20, 1910 / FORT PIERRE, SO. DAK.
TO MRS. M. M. COREY

Dear Ma,—Mr Stone is thinking of going to town Saturday so if I write a few letters tonight and give them to him tomorrow they will get started Saturday perhaps. Your card of the 11th inst received last Sunday—Blumgreens brought the mail over. Was very glad that I didn't go to town with them last Friday as by noon it was storming something fierce—we had no school in the afternoon—then we all came down with bad colds except me and we didn't have any school Mon. have had school since but not a very large attendance. Myrtle [Stone] has started in again.

That registered package must have been in town some time before I got wind of it. Then when Mr Speer went down he was going to sign as my agent and get it but they wouldn't let him have it with out a written order signed by me so I had to wait till he went down again which was some time which caused the delay you mentioned but you must have rec'd a letter ere this telling of it. Baird better not go after the old boy too hard or he will be apt to get a swift kick[.] What did your school maam stay out of school for? She says evergreens don't freeze. I tell you though we sure have weather up here—the snow doesn't pack like it does there in Iowa and even when it does its worse yet for there are no trees to stop the wind and it tears up the bigest drifts and stacks them some where else just to move them over a few pegs the next day. A few feet of snow and a wind as cold as my mother-in-laws breath a howling down the pike a whistling at all the corners makes weather for any one out here on the prairie with nothing to stop it. You folks are not the only ones that have roads and weather. Monday Mr Stones horses were both down twice just between here and the school-house.

The last two or three days it has thawed a little in the middle of the day the first time in weeks and weeks. When the sun shines it is fierce—you can look over miles and miles of snow without a speck of color to releave it. Will be most mighty glad to get that gun—what kind is it? Howard says its going to be one of these little air rifles—Glen and I think its a 22[.] Have shot a few times with Glens but I couldn't hit a flock of barns—am practicing up in hopes of getting a few of the Dutchmen as there is a big bounty on them and Mr Stone says he will raise it.

This little Ruth [Speer] is what Bess called Verl I do believe. For of all the imp mischief you ever heard of! I say she is the limit. She was pinching my arm one morning in bed because it was fat and I asked her if she didn't suppose fat could feel and wouldn't Rob have laughed to hear her say tonight "Darn you Dutch, don't you spose fat can feel[?]" or something of the sort. And once when she was sleeping with Fannie and I[,] I did something to tease her and she said "One of you kids will get slapped the first thing you know[.]" I said I wondered which one and she said "Fan."

Am not as stiff in the joints as I used to be but do not indulge in foot races yet as the snow is too deep. I dont get homesick—not when I'm awake any way though they say I sometimes cry in my sleep and talk to you but oh how I wish sometimes that Toad and his violin were here—I get so lonesome for music.

Well I guess I better close as I have a lot of other letters I aught to write[.] Wish the kids would write to me—I like to hear from them though I don't write often now I'll answer later when I have more time.

The four of the younger children sleep here in this room and I have just finished a tussle with Glen who has been biting them so they couldnt sleep[.] Have shut him in us girls room as Howard had gone to bed—there has been an unnatural stillness for some time—Mrs Speer was afraid he had gone to roost in our bed but guess he hasn't—

Will close now as it is most time to hit the perch

With Love—Bess

* JAN. 28, 1910 / FORT PIERRE, SO. DAK.
  TO MRS. M. M. COREY

Dear Ma,—A week ago today the Scripters[1] were going to the river after wood so Florence [Scripter] rode with them up to where the trail passes half a mile east of the school house and walked over and visited school. After school I decided to go home with her so she went with me down to Speers to get some clean handkerchieves. By the time we got back to the school house we could see her brothers comming so we had to hustle to meet them at the trail. That made a mile and a half at a stretch and we were about all in when we got there. The boys wrapped us up good in a fur coat and two fur robes so we got along pretty well till the horses—or one of them rather—played out then they decided to come back for the load next morning. (Say one of the By Yinks[2] came just a few minutes ago and those wonderful eyes looked round and round me as I write which causes a peculiar scattering of wits[.]) We were about half a mile from their home—no I guess they said it was a mile—The boys wanted us to ride the horses and as Florence was about all in they just picked her up and put her on one of them but I persisted in walking so Erle the married brother took the other horse and Art and I walked—didn't go the same road they did either—Yes I've begun to appreciate Art and make no more remarks about Lida—Will study the subject whenever circumstances afford opportunity. Was nice and warm when we got there but Florence was almost froze and was sick most of the next day. I had a splendid time and Sunday afternoon they brought me home.

When I got home I received yours and the boys letters[—]was glad to hear from you all. Tell Rob I will write to him and the rest of the kidlets when I can and tell him I think Howard would write him if he would write the first letter but he draws his line at *first* letters—he wrote a letter to a young fellow a while back and the young fellows mother answered it which about scared him out. Howard drew that map Rob wanted the other day but I toasted bread on it yesterday and I dont know if he will make another or not. Glen never writes letters. Rob asked if folks ever caught anything out here and H says he will tell him he dont believe I've caught a man yet anyhow. His ma asked him how he knew so much and he has been mum since. [One sheet of letter missing here.]

Great Scott! In Marne? Ft Pierre and Bug juice! What next! Suppose she was visiting her cousins—The young gent was her chrysanthemum. Didn't he look like he might be the flower of a flock?

So Hugh[3] is married! Well! well! Let's see it took between four and five years for the complete cure didn't it? Well perhaps his was a *bad* case—it must have been or Dakota would [have] affected a cure in less time than that—Even I am improving—though slowly. Well good luck to the young married folks and may all their troubles be little ones.

Aunt Thettie[4] would sure feel bad if Uncle Walter used stamps like I do. Its up toward five dollars worth since starting for S. D.

Have paid my lumber bill and when I get these two orders signed I can pay that other note then I'll just have to pay Stones and my board—will have $140 for that and to last me through the summer—will have to have a lot of new duds befor next Sept—will have to attend Institute [and] am thinking of going to Mitchel[l, S.D.] and attending there[.] I wanted to have 25 acres broke this spring so as to raise something of a crop next year for I may not always teach school but there is no use trying to do anything of that kind until I get fenced and a mile and a half of fence costs some thing for material and work and breaking is $4 per acre so will have to give up some though I hate to and there is the dam too[.]

Must close for now love to all Bess

P. S. Would like to put a porch on the east side of my house and cover in with screan wire so it would be snake, fly and mosqueto proof—there would be more comfort in that than a dozen rocking chairs and all the skeeter skute in the state—B.

✱   FEB. 3, 1910 / FORT PIERRE, SO. DAK.
TO MRS. M. M. COREY

Dear Ma,—I dont know when any one is going to town and I left your last letter at the school house but will write you any way as I have a little time.

I dont want anymore of the tin[1] as I think [I] will only have ten acres broke and fenced this spring—the rest can wait till next fall. and you dont want to give up that plan about the house as you know I told you I'd come home if you ever needed me. My school closes about April 20th I believe and I dont think they hold Institute[2] till August. My car fare both ways wouldn't be much over twenty five dollars and if I staid in S D it would cost me that to live. I think I can get a two or three months leave and get to Marne by June 1st or perhaps sooner if you wish and perhaps could stay till the last of August and attend Institute in Harlan.

I could be there during the fruit season and can do three times the work in the same length of time I could when I left Iowa and you know I managed the work pretty well a year ago last summer when you were away and Ethel is older now so I think we could get along pretty well

Stopped and rocked Edna to sleep then before we were through supper Mr Walton came—he brought my warrent and a letter—has just gone—it is ten o'olock—the boys have gone "a piece" with him I guess.

Howard kicked me under the table when he came in so you know what I'll get later. Mr Walton got to Stones Tuesday eve while Speers were there and he didn't send it (the letter) down even after they suggested it and Mr. Speer was there again yesterday but still he forgot. (?). Tonight I was cleaning my face with a brush and Glen asked if I was expecting one of the Dutchmen[3] this evening—The rest goes without saying.

Plague take the luck! I cant work the men "like I used to could[.]" There are those two warents to sign and there is that teachers meeting Saturday and Governor Vessey[4] is to speachify and Oh! Plague take the men any way! "If I cant get a red bird and [any?] blue bird will do or even a blue jay" (?)

Am busy most every minute—if it isn't school work it is something else. Last evening when I got home from school I washed—rocked Edna [Speer]—then mended my coat, ate supper, cleaned the gun, mended Howards mitten, by that time Ruth was fussing for me to undress and rock her—as soon as she was asleep I was asked to "favor" them with a few more chapters of "With Lee in Virginia"—that lasted till ten o'clock—then fire and light out we hit the perch.

Oh say[,] I have great times shooting—Glen has a rifle like the boys and about the first time I tried I hit a tin can six out of nine times—just happenstance you know—suppose next time I couldn't hit a flock of barns. I had said I knew nothing about shooting and the first thing I knew Glen was telling about my shooting here the other evening before Reeses and asked how six out of nine was for one who claimed to know nothing of guns. Haven't heard from the gun you spoke of having expressed to me.

The last time I wrote you the kids were around here and they just make the table fairly dance—first Ruth then Clayton then Herbert[5]—so I promised each a penny to keep away till I finished then every second minute Ruth would shove my elbow and want to know *when* I was going to give her that nickle—when she got it her ma asked her what it was for and she said "For jogging the table when Miss Corey was writing[.]" She still hides my clothes in the day time and kicks my ribs loose in the night time but we get along fine.

Did I tell any of you about Clayton? You know he is one of the kind who studies his words c a t c a t c a t with out pronouncing them. I had him almost broke of it once then he got at it again and one day he spelled *some* p l a y and that was too much—I started to talk to him about it and he stood there looking up at me with his big blue eyes amost as large as dollars. I thought while he was so attentive a listener was a good time for a lecture on the error of his ways so just led it off—was just slinging off the closing remarks when he exclamed with a big breath "My but your eyes are big[.]" Oh! what a jar to ones conceit. I told him to "take his seat" in no very gentle tone and he did so rubbing his fist in his eye in a way calculated to "touch the heart[.]" I started to call the next class and was so amused at their looks I could not conceal a smile. Clayton peaked around his fist to see how I was coming and caught that smile and his red head got clear away with him that time—his freckles stood out like ginger snaps and his eyes blazed as he shook one dirty little fist at me and exclamed between his teeth "smell that for a while[.]"

The other day I cleaned the school house—swept down the walls and ceiling, washed the windows, black-boards, desks, seats, wash stand, scrubbed the floor and porch. The floor I scrubbed first with a broom then got down on my knees and went over it—quite a job but I felt hardly tired when I got through and my shoulder hardly ached a bit.

Love to all—must close—ten after eleven—

Bess

Dear Brother Olney, Yours of almost two months ago was very welcome. I just get so mixed on who I owe letters and who I dont owe letters I hardly know where I'm at—Just know I owe a lot of them as I got my mail last evening for the first time since the 16th receiving nine letters and four cards so will have to get busy.

People have lost some cattle and young stock but not as much as you would suppose—in this neighborhood at least, but they say that 75% of the range stock in the great north west (which includes the Dakotas) will perish ere summer comes again. Some are starving but it is impossible to get hay to them and they are too weak to get to a station to ship out. We have had a hard winter but it can't last always. We have about one bad cold snap or storm every week but a few warm days now and then have reduced the snow on the sunny slopes so there will soon be forage to keep the range stuff alive till summer[.]

People who put up plenty of hay are alright, it is the ones who trusted to an open winter that are all in but their shoestrings. We—I mean Speers—have lost a calf or two and several lambs that came this last cold snap.

Does mamma worry as much as she did? I suppose there is lots to worry her along now. Have they a new buggy yet? Ma wrote about the smash up[1]—I didn't get it all straight but most of it—He must be some sort of half baked guy that dont know as much as Dicks hat band[2]—I'd like to hand him such a bunch he'd land where potatoes are four dollars a bushel.

Was so glad to hear from Fuller—he writes so seldom[.] What did he go to Harlan for? I hope he is earning a few cents now and then[.] Am getting along nicely myself. Have paid my lumber-bill and relinquishment note—have board bills left. Mr Stone brought out some coal for me last night—don't know when he can get it over to my house—its paid for any way. And I will have enough to hire ten acres broke this Spring, replenish my wardrobe and enough to start me well next fall—that is to last till I earn more even counting trip to Iowa if ma wants me to come and help her for a few weeks.

You see its this way I could stay alnight at home the first night in May then hit the trail for Iowa. I could stay eight weeks about, then get back in time to stay the last night in June at home so as to be on my claim one night in each month. Have to be a little carefull but if any thing in pants jumps my claim he'll have a lot of jumping to do before he gets through with it.

Don't say anything about my returning to Iowa, even on a visit, to any one as every thing is uncertain as yet. It all depends on whether ma desides to build or not.

A week ago today and evening I had a—what do girls in society say? an experience? or is it a scene? *I* think it was both. Guess my nerves have settled enough so I can tell you all about it and you can let ma read this letter[.]

When I first came out here I met a girl and a gentleman who was, and had been for some time, paying her some attention. I wished to consider them both my friends. I met the gentleman frequently and we had jolly times. Before long he ceased to pay the other girl attention and I was soon informed that she atributed the fact to my presence in the neighborhood. At first it seemed laughable then it came to me that it was just possible that the ones so quick to tell me might also have told the other girl things that would make her jealous[.] The thought made me furious and I declared I'd never speak to him again. They then taunted me with the fact that circumstances compelled us to meet frequently which of course soothed my feelings(?) I treated him so horrid the next time we met that I was afterward so ashamed of myself I begged his pardon. In spite of fate it seemed that everyone far and *near* would hook our names together just as if they had a right to. Its a wonder I didn't hate him to death. Well last Sunday Jennie Speer and I went up to Stones—Howard took us up in the forenoon and left us to walk home. On toward supper time the gentleman in question was going through the yard and Mrs Stone told Myrtle to go out and tell him to come in to supper and then walk home with us girls and Jennie said for her to tell him to come in to supper and walk home with me. I declared I would go home at once but Mrs Stone said for me to stay alnight so I staid to supper. After supper the gentleman went home to get my flagelette[3] which he was to return and Jennie began to tease me about him saying I didn't mean what I said and wouldn't stay over night. I said I would—she said if I staid she would too. I knew Stones couldn't keep two of us very easy so I hustled into my wraps and started out. They said for me to go by his house so he could walk down with me. So I took the hay road which went throug[h] the field—hadn't gone far when here he came taking the short cut. What was I to do? I could think of nothing but how I could get roasted. It didn't take him long to find out something was wrong and he can cross-question to "beat two of a kind[.]" I was kind of tongue-tied—was afraid to say any thing for fear of saying too much so said nothing but still I fear said too much. He soon knew all he needed to know. I had thought myself in a glorious temper but heavens! I soon felt as if I was no where; he said he was sorry and would "put a stop to it." He is a perfect gentleman and speaks so quietly but his tone fairly froze me with terror. I asked him "how" and he said he would tell them "to cut it out"[.] He said he would promise me that none of them would ever anoy me any more. He was in such a lovely rage I was almost scared to death. I succeeded in getting him to promise to say nothing about it as they likely meant no harm. He promised rather reluctantly then tried to find out more about it but I was mum as an oyster. His being so nice almost killed me. I almost believe it would have been a relief to hear him swear a little though I dont approve of swearing. He "sincerely hoped" we might be friends. And not till he was gone did I realize that I had that confounded toot whistle in my hands. Sooner or later I'll catch it but no one has thought of it yet. I've been about ready to go to Yankton[4] all week. My nerves are a little nearer settled than they were so I guess its nothing serious though I have a sneaking idea that it hasn't ended yet.

It has been very warm the past two days and if it lasts much longer I will have cause to be thankful my house is on high ground. else I might take a trip by water down to Omaha. It would be like a verse in the paper when the Mississippi levee broke—"The hul family a roostin on the gable en's with the hen coop full of water and the tree top full of hens[.]"

"Oh say" I most forgot to mention that one night, I believe it was the evening after the *scene*, the gentleman was taken very ill. He got up to Stones some how and they worked all night with him. They thought he was going to "croak" before morning but he pulled through and yesterday went to town with Mr Stone and did not return. No one knows when he intends to return.

Am studying Art[5] very diligently—the lessons are few and far between but well studied. Took another lesson Friday evening.

The next county teachers meeting is to be held in Ft Pierre March 12th. Come up—I'm to read a paper on "Devices by Which to Hold the Attention of a Class." There will also be a spelling contest. I'll be Johnnie on the spot when the bell rings if—as the bird said—"If the fates are willing."

I am

Lovingly your Sister

Bess.

P. S. I dont know who *Francis* Copley is. Guess the first name is bogus.

＊ MAR. 15, 1910 / FORT PIERRE, SO. DAK.
TO MRS. M. M. COREY

Dear Mamma,—I haven't had a letter from you for a month or so and only one card since then. What is the matter? I answered your last letter, Im sure, and have been writing to the kidlets since, trying to get theirs paid off.

The snow is all gone here. except a little on the north side of some of the largest hills. It went so fast when it did start that it just made things howl. It is like summer here now.

I guess I'm home to stay now. Howard brought me and my baggage over last Friday evening [and] Saturday morning I was sick as a dog—The severe cold I caught a week before was to blame I guess. am feeling pretty good now but am as "tired as a yaller dog" tonight.

Last Saturday I was to read a paper at the Teachers Meeting but as I did not feel equal to a swim in Bad river or a walk from Teton I staid at home. Have the paper, roughly written, and will send it if you care to read it. It would have taken lots of nerve to have read it.

I sewed my carpet and put it down Saturday—am working on a rug now between times. It is getting so cozy and homelike here I cant stand it, hardly[,] to be away long. This last time I was so homesick at times that I hardly knew whether I was a foot or a horseback.

Do you know what a pack rat is? Well you don't want to know. They are making me the kind of a time that Mr Pingle makes for the school ma[']ams. They ate the green feathers off my hat—I hope it gave 'em an awful stomach ache.

Mr Stone tried to straighten the little mansion (did I tell you) and had to give it up till later on. He told Mrs Speer that "It beats the devil." Says it must have been an experienced hand who roped it—to have pulled it up by the roots so.

By the way—I found the contents of my cellar in what seemed to be an over ripe condition. I started to carry them out Saturday but gave up before I got through. I finished tonighed [sic] and found that in the farther side of the sack of potatoes were some that had not been frozen. I dont see how it happened some had little sprouts on an the rest all mush. Have about a peck of good ones I believe. That will last me a long while. Some of my onions were alright too.

If you have decided not to build this Summer I would like to know as I want to send you the cost of my trip to go toward a new buggy as a birthday present. Now dont say anything. A fellow wants a little fun once in a while and it might be best for us both that way.

I have some dandy candied citron—will send you some if you care for it. I don't care for it myself but Mrs Speer says its fine. I gave her some and she used it for cake.

Have an invitation to a party next Monday evening—also a way of going if I want to but haven't promised yet. Dont know as I'll go—its school-day night.

Who is it sends me that paper? I never saw a Daily I liked as well.

Seems queer—no one had jared the table once tonight.

Its bedtime and I'm *so* tired. I may add a P. S. befor mailing this.

> Good Night. Lovingly—
> Your Bess.

✳ MAR. 22, 1910 / FORT PIERRE, SO. DAK.
TO MRS. M. M. COREY

Dear Ma,—Last Wednesday I took that last letter I wrote you to school and that evening after school Adolph came down. He had come out from town horse-back and brought the mail. He staid and talked more than half an hour and I gave him those letters to mail. I went home with Myrtle [Stone] that night for over night. Had a fine visit.

Saturday I did a big washing I have to carry water from the neighbors pond now. It isn't half a mile but it gets heavy just the same. I also scrubbed my kitchen. Was glad I did as I had lots of callers the next day. To begin with one of "Dose By Jinks" rode up to the door—the one the boys bother me so much about.[1] Oh if you could but see him!! He is as suple as a bear, mounts as easily as an elephant and rides with the grace of a grasshopper. He didn't dismount Sunday morning but watched me through the open door and Talked. He told Howard a while back that he might get married next fall if he got a good crop. Well while talking the other morning he said the first year he was out here he could hardly get hay enough for his team but it got better every year and this year he expected a good crop. Of course that was too good to keep. I had to tell it and the Speer boys nearly went up the flume. Guess I wasn't quite nice enough to the old cuss for yesterday morning I met him and he was mum as an oyster. I don't blame him for being mum for down the trail a way he hadn't done a thing but dump out some dead chickens. Must have been too ripe to suit the coyotes for they were there this evening yet. If I was a man I believe I'd thrash that dutchman till the slack in his pants would drag his tracks out. It would be good enough for him if some one would tie him hand and foot and pitch him out among those chickens to meditate on the error of his ways.

Sunday afternoon two of the Wiseman girls [2] came over and before they left Mr & Mrs Speer and four of the girls stopped here. They said that Browns from down on War Creek [3] are coming up to spend Sunday with me some of these days.

Last evening (Monday) I attended that party down the line five or six miles. Never had such a howling good time befor in my life. They got to dancing. I worked like a good fellow to keep them from dancing and didn't mean to "preform" if they did but the music was so good and Art insisted so I was like Shiner [4]—when I couldn't keep the cats out of it any longer I went in for my share. All three of the young Mr Scripters were there. The married one had just received word from his wife who has been spending the winter with her folks in Nebraska that they had a little son but that didn't keep him from the dance. No you bet, thats the man of it. He paid me more attention than he ever paid his grandmother—but he was "just keeping the other fellows away for his brother who doesn't dance much." Guess if his wife had come in sight about that time she'd have scratched our eyes out sure.

I danced the sole about off my shoes—they are beyond hope I think. Got home in time for two or three little hours sleep this morning.

I got to school in time and Myrtle brought my mail (The goose-kicked Irishman brought it out Sunday but she forgot it yesterday morning.) I hadn't finished yours and Teedee's letters when the Co Supt [5] drove up. Of course under the circumstances I was prepaired for a heavenly time. Got off slick as a greased pig.

I didn't feel much like work tonight so thought I'd start a letter to you and add to it from time to time till I get a chance to mail it.

I almost lost my social standing the other evening—came near taking a double header into the pond which would have been a joke on the pond and the bugs, frogs and water snakes therein. See what Toad is coming to.[6] He'll soon get used to it and eat snake soup with the rest of us and say with Will Stone "Might as well eat the devil as drink his juice."

Was glad to hear that Fuller had another horse[7]—what kind of bargain did he get? Why up here he would have had to pay that much for an old skate that would need sharpening every day.

FRIDAY, MAR 25 1910.
Am at Stones this evening will finish this so as to mail it tomorrow as I am going to town—if nothing happens.

Mr Stone doesn't think it wise to bring very valuable horses up here as there seems to be some kind of disease or other that there doesnt seem to be any cure for and beside thay have to get acclimated.

Wish Chall would come out and be my little nigger for a while—the sun would soon blacken him out here[.]

Ethel must be putting on lots of style with all those new duds[.]

Its too bad about that baby. I hope it isn't quite so bad as that.

Good luck to Frankie & Pete.[8] If I didn't have so much to do I'd write them. Tell Frankie to drop me a card when she gets settled and I'll send her my best wishes.

Please give Mrs Curtis[9] my best regards.

How do you ever get along with out one *buggy top*?

Tell Toad not to tear his shirt. If there isn't hay enough here we will ship in som Canada thistles for *roughness*. Does he know anything about fence prices out here? Cedar 3 in[ch] posts .18 apiece and wire $3\frac{1}{2}$ cents per pound. Have just struck a bargain—bought or have as good as bought 250—3 in ash posts at 5 cents—will have them hauled up to Stones soon as possible and left to weather this summer and Toad can put 'em in in the fall for "knitin' work." Expect to hire a man this fall. Am running a little short so may have to give up my trip or work some good looking fellow for a loan befor the Summer is over. While I think of it—I must be in Ft Pierre for two weeks begining with July 5th so plan according as I would rather attend Institute here than in Iowa under the circumstances.

You can send the pieplant[10] any time—much obliged for same.

Mr Stone broke for me yesterday—started with a strip 72 rods[11] long which will lengthen to 100 rods as he gets past the west draw.[12]

Must close in haste—good luck to you—write—Bess

✱ APRIL 4, 1910 / FORT PIERRE, SO. DAK.
TO MRS. M. M. COREY

Dear Ma,—It is quite late but will write you a few lines as I may
get a chance to mail them tomorrow. I have not heard from you for
some time—the last was a card.

I went to town a week ago Saturday with Mr Stone—we had to go
the long way and it was a fright of a day—the wind was so strong it
almost blew us out of the wagon. We started at six and got home at
nine in the evening.

While in town I had to see about a box at the Post Office as I'm
taking a daily now. My box is 485. I don't suppose I will get my mail
regular for a while as every one is used to my mail being put with
Stones and the few who know I have a box are apt to forget to ask for
my mail.

Am sending Olney under separate cover a few pieces of mica and
the latest thing in neck ties—hope he will be pleased. He is like his
Ma its so hard to get a present that will come within gun shot of pleasing him. I seldom have the courage to try tho I so often want to.

Did I tell you I've several new pupils? and all are doing very well.
Miss Reed the Co. Supt told me Saturday she was pleased with my
work.

I've had invitations to three parties in less than two weeks and
ways to go to them all. The first one I went to, the second I turned
down and the third fizzled. I hated to miss the one Friday evening but
I felt as if a certain girl was trying to shove me off on her brother and
of course that started the crank to turning tho I rather like the fellow
in question. I don't like things so cut and dried. I guess his sister is up
to such tricks—they are all hit with the same club for that matter and
they would tell the poor fellow afterward how well Miss Corey likes
him. As Mary says[,] such things make me feel sick to my stomach.
Jennie [Speer] and her beau spent one evening with me last week and
Mrs Wiseman and her children were over one evening.

Mr Stone has been breaking for me part of the past week. Saturday Mrs Stone and pebbles came with him. We had a fine visit but
Baby Fred showed us a merry go most of the time. You auto have seen
her—she cleared of[f] my dressing table and camp stool—threw my
pomade bottle in the water pail and would have followed suit with the
ink bottle but was prevented. She put on a pair of my rubbers and
planted my lawn to corn meal. If I get a good crop I wont have to buy

meal for years to come. I didn't get hardly a thing done all day but bake my bread. If I was like Lida [Smith] I would likely say "Thank the Lord they dont come often" but I'm not Lida.

I lacked about a rod or a little more of being in the little mansion when it blew over the other morning. Mr Stone put it up and made it very solid once more. I met him on the road and told him there was some house raising to be done in my neighborhood[—]he laughed and said he had noticed and was taking the tools along. I guess I'm getting to be a fright but it seems I cant help it. Sat. noon Mr Stone was reading that Morning Prayer that Ida [Wever Lay] gave me which I have up on the wall. He looked all around and asked where my evening prayers were and I said "Oh I *say* those." I suppose the whole neighborhood will hear that.

I went home with Stones Saturday evening and yesterday I took dinner and spent the afternoon with Mrs Foutts—had a splendid time.

It sounds as if every coyote in Stanley County was howling for its ma tonight.

My but I'd like to hear from you and know what your plans for the summer are as I can't tell what to do till I know.

I got the ticking for my fourth pillow when I was in town—and have it made now—was making it the evening John and Jennie came over.

I have a sneaking idea I may get left on the post deal but dont know yet.

Well its almost ten o'clock and I'm so sleepy I will close.

Lovingly Bess.

✷ APRIL 10, 1910 / FORT PIERRE, SO. DAK.
TO MRS. M. M. COREY

Dear Ma,—Will start you another letter on the instalment plan. I have had no word from you since the card I received when in town March 26th. There has been several mistakes about the mail and I'm out. I expect to get letters tomorrow as Mrs Stone sent for them Sat.

Talk about "strenuous life"! I'll sure need a vacation if this keeps up. Did I tell you in my last that neighbor Fritz,[1] the rusty headed Dutch on the nor'west was here one evening last week? Stopped with Miss Fonlons bill for wages for me to see to and after talking one arm so near off that it has been practicly useless since he borrowed a book to read. He returned the book when I was not at home and as the door was locked he raised the window and placed it in on the sofa. He is coming Wed. evening to get Miss Fonlons warrent. I may have told you that before as I've had such an awful cold and "gumbile" on my heel that I wrote letters most every evening last week till I had them all ans'd up and I've lost track of what I wrote in some of them. But as I told Ida if "Mrs Grundy" was to hear that I had talked so long to Fritz it would make her awful busy for a spell. (I'm considered, by some, a flirt[.])

Friday some of the chldren said something—about my cooking a little more than usual as they might come to dinner Sunday. (today). So yesterday I almost tore my ———— clothes to get things in shape. I baked a great big loaf cake and covered it with chocolate iceing, made dropcakes with thick cocoanut icing and baked sixty tart shells. Howard stoped for a drink befor they were cold and before he finished drinking the team went on—guess from the things he said about that team he might have stopped to talk had the circumstances been more favorable. He took one of the little cakes and started on the run but slacked up to call over his shoulder "Say it tastes alright—expecting Joe [Bahr] over tomorrow?"

I cleaned my cubboard which was a fright and put oilcloth on all the shelves so it will be easy to keep clean now. I suppose you think that is extravigant but I'm not in Iowa and theres a difference[.] I didn't finish my scrubbing till after dark. I was as tired as a "yaller dog" but started to mend my neither-tackle. My cold had gone to my head and as it is the worst cold of that kind I've had for several years you can guess about how I felt. All of a sudden I heard the deuce of a racket at the door and when I opened it there stood Howard. I said "Come in—all"[—]Howard said he was "all." I asked him how many teams he drove and what made so many shadows around the corner and when they all came in. There were sixteen of them—all young folks. Some of them came from six or eight miles away. They all claim to have had a good time but I'm sure I dont know much about it as I could hardly hold my head up most of the time. They left something later than two this morning—I don't know when they would have gone if it hadn't been for Howard. He usually stays till the last dog is hung but I had caught myself several times rubbing my head as I often do when it hurts and I noticed that Howard was watching me. At last he said he didn't suppose I'd say like the old lady he used to know—"Come on old man[,] lets be going to bed so these young folks can go home" but he thought they better start any how. *And they started.*

I got to bed at half after two and was sick as a dog. The alarm went off at six this morning. I waited a while but as I could not sleep I got up and went to work. My! What a job of dish washing and house cleaning as I had. I got through about half past ten and went to lie down for a while. Had just got a little bit more comfortable when the children came—seven of them. Then there was dinner to get, amusements to think of and every thing else it seemed. I thot my head would burst. And after the children went there was another grist of dishes. I had a pretty good rest then for a while but would have rested better only I couldn't help wondering if the old folk[s] were coming this *evening*. Its too late for them now so will close and go to roost. I feel better—believe I can sleep. Lovingly—Bess.

APRIL 18.
This was started a week ago yesterday—will write the rest on the back of these pages.

My cold was a fright—a week ago today it was so bad that Maggie[2] taught part of the afternoon for me. That evening I took a hot bath which helped me in more ways than one but was rather weak in the joints all last week. Last Thursday it rained so Mr Stone came after Myrtle and I went home with them and the next day it snowed and blowed and froze and was a caution. I went home Friday night in spite of the weather—was wet to the skin from rubber tops to knees and my feet were blue with cold. I changed my duds and warmed my feet in hot water which perhaps accounts for the fact that I suffered no bad effects from the dampness. It stormed all day Saturday and most of yesterday so I had no callers except Speers cows. My cold is much better but I'm so tired. There is no chance of rest either as everyone wanted a picnic and program the last day so I had to "hop to it." Am prepairing for an all day picnic, program and exhibition of school work. There is also the exams this week and reports and just no end to do.

It will soon be four weeks since I heard from you last and then only a card. I have written you several letters since I heard from you. Not hearing from you upsets all my plans—don't believe I could make it much befor the middle of May now.

Must close—There's a mistake about a bunch of invitations and the dickens to pay, Please write if only a card

In haste Bess.

As she indicates at the close of her letter of April 10 and 18, 1910, Bess—no doubt influenced by homesickness—altered her plan to stay in Stanley County until she proved up on her claim. She returned to Marne and remained in the area for probably six weeks, presumably returning to Stanley County prior to the end of June in order that she might truthfully say that she had been in residence on her claim during a portion of that month.

✳ JULY 3, 1910 / FORT PIERRE, SO. DAK.
TO MRS. M. M. COREY

Dear Ma, After Fuller left Aunt Jennies[1] I finished my black skirt and waist and we all hit the perch early. The next morning I swept the sitting room, dinning room and bedroom and put the rugs down. Aunt Jen insisted on my wearing one of her short kimonos for fear I would kill my white waist. I went to church with Mrs Smith and she and Geo Stewart and M C Petersen and I had quite a visit after church. Geo is the biggest guy of a man I ever saw I believe. Sometimes I feel like fireing a shoe at him. I took dinner at Aunt Jennies and spent the evening there. Aunt Jennie said as she was going to quit teaching she wished I would help her wear out her school clothes as she would never get them worn out as long as she lived and she gave me a gray skirt and eight waists. She also gave me that white soup bowl she promised me years ago and a quart of cherries. Mrs. Smith[2] went to the train with me. The train to Carrol [Iowa] was late[.] The conductor said he was afraid they could not make connections with the Sioux City train and I had better wait and go the next morning. The baggage master said if I had friends in Carrol to go on up and take the morning train to Sioux City. Mrs Smith declared that the "North Western wasn't no good" and urged me to go another route which would have taken me over three different roads. She argued and the train men argued and at last I threw back my head and said I'd wait and see what connections I made this trip and would then say what I thought of the North Western. At last we started—the train was an hour and twenty minutes late. The way they ran to make up time would have made a naughtymobile tear its shirt. At every station I heard train men hurrying things and caught such words as "Ft Pierre" "S Dak." "Lady—Claim" and "Hurry[.]" There was more *hurry* than anything else. The train men came and talked to me bewteen times. One was to start July

1st on a visit to his father and brother near Wendte which is about eight miles from my claim. Another had bought a farm about twenty five miles from here. When we got in to Carrol one man rushed up to tell me where my train was, another helped with my suit cases, two others grabbed my trunk and ran down the track to put it on the other train. The conductor came to meet me and took a suit case saying "Where to?" I said "Sioux City" [and] he said "through to Pierre?" I said "Yes" and he hustled me on to the train. I learned later that the train from Carrol to Sioux City "makes up" in Carrol and they held it fifteen minutes for me.

Later I met in the train Miss Minnie Ashton the Superintendent of one of the ward schools of Boone I[ow]a who is a candidate for Co Supt in that County this fall. She was one of the instructor[s] in the Ft Pierre Institute last Summer and was on her way there to fill the same position this summer[.] We came on through together. We spent six hours wait in Sioux City shopping, dinning, attending the Theatre and so on. When I got to Ft Pierre Mr Stone was here to meet me. He had one of the Porters teams. He had told the folks out home that he was going down after "Grandma" if he had to bring her out in the wheel-barrow. Mr Erickson and Jennie Speer went out also. I saw Adolph in town. Was only in town an hour but during that time received an awful shock. You know I heard that Ella Bucholz was married. Well she was married secretly a month before I went to Ia. to Harry Roush one of their roomers. Ella has always been considered almost too good for this world and the other party is a handsome devil. Its the old story of drugged candy, a dishonored girl, a shot gun marriage and now I be-lieve a divorce case pending. Poor girl I am so sorry for her.

Jennie Speer saw me comming and called to me then ran acrossed the street[,] threw her arms around me and kissed me. I was so sur-prised I just allowed it.

Mr Stones mother was there but went on down to Speers. We visited till late that night. The next day Mr Stone was away at work. Mrs Stone was so misserable I started to do her ironing as the clothes were dampened but the wind was so strong we could do nothing with the fire or irons so had to give it up. After dinner we were all going to take a nap but were scarcely asleep before Grandma Foutts came. She had heard I was coming home. The next day (Thurs.) I finished the hammock and made my kimono—I made Freddie [Stone] one just like it of the scraps. She likes it very much and calls it "Feddies komo." She looks so cute and cool in it. Oscar Walton was there that evening.

Minnie Ashton, a county superintendent in Iowa and later principal of Pierre High School in South Dakota, urged Bess to pursue higher education and carve out a prominent career in teaching. Photo courtesy Verendrye Museum.

I had to laugh when I saw him coming for he had trimmed his hat with some of the red feathers the wind had torn from mine. From what I hear I believe that Mr Stone has been all but breaking his neck to make it alright between Oscar and I.

Friday Stones had company[—]it was desperately hot and I was busy all day but got but little sewing done. I walked over home that evening and staid alnight—gathered up what I wanted for Institute and walked back Saturday morning. We had quite a shower during the night. My potatoes and the rest of my garden looks fine. Yesterday forenoon I gathered up my belongings and packed my suitcase and in the afternoon Oscar brought me to town. That was a pleasant trip tho the weather was warm. When we got here we found that Mr Speer had taken our mail out with him[.] We met him on the road and he didn't say a word tho he knew I was to stay in town.

The first thing when we got here was to go to the ice cream parlor[.] I stopped at one dish but Oscar didn't. Later it was fruit and candy. I asked him if he was trying to kill me and he said he was so he would have some place to go later on.

We passed Art Scripter on the street. While I was at the Range[3] doing some shopping for Mrs Stone and Oscar was at the barber shop Art came in and we had a great old visit. He was regreting the fact that his brother was going to Draper[4] the Fourth and had spoke for the driving team so he could not take me to the picnic. But there is a plan under foot for two weeks from now if nothing happens. Art is coming after me when Institute is over and I'm going down there for a few days visit and on Sunday we are to drive to Liers about six miles distant and discover from Altas relatives what has become of her if possible. I guess I'm between two fires again but that is always my luck.

I and a Miss Campton[5] have taken a room in the Yokum building.[6] It costs us $1.25 a week each but is a clean cool airy room with a north window. We will take our meals out and won't have to eat three times a day just to get our moneys worth like we would if we took room and board at seven or eight dollars a week.

Say[,] my horseradish was all spoiled when I got here and the goose berries had worked so the cover was bulged. Mrs Stone cooked the gooseberries up and we ate them—was afraid if we canned them again they would [not] go the trip when I took them home.

Mr Stone was born July 4th 1876 the Centenial year. Tomorrow his friends will present him with checks amounting to enough to buy a team which he has in view. I helped what I could but wish it could have been more.

I hope you are through with the masons and dont work too hard.

I guess I had better close[.] I dont suppose you will get to write me very often now but a card once in a while would be alright.

Tell Rob the knife is O.K. I dont suppose I could keep my house without it now.

Lovingly Bess.

❋   JULY 21, 1910 / FORT PIERRE, SO. DAK.
TO MRS. M. M. COREY

Dear Ma—Will start a letter and finish it sometime—I dont know when—I've been sick and the pencil gets so tired after I've used it a while.

Lets see I havent written you a letter since two weeks ago Sunday—will begin there. I took a room at Mrs Bucholz[1] and then a bachelor girl about 59 years of age went in with me for a week. Gee the fun I had with her. She has a claim about a hundred miles out of Ft Pierre and came to town with her niece and husband Mr and Mrs Howel who attended institute. Miss Kempton, when on her claim, lives all alone with her old grey cat. I declared that she was so used to talking to her cat that she sometimes forgot herself and went around saying "Nice kitty" to me. I would go on just the way Aunt Mary[2] used to talk to the cat till I convinced the dear lady that she realy had forgotten herself and then I would almost drive her frantic by telling of it befor others while the Bucholz would laugh till they could laugh no longer. Mr Howel had an uncle in Pierre who came over to visit him (?) quite often. When we got "Uncle Clarence" and "Aunt Debby" together Mrs. Bucholz needed to have a cord on the boys and I. Of course Aunt Debby didnt own either face cream or powder but she made good use of mine. She always wanted me to put it on when she was expecting "Uncle Clarence" and I sure did. I dont see what made the hammock break down—there must have been too many in it for I'm sure we didn't do nothin to it.

Institute was fine and I guess I didn't miss a day that I wasn't treated to ice cream and such. I guess I mentioned that one afternoon we went through the Capitol building[3] in Pierre. The first Friday evening we attended the eighth grade graduation exercise and a reception afterward—came home in a tearing rain—it was so dark we could hardly keep the walk and some places the walks had sunk till we went ankle deep in water. We ran slap dad against a man who said "Why how do you do." I wished afterward that I had told him I would try to swim if it got much deeper.

Miss [Faith] Hunt came the 8th but hurried out to Stones so fast no one saw her. Sunday I attended church and had an invitation out to dinner which I gladly accepted—am going to rest.

Friday morning—am feeling fine—got up at six and didn't have to stop to rest till twenty minutes to eight. Its a quarter after eight now.

On Monday the 11th Oscar, Jennie [Speer] and Miss Hunt came to town. The girls came to see me about the party Mrs Stone was to give for Miss Hunt. She wouldn't have it till I could be there. They decided on the 16th. That afternoon I went up to Miss Reeds office. She was praising my school and I said that when visiting my school she made no criticism and as I as a teacher must have some faults her criticisms would help to overcome them. She leaned slightly forward in her chair and said "Miss Corey I made no criticism because I found no criticism to make. I was much pleased with your work and if there is any school in this county you would like this year let me know and I'll do all in my power to get it for you[.]" Why I felt as if I had a feather a yard long in my hat. You know that I applied for the Klemann[4] school—well I find out that the Speers and Klemans are awful thick and Mr Speer told Mr Klemann a big pack of lies. When I saw Mr Klemann and asked him about the school he said he didn't know yet whether he would be director or not but he had been enquiring about my teaching.

At the school meeting Mr Porter[5] recomended that they hire me and pay me $45 per month (five more than last year) and Mr Kleman didn't want to hire me because Mr Speer had told him————etc———— so Mr Porter (who pays Miss Reed lots of attention) went to Miss Reed about it and Miss Reed wrote Mr Kleman a letter that just whipped him right into line. Prof Galaspie[6] who taught the Kleman school last year is Supt of the Ft Pierre Schools this next year and he has been helping me like a good fellow. He had a talk with Kleman and told me later that Mr Klemann was in the notion of hireing me. Mr Galaspie says its an awful hard school but thinks Ill get on alright if I can keep my nerve up. Of course I'll have to teach the Jones youngsters—you know about them dont you? Their dad[7] is a widower and has fallen dreadfully in earnest—I dont know what I'll do with him if he dont stop telling folks what a "mighty fine little girl" I am.

Oh lets see I left off Monday afternoon—well that evening Adolph and I went to Prof Thompsons[8] lecture—in the course of the lecture he told us just exactly how a tiny baby should be fed—poor Adolph—we scarcely looked at each other all evening. It must have been interesting to him(?).

Tuesday afternoon there was an extra session at the school house after which the teachers were taken in autos out to the buffalo pasture where we saw the three hundred feeding—such fun as we had. Most of the way back we came at the rate of fourty or fourty five miles an houre. They wanted to get into town befor some of the others who started first. It almost blew the hair from our heads[—]some of the girls hung on to theirs with both hands and one of them said "Gee but this is rough on rats[.]"[9] A coyote crossed the road ahead of us and stopped so long to look that he most got run over. We beat the rest back to town and when we got out I started to thank the driver and he said "Oh that's alright I owed you a debt any way." How his eyes twinkled at my amazement when I asked "How so[?]" He said that I treated him to ice cream last spring and then I recognized Mr Geron who took my school for an auto ride last spring. That evening attended an ice cream social[.] The next evening we attended another and Thursday and Friday I wrote exams[—]got through early Friday afternoon— have no idea how I'll come out but am not going to worry as my cirtificate is good yet you know. I caught a ride out to Stones that afternoon with Wisemans and was there till Sunday evening. I worked pretty hard Saturday helping Mrs Stone. of course Miss Hunt was there but her friend *Mr Harris* came in the afternoon to stay over till Monday so Miss Hunt couldn't help much. We froze three friezers of cream and I did the turning—I also churned, washed dishes and a few other such tricks. The party lasted till daylight. I didn't like that as I got too tired. I helped serve the supper—there were thirty six in all. Must rest awhile.

Sunday evening "Mr. Harris," Miss Hunt Mrs Stone and Freddie brought me and my belongings home. It was quite late but as I was thirsty I went over after water and then began my troubles—before morning I felt badly—by noon I felt worse. Mr Stone was over Monday afternoon and put up my screan door and other odds and ends. Tuesday morning May Wiseman [10] was up for two or three hours[.] I boiled some water and put it to cool. In the afternoon Mrs Wiseman and three of the children were up and I wasn't able to sit up. From then till Wednesday noon I thot I was going to croak. Mrs Wiseman sent up medicine and had the kids carry water for me. I haven't been in any violent pain since Wednesday noon but it seems as if I'd never get my strength back—if I work hard for five or ten minutes I'm so tired I can hardly move for an hour or two. Yesterday morning I thought I would go down for water while it was cool. The water is low and hard to get. I don't suppose it is more than five or six feet deep in the deepest place. Well of course the landing gave way and again I lost my social standing. I went in feet first—if I had gone in head first I wouldn't be writing now for I hardly had strength enough to get out as it was. I rested a while then came home and changed my duds then rested some more. I went down again and dipped it out with a little pail on the end of the hoe so you dont need to worry about my falling in any more. I was no good the rest of the day. Had hardly got home when Miss Hunt and Jennie came. They were here an hour or so. Mr Stone & Stanton were here the forenoon—brought the mail—a note from Miss Kempton, a letter from Grandma and cards from you and Mary. How I did laugh over Mary's card! It is a picture of a scrawny dog with corkscrew curls and a big bow of ribbon and says "I guess I'll be a darned old maid[.]"

I have my hammock up now—you *measley* folks can have a swing.

Guess I am proof against measles. I never could catch them.

You said Mr H was sick—who did you mean? [11] What is finished—the house? [12] Suppose you will all be having a fine time about the time you get this. Gee I'm in for it again. You know Art went to town for me Saturday and found I had caught a ride out to Stones. Every one wondered why he wasn't at the party and I didn't say anything. I haven't seen him since. That's always my darn luck—Im just like a fly in the molasses—when I get out with one foot I get in with the other.

Say the Speer school has no teacher as yet. Miss Hunt is to be principal of a town school and when they offered it to Miss Foulon she said if Miss Corey wanted it she wouldn't take it and if Miss Corey didn't want it there must be some good reason for not wanting it and she didn't believe she wanted it either. They are awful short on teachers and Mrs Stone is afraid they wont get one—I don't believe Miss Reed will hurt herself to get them one.

No, I've heard nothing from Alta.[13] I'm not going to fence this fall—have spent most of the post money already. Have done all I need to do and more too to prove up and I think I will prove up a year from now—Miss Ashton urged it for the sake of my education—she says I can get better wages and do better in every way if I am free to come and go to suit myself. And Mr Stone thinks so too. He seems to think there is a chance of some one contesting me. He says they could do nothing but make it cost me two or three hundred to fight it. Now I'm going to teach so far away I dont want to be bothered with a horse and so have [remainder of letter missing]

* AUGUST 7, 1910 / FORT PIERRE, SO. DAK.
  TO MRS. M. M. COREY

Dear Ma—Your card rec'd last evening. Have been afraid you would do too much while the kids were sick and be down yourself by the time you got them welled up—and I guess that's just what you've done. I would have wished to have been there to help you only I know I could not have resisted the temptation to "do likewise" about the time the rest were down and you needed me the worst so you were better off without me.

A week ago last Monday I cam over to Stones—staid alnight—went over to Grandma Foutts' the next day—came back to Stones in the afternoon—went home with Mr Share when he came along from town—staid all night at Shares and Mrs Share and Ben[1] took me home Wed. afternoon. While at Shares I helped finish of[f] picture postals[2]—its lots of fun—we started after supper and kept at it till two in the morning[.] Ben is going to come up some morning and take [a photograph of] me and the house—wont that be fine? Oh! a wandering Jew is alright in the right place—just keep him wandering—thats all. Ben and Mrs Share staid to lunch with me. I made *tea punch* which Ben pronounced "swell dope" the best he had tasted in this country.

The next day I made a patern for a princess dress and the next two days I cut it out and put it together. Last Monday I came over to Stones again. Tuesday Miss Hunt went home and I staid with the pebbles. Mrs Stone had some dental work done and can hardly eat yet. I've been here ever since and this is Sunday. Have finished my dress[—]it fits fine and is the most becoming thing I ever owned. I wore it yesterday[.] Mr Stone went to town and I went along as far as Klemanns and staid till he came back. I am to teach the Klemann school and board at Klemanns at $10.00 *per mo.*[—]will have a room all to myself[—]isn't that swell? They say school won't commense till October so if Fuller comes in September it will be O.K.

(This is great writting but I'm on the bed[.])

Jennie Speer just filed on the claim that I wanted Fuller to take but there are a few hills left that are good for pasture. The land about here has taken up awful fast this last six months—at least ten claims filed on and some of them *all* hills[.] I sent Fuller a card—if he answers it I've got a peach of a one to send him and the third is the peachiest ever.

Say Miss Hunt and Miss Reed together have sure cleaned this neighborhood up proper. Miss Hunt flew off the handle and told Speers they "lied"—she roasted them on one side then turned them and roasted em on the other. They have been "so meek as Moses" ever since. Miss Reed has been telling that I'm one of her best teachers—that I'm one of the most thorough teachers she ever saw—that she took particular pains to inquire of the institute instructors concerning me and they *all* praised me and my work.

I have more to work with this next year and hope to keep up my reputation as "one of the best." Miss Reed and Miss Ashton seem to think I auto prove up on my claim in order to go on in the educational world. My! if I had the education some have couldn't I just go it. They seem to think that its not the education I *havent* got but the way I make use of what I have that counts.

Last night we had a real good shower which saved the corn crop for some and helps with the hay.

I can't plan very well with Fuller on paper—can do better when he gets here. He must not plan on a farm at what they cost this way amounting in the first few years to as much as an Iowa farm worth $150 per acre. Tell him that I heard a few days ago that the blacksmith over south here is getting old and talks of giving up his trade and that it would be a splended field about here for a younger man. I don't know how much it amounts to but it will do to think about.

If I can get some buffalo berries[3] I will have quite a bit of jell and stuff for Fuller to take back with him which will help you out this winter. Two or three gallons of such stuff goes quite a ways.

You might start a list of things I forgot. Take good care of yourself

Lovingly—Bess.

> Knives and forks
> My hair in sitting room bookcase.[4]
> Peppermint
> Banana
> Daylillies[5]

* SEPTEMBER 25, 1910 / FORT PIERRE, SO. DAK.
TO MRS. M. M. COREY

Dear Ma—I dont know when I wrote you a letter last but it must have been quite a while ago—it seems about ten years.

The week before school began I was so busy I didn't know half the time whether I was a foot or a horseback. That Monday I put the cotton in my comforter and got it ready to tie. Tuesday morning bright and early Mr S—— and Weltha came over and before I got my dinner started Mrs Foutts and Mrs Blumgreen came over to spend the day—that was a busy day for me. Weltha was always wanting something and she always wanted it right away quick—and I tried to visit and get dinner at the same time. I got throw pretty well considering. The ladies started home about five oclock but I got supper for the others. After they had gone I gathered my squash and put them down cellar. I tied my comforter that evening and hit the perch about half after twelve I think. Mr Stone was not to work on the cistern[1] the next day as it was the day of the school meeting and they were to go. I was finishing my comforter Wednesday noon when I heard someone calling and going to the door I was much surprised to see the whole Stone family and Mrs Foutts and Max. They wanted me to go along to the school meeting with them and I hated to refuse when they had driven over after me so I went over to the War Creek School House and listened to both factions chew the rag. Gee such a time! I dont want any more school meeting in mine. Julius Barr got on a rampage and cussed till he was almost black in the face and no one could stop him so they filed a complaint and he was arrested later and is now out on bail having been bound over till the Oct. term of court.

Then Thursday Stones came over. Mr Stone finished the cistern and that afternoon after they were gone I made over a white waste and started my washing—was rather late but thot I would put out a line of colored ones and put the rest out Friday morning. The first next thing I knew the Speer young people and their new school ma'am were there for the evening.

It was rather late when they left so I went to bed. The next morning there was a fog so thick you could slice it for sandwiches[—]and my washing, ironing, scrubbing, mending and all sorts of things to finish befor school commenced. I finished my washing and it cleared off so I got my duds out just before noon[—]they dried quickly. I ironed in the afternoon tho it was blistering hot.

It was after seven in the evening when I finished and started for Stones with a large package of books. It was soon dark—no it was moonlight—the last two miles. When I got to Stones garden the package was so heavy that I left it and went on to the house. Mr Stone and Oscar W[alton] had gone to town with hay. Mrs Stone did not expect them home till ten or eleven o clock anyway and perhaps later. Mr S—— had said if Robert and Fuller were in town he would bring them out. We waited impatiently till it seemed we could wait no longer—then they [Stone and Walton] came [back]—both in one rack—had left the other in town—no sign of the boys but a letter. I stood by the rack and talked to Oscar—gee! but he was blue or at least he seemed to be. He misses his five sisters as much as I ever missed my brothers. When he started home I went as far as the garden for my books. We stoped and talked. The evening was as beautiful but not so cold as that evening last February when we met in the hay road. We talked it over from start to finish[.] It seems the blowing up he got that evening completely stunned him—he knew there was something wrong but the promises I had exacted made it almost impossible for him to find out what the trouble was. It seems he didnt rest tho till he had unearthed everything. Its alright now and this time *I didn't refuse to be friends.*

I went back to the house and read your letter. You will never know what that letter meant to me. Why didn't you hint before that perhaps they would not come? I gave it up when I was down to your house last Spring and then your letters sounded as if they were coming and I planned *so much.* Then just as I was to enter a new neighborhood where I had reason to believe an evil report had preceeded me—just before beginning a school that every one told me was a "fright"—just as Mr Walton and the Stones and every one else I cared for were about to prove up and move away I received your letter saying the boys were not comming at all and telling of your plan of selling the old home. When it is in the hands of strangers I will never care to set foot on Iowa soil again never. To think of going back to Iowa without going through the orchard or down the creek, without sitting in the hammock or playing catch on the lawn, without the cream to take care of down cave[2] or the hundred and one little things to do to make the house more comfortable that I had planned—well that's the limit.

But I suppose if it cant be helped it cant thats all. I know you are not strong enough to stand it there and I did wrong to encourage you to build last Spring but I thot if you could hold it another year or two—then the Dakota home would be ready—it must be fenced—a big dam put in[,] the house made larger[,] a barn and chicken house built and then with a team—a few cows and chickens—you wouldn't get rich but you could live comfortably with no great care or burden of debt and then if Fuller liked Iowa best he and I could have tried to save the old home. We could have done it too. I could teach and keep house for us two and $350 cash in the year would be quite a help you know.

Well I had expected to go to town the next day but your letter saved me that. I stayed at Stones and when Mr and Mrs Blumgreen stopped in the evening I got ready and came with them to the dance here at Klemanns. Had a great time—danced quite a little[.] The goosekicked Irishman was there. I waltzed with him four or five times and went down to supper with him. He wanted to know why the boys were not there and when I told him he said he knew just how I felt and was so nice to me I could have hugged him on the spot only there were too many "lookin." Then there was a young college man and Oscar Klemann and his daddy. Oh I had a good time and intend to have more good times too. I sure could have a dandy time if I didn't care for the conseqences. Say I know a fellow who can "get around" *without chalk*.[3] My but his arms are long.

Last week the goosekicked Irishman stopped here one evening, was here to supper another [evening] and supper and spent the evening another evening, and Saturday I washed—ironed and all such tricks—climbed the big hill—had two horse back rides last week. Sunday I was invited to play cards and drink beer but declined. Have been passe-par-touting[4] pictures for my school room.

Am doing my hair up a new style—it cost me more than a dollar to get the dodads to fix it up fancy.[5] Hope they will last a while. The boys say its all right.

I cant think of much tonight because there is "great doings" going on here.

Board has riz to $.50 per day and we roost two to a perch[.] It rained most of last week and cleared off today (Sept 26)[.] I couldnt get home over Sunday and had to wade mud ankle deep in patent leather shoes—slippers. Came home one night almost drowned and as my dress trunk had not arrived I had [to] dress for dinner in a kimona. Every on[e] else had about the same luck and it was rather hard to get all the duds dry. Rudolph [Klemann] watched me clean my skirt—thot I was in hard luck—said to never mind—just wear my kimona to school.

Must close and hit the perch—write when you can

Lovingly—Bess

P.S. talk about postponements! I beat my time a week and feel accordingly[.]

Julius [Klemann,] the one who attends high school and plays foo[t]ball[,] is working partial payments—me too—see[.] I feel like the dog who said "Life is just one d—— thing after another[.]"

Oh well[,] things will turn out alright I guess. If Toad came out here he would get to bawling for his ma sure. Now I haven't any brothers any more I can flirt with any old cuss I want too.

I have given up Summer School next summer—it will take all I can earn these next two years to get my claim around in shape.

Bess

At last, drawn west by his own curiosity and by Bess's persistent urging, Fuller Corey, newly turned twenty-one, arrived in South Dakota to stake his own claim to a piece of free land in Stanley County.

✳ FROM FULLER COREY
OCT. 2ND 25 TO 7 P.M. 1910 / FORT PIERRE, SO. DAK.
TO MRS. M. M. COREY

Dear Mother—I am now alone in Besses house and felling rather blue. I walked out too Besses school Friday morning. Arrived at recess. The door was open. I walked up and looked in. There sat Bess reading your letter you wrote before I left home. She had her side to me but did not see me. I watched her awhile and then asked her what she had. She was pretty much surprised. She said you had said I wasn't coming but she had not finished that letter.

When I was at the Post Office Friday morning, writing the card a fellow came in and called for their mail, I didn't listen to him. Then he called for Miss Corey's mail. I heard that. He was on horse back. It was Oscar Klemanns and he left the mail at the school house when he went home.

I stayed at the school house all day and stayed at Kleman's that night. I slept with Oscar in the bunkhouse. I told Bess afterwards it was my last night at Kleman's because I was one big blister of bed bug bites. We went to town Saturday forenoon and I saw the football game in the afternoon. Bess rode out with Mr. Stone. I went with Mr. Speer. We left town about sun down. We arrived at Stones' $\frac{1}{4}$ to 9, left Stones at 9 walked $2\frac{1}{2}$ miles carrying 75 lbs. Arrived at Bess's house half past 10 Saturday night. Bess had not been home for two weeks, on account of rain. Her bed clothes were folded on top of the trunk in the north end of the house and were kind of damp from the rain blowing in. So we were kind of coverless that night. Bess slept on the couch and I slept in the hammock in the kitchen. Got up about 8 o'clock. Bess got dinner at 12.

OCT. 3, $\frac{1}{4}$ TO 8 P.M.

Well I have just got through eating my supper. I went around Bess's land this forenoon. She had about 35 or 40 acres of level land and the rest are hills although some can be farmed. All the young people are going to leave here in the next two months, or most all of them.[1] I went over to Stones this afternoon and helped him pick up potatoes and got home around sun down. Built a fire and baked some brickbats[2] for supper and they were dandys. I am planning on going to town in the morning if I get up early enough. I'll walk unless I can catch a ride. Hope everything is going fine. How is Fred and bab?[3] Write. Your son Fuller.

Bess got straightened around for school the next week. Taking the water pail at 3 we went over to Stone's. After being there half an hour Bess went on to her school and I got the pail of water and some other stuff. I went back home over the hills $1\frac{1}{2}$ miles. Ate my supper and commenced this. Some of this country looks nicer than any country I ever saw, level as a floor. But the mountains, or the hills they call them, are like our big hill only about 15 or 20 times as high and some are straight up. There are some of the same in Iowa but I didn't know it before. Bess has a good place but it's too lonesome out here. I like to see more people. This is all tonight. I'm going to bed. Half past 8.

✳ FROM FULLER COREY
OCT. 6, 8 P.M. / FORT PIERRE, SO. DAK.
TO MRS. M. M. COREY

Dear Mother—I got your letter Tuesday. I hope you are feeling better now and everything's all right. I walked half way to town Tuesday, then caught a ride. Got there about noon. Bummed around awhile then walked out to Bess's school. Talked with her awhile, then found I had forgot Stone's mail. So went back after it, expecting to ride out with the same man I rode in with. But he had made up his mind to say overnight in town. I was too near broke so went on out a foot. Caught a ride about two miles with some Indians. Arrived at Stones about ½ after 8. Got over to Bess's house ½ past 9. 24 miles. Wednesday morning I went over to the river with Glen and Howard Speer after drift wood. About 4½ miles. Got home at two. Ate my dinner then went down to Sunshines with the Speer boys after water from the big well and saw the snake den. Ate supper at Speers. Went over to Sy's with Glen, Howard and Oscar and played cards. Got home ½ past 12. Got up 9 o'clock this morning. Went over to Stones after some water. Came home got my dinner. Cleaned the gun and went rabbit and land hunting in the north and northwest. Shot one prairie dog and haven't got the heart to kill another. Went home. Washed the dishes. Baked my 3rd batch of brickbats and ate them all up for supper. Life is just one damn thing after another.

I saw a coyote (kioot) when going to town Tuesday. They are yellowish brown. Those down there are gray and much larger. 9 o'clock. Bedtime.

CONTINUED BY: ELIZABETH COREY
OCT. 7
Fuller says he cant think of any thing more to write. I wrote you a card this morning and Toad got a card from Glen this afternoon—its a hun I assure you.

Fuller went over to Stones and back this foreno[o]n after water—hunting jack rabbits—went back this afternoon and helped Mr

Hand-drawn map of the Klemann School area sent to Iowa by Fuller Corey in October 1910. Fuller's plea for secrecy reflects his fear of claim-jumpers. Photo courtesy Cultural Heritage Center, Pierre, S.D.

Stone dig for his cistern and this evening drove Mr Stones team down after me. We got to my house about 9 P.M. Fuller built the fire and made "brick-bats" as he calls them and I opened a can of tomatoes and we had supper. Gee but the boy can cook! Has been living high all week but wont try cake yet.

I'm having the time of my life this term—between bedbugs and lice I agree with Fuller that "life seems on[e] ——— thing after another[.]"

Fuller is going to town with Oscar tomorrow and file if all is well. We are going to a party-dance in the evening.

Be careful what you write me.[1] It is late[—]we must be up at five[.]

Lovingly Bess,

What ails Mary Lanigan?

✳ OCT. 27, 1910 / FORT PIERRE, SO. DAK.
TO MRS. M. M. COREY

Dear Ma—Have a letter partly written to Alta but will leave it and write you a note so you will get it Saturday.

Your two cards received last week. Have been possessed with the idea that something extra ordinary was taking place in Iowa ever since Tues. evening and can hardly wait to hear from you.

Had a dandy school last week. Friday evening as I was leaving the schoolhouse the schoolma'am from Speers went by and asked if I was going to attend the Reading Circle[1] meeting in town the next day. I thot she was mistaken in the date but she said not so instead of walking out to my claim that evening I staid over and went to town with Mr and Mrs Klemann on Saturday. Gee! What a time! Mr Klemann was only going to be in town a few minutes but never left town till half after six[.] There was no meeting so I had time to visit all my friends. When we did leave town it was on top of a load of lumber and feed—it was dark and the driver was ———[,] had killed a few too many[.][2] The team were goers and we hit all the high places and hit 'em hard[.] I hung on like grim death to a sick monkey and *then* nearly got dumped. That sure was the ride of my life. When we got out to Klemanns the young people were ready to start to the goodbye party for Sham[.][3] I went along. Thot I'd die before morning—too much excitement I guess.

Have great times I assure you. One old maid gentleman gave Mrs Klemann a large red apple "for the schoolma'am with his complements" and Fred Dike (Fuller knows him) sent me a bottle of beer which Mr Klemann drank for me.

Was treated to gum by three different ones in one day and candy every twice in a while.

Was invited to spend this next Saturday and Sunday in town but "circumstances prevent." Have also an invitation to a dance next Saturday night but do not expect to attend.

George Stewart wrote me a card this morning after he saw Fuller and also inclosed one of the cards with his picture on. I showed it to Oscar Walton and he floped it face down in a cup of water and said "All Irishmen auto be drowned[.]" I asked how about himself and he said he auto have drowned himself in the river long ago.

Mrs Foutts and Mack have gone for good—moved Tuesday— Oscar took them down. Mrs Foutts left me her rocking chair which is one like that old one of papa's only smaller.

Had a letter from Anna Stewart[4] a few days ago.

Please tell Jennie[5] I'm going to write her next. and what the deuce ails Mary L[?]

When Fuller comes back please dont forget to send that hair of mine which is in the drawer of the sitting room book case.

Have a new pupil—Clemens Nagel[—]not yet five years old. Yesterday they were playing a game and when one side began to loose they missed a man and one called "Where is Charles?" and back came the answer "He's in the backhouse."[6] Ah me! Such is life in the far west.

School time—must close[.]

> Write
> Your Bess.

✳ POSTCARD / NOV. I, 1910 / FORT PIERRE, SO. DAK. TO J. OLNEY COREY

Was twice glad to hear from you—have had only cards for so long am anxious to have a letter from some of you. Have had letters from every where but home it seems. Last night—(Halloweén)—was "Great doin's" in our town. of which more later[.]

Am getting all the enjoyment (?) I can out of life—could greet Mr Pingle almost lovingly now.

Went out home Friday eve—spent Sunday at Speers. They brought me down in the evening[.] It rained and snowed last evening.

Write—I am your

Bachelor Bess [1]

✴ NOV. 7, 1910 / FORT PIERRE, SO. DAK.
TO MRS. M. M. COREY [AND ETHEL COREY]

Dear Ma and Ethel—Yours and Ethels received. I cannot understand why you have not heard from me as I wrote you a card last week and a letter the week before.

I was terribly shocked to hear that the Lanigan boys had left home. [1]

Say ma please dont let those girls go to town that way again—it almost sets me wild. All that Wednesday I had that awful feeling that some thing was going to happen. I began to feel that way Tuesday and by Wed. evening I was almost off my base. I began to feel better about eight o'clock. I guess that was after they got home. Mamma, you dont know and I don't know—perhaps we will never know what—but I feel sure that Ethel was in some awful danger. I suppose you think I'm foolish but I can't help knowing that there was a "Nigger in the fence" some where at that time.

I wrote you about Sham's party two weeks ago last Saturday evening didn't I? I went with the Klemann young people and felt so bad I didn't go on over home after the dance but came back with them so a week ago Friday I had to go up home instead of going down to Mrs Gordon's to spend Saturday and Sunday as I had planned.

Last week I made a plain guimpe[2] and put in my gray panama dress—will send you a sample of the stuff if I don't forget. It looks quite right for evening and I wear a band of the braid to match in my hair.

I didn't go home last Friday evening but helped get ready for the dance which Mr Klemann and Sham had goten up. It was held in the school house.

I had a good time. Emma, I and our partners served the supper. Such a crowd of hungry creatures! We got them filled up to the neck

I believe at last. My partner, who does not enjoy the best of health[,] went home immediately after supper.

Oh, tell Fuller I had the pleasure of meeting the Terry girls and learn[ed] that their father is the blacksmith he met and liked so well.

Oscar K—— was in school again today and did pretty well for him.

My! it is getting dark and I haven't done any of my school work yet.

The wax on the floor[3] makes the sweeping easy. I wish to prepare for the part I'm to take in the program at the teachers institute meeting next Saturday. I will go if possible as I get $2 if I go and pay $1.50 if I don't. I expect that before I get through with it I will wish I was home and the yaller dog was there barefoot.

Would like to make my coat this week but will have to make it by hand as Mrs is afraid it will spoil her sewing machine.

Tomorrow is election—please let me know at the earliest date if Geo Stewart is elected as I have a card to send.

I had just begun to boast of having my letters about all answered when they began to come thick and fast—would like to get these last ten answered before I get any more. I even got one from Louie W. Lida made her a worse time than she made me I guess.

About Mauds[4] letter—yes. She seems to think as much of you as you did of the "little Irish Rosa" so I dont care how much you think of her—treat her as you'd have another treat your daughter.

I guess I'll have to play this letter is for Ethel too as I've no time to write her now. Wish you would start a list of things to send me when Fuller comes home—there is my hair, the extract, day lily—wish you could send me three small ones. And when the Raleigh's agent[5] comes I wish you would get two bottles of that face lotion. I'll make it all right. Emma and I both want some and cant get it here.

Did the plum stuff spoil? You never said and I worried about it.

Did Fuller give all the cards away? They were for Grandma [Corey], Aunt Jennie [Dunlavy], Mamma, Mary [Lanigan], Valerie [Harris], Jennie [Noon], Maud [Hemsted] and Mrs. A[rmstrong].

When is Fuller planning on starting back? Or hasnt he started to plan yet? Perhaps he better not start till after Xmas for I can stand it some how and he wont be so apt to get homesick. If he has any money to spare I wish he would send it to me and I'll make it right later. Am suffering worster every day for it.

What was the surprise you expected to have for me when you wrote? Have been anxious to know all these weeks.

Please write often as you can and tell Ethel I'll write her.
Its dark. Must close. Your Bachelor Bess.
[P. S.] Nov 8th
Hades broke loose this morning.

✱ NOV. 15, 1910 / FORT PIERRE, SO. DAK.
   TO MRS. M. M. COREY

Dear Ma—Tomorrow is the 16th[1] and I wonder if I will hear from any of you. Am afraid I'll cave in if I don't.

Did I ever tell you about the trick I played at a party a while back? The day before Shams party he was in town and through some foolishness or other drew a set a teaspoons. I don't know what kind of metal they are but it is some mixture that will wear. That night at the party I faked one and sent it to Pierre and had it engraved. On one side of the handle are his initials OCW[2] and on the back is the date of the party 10-23-10.

Friday evening after school I walked into town and staid over for the institute meeting Saturday. Mrs Gordon, Mrs Hess and I were up town all evening—had lots of fun—attended the Majestic—it was fine. Staid all night at the Huston House. It was late when I got there—the night man was there. He showed me to a room and before he got down stairs I found that the key wouldnt lock the door so I went down and stired him up. He came up and fixed it. before he got there I discovered that the bed linen was soiled so I spoke of that. He said "It was jest the Jedge" had that room the night before. Imagine how I turned and looked at him. He began to back down the hall assuring me that he would bring the clean linnen at once if I would change it as the girl had retired. It was about eleven when I hit the perch but I slept till eight the next morning when Old Hirmen left the hot water at my door just as he went off duty. I wasted about an hour dressing then went right down town.

About the first person I met was Daisy Hamm[3] who was on the same discussion as I was. We were together all day and had great times. I started to walk out but it was almost dark when I started as I never left the High School Building till five o'clock and was detained down town. I got out about a couple of miles and met the Wandering Jew[4] and his sister-in-law. They told me to get in and go back to town with them and as soon as they got the mail they were coming back out again and I could ride clear out to Speers where the party was. So I did. When we got close to the Speer schoolhouse I got out and walked the rest of the way and they went on. They agreed not to tell how I got out and we were going to have some fun and we surely did too. Of course it was quite late and after Klemanns got there with out me they were sure I wasn't coming.

I had a good time and the next morning rode over as far as my place with Howard. After dinner I went over to Stones through a snow storm and staid there till almost dark and walked down in the moon-light. Stopped at Carlisles[5] for the evening and the boys brought me home[.] It was half after ten I guess when I got here and I slipped in so quietly that no one heard me tho I had to open and close three doors. Margaret[6] never knew when I got in bed with her. The next morning Emma called Margaret and after they had both gone into the kitchen Mrs Klemann looked into our room and as she didn't know that I had returned tho Marg—— was in bed yet. She began to beat me about the branches telling me to get out of that bed at once. I dreamed I was in Avoca[7] till I recognized [her] voice then I woke up exclaiming "This is me if you please." The poor old lady almost fainted.

Say I believe the Klemanns are some relation to the Pingles. I only write you a little but there is really a great muchness.

Tell Fuller that we were a little to late in writing about the shack—Strommy got it. Am going to try to get another.

I seem to have a worse cold in some ways than I ever had before in my life. About every third person I see says "Your going to have pneumonia the first thing you know and large as you are it will go hard with you[.]" I weigh eight pounds less than when I came here and have on heavy clothes now too.

I believe they will fix that school closet[8] some time in the course of human events—they have made a start. I had to just "howl" before they even did that much. I dont have to go out often but when I do go—be darned if I want the whole country to know which side my pantz button on.

There are great things to happen but at present I say each night "Another day gone, thank the Lord." Have finished my second month of school—wish it was the last. I owe so many letters but am so awful busy and—more later[—]love to all from your Bachelor Bess.

WEDNESDAY MORNING — FIVE TILL NINE. This is my birth-day and m[a]y be the worst ever tho it is a beautiful day and bitter cold.

I wrote under disadvantages last evening—didn't tell you anything I guess. Say that spoon—Jennie Speer gave it to him[9] the night of the party telling him it was to remember his So. Dak. friends by. I hope he never knows the rest. I can't help it[.] I just get so angry at him I could almost heave a brick at him—didn't know he was such a snob till the way he treated two or three at the last party.

I may be forced to change my boarding place soon—its hard—I never had to do such a thing before.

I hope Mr Stone goes to town today[.]

Lovingly—Bess.

✱ NOV. 25, 1910 / FORT PIERRE, SO. DAK.
TO MRS. M. M. COREY

Dear Ma, Will write you a few lines, though it is now nearly eleven, as I will have a chance to get it mailed tomorrow.

Monday forenoon I expelled Margaret Klemann. She is back now but does not give me much trouble. Monday morning Louis brought me word that Mrs Divine wanted me to come over to stay all night with her so I went straight from school and didn't go near Klemanns. Tuesday the old boy[1] was at the school house before I got there. His dutch was up—there was a strong odor of whiskey. Great Gun! If some of you folks had heard him talk I think that you'd have knocked him down. I kept cool and handed him back handfull after handfull till he found that the school ma'am was no easier bluffed than squeezed, so he rung off.

Tuesday evening they were all very nice to me and Wednesday I walked into town after school and out to school this morning and as Mr Blumgreen came along tonight and brought me up to Mr Stones they only get one dollar out of me this week.

I had a high old time in town, attended the theater both evenings and a ball last evening but only as a speckled tater as I dont dance you know (?) I dined at the Royal Hotel as the guest of Mr and Mrs Gordon[2]—the swellest meal I ever ate. Another young gentleman[3] dined at the same table. He vows he will have my box at the social a week from tomorrow if it takes every cent he has. Wonder if he means it.

Had midnight supper after the ball—guess it was past midnight some.

There is a party tomorrow night and a big dinner here Sunday so I must not be up much later.

I expect that ere this reaches you I will have purchased a team. Can get them at a bargain. Perhaps Fuller remembers Mr Blumgrens blacks—they are for sale as he is going away. They are both black—Kate and Nellie—about eight years old and the best team I know of. Mr Stone thinks their colts would more than pay for them in two or three years if we had them raise coalts. They are full of life and go and perfectly gentle. Every one about here knows the team. I can get team, harness and buggy for $250. so I think I'll take it and risk Fullers disapproval. Would like to have him send me all the money he can. Will make it good later. Well guess I will close for tonight[.]

> Lovingly your
> Bachelor Bess.

* DEC. 5, 1910 / FORT PIERRE, SO. DAK.
  TO MRS. M. M. COREY

Dear Ma, Your card received and it almost broke me up in business. Perhaps there is no "real hurry" but if you wait till you get in a "real hurry" what for a bargain do you reckon you would get? A person might as well go to Ft. Pierre as go to his relations when he's in a pinch. Suppose I'll have to go to town Saturday and see what I can get on my face.[1] Will have to work some poor cuss. I dont blame the kid for not wanting to loan his money. When a fellow is just starting out he hates to put his money where he may never see it again. Of course I generally pay my debts but thats no sign I always will. If a fellow is going to start out on that line of course he wants to begin with his relatives. I told Mr Stone what you wrote and he said "Well he'll never get a bargain to beat that I'll tell him that." I hate to let them go back now but I don't know how I'll get the mon as I've nothing to mortgage. They would wait for part of it but would want part and perhaps a note for the rest.

Was glad you liked the handkerchiefs—thought you girls would like a little something to blow in along about Xmas time.

Am glad you heard from Maud—will write her soon—intended to ere this but was not sure of her address.

Am glad the boys have finished their corn and hope they get a good schoolma'am soon.

Yes I imagine the boys are busy. The tinkering and straw does not appeal to me but the wood, pumpkins, fish and rabbits make me hungry and thirsty and all the rest. Will write more later.

TUESDAY DEC. 6TH

I suppose you will think I'm crazy—am at the school house and its almost dark but I wanted to finish this letter and didn't want to finish it down at the house.

Last week on Wednesday I sent Oscar [Klemann] home. Gee! such a time as they made for me that night. The next morning I left for school before Mr K was up and left word for him to come up to the school house as I wished to see him on business. He stopped on the way to town—Mr Bertram[2] was with him. I went out and told him a few. He said he would have a talk with Oscar. That (Thurs) evening the young people went to a "swell doin's" out at Moultens[3]—Oscar W[alton] and Howard S[peer] took the girls. They got back just as I was starting for school. The boys told Mrs Stone that Oscar [Klemann] wanted to stay home and sleep but Mr Klemann went after him proper—told him that he not only had to go to school and finish the eighth grade this year but that he had to behave himself or he (Mr K) would knock his block off. Consequently O came to school Friday morning and told me he was going to do better and that he had had a talk with his father.

Friday evening I walked out to Stones—was going on over home but Mr Stone said if I would wait till morning I could ride Jack[4] over and then ride him back in the evening and go to the social with them so I staid. In the evening Mrs Stone and I trimed the boxes. The stuff I sent for cost $.25 and was plenty for our four boxes. Mine sold for $1.80. I never told young Porter anything about it. Mr Stone got it and another one beside so when they got through and there was one or two without baskets he sold mine to Dr Fletcher. Gee such a time as we had! And if the Dr could have danced we would have had a greater time. There was no program—they just danced till they got hungry then had supper and danced some more. The proceeds are for the Xmas tree[5] and they took in $26.

About the time the crowd was ready to go home they found the ground was white with snow and it was still coming down fierce and so dark it was not safe to venture away from the buildings so we had to stay till morning. Oh! how tired we all got. I sat in a seat with my elbow on the desk behind me and my face in my hand and slept.

Dr Fletcher sat there also with his arm kind of around me. Oh its alright. His wife dont care—she says I can have him if I want him and he has promised me one of his photographs. He kept the card with my name which was in my basket.

The Teton crowd took me as far as my claim and the Dr helped me out and was very nice.

Oh! I forgot to tell you about Jack and it's dark—so long.

WEDNESDAY MORNING DEC 7TH

Mr K—— is going to town today so will try to finish.

Saturday morning Mr. Stone put the saddle on Jack and brought him up to the door. After much trouble I mounted tho Jack did not approve and showed his disapproval in various ways[.] Mr Stone said afterward that he knew at once I could never ride him as soon as he started to act up. I did not intend to get off but at last the old boy went down on his knees—that bit of unexpected gallantry caused me to change my mind and I alighted at once and I'm not sure that I landed right side up either. It was done so neatly I had to laugh—just sat there on the ground and laughed till I cried. Suppose I could have staid on but how did I know he wouldn't roll and I didn't want to get hurt so pulled my feet from the stirrups and moved on.

Sunday I walked over to Stones and John Porter took me down as far as the ranch and Howard Speer who is to work there brought me on to Klemanns. Everything seems peaches and cream now. Mr K—— went after them about my wages—got last months order and the one for this month ready for me Friday evening.

The thoughts of Xmas make me sick when I'm in debt so deep and nothing to give.

Must close as it must be almost school time.

I slept under a feather bed this last night and almost got a thrashing this morning[.]

Lovingly your

Bachelor Bess.

✱ DEC. 12, 1910 / FORT PIERRE, SO. DAK.
TO MRS. M. M. COREY

Dear Ma,—Yours received last Friday and caused me heaps of grief for a few hours but its alright now.

My cold is better—I didn't mention it last time as it was so bad that—well it seemed that every one was hollering "consumption"[1] and "pneumonia" at me till I was almost ready to croak. I kept going though I had to hang on to things when I started to cough. You don't need to worry though now as I'm O.K. now—that is it dont hurt me to breath[e] and I dont cough so much. My work is very heavy at present and no chance of its being lighter and no vacation at Xmas.

Say about that school down there—"Dont start anything you cant finish" and if you start into anything to "even up" you'll fail sure.[2] You'll get even quicker by taking it as it comes and letting folks think you like it. Now the corn is out[3] you better quit active labor and turn "boss"[—]the boys are dandy hands I'm sure. Take things easy and dont worry.

Say I'll tell you a joke. I've only contracted for seven months and will be through about Mar 10th or if I teach the extra month Apr 7th and if you dont get a teacher before that I'll come down and take a three or four months term and stay long enough to clean your house from stem to stern. How does that suit you? Or dont you think you could stand it?

I staid over Sunday this last week and spent Saturday in town. Got my "mon[,]" paid my board up to date[,] made another payment on the cisterns—only owe $25 on them now—bought some warm duds— union suits, woolen stockings, knit peticoat and stuff for three waists— worsted—so you see Im going to be warm for the rest of the winter anyway.

Guess I've made arrangements for paying for my team. My team may be *twenty eight* years old but if they can go sixty miles without whip in a day without hurting them and still be fresh they auto raise a batch worth having dont you think[?]

If I could make connections on a spring term of school I could almost pay for my team couldn't I[?]

I rather expect to go to town next Friday evening and stay over Sunday—perhaps.

"Jiminie frost"! I'm going to hit the perch. Its almost ten and I didn't sleep much last night.

Well take good care of yourself and dont worry about me. I'm OK now[.]

Lovingly your
Bachelor Bess

✳ DEC. 24, 1910 / FORT PIERRE, SO. DAK.
TO MRS. M. M. COREY

Dear Folks,—This is Xmas eve and about 10:30 o'clock. Before I finish it will be Xmas day. I wonder where you all are and what you are doing.

Yours and Fullers letters were received two weeks ago last evening. I was in town the next day and sent Fuller a card. If I have written any of you since then I don't remember who or what so guess I better begin there. I was very glad to get that check. The $1.00 I spent for a black hair ribbon. The $10.00 purchased coal and other things.

Did I write any of you about [George] Jones? A while back I was feeling blue and said I'd marry the first man that was fool enough to ask me just to get out of teaching school but I tell you I caved in when Jones hove in sight. I guess I dont want to be stepmother to seven kids—not when they are Joneses anyway. The worst of it is—he always talks everything over with the kids so the whole country knew what was up before I did and almost before I received his letter I heard some measley boy singing.—"When Jonesie married Bessie, A wise old owl was he." Gee! I could have skinned him clear over and half way back.

Was in town a week ago yesterday—got out in time to go to Porters dance. The next afternoon the young folks were going skating and asked me to go with them. I did not wish to go but they set up such a howl about it saying that I wouldn't go because Rudolph [Klemann] wouldnt go and Rudolph wouldnt go because he thought I wouldn't go and Mr Bertram coaxed like a good fellow so I went.—Got cold feet and went back to the house in about ten minutes. That evening I wanted to go to bed early but the girls wouldn't let me so I thought I'd put a stop to their deviling Rudolph and I. I didn't stop to think *how* but went into the sitting room. Just as I entered the room Mr Bertram looked at his watch and I said "Oh Mr. Bertram how will you swap watch chains?" He said "Even" so I swapped my gold fob for an old piece of "whang" that had been used three years[.] Then we kept on swapping till Mr and Mrs Klemann laughed till they almost cried some of the trades were so ridiculous[.] We traded almost everything back the next day and I'm one stick pin ahead.

I worked like the deuce all week to get ready for the doings[1] Friday. Friday was a nice day and we had a good crowd. The program

began at two o'clock. There were six songs, two readings and ten rec-
itations. All did very well. After the program we had Xmas pie which
was also a success. Then last but not least came the eatables. Cookies,
popcorn-balls, nuts and candy—all every one cared for. After the feast
we adjourned.

One remarkable thing about the "doin's" was the fact that almost
all the grown visitors were gentlemen. Mr Flagg Carlisle[2] was among
them. He is home for the holidays from the University of Nebraska
where he is studying and also practicing law.

I have received quite a few Christmas presents. Everso many
cards—haven't counted them up yet—an apron, a jabot,[3] sachet bag,
a beautiful box of the most delicious candies I ever tasted and a swell
box of stationery of which this is a sample. The apron was from Mrs
Klemann, the jabot from Katherine Carlisle,[4] there were several cards
and also the candy from Carlisles—every thing was tagged but the
candy and it had a Sioux City stamp on the box. The stationery was
from Mr Bertram. Gee! I wish you could see the box. I tell you Fritz is
no cheap skate. I'd set my cap for him only he is sawed of[f] so short it
just makes my feelings ache every time I think what a landscape we
would make walking into church together.

Mrs Gordon invited me into spend Xmas with her—would have
liked to have gone but wanted to get home once more. Mr Stone drove
my team to town Friday afternoon and stopped for me when he came
back. I went to the Xmas tree at the Speers School house with them
last evening and came over home about noon today.

I straightened up the house, washed out my handkerchieves and
a few other things.

I wish I had spent my dollar for a new post card album instead of
a hair ribbon as my album is full and I have quite a few laying around.
I had Xmas postals from Ethel, Chall, Paul, Anna Stewart and Jennie
Noon last week.

Well there is so much to write I can't think of anything so will
close for now and add some later. I intend to sleep as long as I feel like
in the morning and am invited over to the Stones for Xmas dinner.

Oh! I almost forgot to tell you I retrimmed my blue plush waist
this afternoon—will inclose a scrap of the trimming.

MONDAY DEC 26 1910
Yesterday morning I slept till almost nine and it was after one
when I got over to Stones. Dinner was very nice and Mr Stone brought

me down in the evening. When we got here they had all gone to the Indian "pow wow" except Mr Klemann—he was waiting for me. Wanted to know if I was going to the "doin's" with him and I said no that I couldn't afford to be out late when I had to teach school the next day so he told me that he would give me today if I would go. We waited till the young people from the south got here and went over with them. Gee! I had the time of my life. There was an awful big crowd. Several auto loads from town—all the high school boys and lots of others. Had introductions to quite a number—several asked for introductions in my hearing. I wore my plush waist and black skirt and felt as good as the best and in for a time. I sure had it too.

Mr Murphy[5] wanted me to try the Indian dance. For a wonder I caught on to it at once and the compliments I received were not a few. The squaws came and patted me, pointed to my feet and talked but of course I couldn't understand them. At last Mrs Spotted Hawk who is a negress told me for them. I tried to drop out of the dance but Mr Whirling Iron came after me twice and once a squaw danced with me. She put her arm around me and mine around her. They take hold of hands and dance around and round in a circle to the noise of a great big drum beaten by four Indians. The Indians dressed in their costumes and looked like real story book Indians. Oh how I wish you could all have been there!

I ate supper with them—of course—the dog sausage[6] was delicious—beats all your pork and beef all to pieces.

The Indians were much pleased with my dancing and were very nice to me.

I have been resting today. Mr Bertram and I played "Old Maid." Well I guess this is all for now so will close. Hope I'll hear from you soon.

> Lovingly
> Your Bachelor Bess.

✱ JAN. 16, 1911 / FORT PIERRE, SO. DAK.
TO MRS. M. M. COREY

Dear Ma,—I hadn't auto attempt a letter tonight my head aches so, oh *so* bad. I can't read and whats the use of going to bed—I couldn't go to sleep for hours if I did—I never do. I received Ethels letter also—was glad to hear from you both—don't see how it happens you both write at once[.] Suppose the kidlets were disappointed in finding those envelopes did not contain letters—perhaps they thot I had been to another Indian pow-wow and was sending a sample sausage. Dont care how you choose or anything about it—I thought I wrote the names in them.

Yes I knew you were angry[1] and was waiting for you to cool off a bit—how's the weather down there? What the deuce is the matter with my way of reasoning any way? You wrote as if your main object was to spite certain persons and you know that when a fellow starts out to "even up" with someone, even if its the devil himself, he is apt to get left—"The Lord saith vengence is mine" and aside from that I know and Olney knows that you couldn't stand it. You think you could[2] but I believe you will notice if you stop to think that no one who has taught school in the last ten years has ever suggested such a thing. It isn't like as if you had been teaching right along or as if you had no children or housekeeping or farm work to think of and you know you *would* think of them. It would be a change—that is true—but in a week or so when things settled down you would find it an aditional weight—a change for the worse. I suppose I should not have said anything but I couldn't lie to you and so "If cussing me will ease your spite, Go off some where and do it right[.]"

I know you are working too hard but what can I do? I suppose I should not have bought that team but it seemed a shame to let such a bargain go. Say they can't be so very old as Mr Stone looked at their teeth and says neither has "lost their cups"[3] yet.

My cistern is paid for and $5 on my team. I dont intend to teach but seven months here if I can get out of it and I think I can. I expect to pay the mortgage by the end of the term—pay back the ten you or Fuller advanced me and have enough to get back to Iowa if I deside to go. I don't want your home school but will try to get a three months term some where in the county.

Well what the deuce do you want me to do—would like to please you once but it seems as if I never could. If there is any thing in particular you want me to do just let your wants be known—don't wait till its too late and then tell me. I'll give up any thing or do any thing you say.

Oh gee! I just itch to get into that house [on the farm] and not have to think of school or institute or examinations or anything for a whole summer but house work and fruit and such.

Hope Ethel is better now. Hope she can finish the eighth grade this year.

And Fuller, too, you said he was poorly—how is he? When does he think of returning to Dakota? Has he sold Nell yet? Well good luck to him. I haven't found a house[4] for him yet.

You will have to get an extra milk stool to use for a wash stand—that would do for the wash-bowl wouldn't it? You want to take good care of that cold of yours. My cold is all gone now—only a little cough left. For sometime the folks here planned on putting me under the sod but as I told Jennie Boob they have postponed that indefinately now.

Guess I told you—did I not? that I was up to Stones New Years day and walked down in a storm. A week ago Saturday evening we were up to Carlisles for the evening and partook of a splendid oyster supper. Was invited to a dance last Sat. evening but did not go. Oh yes was invited to go with the crowd skating this evening but declined. The crowd has just returned.

Next Saturday I'm to read a paper on "The Most Successful Method of Teaching Spelling" at the teachers' meeting in Ft Pierre. Have my paper all written—will send it to you later if you wish.

I had a long letter from Alta [Brown] the other day—sounds as if she was a little sick of school teaching—says she has had some trouble but if they don't want her all they have to do is to let her know and she will go back to Ind. and take the position waiting for her. Gee! I wish I had a beau like the other girls have! Gee I'd cut out this darned school teaching in about no time. Oh! wait till next year—leap year—then I'll show you a trick or two.

This sure is "punk" guess I better close—suppose you'll be so mad when you get this you wont write for another month or two. Perhaps if you knew that you came near starting in the New Year with but one daughter you would find it easier to forgive the many faults and mistakes of your

Bachelor Bess

＊ JAN. 25, 1911 / FORT PIERRE, SO. DAK.
TO J. O[LNEY] COREY

Dear Olney,—I suppose mamma received my letter and is so angry she wont write me for another month or so[.]

I sent Paul a Jungle Book and ball game and inclosed the paper I read at the institute meeting last Saturday[.] There was not a single criticism made on my paper—perhaps that was because it was near the end of the program and they were getting tired.

Gee! Kid but I'm sick and I dont know what the deuce ails me—am keeping up pretty well. You know that Emma [Klemann] was sick a while back—the first week in January—well I've got the same thing and seem to have it worse in some ways though I haven't given up. A week ago yesterday I had such a head-ache, earache and throat-ache—it seemed to ache from my ears clear down my throat and my throat swelled so that at times I could hardly breathe[, not to] say any thing of swallowing. I felt just horrid but didn't start to break out till Monday and am now covered with a kind of rash from my neck to my knees tho it doesn't show on my face. I never realized I had the same as Emma had till Mrs Klemann said so and then I thought it was no use to stop school for if it was contagious the pupils were exposed already so I'm going to stick it out if I can. I kind of wish I knew what it was. The rash is like millions of pimples—the flesh seems to puff up and become a peculiar red and it itches some thing fierce. Last night Mrs Klemann came to see how it was when I went to bed and she started back as if I had hit her a biff[,] exclaiming in German "My God! My God!" She came in before I was up this morning and wanted to know if I was going to school today. I had a pretty good school today. Margaret is sick with sore throat or something and Oscar was as good as a boy can be. Of course Adelbert Jones had to act as ornery as he knew how. There is always some little son of a biscuit eater who has to do his best to spoil things.

I guess I've received the last of my 1910 Xmas presents. It was a beautiful back comb from Mrs Gordon. I walked into town last Friday evening and came out Sunday evening with Basil Carlisle[.] [1] Oh! yes, Basil and I are quite good friends[.] I was up there one evening and he walked down with me. Little Charles [Carlisle] was going to come too but Basil wouldn't let him.

I attended the theater both evenings I was in town and Saturday evening I had a nice little visit with Mr Bertram[.]

Well it is getting dark and I must sweep and go home to supper. I feel ever so much better now.

Say perhaps instead of going back to Iowa after school closes I better live on my claim and send Ma what my car fare would amount to to help in the furnishing up.

I wish I knew some of Fullers plans—suppose he will be here by the middle of March any way so as to get to living on his claim[2] by the 8th of April.

We are having lovely weather here. Will close-write soon[.]

Yours

Bachelor Bess.

P.S. JAN 26 Didn't get this mailed today so will add a line.

When I got home from school last night Mrs Klemann asked how I was and I answered briskly that I was pretty well thank you. She looked at me for about half a minute and then said "You can stand the most of any one I ever saw[.]" I can't stand the heat tho—it makes the itchiness so much worse.

I feel good tonight and marked another day off the calendar—you can't imagine the little thrills and quivers of joy I feel every time I cross off another day.

Well I must close and answer those other letters.

Lovingly yours—Bess

✳ FEB. 6, 1911 / FORT PIERRE, SO. DAK.
TO MRS. M. M. COREY

Dear ma,—Will write a few lines. You read that letter I wrote Olney if you want to.

Guess I was feeling pretty bad when I wrote before but I don't see what I wrote to make you worry so. I am all right—just grunting a little you know[—]but I tell you ma[,] I appreciate your letter. You must never think of coming to take care of me if I do get the measles, or small pox or anything for there is *all the rest* at home and your duty to them is far greater than your duty to me[.] Besides if I was sick enough to need your care I'd need so much care that with the hard trip out here you would be sick yourself.

I'm about alright now so you [can] stop your sweating and if you will agree to keep cool I'll promise that *if I'm ever very sick* I'll keep you posted and have some one send for you if I'm seriously ill but if you are going to pack your suit case and hit the pike the first sqwak I make I'll just never tell you when I am sick till some other time even if I'm dieing.

I don't hardly think it was measles I had but I'd like to know what it was. I'm pealing off now—ugh!

They say Oscar W. has the smallpox awful bad—and the crazy bat wrote a letter to Mr Speer now while he is so bad—said he could only write a few lines and then lie down and rest and then write a few more. I dont think they should write letters when they have a contagious disease.

Mr Stone went to town Saturday[,] no I mean Friday[,] and he took me out to the ranch after school. Saturday evening I went to Art Scripters birthday party (am studying "Art" again) [and] had a lovely time. About the time to start home it began to storm so we couldn't go home till daylight. George Rovang[1] and I danced half an hour straight—wasn't that a fright? Well it was a dandy waltz and I hated to stop. Guess the exertion was about enough as Ive been celebrating ever since.

I ate supper with Mr Frank Hamilton the gentleman that Mrs Blomgren dreamed about. Wonder if her dream will come true. I surely think he is about right.

Mr Stone brought me down yesterday afternoon. I asked him if he wasnt sorry I came out and he said no he wished he had come down after me two weeks ago. I wanted to walk part way back and he told me Id "play ——— walking" and was [so] grouchy I had to keep still.

Did I tell you that Stones sent Myrtle back to her grandpa's and Mrs Stone is teaching Stanton at home so the Speer school is reduced to four pupils. Margaret Klemann is in Pierre. I dont know for how long. Mr Klemann said for the rest of the year.

I'm afraid I cant make a go of that spring term in Iowa as I rec'd word today that institute is from May 29th till June 9th and certificates will be revoked for non attendance.

I think I'll work some in town perhaps, and save a little that way. I wish I could help you out some with your furnishing up but I'm paying quit a bit of ten percent intrest at present—will try to help you out later on.

Good night will write more later.

FEB 8
I intended to finish this yesterday morning at school but found I had no envelopes so sent a card.

Tell Paul I was glad to get his letter and will answer it some time but I always want to write to you and its hard to write them all.

When is Fuller coming back? Wish I knew something about it. I cant get a shack for him any where so he'll have to build. Mr Stone seemed to think it would be about as cheap[.] Mr Stone is not using his team for hauling as so many mares all over the country are loosing their colts[—]he was afraid to risk it. Guess Nellie is all right any way.

Tell Ethel that a "wennie"[2] would taste good for a change tho I'm desperately fond of dog. Must close[,]

Lovingly your Bachelor Bess.

FEB 9 1911

Dear ma[,—]it is just five o clock and I havent started to sweep yet. I just feel too lazy for any use. Have been feeling pretty good the last few days and the school work is going on fine[.] I begin to wonder what is going to happen—it seems to good to be true—perhaps 'tis because Margaret is gone but it seems so quiet I cant help but think there is a storm brewing.

Thought I'd get that letter mailed yesterday or today but didn't so I thought I'd open it and write some more. Am reading another book evenings.[3] I know auto be sewing but thought I'd wait till next week for fear the noise might bother the sick folks. Julius [Klemann] is still in bed and quite bad.

I shouldn't think Grandma's would say any thing about Maud's slang[.] I put so much in my letters to them that the envelopes will hardly stay sealed and they have lots to say about how they laugh over my letters. Grandma did accuse me of "getting wild" though, and the way I let out in the next letter was something fierce.

Well I must sweep—will get this mailed—sometime—perhaps

Bachelor Bess

FEB 10

Yes there was a storm last eve and it wasn't snow or rain but you might call it "thunder." Oh how I hope Mr Stone will go to town today so I can mail this[.]

✳ FEB. 21, 1911 / FORT PIERRE, SO. DAK.
TO MRS. M. M. COREY

Dear Ma,—Heard from you a short time ago but have forgotten most of what you wrote but I guess you all didn't feel very good[.] Gee! I wish I could be four places at once—I'd attend Summer school, stay on my claim, put up your fruit this summer and go visiting all at once.

A week ago Friday evening I walked out home and the next day did my washing and finished putting that quilt together and got the cotton in it. I walked out last Friday evening and Saturday I tied that quilt and did some washing and ironing. Sunday evening I walked over to Stones and yesterday morning Mr Stone brought me down on his way to town. Last evening I walked into town to have my foot looked at. Am pleased to inform you that it is just a "gumbile" and not the gout as I feared. The Dr opened it—cut off the corn and dressed the thing and told me how to treat it—guess it wont have to be amputated if I take good care of it. He only charged me $1. He says it was scarlet fever which I had a while back and if he had known of it I'd have been quarentined[.]

After supper I went to the Majestic—went with Mrs Gordon but Mr Gordon and Mr Berg[1] brought us home. Mrs G's feet were cold so she made Mr G hurry in a way quite impossible for a person with a "gumbile" so we got there later with more dignity if not style.

You know when I was down before I wore my black skirt and velvet waist with dutch collar and cut quite a swell. Mr B[erg] is under the impression that I'm the only heir of a "wich uncle in New Yawk" and he seems hard hit and as Chall writes that you will disown me if I marry an Indian I thought I'd see how you'd like a change of color and decided to accept the attentions of "Dago Harry[.]"[2]

Mr Bertram sat by me during the show and talked so much I didn't half see the pictures and Mr Berg looked like a thunder cloud every time he passed that way.

Poor Mr Walton! He is recovering but the house is still under quarentine as the family have it now. They say that when Oscar was so awful sick he cried a great deal and when at last they found out the reason were amazed to find it was because he was "afraid he was going to die." They say you couldn't touch his face with your finger without putting it in a pit.

The mad dog scare is about over and no one has been killed right lately and the town is out from under quarentine and its awful dull. Am getting so good I'll be good for nothing pretty soon.

I'm coming down with something now—I don't know if its smallpox or a bad cold but I think the latter so don't worry.

Am sorry I didn't get a letter off to Chall on his birthday—perhaps I'll do better next time.

Well I must close[.] Stones have listed their place for sale and expect to move soon.

Lovingly yours
Bachelor Bess.

✻ MAR. 6, 1911 / FORT PIERRE, SO. DAK.
TO MRS. M. M. COREY

Dear Ma—When did I write to you last? Wasn't it right after I had that "gumbile" operated on? The doctor told me that evening it was scarlet fever in a light form that Klemanns and I had[,] I think it must be what some people call scarletina. A week ago Thursday—no Wednesday[—]little Katherine [Carlisle] went home sick[.] They went to the doctor and he quarentined them. That Friday I came up to Stones and went with them to the party at Drubneys[.][1] The crowd split and part of them staid there and part of them went to the school house to dance[.] I went to the school house and have kicked myself every time no one was looking ever since because I didn't stay at the house. The crowd I was with were the worst bunch of soreheads I ever saw. It was one continual quarrel and I hardly dared breath[e] for fear I'd get myself into it. The next day I spent at Stones and helped Mrs. Stone with some sewing as she isn't able to run the machine this Spring. Mr Stone drove my team to town that afternoon and got the mail. I thought the card you sent a beauty and was so glad that Fuller was about to start that I could hardly think straight. Then too, you said once that if you ever got a good chance you would send me my cow and I thot perhaps Fuller was coming with a car[2] clear through to Pierre or Ft Pierre.

I came over here a while Sunday and then went back to Klemanns half expecting to find the school closed on account of the scarlet fever scare but it wasn't[.]

Paul Nagel, a brother of the two little boys that live at Klemanns[,] is visiting there. He is from St Paul and is a blue racer[3] or leastwise he is might[y] swift. I have to admire his nerve for I dont see how anyone could keep up the pace he does after the way Emma and I called him down. I almost believe he has rooms to let in his upper story[.]

School was going just lovely last week. Wednesday we started to write the sixth month test and such good grades! Some 98% and 100% in arithmetic but as Paulie said on his birthday "I just knew something would have to happen." Thursday morning about half after nine word came that I was not to let anyone who had been near scarlet fever go to school and if I was not satisfied to report to Dr. Lavery[,] [4] Chairman of the Board of Health in Stanley County. I dismissed school and went at once to Dr Lavery. I wanted him to come out and make sure that it was scarlet fever but he said he was already satisfied and closed the school till March 27th[.]

That afternoon I received a card from Fuller written in Council Bluffs saying he was on his way but didn't know when he would get here. Also had a very pretty card from Mr Bertram.

I saw Oscar Walton that afternoon. Oh! What a face he has on him! Great red pits as large as my thumb nail all over his face. I staid all night with Mrs Gorden and Friday I received your card and left town soon after. I got as far as Stones and staid all night. There was a big Hard Times party [5] at Speers that night but I didn't go—neither did Stones[.] I took the mail down Saturday forenoon and the weather got kind of bad so I didn't get home till evening.

I was sick most all day yesterday and last night and didn't get up till most ten o'clock today. Then I got something to eat and finished off that comforter around the edge. Gee! its a "whopster"—so big and soft and warm—has about eight pounds of cotton in it.

Did you ever hear of the fellow with the artificial limb? It was jointed at the knee so as to move like a natural limb but he had it for years and it wouldn't take a step. One day something happened to start it going. The old fellow was much pleased and walked till he was tired but when he got ready to stop the limb kept going—when he tried to sit down it kept on walking—when he tried to lay down it kept right on walking. He walked till he died and when they buried him the artificial limb was still walking. I've found I'm some what like that limb[.] It takes me quite a while to make a start but when I once get started I'm apt to keep on going. I was going to move some of the things out of the kitchen and clean it up a bit—have been "going to" all winter. This afternoon I started to move things out and I kept moving and moving till the kitchen was cleared and then kept right on moving till the sittingroom was cleared then I gave this house such a cleaning as it hasn't had since I moved into it. I have every thing back in and everything straightened up except the magazine cabnet.

Thought I'd write a letter or two this evening and take them over to Stones in the morning as Mr Stone is going to take Mrs Stone to the doctor.

My! I've so much to do during this unexpected vacation that I dont know what to do first. School closed two days before pay day leaving me just $1.32 to live three weeks on and I am out of every thing. Say Mrs. Gordon gave me a pat of butter and a pint jar of buffalo berry jelly.

Wish it was going to be Xmas next week so Fritz would give me some more stationery. This is about gone.

It is quite late—must close and hit the perch—hope you are all well and that I will hear from you soon[.]

Your Bachelor Bess.

MAR 9TH Missed Stones. Your card received. F[uller] not here yet. Am to drive my team down today. Jennie and "Brothe[r] Billy"[6] are going along[.]

A happy birthday[.]

✱ MAR. 13, 1911 / FORT PIERRE, SO. DAK.
   TO ETHEL COREY

Dear Ethel, You think you are smart, having two kinds of measles but I dont care[.] I've had the scarlet fever and that beats the Dutch or any other kind of measles[,] so there.

It was a week ago tomorrow that I wrote to ma—no it was a week ago today. The next morning I didn't get up till almost noon so I didn't get the letter mailed. I went over to Stones Tuesday evening after flour and waited for the mail. Then Jennie [Speer] wanted me to go on home with her and go with them to spend the evening at Greens so I went down with her but Howard wouldn't go so we had to stay at home. The next morning I went back up to Stones for the flour but Mrs Stone would not hear to my coming home. She said as I was going to town the next day there was no sence of my making the trip over and back again for nothing so I staid and worked on some aprons for her.

Mr Stone tried to bother me by telling me I'd have to catch my own team in the morning. He said I never took him riding and he'd be ——— if he'd catch a team for me to take "Brother Billy["] riding[.] He didn't think I'd try it but I did and caught Kate and Nell followed her in and Mr Stone caught Nell. Of course he cussed the whole time but he wouldn't be Mr Stone if he didn't.

Mr Speer did the driving—Jennie and I sat in the back seat. Mr

Speer is used to pushing on the lines and Honest to John I believe he was afraid of that team. He just held them in till his arms were numb. We had a big day of it and Mr Speer brought me over and took the team back. Jennie staid all night with me and every little bit she would say "Now what will you do if Fuller comes?" She went home about ten o clock Friday and as I had been sick since I got home from town I went and crawled back in bed again[.] I had just got to sleep when Fuller rapped[.]

He unloaded his junk and took Nell[1] over and put her in Erickson's barn. He had stopped at Speers as he came by and they gave him a sack of hay. Late in the afternoon he rode Nell over to Stones and didn't get back till seven o'clock. Fuller was so tired we decided to hit the perch early. Fuller was asleep and I had just started to pull my hair down when a half dozen young people came in to spend the evening. Among them was Oscar Walton—just out from under quarentine. I was so glad to see him I could have hugged him. Yes, I know that sounds scandiculous and I suppose if I had tried it his toe head would have disappeared over the hills as if something worse than small pox was after him.

The four boys played cards and we four girls made candy. The boys seemed to have great fun but we girls were just dead in the shell. I wish you had been here to liven us up.

My! How glad every one was to see Fuller and they are so disappointed because he has no violin with him.

Saturday he went to town. I went as far as Stones and staid till he came back. We went into a chuck hole and broke a cart spring. Fuller had it mended and it broke again going home. Yesterday morning he rode Nell down to the river to water and got an ash stick for a spring[—]say[s] he will get another and fix the cart himself.

After dinner yesterday we went down to Speers. Fuller went up to Stones a while in the evening and has been there all day helping Mr Stone. They are going to exchange work this spring for mutual convenience. They are going to town tomorrow.

Fuller is going to put my breaking in oats. The seed will cost about $9 and if we [are to] have any hay for next year we will have to fence at once. I am still in debt close to $200 so we have to pinch every dollar till it squeals. I hope you come out well on the exams and am glad you have a nice pretty teacher—*pretty* teachers are usually scarse tho most of them are *nice*.

Ask Fuller about the Rays? He says he doesn't know anything.

Had a letter from Grandma telling of her happy birthday. Also had a letter from Fridtjof Erickson—will enclose some samples of his art.

Will you send me Aunt Daisy's[2] address? Tell Rob I dont think its fair for you to have *two* new skirts. I've only got two skirts fit to wear away from home—the black one I made last spring and the one Aunt Jennie gave me which I made over and washed and pressed. The two skirts I've been wearing to school are patched and darned to a fare ye well. The gray is the best and it caught itself on Stantons little wagon and now I have a three cornered place at foot each way to mend befor I go back to school.

Fuller had a very good trip. The weather was fine while he crossed the country. Every one was very good to him. He only stopped one place where they would let him pay for his lodging. The rest all invited him to stop again some time and regreted that they had nothing better to offer him.

He had some bother in crossing White River[3] as the ice was rotten and they had to cut through the channel. He hired a man to help him. It took quite a while. He had to lug every thing over [on] horseback then hitch to the cart and ride Nell. The water went into the cart seat and Fuller got his feet wet. Nell was in the cold water so long she was just numb at first but warmed up driving. Fuller says he thinks Nell has been on the prairie before. You auto have seen her the afternoon after Fuller got here—she was like a kid just out of school. She doesnt like the wind but she will get used to that in time. I rode her down to Speers Sunday and Fuller walked.

I certainly appreciate the stuff ma sent. What should I do with the beaf? Fuller is here so little and I don't like to cook it when he isn't here. Will it keep? Should I put brine on it? Gee! Ma must think I'm a dirty thing. She always sends me soap. Will be glad when Fullers good duds get here. We've turned down three "doings" already and now there is Johnnie Skipabouts party Wednesday. If Fuller don't go I've a notion to go with Howard.

I sent Fuller down cellar till he changed his mind about that water barrel. Gee! I wish it wasn't so much bother[,] I'd ask you to put the odds and ends in it with a few potatoes on top and label it potatoes and send it. I'd be glad to pay the freight. Fuller said if the head was sent he could make a cover so the water wouldn't slop. I did want that hair of mine[4] so—but that could be sent through the mail.

I'm lots of bother to you folks but I'll make good some time if I live long enough.

I must close now and write Fritz [Bertram] a note. I'm going to use a half page of paper and excuse the shortness of the note on the grounds that I am out of paper—perhaps I'll get another Xmas present.[5]

Lovingly Your Bachelor Bess

Will chase Fuller in to write to ma the first time he isn't so busy.

* FROM FULLER COREY
MAR. 19, 1911 / FORT PIERRE, SO. DAK.
TO MRS. M. M. COREY

Dear Mother: How are all you[?] I got out of Marne about 9 o'clock that night. Got into [Council] Bluffs [Iowa] about half past three and didn't get out till 6 that evening, got into Norfolk [Nebraska] half past 5 in the morning, left there half-past 10 that forenoon. Got to Bonesteel [South Dakota] about three o'clock the next day. Got to Dallas [South Dakota] 4:30, and there saw Chris, and didn't get to Col[o]me [South Dakota] till the next morning (Saturday) about 8 o'clock.[1] We got the horses and cows unloaded about 9, and they were pretty stiff. We unloaded the machinery that afternoon, Sunday morning we hitched Nell to the cart and drove out in the country about 4 miles to see a man to freight for him. The next morning we loaded the fellows wagon (6500 lbs.) all the stuff in the car, except some of the machinery and the stock, charged 45¢ a cwt. We started out that noon. Hooked my cart on behind Chris's wagon and I drove the cows. Got to Winner [South Dakota] that night. Started on the next morning got to Thompson place about 8 that night, about 40 miles from Col[o]me.

Chris had rented the place from Thompson and had not seen the place. He don't seem very well pleased. I asked him the next morning if I could help him any more, but we had been told that the [White] river might rise and a person wouldn't be able to get across so he said perhaps I had better go on. He paid nearly all my expense and $5 besides. I told him I thought I owed him, but he said no. And if I wanted any more he would pay it to me and if I was down in that country to come and see them. (Mar 20) So I started for the [White] river Wednesday morning, got there (Cavite) about 10, the ice was soft so it would not hold up. I had to give a fellow $2 to help me break a channel through the ice. The river is 8 or 10 rods wide. I got across 1:30.

Nell got scared at a tumbleweed that afternoon and nearly strung me out. I stopped at a place 8 miles south of Vivian [South Dakota].[2] The folks name was Rose. Just the man and his wife and a little boy (Joe) about Paul's age. They would not take any pay for my lodging and she says she was sorry they didn't have more to eat, and when I hitched up she came out to say goodbye. The man looked like Lincoln, he was less than 10 feet tall. He had a large gray wolf skin. One he had killed.

I got in about 9 miles of Bess's house that night and stayed with a bachelor. I got to Bess's house about noon, Friday.

My lunch lasted till I got to Col[o]me, but it got pretty strong, it smelled like limberger.

I carried most of my stuff across White River horseback. How is Beauty?[3] Did Rob pull her shoes off? I haven't got my trunk but expect to go to town tomorrow.

> Ever so much obliged.
> Your son H. Fuller Corey.

ADDITION BY: ELIZABETH F. COREY

Dear Ma, I've just finished reading that boys letter and he has gone to bed.

I'm going to town with him tomorrow—am almost afraid to let him go alone for if he was as full of the Old Nick as he has been tonight I'm afraid he might get run in. I never saw him act so—he has kept me laughing so much of the time I'm quite tired. He says he has homesickness so bad he cant be good.

Mr Stone helped him one day and they found the corners[4] of our land so it wont have to be surveyed and today he finished the digging for my barn.

Mr Bertram was down yesterday afternoon. Fuller don't seem to love him very much[.] I don't know whether its his big feet[,] his bow legs[,] his rusty hair or red nose or what but Fuller don't seem to think much of him and when Fuller found out the trick I've been playing him he just grinned instead of roasting me as I expected.

Mrs Speer gave Fuller a cot like the one you got only stronger, I gave him my big "Ruben Blue" comfort that I made last fall and Mr Stone gave him a rocking chair[.] I've written Mrs. Foutts about a little table that was left in Macks shack and I've got to get a larger stove then Fuller can have this one so I think he will start out well—better than I did—oh yes, I gave him my largest rug. He can nail a box up in one corner for a cupboard and the trunk for extra seats will about fill his 8 × 10 shack.

Fuller has the cot and the rest of his stuff up in my attic and is snoring now so the stove pipe rattles.

There was some one prowling around the house again last night but we didn't find out who it was. Are sure it was a person.

Well its ten o'clock so I must close or I wont feel like getting up in the morning.

Lovingly Your
Bachelor Bess.

✱ MAR. 29, 1911 / FORT PIERRE, SO. DAK.
TO MRS. M. M. COREY

Dear Ma,—The day after I wrote you last Fuller and I went to town. Jennie Speer had gone in to work but was taken sick so came out with us that night. Florence Scripter also came out with us. Before we got back to Stones John Porter rode up behind us on his way out to Speers. It was late that night when we retired and the next morning before I had the dishes washed John Porter came for some medecine for Jennie. Fuller had gone to haul water so was glad that Florence was there to entertain John. Fuller was late for dinner and went to take the wagon over to Stones shortly after dinner. John staid till about half after five. The next morning Fuller gave me a note that Mrs Stone had sent saying that she had Weltha's and Fred's dresses ready for me to sew so Florence and I went that far with Fuller when he went for a load of poles. I did the machine work while Mrs Stone and Florence did the hand work so we got through early. The next day I baked bread and washed—had an awful big washing—and in the evening Arch and Fern Scripter came up after Florence—we had lots of fun. Arch has been wearing Fritzies scarf pin since. When Fritz[1] finds it out wont his red hair just blaze through?

Fuller bought the Ella Bucholz shack and Saturday Mr Stone and Fuller moved it and that evening we went to a dance at the Berry School house. We drove my team as far as Scripters—Jennie [Speer] and John went along—then we left my team and took Arch's team. Jennie, Florence and Fern took the back seat, Fuller and John the middle one and I rode with the driver. The trail was a fright—full of ditches and wash outs and it clouded up dark as pitch. We got off the trail and poor Fern had to hot foot for miles before he found it. We almost upset a dozen or more times and I would have gone out as sure as shootin if—well if Arch hadn't had his arm around me. Once we came near going down a seventy foot slide.

Fuller says he thought several times we were goners. At last we found the trail and Fern sat on our laps and drove as his eye sight is the best ever. Shortly after that it began to rain. The rain didn't amount to much but Arch put the tarp' over me and held it around me so the wind wouldn't blow it off. We got there at last and I danced till I couldn't see straight hardly and the rain changed to snow and the storm raged all night and was still raging when we started home at daylight. We got to Scripters for nine o clock breakfast and home for late dinner. Monday Fuller brought me down to school and went on to town[—]he got a letter from home but didn't open it so I wont know what is in it till Friday or Saturday.

The Co Supt[2] visited my school Monday. I expect to close about Apr. 22nd. What chance of a school is there in your part of the world—have written to Mrs. Parker[3] as our institute is postponed till July 11th or there about.

Klemanns dont have supper till seven or seven thirty so I've been staying at the school house till late but I'll have to get into the grub line pretty sudden now or I'll feel thinner than I look before morning.

I received letters from Geo Jones, Alta Brown and Mrs Foutts the other day and I've been oweing Grace Haynes one this long time[.]

It is most 6:30 so will close and sweep.

I am Your
Bachelor Bess.

❋ APRIL 2, 1911 / FORT PIERRE, SO. DAK.
TO MRS. M. M. COREY

Dear Ma,—Fuller went to town Friday and brought me home with him[.]

We spent yesterday fixing up his shack and he has just gone to spend his first night on his claim. Fuller had been working at his shack all week and gave it up and though I had so much to do I couldn't see straight hardly he said I'd just have "let it go["] and help him. I pasted cloth over every crack and got about half of it papered with newspapers. We are going to finish papering it with newspapers

and then paper it with plain green wall paper. Yesterday was the
first time I had ever been up to his place. His shack is 8 × 10 tar
roofed—faces the east—is covered with blue [building] paper on the
out side and set in the side of the hill so the dirt comes half way up the
west side and pretty well up the ends. There is the door in the east, a
window in the west, and a board window in the north that can be
removed in warm weather. I baked t[w]o ovens of bread and one of cin-
namon rolls yesterday and that dont go well with paper hanging. We
went back after supper because Fuller wanted to get it fixed so he
could spend the night there. It was late when we got ready to come
home and so dark you couldn't see a thing and was sleeting from the
east. I dont know how many miles we walked before we got here but
it was twelve o'clock when we did get here and Fuller didn't try to
go back.

Mr Stone is going to take the black team to work this week some
time and perhaps Mr Speer will take Fullers Nell so we wont have to
think of hauling water or buying horse feed.

You have no idea what it costs to live out here. We could make out
pretty good this year if we could only fence but this is how we are
financialy[:]

Fuller—cash	$6.30
Me "	0.50
2 Mo. wages @ $40^{00}	80.00
10% withheld till term end	31.00
Resorces at end of term	$119.30

Fullers shack	$18.00
My board	18.00
Bal on mortgage & *int.*	74.00
Note due in July	150.00 and int.
	$260.00

Of course if I get a spring term in Iowa it will help a little but if
we are going to fence we auto be at it. I'm hard up for clothes too but
I didn't reckon that in.

Our west line of fence will cost at least fifty dollars[,] our east line
not quite so much because Mr Speer will help on ½ mile of it.

You made Fuller some kind of a money offer but he hasn't the
nerve to go in debt any deeper—he says he owes you enough now but
I'll tell you what [—]if you can raise me a little mon—anything up to
$300[—]I'll pay you *10%* same as I have to pay here. I couldn't give

you any thing but my note at present but if I lived I'd pay it and if any thing should happen to me you, as my heir[,] get what property I leave so you couldn't possibly loose out.

Well its almost nine and I've got to take a bath and I've enough other work to last an hour an[d] I have to "stand up at five"[1] in the morning. I expect to teach next Saturday—attend school meeting the next and close school the following Saturday and if I schould get a school in Iowa I will leave Ft Pierre on the afternoon train the day my school closes and by going via Council Bluffs will be with you in less than twenty four hours.

Say I had a note from Ethel the other day in an envelope you had directed and it wasn't ceiled at all nor hadn't been—will answer when I can but am so busy now both in school and out that I hardly have time to eat.

Lovingly your
Bachelor Bess.

* APR. 6, 1911 / FORT PIERRE, SO. DAK.
  TO MRS. M. M. COREY

Dear Ma,—I was going to write this before going to town yesterday morning. Emil came along just as I got it started and I was so busy in town that I just let it go.

I received your letter with the radish seed alright. Paul Prairie Chicken[1] brought it out. There was no extra postage.

My! Ive been so busy and I will be busy with final tests and reports and the last day and all.

Please hurry up the mon as we will be running the grub line[2] in less than two weeks unless some thing happens and I'm not in very good condition for running as I had that toe operated upon again yesterday. The doctor declares it is a serious matter but I think its just a "gumbile" and swore of[f] chewing gum last week when Rudolph swore off smoking cigaretes. Like every thing else it takes the mon and I havent been able to get my wages for ten weeks and can't now till after school is out and its all spent now but a dollar or two. Fuller has had to spend his for grub, fuel and horse feed and the like.

Fuller gets so blue when he is here alone all week that its an all day's job on Sunday to bully, coax and feed him into shape for the next week.

Bess Corey's Indian friend and neighbor Paul Prairie Chicken during a thinning out of the herd at Scotty Philip's buffalo ranch. Photo courtesy Verendrye Museum.

Three hundred will fix every thing hunkey dory if it gets here quick enough.

We have been using Ericksons barn half a mile from here but Fuller has started to build me a pole barn just below the garden.

I haven't been writing you folks on your birthdays but I have some things I'm keeping for you till we come home a year from next Xmas.

Tell Ethel if she will remind me of it later I'll send her two flannel waists, one red and one green[;] they shrunk so when I washed them that she could make them over to fit her in half an hour and have two school waists for next winter.

I have a piece of red pipe stone[3] that Rudolph picked up on Willow Creek. It was dropped by some Indian I suppose. Was going to send it to Olney but it was so heavy I thought I'd let it wait.

Fuller got him an auto harp[4] yesterday[—]it didn't cost as much as a violin and he had to have some thing to keep him from getting lonesome. He kept it busy most all day. He went over to Stones a little while ago on an errand.

It is such a lovely evening and I'm so uneasy I can't write so I guess I'll close and go out doors. Perhaps I'll add a P.S.

Lovingly Your Bachelor Bess

* FROM FULLER COREY
  APR. 27, 1911 / FORT PIERRE, SO. DAK.
  TO MRS. M. M. COREY

Dear Mother—Mother for God sake, don't send anymore money up here. If you do, Bess will just go that much farther. This morning she has went to the river to buy posts (640) at 5 and 10 cents apiece. She couldn't stop at just fencing the west side but she is going to fence her's all. She only owes $150 on her team and I think that is about enough in debt.

You wanted to know if I had a violin yet. No I have not. There was a dandy in Ft. Pierre for $6 once but I was low on change and now it's gone.

When I got here Bess was out of change and helped me spend mine and when I bout my house she said guess I would have to pay for it. But I didn't. The work is vary scarce but if I say anything about it, she dont want me to get a job. If I don do just as she wants me to she gets mad and hasn't got any sense and would injure herself to make me worry. Mother for goodness sakes don't let this worry you. I just wanted to put you on your guard. I'll take care of myself. If I could sell my belongings I would soon settle this matter. How are you and how is everything else. I have even forgot what hogs there was on the place when I left. It just came to me last night that you's should have some fall pigs. Is Rob nearly ready to plant corn. Questions—I run out of past and strength. I'm using the little lap, I have a bed, a chair and a table, didn't cost me anything. But the table I had to tie up to make it stand till I got it doped. I hope to go to tomorrow and buy a gasoline stove. Bess won't have her roof painted and spouted.[1] Don't you worry about Mr. Jenner.

Fuller

* APRIL 28, 1911 / FORT PIERRE, SO. DAK.
  TO MRS. M. M. COREY

Dear Ma,—It is quite late but I must write you a few lines anyway. A year ago now I was on my way to Iowa.

My school closed last Saturday. We had a fine time tho it rained a little. None of us shed many tears at parting—I would have, only I forgot to put the onion in my pocket. They had things all fixed up so I could get my money that day so I signed the order and let Fuller draw the mon. Payed the mortgage on my team and after paying for Fullers shack and my board bill had a dollar to live on. Fuller rec'd yours and the ten spot so between us we have $11.70 and only in debt $150 altogether. That looked so small it made me feel bad so the other day I went down to the saw mill to see about posts. Made a bargain—can get all I want and when they get through hauling I'm to give my note for the amount which will be about $45. Tomorrow Im going to town and see if Rowe & Co.[1] wont trust me for the wire which is about $45 more. Then I've got to get a job for Fuller worries all the time about not having more money and like Rob he insist[s] that you mustn't get that for me so you'll have to let it go. There is quite a demand for kitchen help so I'm sure I can get a place but gee! I hate to. I never wanted to stay at home so bad in my life. We have [put] in quite a garden and a little of the lettuce is up already.

Fuller is home too close to find a job and I don't know as he would feel like working if he had a job. Guess he will help Mr Stone put in my fence but I just can't tell a darn thing about him. You see he is just getting acclimated and he feels ornery—almost as bad as he acts I guess. He'll feel better by fall. I dont know what he would do if he had come out here and got knocked around the way I did the first year. You folks thought I auto write home about three times a week and I was at work all the time and I didn't feel any better than Fuller does.

We had a glorious shower Monday night and Tuesday forenoon— it helped the hay and grain but wasn't heavy enough to put any [water] in the ponds. Mr Bertram was down Sunday and he said I didn't need to worry about getting a dam in as his is now as large as Browns and if it rained enough to put water in it I was welcome to use it. Wasn't that lovely? Even Freddie Stone has got to threatening me with "I'll tell Fritz[.]" Say that Freddie Stone is a stunner. She likes eggs so well the hens can't lay them fast enough to suit her. The other day she said she wished she was a hen so she could lay eggs too. I had a hand full of letters the other evening and Mrs Stone asked me who one of them was from. It happened to be from George Jones and Freddie began "A letter from Jonesie. A letter from Jonesie[.]"

I guess my toe is going to get alright. I stopped chewing gum and that fixed it so that proves it *was* a "gumbile[.]"

Well its getting on towards eleven and I've got to get over to Stones bright and early in the morning so I better close.

You folks might write to me once in a while if you have time or would you rather I'd turn the correspondence over to Fuller—

Lovingly your *Bachelor Bess*.

P.S. It rained again last night and is raining still this morning. Fuller is going over to Stones and if it clears off perhaps they will go. I'm not going to try to go.

✻   MAY 5, 1911[1] / FORT PIERRE, SO. DAK.
TO MRS. M. M. COREY

Dear Ma, Yours of the 22nd at hand. Fuller went over to Stones last Monday morn to see when Grant was going to town. Howard came along driving his Nancy and Fullers Nell and Fuller and Grant both went to town with him.

It was quite late when he got back. He brought letters from Ida [Wever Lay], Jennie [Noon], Mr C M Corey[2] of Wendte, and you.

I have given up teaching a Spring term so you need not expect to see me in Iowa again till Xmas 1912 when we want as many as possible of Grandmas children and grandchildren to be with her for the kind of Xmas we used to have. I rather think Fuller will husk corn in Iowa this fall if nothing happens to prevent.

When I read your letter Fuller said I just had to give him money enough to get him a violin the next time he went to town or he was going to take to smoking so I presume he will be playing the violin tomorrow evening unless it rains again as it threatens this evening. Fuller said the other evening that I would have to furnish him with money and see him through with this deal and I didn't need to expect him to pay it back till he got out of Dakota even if he did get a job[—]then the other day he heard about Briggs[3] wanting to lease it and he was planning how much he could sell to B—— for as soon as he proved up. I told him I thought it would be a mean trick for him to sell to someone else and not give me a chance when he expected me to see him through with it. He says I can have it if I pay more than any one else but he will let the ranchers run it up first.

Fuller is just too tired to move out of his tracks almost. He reads most of the time it seems to me. Yesterday forenoon he cut a bushel of potato seed and in the afternoon went after the team and plow and put them in. Today he hasn't pretended to do anything but write a letter to Rob and wash his neck. Mr Bertram was here to dinner and Fuller said he was so tired he was taking a day off today. Oh yes Fuller has cleaned his overcoat today. Fuller is lonesome but he wont go anywhere cause he says his clothes aren't good enough. He has been quite jolly the last few days though—thinking about the violin I guess.

I've been trying ever since Fuller came to find out what he was going to put in on my ten acres and at first he said there was no use to put in anything till I knew for sure I was going to fence and lately he would just say "I du know." Tonight I told him he auto make up his mind and he said some thing about waiting till next year. I told him if he didn't want to bother with it, to say so, so I could have some one else put some thing in. He said I better get some one else to put it in then. Perhaps I can get Mr Stone to put it in corn as it is late for most anything else.

I went down and cleaned house for Fuller Wednesday. He certainly has a neat cozy little home. He picked up a two burner gasoline stove some where and cleaned it up. It works fine. Today I made him a supply of dish-rags, dish-towels, scrub-rags and the like.

Our garden is comming up some now and—Oh say! Fritz says the cold snap didn't hurt the fruit any.

Have been working at the mending and sewing to beat the cats this last week. Wish I had another week at it but if I can get work in town tomorrow I'll let it go as Fuller is about out of shoes.

I wrote Mr and Mrs Stewart a letter of congratulation.[4] I came near making it a letter of condolence—might even have shed a few tears over it had I not feared they might think that I, like Joneses young hopeful, had let "my nose drip on it."

Am glad your seed corn tested so well. Hope the 8th graders do better this time[.]

How many little chicks have you? You have hardly mentioned chickens since you set the first seven hens.

Yes, we put in a quart of onion sets.

"Yous fellers" don't want to get homesick for me. If I was there you would soon be wishing I was in Dakota again and don't worry about me for I'm going to make good if I just keep my nerve. I sometimes feel as if the "weeds was a gettin' ahead o' the corn" and my head begins to itch and it seems as if forty kinds of bugs and buglet[s]

were running up and down my back and my hands and face begin to
burn then I go out and take a run or else I sing that good old song—

> Nothin ever worries me
> Nothin ever hurries me
> Slow but sure is the safer gait
> All things come
> To those who wait
> So let the foolish people weep & sigh
> Whats goin to be is boun' to be
> So nothin ever worries me.

And then I'm alright again.

Well I must close as it is twenty minutes of eleven and I must take
a bath and care for my pet toe yet.

What ever you do don't worry about me[.]

> Lovingly
> Your Bachelor Bess

✳ MAY 11, 1911 / FORT PIERRE, SO. DAK.
TO MRS. M. M. COREY

Dear Ma, We went to town last Saturday. The Stone man went
along. I was so busy I hardly had time to eat. I ordered the wire and
they threw in the staples so it came to $47.50 including smooth wire
for braces. Fuller got his violin for $7.00. Of course he isn't satisfied
with it but it was the only one in town and—well that is all I can put
into it just now. I got a place to work and then took my toe to the doctor
again. He said if I was on my feet much inside of two weeks that that
toe would lay me up for the rest of the Summer so rather than loose
the little cuss I gave up my job and am at home barefoot. Have been
feeling horrid all week and having to soak that toe in hot water every
night dont make me feel any better.

You know when Mr Speer took Fuller's Nell to work her eyes
seemed all right[—]well he worked her right along an let her go clear
blind as a bat before he said anything to Fuller about it and then as his
mares with colts were so he could work them he told Fuller Monday
he could take her home. She looks awful thin and acts starved to
death. Mr Stone let Fuller turn her in his pasture. Fuller has been
helping at Stones since Sunday and he seems more cheerful than any
time yet.

Yesterday afternoon we had quite a little shower—enough to help the garden some.

I haven't had much fire of late—am burning cow chips[1]—had to come to it as there only a few little chunks of coal left. Am going to bake bread tomorrow.

Day before yesterday was blistering hot. A young cow boy stopped here for a drink. He saw my bare foot and it bothered me so I couldn't talk straight.

You know Rudolph [Klemann] quit smoking cigarettes and I quit chewing gum. Saturday we stopped there on our way home from town. Paul Nagel[2] was standing leaning against a porch post making fun of my leather gloves and Rudolph came up back of him and put his arms about twice around the post and Paul and held him while I boxed him clear up to a peak. Paul was bound he would get *even* so Rudolph had to hold him all the time we were talking and until we were part way up the hill. Paul vows he will get even if he has to poison me in candy[.]

While we were talking Rudolph took a drag at Paul's cigarette and I said "O Rudolph!" Rudolph said that "honestly" he hadn't rolled or smoked a cigarette since "we quit"—that he had only taken a "drag" at one of the boys once in awhile. My how it did tickle Mr Stone when Rudolph said "since we quit" and he likes to say something about it "fore folks" too.

Mrs Porter[3] and Mr Carlisle are trying to patch things up so I'll take that school next year. I haven't applied—am waiting developments. Mrs Porter says she is at a loss if I dont take it. There is Daisy Hamm but she had more trouble in a quiet school than I had with my "outlaws[.]" Daisy told me if she took it she would expect Klemann to poison her about the second meal she ate there.

Malcolm Carlisle, my seventh grade pupil[,] passed his final examination and enters the eighth grade next year.

Please tell Mary L—— that the patch she sent for my feelings didn't half cover the place so she better come on with that letter.

Well I must close for now—perhaps I'll add a P.S.

Lovingly Your

Bachelor Bess

P.S. Fuller wanted to write but has been at work so hard he hasn't had time. Grant is going to town tomorrow (Saturday) but I guess Fuller wont go. B.B.

✳   MAY 14, 1911 / FORT PIERRE, SO. DAK.
TO MRS. M. M. COREY

Dear Ma, We got the mail last evening. You folks all write as if you thought Fuller was being "skinned[.]" When you reckon things that way it looks as if you must always keep your quid on the same side o' your mouth. When he got here he had about $23. You sent him $10 and I owed him $10 that makes about $43 altogether. Well his shack cost $18, violin $7, zither[1] $1.50 half the groceries $15[,] about six .25 dinners and two or three trips across the river, tinware and gasoline for his shack beside horse-feed. It will amount to $50 or better so I dont see where he has been skinned much. And as to paying him for his work—How much do you think I auto pay him for working a little in the garden when I paid for all the seed except what you sent and helped put it in and how much should I pay him for hauling a few barrels of water with my team when the water was used to clean his house and clothes as well as mine? And the fence—there was no hope for a crop of hay or anything else unless we fenced. Fuller wouldn't borrow a cent so I bought the stuff with the understanding that he need never pay me. Grant [Stone] has told me several times he would gladly help put in that fence for nothing for the sake of keeping the ranch stock from the west[2] out of the neighborhood. Now how much do you think I auto pay Fuller for putting in his part of the fence for which I've furnished the material with 10% money?

My team, harness and buggy cost me $250 and havent cost me anything since. They have saved me walking several hundred miles and a good many dollars board. They have made several trips to town that would have cost me $5 a trip otherwise. I expect to hear that Nell has a colt any day now. Last fall one of Mr Stones mules gave out and he got a gray mare named Dolly. Before Spring he found that the other mule, little Joe, wasn't heavy enough to draw big loads of water up the big hill so his Dolly and my Kate have been his standby team ever since. When spring work began Joe made the *third* and when four horses were needed he used my Nell and old Jack against each other for the *fourth*. So many have had a time with their mares this Spring that Mr Stone has been very careful of Nell only using her what he thought was necessary for her good. Without the team it would cost me $5 a load for wire and posts and yet Rob thinks I should sell my team and pay my debts. Thats alright but why dont they talk nearer home? A man in town told Fuller he thot he could get $110 for his

Nell when he first got here but he would rather buy feed for her than part with her and now she is blind as a bat. You keep Beaut[y][3] for style and go just as your neighbors keep their "Ford" or "Jackson" or "Maxwell." They write that one fellow would "give almost anything" for her. You could sell her with out taking bread and butter out of any childs mouth but you don't and I've never made any remarks about it either.

A week from now I expect I'll be working in some bodys kitchen, earning money to get Fuller hat[,] shoes and good trousers. I've got to have a few things too—my only corset looks like a Chinese puzzle and Im still wearing woolen stockings because I've only three pair of Summer ones and they are about the darndest things I ever saw so I know they wont last long. I suppose if I should sell my team and pay my debts I wouldn't have to think about that.

If nothing happens I'll check back to you the $90 that is left of what you sent me[—]you can keep the note until I can raise the other $20 and interest. I expect you do need it with all that bunch to feed and clothe and I can get along with out it. I suppose Rob is suffering agonies because he cant have his shirt tails shortened and embroidered around the bottom as I hear that is the latest. I dont know what its for unless its to look pretty if they happen to slip up too high. I'd rather have some of these poor devils getting thin for want of the money I owe them than to inconvenience my relatives.

We had a great rain last evening. Water ran eight feet deep in Bad River so they say.[4]

Last night I received letters from Grandma and Aunt Jen and a picture of Alta and Nourmal's[5] little girl. My! but Alta is a fattie.

I am getting so I like the zither just fine. I can play on it a little now.

Last night I saw a young rabbit in the garden. He seemed doubtful about staying. I had to give him a little persuasive gun talk to get him to stay for dinner today. He was very good.

MAY 27TH

Quite a while since I started this letter and lots of things have happened since then. I came into town last Tuesday and am at Gordons[—]expect to be here a week yet. I would like to stay all summer—she wants me to but can only afford to pay $3 per week and so I'm looking for another place.

I shot two squirrels the week after I shot that rabbit.

One day Mrs Stone and the kids and Glen Speer were at our house for dinner.

A week ago today Fuller went over to Stones and I wanted him to bring me back some eggs as we were mighty short of grub[.] I was sick and crawled back into bed as soon as he had gone. He got back about noon but didn't bring any eggs[.] I said "Darn it I've a notion to go after some" and that made him sore. He said if he had some money he had eaten his last meal in my house. So I wrote him a check for $10 for his saddle—that was what he wanted for it—and he bawled and gathered up the rest of his junk and went home. That afternoon Fritz came down and I was so blue I didn't care a darn what Mrs Grundy had to say[—]I just asked him in and he staid a couple of hours. When Jennie Speer gets ahold of that she will raise Ft Pierre and put a block under it.

I came to town Tuesday with Mr Stone when he came for Myrtle and his "stepmother-in-law." They were out of grub and out of money and poor Mrs Stone was at her wits end. Mr Stone and I got to talking about guns and I said I intended to get a shot gun sometime and he said he had just the thing—a little shot gun lighter than Fullers that he would guarente to be alright and I could have it for $2.50 so I wrote him the check. He thought I auto see the gun first but I told him I'd take his word for it. My! you should have heard him sing and whistle the rest of the way to town. I had an invitation to spend tomorrow at the Judge Holms[6] residence in Pierre where Louie Wilcox[7] is visiting but I declined—expect to see Louis soon[.]

My how I wish I could stay on my claim this summer—this working out feeling the way I do is like sandpapering ones fingers clear to the bone.

Say what is the matter with you and your arm—no one will tell me.

My toe still bothers me and I suppose I'll loose it eventually and limp for the rest of my days. Gee I'm blue tonight.

Lovingly Yours B.B.

✱ JUNE 15, 1911 / FORT PIERRE, SO. DAK.
TO MRS. M. M. COREY

Dear Ma, Yours received—also the ones that you and Ethel wrote Fuller[.] I opened and read them all as Fuller hasn't been in town since a week ago Monday. Have written you but always give up sending the letters and wait to write better ones. I wrote you a card the other day and gave it to "Cousin Carl" to mail tho he declared he'd never mail it.

And you are still roasting me—well I suppose I auto get used to it sometime.—About the team—Fuller talked last fall that he didn't want to sell his team and he didn't want to bring them to Dakota. I knew if he brought horses from Iowa they wouldn't amount to much the first year and if he waited to buy this spring the chancers were they [might] be out of sight so I took a bargain while I had the chance. Every one thinks I got a bargain unless it is some sore head who wanted the team themselves. I guess I wrote you that Nellie had a little colt. I dont want to name him till I see him. I thot I was doing what was for the best but if you folks cant get over it I'll sell them the first chance I get. I kind of hate to tho as I think so much of them. You say I expected Fuller to get rid of his team.[1] You are mistaken. I merely understood that he thought them too expensive to bring into so different a climate and when I got this team I thot he could pay half and have one of them and then when he was ready to prove up I could buy it of[f] him and have a team of my own but when you all gave me the devil about it and talked about my expecting so much help I tho[t] I'd go it alone. I'd hate to have Fuller sell Beauty as badly as any of you but I can't help feeling sore about the way you all act about my team. Haven't I a right to own any thing unless some of you pick it out and try it first and give your consent? Fuller wouldn't have so much team if one wasn't as good as given to him and whether you believe it or not my team is worth as much as his and tho I owe some on them yet I'm the colt ahead. If you want me to sell them why dont you say so and be done with it. You are all I've left to live for and I've tried so hard to please you these last few years but every attempt meets with the same kind of success[.] You always misunderstand me and roast me for something. Do you suppose the money is anything to me? If I had all the money there is would it bring back all that was so near and dear and is now gone forever?[2]

You roast me for helping Stones or rather for boosting them a little[,] while on the other hand Fuller was at me twice if [not] more times to help them more and all I could do was grit my teeth and remind him of the 10% int.

I, too, expected to put money against Fullers work but the way I had to work to get him to work would make a preacher almost cuss. The barn he was to build for me had two corner posts erected the last I saw of it and the last I heard it was the same and that nine acres I was so anxious to have put in—he wanted [to] put in millet—said it was only good for calf feed so I couldn't see any advantage in that as our neighbors raise their own calf feed and we had no calves. I talked and urged and coaxed and at last when all the wheat and oats in the country was up and part of the corn in he at last said he didn't care to bother with it. So I asked Mr Stone to put it in corn and he set Fuller to disking it. I don't know if its in yet or not.

Fritz gave me troughs and spouting[3] for my house and if it had been put on the cistern would be nearly full but Fuller didn't get around to it till after that last rain so I don't know what he'll do now the dry weather is on.

You talk as if I were in the habit of scolding Fuller day and night but he can't tell you of more than three times that I as much as spoke cross to him.

I thot he would be interested in the garden but he wasn't. One morning he played the violin till I finished my work and we went to the garden together about ten o clock. At eleven he was ready to quit and when I wanted him to work a while longer he got mad and cussed. That settled it. I never asked him to work in the garden again. I just told him I'd give him 15 cents per hour for all the time he spent in it. The onions were large enough to eat before I came to town. When Fuller was down I asked him how the garden was and he said he didn't know as he had hardly seen it for a week but that Grant and Fritz said he auto be eating the radishes before the[y] got woody.

Fuller will tell you himself that I dont owe him any thing so I don't see why you make such a noise about his working for nothing and boarding himself.

As to my injuring myself to worry him—He said one day "One of us has pretty near got to go to work and I cant get a job[.]" So it was up to me. He said he didn't think the work would hurt my foot if I'd just take care of it. He has said all along that he wouldn't take a cent from you as you needed all you could get and that I must foot all his bills if he couldn't so now when he gets the little check I suppose I'll be in for another dose. I'm not writing all this to run Fuller down but simply because I cant stand this sort of thing much longer and I thot perhaps you could more "fully appreciate" the things Fuller writes if I wrote some too.

Yes, I suppose I haven't done every thing that was right but perhaps I'm not the only one and with all my "puffing" myself up I cant manage to weigh more than 189 pounds these days. As to getting along with Fuller I got along with him alright—that is we never had a racket—when it got to[o] thick I cleared out and came to town[.]

What about the writing paper? I did borrow some of his but paid him back. And suppose I hadn't—I've been furnishing him with stamps and I dont expect him to pay me back either.

I have been presented with two lots of linen paper since I came to town—one box contained twice as much as the Xmas box and the other not so much[.] I would like to know what *gift from my kin* you refer to that I didn't appreciate.

I've been in hot water ever since I received your letter. I feel as if I packed my suitcase and left for Iowa at once that befor I had been under your roof twenty-four hours someone would be saying I came with out being asked just to see if I couldn't squeeze a little more money out of you and if I didn't go [to Iowa] the chances are that you would always feel hard toward me for not coming when you needed me. You are bound to misunderstand me any way—you always do. *If you want me, just wire and I'll come on the next train.*

I am working for Mrs Holland[4] now. I have a dandy room all to my self—the work is easy and I have time for sewing and may can all the fruit I wish for myself so she says. Am to can some for her next week (*$4 per week*)[.]

My moccasins are dandy. I couldn't get along without them as my toe still swears when I wear a shoe.

I have a "steady fellow" now it seems and he isn't afraid to spend his money either. He is several years older than I[.] Guess he is about twenty-seven or eight. He's one of the best men I ever met but I don't like him a little bit. I dont know why I dont like him but I dont. Why if his hand touches mine I just have to grit my teeth to keep from knocking him down. You wouldn't think it tho to see or hear us together. I started going with him just as I wore Mr Folks ring (on a dare) and now I find Ive started something I can't finish so very easily.

A bunch of us went to gather wild roses the other day—we not only got roses but fleas also. They are the darndest things. I felt one on my knee and slapped my hand down quick but about the time I thot I had him he bit me on the back of the neck.

It is one o clock and I must close. Please write and tell me what you want me to do.

Bachelor Bess

For the two months between June 16 and August 18, 1911, there are no letters from Bess. She appears to have stayed in Fort Pierre, working for Mrs. Holland. She also had to attend the institute for county teachers, and her foot continued to bother her. She had other ailments as well.

✳ AUG. 18, 1911 / FORT PIERRE, SO. DAK.
TO MRS. M. M. COREY

Dear Ma, It has been such a long time since I wrote you a letter and I dont know where to begin.

Im feeling ever so much better today than I have for a long time. I think two weeks perfect rest on the claim will fix me out about right. You know when I started to work last Spring my toe was quite bad and when it got better my ankles were a fright. They were both better after institute[1] but it was quite a strain attending institute and working too and that darn kid getting sick didn't make the work pleasenter or lighter. The Friday after institute closed I cleaned the kitchen[.] There was about fourteen different kinds of linoleum on the floor and it was all in rags and had to be taken up. The dirt had to be sorted ever so many time in hopes of finding the Mrs diamond ring which was lost some months back. It was an awful job and when I got to the stove I wanted help but Emma had some thing else to do and Miss Hart[2] was afraid she would get her dress dirty and when I spoke of asking Mr Holland the Mrs said he couldn't stand it to lift so I had to do it alone so I lifted the stove and had the kids pull the stuff from under the legs and I guess I lifted too much. That night I felt bad and I noticed it more or less of the time after that. The following Tuesday when I began to "celebrate" I was awful sick—didn't work a whole day that week. I hated to go to the doctor. Darn the doctors anyway[.] Dr Walsh[3] has said several times this summer that I aught not to be at work. I went to see him a week ago Tuesday—he said I had strained myself and caused a misplacement[4] said he could do nothing for me while I was at work—said that at my age he thot two or three weeks of perfect rest would right me up and if not something would have to be done. That Tuesday finished my week's work but the Mrs didn't want me to go and I knew I couldn't live on $4 till school commenced so I told her I would try to stay two weeks longer[,] that would be till

Aug 22. So she started in to have me do up her fruit and pickles and stuff and clean her house in those two weeks. I could see I was going to drop in my tracks at that so when Jennie Speer was in town Saturday I insisted that she hire her so I quit the 15th and Jennie took my place and that left me the sum of $8 to pay the doctor and live on till school commences. Am afraid I'll have to borrow like I did last year.

Mrs McGuire wrote me I could depend on one of the Leslie School[s][5] and I wrote asking which one and when they wanted school to commence and haven't heard from her since. Mrs Porter sent me word to apply for the Thomas[6] school and Mr Luco is going to see their director and let me know about their school tomorrow. So Im still in town. Have a room at the rate of $1 per week and am batching till I get things settled and if I get a school closer than Leslie with as long a term and as good wages I'll be glad to cut out that long hard $5 trip.

Am so anxious to know if you are going to send the apples. Mrs Stone is comming back a week from tomorrow (Aug 26) and Grant said he guessed he could pay the freight for one bbl.

The season seems so early[.] They have been bringing wild grapes and plum[s] from up the Missouri into town by the bushel but Jennie says there are but few out our way. They would make up fine with apples but I'm short of money now and dont know where Im at any way.

I was over to the Land Office in Pierre and found out some things that I wanted Fuller to inquire about before he left town. Tell him he will have to live on his claim *fourteen consecutive months* from the time he gets back to Dakota or else swear to a lie when he proves up. Of course most of them swear to lies when they prove up but I dont intend to and I didn't think Fuller did. I found out a whole lot but it would take too long to write and I'm so tired. I'll write you a whole lot when I get livened up a bit.

I believe my hair is thinner than Aunt Rate's[7] now. I wish some of you would send me that bunch I had cut off.[8] Its in the drawer of the sitting room book case. I'll pay you for the postage and the bother when I send you the interest on that note if not before[.]

Are there any vacant schools around there? If I go up to Leslie I'll have to get a leave of absence [from my claim] and if I do that I might as well teach in Iowa and visit up at the same time. You can only get a leave of absence in case of failure of crop. I can get one this year[9] and perhaps I couldn't another time.

I just dont know where I'm at you see. You must not worry about me. I think a few weeks rest will rig me up fine. It has been so long since I got your last card.

> Lovingly Yours
> Bachelor Bess

HOLLAND THE TAILOR
Will make your clothes
Order your clothes
Or Press your clothes

✱   AUG. 20, 1911 / FORT PIERRE, SO. DAK.
TO MRS. M. M. COREY

Dear Ma—Am in town yet. Darn the luck! Well I have some news for you any way. We got Daisy Hamm to take the Kleman school and I've contracted for the Thomas school—the other school in the same dist. Its a huge joke, I think, for Kleman didn't have anything to say about it. In fact he knew nothing about it till afterward[.] Mr Thomas [1] came to see me about taking his school and I said I wouldn't contract for less than eight months so he and Mr [Frank] Carlisle got together and decided to have eight months school even if Kleman didn't want but six. Then Mrs Porter and I rounded up Daisy and by using all of our persuasive powers got her to take the Kleman school and the contracts were drawn and signed right there and then by "two members of the board" so its all settled. The school I am to teach is a mile or so east of the railroad dam. I guess Fuller knows where that is. My school begins two weeks from today and I get $45 per month and no discount.

I had a letter from Alta Brown Saturday and she said Uncle Chall [2] was visiting you so I suppose that is why I haven't heard from you.

Have half a notion to tell you some of the mischief I've been into this summer though I suppose you will give me the dickens for it. Last spring Fuller roasted me for treating the boys so hateful—said I'd think I was killed if they treated me half as bad and so just to get even with him and others I started to go with Fred Bertram and I made him (Fuller) so sick of it I guess he wished we were both in Canada. Well Fred began to get rather—well—what you might call sentimental and so I treated him just horrid and we had the kind of a time Mr Pingle tells about. Daisy [Hamm] dont like Fred—says I auto go with a tall dark man (like her brother) and the other after noon when I was up to see her she said if she ever caught me on the street with him she would take me by the neck and boot me down the street and around the corner. I thought that was putting it a little strong so when I was down town in the evening I gave him a chance to speak to me and then we walked up the street untill we met Daisy—we didn't stop when we met Daisy either. Fred said he was comming to see me and I'm afraid I'll have another deuce of a time with him. It makes me so mad to think I made such a darn fool of myself. I'm always getting into it just because its so hard for me to take a dare.

I didn't sleep much Saturday night or last night either so as it was nice and cool this morning I thot I'd just stay in bed as long as I felt like it and get my sleep out. About half after nine Jennie came up and said there was a gentleman from Leslie here to see me so I had to get up. It was Mr Hudsons brother-in-law[,] a young widower who lives with them. He was in town and as Mr. Hudson thot I was to teach their school had him stop to see if I didn't want to go out there with him. Gee but that would have been a fine trip—wouldn't I have enjoyed it though?

Charles Hurst who has been up on the Cheyenne is in town and called later. He is the fellow who sent me the fruit last fall or winter.

I thot I was going out to the country Saturday night so I purchased my provisions which left me 26¢ and enough to pay my room so if I get out of town today or tomorrow I wont have to borrow as school begins two weeks from today.

I met Mr Stine on the street and he said if I wanted wild plums to go down to the Moore Boys pasture and get all I wanted and if anyone said any thing to just tell them he said for me to and it would be all right. I'm going down if I get a chance but I'll just can them and make them up later when I *have the money to buy* sugar.

Mr Stone is in town this afternoon and I'm going out with him. Have had dinner at Calisons[.]

The wind is blowing to beat seven of a kind so I don't suppose I'll enjoy the ride on a hayrack[.]

Please write when you can[.]

Lovingly yours
Bachelor Bess

✳ AUG. 25, 1911 / FORT PIERRE, SO. DAK.
TO MRS. M. M. COREY

Dear Ma,—Guess I mentioned in my last letter that I was coming out with Mr Stone. I got every thing packed and ready and then I began to feel just horrid—began to celebrate—always have to beat my time when there is something extra. Mr Stone wasn't ready to start as soon as he expected and I felt better by the time he was ready. I rode out as far as Carlisles with Malcolm and had a good old visit then came on with Mr Stone in the [hay] rack.

The country is looking fine.[1] They have had heavy and frequent rains ever since Fuller and Mrs Stone left almost. Guess they "saved the nation" by going. Mr Stone is anxious for Fuller to get back as haying will begin in a week or two and they were to work together[.]

Gee if Fuller was here this minute he would get excited! There's a wolf a quarter of a mile south of my house—seems to be investigating some thing. I'd do a little investigating myself only I have nothing but the "Little Son of a Gun" and only one shell for it.

There was a cyclone[2] through here a week ago yesterday accompanied by a cloud burst. Two houses and numerous other buildings at Wendte were completely demolished. Ericksons barn is an armfull of kindling wood scattered down the side hill. It swerved enough to leave my house—just took the top length of pipe from the roof jack and unhinged the door of—my grandmothers shack[3] out here. So you see the Lord is still good to me.

My corn was fine two weeks ago and promised a good crop[.] Then ten head of cattle got in and have lived in it ever since. Mr Stone saw them twice and came over and put them out—says he cant find where they get in. Grant has to work at such a disadvantage. Mae being gone he has to hitch up a team and take the kids every time. Julius Bahr put them out about five o clock one afternoon and they just disapeared but at twenty minutes of eight here they came up the draw from the north. I went out three differant times to scare them away but they didn't scare—and I did. Well laugh if you want to. I can't help it. I seem to have lost a great deal of my animal courage.

Monday evening when we got to Stones Mr Stone put the team to the buggy and I brought my baggage and groceries over. There was no key to be found high or low so I left the stuff in the yard and took the team back and left it and got a screw driver. I crawled in the window and took the lock off the door. It was quite dark so I came via of the road. It was awful cold and I thought when I left Stones "Well there's some satisfaction in its being so cold—I don't have to think about snakes." That was once I missed it. I was about half way across the Cornel quarter—was walking in one wheel track—and braer snake came down the other wheel track—was a buzzer too. I shied out of the road and Mr snake went by without saying any thing and, believe me, I kept pretty mum my self.

SATURDAY MORNING AUG 26TH[.] I started this yesterday afternoon a little after one o clock and then Mrs Speer came over. She staid all afternoon and for supper. It was quite a bit after seven when she went. By the time I finished the supper dishes it was dark so I didn't try to write any more as I have only the nightlamp—F—— has my other lamp at his house and his door is padlocked. I tell you what, between Fuller and Fred I came near starving this time not only for want of grub but for want of something to cook it in.

Does Fuller know that Ella Bucholz Roush got her divorce this summer? The whole family leave for Brookings[4] soon where the boys are to attend school. Oh! yes! Tell him that "Pig," that noted horse thief and sort of all around devil is at large again. He broke jail I guess and when the deputy went after him he swam his horse accross Bad River (The day after the cloud burst)[.] They say he rode up on a little hill and jeered the deputy—called him a "white livered" something and dared him to come after him. The deputy had no long distance gun and gave it up. He ask a fellow if he supposed Pig had a gun and the fellow said "Lord! man, he's got two of 'em[.]" So the County says "Good ridance and lets him go."

Well the sun is coming up so I guess I better close and go over to Stones—have to go via of Jennies shack as she said for me to send her some things she wanted.

I dont feel equal to the trip to town but I think I'll wait till they get back and see if I dont hear from you as it is about three weeks since I got your last card.

Lovingly Yours
Bachelor Bess

I paid my taxes the other day

✳ SEPTEMBER 1, 1911 / FORT PIERRE, SO. DAK.
TO MRS. M. M. COREY

Dear ma and the rest,—Mrs Stone got home alright and the baby is pretty good. I got your letter and card and the hair—much obliged. I came home that same evening and was sick that night and the next day and the next night—dont know what it was—at times it seemed to be only a sick headache then again I had such a fever I didn't know exactly where I was or who I was—the room seemed full of those little wiggle twisters of imps that dance and caper and crowd up around one—when I'd wink hard they would scatter away but they came right back again.

Monday afternoon I felt better and did some sewing and mending. Tuesday I tried to wash but only did part of it—gave out and quit. Tuesday evening I was out in the garden and killed a rattle snake. It had eight rattles.

Wednesday forenoon I walked down to Speers and in the afternoon I made a black underskirt—its a dandy—black sateen with a heatherbloom flounce. Running the machine didn't agree with me very well either. Mrs Green came over late in the afternoon—said she stopped on her way over to my house—wanted to know if I would go down to the river after plums with her Thurs. I decided to go so staid all night at Speers and she stopped for me Thursday morning. We had a fine time—took dinner at Wheelers. We were too late to get many plums. When I got home I found Fuller here waiting for his supper. I put in quite a spell today cutting his hair and scrubbing his head and neck.

Gee! I'm so sleepy. I didn't sleep hardly a bit the other night at Speers and last night I ached so till nearly morning.

Have my plums put up—seven quarts. Fuller brought me yours and Ethels letters also a letter from Aunt Jen and a card from Mary L[anigan]. Fuller and Grant are going to town tomorrow and then up the Missouri in search of grapes—hope they get some.

I've got to bake bread and do a little washing, ironing and scrubbing tomorrow—am going over to Stones Sunday.

My school begins on Tuesday as Monday is Labor Day. Guess Grant will take me over on Sunday and Fuller will come for me on Friday. Then Fuller is going to get his Nell up and have his cart fixed so I can drive over Monday mornings and back·Friday evenings. He admits she is tricky but thinks I can manage her if I tie her every time I stop to close a gate.

Am glad you are in no rush for the mon—the Blumgren note comes due Dec 17th[—]thats $150.00 and $15.00 interest. I may get a few dollars damage for the loss of my corn but I dont know yet.

Glad to hear that the hose made your feet grin—thought they would.

It seems as if all the rest are having their vacations—when do you and Paul take yours? Tell Paulie to come up and spend his with me. Will find a nest of pack rats and tie strings to their tails and drown them in the cistern and use them for coyote bait. The coyotes are quite numerous around here. If we catch one Paulie can tame it and take it home to catch rabits for him next winter[.]

Fuller wanted to write but thought he better wait a little. He is pretty busy and will be right along I guess.

Ethel writes dandy letters now—tell her to write as often as possible and some day I'll make up for lost time[.]

Must close[.]

Love to all

Bachelor Bess.

Apparently in response to a direct request from Margaret Corey, the ever-helpful Grant Stone, who had broken the sod and built the house on Bess's homestead, now undertook to act as agent in the marketing of apples to be shipped to South Dakota from the orchard at Corey farm.

❋ FROM G. H. STONE
FORT PIERRE, SO. DAK. / SEPT. 4, 1911
TO MRS. M. M. COREY

Dear Madame. yours of the 26th inst at hand. 2 Bbls of the apples arrived all o.k. last Saturday but the Smallest one was missing. it may be there now. but have not heard from the office yet. Fuller thought we had better keep these two so if the others did not come [we] would have some anyway. The freight was $5.95 on the 3 Bbls and I think Fuller said there was 10 Bu so you see it cost about 60¢ per Bu Freight. Now if we had them now they would easly sell for $1.25 per bu making

65¢ per bu for them. May be able to get more. So if you want to Send more, I will be Willing to Sell them for Bess and Fuller. if you Ship, Ship as Soon as possible before they begin rushing in the new crop. You Should be sure to Nail boards in the head of the bbls as it is a easy mater to cut the burlap, as one that came was cut and Some taken out. Most all the apples that we get out here comes in 1 Bu boxes, or in car loads.

Fuller and I went picking wild grapes last Saturday and Mrs Stone and Bess put them up this forenoon when I took Bess to her School[1] this P.M. her school is about 15 miles from her place. Hoping to hear from you soon, in regards to apples I remain your Friend

G. H. Stone

Will drop a Card when the other apples show up if they do and I think they will all right.

---

* SEPT. 5, 1911 / FORT PIERRE, SO. DAK.
  TO MRS. M. M. COREY

Dear Ma, Fuller and Grant went to town Saturday and then over on the river for grapes. They got a tub full and a pail full beside. Two barrels of the apples got here O.K. but the little bbl came up missing so Fuller didn't want to sell any and they brought both bbls out.

You know Glen Speer is such a shy bashful fellow[—]well the other day when I was down there he almost knocked my wits sideways by replying to my invitation that he *was* coming up "sometime". I was telling Fuller about it and after his first surprise he grinned and said "Yes but I bet it'll be a long time before he comes unless he knows I'm here[.]" I thought so too. Was much surprised when he stopped there Saturday forenoon—had been looking for cows over in the hills—was on his way home—had his gun and four rabbits. We talked for more than an hour I guess. Then he saw a rabbit and wanted me to shoot it with his gun so I tried it—got it too. We went after it but it squirmed and quivered so he had to carry it to the house for me. It was about half grown or a little better and made dandy eating. Fuller didn't get up to my house till Sunday morning and after our fried rabbit breakfast he went over to Stones for the team and brought the groceries and stuff over. I packed my suitcase while he was gone and then drove the team back. Stayed alnight and helped Mrs Stone with the grapes yesterday. I couldn't do any for myself as Fuller failed to get me the fruit jar rings even though they were on the list. Mrs Stone is so miserable and has *so* much to do she appreciates a little help. She was finishing the grapes when we left yesterday afternoon. She just sealed up the juice and will make it up when sugar is cheaper. She had over thirty quarts but I don't know exactly how much.

Grant brought me over[1] yesterday afternoon. Its about ten miles from his place but we didn't know just where we were going and drove a great deal farther than that. It didn't take so very long though as we drove my team. Mr Stone caught up Nell one day when he wanted to plow and Billy Deuce[2] ran back in the pasture so he let him go. He seems satisfied so they just left him and he has weaned himself. Its a good thing as Nell was getting so thin—everything she ate went right to the colt and he is a bouncer. They say he can't be beat by any on the flats—not even by colts from big eastern mares. He'll be worth $48 by the 1st of October. Grant says we must brand him early in the Spring as there is so much rustling going on and he is such a dandy. (Even Fuller says so[.]) I hate to have him branded but it cant be helped. Mr Stone says a small brand on the shoulder wont be very noticeable. Billy Deuce will be the first to wear the brand of the E Bar C

which will be E-C or $\frac{E}{C}$ wonder if Circle E $\textcircled{E}$ wouldnt be better[.]

I dont know how I'll like it here—have a room all to myself—it contains a wardrobe, small bed, comode, dresser, chair and sewing machine. It has two windows and no door so everything can come in that wants to and that darn dog Gumbo, *will* sleep under my bed and he is just full of fleas *so I've* had a lively time the past twenty four hours.

There comes Emmie Lou[3]

x x x x x x

This is Thursday evening. I went home with Emmie Lou and staid all night. We stopped at Atkinsens to get the classification but she said it was over at her shack so I had to do the classifying myself—the dickens of a job to as there are twice as many pupils as last year and they are from different schools. Have things all straightened out now I guess.

Emmie Lou and I had a fine time. It started to rain after we got there and rained all night. It cleared off in the morning or rather it stopped raining for a while and Emmie Lou took me to school then she staid here at Thomases[4] last night.

It rained all night last night I guess and is raining again tonight.

MONDAY MORNING SEPT II Fuller came for me Friday eve and brought me back yesterday afternoon. I put up fourteen quarts of apples and six quarts of juice. Fuller didn't even sort the apples—let them stand in the kitchen all week but they were in pretty good shape in spite of that.

Fuller is the bluest thing I ever saw. I tell him he better give up his claim and go back to Iowa if he cant do better than that. I guess he is kind of sore at Mr Stone—I think it's about his Nell. Mr Stone tried to cultivate corn with her last spring and she was determined not to go and when she did go she discribed all kinds of circles in the corn field and Mr Stone said he would never put the harness on her again. You know Fuller wanted to catch her up and let me drive her back and forth [to school] and I guess Grant didn't think I auto. Grant said she wasn't safe for any one to handle and that makes Fuller sore for he dont hardly dare let me drive her since Grant said that. I told him I'd drive her if he would get the cart and harness fixed up strong but I won't drive her to a buggy as I have several gates to open and some crazy roads to go over but I know she cant hurt me in a cart. Well I must close and go to school[.]

> Hastily Your
> Bachelor Bess

✳ FROM FULLER COREY
SEPT. 20, 1911 / FORT PIERRE, SO. DAK.
TO MRS. M. M. COREY

Dear Mother:—I hope this finds everybody well and happy and expect this will find Rob home.

Well I'm sorry to hear what's been doen down there.[1] I am afraid your neighbors will never love the Coreys anymore.

I can't come back to Iowa this fall. I will have to wate till I prove up. Have Rob tell Pete D.[2] I wish you's would ship my clothes when you get time and put that collar in I got ready for Nell and forgot, and don't forget that horn that goes with my shoes. My violin's health has been getting better.

I've got Nell running on my own clame now. Glen said she pretty near killed J. Bar.

I killed a rattlesnake half an hour ago, makes the 3 since I came back.

Fuller

Shot two ducks Monday

* SEPTEMBER 23, 1911 / FORT PIERRE, SO. DAK.
TO MRS. M. M. COREY

Dear Ma,—Yours of the 17th received. I believe I told Ethel that the little bbl of apples came and were in good enough shape so that Mr. Stone accepted them. Fuller brought the sweet apples over last Sat. and I made two pint cans of sweet apple pickles.

You are mistaken about Glen[.] He isn't that style at all at all. Fuller and I both like Glen better than any the rest of the Speer tribe.

My! I do hope you all get some time to gather walnuts[.] I'm almost starved for some—There! you see I'm getting the southern "you all"[;] I hear it so much here.

Am glad you are doing so well with your fruit. I auto be at home working with mine every Saturday but Fuller didn't come for me last night.

I didn't know Mr Stone was sore at Fuller—neither of them said any thing to me about it but Fuller was sore because Mr Stone doesn't think I auto drive bay Nell.[1] He surely had no personal interest *there* for if I don't drive Fullers I'll drive one of mine and he can make good use of both of mine.

Yes, you have always said I was selfish so I suppose I am but its this way—I have three head of horses and Fuller has one. If there is any work for a team its apt to be up on my flat not down in his hills and he hates my team so he wont treat them decent and I'd like to have them where I could take as much care of them as possible and so long as I pay for the lumber and the building I felt as if I had a right to have the barn on my place. I don't care how many barns he has only I *need* my barn *now*. There auto be lumber enough in that lot to build us each a barn.

That fence of mine—When they finished it Fuller told Mr Stone that he would see to the draws and Mr Stone thot he had and Fuller went down to Iowa and left one or two draws where a full grown critter could almost walk under—of course they did and cleaned up my nine acres of corn so it looks as if the corn had been cut and hauled off beside all the hay they ate. yet Fuller thinks I auto not mention damages to Mr Briggs because it was the fault of my fence that they got in. What I lost *there* would have built a barn. The first week of school he sat around bein good and let the cattle even get into my house yard when tightening the wire would keep them out. They tramped over the top of my cistern and bulged the top down some. You have settled my mind on one thing. I'll not pay Fuller an[y] $10 per month regular[—]I'll pay him just what he earns. If he wants to do some of the work I want done I'll pay him as well as any one else would. He can make it amount to more than $10 per month if he wants to. As to the *"encouragement* and *backing"* I *"owe"* him—I wish you would figure out just how much that is please. When I try to encourage Fuller he is apt to tell me if I could let him have fifty dollars he could do thus and so. I'd like to know where you think I get my backing and encouragement from. My encouragement was in the corn and hay that the range cattle got and in knowing last summer that Fuller was back in the old home while I was working like the dickens to keep from going farther in debt. My backing was in working hard all summer contrary to a doctors advice and in teaching school at a little old $45 per month and 10% of that is withheld till the end of the term.

Fuller turned down all kinds of chances to work because he wants to "live steady on his claim and prove up." Don't you suppose I ever wanted to "live on my claim steady and prove up"? I can't because I've got to earn my way. Don't you suppose I'd like to go back to Iowa just as well as Fuller? If I sit down on my claim and fold my hands who do you think owes *me* the *encouragement* and *backing* to stick it out for fourteen months?

You seem to think I never have occasion to feel blue. How about the time this summer when I didn't have $10 or any way to get any and it seemed almost a certainty that I'd have to have an operation of some kind way out here and all alone and there was little chance of my being able to even earn $45 a month this year. When you were my age a little thing like that wouldn't have made you blue would it?

Oh! well never mind I'm some better now and next Friday is pay day. I've got to spend some of it for clothes though as the best I have are hardly fit for school.

Fuller was feeling pretty good last week so you don't need to worry about him.

I must close as I have quite a bit to do this afternoon and I dont feel very good. I am Your

Bachelor Bess.

* OCTOBER 7, 1911 / FORT PIERRE, SO. DAK.
TO MRS. M. M. COREY

Dear Ma, Yours of the 28th ult. received.

I think we might as well have some kind of understanding. Its just this way—When Fuller gets blue he'd drive the devil crazy and when I feel so horrid I can't stand such a great sight and as Fuller says—if either of us make a careless or blue remark in our letters you just think about it till you imagine its worse than it is and then you give me the dickens which of course keeps a good thing going. Well the first week or two after he came back he was so blue it was enough to make all his friends and relatives ashamed of him if nothing more. When he came over after me he saw lots of land a quarter section of which was not worth ten acres of his and he was rather surprised to find that people had paid from one to several hundred dollars to be located on even such land as that. Well the more he thought of it the more he realized how well *he* had done. At last he told someone that he thought it a wonder that I, a girl alone among strangers, had done so well—better than most of the men had done. They told him yes and they thought I was pretty shrewd to have done so well. Fuller has just been feeling better and better ever since.

Fuller came for me last Friday afternoon. I had told him *not to* but he said he sposed he had been thinking of something else when I told him. I was sick with a cold—could hardly hold my head up[—]so he took me as far as Stones and I staid there. We had birthday dinner for Fuller[1] at Stones. It rained Friday night and has rained most of the time since. Fuller and Mr Stone hunted some and Fuller brought me over Sunday. My cold is some better now and otherwise I'm better and worse by spells—at present its worse.

Erickson wants $18 for the barn lumber[2] and I told Fuller we'd take it so he expected to begin work Monday. He is decidedly all alive now and doesn't even say any thing against my team any more.

I don't think your idea about the horses would suit Fuller any better than it would me. I wish you wouldn't try to manage things out here for you simply know nothing about things here and beside you know if I merely make a suggestion about any thing down there you get into a glorious temper about it.

You say I talked Fuller into the notion of filing up here. Your off your base again. I didn't and Fuller will tell you so himself. You've got a letter from me somewhere in which I said if Fuller didn't think he'd like it out here he better not come. And I told him before he filed that he better not unless he thought he'd like it here.[3]

Mrs. Atkins left her baby here today. I've been helping take care of it. It is crying now so I guess I'll close. My first months wages are drawn and spent. I may feel more like writing next time.

Your Bachelor Bess

Am reading "Lorna Doone."[4]

* OCTOBER 14, 1911 / FORT PIERRE, SO. DAK.
TO MRS. M. M. COREY

Dear Ma,—Am sorry you have not been well—hope you are better ere this.

I'm feeling better today—just a little lazy but thats usual you know.

Last Saturday evening a man got lost on his way to Vivian [South Dakota] and staid here all night. He was pretty well organized and had plenty along.[1] Mr Mitchel swiped a bottle from him and hid it and Sunday morning, after the man was gone and before Mr Mitchel came back from his sisters, where he had staid alnight, Navaho, as they call Mr Barnett, told us that "Mitch" had hidden the old fellows bottle. Mrs Thomas and I didn't want Mr M to have the bottle so when there was no one around Mildred[2] went to the barn to hunt eggs and I went along to hunt eggs (?) also. We found nothing about the barn but in the corn crib we found the flask under an innocent looking grain sack on a shelf in one corner. We couldn't take it to the house with-out a chance of being caught in the act so we pushed a lot of old irons under the shelf and jerked the sack off—the rest goes with out saying. We fled as if the old mischief was after us and I guess Navaho who was writing letters and smoking cigarettes up stairs must have seen us for they seem to know all about it and they have been roasting us and playing tricks on us ever since.

One of the boys told me at school the first of the term that he brought his rifle to school last year and when the teacher told him to take it home and leave it there, he took it part way home and hid it and later he brought ammunition and the boys had their fun in spite of her. Last week he tried it again—brought his gun and was going to put up a target. I took possession of the gun and told him he was to take it home that night but he left it at the school house till after I was gone and then came and hid it in the boys closet. I heard about it Sunday on the way home from church and late Sunday evening I went up to the school house and got it. I have it hid in my room and the boy thinks some one stole it. I won't enlighten him till school closes either.

When the men found I'd been some where Sunday evening they said if they had only known it they would have had some fun. So when I went for the mail Monday evening I persuaded Mildred to go along. The boys slipped out while we were getting our wraps and beat us to it. When we got almost to the mailbox I saw them coming back. They cut across the pasture and Mildred called and asked them twice if they got my letters but they didn't answer so we went on to the mailbox and then I coaxed Mildred to go on up to the school house after some books so we were gone quite a while and the boys laid out here in the corn field, waiting to scare us, till they were most froze stiff and then they decided we had gone around through the pasture so they gave it up and came to the house. We got here a few minutes later looking "so meak as Moses[.]"

Last Thursday evening we went to the literary society and while we were gone the boys fixed a cow bell under my bed with a coard through my window and through their window up stairs so they could call me in time for breakfast but I found it by accident the first thing when I got home and cut the string. Mrs Thomas says they feel cheap to think I have found them out every time. They are planning something else now[.] I can't imagine what. They expect me to get even with them for when they went up to bed last night they were both singing "ting a ling a ling[.]"

Last night after school I went over to Obele's[3] and staid for supper. I stopped at the mail box on the way home. They all supposed Fuller had come for me so when I walked in about eight o clock they were most froze stiff with surprise. I just handed over the papers and remarked that the "mail was late[.]" Will close as dinner is most ready[.]

Lovingly Yours B B

✴ OCTOBER 24, 1911 / FORT PIERRE, SO. DAK.
TO MRS. M. M. COREY

Dear Ma, Haven't heard from you for quite awhile—at least it seems a long while to me.

I wrote you a week ago last Saturday didn't I? Well last Saturday evening a week ago the men took a notion to go to town and after they were gone we worked for about two hours trying to fix that cow bell in the boys room so we could call them Sunday morning. We gave it up at last, as a bad job. They all got home sober, for a wonder, at some crazy time of night and Mr Mitchel and Navaho slept so sound next morning that we called them to breakfast with the bell after all.

Emmie Lou and I were going to Sunday School that day if we had to walk but it rained all day so we didn't.

Alta Hoyle[1] staid here last week and went to school but her folks thought they couldn't stand the price so she took her books today. I was sorry to see her go and she felt badly about it too.

Mr Thomas shipped his cattle last Friday.[2] I told him Thursday evening that if he didn't send me a card when he got to Chicago I wouldn't be his school ma[']am anymore and Friday morning when I started to school I wished him "good luck" and he said he'd surely send me that card alright.

Friday evening Mr Mitchel took us to a "doin's" at the Peterson School House. We didn't get back till after twelve. Had a good time.

Saturday afternoon I went home with Emmie Lou and staid all night—came back yesterday morning. And after driving over to Obeles on an errand I spent most of the rest of the day in bed. Miss [Lydia] Taylor[3] was to have come over to spend the afternoon but she didn't come. It was a miserable day.

I guess there were not as many in to hear Mr. Taft[4] as was expected[.] Mr Kitchen was down and he stopped here for supper on the way home and told us about it. He says Taft is as large as "chicken."[5] Do you know "Chicken?" His real name is Chas LaMoore and he comes to see Mr Thomas on business when there is no one at home but the school ma[']am. My fondness for chicken is much remarked upon—of course.

Well its after eight oclock and the water is hot so I guess I'll do my washing.

Hope I'll hear from you soon. They have no day trains in Ft Pierre at present[.]

Lovingly yours
Bachelor Bess

✳   NOV. 2, 1911 / FORT PIERRE, SO. DAK.
   TO MRS. M. M. COREY

Dear Ma—Where did I leave off? Did I tell you about the cards Mr Thomas sent me from Sioux City? He stopped there and sold his cattle. He sent me one—a crazy thing—lover's lane[.] Told me to give his regards to "Charlie"[1] then I guess he was scared to come home so he sent me another. Its the cutest thing—a spotted kitten and a mouse and it says "I was only teasing you."

I went to town Saturday with Mr Thomas. Got my suit[.] Its fine. Got some woolen hose and other necessary things for winter. Met Howard Speer and desided to go out to Stones with him in the hay-rack—found out that Mr Speer and Mr Hyte were in town also but I went out with them just the same. I paid Fullers freight bill and we took it out. It turned so cold I thought I'd freeze to death though I was dressed warm. Mr. Hute had a box of freight also. He opened it in the dark and got out a fur coat and put it on me and then the men walked to keep warm. Gee such a time! And the deuce of it is I left one of my best linen handkerchieves in that fur coat pocket—a clean one to[o]—plague take it.

Fuller was at Stones when we got there and as he had moved my stove down to his house I staid at Stones and Stanton[2] and I drove over Sunday morning and got the rest of my winter clothes and wraps. We drove on down to Fullers to see the new barn[.] Its a dandy and surely does make one think a little of Iowa. I like Fullers new horse very much. Its pretty and seems perfectly gentle. Mr. Speer said it was an outlaw but I dont think so—at least it never killed a man, though I guess its a pitcher when it takes the notion. We took dinner at Stones and then Fuller brought me over here[3] in the afternoon. He is getting so well satisfied now that I dont think he will ever want to dispose of his claim. He has been having lots of company and is working between times. He certainly has enough to do to keep him busy all winter.

Say if you ever want to get word to me quickly telegraph directly to C. H. Leggett.[4] They have a telephone and can get word to me at once.

Leggetts were over for the evening Sunday but I had the figets I guess—didn't enjoy myself a bit.

Mr. Mitchel is gone now. It seems kind of lonesome just to know he has gone to stay. Back to Iowa. Mr. Higgens is here now—ugh!

There was to have been a Hallowe'en Social—no—a pie Social[—]Tuesday eve but Mr Thomas was sick and the *Butler* (Mr H) was out of sorts and the weather was bitter cold so we couldn't go. It was a good thing we couldn't for it was postponed till last evening. We all went. It was a beautiful evening—clear as a crystal but bitter cold. I had a fine time.

Oh say, did I tell you about [George] Jones? He proposed to *three girls* in one day. Said he "wanted a mother for his (seven) children and one thing er another[.]" Talk about a proposal of marriage being an *honor!* Suppose it might be from some but some have formed the habit and that's different.

Just been down to see the fire and then didn't see anything. Thomase's have a big cave down south of the road. They dug potatoes last week and put them in it. Some one left the door open and some of the potatoes froze so today they sorted them and put a stove down to warm things up and they just discovered the whole thing was on fire. They are working with it now. Reckon we all will have to eat baked potatoes the rest of the winter.

The Ladies Aid Society are to meet here a week from today. I guess I will dismiss school early and come down—am on for a reading or something.

Well I must close. I have so many things to do I dont know what to do first.

I have a couple of waists to send Ethel—will try to get one off tomorrow.

Hope your apples didn't get frosted. Wish you could send Fuller a couple of bbls. They mean so much to him and he could put them in

Stones cellar if he hadn't mine fixed. I dont think they would freeze and if you let me know when you ship them I'll go down and smile at the agent so he'll take good care of them till some one takes them out.

You must stop working so hard it almost worries Fuller to death and me too. "Take keer o' yourself[.]"

Your Bachelor Bess

✳   NOV. 19, 1911 / FORT PIERRE, SO. DAK.
    TO MRS. M. M. COREY

Dear Ma,—Your card of Nov 4th reached here shortly before your letter—some one got the mail and left it at Brown's barn[1] in Ft Pierre so its a wonder I got it at all at all.

A week ago last Wednesday the Ladies Aid met here with Mrs Thomas. I was to dismiss school at noon and come down to help entertain but at the last moment my conscience wouldn't let me so I got home at the usual time—just as the Ladies were leaving.

A week ago Friday I had an attack of something the like of which I never had before. I just couldn't keep my mind on my work for the life of me—I kept thinking of Iowa—of the cornhusking, the snow, the sleighrides, the coasting, skating, the evenings with stories and popcorn and nuts and apples, the Xmas time, the spring when it is breaking up and the creek is out and later when every thing is green and we are putting in garden, taking care of little chick[s] and pigs and things and summer when the boys play ball in the creek pasture and then when we are putting up fruit and stuff and getting things in the cellar and—oh everything and my throat ached and I could hardly hear the classes recite. I dont know what you call it but its a bad dose and lasted an hour or so. That night we were to attend the good bye party for Emmie Lou but the weather was so cold and threatening we didn't go and weren't we glad we hadn't gone when we awoke next morning with that old blizzard a howling! It began Friday night and lasted till Sunday morning. I didn't suffer much as I did nothing but hug the stove to keep warm. The folks moved their beds down into the sitting room so we just about all live in one room as there is but the curtain between. Gee but that was a storm! some folks haven't found all their stock yet that was driven through the fences. They say there were about five hundred head of cattle in the streets of Pierre Sunday

morning—driven in from the hills north. Poor dazed frightened creatures it must have been hard to do any thing with them. Sunday was
clear and bitter cold but the men were out all day hunting stock. The
snow was in heaps and streaks and it didn't even thaw in the sun
Monday or Tuesday but Wednesday afternoon it turned warm and
about four o'clock it began to snow and several inches of snow fell
without a wind and such fun as the children have had since.

The evening before my birthday I sat up rather late. We did
some house cleaning in my room and I had the windows open till
most twelve o'clock to blow out the—the—well it was not attar of
roses—perhaps you might call it attar of cats. "We aint killed the cat
yet but we're going to." While I was sitting up I knit on the socks for
Baby Blanche [Stone] the smallest pebble. I sent one pair yesterday.

I received seven birthday cards. The one in the Red Book[2] was
broken clear through the middle—in two pieces. I dont know much
of the Red Book yet—am almost burried in reading. I am also helping prepair a program for December 5th. We have a week off next
week—am to attend the State Teachers Association meeting in Pierre
the 27th, 28th, and 29th.[3] I'm trying to do some sewing and mending—also have another pair of those socks to knit.

I take three current events papers, three educational papers beside the McCall Magazine.

We attended the Farmers Protective Association meeting last Friday. They want me to join that but oh gee! I've enough on deck now.

The Literary Society is to prepair a program for Xmas. That means
more work for me too. Yes, that registered letter of Fullers was in town
that day I was there but I didn't know it till I got out to Stones as
Howard got Fullers mail. I'm expecting Fuller over after me next Friday evening and can hardly wait as I've neither seen or heard from
him since I was over there—dont even know how they stood the storm
over there. I expect him to come early as I've bought Emmie Lou's
stove and we are going to take it over home. The stove is a little sheet
iron four hole cook stove as good as new and cost me $5.00. It bakes
nicely too.

I think Fuller did exceptionally well in his dealings with Seun-
schine.[4] I only hope he wont be tempted to have anything more to do
with him for I guess he is about the worst ever.

You must take care of your self what ever happens. Fuller will
prove up as soon as possible and then he says he will stay with you if

you need him till I prove up. He thinks I auto prove up and go back to Iowa.

Had a good letter from Mary L[anigan] the other day. Must close.

Lovingly yours
Bachelor Bess.

✳ DEC. 8, 1911 / FORT PIERRE, SO. DAK.
   TO MRS. M. M. COREY

Dear Ma—Back in school? Yes. Busy? I should say so!

Friday Nov 25th I finished my third month of school—finished exams and reports—also drilled my pupils for the entertainment Dec 5th. Fuller came for me and we went over to Emmie Lou's and got the stove.[1] Fuller thinks my little stove is about *it*. Its a little sheet iron cook stove. When we got home we found we didn't have stovepipe enough so we had to put it up on the table to make connections. Its some joke this getting supper on a stove above your head. It was about eleven o'clock before we had supper. After supper I had to take a bath and hunt up some duds. The next morning I went down to Fullers place for breakfast and we went over to Stones. I went to town with Mr Stone and Mr Murphy. They almost drove me crazy with their tormenting. Those men paid me $25 for the damage of my corn crop and Mr Stone went over to the bank and got it for me and borrowed five to start on.

The ladies of our lodge were having a cooked food sale and I was there most of the afternoon. I staid all night with Mrs Gordon and we spent the evening at Mrs Angle's and helped her serve the supper for the party given in honor of her son Edgar.

Sunday we fooled around all forenoon. We were going to church in the afternoon but it stormed. In the evening Miss Lidia Taylor and I crossed the river and engaged a room at Wm Kemps till after the State Teachers Association Meeting. We went to church in the big Methodist Church and heard the big pipe organ—My! Its a fine one—seventy one pipes. They say there is still a mortgage of $30,000 on it (the church). Monday forenoon we did some shoping and joined the Association and got our badges. There were lectures and meetings forenoon, afternoon and evening from then till Wednesday evening. We took in every thing up till Wednesday evening. We met Daisy

Statue of Gen. William H. H. Beadle installed in the rotunda of the
South Dakota state capitol. Here Bess Corey shook the general's hand
in November 1911. Photo by Philip Gerber.

Hamm Monday afternoon and she went in with us and we just had a time.

The reception Monday evening was fine. It was in the State Capitol Building.[2] We saw the Statue of Gen H. H. Beadle[3] unveiled. Also met Gen Beadle and shook hands with him. Daisy [Hamm] sent me one of the souvenirs and a—someone from Sioux Falls sent me one so I'll send one to you.

Wednesday afternoon we came over on the five o'clock dinkey[4] and was told that Corey and Stone had got tired of waiting and had left town about five minutes before. I was so darnfounded sore I just grit my teeth till I broke a filling almost. Then I started out and walked out to Stones—eleven miles. Was a little tired when I got there and Fuller had just gone so I staid there over night and the next day. I made a batch of cookies for Mrs Stone while I was there.

On Friday I did Fuller's washing. Gee! but it was fierce. He hadn't washed since school began and you know he had that skin disease and had to use some kind of salve and there was so much of the salve on the clothes that I could hardly do any thing with them[.] I tried to use Mrs Stones washing machine but it was no go. I run the sheets for twenty minutes in a machine of rain water and *two bars* of soap and it never phazed the dirt and never made a suds.

Saturday I cleaned up and made bread, doughnuts and pies. I made four plum pies and two loaves of bread for Mrs Stone as she was going to have the crowd there Sunday and the baby was kind of cross.

We took dinner at Stones Sunday and Fuller brought me over here[5] on towards evening.

Last Tuesday evening was the program by the three school and my pupils came out with flying colors—beat the other schools all to smash—am rather proud of them. Tomorrow I expect to attend the Reading Circle meeting in Ft Pierre and am going home with Lidia Taylor for over Sunday.

Next Tuesday eve is the social at Miss Whalens school house—a carpet rag social. I dont know whether I'll go or not. And next Friday is the other Association meeting at the other school house and the next week is tests and a "Xmas doin's" the Friday before Xmas and the Literary Society has a meeting and annual election of officers Jan 5th and various other things that I haven't the dates of yet.

We are to eat Xmas dinner with the Speer tribe and I expect to greatly enjoy myself for I expect Mr Hyte will be there.

I expect you are very busy and short of cash so dont plan on any

Xmas present for me but all of you write to Fuller. If you write me inclose it to Fuller as I wont get any thing here after the 18th till the first week in January.

I just had a card from Everett. He is at Linn Grove Iowa at present.

Am feeling fine but having a severe attack of eye strain and an acute attact of laziness up till the past few days.

It is late so must close with these few lines.

Yours lovingly Bachelor Bess

* JAN. 4, 1912 / FORT PIERRE, SO. DAK.
TO MRS. M. M. COREY

Dear Ma,—Where did I leave off? Guess it was the Saturday I went to town with Mr Thomas and then went home with Lidia Taylor. Say I had a time! We rode out with Guy Jacobs. Ray Harland came out in the evening and we made candy and ate nuts and candy till we couldn't see straight. He was down to dinner the next day also. I reached home late that evening. The next Tuesday eve I attended the carpetrag Social at Miss Whalens school house. I went with Mr Leggett but Mr Sylva[1] got my carpet rag ball and I do dislike him so.

The next Tuesday evening I walked down to Lidias school house after school and went to supper with her. We attended the Farmer's Association Meeting in the evening and I staid all night with her at Curreys.[2] The next day we went to town. I had some of my duds in her suitcase. We left it at the office of the barn w[h]ere the horse was. A fellow with a similar looking suitcase left town on the Deadwood trail and took ours by mistake and when we got home that night we had a locked suitcase and no key to unlock it. I've lived in mortal terror ever since for fear Mrs Flint would find it out and put some thing in the paper about it. But what hurt me most was to think I had to sleep in my neither tackle while some long-legged lop-eared squint-eyed bat was likely wearing my prettiest kimona. Lidia stopped here last Sunday night and told Mrs Thomas that she had her own suitcase again. We'll never hear the last of it though.

The Friday before Xmas we had a taffy pull at the school house also Xmas pie and a program.

Fuller came for me about three o clock and we started home about half after three.

The Rutterford children[3] gave me a beautiful collar and the Thomas children gave me a beautiful head scarf. They must have cost considerable.

It was quite late when we got home that night and I was some frosted though I was much wrapped. My fingers pealed off and are sore yet.

The next day Fuller and Grant went to town and I baked bread and pie and sausage turn overs. (Mrs Thomas gave me a quart can of sausage for Xmas[.]) My head ached a little when I got up and it ached worse and worse till it was a regular sick headache[.] I couldn't walk across the room with out offering up my boots.[4] It was late when Fuller got there but he had the barrels[.] Much obliged for every thing. I am now wearing a fur cap every day. The apples got frosted in one end of the barrel but thawed out ere they got here. As soon as they thawed they settled down so every time the bbl was moved the walnuts bruised the apples in the other end of the bbl. I had to can up some—twenty-two quarts and about two quarts of pickles. The walnuts went to the right spot so did the chili sauce. I told Fuller he might have the other meat dope because he can't eat chili sauce—it always gives him a pain in his saw dust you know.

The next day we went down to Speers for Xmas dinner. Mrs Speer had started to make me one of those pretty work baskets but didn't get it finished. The girls gave me a pretty pin cushion and Jennie gave me a framed picture. The girls gave Fuller a picture too. Mrs Stone gave me a pound of butter and Fuller a handkerchief[.]

On Xmas day Fuller put down my linoleum—it is a beautiful patern—and Tuesday I washed[.] The weather has been getting worse and worse ever since Xmas. I had to burn wood and almost froze to death. Fuller and I both had a big wash and I had to dry everything in the house. I had quite a bit of mending to do for Fuller and I made up the plum jell and some of the grape—had about two quarts of each also made about a gallon of mince meat.

I had to take my foot warmer to bed with me every night and one night I didnt get it warm enough and in the morning my feet were so cold they hurt for quite a while.

I went over to Stones Friday evening and Saturday worked on my sheep skin lined coat. Didn't get it finished but wore it any way.

Sunday we went down to Scripters for the day. It was awful cold. I got my switch[5] and am not pleased with it a bit. Fuller brought me back to Stones and I staid there all night again. Freddie beat me up in the morning and says "Auntie Bess is wazy." Fuller brought me over here[6] New Years day [—]was here to dinner. They had a crowd here for dinner. My heels were both frosted and I was most crazy with them—didn't have my feet far enough on the foot stone.[7]

I found a bunch of letters and cards here waiting for me. One contained a beautiful crocheted jabot from Aunt Jennie and another, pictures of Alta[8] and her hubby and their house.

Blomgrens can't wait longer for the mon so will have to mortgage my team again. The Xmas box from Atlantic[9] contained holly and a half dollar for each of us. My half dollar finished up my little debts and leaves me twenty cents. Fuller still has some money left. And he is lucky too for he has the warmest house in the neighborhood—it hasn't even froze potatoes there for him.

This morning the government thermometer registered 26° below and yesterday it registered 30° below. I do hope it will moderate soon for the snow is so deep the prairie will soon be strewn with carcases of the poor cattle.

There is to be a debate at the Petersen school house tomorrow night on "Resolve that the United States should have Parcels Post[.]" Mr Thomas and Lidia Taylor on the affirmative and C. H. Leggett and myself on the negative. I stayed allnight at Leggetts Monday night. They were out making New Years calls and I went home with them. We found quite a bit of material [for the debate]—I have five good points and "me fightin' pal" has about eight. I don't know which I prefer[,] prepairing a debate or drilling my pupils for a program. One of my pupils told his dad before Xmas that he "sure had" his piece. He said Miss Corey had drilled him till he could "say it either up or down[.]"

Mr and Mrs Atkins went to town yesterday and left the baby here. It was storming so when they got here in the evening that they staid all night. The baby is about six months old and such a spoiled little rat. He will be good for me sometimes when he wont for any one else. I got him to sleep at bed time and once in the middle of the night.

Did I tell you that I took supper at Harlands a while back. I like them very much.

Well I guess I must close. Am getting along quite well with my school work and have some new pupils. They gave me New Years Day and I only have to make up four days of Xmas week. So that makes five days they've given me so far.

Well I hope I'll hear from you soon[.]

Lovingly Yours
Bachelor Bess.

✳ JAN. 28, 1912 / FORT PIERRE, SO. DAK.
TO MRS. M. M. COREY

Dear Ma,—Your sad message received[1] and I've written to the folks. I got your letter the same time I got the telegram but I believe that Fuller and I both sort of knew *something* was coming before we heard. At noon Friday I couldn't eat my dinner and when supper time came I was walking from one room to another—you know, the way I do. The telegram reached Ft Pierre at 1:48 and Mr Leggett received it about 3:00 and he brought it and the mail out about 6:00 so it made good time. I came to town with Mr Thomas yesterday and Fuller came in a little later. We talked it over and thought we couldn't stand it to go back for just a day or two and it was too late for our going to be any comfort or pleasure to Grandma and we only had a little over three dollars between us and my team is already mortgaged. We thought, too, that we would rather remember Grandma as we saw her last.

Fuller says that Friday morning he never heard the alarm and overslept—said it must have been half after seven when he awoke and he had been dreaming that he was in Atlantic—said he went down horse back and was visiting with them all. Was not that strange?

Fuller feels badly because he did not make a longer stay in Atlantic when he was back and I wish I had written a longer letter to grandma last time even if my fingers were sore from the frost. And Grandma and I had so wanted that we could all be together Xmas once more and its too late for that too.

Fuller is more eager to "prove up" than ever. He has nine months longer to stay now.

They say his patent[2] is worth from $5000 to $10,000 and as he is very cautious he may realize something out of it and if he does it will be possible for me to take up "continuous residence" May 1st and in less than two years will be back in Iowa for an *extended visit*.

I told Mr Thomas I would not teach Monday and am staying with Mrs Gordon. It's so quiet and restful here and the Thomas kids almost drove me crazy. They have no doors at Thomas' and the youngsters would run from one end of the house to the other—back and forth, back and forth, shouting a spelling lesson at the tops of their voices and between times telling me about all the dead folks they had ever seen or heard tell of till I was positively sick.

I dread going back Monday but I'll have to[.]

You must take good care of your self. I should think Ethel would stay out to help you more. Fuller worries about you continuely.

Say ma you know there is eighty acres east of me and a hundred twenty east of Fuller.[3] Do you suppose Aunt Hat[4] and Aunt Rate[5] would care to file? They always seemed to kind of want to live on a farm again and I think they could live on it and prove up for $200 each. It is good for hay and pasture. They could build so one of them would be half a mile from me and just a few rods from Fuller and the other would be about eighty rods from Fuller and about three quarters of a mile from me.

There is a fellow going to file March 17th if it isn't taken by that time.

They might like the change but I dont like to write them and there is only six weeks left.

Must close[.]

Lovingly—Bess

P.S. It seems awful to have written about land but I just thought of it and wrote[.]

✳ FROM FULLER COREY
FEB. 4, 1912 / FORT PIERRE, SO. DAK.
TO MRS. M. M. COREY

Dear Mother, Sister, and Brothers. How are all you's. I am well, but the last few days I felt as if there was some-thing going rong back home. Mite be, its cause I've been a little bit homesick. I have'nt had the mail since a week ago yeasterday. If somebody dont go after it pritty soon, I will. How has everything been going back home. How are the horses and the rest of the stock been standing the winter? How is Beauty[1] do you use her any? What's Rob doing. Is he hauled any ice yet.

The weather has been pretty mild lately up til Fri. It snowed some

Fri. and then turned cold again but it did'nt snow enought to help sleding any.

Week before last, Grant and I filled Besses sistern with Ice.[2] My team broke Grant's dubble-trees,[3] one time when the boat[4] was froze done. we riged up another we puled of the ice, but had to go up hill accross a bear spot, we got stuck good that time. we had close to a ton on I guess.

We had to unload and go back after another load and take a new rout. I havent used the team any last week. I only feed hay and its nothing extra, and Sandy is a getting a little bit thin. I've got to haul some more wood this week I wish the sleding was a little better. Well its my bed time.

FEB. 6TH. Well I was hopeing to go to town tomorrow, but I'm affraid there's a blizzard on, its a snowing a little and the horses are all up around the barn. the wing is in the north west and pritty cold. I caut Sandy up this after noon so to get him filled up with hay cause I cant aford to feed done town, I thought I'd go horseback.

I have'nt been feeling very good to-day. I belive the cause is from some dumplings I made Sunday.

I made to many for the gravy there was, and they did'nt cook good. I'll take a half pound of *slats*,[5] in the morning, if I dont for-get, and see if that dont do some good.

I have'nt seen a human being far or near since Fri even. I been a cuting wood today. yeasterday I lade around.

Well I belive this is all this time. hopeing you's are all well, with love

Fuller

※ FEB. 13, 1912 / FORT PIERRE, SO. DAK.
TO MRS. M. M. COREY

Dear Ma,—Say ma I'll tell you something—you know I wrote you that I was sick when I got that telegram. Well I'd been ailing for several days—had quite an itching sensation at times and quite a high fever most of the time. One night after I was in bed I thought to myself "This is most equal to Scarlet fever in its lightest form[.]" I didn't think much more about it till I went to take my bath and found I was scaley as a fish in places. I'd like to know what it really was and if I'm to have an *anual attact.*

I was glad to get your letter and am sorry you were planning so much on our coming. We just couldn't, thats all.

Fuller will be down in the fall and I—oh well—it doesn't make so much difference about me but tell Rob to get the biggest walnut he can find and put it in his best over shirt pocket and when it wears through I'll come down and eat the nut and mend the pocket. He is to give the walnut no assistance or the charm wont work.

Did I ever tell you that one of my pupils, Alta Hoyle, and all her folks are Christian Scientists?[1] I was over there to stay all night last week and saw a wonderful demonstration. In the morning Alta went out to the barn—she is used to petting the little broncho team—and went beside one of them and he whirled and kicked her three times. She slid over the pole and tried to get out and the little rascal gave her some very able but little appreciated assistance which landed her in the corner. She came to the house crying. Her mother treated her and a few minutes later we went to school. Her mother asked her if she wished to say home and she said "Well what would I want to stay home for?"

I was in town last Saturday and spent some time in the Co Supts office. She certainly did laugh at me. Says she is coming out to visit my school soon.

I met Mr Hyte in town and didn't know him at first. You know he is the one who insisted on my wearing his coat to keep me warm and he walked. I wrote seven letters Sunday evening and tonight my wits are so addled I cant write one *good* one.

I've felt fine ever since I was at Hoyles—guess I need to get busy myself.

Say they have a sanitary couch[2]—one of the best—it won't tip and is good as new. They are going away soon and if they sell it I can have it for $4[.]

Well I must close hope I'll hear from you more often soon[.]

Lovingly Your

Bachelor Bess

P.S. I had a letter from Fuller.[3] He does write the greatest letters. Always calls me Lizzy—the sardine.

I just itch to know how the Erickson bill will be settled.

E.F.C.

* FROM FULLER COREY
FEB. 20, 1912 / FORT PIERRE, SO. DAK.
TO MRS. M. M. COREY

Dear Mother Sister and Brothers:
Well how are you's. I am well[.] Grant cut my hear Sonday and I guess I caut a little cold. Its been pretty worm lately and the snow is getting kind of thind out.

That letter from England I never got. ———— only knows where it went to.

I have got better then two dozen letters and cards, and there isnt a buyer in the bunch. but a good meny sellers that wonts me to send them from one to $10. to start on.[1]

I'm afraid maybe I hant a going to sell it but I hope so.

Well why I was so anxious to hear from yous was becose I was a little home sick I guess. If Bess had kept her word, and had enough money in the bank to pay her way home we may of been there.[2] That night all the way home from town I tried to think of some way to raise the money if I had of I would have caut that morning 3 o'clock train at Teaton and came, and got there Monday morning. But I new that no body in the country around there had enough money. Every body has there troubles, it han't my place to kick, I'm getting so I belive the weather before I believe Bessies promises any more. Every body has their faults though. I've quit makeing bakeing powder pan-cakes and am makeing soure dow pan-cakes. Save owt a cup of soure dow from the yeast when making bread and at night mix flour and water, a little salt and cup of dow. In the morning take out another cup of soure dow fore the next time before puting the soda in. M's Stone gave me a cup of dow to start with. They make pretty good cakes.

Yeasterday I had to bake biskets but they turned out cake[.] I put in sugar, cocoa and banna flavering, extra.

FEB. 21. Well I have just read your letter over again of Feb. 7th. Now if some of you's were away from home and couldn't get back and some of your relations die, maybe yous wont to hear from home pretty bad to.

If there is any more of that kind of mail comes for me, you dont need to send it to me unless you think its a buyer.

When I got to looking over my model[3] I found that mistake is all right.

It has been quite a while since I studied any arithmetic, but I cant see how 8 cows have 9 calves with out some of them having twins.

That butter was strong[4] when it arrived. You covered it to tight.

Grant cleared off some land down on the river for the woods that was on it and I helped him.

I hope I can be back there next year. I hope to get to town tomorrow.

> Good luck and Good by from
> Fuller

* FEB. 27, 1912 / FORT PIERRE, SO. DAK.
 TO MRS. M. M. COREY

Dear Ma,—Gee but its cold tonight. Alta and I frose out and went to bed to get warm. Alta[1] has been in most an hour and is still like an icicle.

Last Friday evening we went to a doin's at the Whalen school house and I went home with Curries[2] and staid all night with Miss Taylor. The next morning we went to town with Mr Currie. I dont know what ailed Fuller. He seemed awful blue and wouldn't take any of the money—said he could get along but I know he has been in debt at some of the stores since the first of January. I'm awful short of money myself but I know he is clear out so I gave Frank Murphey [at the Range Mercantile Co. in Fort Pierre] a dollar just befor I left town and told him to please give it to Fuller.

I went out home with Lidia Taylor and went to the party. Raymond came for us and took us home. There were twenty two there and the two Harland boys made twenty four.

Lidia and I came over Sunday evening and Lidia staid all night with me.

There is to be a something or other at the school house next Friday eve and March 15th the gentlemen give the ladies a spread.[3] But as every lady is to bring an escort or something of the kind I guess I'm out.

My fingers are cold so goodnight[.]

> Your Bachelor Bess.

Im so homesick

✳ MAR. 8, 1912 / FORT PIERRE, SO. DAK.
TO MRS. M. M. COREY

Dear Ma,—Me? no I "aint got" the blues. You'll have to scuse the pencil as Im sitting by the washstand and barking like a coyote.

I was glad to hear from you and to get that statement of last years business.[1] I think you've done pretty well and I wish you would get that fur coat if you want it so. I'd feel good next winter to know you had it.

I'm not planning on visiting you till after the fourteen months on my claim but that plan of yours about coming up next August is O.K. only make it at least *two weeks*[,] *strong two weeks,* whether Aunt Thettie comes or not. Ethel can surely go it alone for two weeks. Why you left me when you went to Mrs Sagers[2] and I wasn't nearly as old as Ethel. I've purchased that couch and its paid for. I have a picture of you sleeping in a hammock. I'm afraid you'd be like Stanton.[3] He went to bed early and rolled out three times before I went to bed.

Yes I knew you had some pride and so did pa and that accounts for my pride being so big, you see its a cross.

You really must get that coat—get it quick while you are in the notion and then you'll have it.[4]

If I go to my claim as soon as school is out, that will be about April 27th, I can prove up in June 1913 so you can go back east for a long visit. But you must come up for a couple of weeks next fall so as to get into the swing you know.

Where does Ethel wish to attend high school? It seems to me that Harlan and Atlantic are both impossible but Walnut isn't so bad. She could stay with Mrs Crow[5] and Mrs Crow would be good to her I know. If she doesn't get to go to high school perhaps she can go to St Louis with me. You know they have a college there that is run by [Christian] Scientists. And one doesn't have to have a high school education to attend college.

No, I can't tell you, now, what the Co. Supt. laughed at me about—some other time I will.

No, Erickson didn't get spanked. Its I who am to receive "paternal correction" from the dear *gentleman* himself I guess from the letter I received from him this morning.

I belong to the Royal Neighbors[6] but dont think I will much longer.

Tell Paul I was glad to hear from him and hope he'll keep a cord on Twigs when I come back to Iowa for he came near enough to eating me last time I was there[.]

Where are the DeSpains and have they more than the one boy?

Yes I got those letters to Fuller. And what is bothering me is the way he acted that day in town[.] I can't account for it yet. Suppose he was just *blue*. Am sure he has long since cashed his last check. You better ask him about it.

We've had an awful week of weather out here. This was the first fair day in March and it has been bitter cold at that.

I have just seven more weeks of school and Im glad though the work is going fine.

Well I must close wishing you many happy birthdays

Lovingly yours
Bachelor Bess

*   FROM FULLER COREY
MARCH 17, 1912 / FORT PIERRE, SO. DAK.
TO MRS. M. M. COREY

Dear Mother: I hope you are feeling better by this time. But dont you be planing on me seeling[1] my patent, cause maybe I wont but I hope I can. And if I should you are that much a head. I dont think much of that valueing Co. They dont show how they get ther bases or principal to work form, or how they do it, and so I belive I can do that good. And if I have got 3.00 or $5.00 in my pocket-book I kind of think of my stomach.

Most of the litters that I have receved, they wont a little haul[2] out of it.

Bess has forwarded some litters to me but I dont know weather they are the right ones or not.

Besses colt is'nt branded yet its over to Stones with his mare and colt. I think he expects to brand them. Hope every body is better.

With love
Fuller

the weather has been pritty cold tell yeasterday.

✳ MAR. 22, 1912 / FORT PIERRE, SO. DAK.
TO MRS. M. M. COREY

Dear Ma,—Guess its two weeks since I wrote you.

Was going to town last Sat. but changed my mind and sewed. Made the waist that Mrs Thomas gave me—will enclose a piece of it. It is made perfectly plain—not a tuck or pleat or gather in it not even in the sleaves. If Fuller is ever short of shirts I can loan it to him.

Mr Leggett stopped at the school house the other morning and said they wanted to have another meeting of the Literary Society next Wednesday the 27th and as Miss Taylor isn't back he wanted me to go ahead with the program. I don't like the job but will do the best I can. Its pretty hard to do much on such short notice but we decided to give a Eugene Field[1] Program and it seems to be coming on fine. The children like Field's poems well and know so many of them. Of course it will storm that evening[.] We've hardly had a good evening for anything since Xmas.

Mr Thomas is in Pierre. Will open his store[2] soon. He went last Tuesday. That Atkins family moved in last Monday and Chas. Feezer is here working again.

Last evening we played "Five Hundred" and I guess Charlie thinks I'm a hopeless case but I don't care much for cards you know and I played worse than when "We and us"[3] played "pitch."

I wrote Mary Lanigan Monday and told her how I was enjoying the spring weather and then Tues. we had a whooping, howling blizzard. Its beginning to melt off again now.

I had a nice letter from Emmie Lou this evening and one from cousin Alta [Brown] a few days ago. Alta is like her Aunt Maggie[4] in some ways I guess. At least I can't mention a bloomin' man creatures name without she begins to think "he's the one" and wants to know all about him. After this, when I write to her, if I have any occasion to speak of a gentleman I'll put—(he's married) after the name.

Say the other day I received the last lot of returned checks and a statement from the bank showing I still have a balance of $6.00 there and I didn't think I had a cent. I've gone over the checks, the statement and my check book and I cant find where I've made a mistake or where they have and I can't see where that six dollars comes from. Oh I'm not objecting at all at all for that six will help me out fine.

I believe I'll go to town tomorrow if nothing happens. I wanted to go out to the claim but I suppose that's not to be.

You must plan big on coming out next fall—August—for I'm banking on it now I've given up going to Iowa.

Guess I better close and hit the perch. I'm so sleepy I cant write straight.

Lovingly yours
Bachelor Bess

❋ APR. 8, 1912 / FORT PIERRE, SO. DAK.
   TO MRS. M. M. COREY

Dear Ma,—This is Monday evening and I'm going to write you at least a few lines before I go home to supper.

You know I've wanted to go over to my claim for so long and Fuller hates to come after me so that every time I suggested it he found some excuse. I was in town two weeks ago Saturday and wanted to go out to the claim and he said he wouldn't bring me back if I did—said the team were too thin for such a trip. That scared me almost stiff, for the horses around here that have been roughing it all winter are in splendid condition and I couldn't see why mine were not. I wanted to give him some money for feed for them and he wouldn't take it. He also said that Kate was badly wire cut. After I got back to Thomas' place I kept thinking about the team and I made up my mind that if Nellie was with foil [sic] and as thin as all that I'd be apt to lose her so I wrote a note to Mr Stone asking him to get some grain and feed them and enclosed a check.

The next day I went down to Leggetts and went to Sunday School with them and we desided to have the next Literary Society meeting Apr 3rd. That evening "We an us" was up for the evening. Guess I'll smile at him a little. What do you think about it? He might be a handy man to have around some times—that is he might "save me quite a few steps" you know.

A week ago last Saturday Mrs Thomas and the *kids* were going to Pierre to stay over night so I went to town with them and staid with Mrs Gordon. Just as we got the mouth of the canon[1] going in town I saw a wagon with four men starting out on the Big Road and said, "Oh Mrs Thomas thats my team or at least one of them is mine[.]" So she drove across and sure enough it was. Fuller hardly spoke but Mr Stone jumped out and came over to the buggy. He said he received my note and was taking out some feed and that my team were looking very well—that Sandy was a little thin but not bad and that he was coming over after me the next Friday evening.

Mrs G—— and I went to the picture show[2] that evening and I came out with the folks the next day.

The meeting and program last Wednesday evening was a success. My school did better than the rest as usual and I received more than one complement in their behalf. The supper (served by the gentlemen)[3] consisted of bread and butter, raw onion, weenies and sourkraut piping hot and coffee. Wasn't that a regular bachelor supper? I ate supper with Chas Doren. I did it just for meanness. There were three young men who I believe thought I'd ask one of them and I think they had bets up. Mr Doren (he's married)[4] is neither young, educated or handsome though you might call him picturesque. He is running for nomination for Register of Deeds in this County.

The Schomers[5] had moved back to the country and the children are in school again and seem tickled to death to be here. They are way behind the rest now. Mrs Schomer says they kept saying all winter that they could do much better if they were going to school to Miss Corey.

I was down to Rutterfords a week ago this evening and Mr Rutterford wanted to know if I was going to teach next year and I said I supposed so. He wanted to know if I would take this school again and I said I didn't know if I was giving satisfaction. He said that every one was very much pleased with my work except Thomas' and they are going away. He said if I wanted the school next year that he would see that I got it. Of course I was much pleased to hear that.

I have no sixth grade now. Edgar[6] ran away from home over a week ago. Went down to McClure[7] and got a job and his folks are going to let him stay.

You know I wanted to live on my claim this year and prove up in Aug 1913 but Mr Stone says that is foolish now I've staid this long. He says I better teach here next year and then prove up in Aug 1914—that would a five year proof and save me eighty or a hundred dollars beside taxes. The mortgage on my team is due May 1st and it looks as if I'd lack about $30 of having enough to pay it. God always has met and always will meet every human need so I suppose some thing will turn up. Perhaps Grandma's estate will be settled up and there'll be a few cents coming to me.

When Fuller found that Mr Stone was coming after me Friday he said he'd come. We got to Stones about seven o'clock and I staid all night. I didn't see Fuller after that. He said he was going to town Saturday to look for work.

Weltha and I went over to my place Saturday and Sunday I went with Stones down to Drubneys[8] for dinner and Mr. Stone brought me over here in the afternoon. My cistern is full of ice and Fuller and Mr Stone worked one day on a dam on my place. It is quite good sized and promises to be a dandy. It has about a foot of water in it all ready.

Last evening when I got here I found a card from Mary L——, it says "If money makes us happy—Dern me—but I'm an awful case of misery." Also the letters from you, Paul and Uncle Walter. I know now why Uncle Sherman[9] has been in my thots so much the past few weeks. One day I thought of sending him a postal but he hadn't answered my last so I let it go and wondered if I'd ever be sorry I didn't.

Did I tell you that Ida [Wever] Lay has a little boy? Born last December.

I agree with Ethels teacher that [the] principal thing to consider in desiding on a high school is the environment and not the efficiency. I think I could name a good dozen things in favor of Walnut.

Tell Paul to write often and to get a hustle on him. My third graders write better than he and use *ink*. How is Twigs? Did he croak? What was the matter with him?[10]

Well I must close and hurry home—am afraid I wont get much done this evening. I'm helping the Mrs [Thomas] a little. Mildred is to have a pale blue linen dress embroidered in white. Its a pretty thing. I'm doing the embroidering.

Lovingly Your
Bachelor Bess

[Enclosed in the letter is a penny postal card mailed from Fort Pierre and addressed to Miss E. F. Corey]: 4/8/1912

Dear Friend—
Came in after seed grain to day but the Blooming Stuff is not here yet. $35.00 is the best I can do in here for the Colt. So think you had better figure on keeping him for he is worth more money [and] may do better some where Else[.] Will let you know Later.

Yours
G H Stone

✳︎ APR. 19, 1912 / FORT PIERRE, SO. DAK.
TO MRS. M. M. COREY

Dear Ma,—I wrote you a day or two ago—guess it was a week ago Monday—thats most two weeks. Well the following Wednesday afternoon I let school out early and came home. The Ladies Aid met here—there were seventeen of the ladies here. Don't you wonder how they managed to round up that many? I had some fun but seemed awful tired when it was over. The Atkins baby wanted more or less attention and I took the job—had to take care of him at lunch time and Mrs Flint thought she was going to have some fun at my expense but she got left.

Last Friday evening—a week ago tonight[—]there was a dance not many miles from here[.] I went and I dont care if I never attend another—thats what I said the last time, you know. I was going to wash last Saturday but the weather was a fright and I felt—alright—only it was the day after the night before. Sunday and Monday we almost froze to death and Monday evening I came home early from school to do my washing and then decided to only wash a few pieces and the next morning we got up awful late—it was twenty minutes after eight when I was at the breakfast table and when I was about half way to school I saw the Co Supt and her husband[1] drive up and the floor wasn't swept even and "Gee!! but I was skeered[.]" I started the fire and by that time some of the pupils were there and I swept while one cleaned the black board, one cleaned the wash basin and bench and another put the desks back in place and then while I entertained the guests some duested erasers, some dusted desks, some put the book case in order and as soon as they had finished they went out to play. They were so quick and quiet and neat about their work that the Co Supt was charmed with their training and my generalship. She found so many things to praise and went away and said nice things about me and my school. I went down to see Miss Taylor a while after school that evening and she said that Mrs Porter was their only about twenty minutes and she talked about me all the time she was there. She said I was a splendid primary teacher and that if Miss Hall didn't take the primary room out at Midland next year she thought she would speak for the place for me. Isn't that great? Dont say anything. This suits me pretty well here even though I did have a tiff with "We and us" the night of the dance.

Oh by the way there was a fierce hail storm here the 12th the hailstones were as large as walnuts and broke windows and tore up things some. I had to dismiss school two different spells and you should just see the holes it left in the ground.

Next week is the last week of school and it is crowded to the brim. Tuesday evening Mrs Rutterford gives a party to my pupils and I, and on Thurs Mrs Schomer gives us one and Saturday is the *"Last Day"* to be celebrated with picnic dinner and program and of course there is the usual amount of exams and reports. My pupils are *just as good as they can be*—just ornery enough so I wont expect 'em to die young.[2]

Mamma, I've had just loads of complements lately and you know the failing of our tribe. I frequently take myself to one side and draw my face down to a remarkable length and remind myself quite severely that "Pride goeth before a fall" and be plagued if I dont have to grin every time before I get it finished.

I've finished that blue dress of Mildreds—will send you a piece.[3] I've got that coat to embroider next week when I've nothing else to do.

Well Im sleepy guess I'll close. Suppose the next time you hear from me I'll be on my claim or at work in town. I guess the Harlan H.S. would be alright if Ethel got in with the Stewarts. I haven't heard from Anna for a long long time.

You must plan big on coming up in August cause I am

       Lovingly Yours
       Bachelor Bess.

✱ MAY 6, 1912 / FORT PIERRE, SO. DAK.
 TO MRS. M. M. COREY

Hello Ma! Here's where I play hooky.

Guess I told you what all happened the last week of school but I suppose you want the particulars. The Saturday before school closed I went to town with Mrs Thomas and the kids and staid all night with Mrs G[ordon]. I got the mortgage on my team renewed—it is for only $60 now and if I cant meet it when due they will renew.

I went home with the folks Sunday evening and Mr Ketchen[1] was there for supper. Monday evening I worked at Mildred's coat—the one I was embroidering you know[—]and Mr K was there for supper again[.] Tuesday we had no recess and only half an hour noon and got out at three on account of the party given for us at Rutterfords. Had a swell time and such a glorious supper. Got caught in a shower going home and it—Well I suppose a dr. would have given me a hot drink and put me to bed but I was alright again in less than fortyeight hours and I didn't get to bed till late and Mr Ketchen was there for supper again that night. He excused himself to his sister for saying it was "The last week of school you know[.]"

Wednesday we had exams and in the evening I finished that coat and packed some of my stuff. Didn't feel just right all day—was to much tanned to look pale but one of the girls said "My goodness Miss Corey you look like you'd been dipped in yellow paint" and I guess she was right. Thursday we were to be ready to dismiss early on account of the party at Schomers but the Schomer party was all a ruse. They had a surprise party on me instead. Just as I was about to dismiss here they came—Miss Taylor and her school and the ladies of both neighborhoods. I surely was surprised. We had our last day program and the ladies served a supper that beggars description and when we went home at rather a late hour Lidia went with me to spend the night.

Oh say at the school house when the children were speaking their pieces the Atkins baby would clap his hands and shout like the rest did and some times he didn't even wait till they got through speaking. It was so cute. He will be a year old the *8th of July.*

Friday evening I went down to Schomers to stay all night and we went down to the Farmers Association meeting. They gave me a nicely bound book—the report of the Agricultural Experament Station of S.D. or something of the sort and several packets of seed. I made a mislick and left it at Schomers the next morning and Sunday I saw Mrs S[chomer] and she said Fergie opened it—Guess he is handy at more than throwing kisses—ugh.

I went to the school house Saturday to make out reports and gee! how it rained! I got almost drowned going home and of course no one could come for me till Monday and it was Monday evening before I got home and then my whole forehead and cheeks and nose were blistered from the sun and wind. Have my couch home and it rests fine, or rather, I do. Tuesday I worked all day trying to get things straight and baking bread. My! but the cleaning was slow work. It was all so dirty and pulled up there was no place to begin.

Wednesday I went over to see Mr. Stone. He was in the field so I staid to supper and then as Frank was going over to Fuller's to stay alnight I staid alnight at Stones and helped Mrs Stone a while the next day. She had the baking to do for the picnic and the whole family have such colds and the baby was so cross. I helped do up the work and made a batch of cookies. Then I took a note down to the school house for Mrs Speer and got home about half after twelve. And I washed a few pieces and did my baking for the picknic after that and I had to go down to Fullers for the boiler and flavoring extract too.

I made a walnut cake, iced a box of graham crackers and took a jar of sweet apple pickles. Today (Friday) the big event came off. It was down at Browns. There was a big crowd and we had such a good time. And the compliments on my cooking! well they were too many to suit me. A few is all right but a few too many make me want to take a sneak.

By the way, have you noticed my new stationery? Look at it close now for it is the prize I won. On the bottom of the box it says "Winner of 100 yard dash" and I wish to state that I won it fairly and squarely and that hence forth and forever I shall strenuously object to being considered the slow guy of our tribe. A little while after the race I overheard some of them talking and some one said "Oh Miss Corey's had training, she's had practice[—]you could tell that from the way she runs[.]" I was kind of sore for a minute but now it makes me grin.

We hadn't been home half an hour till it began to rain and is still raining at eleven oclock. That is why I'm writing you a letter instead of prepairing a paper on Sight Reading for the teachers institute meeting tomorrow afternoon.

You know the bulbs Aunt Rate sent me for Grandma last spring— the blue bell are all up—every one[—]and there is one bunch of blossoms. Some of the lillies are up too. Will close—

Lovingly Your Bachelor Bess

❋ MAY 12, 1912 / FORT PIERRE, SO. DAK.
TO MRS. M. M. COREY

Dear Mamma,—This is Mother's Day and I'm not wearing a flower but I would if I had one. I'll write you a letter any way.

I wrote you a week ago Friday evening when it was raining to beat seven of a kind—and it rained the next day and was none too good on Sunday. Fritz came Sunday afternoon and staid for supper. Gee! such a time! You know he had been converted and is now a good Catholic and he was telling how *awful* good he was. I told him not to loose any sleep over it that it wasn't noticeable yet. He was quite proud of the fact that he hadn't drunk to excess for *two weeks* and there he didn't drink for more than six months when he was shining around me. He was croaking about the weather as usual—said it would soon be to dry again but when he got to be a saint he'd send us lots of rain. I told him I was afraid we'd have a mighty long drought if that was all we had to depend upon. We chewed the rag the whole while he was here and Fuller almost grinned his head off.

On Monday we came to town—Mrs Murphy,[1] Fritz, Fuller and I[—]and Fuller went back alone. I started in to help Mrs Gordon a week house cleaning and am then to go to Mrs Douglas[.][2]

MAY 19—Will try to finish. I started in at Mrs G's on Monday and on Tuesday I went to Fritz[3] wedding. Poor little Frances! If she knew him as well as I do she would rather be shot than marry him. It was quite a swell affair and I think I'll have quite a nice little neighbor.

On Saturday Mrs G and I went to Pierre to do some shopping. I got three striped one piece house dresses and three check aprons already made[.] The dresses are quite light but I wore one a whole week and Mrs Douglas said this morning that she couldn't help but wonder how I kept it so clean. I also got a lavender and white striped lawn trimed with white for Sunday wear. They all fit me quite well. I have a new suitcase but as long as the old one will hang together I'll use it for rough wear. One end of it is nearly all out. Saturday evening Mrs Bates and I went up and I got a new hat—it is all black and has no trimming except a little bunch of small pink roses. It is very becoming so they say.

Monday evening I finished at Gordons and came up here.[4] Mr G[ordon] carried my suitcase and I was glad to have him as it is most a mile and up hill.

MAY 22ND—Well I've been here more than a week and like it fine and they seem to like me. There are no children here—Just Mr & Mrs Douglas and the boarders. The boarders are all nice young people[.] They call me Miss Corey as if I, too, was a boarder and not the *cook*. They've had so many poor cooks that even my cooking tastes good to them. The first evening at supper one of the girls called out "Miss Corey youre all right" and one of the boys called "Yes and you'r cake's alright"[;] one of the other boys said yes they were going to keep me and another said I might stay. They just rave over my cooking and they're getting up glorious appitites.

Miss House the music teacher and Mr. Robar[5] the jeweler come down [to] the kitchen to visit quite often. Miss House[6] baked a cake for me this afternoon and Sunday Mr Robar was going to fill the water glasses for supper for me and came near giving them hot water instead of cold.

My feet are better now but the first few nights here they looked like a couple of hams they were so awfully swollen. They say I have heart trouble—leakage of the valves or something but I dont believe it.

I expect you've heard from Fuller before this. I've neither seen or heard of him since he brought me to town.

I arranged about that mortgage and had money enough left so I could go back to Iowa for the summer but when I got to the claim I found Fuller didn't have a cent and not a meals victuals so I laid in a supply of grub about $7 worth and told him if he'd put in the rest of that fence, he was to put in last year but didn't, and put in my crop and take good care of it and the horses I'd run him through the summer and here I am working like the deuce. Some times I feel as if Im a big fool to give up so much and work so hard when he wouldn't even come over after me when I was teaching untill he found Grant was going to come and the neighbors would talk.

It is so hard to give up for this is the last chance I'll have till two years from August after I've proved up and that is so long and I'm *so* homesick by spells. It seems as if I always have to give up what I want but I suppose that is just my selfishness you are always roasting me about.

It sounds queer to hear of Ethel cleaning house. It would seem something like heaven to go home and find the house cleaned.

Well it is half after ten and I guess I better close. Take good care of yourself and write when you can.

Lovingly Your
Bachelor Bess

* MAY 28, 1912 / FORT PIERRE, SO. DAK.
  TO MRS. M. M. COREY

Dear Ma,—It isn't nine yet but I've had my bath and my hair took down and I'm going to sit here in bed and write you a few lines.

Say we're going to have a new boarder—the deaf and dumb printer—wont that be fun? The boarders are so nice to me. They show me as much consideration as if I was one of them and they always call me Miss Corey tho they called the last cook "Mary"[.] I don't know why it is unless its because I'm a transplanted schoolmaam and they happen to like my cooking. Tonight one of them came down early—maybe he smelled the strawberries and was hungry—and filled the water glasses and rang the supper bell and the one who came to supper late brought me a beautiful rose to "pay for the bother" and staid to wipe the supper dishes.

Every Saturday evening I get a check which reads "Pay to the order of Elizabeth F. Corey—Cook" Fuller was up for an hour or so Saturday he says there's an addition to my family—a bay feminine gender—third person—singular number and objective case—obj of admiration.[1] What shall I name her?

Fuller has my corn and taters in and my *four* head of horses over to his place. He says I'll have to work here till school commences for he has to have $10 per month to live on. That leaves me just $10 per month of [*sic*] clothes and institute and Fuller said I must pay Mr Wheeler[2] $10 for the colt as soon as possible.

I suppose you think its my selfishness makes me complain so much but I tell you *it is* hard. One girl staid here three months and her feet were actually blistered when she left.

I went to the commencement exercises[3] Friday evening. They were fine.

Mr Robar the jeweler is so much like Rob I almost call him Rob sometimes. He says things so much like Rob does. The other evening he and Miss House got to arguing over which was the taller and they wanted me to settle it so I got a pencil and we lined up against the wall. I was half an inch taller than Miss House and Miss House was half an inch taller than Mr Robar.[4] We were all laughing at him and he straightened up and said he'd bet if we all pulled off our shoes and stockings and washed our feet he'd be the taller. I thot Miss House would mop the earth with him.

Oh gee! I forgot to start my bread. ——— There I've got it started. Will have to scrub, bake and churn tomorrow so will hit the perch. My feet are lots better so dont worry about me[.]

Your Bachelor Bess

Dear Ma,—Please scuse pencil again but I haven't ink. When did I write to you last? Did I tell you what a deuce of a time we had while folks were on their trip to the hills?[1] Guess I did.

Last Tuesday Mrs Drubney came up to see me. While she was here I fell down the back stairs and landed on—on—well if I was a boy I'd say the west end—being the side the son sets on—but being a girl I dont know just how to express it. Perhaps I better say out by the old black hen's coop or on the sharp edge of the lower step. It left a purple spot as large as a pie plate and about two inches thick. I wouldn't mind the looks only darn it all! I hate to have folks think I never get my bustle on straight.

I quit work Saturday and went out with Grant and Fuller. We stopped at Stones for supper then Fuller took me over to my place. I didn't get up till about ten oclock the next day then I swept and went over the Sundayschool lesson and went down to Fuller's for dinner. One of Fuller's cats is gone. He said he hadn't seen it since the night before the fourth—said he guessed it went away to spend the fourth and hadn't got back yet.

After dinner we went up to my house and I cut Fuller's hair and shaved his neck. He got to laughing so we like to have never finished. It took considerable cold cream and stuff to "cover up the blemishes" as he said. I went over to Stones to supper and staid all night and yesterday Fuller brought me back to town. I am now attending institute and am not working for my board either but am living on tick. Mrs Douglas declares she will not charge me as much as the others but I dont know. Am so glad Im not working for I don't feel extra good and there is more or less going on and of course there is the exams next week—but I'll feel better by then I suppose. Am invited to spend Saturday and Sunday in the country but I dont know yet if I will.

Gee I wish Mary L. was at home! I wanted her to help us girls get a joke on a fellow here—think it would work fine and it would get even with him for all his meanness. Am glad your stock is doing well so is mine. Wish you could see them.

We had lots of rain last week and a big rain storm last night. It drove in the windows till we had to work all hands wiping it up.

Don't believe I'll have much fun this institute. I'm tired of girls and I seem to be too slow to work a single darned man tho one kid is quite nice to me.

After supper they phoned for me to attend lodge meeting and then Lydia came before I got started and she walked down with me. I'm receiver now and had over eighteen dollars in silver[2] to lug home. Silver is heavey stuff isn't it?

I've got to hunt up a place to go to work after institute for there's my board to pay and nothing to pay it with and nothing for Fuller's next batch of groceries and I've only a dollar or two left. I hate it too for I did so want to go out to the claim after institute and rest up. There is only one thing that could happen to help me out and that is if we should get the money from that estate[3] but I suppose that is impossible. so its work work work.

Its late and I'm so homesick I guess I better close for tonight[.]

Lovingly Your B.B.

* JULY 28, 1912 / FORT PIERRE, SO. DAK.
  TO MRS. M. M. COREY

Dear Ma, I just cant remember when I wrote last but suppose it was some time during institute. My time was awfully filled those two weeks—something every evening—and two mornings we got up and went down to Rev. Roberts to look at Saturn and then that Christie got to raising the devil—that sounds rank but nothing milder would express it. She sure put [Jay] Robar and I on the outs for good. I knew she was up to something but couldn't find out what and my nerves seemed stretched tight enough to break.

On Monday evening of the second week of Institute we heard Rev Roberts lecture on "The Dead Man In The Moon" illustrated by lantern slides and Tuesday eve was the reception by the Woman's Club—that was swell. Wednesday afternoon there was a boating party given by the Co Supt. There were a hundred or more of us in three large boats. We were out most all the afternoon and had a swell time. Mr Warner[1] invited us[—]L[ydia]and I[—]to go again in the evening but I did not as I was tired and had to write exams the next day. I haven't heard from the exams yet and am worried about S D History but Mrs Porter thinks its alright[.] I didn't study a lick during the two weeks and I surely had some fun. I know a good many of the teachers and was acquainted with all the instructors and I never entered a class or assembly room without a four inch grin on my phiz and I managed to keep every one around me going some, except during recitation[.] Did I tell you what Miss Appleby[2] said about my being an inspiration? and did I tell you what Dr Taylor[3] said about my eyes?

Saturday I went down and had the mortgage on my team made up to a hundred which gave me forty to go on till the end of the first month of school. I paid my board and got a big supply of groceries and sent for Fuller to come for me on Monday. Sunday evening Jennie [Speer] and I went to church. Monday Fuller came for me. Weltha [Stone] went over with us to stay a few days and the next day I baked bread and put up four quarts of sand cherries. Do you know what sand cherries are? They look like tame cherries—have pits and stems like them—grow in twos and threes but they grow on little bushes right down close to the ground. Just as we were finishing supper Tuesday eve Fuller came in with eight quarts more he had picked that after-noon. He sat down to eat and I was just saying I was going to scrub floors wash windows and a few other things yet that night when we heard an auto. It was Mr McPherson[4] and one of the little girls. Mrs. Mc had found cause to discharge her hired girl and was in need of help and so I hastely repacked my suitcase and came back to town with them. They came the long way so I had about a twenty-five mile ride in the cool of the evening. There are ten here to do for beside myself so I guess I'll earn my $5 per. There is Mr. and Mrs. Mc and the three children—Esther aged ten[,] Ruth aged seven and Dean eighteen months old—also Grandma Allen[5] and four hired men. Two of the men are married and the other two are young fellows—one named Mahutga[6] promises to prove interesting. He seems positively to freeze stiff with fright every time I glance at him or speak to him so I keep him froze stiff most of the time he is around the house. Gee! hasn't he a cute name—te! he!

Mrs Allen sends you her best regards and says she is a Grand-mother from Iowa and thinks it about the only state.

Say ma when are you coming out? Can't you make it the last two weeks in Aug? I could work right up till that time then. I need some vacation before school begins but the folks here want me to stay till Sept 1st if possible and will want to know soon how long I'm going to stay so they can get some one to take the place. I don't think I can stand it here long any way and I do so want you to come for I'm not sure about getting home Xmas for Fuller is talking of proving up on the three year plan they say and if I have to "grubstake" him much longer I cant possibly get home till two years from this August.

Would like to write about a hundred funny things but will save them till I see you[7] which I hope will be soon. Please write at once so I'll know what to plan on. Big wash tomorrow.

Yours
B.B.

P.S. This is Wednesday and I've just received a letter that is *so interesting*. What would you say if I was to get married? Te! he!—A German—sunny side of sixty and *real spry*—has six children—all married—married young you know—he has dark eyes and black hair streaked with gray—is six ft tall or more and *not* slender. He lives in the eastern part of this state where it is like Iowa. Has a farm of over 200 A with fine buildings and all paid for. It would be for me to deside whether we would live on the farm or rent it and live in town. I met the gentleman some time back and thot there would be fun in the correspondance but I may have started what I cant finish easily. I'm tired of this working around and taking care of other folks kids and I've heard that it is better to be "an old man's darling than a young man's slave[.]" I believe I'd prefer being a darnd old maid to being either.

This is the last of July and I've decided to stay here three weeks longer—if I can stand it.

Well I must close. Can't you come about the 21st and stay a couple of weeks—If you dont I'll be tempted to give up the claim and marry some darned old cuss just to get down to Iowa once more for a wedding trip.

Will try not to do anything rash.

Lovingly Yours
Bachelor Bess

❋ AUG. 11, 1912 / FORT PIERRE, SO. DAK.
TO MRS. M. M. COREY

Dear Ma,—I havent heard from you yet but I suppose I will soon—saying you are not coming on that visit. I've got lots to write but its awfully mixed—you'll have to sort it as you read for if I try to I wont get anything written.

Fuller was here again yesterday—had been over to the Land office—says he may advertise [his claim for sale] next Saturday and then go to the harvest fields for a few weeks.[1] That will give me time to draw my first months wages before he proves up. I think I can make a raise of sixty-five or seventy dollars for him and if he goes to the harvest fields he auto raise the rest.

I received my new certificate last week with the following grades

Reading 99	Physiology 74
Writing 75	U.S. History 83
Orthography 92	Civil Gov 88
Arithmetic 95	Didactics 100
Geography 83	S D History 69
Grammar 80	Drawing 78.

It could have been better[—]still "it might have been worse[.]"

Is there any chance of their settling up Grandma's estate soon? My! how that little bit would help me out[.]

I'm just so tired and sleepy I'm going to quit[.]

Please write

your Bachelor Bess

I hope Ethel can board with Stewarts [in Harlan] this year.

AUG. 14, 1912

Dear Ma, have just discovered that my letter didn't get mailed so will write some more.

I received your letter—am very sorry the Corey tribe are all fuzzed up again and just over a few little old dollars. It was only while Grandma lived that I planned on going straight through to Atlantic when I returned to Iowa and then it was partly to save time. You see the shortest way is by Omaha and I could go straight through to Atlantic and phone you folks and then I'd have it over with and save lots of time on the road if the stay was limited to a few weeks—see? But I suppose any of them are able to come "part way" if they care to see me.

I was to lodge last evening—there were too few of us to have a meeting. Miss Crites was here twice this afternoon to see about the books. I'm going over town tomorrow afternoon—if nothing happens— to put in some lodge money.

Im sorry I wrote anything to work you up so—lots of time I dont write just for fear I will.

I suppose it's so about my not studying during Institute[1] but I thot that a *perfect* attendance and class record was enough after I'd taught all year and cooked all summer and that was the only chance of a little fun in a whole year. You know we had a frightful two weeks of weather for institute [—]some times it was *cold*—down to within one degreee of frost and then so frazzlin hot you could take off your shirt and wring out buckets full as that dutchman said and part of the time it rained.

Miss Appleby said that no matter what the weather or how things went I always seemed so cheerful and happy and always had a smile ready—that it seemed I just radiated happiness where ever I went and was a perfect inspiration to her. I suppose that was an exageration but I guess there was something in it for I always seemed to be one of a "bunch" and it seemed to be a jolly bunch *always* and several of the middle-aged and married women whom I didn't even know the names of for a time called me by name and joined in. And not a half day passed but what some of the instructors came to laugh and joke with us.

The Dr Taylor I spoke of is a very extra ordinary oculist. Every one else was having their eyes examined so I thot I would too just for fun so I sat down and said "Any thing the matter with my eyes?" and he said "Yes they are just chuck full of mischief." He didn't recomend glasses but Flag[g] Carlisle says he should have recomended dark ones.

I guess I haven't been cultivating a "cheerful countenence" this past year for nothing.

Well its getting late and I'll have to be up in the morning. I have to "stand up" ant [*sic*] fifteen till five so must close. I hope you'll let me off easy for not studying this time so long as I didn't fail. I do hope Ethel wont have to give up the H.H.S.[2]—that is what worrys me so about being so tied up financially. If she can make the start I'll help later.

Your Bachelor Bess

✳   AUG. 25, 1912 / FORT PIERRE, SO. DAK.
TO MRS. M. M. COREY

Dear Ma,—Yours and Ethel's letters received. Would certainly like to be in Iowa for a few weeks but have less than $2.50 to last me till the first of Oct.

Last Sunday I went up to Mrs Douglass' to see Miss Hickey[1]—was there to supper and then as the storm was coming up so fast she came part way home with me. I just got home before the storm broke.

My time was up at Mc[Pherson']s Tuesday evening so after the work was done up I packed up and changed my duds and went over to Mrs Gordon's for the night. The next morning I paid the rest of that fence bill which was $17.50 which left me $4.75 as Fuller had to have a check before starting to the harvest fields the day before. Of course after doing some shopping I hadn't much left. I went up to dinner with Miss Hickey and we sprung that joke on Robar. We've got him to going some sure nough. Wednesday evening I started out with Mr Stone and Mr Carlbum in a hay rack. We got to Porters crossing and found it too high to ford and still rising. I staid over night at Carlisles and Mr Stone staid at Porters. Mr Carlbum swam a horse across to let the folks know what was up. He was in to his neck—the horse swam most of the way. The next day Grant took Carlisles buggy and we went back to town and came out the long way—got here the middle of the afternoon on Thursday.

Mrs Stone's stepmother who was here visiting was down to Speers so Mrs Stone went down after her and I went along then they took me home[.] I wish you could have seen my house it surely did look as if the devil had had a dance in it. I found that my broom and clock and all the salt was down at Fullers.

I slept late Friday morning and have no idea what time it was when I went down to Fuller's but I forgot the key and came back with nothing. Then after I had rested I went down again only to find the key wouldn't work so I had to go back for the hatchet and that time *I got in*—anybody or his dog could get in now I guess.

In the afternoon I cleaned up some and on towards evening Fritz stopped to borrow some flour and salt and I gave him a big mess of lettuce. My! I've a swell patch of lettuce and the onions are quite good sized, also plenty of potatoes and summer squash.

Saturday morning I started to clean house—was just taking up the sitting room carpet when Stanton came with a note from Mae [Stone] asking if I could come over that evening to stay with the children the next day while they went plumming. I told him I would and then nearly tore my clothes to get the room finished before dark. I got the room cleaned and the carpet cleaned and down and most of the big things cleaned and back. Then I read for an hour and came over to Stones.

AUG 26.

The folks started early and took the baby so I had four of Stones and the four youngest Speers. After the work was done I dropped down on the bed a few minutes to rest and the first thing I knew the girls were all down playing in the pond. I sent the boys after them[.] They sent the girls home but staid themselves. I asked the girls why they went after the folks had forbidden their going and one said "You see we thought you were asleep[.]" After a while the boys came up—two of them looked amused the other one rather silly—they had been jumping across a narrow place and the one went in most to his shoulders. I suppose I should have put him to bed and hung his duds on the line but the beds were all made so I sent him out doors to play in the sun.

I thought I'd cook a whole lot of stuff for dinner and then just warm things up for supper but my stars! They ate up *every thing*— hardly left a scrap of bread for the cats.

Before I had the dishes finished a bunch of horses went past. The driver, a tall, sunburned, rather handsome young fellow stopped for a drink. I imagined he looked amused—perhaps he was trying to figure out how many pair of twins I had. I believe all eight of the children were about me.

About the time I finished the dishes the boys came in—My patience! *They had all been in the pond.* Played their clothes was their bathing suits they said—didn't even take off their shoes. Went in clear over. The sun was hot enough to blister so I sent them out in the shade to dry that time. I didn't punish any of them—just looked at them and thanked the Lord I wasn't the mother of any of them and from their looks they too were thankful that I was not. I only punished one youngster in the whole day and that was the one who was bound to eat raw bacon. I made her sit in a chair. Gee! how she howled.

They didn't play together very well and I didn't pretend to keep track of the spats I was called upon to settle. It was soon time to get supper and about dark the folks got home with about five bushels of plums of which I'm to have a share. I retired early and as tired as if I had worked all day and in my ears was ringing Bernard Vessey's[2] beautiful voice singing "—the end of another perfect day[.]" I believe I dreamed of throwing bricks at him.

This morning I went over home after some things Mae wanted and my dirty duds—we are going to do our washing together tomorrow. I drove Nancy. Do you know Nancy? She is an old grey and awfully tame—that's why they let me drive her. She will go some—if you push on the lines. She went lame and got worse and worse. At last I got out and looked at her foot. There was a small iron knob with quite a long projection in her foot. It was in so tight I had to pull and pull to get it out. She flinched and trembled so it made me feel kind of sick but I got it out.

It was awful late when we got back and Grant was all fuzzed up but he didn't scold me.

The folks are over to Drubneys this afternoon and I auto be working at the plums.

Tell Ethel I will try to get home for a week at Xmas and wish her all kinds of success.

Well, must close. Write soon and "take keer o' your self." And believe me (?) I am enjoying my "two weeks rest and perfect quiet on the claim."

Your Bachelor
Bess.

❋ SEPT. 25, 1912 / FORT PIERRE, SO. DAK.
   TO MRS. M. M. COREY

Dear Ma,—Hope you are through with the threshers and were all ready for the freeze or didn't you get one down there?

Last Friday Dorothy Rutterford and I went out to the farmstead.[1] We intended to drive a little bay of theirs. He hadn't been hitched single since they got him over a year ago but they thought he would go—and he did. Just like a rocking horse—first one end up then the other but he didn't get over much ground so we gave it up and drove old Shy. I pushed on the lines and Dorothy used the whip. It was cloudy and damp. By the time we got to Frank Obele's I was almost frozen so I borrowed an over coat and mittens. When we got to Stones it was dark and the teacher[2] was gone so Mae wanted us to stay alnight. We staid and didn't get over to our place till about eleven o'clock the next day in the rain. Dorothy got dinner while I took Shy down to the barn and got some wood. We had mashed potatoes, squash, and roasting ears.

The next day we had an early dinner and started back. I cut all the lettuce. There was a mess for Stone's, Speer's, Andrew's[3] and Obele's beside all we ate for dinner. Dorothy took some squash home with her. Some of my corn was dented but most of it was right for roasting ears so I suppose this cold snap finished it.

Sunday was a beautiful day and we got back about dark. The geese were going south all day Monday so the children say though I didn't see them. Mon. night it rained and yesterday morning it turned to snow and snowed all day to beat seven of a kind. Last night it cleared off and froze up—even large ponds were frozen over and the ground was hard as cement though I don't know how deep it was frozen. It turned warm this afternoon and the snow is nearly gone.

Friday is pay day and Im going to put most of it into clothes.

Have had several letters and cards from Fuller or "Henry"[4] as he calls himself. He expects to get back soon.

Have you decided which coat you like best?

I expect to change my boarding place soon as Obele's are talking of going away. Perhaps I will board at C. H. Leggetts. Its three or four miles but would get to ride both ways every day. If I got along with them for seven months in such close quarters I'd be the first ever.

Must close[.]

Sincerely
Bachelor Bess

✱ OCT. 13, 1912 / FORT PIERRE, SO. DAK.
TO MRS. M. M. COREY

Dear Ma,—Your card received last evening—was glad to hear from you—had a letter from Ethel a long time ago and a couple of cards since. She can write the most and say the least of anyone I ever saw. I dont know if I answered her letter or not I cant even find it now.

Two weeks ago today we went over to Frank Obele's. Had a good time. I believe I'd know it was Emy Lou's[1] house without being told. It looks just like her.

Have been to town every Saturday for three Saturdays—do hope I wont have to go next Saturday.

Week before last Obele's desided to move and I had a great time trying to settle on a boarding place or shack. The only comfortable boarding places were three and a half and four miles. There were three shacks under consideration—or four rather—one would take a months wages to make it inhabitable, one would have to be moved and repaired, one was small and a long way from school and water and the other was the Andrews shack—near to school, road, and water so I took it. Mrs A left a week ago yesterday and I went to town and sent out coal and provisions by a neighbor and went out to Stones with Mr Speer.

Fuller dug me most a bushel of potatoes and brought me over on Sunday[.] He was much disgusted with my lay out—said it made him feel like cussing. I don't know what he'd have thought if he had seen some of the other places.

He put up the stove, wired up the old bed stead, proped up the table, helped me move the cupboard, and made a door into the kitchen part which Im using for a coal shed. He also patched up a few of the largest air holes.

Was at it hard all last week cleaning and fixing things and will have another good week of it. Am going to tack heavy blue building paper on the floor for carpet[;] it will be warm, save scrubbing, and easy to sweep. The Obeles moved to town the same day I moved in here. They were out today for the last of their stuff and Mrs Obele came down a while she says it looks cozy already. She says I'm getting thinner and I guess its no dream for I ordered a bill of stuff from the "National" and they didn't have the coat I wanted. I found when I came to reorder that my bust measure was reduced enough so I could wear a coat a size smaller. (The size I wore last year).

Oh! I'm not working myself to death by any means. But along with the rest of my troubles I got a letter written the latter part of Sept. from that party at Fulton[2] saying that he should like to make visit to Ft Pierre in October and asked if he might drive out in an auto Friday eve and take me to the home of a mutual friend[3] for over Sunday and would I answer at once.

Well I wouldn't have thot much of it only I was warned by the "mutual friend" that he was getting "a little serious." I didn't know whether to tell him "yes" or "no" or leave the letter unanswered. I made up my mind some fifty times or more and changed it as often. At last I made up my mind I was a conceited phool and wrote him that I'd be pleased to have him visit my school some Friday afternoon. Guess that leaves us both a margin. I let him wait most three weeks but that is good for what ailes him.

By the way I saw a card a while back that Ethel sent Fuller and I cant say I admire her taste in the selection of post cards. Another party picked up the card thinking it was mine and remarked "That sure is suggestive to say the least[.]" She is such a careless mortal she might send such a card to most any one and never think.

I tried to work Fuller for a little change but he was like the fellow on a Dutch post card I saw the other day "Long mit luf un short mit money[.]"

Guess I'll close and perhaps I'll feel more like writing next time[.]

Lovingly yours
Bachelor Bess

P.S. A certain person said he did wish Miss Corey wouldn't sign her letters Bachelor Bess[.]

＊ OCT. 27, 1912 / FORT PIERRE, SO. DAK.
TO MRS. M. M. COREY

Dear Ma,—Was in town a week ago yesterday—saw Fuller and he said he was to start for Iowa last Wednesday so suppose he is with you ere this.

Have the building paper on the floor now and it makes it quite warm.

Have been having lots of company. Lydia was here las[t] Sat forenoon, Miss Hickey came out Saturday eve and staid till Monday morning, Mrs Rutterford came up Thursday eve and the gentleman from Fulton S. D. was out Friday afternoon. Mrs Gordon came along as Chaperon and he wanted me to go down to Mrs G's for over Sunday but I told him the jolt of the auto would hurt my skinned knee. That was awful wasn't it? Mrs G and the driver went for a pail of water—I didn't like that a bit—had a notion to go along only Mr K[rug] would think my skinned knee a fake. They staid till almost dark. Mr K[rug] looked as if he felt badly about something when he went—perhaps I didn't treat him nice enough—guess he wont come again. I hope not for "If troubles neffer come single for why should I get married?"

Have been having good school work[.] The children have been making wiches on broomsticks, black cats, and jack-o-lanterns to decorate the room with.

Please ask Fuller how many potatoes I had and what he branded the horses.

Am expecting company so will close—

Lovingly yours
BB

✳ NOV. 3, 1912 / FORT PIERRE, SO. DAK.
TO MRS. M. M. COREY

Dear Ma,—As I've had no word since Ethels letter written last Monday I presume Olney must be well or a great deal better and as I expect to start in school again in the morning Ill write you more of a letter than I did last time.

Two weeks ago yesterday I went to town to see Fuller as he expected to start for Iowa the following Wednesday. I saw him and Grant as I mentioned before. I was going to ride out with Mr Feezer and after getting into the wagon discovered I had left my fur in the store. I started to jump from the wagon which is an awkward home made affair and Mr Feezer told me to be careful or I would tear my dress. In taking care of my dress I forgot my feet and caught my right heel on a rod which threw me rather violently to the ground. I landed on my right knee and left hand. I jumped up saying I was unhurt and went into the store for my fur. Mr Stone and Fuller were in the back part of the store and Mr Stone called "Hello Grandma! back already?" I laughed and told him I was glad he was inside but didn't mention what had happened. Before we were half way home my knee seemed to ache like my shoulder used to once upon a time and I decided I had a fractured bone.

Miss Hickey came out that eve with Mr Leggett and staid till Monday morning. I felt little inconvenience from my knee Sunday but walked quite a little and Sunday night I didn't sleep much. I tried to teach Monday but caved in about two o'clock and came home and went to bed. Tried it again Tuesday and Wednesday but didn't stick it out till four either day. I went to bed Wednesday afternoon and wasn't out again till this week. Was up and dressed a little while Monday evening and a little longer each day since till now I'm up for all day and start school tomorrow. Have been walking all about for two or three days though I limp some yet. You can lay your finger between the two pieces of the knee cap though they seem gradually drawing together. Have had no help except the reading of "Science & Health" [1] and those who have visited me speak of my recovery as a "mystery" and so on but advise me to visit a doctor for fear of—I don't know what.

I didn't write you for fear you would worry and I didn't write Stones for fear Fuller might hear and tell you. If you folks had known it you would all have suffered more than I did. Tho I went through quite a bit in some ways.

So you see why I didn't take the car ride with Mr. Krug.

People have been coming and going all day it seems—began before I was up this morning. Will be glad when you are not so busy as Ethels letters are rather unsatisfactory.

Say, if I come home Xmas will we have a tree or hang up our stockings in the good old way?

Mamma I'll tell you a joke. I hear I'm becoming remarkable for my "cheerful disposition" my "sunny smile" and "mischievous eyes[.]" Do you think you will recognize me at Xmas time? Ha! ha!

Well I want to write a few lines to Rob and must write a note to Mrs. Stone so will close. Now *dont* worry about me for I could beat you in a foot race this minute. Hope to hear from some of you soon as I don't know where Fuller is.

Lovingly your
Bachelor Bess.

✳ NOV. IO, I9I2 / FORT PIERRE, SO. DAK.
TO MRS. M. M. COREY

Dear Ma,—Received a letter from Ethel the latter part of the week.

Yes, I've had a good week. My knee is fine. I hardly limp at all. The pieces of the knee cap have gone together so they touch now.

Say[,] I've changed my politics. I'm going to work for "Woman's Suffrage" tooth and toe nail and then I'm going to have 'em make a law that all proposals of marriage *must be verbal*. You needn't laugh. Its no joke. The other two tried it that way and never got it all said but this last one went home like a big "It" and wrote. And when they write they just say every thing and you can't stop them. Of course he is nice and old and honest and honorable and wealthy and all that but as I'm not yet twenty five and hardly old enough yet to consider matrimony I wrote and politely but firmly refused to consider it. So *thats* settled.

What did Fuller brand the horses?[1] Did you folks have any apples this year? How much oats and wheat? How much corn to husk? Have they started husking? Is Fuller husking at home? What was the matter with Jim?[2] Did Fuller let down the fence so Brown's[3] horses could feed on my claim? Should I give him that privilege for caring for my horses? Or am I free to lease it?

Have had company yesterday and today.

This has been a beautiful day but it is clouding up now and looks like rain. It has been *so* warm.

I'll be pretty busy this week getting ready for the institute meeting next Saturday. Have to prepare a discussion on Miss Taylors paper "How to Present "The Great Stone Face"[4] to an eighth grade class[.]" Have had no eighth grade last year or this so am rusty.

Will close and give this to Edgar [Rutterford] to mail.

Hastily your
Bachelor Bess

From at least November 3, 1912, when she asked her mother, "Do you think you will recognize me at Xmas time?" Bess was making plans for a holiday trip to Marne. It had been eighteen months since she had been in Iowa and, as her first letter of 1913 indicates, she used a good portion of her time renewing acquaintances in Harlan and taking care of some essential dental work.

✴ JAN. 6, 1913 / FORT PIERRE, SO. DAK.
TO MRS. M. M. COREY

Dear Mamma,—I didn't let Dr Brandt[1] use cocain when he pulled that last tooth and it bled much more. It stopped once and then an hour or so later it started again worse than ever. It almost frightened me for I thought if it acted like that on the train it would be dreadful. It bled a little once in the night—just enough to soil a handkerchief badly.

I got to see Valerie and George[2] in town also Emma Schief, Dave & Henry Lamers, Mrs Cook, Marten Peterson and several others.[3] The west bound [train] was late enough so we had but a short wait in the Bluffs.[4] I saw Mr. Lana[5] on the train—guess he didn't know me. There was a young fellow accross the car from us who was telling a little girl in the seat ahead of him of his wife and "very, very little girl." He also told her that Minden was a Dutch town and that his brother-in-law was teaching there.

We ate our supper in the Bluffs. We both slept most of the time after leaving there except when it was too awful cold. We were left on the train in Sioux City till we were most frozen but of course we didn't dare leave the car. We got into Huron at 8:10 but the trains were all late so we had to wait till 11:30 and the waiting room was so cold we had to walk to keep warm. We just hit Dakota in time to get the benefit of the first severe cold spell. We got into Pierre in time to miss the three o'clock bridge train so we had to wait till six. While there Frank Murphy and his sister[6] came in. Frank said Grant drove my Kate to town single Saturday and she went fine. If he gets her broke well single I'll hate to sell her worse than ever.

It was 6:20 when we got off at Ft Pierre and I took my suit case down to Mrs Normans.[7] I also left my sweater and overshoes as I could walk better with out them. By the time I had them off Mrs Norman had a bowl of hot soup, a cup of coffee and crackers and cake set out for me—so much for natural gas.[8] It surely makes the quick heat.

I left town about a quarter of seven and stopped at Rutterfords quite a while. Dorothy [Rutterford] came up and staid all night with me. We got here[9] about 9:20. I went down for a pail of water but found nothing beneath the ice but mud[10] so had to bring ice up and melt it. Thats slow too when you are thirsty.

There is no sign of snow here and no wind to speak of the past two days. The weather is clear and bright but oh so bitter cold.

Tell Paul that old Santa remembered me out here too. Received a box of linen stationery. He said he would rather have given me a ribbon but thot there was more chance of my using the stationery.

Dorothy gave me a tie similar to the one Mary [Lanigan] gave me only smaller. It has pale blue velvet ribbon and the rest is made of very fine silkey thread which makes it *very* dainty.

Edgar Rutterford started in school this morning after changing his mind about it some forty times. I hope he stays with it this time till spring.

My trip to Iowa already seems like a dream. I can hardly make myself believe I was really there. It might all have been different but for my selfishness and neglect. At the end of the month I hope to be able to place in the bank money enough to buy a ticket to Marne so it will always be ready if you want me. And if you ever invite me there again I'll try to show you that I can take *any thing* without saying anything and not give my opinion unless it is asked for.

It is getting late and even colder so must close and hit the perch for Ill have to get to school early tomorrow. I wish my overshoes were here. I frosted my feet this morning going just that little way.

Lovingly yours—B.B.

✱ JAN. 13, 1913 / FORT PIERRE, SO. DAK.
TO MRS. M. M. COREY

Dear Ma,—Yours received last eve. If you will send me those books I'll send you the postage—and be very much obliged to you into the bargain.

The bag Cousin Sue[1] sent is evidently an opera glass bag as it is a trifle small to be one of the up-to-date hand bags. To match it you will need a gown of white brocaded satin abbreviated at neck and sleves and trimmed abundantly with fur. Also an opera cloak lined with white satin and trimmed with fur. A most useful article, certainly—that bag.

Do you make the beds upstairs when Ethel is away? I was wondering if you could put the feather bed on the lounge and make a more comfy place for you and if the cot in Ethels room was in the sitting room for Rob and the little boys slept in your room. You would have them all down stairs for a couple of months while it is cold. I suppose the boys can make beds though as well as any one.

I left a C.S. Journal[2] with the magazines on the sitting room floor. If you look up that testimonial of Mrs Singleton's you will find her address. There is no street number but perhaps a card or note would reach her. I'll try it if you like.

Fuller put that money to your account but forgot to get the account slip so he said—at least that is what I understood him to say.

When we were coming out Fuller asked if I wanted to lease his place. I told him "No[.]" He said he wanted to lease it to me and I could have [use of] it for [paying] the taxes—He said [Joe] Bahr and [Fritz] Bertram both wanted it and he didn't want them to have it and if he leased it to Grant [Stone] they would be sore at him so he wanted to lease it to me and I could lease it to Grant. So I took it. *Somebody* has to be the goat.

I started to walk to town Saturday but caught a ride with Mr Morton—lumber wagon—no robes—cold as—as I dont know what. I didn't get thawed out till most four o'clock I was so chilled. Fuller and Grant came down. I sold my horses.[3] Fuller didn't like to assume the mortgage but there was no way out of it as I couldn't handle the mortgage and let him have the team without payment.

Grant wanted to know when I was coming out to make them a visit and I said I didnt know. He said if I'd come out from town some

Saturday he'd bring me back on Sunday—said he was short of horses since I sold mine but he could drive Doll single. Then he grinned at Fuller. He knows that Fuller will either come after me or take me back now without kicking—after his saying that.

I staid in town Saturday night—went to the show—had oysters and a very nice time and its my own fault I didn't have more fun for I passed Mr Blair three times and never spoke to him.

I wondered why Harry Berg didn't make an effort to be agreeable but he told Mrs Gordon, on the side, that he wanted to go and talk to me but he wasn't dressed up much and had been having some dental work done—had some teeth out—one corner one that caused an impedement of speech. Just wait till next time.

Had a nice ride out Sunday evening—plenty of [buffalo] robes and a dandy team. Though of course it was cold. It was 18° below Sunday morning and it will beat that a long way tomorrow morning. I am at the school house—have a big fire and have moved my desk down by it. It is not only cold but there is an ugly southeast wind that seems to cut clear through. The weather has been clear ever since I got here except Friday which was blustery. And this is the first windy day. I'm not going home till dark—I might as well save that much coal.

I sleep very snug and warm but have to keep my nose under to keep from freezing it and I dont like that.

I think my dental bill was $3.50. He has it separate from the rest so you can easily find out.

Well it is getting dark so I better make tracks.

I wonder what you all were doing between 6:30 and 7 o'clock last evening.

Must close—Lovingly yours

Bachelor Bess.

P.S. Since I sold that bunch of horses I feel like old man Backsen[4] did after he had "skinned Bill."

＊ JAN. 19, 1913 / FORT PIERRE, SO. DAK.
TO MRS. M. M. COREY

Dear Ma,—When I wrote you last Monday eve it was bitter cold but that evening it turned warm and for three days it was just like October weather—so soft and warm. The ice on the ponds got rotten and was covered with watter—we could hardly get watter or ice without getting our feet wet. Thursday eve we had quite a little blizzard but there was no snow on the ground and it didn't last long so didn't amount to much.

This has been quite an eventful week in a way. You know that little George [Rutterford] who I told you was such a figety youngster—well he was going around the corner of the school-house and had a collision with one of the others. He jumped up and said "What did you run into me for?" and then he had a spell. Edgar thot he would put his finger in his mouth to make him gag so he would stop holding his breath but the teeth closed on it and bit it dreadfully. I didn't realize any thing was wrong at first, till the little ones screamed so. He was limber by the time I got there. He seemed quite sick afterward and I sent for Mr Rutterford to come after him with the buggy.

The other evening just before dismissal I told Edgar to do some thing or other and he said he wouldn't. That stirred up my English. I arose from my chair to such a prodigious highth that I broke three hose supporters. I looked at him an instant then stated a couple of facts that worked like magic. He assured me he was willing to do anything on earth I might ask him to. I happened to think of my hose supporters just then so sat down and dismissed as usual.

Did I tell you that Miss Hickey is one of the stenographers in the Senate at $5 per day? I should like to spend one Saturday there with her during February. Wouldn't that be great? Will have my new dress by that time. Fuller placed $10 to my account till the end of the month so I could order at once. I didn't suppose he would but thot it wouldn't hurt to ask him and he did. Its blue serge and velvet. Hope it fits well.

I went down to Rutterfords Thursday evening and we made crackerjack of some of that popcorn you gave me. (My! how I've enjoyed the stuff you gave me—have meat enough for this week I think.) While I was there that little blizzard started so I staid all night.

Went to town Saturday P.M. and came back this evening. It was so warm when I went and I thot I might have to walk all the way so I left my overshoes at Rutterfords then it turned bitter cold and I most froze my feet off coming home tonight.

While in town I went to a show and a lodge meeting. I've surely got Harry Berg to "goin' some." I'd have a heap of fun with him only they say he takes things so seriously he might spoil it all like Daddy Krug did. Guess I'll smile at the butcher—might help solve the "high cost of living" problem. That would be something. They say he "has a girl" but ———.

Say I sent that second mitten of yours the other day. I left the mate to it under the workbasket on top the safe. I wrapped some yarn for darning about the one I sent.

That "Walnut Bureau"[1] received. Where do they hold school now?[2]

Lovingly yours
B.B.

✳ JAN. 29, 1913 / FORT PIERRE, SO. DAK.
TO MRS. M. M. COREY

Dear ma,—Your and Ethels cards received—was glad to hear from you. Glad Ethel is in school again and fancy she is laboring under difficulties from what she said. It was the best card she ever wrote me.

Am glad you can make use of the mittens. They are warm but not as nifty as gloves. Have finished a pair for myself since then. And one of the cuffs for Ethels coat sleaves. Hope it is all right—if not let me know. Have the other started and will send it next time if they are O.K. She wears her sleaves so short—I thot they would keep the wind out.

Am making another school waist. It is kind of cute. Will go down to Rutterfords tomorrow eve to finish stitching it.

Have you printed off any pictures yet? Am afraid if I had a camera that photography would soon be a mania with me.[1]

Yes I think I have a good postal picture of the Walnut H.S. building *that was.*

Went over to Taylors[2] last Friday evening for over Sunday. Little Dorothea[3] is a captain I tell you. She isn't three years old yet and Saturday morning she said "Grandma dont you suppose Miss Corey would appreciate it if we'd scrub this kitchen" and another time she said "Miss Corey, Dorotha would appreciate it very much if you would tell her a story[.]"

Guy[4] came home unexpectedly—got there before breakfast. Later on I heard Dorotha say to her grandma "The first thing Guy did was to go in and kiss Aunt Lydia and Miss Corey." The little wretch knew what she was telling and had the grace to hide her face when I turned and looked at her. When they asked her at dinner what Guy did first when he came home she looked first at him and then at me—her eyes just danced—then she gave a little scream and put her apron over her mouth.

Had a note from Mae [Stone] this morning. She said they had finished the ice and that my cistern is full. She said Grant told her to tell me he'd be over after me Friday evening if nothing happens. I hate it awfully. If Fuller were not in the country it wouldn't look so bad but so long as he is and has two horses to Grant's one it *looks like the devil*. I didn't intend to use any more slang but nothing mild would express it. Mrs Stone has told me several times that she was of a very jealous nature and in this rotten country where there are so many ready and waiting to start something. Suppose some one starts something. Can you see my finish? I can and so can Fuller but it is evidently alright with him.

Grant Stone is a fine man. I like him very much but there are a good many shadows in his past. Isn't that enough?

Oh say I have an invitation to spend the summer at Bemi[d]ji, Minn.[5] Its right on the lake. The lake is about six miles long and two or three wide. They talk of a log cabin with a fire place and lots of fishing, hunting, boating and bathing. They say they wont take "no" for an answer but I suppose they'll have too. But wouldn't it be fine?

Lovingly yours

Bachelor Bess

* FEB. 3, 1913 / FORT PIERRE, SO. DAK.
  TO MRS. M. M. COREY

Dear ma,—Six weeks more winter! For the groundhog surely saw his shadow yesterday.

Grant came for me Friday evening and we went back by way of town. Had a good visit with Mae, and the girls went over to the claim with me. Fuller brought me back last eve. He said he would have come after me but he was working down on the river. The new date for his proof is Feb 27th and he said he would be over after me the day following if the weather would permit.

Horses are going up sky high here it seems. Guess Fuller got his plenty cheap. Grant said he could turn them in the spring and make a good thing on them. He *may* drive Kate and Sandy through.[1]

The enclosed check for ($8) eight dollars is for the following:

Dental work	$3.50
Post cards	.30
Olney for periodicals	1.20
For making the blue silk	3.00
total	$8.00

I haven't that laundry bag quite finished yet and I thot Ethel didn't seem to like it very well so, if she would rather, I'll keep it and send her a dollar some time soon to get her something she does like. Will you find out which she would rather, please? I dont like to ask her.

Fuller and I had quite a talk on the way over here and I found out where he couldn't depend on me. He doesn't like it the way I've done several things. He doesn't like it because I taught this school again. It is considered to a teachers credit to teach more than one year in the same place and I promised to take it last spring because I thot I could give satisfaction here. The school he wanted me to teach was only about eight miles from my claim and I could have walked that. It was about twelve or fourteen miles from town and *I couldn't have walked that.* The school was run down and I couldn't possibly have given satisfaction but he doesn't think that makes any difference. He said it wouldn't hurt if I had broken my promise to teach here as I was used to breaking my promises. He said the first summer he was here I promised to pay him $10 per month to do my work and that afterward I would only give him 15¢ per hour. He had forgotten that he had said afterward and before I went to Hollands that he didn't want to do my work, as he had nothing to work with, and I better let Grant do the work[,] that Grant needed the money worse than he did, tho I could tell him the very day and where we were when he said it. Furthermore *he didn't do my work.* I purchased the poles for him to put up a pole barn for me and *it isn't up yet.* If one party breaks an agreement have they any right to expect the other to keep theirs? He said I had to back him and he'd stay fourteen months then prove up and back me so I could stay on my claim and prove up. If he had done that he'd have proved up last summer as it is he hasn't proved up yet and I had to work like a slave two summers when the doctor advised "perfect rest." Fuller says that it dont make any difference about *my* staying out here that I've always said I liked it. Says I could have proved up and left long ago if I'd wanted to. I don't know how he figures. If a person dont keep up a continual howl everyone thinks he's got a snap. I suppose ten years from now when Rob has a little ahead the others will say—"Thats always the way. See what Rob's got and he never did a darn thing he didn't want to do and we've had to work like niggers and aint got nothin."

I've always been the biggest misfortune to the Corey tribe and I guess when Fuller gets out of here I'll play I've croaked. So if you ever fail to hear from me you dont want to worry. I'll take care of my character and *my* reputation will have to take care of itself. You could get word to me via. of Stones or some one if it was necessary.

I think perhaps I'll go over to Lydias Friday. There is an institute meeting for the Saturday a week later.

What were the pictures you all finished? Have you printed any? I think I'll have to manage to get a camera of some kind if I go to the [Black] Hills or to Bemiji next summer. I told Fuller about Bemiji and he said "By jing I'd pretty near go if I was you!"

How did Rob come out with the hogs? And how is Viola?[2] The Stones have several pretty valentines they have made to send her. I'm going to start the doll mittens for her as soon as I get the material.

Will you ask Paul what her doll's name is please? Must close.

Lovingly Yours
Bachelor Bess

**✳ FEB. 9, 1913 / FORT PIERRE, SO. DAK.
TO MRS. M. M. COREY**

Dear Ma, Am sorry I wrote you such a horrid letter last time. Will try to do better. Have felt that way a good many times but usually I just write a card and say I'm very busy and write later. I suppose if I were either an angel or a devil I wouldn't have so much to contend with. I haven't a relative I don't feel alright toward now. And in some ways I can depend on Fuller a little better than any one else I ever knew. (Changing his mind, for instance.) I never did believe in having to go outdoors to change one's mind but—my stars! Mamma, Fuller changes his mind right before folks without a blush.

Will write to you always no matter how much you scold or how blue I get unless you should wish differently. And if I dont write to each of the others while they are at home they aught not mind.

We had exams this week—that makes some extra work you know. I also read two book[s] "Freckles"[1] and "Poppy."[2] "Freckles" is a splended book. I wish the boys could read it. I fancy Rob would laugh till he almost cried over the "licking" Wessner[3] got. "Poppy" is all the rage, they say, in Sioux Falls and larger towns. I dont like it. It is very fascinating but the influence is all on the wrong side it seems to me.

The corn on the small toe of my left foot has a gathering[4] under it. I dug a hole in the center so the pus could get out. Guess it will be alright soon. Thought I'd stay home for over Saturday and Sunday to do some reading and write some letters. I dont feel much like writing—just got through dinner and am a little sleepy. Had beef soup, crackers and pickles with cookies and black coffee for the finish—am still sipping black coffee between times.

Wish you could see the red wool lace I am making for a petticoat. Have most a yard of it done.

I brot my little "son of gun" over here and I haven't seen a rabbit since.

There is another Institute meeting next Saturday and as I'm not on the program it will be an easy $2.50 for me if I get to go. Lydia is on but says she is going to study up and write the paper herself this time so I draw a breath of relief.

Am anxious to hear how Rob made out with his hogs.

Oh! How sleepy I am! Guess I will close.

Lovingly Yours
Bachelor Bess

✳ FEB. 20, 1913 / FORT PIERRE, SO. DAK.
TO MRS. M. M. COREY

Dear Ma,—Will write you a few lines while my supper finishes cooking. Am going to have fried cotton tail with brown gravy and a little onion in it.

Edgar has been promising me a cotton tail all winter. The other noon he saw one—ran it down, wrung its neck and dressed it very nicely. I hardly found a hair on it.

Last Friday eve Dorothy staid with me. The next morning we got up early enough to get down to Rutterfords a little after eight and went on to town with Mr. R——. I staid over Sunday—attended the institute meeting. Fuller was in town but I didn't see him. He mailed me your letter but didn't add so much as a pen scratch. Wonder if I've done something more he don't approve of.

My new dress is pretty nifty I tell you. One gentleman remarked that it was just his idea of a beautiful dress—simple and very becomming.

Mrs Gordon's paw gave her a beauty of a driving horse. He just got here last week. She was going to bring me out Sunday eve but was ill so sent some one else. Said if she was able was coming after me Friday eve and Mr B.[1] could bring me back Sunday. Perhaps it will storm so she cant come. It has been stormy all week.

Well I've finished my supper and there is still a little oil in the lamp so will finish.

Last night I had soup for supper and there was some over. This morning the fire didn't want to burn and it was rather late so I drank a little and put the rest in a jar and took it to school for dinner. This noon I heated it up and had my mouth just fixed right when between Lillian & I it was upset—went to smash—the whole shootin-match. The children had brought me a loaf of bread and a quart of milk so I had bread and milk for dinner and that after two meals of soup left me hungry for supper tonight. I could have eaten a raw dog without any salt I believe.

Will enclose a clipping that I thot might interest Chall if he is within the age limit.[2]

Have you all one of those measures for measuring the hand for gloves? If there is a number 8 hand among you let me know. Measure snug without bending the hand[.]

Am going around with a big piece cut out of my shoe. Have a toe—You'd be skeered if you saw it. Guess it will be alright soon. Looks kind of rotten in spots. Thats a fact if it does sound bad.

Well I must close before the light goes out. Dont be surprised if you dont hear from me for a week or two am *dreadful* busy[.]

Good luck to you all.

Lovingly yours
Bachelor Bess

❋ MAR. 4, 1913 / FORT PIERRE, SO. DAK.
TO MRS. M. M. COREY

Dear Ma,—Am very sleepy but must write you a few lines any way.

Last week I found that I just had to be in town Saturday—no I mean Friday night[—]so I sent Fuller a check for ($30) thirty dollars and told him not to come for me Friday eve and I'd see him in town on Saturday but he wasn't in town Sat. At least he hadn't been when we left in the afternoon. I got your letter and read it then gave it back to Bogus[1] and told him it was for Fuller. He put it back in the box and said he'd give it to him. I haven't heard a word from him since I was over to the claim last and know no more of his plans than the man in the moon. I rather hope he decides to ride through if horses are so dirt cheap down there for Grant needs Kate dreadfully this spring. If I buy the horses back I could put a plaster on them big enough to pay you what I owe you and I guess I can earn enough working out this summer to put me through the six weeks Summer school. So I'll come out all right I guess. I'll have to teach next year any way—or get married.

I staid at Normans when I was in town. Jing but I had fun! John Norman[2] is just a school kid you know but he is six foot tall and about Fullers weight. He had been planning big on a class meeting or something of the sort that evening then changed his mind and didn't go. We spent the evening working catch problems.

Mr Norman started up town and stopped at the door and said "John you kind of hang around here and—" John interrupted him with "Yes, yes Im going to[.]" Mr. N. looked rather amused but went on. Mrs N and Pearle[3] just laughed and laughed. I asked what was the joke. Pearle said "John is going to 'hang around' alright but he hasn't the slightest idea what papa wanted him to hang around for."

I went out home with Lydia Saturday night and we all went down to Thompsons for the evening to play cards.

Lydia didn't teach today as they held precinct election in her school house. She came over here last eve and staid all night with me.

March came in like a lion all right didn't it? It stormed here Friday and Saturday forenoon but has been warm ever since.

I canned Edgar Rutterford about a week ago. Told him to do something and he said he *wouldn't* so I sent him home till he *would*. Dont think he will come back. Dont care either.

Am so sleepy—must close.

> Lovingly yours
> Bachelor Bess.

✱ MAR. 10, 1913 / FORT PIERRE, SO. DAK.
TO MRS. M. M. COREY

Dear Ma, Tomorrow is your birthday and I should have mailed this Saturday so it could have reached you.

Fuller came for me Friday eve. I staid at Stones that night and the next evening Myrtle and I went over to my place and staid all night. We read part of "Cujos Cave"[1] while there. Fuller and Weltha came over after us on Sunday. We all went down to Fullers house and had dinner.

Fuller brought me over last eve and was to stay over night in town. It showered some on the way over.

He expects to ride through. I bought the horses back[2] and have let the land for this year. Its a relief to know its all settled.

I don't know when Fuller will start or how long it will take him. We got things settled pretty well between us.

I'm to have Fullers land for the taxes and Grant is to have the whole 320.[3] I furnish the seed and get half the crop and a third of the hay. Grant works the horses for their keep and grains them when he works them.

Have almost as many irons in the fire as usual.

Will you figure out what I owe you some time when you have time? I don't know that I have it all.

Hastily yours
Bachelor Bess

I think the wall paper samples very pretty. I wouldnt mind having my house papered like that.

✱ MAR. 16, 1913 / FORT PIERRE, SO. DAK.
TO MRS. M. M. COREY

Dear Ma,—Last Monday and Tuesday were very warm and Wednesday was misty. Thursday it was mist, rain and snow by spells. By five o'clock it was storming to beat seven of a kind. It grew worse and worse and by Friday morning it was the worst blizzard I ever saw and I never expect to see a worse one.

When I get up in the morning I just get already then jump out quick and throw the covers back over the warm place, run and build the fire then crawl back in the warm place till the fire burns up good. Well Friday morning I jumped out of bed right quick and landed in a snow-drift. Thats once when I yelled now believe me. I just screamed "Golly!" at the top of my voice and made another jump. I didn't go in quite so deep that time and the next jump landed me on the rug before the stove. I couldn't get the fire started for quite a while. Then I looked for the broom to sweep the snow aside before crawling back in bed but Oh grief! there it was on the other side of the drift so I had to go through the snow again. I got into bed and warmed up but my fire went out and I had to build it over again. It wasn't very cold then but kept getting colder. My fire didn't amount to much. The wind blew down the chimney or something so I staid in bed most of the time to keep warm. The storm let up some about five or six in the evening. Yesterday was clear and bright but cold with a sharp north wind. Its the same today.

Mr. Rutterford stopped here a little while ago. He said that he and Leggett went to town yesterday and didn't get there till four o'clock on account of the roads.

Well its time for my lesson so guess I'll stop for now. Haven't heard from you since Mar 1st[.]

Must get down to Rutterfords this afternoon for some grub so this will get mailed tomorrow.

Lovingly yours
Bachelor Bess.

There are drifts that would cover acres and higher than a house in places.

✴ APR. 13, 1913 / FORT PIERRE, SO. DAK.
TO MRS. M. M. COREY

Dear Ma,—Dont know whether I can write any thing or not. I dont feel much like it. A week ago Friday evening I walked over to Taylors. The walking was good in places but there were torrents of water in the draws. Several places I had to follow along the bank to a fall. Just below the fall the stream would be narrow and deep and the banks dry. One place I made a jump and shortly after the bank where

I had stood caved off. It had been undermined but of course I never thot of that. If it had gone a little sooner it might have thrown me into a narrow canyon six or eight feet deep. When I looked down into the whirl pool below it gave me a kind of creepy feeling.

Lydia got home from the dance before I was up the next morning. In the afternoon we went to town. Sunday I came back to these diggings.

Monday was rainy—none of the children came. They were there Tuesday, Wednesday we had a snow storm. The wind wasn't cold or very strong but the snow came down in big wet flakes. I went to school. Some places I went ankle deep in slush and most to the knee in that wet, wet snow. The children were not there and Mr R[utterford] says I must teach another day to make up for it. He threatens to take it to the school board if I do not. He knows Klemann will side in with him for a whiskey or two. "But I aint dead yet[.]"

The snow is nearly gone again and there is any amount of dam work to be done.

There is to be an institute meeting next Saturday. Have my work most ready for it and sent Lydia the book so she can prepair hers. I was to have gone over Friday evening to help her prepair for company today but I taught yesterday to make up for that first blizzard.

It is lovely weather. The gophers are working, the frogs are croaking, and the bed bugs are biting. The grasshoppers were here before the last storm. After the storm the children had great sport chasing them, to make them jump into the snow drifts. My how they'd kick.

Do you know why Fuller didn't pay his taxes? I gave him three dollars to pay them with and that auto be almost enough if he worked his poll tax. My taxes were only $4.59 and I have more stock than he. He kept the $3 and I supposed his taxes were paid till I went to pay mine and they told me his were unpaid.

I agreed to take his claim for the keeping up of the taxes but if he leaves his personal [taxes unpaid] with the incurring penalty to go in with it I'll have quite a bunch to pay.

Am working hard at my clothes all the spare time I can get for I cant afford new ones and if I have to work this summer I'll have little time to see to them you know. Its hard work when all my Saturdays are taken and no sewing machine.

How long did Maud and Jack[1] stay? How is Ethels cold? When is her school out? When is your school out? How many little chickens

have you now? How many little pigs? Will you have any more? Has
Fuller a steady job yet? Any garden in yet? Hope you are feeling better
and can send that bill soon.

Will close for now. Love to all

Sincerely yours
Bachelor Bess

✳ APRIL 21, 1913 / FORT PIERRE, SO. DAK.
TO MRS. M. M. COREY

Dear Ma, Guess I wrote last Sunday eve—a week ago. Well the
evening following I had the three little Rutterford boys to dinner. I told
you did I not that they asked me to "Please invite us to dinner some
time soon before all that jam and pickles is used up?" I noticed Monday that they put almost all their lunch back in the pail and I made
them hustle it out and eat it. I heard one remark to the others shortly
after wards that "Maybe we aint going to get much for dinner at
Miss Corey's" and one of the others said "Aw! I know better en that.
We always have lots of good things at Miss Corey's." They started eating before half past five and the last one finished at fifteen past six.
Guess I got 'em filled up tho I only found one button that burst off and
none of them were ill afterwards.

Tuesday evening Lydia [Taylor] came over and staid all night. The
thots of walking back in the morning gave her an acute attact of indigestion. Soon after she retired she became quite ill and went to preside
over the slop bucket. She hadn't been there long when an impudent
mouse ran across her bare foot. Jing! but she let out a blood curdling
yell. I think the roof raised three inches but as there was no wind it
settled back in place again. Between Lydias gagging and my laughing
I began to experience a squeemish feeling in the region of my tummy.
I put both hands over it and tried to hold it down as long as I could but
at last I told her to get through with that bucket quick cause I wanted
it. She said I couldn't have it more than a minute so I rushed out doors.
The first time there was a lull I called and asked her how she felt. She
said "A little better." Then we went at it again. First time she had a
chance she called nerveously to ask if I was there yet and I told her
"Yes what's left of me." We kept things going till about one o'clock.

I had Edgar take Lydia out to school the next morning. Wednesday evening I went down to Rutterfords to stitch the hem in a skirt. Mr R kindly told me that the school board said *I didn't have to* make up that other day—Whoopee! Lillian [Rutterford] came home with me and staid all night.

Thursday eve I brought "The Girl of The Limberlost"[1] home and read it.

Friday eve I walked into town. Mrs Gordon was going to a party so Pearle Norman and I went to the show and sold tickets. Had lots of fun. I staid all night with Pearle.

Saturday was the Institute meeting. There was quite a crowd out. Miss Whipple one of the noted educators of the eastern part of the state was there. *For the first time* in the whole four years I've been here a rural teacher was asked to take the chair. It happened to be myself and I was so amazed I almost collapsed for an instant. I regained my composure before I reached the front of the room and it wasn't for long so I got along O.K. I saw Grant. He says the dams held and are full. He took out the seed potatoes and will get the oats next Saturday so I'll have to be in town again. And the Saturday following is moving day. Lydia wanted me to come out there for over Sunday but her mother was along and I was afraid(?) of their buggy so I rode out with Harold Hoisington[2] and his sisters. Say! but we had a time. I swapped pocket knives with Harold till he gets mine sharpened. Hope he wont be long about it for his weighs a ton almost. Sunday I slept most of the day and we had supper and spent the evening at Thompsons.

Tonight I've been fixing a hat. Do you remember that 25¢ sailor that Ethel wore for good for one summer? I've been wearing it to school spring and fall for the last five years I guess. Have cleaned it and put on a new band occasionally but this time it looked utterly impossible so I cleaned it and gave it a coat of "French dressing" (not salad dressing). It looks as if it needed anothe[r] coat and a shirt or two.

There is to be a big reception in town tomorrow evening. I hate to give it up but guess I'll have to. Tomorrow is "Arbor Day[,]" Thursday is the surprise on Miss Folgers school and Friday evening a ball. Mrs. Schomer said she would send for me Friday evening and see that I got to town Saturday.

Next week is the last week of school and things will just fall over them selves. The atmosphere seems already to be charged with something unusual tho I can't tell what. Will be very busy so if you dont hear much from me dont worry.

Please tell the boys I rec'd their cards and appreciate them. Will be glad to get those papers to sign also that bill. Money is getting awful tight here.

Tell Fuller that eighteen or twenty head of Roy Rothrock's[3] horses died with "Texas itch" in the pasture in front of Frank Obele's house. Frank [Obele] ask him to burn or bury them and he said Frank would have to thrash him first so Frank thrashed him almost to a ravelin' I guess. Frank came down with the appendicitis the next day. He was to undergo an operation today. They said it was serious.

O[scar] C Walton is also ill.

Well this seems about the last of the paper so will close and hit the perch.

> Lovingly yours
> Bachelor Bess.

✳ APR. 26, 1913 / FORT PIERRE, SO. DAK.
TO MRS. M. M. COREY

Dear Mamma,—Your card and letter recieved. It was hard work and worry that ailed Mrs Ed Fick.[1] Perhaps that is what ails your eyes. Something must be done. What ever you do, *don't* worry about me. I'm no worse off than I've been before and will be again. Am ready to do any thing you say about the accounts. I think they just about balance and if you wish it that way and think Fuller would be satisfied that way you can send me a receipt in full and I'll send Fuller a receipt in full and then when I get the last of my wages I can pay the remainder of that mortgage and be out of debt and if they send those papers and hurry up the mon I can pack my suit case as soon as school is out and come over and wash dishes for you this summer. That will make it a little bit easier for Ethel too for the rest of the term. It must be pretty hard on her keeping up with her studies and riding so far. I'm just itching to raise chickens and garden and put up fruit. I only have to attend institute two weeks and they say if I attend there they will accept my attendance certificate. Or if you would rather have the money—if it would help you more that way—I'll pay off that mortgage and then I think I can put on a plaster for enough so with that little bit from the estate—if I get it—will pay you what I owe you. I can get work enough here to put me through the summer. Fuller knows he doesn't have to worry about paying me. In fact the "hard luck tale" I've been giving was mostly for self protection—sort of a "counter iritant" as the monkey said.

I want to teach as near the claim as possible this next year so I can prove up. Mr Reese and Mr Stone want me to take that school. They say no one wants Ada [Hoisington] again. It's her first term you know and she had plenty to contend with. I like her and all the rest of the family that I know. I dont know a thing against any of them except their extravagance. Oh their father is a bad one but they are not to blame for what their father is. I guess I know more of him than most folks but I wont tell.

You never heard me say any thing against Billy Speer[2] did you? He's almost a "brudder" to me when Fullers gone. He's quite a nice old cuss when you know how to take him and he knows how to take you. He sure knows how to take Fuller all right.

Say dont send any more stamps. Keep them to even up on the postage on those books you send. These came in mighty handy as I didn't have a cent and was clear out of *ones*.

Does Fuller know that Dave Bull[3] is being very nice to Lidia? I hope she makes him change his name.

We all went to the picnic Thursday afternoon and I went to the Dance Friday evening and to town yesterday afternoon. Those papers were not there yet. Grant got the seed oats—says Nell will not have a colt this spring so I'm out that much. He put the team in the barn to grain them up for spring work and they got so full of life they kicked the whole south side of the barn out. He has my potatoes in—said the ground was so mellow he could hardly plow it—put the plow clear in to the beam and it was moist and nice clear down. Auto raise taters—think?

Am at Taylors again for over Sunday. It will be the last time for a long while as I move next Saturday if nothing happens. I'll miss them awfully. They have been so kind to me.

With love your
Bachelor Bess.

* MAY 9, 1913 / FORT PIERRE, SO. DAK.
TO MRS. M. M. COREY

Dear Ma,—Dont know when I wrote you last. Did I tell you about the surprise on Miss Folger and the Schomer dance and staying over Sunday at Taylors? The Monday following I was invited to dinner at Rutterfords and Tuesday evening Mrs R—— and Alice took dinner with me. Wednesday eve after school Edgar brought me that deed so I walked down town[1] to get it signed[.] Caught a ride of a mile or so. I only had eight and a half or nine miles to walk. Its nice to have a nice Notary friend then it doesn't cost any thing to get papers signed up. I made a mistake in signing my name. He thot that the worst ever.

I dont suppose Fuller has heard of the kid house-breakers in Ft Pierre—William Murphey, Paul Burns and the McQuay and Crawford boys. They broke into Weeds, Rowes, Fergusens[2] and the Pool Hall—broke into one store three times. They swiped a lot of gum and were giving it away in school which led to their detection. Dont know what they will do with them. Had them under arrest that day I was in town.

Friday Mr Rutterford said I need not teach in the afternoon as they were going the next morning and so was I and we'd take the time to pack. I went up to Atkins that eve and staid all night and came back to finish packing in the morning. Mr Stone got there in time for lunch. We took the stuff over to my place and I came back to Stones for over night. That night the kids were all sick. They are about O.K. now but the baby is still cross. Sunday I went down to Speers and when Harold brough[t] Ada[3] up he brought my suit case down and we swaped knives back again. Mr Stone said to tell you your prospects out here were fine and if you didn't know what he meant to ask Fuller. Harold told his mother she would have to become reconciled to the Coreys and you may have to do the same with the Hoisingtons.[4]

Monday I helped Mae [Stone] wash[.] Tuesday morning I went home and cleaned house. Even had to move that haystack that Fuller had down cellar to pack the potatoes in.

Ada came over that night for over night and we went down to Fullers house and broke in. We smashed the lock and couldn't fix it so we nailed up the storm door again. It got dark or we'd have smashed into the barn too, after the tub[.] You see Fuller does like some [of] the rest out here—b[o]rrows every thing he can to save buying and tells 'em any time they need it to just come and get it. Fullers dam has some water and mine is about full. Tell Fuller that Sandy[5] is looking fine. Glen surely must take good care of him he looks so sleek.

I sent for the mail Wed. but got no word from you—think you might write a card so I'd know what to plan on.

Attended Ada's last day picnic Thursday. Surely had a good time. She did very well. The program was splended.

If nothing happens I'll go to town with Mr Stone tomorrow and if I dont hear from you will clean house for Mrs Gordon next week but Gee! how I hate to.

If Ada doesn't want this school next year I'm going to apply. Don't know how I'll come out. Its $400 per year now. They want me to try for the Hoisington school but that is so far from town.

Stones got Fullers letter. My! I do think some of you might find time to write me a card any way when I'm so anxious to know what I'm to do.

[Unsigned]

✳ MAY 10, 1913 / FORT PIERRE, SO. DAK.
TO MRS. M. M. COREY

Dear Ma,—Yours both received today. My suit case was packed and I had intended to take the four o'clock train but the stuff is all off now.

When school closed I had just enough to pay the mortgage and eight cents left. I paid the mortgage and put another on for fifty dollars to get some duds and pay my expenses this summer for you all are enough ashamed of me with out my wearing shabby clothes. The draft for $35.75 made it about enough to get through the summer comfortably.

You say I can get along alright with other folks but not with my relatives. Perhaps if my relatives showed me the justice and consideration that most "other folks" do I could get along with them as well. The whole bunch of you will sit and see Ethel sandpaper the skin off me clear over and half way back and tell me that I'm foolish to pay any attention to her as she means nothing by it or "only half what she says" and when she makes a big howl about something I've said with out the slightest thot of offending anyone you go after me rough shod for "*brushing* Ethel so *rough* the *wrong way*." You say Ethel gets all boss-ing and no petting from me. Can you or she mention a single place where I attempted to "boss" her when I was home at Xmas? As to petting—who wants to pet a cat who does nothing but spit and claw in return?

By what law of nature does a "little sister" require more petting than other people? She is petted by the whole family and as far as I'm concerned she is welcome to it. Do you remember how I got my petting? Every mistake was considered a fault and was punished with a "You're just like your Aunt Moll!" and at Grandmas it was slights and slams and "She's just Maggie over again." I suppose you've forgotten all that—forgotten that you refused to kiss me good night when I was a kid—forgotten that once for days (it seemed ages) you never spoke to me unless I asked a direct question before some one and I never got a pleasant look. Of course Ethel never needed punishment or criticism as I did but I can't see that I'm altogether to blame for my disposition. I've tried hard to overcome my faults but there's still a lot of them. And I'll admit I'm still jealous—yes even of the dogs and cats for most of them belong to someone and I never did.

If I go to Iowa this summer it will be on these conditions. I will share work with no one. I will work for you as a hired girl but without wages[.] I will be bossed by you but by no one else.

I can't promise to do much petting. I never was any hand to slobber over any one but I'll agree not to "boss" or criticize[.] And if I find I cant take whats coming my way and keep my mouth shut I'll pack my suit case and come home.

One thing more. I want some time off on Sundays. If you want me to come on these conditions just drop me a card.[1] Will stay in town till Saturday and if I dont hear from you by that time will take it for granted I'm not to come and go back to the claim.

About that account of Fullers. He told me once that he figured it out that he owed me about a hundred and twenty five dollars. I've reckoned on from that and as near as I could tell it would be between $135 and $150. He was to keep track of it and I thot he had. I was gone so much I never knew what he did or any thing. If he wants to call it the same as the other account its all right with me. You have the other account. If not just settle it any way you like.

Why do you want that receipt made out for $35 and no/100 when the draft was for $35.75.

Will close for now—as ever
Bachelor Bess

Paul Corey with his friend Clifford Armstrong in the orchard at Corey farm, ca. 1913. Photo courtesy Margaret Nelson.

P.S. I dont blame you for the way you treated me when I was a kid or since either only you never under stood me and I dont believe I ever did any thing in my life when you couldn't see some wrong or selfish motive in it no matter what it was. Or how much I sacrificed by the act.

Apparently Bess spent the entire 1913 summer in Iowa—a long stretch of time, considering the abrasive nature of her relationship with her mother. The prospect of several months spent at Corey farm undoubtedly accounts for much of Bess's outpouring of emotion on May 10 and the care she takes in making the stipulations that must govern her return. There seems no indication that Bess's trip was prompted by the ill health of her older brother Olney, who died at the age of twenty-seven on July 16. From Olney, Bess "inherited" the box camera which touched off her hobby of photography.

✴︎ SEPT. 3, 1913 / FORT PIERRE, SO. DAK.
    TO MRS. M. M. COREY

Dear Ma—Am going to let everything go and write you. Have had such a time making plans and changing them—trying to find something that would work. The trip home was a very warm and dusty one but quite a number of funny and interesting things happened. Had a scrap with the conductor in the [Council] Bluffs[.] I was the last one to leave the train—had two suitcases and was at the far end of the car. They must have been in an awful rush for by the time I got to the door he had shouted all aboard and the train was in motion. He was bound to take me to Omaha and I was bound he shouldnt so after a little word battle, in which two of us became angry and another gentleman apeared on the scene, he stopped the train and let me off.

You know that once or twice during Institute[1] I didn't get home at night so had to take notes on scratch paper the next day. Well I had the copying of them for "knittin' work." In the Bluffs I put one suitcase across the seat and used it for a writing desk. Copied notes of several songs and a little later was addressed as one of the ladies of a musical troup whose instruments had been left near by. At my very evident surprise the lady apologized saying she saw that I was writing music and took it for granted I was one of the troup.

Two gentlemen came in. They were evidently father and son and such monsters—neither were nearly as large as Paul. The elder one carried a suitcase about the size of a Montgomery Ward & Co catalogue and the other worked hard carrying an ordinary small sized suitcase.

They left their suitcases and went to the baggage room returning with a couple of savage looking bulldogs. The younger man had his in a leash and it misbehaved so he borrowed the other gentlemans cane to punish it with. The old gentleman said "Thats right, beat him good[.]" That awful *beating* made me smile.

There was some misunderstanding and Stones didn't expect me yet * * * * * (Weltha just got here and is going to stay over night—says her pa is going to town tomorrow. She is going to look at pictures(?) now while I finish this.)

I got to Ft Pierre Tuesday eve and staid all night with Mrs Gordon. The next day I met "Brudder Billy"[2] and spoke to him about the taxes[.] he said he had been neglecting it but would go over and pay them and send Fuller the receipt. I came out to Stones with them. When I was in town last week I found the taxes were still unpaid. Was down to Speers last night. He wouldn't give me the tax receipt—said he was going to town today and would see about it[.] He said he forgot it the other day. I don't know how to get at him. He sure wont give me that tax receipt. He said once there was no hurry till the first of October. I think he means to pay them some time.

I'm to teach the Donahue School—will begin Sept 8th. Have only the three little rusty headed Donahue girls for pupils. Will drive back and forth. Heard in town that a realestate man from Pierre had said it meant five or six hundred dollars to him if I was off my claim this winter.[3] They said he had nothing personal against me but was after the mon and my claim looked good to him. I said, "That sounds to me like old Gunderson[.]"[4] They wouldn't tell me who it was but Stones said Gunderson had been out here snooping around tiwce and Monday he drove by here again. I had a big wash on the line. Wonder if that "Looked good" to him.

Mae wanted to look at the clothes I got while I was gone. She haden't even seen my serge dress. When I came to my white dress Weltha's nose went up and she said "Call that linen? Looks more like flour sackin'[.]"

Maggie Speer came home yesterday. She said Fuller better look out or he'd loose his girl as Ada is going with some crooked legged fellow[—]I've forgotten his name. I just laughed and didn't know any thing.

Mrs Speer was telling a woefull tale of how Grants[5] wont board Ada and Ada wont board at Reeses and she doesn't see how she can board her for Ada declares she cant and wont sleep three in a bed. I laughed and said "Tell her she can board with me if she wants to[.]" Mrs Speer seemed to take it seriously so I may have to board her or back down. Dont know how I'd like that.

Had that mortgage raised twenty five dollars and its all gone but fifty cents[—]am going to try to live on tick till next pay day. Kind of hate being short just now too, for Deans[6] have an erigated garden below their dam and they have so many tomatoes and cucumbers they're giving them away to their neighbors. I'm not very well acquainted but I'd try to buy some if I had the mon. Say I bet I could swap apples for vegetables dead easy. Vat you tink?

I havent heard directly from the Hunts[7] since I got home. Mr Hunt has been troubled with rheumatism for years and he got so much worse he went to some place in Minn. to take the mud baths and Mrs Hunt has gone to take care of him.

I asked Grant if you sent me some slips[8] if he'd set them out for a share and he said "God! yes, I'd like to get enough stuff like that to set out the whole garden patch[.]" I thot after the dam was fixed up in good shape I'd have a patch broken below it and fix it like Deans vegetable garden. Then some time when you werent too busy or some time when Fuller was coming home you could send me slips of any kind you could spare.

Weltha just said her Uncle Will didn't go to town today—that Maggie and Howard went instead. So if Fuller don't get his tax receit soon he better plan on coming back befor Oct 1st.

I've never heard of Gunderson being about Fullers claim but he has Howard's and Jennie's.[9] The mice have surely taken liberties with Fullers belongings[.] I had to darn four holes in his wool blankets before I washed them. All the clean dish towels and clothing he left were badly stained and full of pop corn and mouse tracks so I washed every thing I could get my hands on most. Am going down to scrub out the shack when I get time[.] I'm going to put his clothes and stuff in that old suitcase he took when he went thrashing. I dont think the mice will get into that and I'm going to take the mouse trap down when school begins for Im going to keep my horse in his barn till I get one built and I can set it night and morning. Have the trap down cellar here and have caught five.

Am thinking of buying three cows tomorrow if I can make a raise of $140 cash. Next spring I can sell two of the cows for that much and have a cow and three calves left.

Well I guess I better close. How is Pauls heel? What is Ethel doing? When is the next League social? Have the boys thrashed yet? Have ordered the negative or film developer.[10] It auto be here soon.

> As ever
> Bachelor Bess.

✻ SEPT. 11, 1913 / FORT PIERRE, SO. DAK.
TO MRS. M. M. COREY

Dear Ma,—Went to town last Thursday with Grant, Stanton and Weltha [Stone]. Weltha nearly drove me crazy of course. Am in debt $225 now as I bought those three cows. Am living on tick at present. Robertson[1] said I could get lumber & coal there and pay when it was convenient. Fischers and Weeds both said I might run credit accounts there so guess I'll make out some how. Dont suppose I should have bought the cows but it was a bargain and I couldn't resist the temptation.

Myrtle [Stone] went home with me Thursday night and staid till Friday evening so I didn't get much done on Friday. Saturday I ironed and baked in the forenoon and cleaned Fullers shack in the afternoon. Sunday afternoon I went over to Stones for the horse and buggy. Grant had the buggy in the dam soaking up.[2] He hitched up Nell—first time she was ever driven single that anybody knows of but she went pretty good. I found the drive a good six miles and four gates to open. The first morning she got "skeered" at a plow and road scraper in the draw at the foot of the bad hill and almost ditched me. I look at those tracks every time I pass and wonder how it happened the buggy didn't turn over. The next morning just as I was going down the second pitch of that same hill the buckle on the what you call it—belly band? [—]came off and the shafts flew up and the buggy seemed to run on to the horse. Nell was so interested in getting the buggy stopped she forgot to shy at the plow and scraper. Had an awful time getting it fixed but succeeded at last with a bit of twine and wired it with a hairpin.

Donahues saw me go down the hill and got scared because I was so long in the draw (Porcupine).[3] Mr Donahue was just starting over on a saddle horse as I got in sight. He waited to find out what was the trouble and mended the harness up right. Last night I stopped there

Fuller Corey in the orchard at Corey farm, ca. 1913. Photo courtesy Margaret Nelson.

to greese the buggy and Mr Donahue came and greased it for me and put another bolt in. I told him I thot it very nice to have a repair shop on the road. He says that buggy is awful shaky.

Monday eve I developed those two films. It was eight o'clock when I first thot about it and I had them both drying at half after nine. The church was a failure—just a blur—looked like you could see one man—a tall one—must have been Mr. Kevan[?][4] Tuesday eve I printed off some. can print a dozen in an hour if the negatives aren't too dense. I can't print any more till I get the "acid hypo" for the fixing bath and I can't order that till after pay day.

Those out here who have taken pictures think I have a "knack" for it, to do so well with so little experience. I'm clear buggy about it. I'd rather fuss with those pictures than eat or sleep. Ask Fuller if he'll take pictures in exchange for the dollar I forgot to pay him.

Fuller would take a good picture if he could keep his mouth shut.

I think your picture is quite clear but you look like some one had just handed you a lemon.

The picture of my team isn't good. Either it was an awful dense negative and needed longer exposure or else the negative needed more developing than it got. Mae told Grant that Fuller wouldn't know him without his pipe in his mouth and he said he didn't dare have Fuller see a picture of him with his pipe or he'd be after him for that quarter.[5]

Well I must close and hit the road. What is Ethel doing? When is Fuller coming home? Has he his tax receipt yet? Are you thrashed yet?

Mrs Speers Mother sent her a barrel and box of apples and there were three buckets of them clear rotten and lots of spotted ones. They just came from eastern part of state.

Yours for hairbreadth escapes

Bachelor Bess

P.S. Will send you some of the pictures. Was going to send you the best ones but they are up to Stones—guess Mae forgot to send them back.

❋ SEPT. 26, 1913 / FORT PIERRE, SO. DAK.
TO MRS. M. M. COREY

Dear Ma, I got half way down to Fuller's this evening and met him coming up. He said he'd take Nell and for me to come back and write you a note. He said tell you he has his patent[1] all right and if you can send his quirt by parcels post[2] to please do so *at once* as he will need it by Sat. Oct 4th.

This is three weeks of school gone and the buggy still hangs together—guess Fuller will give it a dose of tonic before I start next week.

My! but I've been busy with my house work and all. Was up to Bertrams a little while last Sunday—had to go somewhere to keep from working all day and Frances wanted me to take some pictures. By the way, did you get those I sent? And what did Paul think of his picture with Fuller and Beaut? I never discovered it till after I sent you those. Its equal to a puzzle picture.

Fuller and Grant finished Grants hay this afternoon and they are going to town tomorrow. Fuller is all decked out to go down to Speers for the evening—is going to try once more to persuade "papa Billy" to give him a tax receipt.

Guess they will work on my dam next week.

Fuller is here and says tell you he got his overcoat O.K.

Fritz & George R[ovang] are putting up hay here on my place. The whole bunch of them are to dine here Sunday.

Must close in haste
Bachelor Bess

* OCT. 8, 1913 / FORT PIERRE, SO. DAK.
  TO MRS. M. M. COREY

Dear Ma—"Rains so much"—same here. Have had three good muddy spells in the past four weeks and its fixing up for another today. Have crossed Porcupine every time but one—when I staid at Donahues. Couldn't get to town last Saturday so havent any money yet. Will go with Grant next Saturday if it doesn't storm.

My barn is nearing completion. Have kept Nell in it since last Saturday. Am watering her at my dam which is nearly finished—lots larger and stronger than "Brother Billy" made it. Has a fine lot of little trees about it if they only live.[1]

Fuller has been working for Bob Jennings[2] since Oct 1st. Suppose you've heard from him. He got the quirt all right.

Friday evening when I got home "Brother Billy's" horses (12) were in Fullers dam—its sure dam water now. They seemed to want to fight Nell. Had a peach of a time getting them out. They hadn't got to the hay yet but dont know how soon they will.

How long did it take that "Auto hearse"[3] to make the trip and why didn't they send the body by train? Some how that seemed to "queer" me. Have dreamed of an auto hearse every night since I guess. Such wild dreams too. Perhaps Im getting like the old Quaker that Lydia tells of. He was a long way off his base and thought every one crazy but himself. He used to tell his wife "Every one is queer but me and thee and thee is a little queer[.]"

Its too bad about that survey. How did it turn out? All right I hope.

Yes, I sent Dolma a card a long time ago when I sent cards to the other girls. Belle is the only one who answered. Where is Dolma going? Thot she was there to stay.

No, I haven't sent any of those pictures to any one but you. That batch took the last of the Acid Hypo and I can't get more till I get some money so cant develope any more negatives or print any more pictures for several weeks yet. Have orders for several dozen pictures if I ever get the stuff.

The other day I brought the camera to school and snapped the children. At noon went over to Donahue's and took the family. The middle of the afternoon the Co Supt[4] called. He was asking some thing about it and I showed him some of the views I took in Iowa. You should have seen him when he came to the picture of Beaut. He said he had a picture of his brother and his saddle horse that looked just like it—said Oh how he wished he had the picture here to show me. I said it was a picture of Fuller and his saddle mare taken in Iowa. He said "Yes, 'Kentucky Whip'. Is that the stock?"

Mr Warner seemed much pleased with our work. I told Mae that he said a lot of nice things but I didn't know if he meant them all or not. She said he probably did for at the Speer school he roasted them unmercifully.

Some one was in my school house again last night. One of our sash curtain rods is a little loose. It had been knocked down. They had evidently tried to put it up again and given it up as a bad job. It was left with the curtain shoved to the middle of the rod. I dont know now if I want to camp in the school house during the worst part of the winter or not. Its at least half a mile to the nearest house.

Grant worked at the house the other day—took out the partition and wardrobe and put in the extra studding—worked at all four walls

Bess Corey's friendly neighbors, the Donahue family, on their homestead, October 1913. Photo by Elizabeth Corey.

and the ceiling so you can imagine what it looked like when I got home. Found a card saying that if I'd kindly step sideways he thought I could get in. Had to step sideways all evening.

OCT 10. Last night on the way home Nell was putting on a little style and that piece that goes over the axel to hold the piece that holds the shafts came off and let the shaft down on one side. Both burs that held the piece had lost off and being underneath and out of sight I never missed them. I wired it up with hair pins till I got to Speers (a mile and a half) then Glen put a couple of burs on. Howard said it would hold as it was but I was afraid it would work loose and I couldn't spare any more hair pins.

Wish I knew how to wire things up right. I can make them hold but the men always grin so when they unwire them.

I know *one* reason why Fuller got his tax receipt and why "Papa Billy" is so nice. They want Glen [Speer] to file on that eighty east of me[5] and did I "suppose Glen could buy Fuller's shack?"

Fuller better sell it(?) Glen *might* pay him. Otherwise he'd always have something coming. Of course I didn't know anything about it. They expect to have Sandy again—so they told the pebbles[—]and perhaps they'll lease his (Fullers) quarter. Then I'll almost have to

lease them mine—give it to them rather[.] They wont pay if they lease
it and they'll run their stock on me if I don't. Gee! such neighbors—equal to yours.[6] There's the Bahrs too. Julius is apt to love me
to death most any time—comes over two or three times a week. Joe
doesn't come quite so often. Grant swears by all thats good or bad that
when he went over to work at the barn Saturday that Joe was standing
on the porch talking to me and I was inside with the door shut talking
to him through the key hole.

Must close—Bachelor Bess

Dear Mother:—Well I belive it is about time I was writing yous. I
received my over-coat and qurt O.K. and meny thanks for them. I was
planning on riding Sandy back but when I got your letter saying Pete
had a mar[e] I changed my mind, didn't belive I could stand the ride
any way. Now I dont know when I will get back, it may be Xmas unless
yous wont me back for some reason, then let me know at once. I kind
of wont to go back to Minn.—to pick corn[.] They say the corn is awful
good this year, pay 6 & 7¢ cents and help is scarce. Howard [Speer]
leaves to day, for there. I have been working for a fellow that use to
live there, he is Rob Jannings. his father is going back to[o]. I worked
for Rob 9 days already, I came home Monday morning sick and been
feeling pritty tuff since till to day I feel a lot better. Bess had a lame
back last night and this morning. She got your letter several days ago.
My thats good a bout that insurance, that makes me out of debt.[1] So
the kids are looking for me any time but I'm afraid they will have to
keep on looking for some time yet. I wonted to work a week longer at
Robs yet be fore I leave here[.]

Say! that stock food man that was on the train with me, up from
Winterset, [Iowa,] said that done there where the Corlia [Cholera] was
so bad, that on still nights the air was full of solpher that the farmers
was burning around the hog-pens and sheads.

Rob might use some of it to. Well guess I had better quit. Hope
this finds every body well, with Love

from Fuller.

Fuller Corey on his mount at the dam constructed on his homestead, claim shack in background, ca. 1913. Photo by Elizabeth Corey.

ADDED BY ELIZABETH COREY:

My back is all right—(Plague take that pen anyway)—now.[2] Went out to dig a bucket of potatoes and they're so large you know and I threw out a whopper and dislocated three of the lumbar vertabrae—pretty near—I could hardly navagate last night and today.

I went to town last Sat. and paid a few of my debts—just a few. Lumber, coal, brick, store bills, plasterboard and dam work counts up. Mae says Grant says he dont see how the devil I'll ever make out. I told her I was sure the money would get here when I had to have it. I could almost have shouted when I read your letter.[3] I would seem almost mean to take that money still theres fifty dollars due on the cows Dec 1st and no show as yet of raising the mon by that time. Was in hopes Rob would get a chance to sell that saddle. Which one of the cows shall I say you gave me? Betty[,] Bobs or Biddy? Betty is a little red cow, Bobs is a middle sized black cow and Biddy is the great big red cow.

Had to wear slit skirts on my left arm this week—pretty near. Last Saturday morning was going to drive Nell over to Stones and go to town with Grant. When I went to harness that little imp she tried to throw me in the manger[.] She took hold right on the shoulder—

seemed like she hit every nerve from my neck to my hip on that side. Could hardly bridle her afterward and when I got her hitched up I sure didn't let her waste much time on the road. I "talked to" her "real hard" and I dont think she will do so any more. Grant says no matter how gentle a mare is she's cranky this time of year if she's with foal[.]

The Speer young folks and Ada [Hoisington] spent one evening here and Ada and Howard [Speer] were here again last evening.

Potatoes are 75¢ per bushel here. Think I'll buy some of Stones[.]

Got an order for another dozen pictures the other day. If I dont get the Hypo pretty soon I'll never get caught up.

I cant have the house plastered till spring as it'll be so late when Grant gets to it. The plasterboard will make it warm though. Must close[.]

Lovingly your
Bachelor Bess

* FROM FULLER COREY
OCT. 24, 1913 / FORT PIERRE, SO. DAK.
TO MRS. M. M. COREY

Dear Mother:—Will Im here yet. I worked Monday and Tuesday for Rob Jannings[.] I got *romitism* in the calf of my right leg so I can't hardly get around and my stomach is pritty baddly out of whack, I rode Sandy to town yesterday and got me some medicine. I'm a going to have to leave here as soon as I can and never come back, cause its to hard to get away from here. Bess had some bad luck Monday. Nell lost her colt, dont know what was the cause of it. Grant thought it was something she eat. I see Sandy was some lame this morning, he has a cracked hoof so would have to get him shod if I use him. I would like to bring him back yet, if things would be a little more in my favor, but seem as though things were against it. I haven't cashed your check yet and hope I wont have to unless I have some doctor bill to pay. I havent seen the doctor but expect to tomorrow. I suppose the boys are picking corn by this time. I'm affraid I'm a going to lose out on that, I was hopeing I would earn enough money picking corn to go south this winter. Hope this finds yous all well.

With Love from Fuller.

ADDED BY ELIZABETH COREY, ON OCT. 25, 1913

Dear Ma,—was going to write you some but Ada is here for over Sunday and the house is all torn up and I dont know where Im at.

Nell is looking pretty good again and this second buggy will last about a week yet then the third buggy auto last about a month then I think I shall ride.

Instead of Donahue leaving some of the gates open after he got the feed up he strung up another that makes six gates—Trust an Irishman—

B.B.

❋ NOV. 14, 1913 / FORT PIERRE, SO. DAK.
TO MRS. M. M. COREY

Dear Ma, I haven't your letter here but will write any way.

Suppose you have heard from Fuller ere this. He left here Tuesday the 4th with Sandy for Valley Springs.[1] Have had one card from him. He was then waiting for the boat at Occoma[2] or some such burg.

I wonder when I wrote last and if I mentioned the little neighborhood broil we all had a while back. One week Fuller went to work for Jennings and said he didn't expect to be home the next Sunday and Ada promised to spend Saturday and Sunday with me. Fuller came down with rhuematism and came home the middle of the week. Ada came any way. None of us thot anything. Why should we? But "papa Billy" [Speer] took the trouble to tell Harold [Speer] that Ada had gone over to spend Saturday and Sunday with Fuller. Then the Dutch was to pay. Harold came over Sunday. And that wasn't enough. He and his ma came up the next day and worked the neighborhood over a little. I missed it all but a little word battle with Harold. Guess he'll get over it but he'll never look like any thing. When Fuller got the straight of it he was right fuzzy. He went down to see "Papa Billy" the next day. Neither of us have been near the Speer tribe since. Stones were worked up over it too. The evening before Fuller went away they had Ada up for over night and Fuller for the evening.[3] Dont think Speers or Hoisingtons know any thing about it.

A week ago this morning I went to feed Nell about six o'clock and found I had no more driving horse than the man in the moon. Halter rope was there and snap unbroken. I was skeered. I had to wait till day light before I could do anything. It was awful dark and several heavy showers fell. As soon as I could see I hustled out. Found the little wretch feeding in a draw but didn't get her caught till after eight and then had a circus getting her hooked up.

Mrs Stone and I went to town Saturday. Mae had dentel work to be done and I had to attend the Institute meeting. Yes Stones got those slips[4] alright. Many thanks. They were awful busy at the time and so were we and every one thot some one else had written you. They were in splended shape. Mae put them in a pail of rain water down cellar till Grant had time to plant them and when they went for them some had sprouts most an inch long.

Well I auto close. It is snowing and blowing to beat the cars today and Weltha expects to go home with me tonight for over Sunday. (Oh Joy!?)

Guess I'll have the same kind of birthday I did four years ago.[5]

Will try to do better next time[.]

Yours

B.B.

❋ DEC. 5, 1913 / FORT PIERRE, SO. DAK.
TO MRS. M. M. COREY

Dear Ma,—Your letter received a week ago Sunday and I was so glad to hear from you. In spite of the bad news it contained it was about the best letter I ever had from you. Was glad to receive the birthday present too. It came when I was clear out of money.

Was over to Stones the day I got your letter and took some pictures of the horses. Most of them were good. (Will send you some under separate cover if I get to it.) Went home that evening and popped corn. The next evening I made cream cookies and Tuesday evening I made little pumpkin pies. The next day my school had their Thanksgiving program and luncheon. The children did very well and seemed to enjoy themselves. They helped me serve the lunch very nicely. I brought popcorn, cookies, little pies & pickles. Mrs. D[onahue] brought sandwitches, brown cookies and sour pickles. We made cocoa at the school house.

We invited the other school over and such a mix up! We were going to have our program the Friday after Thanksgiving and Ada

[Hoisington, the teacher] wrote me a note and asked me if we couldn't have it Wednesday as she had Thurs. & Friday off and was going home. So we changed it to Wed. Then she had a chance to go to a social Wed. eve (She is going with Ed Patrick) and didn't want to come over here for fear it would make her late so she fixed it so none of them got to come. Stones were awfully put out about it.

After the program I went over to Stones. They said Mr Brown had gone to town and I staid to supper and waited for the mail. He didn't get the mail but I rented him the claims for winter pasture. Got $20 for mine and $10 for Fullers, cash on the spot, and they take the stock out before grass starts in the spring. Mr. Stone thought that was pretty good as the hay was cut you know. It got so late I just staid all night and went home the next day.

Stanton came over that afternoon and staid all night with me. He thot he had the time of his life sleeping upstairs and using the flashlight (Was afraid he'd upset a lamp up there)[.]

I went over to Stones late Fri. eve so as to be there early Sat morning to go to town. Spent a long hard day in town. We got home late and so tired.

Sunday Mrs Stone had her Thanksgiving dinner. I helped her get it ready. Also helped get supper and waited on the table. About the time the rest started to leave it began to rain and I hadn't had my supper yet so I staid all night. It has been raining off and on ever since. When it wasn't raining there was fog so thick you could cut it with a knife almost. I got to school Monday morning and didn't get home again till last evening and then it was a fright. It has tried hard to clear off today. There has been a faint gleam of sun shine two or three times.

I got a couple of woolen union suits the other day and a heavy knit woolen cap. Did I tell you what I'm wearing for waists? Mens heavy woolen shirts. I cut them off and belted them. No one would dream they were not ladies waists and they are so much warmer. I have a gray one that was a little too small for Delbert Stone and a brown one I sent for. When it gets cold and I wear sweater and leggings that will make three layers of wool all over me. I've sent for five pair of wool stockings.

Its too bad Ethel has such a boarding place. I know just what its like. I fancy there is a nerve strain more tireing than the work, too.

Aunt Jennie was the only relative I heard from on my birthday but I didn't mind it so very much for I got cards and letters from several friends.

Did you know I was hearing from "Sammy"[1] again? He had been sending me the "Christian Herald." He just puts it back in the wrapper and places the stamp over his name. Once the stamp came off and Mr Stone has been roasting me ever since about "Knute" as he calls him. Such things travel. Not long ago some one was asking Mrs Stone about it. Sure now there is "a man."

Must close. Will enclose a bill of lading. Grant shipped Fuller's box.

The wind howls as though it was getting awful cold. Have my foot stone on warming so I wont get cold going home.

> Hastily yours
> Bachelor Bess.

Many thanks for the birthday present.

* DEC. 10, 1913 / FORT PIERRE, SO. DAK.
TO MRS. M. M. COREY

Dear Ma,—Yours received. Many, many thanks. You dont know how welcome that check was. It enabled me (with my months wages) to pay the note ($51.15), the balance of what I owed Grant, what I owed Mae and quite a payment on the lumber bill. Next months wages will finish my lumber and coal bill if I let the store bills wait, I think, so I'm coming out fine[.] Betty the little red cow is the one "My mamma gave me" as I hope to sell the black cow soon—(she isn't exactly what I want to *keep*) and that price wouldn't pay for the other one as she is a great big one—the best of the three. The little one is a good one though.

My school is small but my Xmas work is *heavy* and with my sewing and the little extras that will creep in I am almost overwhelmed so please dont be disapointed if you dont hear much from me for several weeks.

I cant do anything in the line of gifts this Xmas but will surely get some post cards off to you all.

Saw George [Jones?] last eve. He wanted to come over Sunday—. I told him I was going to be at Stones. He said he would go over there then he said he wanted me to take his picture again.

Woodwards want me to come down and take the baby and some other things. Taylors have wanted me to come over there and take some pictures ever since school began[.] Guess I could keep the camera busy for a spell if I had time. They say photography is such a nerve strain that it drives the average photograper to drink and after my *very* limited experience I believe it. Tho it is as facinating as ever to me.

I stopped at the Stones this eve and fell as near down cellar as I could get. Haven't undressed yet to discover to what extent I am damaged but I know its some. I was saying how tired I was and how I'd sleep tonight and Weltha said "Yes and when you fall into that deep sleep maybe the Lord will take one of your ribs and make a man of it for you[.]" I asked her if she thot it was time the Lord took pity on me and she said something to the effect that she thought it time some body did. They all think its too hard—this batching and teaching. But how was that for the speech of an eight year old? Isn't she "the limit"?

Has Fuller got there yet? He must have started over a week ago. I had a card from him Sunday but forgot what day he started.

Mr Donahue thinks Rob's hogs had anthrax. The papers say it is raging from coast to coast. It takes mostly young stock but seldom touches horses and cattle from September till spring. Takes hogs any time of the year. Mr. D[onahue] said if he was Rob he'd vaccinate *everything* before spring.

Must close[.]

Lovingly—Bess

❋ DEC. 14. 1913 / FORT PIERRE, SO. DAK.
TO MRS. M. M. COREY

Dear Ma, Yours received with check for eight dollars. Many thanks to you and Rob. Things are certainly coming my way. I surely am not howling about my luck—not yet—only eight school days before Xmas and only four days yet I couldn't make it on account of the weather.

Will enclose another picture of Ethel—think its a little better than the one I sent her but there is still room for improvment. Will try some of those others when I have material and time. Yes will try and get those extras in and any extras the rest wish if you mention which.

Fright about Rorbeck wasn't it? [1]

Well now if you was some kid I might advise you not to make eyes at any Pat, Mike or Terklesen [2] that came along but seeing you're my mother you have the advantage of years and experience and must know a lot more about the business than I do and if you prefer double harness I reckon its your risk. I guess if *I* made up my mind to get married "He she nor it" couldn't stop me. Wouldn't think Ethel would say anything. Last summer she told how fast she'd land Sammy and his mon, if I'd bait the hook.

By the way I got the killingest dutch card last eve. It says "Ven mine girl goes mit odder fellers, Himmel! How dat makes me chealous" And George coming up today made it look as if some one must have had a "hunch" there was something up.

Its too bad about that ditch. Hope you're kicking hard enough. Grant thinks it should have been $3500 or $5000 to make sure of what you want.[3]

Friday afternoon a car passed the school house (we thot) and a few minutes later there was a knock. It was [Clarence] Coyne. He motioned for me to step out side and asked if any one had stayed in the school house the night before. They were "after a man" and had traced him that far they thot. Havent heard yet if they got him and Grant said there was no sign of either Coyne or Norman[4] in town Sat. Am a little anxious, of course, as I'm here alone and Nell might look good to him if he's lurking about.

Mae made up her mind to go to town with Grant yesterday and left me with the pebbles. They were *just as good as they could be* but I didn't get such an awful lot of sewing done.

The Donahue tribe were at Stones today. I told them what you said about the vacation and they never said a word.

Henry Reese, John Stroup[5] and George [Jones] rode into the yard. George staid and the other two went on to hunt rabbits. Mr Reese came back after dinner and with Mr Stone and Mr Donahue looking on—(The three worst torments that ever lived) George and I hardly opened our mouths[.] After dinner I was trying to take out the extra table leaves to make more room. George jumped up and came to help me. The men all stopped talking and looked at each other and grinned. A few minutes later when I was ready to move the table back I caught hold one side and looked at George and he came and helped me move it back. That was too much for Grant. He said "Gosh!! Got him trained already?" And turning to the others he said "See that? She just looks at him and he jumps." And after that they just kept something going all the time.

Am sorry about Aunt Hat's and Aunt Rate's poor health.

It was Fuller and Ada on the barn[6] but I didn't think it at all nec-

"My barn is nearing completion," wrote Bess in 1913 when she snapped this photograph of Fuller Corey and Ada Hoisington (wearing straw sailor) nailing tarpaper on the roof. Photo by Elizabeth Corey.

essary to ruin the reputation of both of them by publishing the fact. I knew Iowa people would recognize my hat.

I haven't that box yet but it must be in town by this time. I can hardly wait to get it. You don't need to think of that bath robe. I think I have a pretty good Xmas already and *I* have so little to give. You didn't mention popcorn in the box, but I wont cry if there is a little, for mine isn't holding out very well. I never cared much for it before but am just crazy about it this winter.

If you cant get that blue edged ware for Ethels room just take an extra one gallon jar and paint a blue streak around the top. I've got one like that. It's fine.

Mamma, its funny but you and Stones worry more over my debts than I do. I always say "By the time they're due I'll have the money." They had to admit that always had been true in my case but Grant couldn't see "where the devil it would come from *this* time[.]" I said I didn't know but it would be here when I needed it I was sure. I believe my faith exasperated him a little but the rent from the claims and these last two checks prove it. Last night when he caught a glimpse of the check he said "H——! I wish I'd known that was in there![")

Fuller must be there by now.[7]

Must close as it is almost midnight and I must be up at five o'clock.

Lovingly yours—Bess

* JAN. 2, 1914 / FORT PIERRE, SO. DAK.
  TO MRS. M. M. COREY

Dear Ma,—Wonder how you're all making it. Am going to try to write a few lines but don't know how I'll make out.

That box came the Sunday before Xmas and I was so glad to get it. I dont know what I enjoyed most. I received a card the other day saying there was an express package there for me—prepaid. Wonder what it is and who its from.

Our Xmas pie was quite a success. Mr Stone with three of his youngsters and three of Speers were there beside the Donahue bunch. It was very cold and stormy but they all seemed to feel paid for coming. That evening I went up to Stones for supper and went to the tree with them. The next morning I discovered I had left my bill for wages at the school house and thot I'd go over after it while Nell was hitched up. Donahues came out and insisted on my stopping to dinner so I did tho I was not dressed for it. I didn't get home very early that night and slept till the middle of the forenoon the next day. Then I got a batch of mail ready to send and took it over to Stones. On the way home I stopped for Fan and she went over to spend Saturday and Sunday with me. We had lots of fun. Saturday eve we went over to Stones for the mail. Got a card from Lydia urging me to come over to spend New Years Day. I worked around home Monday and Tuesday and came over here Wednesday to Taylors. Stopped at Stones on the way over here[.] Mrs Stone was in bed. She did the washing Monday with the childrens help. She dipped the water from the barrels and carried it in and I guess thats what did the damage. She was feeling pretty good then but will keep quiet for a week or so yet. Grant was doing the ironing—finished while I was there. I never offered to help him.

Lydia has to leave for Weta[1] this afternoon and I'm going to take her down [to catch the train at Teton].

I got quite a lot of Xmas presents—a box of stationery,[2] a turkish towel, a holder, a book mark, four handkerchieves—all from different people and all exactly alike. Wasn't that funny? They are *very* nice ones.

Yes—will write Aunt Jen about the organ today.[3] I can pay her when I draw my next months wages. I know its a good organ but not worth that much as organs go now. You can get the best organ in a piano case thats made for between sixty and seventy dollars. And you can play anything on those that you could play on a piano.

If those pictures I sent don't all go in together just write me the ones you want and I'll print them off for you.

Must close & get dinner as every one is so busy. Mrs Taylor said I might.

There is a dress maker here for a few days. She began on me first and I've sure shown her the time of her life[.]

Lovingly yours
Bachelor Bess

P.S. Tell Ethel I rec'd the tie. Many thanks. Have wished several times in the last six months I had one of those.

P.S. Tell Fuller that Mr. K[rug] sent me a "Christian Herold Almanac" and Arch Scripter asked me to go to the dance New Years Eve but I declined and oh—lots of things.

* JAN. 23, 1914 / FORT PIERRE, SO. DAK.
  TO MRS. M. M. COREY

Dear Ma,—Yours and Fullers received to night—also one from Dolma. Was glad to hear from you. Yes the organ is for Ethels birthday. I told Fuller. Suppose you will get his letter the same time as you get this—Open it if you want to he wont care.

I walked both ways Monday but Tuesday eve there was such a cold sharp wind from the north west I could hardly face it so staid at Donahues. Walked home Wednesday eve—staid at D's again last night and came over to Stones tonight[.]

Have been feeling pretty good and am going to drive next week. I can use my left hand to help the right but there doesn't seem to be much strength in it as yet. You'll have to excuse this writing as the children are playing cards and the table isn't very steady. I can breath alright now any way.

Have been learning how to do tatting the last few days—don't have to use my left hand for that to—speak of. Had some patterns Mrs Taylor made for me and have made some little bits with coarse thread of the plain edging, insertion and "hook & eye[.]" Have run a white thread in to give you an idea of how they can be joined to make lace. I'd like to make enough of it of fine thread to trim a white voile dress next summer but have so many irons in the fire.[1]

Have some duds to fix and extra reading to do. They've started a county school paper and Warner has asked me to write and oh gee!!!

Yes I'm pretty well fixed financially. Have most of my little bills paid except a ten or twelve dollar store bill and that organ and a note for $176.00 and int. due in a couple of months and a few papers and *sich*. I haven't said anything to Grant yet about the work but reckon it will be O.K.

It'll take all this month's wages for the organ and little bills. Would the first of March be soon enough for Fuller or shall I have 'em make the mortgage twenty-five more?

Tell Fuller that Reeses have twins—a boy and girl[2]—arrived Tuesday morning. Didn't get the addition on to their house any too soon. That makes six children living and the eldest just started in school.

One of the girls wrote right away after that party at Corey's so I heard about it about New Years time.

Mae is pretty well now but Grant is still doing the heavy work.

Well I must close. Say what time next summer are you planning to come out. Would like to know so I can make my plans you know.

Yours—Bachelor Bess

✳ FEB. 14, 1914 / FORT PIERRE, SO. DAK.
TO MRS. M. M. COREY

Dear Ma, Goodness knows when I wrote last or when I will get to mail another so will try a few lines. Yours rec'd Thurs evening. Was glad to hear from you. Hope you are better. Dont try to write till your able—just have the kids write once in a while. Please tell Paulie I will send him some drawings as soon as I can get them and get them ready and some other school work which I'd like to have him notice. Was so glad to hear from the boys. Will write them later[.] Am sending Chall a [photographic postal] card but the negative is so marred it isn't *very* good.

Plague take that ground hog! We had such swell weather—was as warm as spring. The last day of Jan they were worrying over not having any ice. The river seemed going out and they say if the ice goes out before the 10th of Feb it doesnt freeze again. But thet ground hog settled that. He put his nose out just the wrong time. Then it kept getting colder and colder till the night of the 4th then we had a howling blizzard[;] it lasted all day the next day and the following day (Friday) I made it to school tho few did. The cold was intense. Grant froze his nose and toes just going to the barn. I made my twelve miles that Friday and only frosted my feet. Saturday was a fright again but it moderated a little and I made it to school O.K. We had another howling storm all day Wed so I staid at Donahues that night. Staid again Friday night in hopes that I could get to town yesterday with Mr D but it stormed to beat the [railroad] cars yesterday and is at it today. They are out of groceries and coal so Mr D is going to try to make it in this afternoon and out tomorrow but its fierce. Thot I'd let you know I was O.K. and wont try to drive till its better.

Have been as lucky as usual. Just think! Never stuck in a drift once and only driving one horse while others have had to dig a lot.

Could Ethel or one of the boys write Aunt Jen a note to tell her I cant get my warrent till the weather changes—am afraid she'll think I'm a fright but I haven't time to write her now.

Am sending Fuller his pictures—am sorry they are not better—they are the poorest I ever put out but those first negatives are fading—guess I took them out of the fixing bath too soon. If there are any he can't use tell him to let me know and I'll replace them. I printed more than five dozen a week ago last eve then had to set up all night to keep them from freezing. Gee! that was fun. But have all orders filled up to date. Am sending a clipping.[1] If you or Fuller dont want it please save it for me. It reminds me of "The Long Ago."

Tell Fuller I don't know about Stones. He better go a little slow. Mae is always telling Grant some thing and she couldn't tell any thing straight on a bet. I've heard her tell him a few when I was there and had gone to bed. She said Grant was "awful sore" because Fuller made that suggestion about paying for the buildings. I asked her "why?" and she didn't know but that Grant was kind of funny about such things. Mae has surely been queer lately. You know I had a time with Weltha the last time she was over to my house and I suppose May thinks I'm "not nice enough to her" as she said of Ada. Weltha told Speers all about Fuller and Ada corresponding and May talked to her "just as hard as she could with out scolding the child[.]" Weltha brags that she "can do any thing and ma won't lick me if I just tell her the truth."

May wanted me to stay with the kids while they went down to Deans for the day yet when Weltha calls me an "old hog" and says she wishes I'd go home as she is too crowded when I'm there, May says I've no right to pay any attention to it as I probably said things just as bad as when I was a kid. Had a notion to tell her that my mother didnt laugh about it when I did.

George [Jones] sent word he was coming over today and Reeses and Donahues are having caniptions about it. Seems like I cant make a hit with any but a Dutchman and they're all ages from kids to grandads.

Tell Fuller that Basil Carlisle died[2] the day his mother returned from the hospital. He seemed to recognize her once. They said he died fighting. They had Coyne and two other men there to hold him that last day. *We* have lots to be thankful for.

Did I tell Fuller that Ben Sylva's have twins. Mighty busy stork this winter.

Well I must close. Dont worry about me.

Lovingly yours
Bachelor Bess

* MAR. 8, 1914 / FORT PIERRE, SO. DAK.
  TO MRS. M. M. COREY

Dear Ma,—Will write a little and if Mr Donahue goes to town to-morrow, as he planned, perhaps you will get it by your birthday.

The weather was just awful all through February. The past week has been regular March weather—windy and raw. The snow is going fast but there is lots to go yet. The roads are just a fright between here and town. From the foot of the big hill they say the mud is eight or ten inches deep. Its almost death to a team. I wanted to go in yesterday so drove up to Stones after school Friday to see if Mr Stone was going. Mr Stone couldn't make up his mind till Saturday and there wasn't room for Nell in the barn unless he turned some of his stock out so I came on home and gave it up.

I don't know what ails Stones. Mrs Stone acts just like Fern[1] did that Sunday the Sunday School class was at your place. She goes out

Sometimes only a horse could haul an auto through the South Dakota gumbo. Photo courtesy Bud Gould.

to help feed the calves and makes the kids stay in the house and such things as that when I'm there and she never used to. She doesn't think Grant charges me enough for work. I paid him up last week and when something was said about the smallness of the bill he said I over paid him something over $3 last time. Some times when she is telling me something he is going to do he'll fly all to pieces and declare he isn't going to do anything of the sort. She says she can't depend on him at all any more and I could almost swear I've smelled whisky on his breath more than once tho I've never mentioned it to any one but Fuller. Mr Donahue said something that sounded as tho he *knew* Mr Stone drank. I'm afraid to go to Stones and afraid to stay away. I feel all the while as if a bomb were going to burst—different from any thing yet. I feel so alone now Fuller is gone for good.

Tell Fuller his gum is on the nail where he left it but its getting kind of dusty now.

Ada writes her letters down at Speers now and they manage to read as she writes. Jennie was telling Mrs Stone something she wrote Fuller. Ada and Ed Patrick have had a smash.[2] Her mamma put a stop to it. She also put a stop to Harold's taking Maggie S[peer].

Mrs Donahue is quite miserable[.]³ I've been helping her some with her sewing so haven't had time to read or write, hardly, for a long while.

Yesterday I washed and today I finished cleaning my barn. The first time its been cleaned since before my shoulder was hurt. I'm awful tired tonight[.] Tell Fuller the Bertram bunch left for the Ozarks Wednesday.

My! This is a horrid letter. I guess I feel kind of punk.

I must write Fuller and Chall soon. I surely enjoy their letters. I wonder if I owe Ethel a letter. Tell her she can send for her organ any time.

Don't mention paying for those post cards. I wrote you a check Oct 8th but have never torn it from my check book for fear of over checking.

Wishing you many happy birthdays

I am Lovingly your
Bachelor Bess

✳ MAR. 22, 1914 / FORT PIERRE, SO. DAK.
TO MRS. M. M. COREY

Dear Ma,—It seems a coons age since I wrote to you.

Gee! such weather! Last Friday it stormed again—all day. Mr D came over to the school house [on] horse back for fear we would be afraid to start out. Am here at Donahues yet—guess the roads are not so awful bad but I havent been home yet. I made a dress for Mary [Donahue] yesterday—got it all done but buttons and finishing the seams you know.

I got my warrent Thursday so of course it had to storm so I couldn't go to town Saturday.

Am sorry you are so miserable. Just wish you would plan on coming out here when school is out—my school I mean—for a few weeks. Our Institute begins about June 15th. They expect a six weeks term and I should like to attend even if I have to make the mortgage larger. If you could come out the first week in May and stay till the middle of June I'm sure you'd get rested up good. When is Ethels school out? Well it don't make much difference any way. I'm sure they could get along. I'll send you the mon if you'll come. I don't think I'll be in debt more than $100 when school is out and I can work for a few weeks after institute if its necessary.[1]

If the weather is at all fit I should like to go to the Co[unty] School Exhibit at Midland next Friday—will have to go on Thursday if I go.

Tell Fuller "The Constable" thinks I'm a "mighty fine girl" and things are apt to be interesting.

Did I tell you folks how Mary [Donahue] started to ride Nell after the cows and the excitement that followed? Mary begs me to "don't tell Paul[.]"

The other evening little Tom [Donahue] pulled off his shoes and stockings before supper. At table the cat climbed up to get the crumbs and scratched his feet. Of course he let out a yell then he said "Ditty 'ants toe jam[.]" Then how he did laugh.

Wonder if I told you how little Lena Reese looked me all over and then said "Why you got wed hair like us has[.]" She always calls herself "us" and her hair would put the sun in the shade.

I'm not in the mood for writing tonight so will close and try to do better next time.

Lovingly yours
Bachelor Bess

**✳ APR. 5, 1914 / FORT PIERRE, SO. DAK.
TO MRS. M. M. COREY**

Dear Ma, Yours rec'd a few minutes ago—first I've heard from you for so long. Its kind of awful about Fuller but as Rob says we can pray and have faith. Am sure he will get along nicely.

Well about me—I went to Midland—started from Donahues Thurs morning a week ago and drove in—stopped at Mrs Taylors and she rode in with me—went right to the Supt's office and Mr Mendenhall phoned to Pierre for the mounting board for the rest of my school work. They couldnt sent it till the five oclock train. I went down to Mrs Normans and she was just getting ready to go to the goodbye party they were giving to Mrs Fergeson and I hadn't been to any of the lodge doings for so long I went too. Had a fine time—got back to the post office just in time to get the mounting board before it closed at seven. Went down to Normans and after John[1] and I got the dishes done we tagged and mounted the rest of the school work. I finished about eleven. Got to bed about twelve and got up at two to catch that train but was taken very sick—dont know what ailed me—but missed the train—went back to bed at three and got up at six to catch the freight. Caught it but they had on bridge timbers, sand and stock that had to be unloaded along the road—so we didn't get there till twenty after eleven. I didn't mind it much for I got in with a jolly bunch from Van Metre and had a good time. It was a very busy day. Heard lectures by Gov Byrne,[2] State Supt of Public Instruction Lawrence,[3] Hon Wagner and Jefferies and attended the reception and caught the night train back. My pupils won three prizes and after the work had been looked over the bunch from Van Metre informed me that they were a school board and their wives. They wanted to hire me for next year. I told them I would prove up this summer if nothing happened and would teach next year where I could get the most mon. One of them said "Well we'll pay more than the other fellows[.]" When they asked what I wanted I said $6o and no discount. They wanted to draw up the contract but I said wait a couple of weeks. Some how—I dont know why—but I had the feeling that I'd never go there to teach. I still feel that way but am going to write for them to send the contract as soon as possible.

When I got back to Ft Pierre I went right to the hotel and went to roost—it was a quarter of four in the morning. I didn't get up till a quarter of eleven Saturday. I did my shopping and saw to a lot of business then went down to Gordons. Daddy K[rug] was there. It was so muddy I thot I'd stay over and drive out Sunday morning when it was frozen a little. That night we went to the show and after the show I ran off and went up to Carlisles[4] alone. Flagg walked down with me. I don't know how Mr K liked it. Sunday morning it was sticky as the mischief—hadn't frozen a bit so I thought I'd drive out to Taylors and stay over night and go on from there Monday morning. Mrs G[ordon] wanted me to wait till after noon. When after noon came both the men were gone. Mr G went up town at breakfast time (he's drinking hard again) about noon Mr K went up to round him up I guess. Mrs G was taken with one of her bad spells and I didn't want to leave till some one came. Mr K came about five o'clock and I phoned down for my horse. I was rather surprised to find that Roy Norman had her out for a drive. It was half past five oclock before I got him located so I waited and drove out Monday morning. There was a very heavey fog Monday morning and I had to angle across a piece of prairie for two or three miles with no trail to speak of and about the time I thot I was accross I came out just where I started. It was ten o'clock when I got to school.

Friday about half past one Mrs Donahue and the little ones came over to the school house. Mr D had gone over to Reeses in the morning and she was taken sick shortly after he went. When he didn't get back to dinner she knew he wouldn't be back till night. (That darned man is always gone when he's wanted)[.] I hitched up—sent the children home—took Mrs D home and hit the high places for Reeses. I sure took the hills on high. Mr Reese took Donahues team and went for Mrs Wendbourne[.] [5] I guess he didn't spare the whip. Mrs Speer said he "Was fanning them horses tails all the time[.]" Mr D went back with me. It was less than an hour from the time I took Nell out of the school house barn till she was back in Donahues barn. Mrs D was *awful* sick. By six oclock another red headed Irishman was complaining about the hard times in this country.

Mrs D is still bad off and Mrs Wenbourne is to take her husband to town Tuesday to be operated on for appendicitis so she has to go home to-morrow. They cant get a girl so I told Mr D this morning I'd take two weeks vacation and stay with them. He said he'd be "tickled to death" if I would and he certainly looked relieved.

I was to have gone to a dance Friday night but of course didn't. I'm at Stones to night. I started over to the claim after supper and came this way to get the mail. They had your letter and card and Aunt Jennies card. They were almost wild to know more—they had read the cards. They didn't know if I was at Woottens, Donahues or my place but Grant would have brought them over to my school house in the morning if I hadn't put in appearance.

Should you wish to wire me any time in the next few months send it in care of *Horace Dean* and they'll get it to me as soon as possible.

I ordered a bunch of flowers sent you last week for a birthday present—it was late I know for that but some how I got a notion you wanted them. I hope they reached you O K[.] If Rob is up you'll send part of them to Fuller[.]

Will hold twenty five dollars in the bank so if you want me, whistle[.] My hands will be so full these next two weeks don't be surprised if I don't write.

Let me know as soon as possible how all are. Every one around here will work to get my mail to me quick.

It is late—must close tho there is a world to write[.]

God be with you all till we meet agin—Bess

✻ JUNE 8, 1914 / FT. PIERRE, SO. DAK.
TO H. FULLER COREY

Dear Brother,—Was so glad to get your card the week before school closed. I could just put my whole mind on my work after that and I surely needed to too. We found that the whole country around seemed to be planning on attending our picnic and there was the program, exams, final reports, the dinner and I had to make a dress for Katheryn.[1] We got all ready then the night before it just rained to beat the cars[2]—the roads were almost impassable in places and it was still raining in the morning. I had a hunch that some thing was going to happen so took all my stuff the morning before and staid at Donahues that night so there were Reeses, Stroups, Donahues and myself. I never saw so big a dinner for such a crowd. They all seemed to enjoy themselves. I staid that night at D—— and went home Sunday afternoon. Oh I didn't tell you that the Sat before school closed I let Speers work Nell because they thot they were so short of horses. They just kept her over and worked her all day Sunday so I dont owe them any thing for the horse they loaned me that day last fall. Well—the girls brought her home between eight and nine Sunday evening and I drove over to Stones for the mail. The end of the flashlight stuck so I took it along for Grant to re load for me. We broke the contact which left me out of a light. Mrs Stone insisted on my taking the lantern for fear I might run on to a snake. Well I didn't meet a snake that night but the next morning bright and early I killed a big one out south east of the house[.] Suppose if he had happened along the night before it might have been the finish of Bessie. That same Monday Grant was over there and killed two more in my garden and the week after school was out I killed one just accross the breaking north west of the house.

The Monday after school closed Mae, Fred, Blanche [Stone] and I went down to Scripters after my seed-corn and drove Kate and Nell. When we were coming home I killed two rattlers between Speers school house and Stones. We didn't have a snake stick so I pulled up one of Brother Billy's posts and kicked the wires off. Mae said she would never have dared to kill them they fought so.

Weltha went home with me and staid over till the next night then she got home sick and I had to hitch up and take her home again. It was so late that I staid the rest of the night at Stones and the next day the whole family went over. Grant put in the corn and after dinner the rest of us went over to see the Wenbourne's. Had a fine time. The next day Myrtle [Stone] came over with her father and staid over till Friday eve. I went over with her and drove Doll[3] back. Saturday I wrote twelve *important* business letters and put in the rest of my garden stuff. Sunday Mrs Sheldonne—Florence Scripter and her baby and Fern and Arch [Scripter] were up for the day. Monday Mrs Wendbourne, Mrs Kole from Pierre who was visiting her, and myself went down to spend the day at Clarence Rovangs on the Sonnenschein Ranch.[4] We had a fine time and took several pictures. That evening I took Doll home so Grant could use her on the disk and killed a great big buzzer on the way. Thats the seventh this spring. Will send you the "trimmin's."[5]

Tuesday I did a big washing and Wednesday, Thursday and Friday I was ironing and mending and getting packed for institute. It rained *hard* Wed. Thurs. and Fri. nights and Friday night the big railroad dam went out—the whole middle of it. Looks like you could set a shack in the hole it cut.

Grant brought me down Saturday afternoon—had to come the long way and Grant staid over night. I have a room at Mrs Wherles and take my meals most any where. Dined with Miss Appleby Sunday and staid all night with her. She is not coming back here next year. She told me some of the nice things Prof. Beckler has said about me as a teacher. Makes me feel good and also accounts for his treating me so nicely.

Institute began today. We recite from 8:30 in the morning till 12 and from 1:15 til 4 in the afternoon and prepare our work outside. Am afraid I won't have any time for cussedness this four weeks.

The night little Katheryn when [sic] home with me she said "Miss Corey are you glad you put your place over here?" I asked her "Why?" and she said "Well I'm *not*. I wish you had put it over beside our place."

Oscar Walton is running the icewagon.[6] He said last night he was in hopes it would keep right on raining now as he was getting webfooted. But tonight he had changed his tune—said it didn't work.

Say my corn and garden sure look swell. The corn has mostly three and four stalks in the hill and Mr Wenbourne said he didn't see a missing hill.

There is no sale for land to speak of out here. I would not know what to offer. I have everything mortgaged for every dollar I can get on it and a personal note for $40 beside. I asked several what your place was worth and they said there was no land selling and they couldn't say. The only way you could get any thing out of it would be to try Oscar [Walton]s way—work some one to take a mortgage on it and let it go. It will pay you well to wait if you possibly can. Am sending you a check for $100 but I can't make it a cent more tho I wish I could. It will help a little any way. You don't need to worry about ever paying it back—play its a birthday present.

If my garden does well I'll make out O K. Will any way for I'm sure I can get a job for a few weeks any way if I need it.

Take the trip east by all means if you can—wish mamma could go too. It would do her so much good. Hope she is feeling better.

> Love to all
> Bachelor Bess

*** JULY 5, 1914 / FORT PIERRE, SO. DAK.
TO MRS. M. M. COREY**

Dear Ma, Will try to write a few lines, and later, in a week or so, when I'm on the claim once more perhaps I can write up everything.

Surely these past few weeks have been busy ones yet I've enjoyed every minute almost and have gained more than from all the rest of the institutes I've attended put together.

Did I tell you of the Dr. W. F. Jones[1] of the State University who was our instructor in Fundamental Principles of Teaching, Games, and Teaching Processes?

He is one of the noted Educators of today and he's simply great. He had with him part of those machines for taking physical and mental tests. I took the tests—came out *strong* in every thing but the fatigue test which was *bad* but he thot possibly sufficient sleep would soon bring me up to my norm. First I tried that machine that records the strength of your grip in pounds. Its a rare case when a woman grips a hundred pounds but I made it record 120 pounds. That was supposed to show strong mentality as well as physical ability. Dr Jones said "That means if you should marry it would be perfectly safe for you to take your husband by the collar should you ever wish so to do." There were only about half a dozen there when I took the test but in less than three days nearly every teacher from the two counties was addressing me as "Miss Corey" and every one in town seemed to know me. Wasn't as much fun as you might think either.

Dr Jones has spoken very nicely of me and my work to more than one. Miss Appleby (one of the Ft Pierre teachers you've heard me speak of) told me what he said at Co Supt Warners one evening when several callers were there. He told some one I was one of the best teachers in the two counties. At Warners he said "That Miss Corey is the best thing we have in the institute[.]" That isn't nearly all thats been said either and I've been offered four schools since I contracted. I want to teach this next year, now I've contracted, then I want to go to the University for a couple of years. If I'm going to stay with it I might as well get ready for big game.

MONDAY JULY 6—Institute closed last Friday and I've been here at Lydias since. Her beau from Weta[2] is here visiting and she wanted me to come out and help entertain. I'm sure doing my share. Yesterday one of Dave's shoes got to hurting so he pulled it off. In a few minutes he went out for a pail of water. Lydia suggested that he put his shoe on but he wouldn't bother so when no one was looking I put his shoe up on top of the organ out of sight. After a while he looked the house over for the shoe and accused Lydia of having it. At last he bet a pound of chocolates that she had hid it so I produced the shoe and this evening am eating my share of the chocolates—gee but they're good.

I've been up to lots of such tricks lately. I suppose they would interest Ethel more than the rest of you. There was one George Coler[3] who runs a resturant who came up to Mrs Werles (where we girls roomed) quite often—we had great times. Then there was Flagg Carlisle.[4] He's been keeping cases on me all summer and I've surely played him a bunch of tricks and between times I've kept Mrs Werle guessing.

Oh! I really must tell you I've invested 50¢ in a box of rice powder *and use it* when I'm going some where. It happened this way. You know here in town Im rather noted for my cheerful countenance and one day in class Dr Jones was giving us a lecture on morality. His definition for morality is "The will to work for the good of the race." He said the long faced, sanctimonious person was not always moral. To refrain from doing evil didn't amount [to] much if one *did no good.* At last he asked which they thot would influence him most for good if he were to go down town, and on his way meet two individuals—one a long faced solemn individual who evidently knew how good *he* was and how bad the world in general was, and the other one a person who fairly radiates cheerfulness and good-will from every pore—one who had a ready smile—one whose face is "fairly greasy with joy." The room was crowded and I was almost in the middle. The rest looked at me and then such a howl. Mrs Werle had been roasting [me] because I wouldn't use cream and powder and when she heard that she gave me no peace till I caved in.

We went to the dance out to the Dean School House[5] Saturday eve but it broke up at midnight so wasn't there long.

There's a lodge doin's tomorrow eve and Lydia and I hope to go out to my place Wednesday. When is Rob coming?

Love to all—more later.

Bachelor Bess

[P.S.] I surely wish you all were here.

* JULY 26, 1914 / FORT PIERRE, SO. DAK.
  TO MRS. M. M. COREY

Dear Ma and the rest,—Here goes for a good old write up—its Sunday eve about eight oclock and its al right till morning. I wonder what I've written and what I've not.

Perhaps some folks are born popular and others acquire it but the Lord knows I've had it thrust upon me. At first it was queer then,—being human, it was kind of pleasant, then it got old in a very short time and now it almost smells bad to me. It started with that exhibit at Midland and then Dr Jones *"There's teaching ability"* and *"There's wonderful teaching genius"* etc. and what he told outside was the finish. Of course my doing so well with those physical and mental tests helped some. At first—Oh! you cant imagine the satisfaction of feeling that these years of work had really counted. That I'd "Risen from the Ranks" in my profession. That I'd won the respect and friendship of those "higher up[.]" Some times I wished you were here— perhaps then you could see why it gets my goat to be where I have to ask "Please may I go with you?" most every time I want to go any where. And to feel that my very existence and presence was a burden to others. Then I began to get the other side—that was different. People who had looked over my head or turned up their noses at me before, began to remember "How much they'd always thot" of me. So many were introduced to me or introduced themselves, others assumed previous acquaintance—some thirty of them are still stranger-in-laws to me—I never found out their names. I over heard such remarks as "Sure its alright Miss Corey does" "Lets ask Miss Corey" and "Miss Corey said ———". I don't know how many came to me to know where I got my barefoot sandles assuring me with many apologies that they could not get them in Ft Pierre or Pierre. First I was surprised but I was so intensely interested in the work and so "full of the devil" (as Mrs Werle says) out side of school that it was not till I over heard a conversation, that I got next to what it all ment. Then the fun ended. A feeling of responsibility as big as a house settled down and nearly squashed me. For two or three days I tried to kind of keep out of sight. I never volunteered a recitation, I sat in the least conspicuous place in the room and all that, but it was no use—in fact it made it worse than ever. One instructor said "Wheres Miss Corey? She's a good authority on this." Another said "Miss Corey, what are you trying to hide for? Haven't you your lesson?" I was more conspicuous than ever—I'm so darned big any way. So after a day or two of intense misery I gave it up. Since then I've tried to act natural, make as few mistakes as possible, I have to be friendly with every-body to keep from "having the swelled head" and mix with it a little of the "thus far and no farther" to keep some where they belong.

The Thursday after the Fourth Dave,[1] Lydia and I went to town—crossed the river [to Pierre], and I had my feet measured and a pair of shoes ordered. The shoeman had knipshuns over my feet— there was over an inch dif[ference] in some of the measurements and over an eighth of an inch difference in the length. The *last* will have to be made for them and that's expensive but they wont cost so much after the first pair and any way the satisfaction will be worth it. You know it had just got to where I couldn't get a pair of shoes any where that fit at all. I went with Lydia to have her picture taken and on the spur of the moment sat for mine. I have quite a few new clothes—a white rice cloth dress made up with net and lace and a flowered crepe made up with Swiss embroidery but I had on that skirt and waist you like to see me wear so I dont care. The girls say its almost a perfect picture—that the position, the facial expression, the hands and all are so natural. It was a frightfully warm day and my waist was some what wilted and mussy but I suppose thats me too. That three cornered grin may be natural but be blamed if I admire it. This having a picture took is like sitting on the fence and watching your self go by. The bracelet is one Dave paid eight dollars for. He clasped it on my wrist before I had my picture taken. I'm still wearing it just to oblige him. It isn't safe to have such expensive junk laying around.

". . . my waist was some what wilted and mussy but I suppose thats me": Elizabeth Corey in 1914. Photo courtesy Paul Corey.

I never got out of town till Friday then I got out as far as Stones and the next day Myrtle and I went down to meet Ella Griffen.[2] We didn't get home till past midnight. The next day we went over to Stones to take the [break in letter here][3] . . . [letter continues:]—she didn't believe we had any out here—she'd been here three days and hadn't seen a one. I said perhaps the seven I killed before institute were the last seven and about that time there was a buzz and right in front of Ella was a black prairie rattler. Gee! you should have seen Ella then. She evidently thot it was her move. She left me to kill the snake.

Wednesday evening we were over to Stones. Wenbournes and

Speers were there. We had a fine time. Thursday eve we went with Wenbournes down to see Joe Bahr and his bride. I like her very much. She is a little chunk of a Dutch woman about your age and size. She understands some English but doesn't speak it. I can understand a little Dutch but dont speak it. She says she is coming to see me. Im sure we will get on famously. Joe told me that "Yulius he once like you putty goot but he no have nerve enough to come up to your shack and ask you would you marry him." And then Joe just laughed till he fell all over himself—the rest of us didn't(?)

Sunday we went to church and staid for the ball game. Miss [Faith] Hunt is here you know. She goes to China in Nov as So Dakota's Missionary[.] She is making a lecture tour of the state to gather funds for her expenses. She is here visiting Stones and I've heard her talk twice.

Monday, a week ago today, Marcus Texley[4] stopped here for a "nice cool drink" and I took his picture. I didn't mind that so much because Ella was here. I didn't invite him in tho. I noticed that he tried the screan door once but it was hooked. He has a claim over the other side of Wenbournes and I've been warned to never make him angry for they say he's a "perfect devil" when he gets angry and always carries a big knife in his belt. Ella went on Wednesday and on Thursday Tex was here again. I handed him out the pail and a glass and let him draw it himself. When he handed them back I took one in each hand and turned to set them on the table when quick as a flash he opened the door, walked in, planked himself down in a chair, and remarked that he thot he'd stay and rest a while. I said "oh bring your chair out on the porch where it is cooler" and picked up a chair and started for the door. He said it was plenty cool enough for him where he was, there in the doorway. For one awful minute I stood there waiting then he got up and let me pass and brought his chair along. Then I remembered that I had a bunch of pictures he might like to see. I got them for him and while he was busy with them I slipped inside, hooked the door and went to washing dishes. My! how I washed those dishes! When he tried to bring the pictures in he found the door hooked. He said "Here's your pictures[.]" I told him to just lay them down somewhere. He said they'd blow away and I told him to put some thing on them so they couldn't. He said he was afraid it would rain before he could get home. I told him I was afraid it would if he didn't hurry so at last he hurried. He was here again this morning. (Monday afternoon—I started writing last night you know) He ordered half a dozen pictures and paid for them. He wanted me to do his washing but I said "Oh my stars! No! I've got so much to do these few weeks before school begins I cant get it half done any way" So he went his way.

Guess I told you about the big rattler I killed in the barn when Ella was here. He was a buster and he fought to beat the band. I killed another up north of Stones when I came home from taking Ella down [to the train]. That makes ten for me since the middle of April.

Some of my garden didn't amount to much. Have had a mess of spinach, lots of onions and my first mess of potatoes. They are late potatoes and small yet but look good. The garden was put in late any way (The last week in May) I have lots of beets and the okra are in bloom—there are lots of them too. The tomatoes are loaded with blooms and little green ones. Most of the other vines are in bloom but some of them gave up the fight. The flea beetles took the tops of the turnips when the largest of them were about the size of a dollar.

I advertised to prove up on Paul's birthday and will make final proof Aug 22.[5] Aren't some of you coming up? Was in hopes Rob would get here soon, as I auto do some entertaining before then and it isn't easy with out a man around.

Where is Fuller? I had a card from him when he was at Uncle Grants[6]—he didn't say how long he'd be there or where he'd go next. I wish you'd send him some of this that you'd think would interest him and tell him to write.

Hope you are all well and having good weather. Its scoarching here and we need rain badly.

As ever
Bachelor Bess

* SEPT 21, 1914 / VAN METRE, S.D.
TO MRS. M. M. COREY (% C. D. BROWN, BOSWELL, INDIANA)[1]

Dear Ma and Paulie,—You card rec'd. Was not surprised. Had told Mrs Stone that you would go back east this summer but that you wouldn't come out here.

They wont let me prove up as I hadn't been on my claim enough. I'm kind of glad for I wont have to pay taxes.

This is my third week of school.[2] I'm very busy and will be all year. Have pupils from three different schools and two counties. Only two of them seem to know the work they've been over. Have six grades including the 9th. I put in the whole first day (with the help of directors and patrons) getting the school house ready to begin school in.

I was under the impression that there were very few men in this neck of the woods but I wasn't twenty four hours changing my mind. The country is fairly lousey with them. At first I had a notion to resign. I felt as though they had secured my contract under false pretenses but upon second thot I made up my mind that men were made to work and be worked so I got busy. Mr Andrew Seieroe[3] took me to the dance last Friday evening and I surely had a fine time. Mr S says that he will take me to Wendte [to catch the train] any Friday evening I wish to go to Ft Pierre and meet me there (at Wendte) Monday morning so watch my smoke.

I board with the Newlins[4] about a mile from the school house and across Bad River. They are a very young couple much opposed to dancing. They live in a two room shack that is 12 × 20 ft. They roost in the kitchen and I in the sitting room which is 7 × 12. Its like this

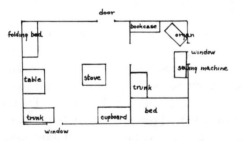

There are three chairs. And the organ stool for company. They are very jolly and I like them. They charge me the highest board I ever paid. I haven't had a good drink of water there yet. I sleep on a feather bed and feel its ribs every night before morning as there are only quilts between it and the slats. I go to Sunday School every Sunday and teach the young peoples class. The first Sunday Virgel Strunk,[5] who will be one of my ninth grade boys later on, came down and went to Sunday school with us and last Sunday Frederick Nordin' and his mother[6] came home with us to dinner and spent the afternoon. Frederick also expects to enter 9th grade soon. After dinner we went into the sitting room and I sat on my trunk and Frederick sat down beside me in the most matter of fact way. The rest were much amused and I was a little myself.

There is one thing about my boarding place that is any thing but pleasant. That is the total absence of out buildings[7] and not a tree, shrub or ditch in side of half a mile. The school house is only a mile away Thank the Lord! But the buildings[8]—I wish you could see them. The carpenter man not being very good at circles used the dish pan for a pattern. Its awful. The vault is deep—a good six or eight feet at least[—]and every time one of the little girls went out I was in a perfect agony of apprehension. I knew I couldn't stand the nerve strain long so I fixed a bunch of tomato cans with pebbles in them to a rope and put it where in case of accident they could pull the rope and call me to their assistance. I occasionly find one hanging by neck and heels but no serious accident has occured.

Well I must close as it is most supper time.

I am your
Bachelor Bess

✳ NOV. 15, 1914[1] / VAN METRE, SO. DAK.
TO MRS. M. M. COREY

Dear Ma,—Its almost nine but Im going to write you a few lines any way.

My school work is mountains high this year. I'd have to work twenty five hours a day to get it all done. I want to last till the end of the school year so have adopted the motto, "Do the duty that is nearest, Leave unto thy God the rest." Sometimes I've been to school in the morning just as the sun came up and most nights for the last six weeks I've worked till it was too dark to see and then done my sweeping etc after dark—have been as late as eight oclock getting home. I declared I wouldn't bring school work home but I have a few times. Of course there are other school duties that creep in. For example the first week in November. On Monday one of the patrons visited school all afternoon and staid till most five. She wanted me to go see Andersons and Parkers[2]—said that I could do more with them than anyone else could (That wasn't the first time I'd been called upon to pour oil upon the troubled waters of this neighborhood) so Tuesday eve Mrs N[ewlin] and I rode down to Andersons for the evening—came out fine—Wednesday eve we rode up to Parkers for the evening—came out fine. Thursday eve we had to have the mail so rode down to Van [Metre] and Friday we rode down again to practice. Saturday I refaced my panama skirt and pressed it and my serge dress in the forenoon and went to town in the afternoon to pay up my bills and see to several things. Sunday we went to Sunday School and went home with Mrs Nordin' for the rest of the day because there was school matters that had to be talked over. We got home after dark and I jumped out and took the robes in. When I got inside the door I called out "My but its warm in here[.]" Then I touched the stove and called "There's a fire in the stove too" Just then I heard some one draw a quick breath and said "There's a man in here for I can hear him breath." I struck a match and started for the other room saying "Come show your homely face and lets see what you look like[.]" I didn't feel a bit afraid but I surely felt silly when Bill Boggie[3] walked out looking like a Cheshire Cat. He got here just after we went to Sunday School—in fact he saw us leave. I don't care, it served him right. I had a note from him the Thursday evening before and he didn't say a word about coming. He didn't even know that Mr Newlin was away cornhusking. He staid all evening and helped me make out an order for Sears Roebuck & Co but of course I didn't get any letters written. He teased me so he almost drove me frantic and he persisted in taking his sweater with him and I've nearly frozen since for mine hasn't come yet.

The past week I've had to bring school work home to make up for the week before.

I was to the dance in Van [Metre] last Friday eve. Such fun! I missed just three dances and got home just in time to start the fire for breakfast. I was some tired tho.

Have had a chance to attend all the dances but have had to cut most of them out on account of my foot. Its much better now. I've worn my shoe for most two weeks steady.

Yesterday I worked on my new fangled skirt will enclose pieces if I think of it.[4] The plaid is the lower part and the green is the upper portion. I want to make me a riding skirt as soon as possible. I surely like to ride. It hasn't made me stiff or sore a bit—not even that week I rode every evening. I ride Jerry, a strawberry roan coming four next spring. He is well broke and perfectly gentle but has a fearful imagination. I get along with him nicely except when he imagines he's a ladies hat tipped down in front and up in the back. I have Wilbur Travers[5] spur yet but I don't dare use it. Did I tell you about that spur? Or when Otis Newlin[6] was down? and the kisses? Or Mr Bell? Or when Maw and Paw Newlin were down?[7] Or when the young folks came here to practice singing?

Its getting colder than Greenland so will hit the perch. Tell me what I haven't written and I'll try to finish next time.

I finely turned that post card over and saw the names on the other side.

> Lovingly yours
> Bachelor Bess

❋ DEC. 13, 1914 / VAN METRE, SO. DAK.
TO MRS. M. M. COREY

Dear Ma, Am going to try to answer your letter which I received last eve but I may not hold out as its so cold I'm almost shaking to pieces. Have one shoe shook half off now and the other is started. If the ink in this fountain pen don't freeze guess I can make it.

Living in a hurry! Well I should say! Did you read Fullers letter from me? Well, the week after Thanksgiving I gave the exams for third month and my seventh grade pupil (Ruth Mathews)[1] failed completely and some of the rest didn't do much better. It almost made me sick. Have been making the fight of my life since. Stay after school every eve and correct every paper and plan every lesson for every grade for the next day. Try to make the plans fit every pupil. Its after eight every eve when I get home to a cold supper and a cold kitchen. The school board are very kind—have given me one of these great big round wick lamps so when it gets dark I draw the shades, lock the door, turn clock on its face and work till I get through. Its going to be a hard pull but I think I'll keep it up till the Xmas vacation and if I get rested up good then I can keep it up till the last of January then I'll have to let up for a spell.

After I had that card a week or so I turned it over and read what it said on the back—then I recognized most of them.

I have one of those pictures for Lona[2] and one for Normal[3] but I thot you spoke as tho Normal had moved back to Indiana and I wanted to know for sure before I sent them. Please let me know.—Gee! such a noise!!!

*   *   *

I think you do mighty well with your left hand but hope you wont have to use it any more.

Good for Rob! Guess we girls never tried to get ahead of him. If he gets to feeling too blamed rich he might divvie up a little.

Upon rereading your letter I discover that it was a *dump* and not a *drunk* they had where Fuller husked corn. That reads better.

Yes, why don't you put a ticket box on Babe?[4] Thats the way Rob's investments hike out and coin for him.

Yes, I know I have no right to worry about Fuller. I throw it off by spells then it comes back so strong again I can hardly fight it off. I'll never feel quite satisfied till I've seen him again. But then I may never see any of you again. I'm running risks of all sorts that would have made my hair raise five years ago.

The reason I didn't say anything about the taxes is because they are not paid. I haven't had the mon and we've just given up all hopes of ever getting track of Fritz [Bertram][5] again. Its about sixteen dollars. Was in hopes I could make it by Jan but that mortgage is due in Jan thats $210 and seven weeks board at Xmas. Will see about it in vacation and do what I can. They are howling about that mortgage to beat the band.

No, I didn't hear about Geo M——[6] being ill again. How should I hear? Have had one note from Ethel in about six weeks.

I   The reason I didn't prove up is because they desided at the finish to allow me no "constructive residence" so the five years of "actual residence" would not be completed till Nov. 12, 1914.[7]

II   I wrote the 1st grade exams in Aug. and they are suppose to give you six months credit on all grades of 90% or over so if you fail in some branches you can write again inside of six months and use the best grades of the two. Well they never gave me credit for one single first grade standing on the standing sheet—put them all down for second grade and I had several good grades too. Got 100% in drawing you know. Am going to send Ethel the questions sometime.

III   My average was low[.]

IV   I hold a second grade certificate good for next year.[8]

V   The wire cut colt can now step on his lame foot but may always limp.

VI   Yes I'll send you another picture of the hog and pigs and several others when I get them printed.

"Ruth Mathews . . . is a real Rancher's daughter and has almost lived in the saddle from babyhood." Photo courtesy Verendrye Museum.

VII I was always crazy about your engagement ring but supposed of course Ethel would have it. I should like to have it if you don't think Ethel would care too much. But I'd rather Ethel have it than know she always wanted it.

VIII I expect to get into Ft Pierre Xmas morning so if you send it you better send it there. Make a big package of it some way you know so it won't get lost easily. If you send it to get here befor Xmas Van [Metre] would be O.K.

IX Ft Pierre for the sausage—sure. Gee! I can almost taste it now.

X Am about three miles from the P.O. Some folks are not as accomadating as they might be about getting things for me.

XI Am about twenty miles from the claim and I know the road now[.]

XII Ruth Mathews is a girl of fifteen years of age in the seventh grade. She is about my highth and light complected. She is long geared and can break most any broncho or steer, in the country, to ride, with out even pulling leather. She is a real Rancher's daughter and has almost lived in the saddle from babyhood. Cattlemen say she beats any man in the country riding after stock. She never forgets a road, a building, or a critter she has seen once. She had ridden from here to Nebraska and back and never lost the directions. She had some stock of her own and oversees the branding of them. She is a strange mixture of womanliness and boyishness. She is rather shy among strangers but chuck full of the old nick when she gets acquainted. There is nothing more dependable than her word. She has quit cussing the last few years but wont hesitate at calling a horse an "old devil" if she thinks he acts like one.

XIII I don't know as I'll prove up for a year or two yet and I may prove up next June.[9] Am thinking some of going to Minnesota or California for a part of next summer at least—I might if I could get enough of my debts paid. My board is fierce—with the washing its between four and five a week and see what I get!

XIV Yes I received the pennants[10] and recognized the receipt of same by cards. Didn't you get the cards?

The house here has but two rooms the largest to the east and a little one to the west. Last fall the little room was my room and the sitting room but when it got so cold they changed and now they use it for the kitchen and we all live and sleep in the big room and its like this

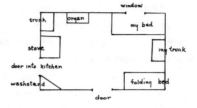

and the curtain goes between the two beds. and the pennants are on the west wall between the stove and the organ. They are like this

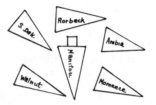

and postcards stuck between[.]

I have Daves picture[11] up over the Manitou.

Boggie came down a week ago Wednesday and staid till last Monday to build his shack. He was here when I put the pennants up. He and the Mr slept on one side the curtain and the Mrs bunked with me. Boggie said I had no business to let Dave['s photograph] stay that side the curtain so I'd take the point of the Manitou and pin it up to Rorbeck every evening befor we drew the curtain and a postcard dog watches him so he dont peek.

Its all right as far as Im concerned about those rings and things but you never gave me the one you refer to—that I know off. I only have a faint recolection of having seen it once.

XV   That insurance business auto suit me all right. It leaves no chance for me to get kicked so its alright with me.

Last Thursday eve Chum, the iron gray mare you've heard me speak of, got on the track and the freight hit her—killed her. So Mrs N[ewlin] and I can never drive Chick and Chum again and have such times as we used to. Sometimes I'd use one line and the Mrs the other and we'd both drive—using the long end of the lines as whips. Chum was the one I drove and we sure hit the high places. She was three years old and Chick four.

A week ago today it began snowing and blowing and sleeting and it has been at one or the other constantly ever since. I had to walk the [railroad] bridge [over Bad River] and it was fierce after night with ice and sleet on the ties. I never happened to meet a train but I fell once and rebusted that knee cap—one part of it you can lay your finger in. My other foot is healed up now so I guess I'm keeping even. I only limped one evening.

My new shoes and overshoes came the other day. I was surely glad to get them. Its awful to have to pay $30 per year for shoes alone but its a great satisfaction to have my feet look as well as any one's and I guess they do or people wouldn't remark on them as they do.

There are a whole lot of things I told Ethel I'd write you folks about if she'd tell me which ones I hadn't written of yet but I havent heard from you all so I don't know what to write. Did I tell you what a nice letter I got from Miss Appleby who taught in Ft Pierre for so long. She wishes to correspond with me. Quite a compliement I think. Also had a letter from one of the girls in Canada and such scads of others unanswered.

Someone said Mary L[anigan] was to teach the home school.[12] Where is she and what's her address, please.

Well I must close. Hope you will be able to write oftener after while. I expect to have two weeks vacation and spend it on the claim and near Ft Pierre.

Have had no time to think of Xmas presents. Much love to all. Hope Chall is better. Thank Paul for birthday card.

Lovingly
B.B.

★ JAN. 7, 1915 / FORT PIERRE, SO. DAK.
TO MRS. M. M. COREY

[Letter lost.[1] Enclosure as follows]

Battle of the Bones.—
How many bones in the human face?
Fourteen when they're all in place.

———   ———

How many bones in the human head?
Eight, my child, as I've often said.

———   ———

How many bones in the human ear?
Three in each, and they help to hear.

——— ———

How many bones in the human spine?
Twenty-six like a climbing vine.

——— ———

How many bones of the human chest?
Twenty-four ribs, and two of the rest.

——— ———

How many bones the shoulders bind?
In each arm one; two in each forearm.

——— ———

How many bones in the human wrist?
Eight in each if none are missed.

——— ———

How many bones in the palm of the hand?
Five in each, with many a band.

——— ———

How many bones in the fingers ten?
Twenty-eight, and by joints they bend.

——— ———

How many bones in the human hip?
One in each; like a dish they dip.

——— ———

How many bones in the human thigh?
One in each and deep they lie.

——— ———

How many bones in the human knees?
One in each, the kneepan, please.

——— ———

How many bones in the leg from knee?
Two in each, we can plainly see.

——— ———

How many bones in the ankle strong?
Seven in each, but none are long.

——— ———

How many bones in the ball of the foot?
Five in each as the palms are put.

——— ———

How many bones in the toes half a score?
Twenty-eight and there are no more.

———   ———

And now, all together, these bones may fix,
and the count, in a body[,] two hundred and six.

———   ———

And then we have, in the human mouth
of upper and under, thirty-two teeth.

———   ———

And now and then have a bone, I should think
That forms on a joint, or to fill up a chink.

———   ———

A Sesamould bone, or a Wormain, we call.
And now we may rest, for we've told them all.

✳   FEB. 22, 1915 / VAN METRE, SO. DAK.
TO MRS. M. M. COREY

Dear Ma,—Yours received, was surely glad to hear from you. I got
Ethels letter but she never mentioned you.

February is surely a busy month[.] We had exams the first week,
Lincoln[1] and Valentine work the second week and last week we got
ready for the District contest[2] which was held in Wendte last Friday.
My pupils did well. Three of them go the County contest held in Ft
Pierre Mar 12th. Today we had Washington's birthday[3] work and the
rest of the week is Longfellow week.[4] Next week is exams again and
then I've all that reading circle work (two books) to get ready in the
next two weeks. You auto see my nose—had a mix with a particular
friend and he smashed me one with a chair. Sure looks swell.

Lovingly B B

Appreciated my several pretty Valentines.

✳   MAR. 6, 1915 / VAN METRE, SO. DAK.
TO MRS. M. M. COREY

Dear Ma,—Guess I better begin to write if I'm going to get a letter
off to you before your birthday.

You never in your life saw such a bunch of weather as we're having. It has been snowing for about a week almost constantly. There hasn't been much wind but I never saw so much snow in my life. Last Wednesday morning it was so deep that Mr Newlin went ahead of me to the railroad gate to break the way a little for me and it was so hard to get through then that I knew by night I couldn't make it so I just camped at the school house. Mrs Seieroe heard about it Thursday so Thursday evening Andrew [Seieroe] came for me. He took me to school yesterday morning but I had no pupils except Peter [Seieroe] and the Mathews. The whole bunch looked like boys for the only way the girls could make it was to put on overalls. Andrew came for Peter and I last evening. We like to never have got here. If this keeps up I don't know what will happen. Stock is suffering now in places. Mr Putnam[1] and Andrew started to walk to Wendte on the track but got in up to their waists and gave it up and came back. Am afraid it will be to much for the snow plows if it keeps on. Wont the river howl when this goes off.

Last Sunday night Newlins other two horses got on the track and the west bound passenger made mince meat of Chick—almost—and they had to shoot Jerry. So Newlins are a foot now.[2]

Mr Putnam[3]

B B

* MAR. 22, 1915 / VAN METRE, SO. DAK.
TO MRS. M. M. COREY

Dear Ma,—Yours received the other evening with a bunch of others. Was glad to hear from you all. Was sure you would get more good out of the flowers now than fifty years hence. I have always longed for flowers so this time of year. Why I've seen cut flowers in Mr Fergusons window[1] when I wanted one so bad I could have cried, but I couldn't aford even one. I do wish I could take the job of dining room girl at your place but of course its me for the claim. And then Mrs Stone wants me for a few weeks as soon as school is out. Am afraid I got myself into it by staying at Donahues last spring. Then there's institute and if I can manage something satisfactorily will try to prove up again.

I just don't know whether to come back here next year or not. Its "the limit." I never saw such a neighborhood. Your hair would raise on

Ferguson's Confectionery in Fort Pierre, in whose wintertime window the sight of hothouse blossoms brought tears to Bess Corey's eyes. Photo courtesy Verendrye Museum.

end if I should tell you some things. Most every one is very good to me and they all seem to want me to come back. They've offered me the same wages as our County Supt. gets if I'll come back. I don't think I can beat it with out getting so far from home. It takes a strong character to make good here—here where other teachers have gone plumb to the devil. Im all the time running up against something fierce.

One day I went over to Mathews to phone to Park[er] and Mrs Van Metre was there (she is Mrs M's mother) She started to tell me about a time she had with Parker. I can't remember whether it was the butcher knife or hatchet she had but she chased him "around that wagin and round that wagin till I fell down—I aint strong I aint—then I got up. I chased him agin. One of his kids was standing there an he says 'Dont you hurt my child' and I says [']it aint your child I want its you you ———[']" Then she just unwound a real and a half of profanity that would make your hair raise and that creepy feeling go down your spine. I've heard men use cuss words but the way she used 'em made me catch my breath a time or two. I was cornered and couldn't get away till she got through. She wound up with "Them's the very words I said to him." I didn't remonstrate with her. I didn't want her to say 'em to me. She's no small eel either. I feel like "Little Alice"[2] in her presence. She seems growing fond of me—had me write a letter for her and gave me a pretty card.

How would you like to be where they fight with knives, hatchets and guns to say nothing of the rocks and clubs. On the other hand the children all like me and folks say they have improved mentally, morally and physically this year. And suppose they should have some young girl for a teacher next year who would go to the dickens herself and take some of the rest along.

I do wish your health would settle down and be better—it worries me. Try C[hristian]. S[cience].(?)

That last time I wrote I was at Seieroes. The roads slowly improved the following week and Newlins got a team to use so we accepted an invitation to Nordin's for Sunday dinner the following Sunday (a week ago yesterday.) Had a fine time. Went out and snow balled with Frederick, my ninth grade boy. In one way it was fun and one way it wasn't. He gave me all the advantage and was so afraid he'd hurt me—he'd almost hold his breath every time he hit me.

MAR. 24TH. Last week was a busy one in school—they all are for that matter—but different. There was a large closet in one corner of the room and I had the boys tear it out. Mr Nordin is coming down some day and put up some shelves that I want. We are going to use some of the boards to make some rug frames so the boys can do some weaving when the mud gets too deep out doors for games. The coasting is gone now and the boys have been at some dam work the past few days. We melted up a barrel of water and put charcoal in it so we'll have some [drinking water] for a while when the river gets bad. Today we planted our lily of the valley roots. I sent to the David C Cook Co. for them. They had shoots on them from one to three inches long. I think they will bloom in a couple of weeks. Thirteen tomato cans covered with white drawing paper and a name on each—makes a window full.

We had another blizzard last Saturday but it turned warm again Sunday and we took dinner at Andersons. Mrs Newlin and I walked the [railroad] track—the snow plows had been through early in the morning. We couldn't have got there by the road. We played we were "a couple of kids once more" and threw stones at the telephone poles and when we crossed the bridge we took turns climbing down and sitting on the girders or capsills or what ever they are beside the water barrels—just played a train was coming. We had a swell dinner. Gee! I can almost taste it yet!!

How is Ethel making it with her school? She never says she likes it or that she doesn't.

I have one of the funniest boys in school. Positively I think some times he is trying to flirt with me. Now I know that sounds killing. But—for instance—he had a dreadful habit of saying "um hum" to me. I spoke to him about it severeal times and at last I said "I'm sure you'd never answer me that way if knew what it meant." He looked so very startled I had to explain by telling him I'd heard it meant "Yes, my dear." I thot that would finish it, sure, but the imp is worse than ever—when no one else is near enough to hear—so I know he does it on purpose. I don't know what to do with him. Frowns and sarcasm do no good—he just laughs. Once he told me he couldn't help it and it was my fault. He is only a kid—about fourteen years of age. Once his ma told me how very much Peter [Seieroe] liked me and I said "Oh he doesnt like me as well as Ralph [Mathews][3] does[.]" She wanted to know why I could say that and I told her that when Ralph got to school before I did he always had a nice warm fire built for me and once Peter got there first and went on to coast. Well I didn't have to build a fire for a whole week so I reckon she must have told him.

Will try to mail you a bunch of clippings and a letter of Mrs Stones soon.

I must hit the perch[.] I'm almost shaking my teeth out.

Am having some sewing done—suppose you think I'm extravagant but I don't seem to have the time and nervous energy.

Love to all
B.B.

* APR. 17, 1915 / VAN METRE, SO. DAK.
TO MRS. M. M. COREY

Dear Ma.—This paper[1] is dreadful but its all I have here—have a couple of pounds [of good paper] in Van [Metre] if I ever get that box of freight out.[2]

Did I write just before Easter? I believe I did but I don't know.

The Saturday before Easter we had an egg roast down on the river. Gee! such a time. The snow was going fast and the river rising. We found a nice dry place and made a camp. There were only thirteen of us but we got away with six or seven dozen eggs. I made a batch of candy and we ate every bit of it. I put lots of peppermint in it so they wouldn't think they had to have a pain in their saw dust in consequence.

The boys played ball. And they set a stake and we watched the river rise. It came up at the rate of an inch in seventeen minutes. It was too high to ford then. Every one had to walk the rail road bridge.

I didn't go to church Easter Sunday—didn't feel equal to walking eight miles the way the roads were.

Monday morning the water was boot top deep between the [Newlins'] shack and the track. Mr Newlin brought the team over and took me down to the track—almost got stuck. He met me there Monday eve and took me home. Tuesday they had planned to move over here to the log house and just before breakfast in walks Otis Newlin of Pierre and one John Michiel of Illinois. I rode as far as the track with the first load of goods and told Mr. N. I wouldn't be back that night. I won't stay under the same roof with that brother of his. He went home last fall and told his folks that he slept with the schoolma'am when he was down to Roy's. They seemed to think it a big joke but I couldn't see it that way. I staid at Seieroes till Friday and they left on the Friday's freight. I was about sick all day Saturday but managed to trim a couple of hats to last till we got some. I decided I better go down to Ft Pierre on business on Monday so Sunday morning I went up to Mathews and phoned to the folks that there was to be a short vacation.[3] I walked to Van [Metre] to Sunday School. Mr Newlin caried my suit case for me. I had three great blisters on my feet when I got there. They put me in to teach a class and I just couldn't get out of it. I took the night train and got into Ft Pierre at four Monday morning. The old shoes I wore down to Van [Metre] were so loose it seemed I could not stand the friction on those blisters so put on my new ones—had only had them on a little while once before so by Monday eve I was completely exhausted. I was to take the night train back so I phoned up to see about the river. It wasn't so they could ford it yet so I'd have to walk that five miles to school. So I just made up my mind Id stay over and go Wednesday morning on the freight and get them to put me off at the school house.[4] Then Tuesday eve I got word there was to be no Wednesday freight so I had to take the night train and walk out after all and carry my suit case. I got here about getting up time. We are in the log house now and there isn't even a curtain between the beds. I found my bed occupied. his folks were here on a visit. I got my bath robe and went out doors and undressed while they got up. I took a good nap before I went to school. It was a blistering hot day. We suffered much with the heat. His folks left before night and I've been putting in big nights since. The river is down so they think we can ford it tomorrow. We surely have had some raise. Mrs Newlin measured up to a bunch of drift in a tree *on the bank* the other day and it was up $11\frac{1}{2}$ feet from the ground. Strunks[5] had to walk out and Mathews were ready to move. * * * * *

The mail just came—a letter from Ethel. I've wanted to write to her for so long[.] And one from Aunt Hat—a long one. Aunt Mary[6] is making numerous threats as to what she'll do to me "if" she ever gets a hold of me. You see she doesn't know what a reputation I have for quick motions. One night I was at Seieroes and Harry (who is taller and larger than Fuller[7]) just tormented me till I couldn't stand it any longer and I just went for him and slapped him clear up to a peak. I'd make a feint and he'd throw up his arm to protect one side of his face and I give him three on the other side before he could move. There was a whole bunch there and they can't get over it. Mr Mathews who is quite a boxer himself is always saying he'd like to have me practice with mits just to see what I could do. Another letter from the Co. Supt.—I'm on the program for the officers and teachers meeting next Friday—more work.

And that reminds me. Can you tell why it is that at eighteen or twenty I felt myself an old maid and now I'm past twenty seven and the men are nicer to me every day? Is it deference to age? Himbel [*sic*] Putnam asked me if I'd go to the next dance in Van Metre with him. Say, he was twenty-five last Sunday, Apr. 11th. When I was in Ft Pierre I phoned over the river about some shoes and Paul Noren,[8] the "shoe man," asked if he might "call to have a little chat" with me. He is just such a fellow as uncle J.D. [Dunlavy] for size and build but very light complected. He has a good education and is spoken well of. And when I 'phoned to Oscar Walton to ask him to witness my application he talked a few minutes and then said "Wait a minute I'm coming down" and he did tho I couldn't see any possible excuse. Thats the way its been going and I have to get new dresses and hats and things.

Well I must close. Love to all.

Yours as ever, B.B.

✳ MAY 19, 1915 / VAN METRE, SO. DAK.
TO MRS. M. M. COREY

Dear Ma,—About that 80—I guess the papers have to be made out all over again—the information was not complete enough. The rulings stating the requirements[1] are not here yet I understand so I don't know yet what I'll have to do. Yes Toad can take up 160 a[cres] but he must "Own and reside on the original claim" at the time of filing and the land he takes must be within 10 miles. Rob could take up 320 a[cres]. School closes the 27th and if Lydia meets me here we'll go on to Weta together for a week then she'll go on to Minn[esota] and I'll get a job some where and go to work.

Am so busy I don't know where I'm at. Am tired to it seems. I should like to lay around all summer but I cant aford to.

7th & 8th [grades] final examinations tomorrow and the next day.

Lovingly B.B.
More later.

✳ JUNE 1, 1915 / FT. PIERRE, SO. DAK.
TO MRS. M. M. COREY

Dear Ma,—School closed Wednesday. Were to have had picnic Thursday. The flood came—biggest in ten years.[1] Some had to take to the hills. We moved. Mud shoe top deep—picnic you bet! Got here with suit case late last eve. Had to leave my trunk. (Cashed warrents this morning and am sending you check for ($34.60) Thirty four sixty.) Will write more later.

Yours
B.B.

✳ JUNE 5, 1915 / FT. PIERRE, SO. DAK.
TO MRS. M. M. COREY

Dear Ma,—Yours received and read and am now lined up by the table with the cripled member on a cushion in the rocker and will try to answer up to date.

I believe I wrote you that a brother of Mr Newlins, of whom I'm not particularly fond, came to stay with them about a month before

school closed so I didn't stay there a day more than I had to. Had so
many invitations that I was gone over every Saturday and Sunday and
one week was there just one night between. Then the weather for the
last six weeks has been fierce most of the time and many a day I had
to wade mud that would occasionly go over my shoe tops. Then we had
planned since Xmas on a picnic the last day. Hoped for a change in
the weather clear up till the last week[.] We got a change but not the
change we hoped for. Van Metre, Wendte, White Clay, and the surrounding country had all planned to join in the picnic and the program
we planned took much time and thot. Then there were the final exams. I had one seventh grader and got notice from the Superintendant
that the pupils from Wendte might come there to write but it was
stormy and they didnt.

I got notice about that time that my application for filing on that
additional eighty[1] was being held for additional information but I
couldn't get off just then. I also had a letter from Lydia urging me to
close school a couple of days early so as to leave with her the 25th for
Weta for a weeks stay with friends. I wrote her that it was *impossible*
but if she would come down on the freight Wednesday morning and
stay to the picnic I would go on with her Thursday night. She got my
letter too late to make the necessary arrangements so went on alone.
She wrote me later to come to Cottonwood Friday morning and Dave
[Bull] would meet Flagg Carlisle and me there and take us the remaining twenty miles. You know the Supt. of the city(?) schools at Cottonwood played out and Flagg finished out the remaining three months
and a half. They like him and he is going back next year so he desided
to open a law office there and sent for his books. Had to put them in
his room for a couple of weeks till he could fit up an office. The night
of the twenty sixth there was a cloud burst in Cottonwood and the
building Flagg was in was struck by lightning and burned. Flagg
never awoke till the windows in the room below fell out and he just
escaped with his life, loosing all his wearing apparel and whole private
library. So he didn't get to Weta either, and he was to have given the
Graduating Address, too.

Well as it was so rainy and bad we desided to have our program in
the schoolhouse and Thursday morning I waded off as usual with a
"change of raiment" in a package under my arm. When I got to the
bridge I found the river risen dreadfully and Mrs Mathews, more
scantily and grotesquely garbed than usual, came down to tell me that
they had just received word of the cloud burst—that Phillip[2] and Pow-

Bess Corey's friend and fellow schoolteacher Flagg Carlisle, who lost his entire law library in a lightning-set fire at Cottonwood, S.D. Photo courtesy Marie Carlisle.

ell were flooded and they and Strunks were packing to move. I asked her to phone to the rest that we would wait and see what another day brought forth and if we couldnt have the program the next day (Friday) we'd call it off entirely. Friday morning about day light the raise got there. Say! it was a sight!

The Newlins loaded up a load of stuff and went over to the shack. Mrs Newlins two sisters from Illinois had arrived the Wednesday before and the younger was almost stiff with fright. When all was ready the team declined to move so the elder Miss Beckett (who is my size) and I got off and pushed up on 'em till we got them started then we walked the rest of the way. When we got there, wet and muddy to the knees and almost starved to death[,] I discovered that those very lovable man creatures had managed some way not to bring my suit case. They thot it quite a joke I guess but some how I couldn't see it at the time I was *so* tired. I walked back over to the log house and stayed alone all day. They had taken all the drinking water with them and what I dipped from the cow steps was too yellow to drink but used it to wash the mud out of my clothes with. I took a bath also and did quite a bit of mending and packing.

Saturday I finished packing. Saturday evening Harry was down to supper and spent the evening. Sunday I went up to the school house to gather up odds and ends. Ruth took my reports up to Mrs Nordin's. Mrs Nordin and [her son?] Albin saddled up and came back with her. Mrs N said she just *had* to see me before I left. Andrew [Seieroe] came down and signed the warrents and Mr Parker came over and registered them and wrote the checks. Its kind of nice to have a school board that comes to you. I signed up and will go back next fall. They agree to move a shack or small house down and partly furnish it—a good stove and such—also build walks so I "wont have to get in the mud at all" and furnish all the wood and water I need—the wood to be cut in proper size for my stove. I also get $65.00 per month and no discount.

Well Monday afternoon I left. Of course I had to leave my trunk but they were to send it down as soon as possible. Did I tell you how I got to Van? The boys took me down to the bridge and drew up my suit case and band box with a rope. I climbed the ladder and carried them across. The boys unhitched and unharnessed and swam the horses across. Then they borrowed Andersons buggy and harness and took me on to town. It was late when I got into Ft Pierre but I wasn't sorry for while I waited in Van I had a long, long visit with Mr Calihan one of the Lyman Co. teachers. He urges me to write an article on "School Luncheons"[—]he says their Superintendant is much interested along that line but it seems she can not get them to take it up. We came out beautifully you know. We had something hot for Luncheon practicly every day and it only amounted to 15¢ per month per pupil—thats only ¾¢ per day you know. We had beans, stewed onions, tomato soup, mashed potatoes and cocoa. But it was mostly cocoa. It is because I have not only recognized the needs of the Rural Schools, but have succeeeded in meeting, in practical ways, some of the needs that others seemed to think could not be met, that my work is being heard of in parts, at least, of five counties.

As for being Co. Supt.—Bah!

Didn't I tell you that some wanted to suggest me for the place when Mr Warner resigned and I told them "*No*, there are others better fitted for that position than I.["] And once John McPherson asked me why I didn't get a position in the Ft Pierre Schools. Of course I hadn't thot of Ft Pierre in particular—just town schools in general—and I replied promptly "For one thing, I don't want it." Once Mrs Gordon asked me "*Why* don't you want to teach in Ft Pierre?" I wondered at the question but explained my reasons. Then Fred Rowe[3] asked why I didn't take a position in the Ft Pierre schools[.] I laughed and said I couldn't get such a position if I wanted it. He said "Yes, you could. They've been talking about it." Then it all came to me. John McPherson is Chairman of the School Board and I had thrown away the chance of an offer that dozens of girls would almost crawl to get. I suppose you think I'm foolish—lots of folks think I am—to stay in the country but I feel that I can really do the greatest good to the greatest number by staying where I am. As for the name—what I've got is alright till my Swede gives me another. I'll tell you, I don't like to lead a mule but I *do* like to get behind him with a ten foot pole and help get him started.

My greatest handicap at present is my inability to handle a typewriter. Put Ethel next so she'll be prepared when she gets to such a place.

Tuesday I rode out as far as Taylors with Mr Stone. I didn't think there was any use going clear to the claim without my trunk.

x x x x x x x x

SUNDAY JUNE 6

That very evening I was going down the cave to help skim the milk and somethink happened. I don't know just what—but it took affect in my left foot. Its getting along beautifully[.] I can put my foot on the floor today but I dont walk. Two nights it was swelled so tight from toes to knee that it was sleck and hard and I couldn't feel the ankle bones. I had to laugh when I looked at it. Some how it made me think of a right fat little pig lying on its back with its legs sticking out.

My I'm glad it wasn't my head or my hands! I've written a dozen letters—all business except the one to Mary[—]and read some. How lucky I am! Just suppose that had happened at Newlins.

Am sorry you lost that cow and calf. Have had a little of the other kind of luck myself this past year. Last summer one of my cows lost her calf, then Rowdy got ruined then I lost a cow and this spring some one stole a yearling steer with out a brand and none of my three mares are with foal.

Say Glen and Howard Speer have both filed just lately—Howard on another quarter and Glen on half a section. They took it in north of Fullers and left some between so they'd get free use of it. Grant doesn't know if they fixed it so as to cut off a chance of Fuller's filing or not. When I get to Pierre I'll look it up. There were seventeen quarters open for filing in the Sonnenschein pasture last fall so I suppose Rob could get a half section there if he wanted it. I think Rob could make out fine up here if he didn't expect to find it like Iowa or let the blue devils[4] get him every time it rained or didn't rain or a cow didn't have twins or some thing went wrong.

There's always a way out of everything and the Bible says "Seek ye first the kingdom of God and all the rest shall be added unto you[.]"

There isn't much chance of my working much now before institute which is to be held between July 13th and 21st and I have made arrangements so I can get along. If all goes well will be free by the last week of July to accept any invitation I may receive for three or four weeks.

Did the boys get the job of building—I mean digging[—]that ditch?[5]

Do you think there will be many apples this year? I surely would like to get some if possible—will be batching again this year you know.

Am glad Chall is doing so well with the chickens.[6] Gee! I can almost taste those fries[.]

No, I hadn't heard before that Rob was farming some for himself.[7] Good luck to him.

How many cows do they expect to milk this year? Mr Newlin was trying to work me in on the milking but I didn't work. At last I told him I would if it were not against my mother's teachings. He wanted to know how that was so I told him before all the rest that my mother thot a person very foolish who would work for nothing and board themselves. He didn't try to pull off any more such deals[.]

Yes, I expect Ethel has had *several* battles to fight but she is so much better equipped than I was at her age. Say, I'll bet my Swede is the taller.[8]

I'll be glad to have Rob come up—Ethel too. Any or all of you are welcome if you ever care to come. You'll find the latchstring out.

So J.D. [Dunlavy] was afraid of the frost—he's wise. Mrs Newlin had one bean that grew twice as tall as the rest and the frost got him.

Paul must have made pretty good time going around that tree but I think he made one mistake. He should have turned and run the other way so as to have met himself face to face. That would have been equal to sitting on the fence and watching himself go by.

Am sorry I forgot to return that note—was so rushed to death just then.

Am also sorry you all do not feel that my cooking is a "clean job." Am used to having my cooking quite well spoken of.

If I could have handled a typewrite[r] I could have had a job on the transcribing force for all summer at $60 per. mo. but they had enough penmen.

Yes, its all right for Aunt Jen to swell up *now* but she was willing to listen to evil reports of me and kick me every time she got a chance when I started in. Am getting the same cash salary the Co Supt does and house rent, fuel and water beside[.] Would have had a higher salary but some of the school board thot they should not offer me more than the Co Supt was receiving. Sh!! I'm going after the commissioners to raise her salary. See?

Poor old Toadie! I should like to see him settle some where where he would not be much exposed to the elements or have heavy physical labor exacted of him. I'm afraid he was not born to lead.

Do wish Rob would write me of his plans—tell him to use a pencil and write shorte hand if he likes[.]

Well must close, will try to keep answered up better after this.

Did I tell you about visiting the Corey's?[9] And how we girls ran Paul down and ate his cooky for him?

I have been home sick to see you all for some time.

Lovingly yours
Bachelor Bess

By summer 1915 it had been two years since Bess's last visit to Iowa. The long summer spent there in 1913 appears to have done much to convince her that her place was in Stanley County. Ties with Iowa were weakening, as they must. And as her younger siblings grew to adulthood, their curiosity caused them to follow Fuller's example and travel west to see for themselves the land and people they had heard so much about from their sister. Ethel Corey visited during July 1915 and was followed in September by Robert Corey. Later, Elizabeth's brother Challenge came for an extended stay.

✳ FROM ETHEL COREY[1]
JULY 11, 1915 / FT. PIERRE, SO. DAK.
TO MRS. M. M. COREY

Dear Mother,—I don't feel very much like writing letters, but I'm going to write some anyway. I'm out on Bess' claim now. I got in Ft. Pierre at about half after two Friday after-noon; and after a time I found Mrs Gordons to find that Bess had gone to the train to meet me for three days and then had given me up or almost had and had gone home the day before. She was to come in Monday again, but it seemed an awful long time, before I could see her.

So Mrs Gordon said she would tell the store keeper that if any one came in from out Bess' way he was to let us know. In a very little bit the 'phone rang to say that Joe Bahr was in and would be going right out. A little while later a knock came at the door and Mr. Bahr was there ready for me. He took my suit-case and wobbled off with it. I thought[,] my, he acts funny and when I got the rest of my stuff together and started up town I met Mrs Gordon coming back and another lady came hurrying down to say that the store-man had asked a chance for a ride with Joe Bahr "before he under stood the conditions" that he was drunk, but his wife was along and that I didn't need to be scared. Well I should say not, I just had a lot [of] fun. To hear him talk is killing funny. I've had lots of funny things happen I'd like to tell you about, but it would take so long that I'll wait until I get home to tell you about it. I walked a half a miles to Bess' house after I got to Bahrs. He said he'd take me clear home, but he had to milk and it was getting late, but he was awfully good and he told me the directions so good that I could walk right to Bess' house. I don't know just for sure when I'll come home, I'm going to Institute with Bess next week; and she says that if I'll stay until a week after Institute she'll come home with me if Rob will come back with her the last of August and help her move. Institute is out the 21st of July. I've seen a snake, but no rattle snakes yet. There is lots of Jack rabbits[.] I've seen 4 or 5 already.

Bess'es foot isn't quite so well as it has been. I don't know weither I'll ever get this letter written or not. Little Mary Donehue is here, oh she isn't so little, but she and Bess they just keep things agoing and of *course I don't help 'em at all.*

I got here Friday night you know and yesterday I stayed home all day and to-day is Sunday and I guess we are going some where to-day if we ever get around to it. Oh, I don't feel a bit like writing and I'll tell you, mother, that this isn't Palmer Method[2] either. I don't know what ever is getting the matter with me, but I'm getting so I can't write at all any more.

I wish I could tell you folks about the country out here just like it really is because it is quite interesting to see the hills and the level country all mixed up to-gether out here. Well I'm going to stop writing for to-day.

Now Mother don't do any hard work, just pile it up and let it set until I get home. And Boys you must all help her lots with the work.

Well with lots of love to you all

> I'm you'r'e little girl
> Ethel.

✳ FROM ETHEL COREY
JULY 16TH 1915 / FT. PIERRE, SO. DAK.
TO MRS. M. M. COREY

Dear Mother,—I'm going to write you right now. Bess and I received your letter this morning and I guess *I was* mighty glad to hear from you. Bess has put in an awfully hard day to-day and is tired and kind of cross and you know what that means for me. Her foot isn't well yet by any means, but it is doing the best it can I guess. When we get to Iowa I intend that she shall rest if my plans don't fall thru like they generally do when I get to making plans of these kinds. We have gotten along just fine so far; but the work she has, isn't the easiest by any means. I try and help her all I can but I don't know so very much. Say, Mother, do you suppose it would be possible for me to borrow $10 or $15 out of my own bank so to speak. I may not need it at all, but again I may. When you write be careful what you say. Just say *if* it will be al-right that "It will be al-right.["] And I will under stand.

I rode out to Bess'es claim with Joe Bahr as I said before. He was drunk, but his wife was along so I didn't get frightened any. I did have

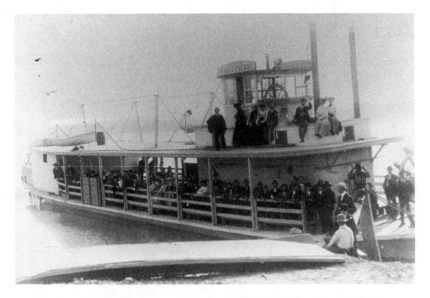

"... *it sure was great crossing the Old Missouri in a boat.*" *Photo courtesy Verendrye Museum.*

a lot of fun too. He started in to entertain me and tell me about the "*tam*" country out here and about the people. I just couldn't help but laugh at him.

It was awfully lonesome at first out to the Claim, but I got used to it finally and it was really better off out there than here.[1] You know what I am when meeting lots of strang[e] folks when with Bess. But she is real patient with me.

I have met all of Grant Stones family; Maggie Speer, she is going to teach next year; Ada and Berniece Hosington; Alice, Virdena, and James Murphy, they are Frank Murphy's sisters and brother. I also met Mrs. Murphy[,] Frank's mother. I like Mrs Gorden just fine.

Last evening Bess and I went over to Pierre on one of the gasoline launch boats it sure was great crossing the Old Missouri in a boat. If it doesn't rain or something doesn't happen we are going over to Pierre again to-morrow. I would like awfully well to see the buffalo's up here before I go home, but Bess doesn't know weither we can make it or not. It is kind of hard to plan so much when she is so busy and has her mind so full of other things.

Don't you worry about Art[.][2] I guess he will be able to take care of himself. He has quite a hard time to decide what to do. Poor Kid.

The buffalo ranch was established north of Fort Pierre, S.D., by Scotty Philip as an aid to preservation of the species. "I would like awfully well to see the buffalo's up here before I go home," wrote Ethel Corey while visiting Bess in 1915. Robert Kolbe Dakota Collection.

How is Marvel coming?[3] I haven't heard one word from her yet. But I've only written her a card. Has Glee come to help Fren [*sic*] yet?[4] How does Ed. like his hired man? Is Fren jealous yet? Did they want Art back when he went to get his stuff?[5] Did Mable teach my class Sunday? How is the League coming on?[6] I got those to letters you sent me alright. If you haven't time to write me and drop me a card now and then tell the boys to get busy. Each one take turns writing cards.

I have just had a glorious time so far. We wont be able to be home before the middle of week after next, but Mother just let the work go as much as you can and I will see to it proper when I get home, as I am geting fat up here, I'll tell you. Now you boys help mother all you can. Well must go to bed. With Lots and Lots of Love to you all.

Ethel.

✳ FROM ETHEL COREY
JULY 21, 1915 / FT. PIERRE, SO. DAK.
TO MRS. M. M. COREY

Dear Mother and the Boys,—I have just a little while, so will try and write you a few lines. I would like to know how things are coming down there awfully well. I got a card from Marvel and a letter from Belle[1] and one from Rob yesterday.

Isn't that awful about Armstrongs? My I think that is dreadful. I feel awfully sorry for Ed. I hope things soon get straightened out. Bess says she is almost afraid to come home now.[2]

I'm sure enjoying myself up here. Did I tell you about our trip to Pierre? We are going over there again Thursday if nothing happens; but it might rain or something. We have had so much rain up here since I came. It has only missed two nights since I've been here. Some folks leave this country because of the dry weather, but if I leave it before I'm ready I assure you that it won't be on account of dry weather.

Thursday after-noon if nothing happens we are to go to Wendt. Bess is awfully afraid something will turn up so we can't go. Two young men stopped here at the school house to see her for a few moments before they went home, that were from her district out there.

Has Dolma been up to see you folks yet? In her letter she spoke of coming. I wrote to her yesterday.

Now Mother be careful and don't work to much. I expect you will have to wash some before I get back but Mother don't try to do all the washing; just wash out a few things that you may need and let the rest go. You see Bess has to go out to her claim once more before she goes home with me. She has to go and come whenever it is convenient for some one to take her and not when she is ready and we have had so much rain.

Lovingly Ethel.

*   FROM ETHEL COREY
    JULY 29, 1915 / FT. PIERRE, SO. DAK.
    TO MRS. M. M. COREY

Dear Mother,—Well we are back from Van Metre. I had a fine time down there, only it rained so much that we didn't get back as soon as we expected. To-day is Thursday and I want to go out to Bess' claim before I come home. I expect you have that card by now to say that Bess isn't coming with me. Well, I'll explain all that when I get home.

It just rains here every night and that makes it hard to get around, you know. I had planned on getting out of here to-day, that is, to start home. But then I thought as long as I was up here I want to see as much of the country as I can, because I don't know when I'll ever come back you see. But if nothing happens I'll start home next Monday, but it rains so much that it is uncertain.

Now, Mother, don't do any more than you have to. I know I really had ought to start to-day, but I just felt this way. I'm up here now and I had better see as much of the country as I can while I'm here, because Iowa is quite away from S. Dak. and I might not come up here again, at least for along time.

Well I wont write any more now, but, believe me, I will talk when I get home.

> With lots & lots of Love to you
> all, Ethel.

✽ AUG. 24, 1915 / FT. PIERRE, SO. DAK.
TO MRS. M. M. COREY

Dear Mamma,—Yours with the enclosed letters received after some delay. I read yours that evening and started on the others but stopped as I had company. The next morning I was *quite* ill. I managed to get breakfast and, as soon as the rest were gone, read the rest of those letters and in a little while was as well as ever. I think my ankle yie[l]ded at the same time perhaps for a few days later I noticed that it was not swollen even after doing a two weeks ironing so have not had the bandage on since and it looks and feels as good as the other. Have thought of writing a [Christian Science] practitianor for help several different times but before I get to it I always get to feeling that sooner or later we must work out our own salvation[.] "Why not now." When I settle right down to work I get on beautifully but sometimes error seems to creap in and I neglect my study times.

Have the lady's address some where and may use it later. I certainly appreciated your offer to foot the bill[.] Thats the biggest thing you ever did for me.

Yours of the 15th says you haven't heard from me since Ethel got home but you must have ere this.

No, I don't believe I've spent a lonely hour since Ethel left—no offense to her—just let me tell you a few. If she were here I'd tell her some things I can't very well write.

Well that night, after Ethel left, the team was pretty tired so the Stones wanted me to stay till Tuesday morning and Tuesday they thot I might as well stay over till Wednesday and go to the Kill Kare Klub with them so I staid and fixed over that grey dress of Mae's that Grandma Stone gave her—and that pretty house dress, that shrunk so, I let down and gave her—also gave her a white waist and finished a sleeved apron for Blanche.

Wednesday I went to the "Klub" and took Mae and the kids. Gee! such a time. There were about twenty youngsters there and as I was not a Klub member it fell to my lot to help Kill the Kares. It didn't seem as tho I sat still three minutes from eleven thirty till six but the ladies assured me that they were "sure the children had a lovely time[.]" So I had to smile and tell 'em not to mention it.

That night I insisted on going home but—Myrtle went home with me. Mae has been wanting me to help her with her arithmetic so there would be more chance of her making her grade next year.

I intended to wash the next day ("Thurs") but slept till late and before we got the dishes done Arch Scripter came. He was looking for some one to stay with his mother[1] till he could get permanent help and Mrs Speer kindly(?) sent him after me. Ethel met the lady when she was here. She is a victim of nervous insanity so the doctors say. She tried to commit sideways[2] last summer but failed. She was taken bad again after Ethel met her (I don't mean to infer that Ethel was the cause of the attact). Its hard to refuse anybody's mother so I consented to come. So from then till Sunday I washed, ironed, scrubbed and mended—teaching arithmetic between times. Sunday Fern [Scripter] came for me and I rode in a lumber wagon behind a slow team and the weather and mosquitoes were fierce. Well the lady was up and dressed on Monday but that Morning Mr S[cripter][3] was taken ill down at the Livery Stable. He was bad enough so they didn't try to move him to bring him home till Tuesday evening. Have had 'em both on my hands since but think I'll get through this Thursday or Friday. Have had to feed the old gent almost every mouth full he has eaten. He generally offers up[4] part of it after ward and often calls me to "look at it." Called me yesterday right after dinner and gosh! I thot I was going to see a yaller dog and four pups before I could get out side. The lady, now is different. Some times its a hunger strike—wont eat because it costs too much—but its a continual worry about something. Its like trying from morning till night to reason with an unreasonable spoiled child of three or four years when they are sick or their ma is there so you can't spank 'em. It would be funny if it were not so trying and so pitiful.

Some of my friends felt badly over my comming here when I had so much sewing and visiting to do but when Weltha Stone was so horribly hurt (see papers) I hugged myself and was thankful I was born lucky instead of good looking.

Bernice Hoisington says ask Ethel "How's Ole?" I told her I would but "Ay tank she been one peach alright[.]" Yes "Ay tank Ole ban pretty good feller[.]"[5]

I wonder what you know that would surprise me. It can't be about Ethel for what she didn't tell me when she was awake I got out of her in her sleep one night at Parkers when I couldn't sleep myself. Ethel likes to load[6] folks but I dont believe she is so good at it when she is asleep.

I wonder if its about Fuller. You know Ethel was talking about him one evening and she said "Well, you know last winter—well Fuller got a bug[.]" That was all Sweede to me but I didn't like to display my ignorance so I asked if it was a "lady bug." Ethel fairly howled but she said it was and thats all I know.

Well I just must close and hit the perch[.]

Lydia came home the day after Ethel left. I had a letter from her beau the other day—if Ethel were here to help her they'd sure load that south bunch right.

Several of my friends have fairly scolded because I didn't keep Ethel here "a month or so longer" and give *them* a chance to help entertain her.

B.B.

✱ FROM ROB COREY[1]
SEPT 3, 1915 / FT. PIERRE, SO. DAK.
TO MRS. M. M. COREY

Dear Maw

Well I dow not no when you got my card and I have been trying to right so no we went out to the clame saturday night and got out there a bout ten and sunday we chined[2] just a bout all day and monday went over to stons for pottoes and staed for dener and then got home In tim to ficked up the old moer and cut a patch of hay so we would have hay for the horses we was using Mike Donhus team.

tuesday we boys went over to stons and hitch up that colt of Besses he went fine and the next day fuller went to work on a bridge and I and sis drove to tallers and staed there over night and the next day we went to vanmeate to see if they had the shack moved down it was not yet so she is not going to start school for a nother week we was at nordins and saw a snake we just got back, and are going out sune I sure do not like this dom cuntry I don't [know] witch to do go west farther or go with Fuler to harvis for a couple of weeks[.]

I have had and Invation to see focks in Yoming how is every thing down there?

Yess it is getting time to leve town tell them all hellow

Your Sarow Rob L

* SEPT. 30, 1915 / VAN METRE, SO. DAK.
  TO MRS. M. M. COREY

Dear Ma,—Yours of the 17th inst received after some delay as it was missent to Van Metre[,] Iowa.

Was so glad to get the fiver. Many, many thanks. I've ordered a sweater to replace the one some one borrowed and hasn't returned yet.

Have been going to write to you all ever since the boys left but have been having my share of battles and don't seem to get to the letter writing.

Have a world of junk to write Ethel—can hardly wait to tell her how near she was right about some things and how wrong about others and how I appreciate the lace, embroidery etc.

I enjoyed the pears tho some of them got too ripe while I was gone. Have the hooks put up in the shack and adorned with all sorts of things.

It was some job cleaning that shack. I tell folks that any one can paper a house but it takes an expert to paper a shack so it looks like any thing. Was to a dance last Friday eve[.] Guess I made a hit with the new section boss—am not overly proud of the fact tho he urged me to put up a mail box so he could bring my mail down every day and hoped my parents would come out and stay with me so he might call on me. I thot that was going it pretty strong for a beginning.

Yes, mamma, I take the quarterly but it comes to Ft Pierre so wont get this one till next Saturday I suppose. Am glad youre receiving so much good. Andrew [Seieroe] is coming—Hastily.

B.B.

✳ DEC. 4, 1915 / VAN METRE, SO. DAK.
TO MRS. M. M. COREY [letter missing][1]

✳ DEC. 13, 1915 / VAN METRE, SO. DAK.
TO MRS. M. M. COREY

Dear Mother,—I got a bunch of cards ready to mail last eve—had been working on them ever since Thanksgiving. Don't know when I'll get them mailed. Thot I'd try and write up every thing once more.

The Sunday after Thanksgiving when I came back India and little Roy came to Van after me. I stopped at Newlins on the way out to see their new baby, a five pound girl who arrived the Tuesday before. It surely was a sweet little thing. I staid till nearly supper time to talk over several things—mostly the meeting that Rev Miller, the State S[unday].S[chool]. Missionary, had called for my school house the following Wednesday evening. My patrons were crazy to hold our school house as the "Community Center" so as not to be divided—part going to Wendte and part to Van Metre. Of course I was in for it, too, and had several letters to get off to both towns, by special messengers, to work the crowd.

I wanted to write you that evening but knew I needed a big nights rest after so strenuous a week and Monday was a hard day and I spent the evening getting ready for Tuesday. My school board and their—how the dickens would you say it? One member and his wife, one member and his mother and the other member and her husband were to spend the evening with me that Tuesday. Mr Nordin didn't come so Mrs N staid all night with me. There was quite a bit of business[1] to attend to and they all seemed to enjoy themselves and the refreshments so much that they never left till midnight so it was one o'clock before we hit the perch and I was surely tired.

The next day at noon Ruth [Mathews] went home on an errand and came back with the sad news that the Newlins baby had passed on. She said they wished me to bring my camera over and try to take a picture of it. I dismissed school and went. I told Roy that I was afraid they would be disapointed as such pictures were seldom satisfactory. Mrs Nordin tried to persuade them not to but Roy and I got her all ready and when I went to take the picture the spring of the camera broke so we didn't get the picture and I'll never get another picture with that camera.

The neighbors had arranged for Mrs. Seieroe to stay all night so I didn't think it was necessary for me to stay as Alec Anderson was working there and Roy's mother was there. I started home about four o'clock and met Roy just outside the door. He said he'd rather I'd stay than most any one else if I possibly could for "You know Perle better than any one else here, and you can do more with her than any one else can" he said. That settled it. I promised to come back. I hurried home, bathed, dressed, straightened the school house and filled the lamp ready for the crowd, took my kimona and slippers and hurried back to Newlins. I sat up all night but laid down at six in the morning and slept till a quarter of eight. I taught that forenoon and then went to the funeral. They left so many little things for me to see to—I don't see why, when there were so many relatives and friends there. It was a large funeral of a little child so they say. Roy's mother and I staid at the house till they came back from the cemetary then I came home and went to bed.

There were a good many people from Wendte and Van Metre here that evening of the meeting but of course there was none of our crowd there but a few of the young people and the Mathews District was thrown into the "Van Metre Community" and the young folks went home firmly believing that "If Miss Corey had just been here it wouldnt have been that way." Well a meeting was called for Van the following Thursday evening (Dec 9th) and Mr Callihan and I were put on to get up a program. Of course there was only a week so Mr. Callihan never did a tap so our program consisted of two songs, a recitation, and an instrumental piece.

Oh I forgot the Saturday and Sunday before. I had been invited out to Sunday dinner with the Nickel's[2] so on Saturday I took my serge dress over to Mathews and finished it and Nickel's stopped for me on their way home from Van Metre. I didn't get back till Monday morning.

We just had to get a double Dutch wiggle on us all week, with back school work, Xmas plans, and practicing for Thursday night.

I knew they were going to organize a society of some sort and I was scared stiff for fear they would put me on for leader in a debate or something. but me oh my! That aint *nothin* to what they *did* do. Mr. Callihan was in the chair and called for nominations for president of the society. My name was up before I could get my mouth open. I nominated Mr Callihan as a last chance but I got every vote but my own. They called it a unamimous vote and I couldn't get out of it with out being a piker. I don't know how I'll make out. I'll have to do the best I can and let it go at that. Of course our crowd are much pleased. They cheered and cheered when I was elected so it may be the means of keeping the crowd together. Its surely going to mean a heap of work and writing.

And another thing—The Superintendant of Lyman County had been trying to get his teachers to do something in the line of warm school luncheons and he can't get a one to try it. Mr Callihan said the other evening that he had me spotted and was going to try to get me to help him get the work started in his county. Gee! Im skeered every time I see a letter coming.

I guess I mentioned on one of the cards about the box social in Wendte night before last. We sure had a time.

Say aren't those cute cards tho? Got 'em in Aberdeen.[3]

Oh how I wish I could make you all Xmas presents this year but I dont see how I can. You may not hear from me again, even till the middle of January so don't worry. There's about four hundred little things I would have written if I kept my correspondence up but as it is I've written most of the big things. Must close

Love to all
Bachelor Bess.

* JAN. 17, 1916 / VAN METRE, SO. DAK.
TO MRS. M. M. COREY

Dear Mother,—Yours received some time ago. Many thanks for the check. I haven't decided yet what to spend it for—treatment I guess.

The week after Xmas I just had to push myself to keep going. Mr Hall, the teacher at Wendte, and his sister visited my school all that Thursday afternoon and staid to supper. I felt better after that. They are C[hristian].S[cientists]. you know. I spent New Years Day at Mathews and the next day Ralph came home from Van with the mail. They got word that Mr Mathews sister wasn't expected to live so Mr and Mrs Mathews got ready and went down to Pierre leaving me with the children. They didn't get back till the following Thursday and believe me, we had some time. It was colder than Greenland so it seemed. They were out of bread so I started some in the morning and put it in a pail of hot water and took it to school with me. I put it in pans when I got home from school and had it baked by eleven, and it wasn't so bad, even if I did slip and chug the whole works to the bottom of a snow drift on the way home from school.

The folks got home Thursday and Thursday evening I baked a couple of big loaves of brown bread for the lunch at the meeting Friday eve. We all went Friday eve and I made out fairly well I guess. There wasn't such a big crowd. It was so cold and a good many were having La grippe.

The next day I washed and Sunday I cleaned up the shack. Just as I was about ready for bed Ruth came over and said that auntie was dead and her folks wanted me to come over.

Mr and Mrs Mathews took Roy [Newlin] with them. They left Sunday evening and got back Thursday evening.

Talk about cold weather! Frozen ears, cheeks and noses were rather the rule than the exception for a few days. The Government thermometer in Pierre registered 38° below last Tueday and it has been colder since.

I was surely glad to get Rob's letter, too. I suppose it is a great relief to have the responsibility of[f] your mind.

The Stone family who live about a mile the other side of Van have the diphtheria so I don't suppose there will be any meeting in Van this next Friday.

The other day Ralph [Mathews] went out to the barn at recess and found a nice two year old steer on his back in the manger. Pete [Seieroe] tore the manger out and let him out. He is all right now I guess but he knocked one horn off with his struggling.

I'm plumb disgusted with this bunch. I certainly have a struggle with the "impersonalization of error" these days. I've got about as far as I can go out here till I go back and finish High school. If I can make arrangements I think I shall go to Wayne, Neb. next year and try to stick till I finish. If I could study up a little between now and then I think I could make it in two years or less. My certificate would give me several credits. The Latin is what will bother me the worst.

Well I must close. Will try to write to Rob and Ethel soon. With love to all I am,

Yours
Bachelor Bess.

She was simply grand. [Note added regarding enclosed program for recital by Mme. Johanna Gadski[1] at Northern Normal and Industrial School, Aberdeen, South Dakota.]

❋ FEB. 6, 1916 / VAN METRE, SO. DAK.
TO MRS. M. M. COREY

Dear Ma and the rest,—I guess I wrote some of you two weeks ago today and there's been some thing doin' ever since. The next day Peter Seieroe was out of school. I didn't think much of it till Tuesday and then I had the Mathews children phone up to see if he were ill. They reported that he was not ill but had quit school for good. That his mother said he was getting too low grades. I knew there was no use going to the old lady for she is very much like Mrs Scripter and I knew if she was prejudiced there I could do nothing with her. I wrote a note to Mrs Mathews. She found out all the kicks and came over. Together we went over the ground and then she persuaded Mrs. S—— to come down the following Sunday afternoon to "investigate."

Well, Saturday I had planned to wash but that morning Mr Tropple brought up the mail and among other things was the book containing that dialogue that Mr Callihan and I were to give at the S[ocial]. S[ervice]. S[ociety]. I had less than a week left to learn it in so thot I'd read it over and then start in to learn it as I worked. (I forgot to state that I froze out in the shack and had been camping in the school house for several nights[.]) Of course my work was progressing rather slowly when Mr and Mrs Nordin drove up about noon. They had the new clock and bookcase. My! but they're swell! Mr. Nordin put them up and also the storm windows—what was left of them. Mrs Nordin was some worked up because the work wasn't done that Eph Mercer had been hired to do at Xmas time. She went over to see Mr Mathews and came back with a list of things that I was to ask Mr. Newlin to get for the school and charge to the district. The list included coal for the shack and seven ricks more wood, ax, hammer, building paper, shovel, screwdriver etc[.] They also decided to allow us five dollars for the cleaning we had done last year and this. So we have that much to put into tools or books. I got dinner for the Nordins and it was nearly sundown when they left so I got no washing done.

Sunday just as I was finishing putting the school room in apple pie order who should drive up but the Newlins. I told them I was to get a "licking" later on in the day and they better stay. They wanted to know how that was and I told them that Mother Seieroe was coming up with the raisor strop but I was sure I could run as fast as she could, so if there was some one there to see that I got a good start I was certain I'd come out ahead if I kept going long enough. That was too much for Roy. They gave up their trip down to the folks and stopped for the rest of they [sic] day. We had a good old visit and after a while Mrs Mathews came over. Then about half after two Mrs Seieroe came—Peter brought her down and then he went on over to Mathews. I think the lady was rather taken aback to find so many witnesses present. She never made a squawk about school work till Peter came for her to go home and then Mrs Mathews said she guessed we better go over those reports—and then such a word battle ensued as I'm sure you never witnessed. I never lost my temper nor even grew excited. I had work, examination papers, and reports from last year as well as this and I proved every assertion I made. I proved every complaint groundless and every accusation false. Even Peters testimony went against her. For more than two hours we had it hot and heavy but I won my point and Peter has been in school the past week. When they were all gone I was completely exhausted it seemed.

When Mr Newlin when to get the stuff for the school Mrs Hill[1] said, "Seems to me that school is pretty hard on hammers and such things." Mr Newlin began to inquire and found that Andrew Seieroe got a hammer and ax for the school shortly after Thanksgiving. He has been using them ever since and I've been using my butcher knife and tack hammer. I suppose the bill went in as "sundries" and the district paid it.

Friday eve after school I went down to Newlins and went with them to the meeting. It wasn't a very nice evening but there was quite a crowd out. The dialogue was a greater success than I ever dreamed. One of my pupils won in the funny story contest. The debate went to the affirmative. The subject for next time is "Resolved that Intemperance Causes More Heartfelt Sorrow Than War." The debators were all young folks this time. Our side has the affirmative and the other crowd has the negative. So I suppose it will be up to me to help the boys what I can.

We are to have a social after the program. The boys are to bring the lunch and have their shadows sold and we girls will do the buying.[2] Dont know how it will turn out.

I staid at Newlins Friday night and got to Mathews in time for dinner Saturday. After dinner Ruth and I rode out north. I'd heard rumors that Roxy was being brutally treated and I wished to investigate. I found that the rumors were mild compared with the facts. She was heavy with foal when Mrs Mathews saw her last before Xmas. They had worked her with every thing they had and pulled her heavy till she lost her colt then they had put her out on the school section to rustle or starve till spring. She was pretty bad off. The only way we could get her home was to bring in about twenty head of Mathews horses to break a trail [through the snow] for her. Then we had to apply the ropes end occasionly. She is in Mathews hay correl and Ralph is feeding her a little grain twice a day. We hope to have her on full feed in a week or so. They think she will never amount to any thing now, but I think she'll come out of it in time.

If I wasn't so busy all the time I suppose I'd put in a good deal of time wondering what was coming next.

I wanted to write the exams[3] the last of February but every minute seems full to the brim and no time for review. I never was so fit to write as at present.

Well I must close and hit the perch so good night[.]

Lovingly—
Bachelor Bess.

**✱ FEB. 29, 1916 / VAN METRE, SO. DAK.
TO MRS. M. M. COREY**

Dear Mother,—I see it plainly now. We'll each have to have a corresponding secretary soon. How shall we manage? Water the stock to increase the dividends?

What does Laura's worser half look like?[1] My eastern relatives don't send me photographs. Guess they've disowned me. I always imagine them with curly noses when they hear of me. I don't know why, for surely they cant smell my feet, or reputation either, that far off. If they could, they wouldn't know it from their own.

I've written to Belle [Brindly] and Art [Erickson]. Am very anxious to hear from them.

Ethel must have gripped it hard.[2] Hope she is all over it now. Perhaps I should not say so, but really Im afraid that, with her school work and Art study both, she is over working. I think she auto drop one or the other, for a time at least. And four weeks straight! My stars! Four hours a week is considered the limit along with other school work. Its so hard on the eyes you know. She'll think I'm worse than an old maid aunty.

Speaking of old maids makes me think. Sunday I was trying my best to get a bunch of letters answered and the Mathews girls came over. I made candy and popped corn for them. We finished the corn and I put some of the old maids in my mouth and bit on them and smashed a tooth. It was a big double one that had been filled. It burst the crown lengthwise, filling and all[,] and split the root on the inner side of the jaw bone. By this morning it was so loose it just wobbled all over my mouth but when I tried to pull it it hung on like grim death to a sick monkey. When Ralph came to school I told him that he'd have to pull it. He tried to rope it but the rope slipped every time. Then he wanted to know if I didn't have some tweezers or pincers or something. I told him I didn't have a bloomin' bit of anything but a new fangled tack puller that came in a box of Sears & Roebuck candy. We got the tack puller and it worked like a charm. I knew all the time that if I kept track of it long enough I'd get my money's worth out of it. (The tackpuller)

Is Toronto, So. Dak. a very big spot on the map? I haven't located it yet. What county is it in?

Well there wasn't any school in Iowa I cared about but Walnut and I knew Ethel wouldn't want me to go there and I know of a fine school in Neb. where teachers who have taught eight or ten years go back and finish their High School courses.

What makes you say "If I was 25 years younger?" Does not "Divine Love supply the body with the eternal fairness and freshness of youth?"[3] I guess that isn't quoted exactly but I don't find the page just now.

Say you haven't plenty of chickens yet have you?

Our society is called the "Van Metre Social Service Society." The chair is as good as new for I stand up most of the time. At the last meeting we had a Leap Year social. The boys brought the lunch boxes and had their shadows auctioned off. We girls bought the shadows. We just had bushels of fun. The river was too high to ford so our bunch walked the [railroad] track. There were sixteen of us. It was strenuous fun. *I* didn't accomplish a great deal the next day. I thot when I planned that social—"Here's *once* when some one else does the work[.]" But me! oh my! Two of the boys came to me for help with the debate and to cap the climax I did all the cooking for four boxes except the bread. I don't get a chance to dodge the work—seems like it comes and stares me in the face.

Am glad you have a watch. I always meant you should have mine but couldn't spare it yet.

Your coat cost more than mine. Mine is black and that thick kind of long haired goods, cost $10.00. Am glad it didn't cost more for that day Ruth and I came back from out north I jumped off the horse and caught it on the saddle. I couldn't get my foot back in the stirrup and my feet didn't touch the ground so there I hung. The rediculessness of the situation appealed to me so strongly that I let out a shout of laughter that frightened the horse and he made a merry-go-round of himself till I caught hold of the saddle with the other hand, raised up and tore the coat loose. Mr Mathews was scared most out of his wits. He thot my foot was caught in the stirrup and I might be kicked or drug. I had a pulled and torn place about fifteen inches long to mend in that coat beside a smaller place. Thats what spoiled last Saturday.

We had two weeks of the lovliest weather but it has been fierce since Sunday. So I guess we wont have to hang the ground hog after all.

Well, I suppose you will have a birthday before you hear from me again. I wish you a happy time. If I were rich I'd send you a rose for every year. My! I get so hungry for flowers in the winter time.

Its almost eleven so will close and hit the perch.

Lovingly yours,
Bachelor Bess.

Why didn't you seal your last letter? Unsealed letters don't reach me so quickly. Have to be read too often.

✱ MAR. 12, 1916 / VAN METRE, SO. DAK.
TO MRS. M. M. COREY

Dear Mother,—Your letter rec'd yesterday afternoon and the butter and lard this morning—many thanks.

I answered Pauls letter but don't know how long it may be on the road so thot would write a line to say that Belle and Art think they would prefer Iowa. If you have any thing else let me know at once as I expect to go to Ft Pierre the 24th and go out to the claim from there. Hansen wants it but I'm afraid I cant depend on him much.

The girls between the ages of ten and thirty met here this afternoon to organize a "Pollyanna Club."[1] They staid till quite late and
each started for home with an apple in one hand and a slice of bread
and butter and honey in the other[.] Am awfully rushed at present, will
try to write soon.

Lovingly yours
Bachelor Bess

✱   APRIL 19, 1916 / VAN METRE, SO. DAK.
    TO MRS. M. M. COREY

Dear Ma and the rest, Here goes for a few lines—closing may be
abrupt.

Several times the gentlemen in the Stock Growers Bank have half
urged me to go on trying to raise stock and have said nice things to
cheer me up when I was discouraged so I thot I'd put them to the test
and it has worked beautifully so far.

Mr Newlin had a letter from them Sunday saying they had purchased twenty head of cows and he was to phone them Tuesday to
make arrangements about shipping them down. I wrote the following
on a slip and had Mr Newlin phone it down when he talked to them
Tuesday—

"Would like to purchase eight or ten head of cows such as you are
to shipping [*sic*] Mr Newlin[.]

"You know my financial standing. Can I make arrangements to
get the cows? If so at what price? And what terms?

"Have a brother staying with me, now, so they would be well
taken care of."

Chall came down Sunday.[1] He went to Van with Mr Newlin. Mr
Newlin phoned the bank and before they left town the Bank phoned
Mr Newlin and made arrangements to send eight head of cows for me
to Wendte with Mr Newlin's. Chall went home today taking Roxy and
the cows with him. Dore Newlin went along to help him.

The cows cost me $58 per and with the first six months interest
the note is $487.80.

Mrs Newlin says they are surely a fine looking bunch so I must
have a bargain. And I reckon Chall will be busy enough so he won't
have time to sit around and look mournful—Hastily—B.B.

✱ APR. 21, 1916 / VAN METRE, SO. DAK.
TO MRS. M. M. COREY

Dear Ma,—Am having what in this country would be called "The
devil of a time[.]" Am well and making a *good* fight. Dont expect to
hear much from me for some time. Chall is doing splendidly I believe.
Had a note from him today[.] Now, mamma, instead of worrying try to
help me to realize that, trusting in the God of the Isrealites, for me, as
for them, the sea of error will roll back leaving my path unobstructed.
Help me to know the uselessness of material weapons, the omnicience
of Love.[1]

Lovingly yours
B.B.

✱ MAY 31, 1916 / VAN METRE, SO. DAK.
TO MRS. M. M. COREY

Dear Ma—Its an age since I wrote you last but it seems I'm always working, fighting, or resting and I haven't any heart for social
correspondence.

The fight is still on. It has been a one sided affair so far but I think
I shall take a hand in it now. I feel that I've reached that place where
patience ceases to be a virtue.

Andrew Seieroe refused to sign my warrents till I had taught two
and a half days longer and as yesterday was Decoration Day[1] I will get
through tomorrow noon. I presume I'll get home Friday morning—
about a week later than should be.

I cornered Andrew in a lie in the dance hall last Friday evening
and produced witnesses to prove it. I can prove a whole lot more, too,
and if there is such a thing as justice in this country the old boy will
have to sweat for some of his cussedness.

Chall was so anxious for me to get home for he had a chance to
work and here I am—held up by that heathen bunch.

I dont believe in fighting but what is a person to do? They've gone
far beyond the law repeatedly just because they thot I wouldn't fight.

Is it wrong? I can't seem to see it clearly at all.

Will try to write you a letter soon[.]

Lovingly yours
Bachelor Bess

* JUNE 25, 1916 / VAN METRE, SO. DAK.
TO MRS. M. M. COREY

Dear Ma,—Your card and letter received. Am going to write a few lines but I dont seem to feel a bit like writing.

I got home in time to get dinner Friday, June second. I walked up from Teton and Chall was plowing in corn. He didn't see me till I was beside him and he was so startled he almost jumped off the cultivator.

The house was surely in a great shape. There was a big washing here to do and I brought several weeks washing home with me. The new cupboard hadn't come yet and the old box cupboard was just running over and I brought a lot more dishes and stuff home with me. I couldn't clean house or unpack till I washed and I couldn't wash or unpack till I cleaned house and I couldn't unpack till I'd cleaned house and washed. It seemed like I did an awful lot of work before it began to show any. Saturday and Sunday I just untangled things. Monday I washed from nine in the morning till about nine at night. The next day, Tuesday, we went to town. I went to Pierre—paid up debts and we got home late with the cupboard. Wednesday I went to the Kill Kare Klub with Speers. It met at Mrs Shaws [1] (who used to be a Corey and is some relation(?) of ours) and they gave a miscellaneous shower for Ada Hoisington who was married last Wednesday.[2] That Klub is just like South Dakota weather. When they start showering they keep it up. The time before that—they showered Mrs Goulds—a hen shower. And then Mrs. Anderson got a miscellaneous shower and next time they meet at Speers, July 4th, and help them celebrate their anniversary with a shower. I never saw such a swad of pretty things in a bunch as Ada got. They were wondering who would get the August shower. Some thot it was between Jennie Speer and I. I told Mrs Speer that if people decided to have me get married again I'd sure keep still till after I got the shower any way. If Ethel is wise she'll be here on her wedding trip the first Wednesday of some month—and let me know a couple of months ahead.[3]

Ever since that Klub meeting I've been working on the Reading Circle work. Had two book reviews to write and they were both fierce. They were supposed to be in by June 1st but Miss Myers [4] said the other day that not a teacher in the county had sent theirs in yet.

Guess we've got our garden all in now but some turnips and late radishes and lettuce. We've just scads of tomato and cabbage plants almost ready to put in the corn field. We have this west of the house in corn—about eight acres. It isn't plowed over once yet. Had to wait for the neighbors to finish theirs first. Our potatoes are looking fine. We've had lots of onions and lettuce and some radishes. There's lots more coming on. Only two hills of pie plant pulled through. I don't know what ailed the rest. These two are surely fine ones. Have two hills of horseradish and three of asparagus.

The hens are doing pretty well. We get five eggs most every night.

The other evening Rox was here in the yard and Chall caught her by the nose to turn her out. She jerked back some way and bumped him on top of the head with her jaw. He went to the barn to get a rope and when he came out of the barn he moved his hat and the blood started to run down his face. He held his head over and it just ran from his forehead in a stream. I pored cold water on it. It soon stopped bleeding but he didn't do any more that evening. He has a bruise as large as two dollars cross wise the top of his head near the pole. The skin is broken clear across. Its not much bother to him.

Chall has rigged him a room out in the barn. We never have horses in only long enough to feed grain. He ties the calf in the other stall at night. One rainy day the calf got loose and got on to the cot. One of the Bahrs stopped here and they went to the barn. Chall thot at first glimpse that Joes big black dog was making himself at home in his bed and he yanked the poor little calf off there before he knew the difference. I don't know who was worse shocked, Chall or the calf. Chall says that's all right but if I buy any pigs I'll have to keep 'em in the shack with me. Well I must close and get supper[.] Where is Fuller now? And where is his breaking plow? I'll have to break twenty more acres before I can prove up on that additional eighty but have till Dec 10 1918 to do it in. Must send Fuller his tax receit soon.

I got Robs letter last eve. Will write him the rest later[.]

Are you coming out to see us this summer?

> Yours with Love
> Bachelor Bess

✳ JULY 29, 1916 / FT. PIERRE, SO. DAK.
TO MRS. M. M. COREY

Dear Ma,—I came to town the 19th inst. and wrote the second grade exams the two days following. I didn't think they seemed so hard but most every one else seemed to think so so I am half scared by spells. I went to Teton on passenger train and Chall met me there. We got home just before noon on Saturday. I forgot to get bread so started some at noon and baked that evening. It was surely good too. I baked a big cake the next morning—a snow cake—one of the kind Chall likes so well. Mr and Mrs Donahue and seven kidlets dined with us Sunday. Little Tom came to his mother the middle of the afternoon and said "I'd sure like to stay here."

Monday it rained and I got some sewing work lined up. Tuesday Chall came to town after the new wagon and I came as far as Taylors and staid till he came back. They are so lonely now. Mrs Taylor wanted me to stay several days—said she would put off her trip to Minnesota for a week if I'd only stay.

Wednesday I washed and Thursday I went over to Goulds[1] and she helped me with my sewing. Yesterday I churned, baked bread, scrubbed, did my ironing, bathed, dressed and packed my suit case by three in the afternoon. Chall took me to Teton and I waited for the freight—yes *waited* is the name for it. I didn't get into Fort Pierre till eleven o'clock. I had quite a bit to see to and Institute begins in Pierre next Monday and closes the 11th of August.

Was so glad to get your letter. It seemed ages since we had heard from you. You better plan to get here the 11th. Institute closes that day and the next day I "prove up"[2] if nothing happens and Chall can take us all out together. We wont be tied to any thing bigger than the hay field from then on and perhaps we can break loose from that occasionly.

Our garden is doing well. The corn is setting full if these hot winds would only stop and a heavy rain or two come on we'd sure have some corn. We'll have fodder any way.

Mr W G Speer has put in the whole fence between Fuller's place and them with new cedar posts—wonder what next.

We still have but the one calf but she is a great one. I remarked the other day that I'd seen her stand in the sun for an hour and a half fanning her self with her ear. Chall said I was getting worse than Mr Mercer. He wanted to know if she wrapped it two or three times about her neck afterward.

Chall has cabbaged on to that little trunk of Ethels. I was going to send it back with you but Chall says he needs it worse than Ethel does so I have all my rug and quilt stuff in the box you shipped and he has the trunk. Why didn't you send his summer underwear?—he needed those worse than any thing else. He is pretty well stocked otherwise—has ten shirts and ten pair of overalls and trousers. Just got him some new shoes. He got a new hat some time ago. Its a good thing the cat wasn't between you and the door when you kicked. I see that you, too, have a belief of *lack of time* to over-come. We must know there is no lack in mind. We will try to attend [Christian Science] services in Pierre while you are here.

I hope to have Mrs C. M. Corey and son Paul of Wendte down to meet Mrs M. M. Corey and son Paul of Marne. We have several invitations out all ready and would like to go up the river while you are here for plums, grapes, buffalo berries and choak cherries. We might get to see the buffalo also[.] Today I had an invitation from Mrs L. Bahr of Pierre to take a ride with them in their new boat some time during institute. They have two boats now.

Last evening I received the contracts from Weta ready to sign. Think I shall hold them for a while. Maggie don't think she will pass the exams. If she doesn't and I do I can have the Donahue school and stay at home.

Don't see why the eastern relatives keep so far from Dakota for when they are traveling. Is it on account of me or the snakes(?). Tell 'em that snakes never attact a car and neither do I and I think my photograph auto be sufficient evidence that we have well filled cupboards and cellars.

Have been struggling of late with a belief of financial lack. I haven't enough to pay my way through institute to say nothing of the $15 to prove up with. Chall did let me have all he could spare and I give him credit for it on one of the cows but he can't work away from home to earn any now. I must know that "Divine love always has met and always will meet every human need[.]"[3]

Did we tell you of Rowdy's latest caper? He went through three fences taking out gate posts and braces. He had one of the gates wrapped clear around his neck. He got out with hardly a scratch through the skin and half an hour later Chall found him in the far corner of the place and led him home quiet as a lamb.

Must close. Come the 11th[.][4] With love.

Bess

Bess's letter of July 29 anticipates her mother's visit to South Dakota. Bess had often urged Margaret Corey to come, and no doubt she yearned to reestablish personal contact with her, but at the same time both mother and daughter must have experienced a good deal of ap-

*prehension. This was to be their first meeting on Bess's home terri-
tory, and she was determined to hold her ground in their struggle
for dominance. Fortunately (although we have no written record of
the visit), all appears to have gone well, perhaps because the visit was
a brief one.*

✳ AUGUST 29, 1916 / FT. PIERRE, SO. DAK.
TO MRS. M. M. COREY
AT HOME, MONDAY 7 A.M.

Dear Mother,—Chall is about ready to start to Teton for a load of
ties. It was too rainy Saturday so Chall took a pail of apples over to
Speers and borrowed some fruit jar rings as I had forgotten to send for
some Friday.

You should have been here Saturday morning to help us brand
the calf. You wouldn't have thot she looked small then. Chall put a
base ball mask on her and turned her out with the cows.

Chall killed another rattle snake the other day.

I have cucumbers enough about the length of your finger to make
a jar or two of pickles.

I forgot to tell you that Mrs Speer offered to pay Chall for the
apples and he said "Oh, no, Mother said if you came over while she
was here to give you a bucket full[.]"

Carl Hansens have a new car. They are setting quite a bunch of
stock around them—a team, a cow, a calf, a hog, and a car.

Joe [Bahr] was here yesterday. He said if Chall would come over
this afternoon and help the rest of the week he would mow for us all
the next week. I suppose he for got that was fair week. He says he will
soon have hay enough up so he can quit when ever he gets tired.

> Must close
> Hastily
> Elizabeth

✳ SEPT. 12, 1916 / FT. PIERRE, SO. DAK.
TO MRS. M. M. COREY

Dear Mother,—the week after you left was a busy one. I washed,
ironed, scrubbed, baked, churned, and put up fruit. I took time to read

some every day and got to feeling much better tho I never got to bed early. One night I thot I was going to, then the Hansens car stopped at the gate. They worked with it some time then called Chall. They were out of gasoline. There was only Mrs Soren and her three kids and Mrs Roy [Newlin][1] and her baby. They started out to walk, each woman carrying a youngster. I told Chall that if he'd hitch up a team I'd take them home so he called them back. Chall was so tired every thing he said sounded crazy. Mrs Soren said she didn't see what ailed that car. they had had six gallons of gasoline in it that day. Chall told her he thot it had a tape worm. When he got the team hitched up he invited them to "come take a ride in our "can't-a-ford" and they gladly accepted. Of course by the time I got home, put up the team, and finished the dishes in [sic] was nearly midnight. I told Chall next morning if any one ever said any thing to me about going to bed early I'd be tempted to hit 'em with a brick.

That Saturday I went to town with Joe [Bahr] and Old Mother. It was a rush trip I had so much to see to.

The Sunday following Mr Donahue and Mr Gould stopped on their way to the river for plums. Chall went with them. They got a lot. Chall had a ten gallon milk can about to the shoulder but I only let him keep what I thot I could handle easily.

That evening when Chall went for the cows the big spotted cow had a little calf—a nice big red heifer[.]

I tried my best to get Chall to go to the fair but he would not consider it. Monday and Tuesday he mowed hay for Mr Donahue and Wednesday he helped Joe. A great storm came up in the afternoon. I never saw a storm come up faster. I finished my fruit, picked the beans and cucumbers (almost a bushel of the latter) and just got that last brood of little chick[s] in when the storm broke. By the way there were just nine chicks in the third brood. My! how it stormed. There was lightning, some hail, lots of wind and torrents of rain. In the midst of it Chall drove into the yard on the run—drove his team right into the barn and unhitched inside.

After the storm was over he began to round up things. It was time to go for the cows but the hayrack had blown off the wagon and turned clear upside down and Chall said it wasn't a good thing to leave it that way and he was going to turn it over. I asked if I could help him and he said "no" but a few minutes later he called me. He had it tipped on the side and wanted me to hold it so the wind wouldn't blow it over hard enough to break it. He went round to the front and told me to let go. I asked if he was all ready and he said, "Yes[,] let go." I let go and he went to step back but some heavy weeds obstructed his progress and one of those 2 × 8's that the rack rests on caught his foot. I could see that he was being thrown under the rack and, quick as thot, I threw all my weight and strength against the rack and with the help of the wind sent it on over to the next corner. It bumped him enough to skin his shoulder and I held the rack till he pulled himself out. He said his leg was broken. I helped him into the house and tried to make him comfortable. Then I shut up the chickens, hitched up the team, put a change of duds and a kimona in a sack, helped Chall into some other clothes and started out to take him to the doctor. It was the "big day" of the fair[;] nearly every one had gone and got rained on. The roads were terrible. I knew the team couldn't make it through the hills and was afraid Bad River would be up so had to go the road north of Deans (the way you went the last time.) That makes close to twenty five miles. It was about half after three when we got to town. The town was so crowded there was nothing to do but go to Mrs Gordens. I put him in the big chair in the kitchen and phoned the doctor. He said he could not set it for some time and for me to elevate the limb and pack it in ice. I did so and then took my team to the barn. If R. T. Parker[2] hadn't happened to be sleeping in the barn I guess I'd never have gotten the team taken care of.

The doctor was down to see him Thursday morning but said he could do nothing till I got the swelling reduced. I worked at it faithfully and helped the doctor set it about
[part of letter missing]
cast on, Sunday morning Mary and I went over home and I put away the last of the jell and plum butter, caught up the chickens, packed Chall's suitcase and mine and did "other things too numerous to mention." We got back to Donahues about half after six and after eating a lunch I drove into town.

I drove out here Monday morning. Was at the school house by nine o'clock to find it locked and uncleaned. I hunted up the Clerk [of the school board] and made a "holler"[;] she 'phoned the Treasurer and they made arrangements to clean the school house that afternoon. I helped around till four o'clock then hunted up my boarding place. I believe its the pleasantest, most comfortable boarding place I've ever had yet.[3] I wish I could settle down and stay all year but I have too many debts so will have to batch as soon as I can make a raise of a stove.

It was rainy this morning so we rode to school. Calvin [Moulton] rode a sorrel shetland named "Lassie" and I rode a chestnut saddle horse named "Snookums."

About the corn crib—Chall says he'll be glad to have it and I think I can make a raise of money enough to pay the freight by the time it gets here.

I asked Dr. Walsh about the bill. He said it wouldn't be less than $30 and he *didn't think* it would be more than $55.00. He couldn't tell yet. Says Chall can't walk for six weeks. My indebtedness amounts to something over $700.00 now. Wish I could teach two days at a time and hurry up the pay days.

Yours—Bachelor Bess

* OCT. 3, 1916 / FT. PIERRE, SO. DAK.
  TO MRS. M. M. COREY

Dear Ma,—Don't you admire my stationary?[1] 'Tis the best my school board has provided me with so far.

I meant to write you last week but had several irons in the fire so let it slide. It didn't worry me much till Friday eve when I got home about nine thirty and met my neighbor Yulius[2] at the gate. Am ready to take any bodys word for it now that he was off his base last winter and I dont guess he has regained his mental equilibrium yet. The more he jawed the louder he bawled and the worse threats he made— and there I sat. I began to think that there were two closed gates between me and the house and the door was locked and I didn't know how long it would take me to find the key in the dark and I'd lost my flash light and I hadn't written to my mother that week and other things too numerous to mention. I told him to go jump in the pond but he wouldn't. Then I told him to chase himself off home he talked too much. He almost jumped up and down but after I had repeated it several times he started out. Guess he was most run down any way by that time. And do you know he never cussed once. Wasn't that considerate of him?

When Mrs M[oulton] found I was going to batching at once they said they would board me for what I could batch for and made several other inducements so have decided to board all year at $2.50 per week.

If you want to send me a great big birthday present you might send me a bbl of apples. Mr Moulton will pay the freight and bring them out. They have a good cave and we kids would have apples for lunch for a long, long time.

Little Don [Moulton] is as talkative as ever. I tried to persuade him to play mum. He said "What's that?" When I told him how it was played he said "Lets wait till after supper." A few minutes later he said "If I just had a mouth organ I'd do a noise on that that would make you mum all right." I'll wager he would too.

Grandpa Moulton is visiting here. He has some great ideas regarding education. He was telling of men who accomplished so much without an education and I said it didn't seem to make any difference how you loaded potatoes. The big ones work to the top and the little ones rattle down. He said "Yes but they are wasting such a devil of a lot of money educating little potatoes[.]" I thot it was time to change the subject before I got in bad.

Must close and hurry home[.]

Hastily
Bachelor Bess

✷ OCT. 20, 1916 / FT. PIERRE, SO. DAK.
TO MRS. M. M. COREY

Dear Ma,—Received your letter a few evenings ago and it is receiving its second reading as I answer.

You think that church bunch wanted some but I think its that way every where. They always want all they can get.

I'd a given a good deal to have been there when Mrs Copley was there. I've thot of her so many times.

I think it is kind of nice to go in together that way to get flowers. That reminds me I meant to write Valerie [Harris Mutim] right away but didn't—it kind of slipped my mind. Have had so many irons in the fire of late.

Please tell Fuller about the two funerals up here this week. Robert Jennings little one was snake bit.[1] They killed two large snakes in the yard and intended to keep the little ones in the house. Bob started to the barn and saw the little one following him. He called to his wife to come and get the child. She started and saw it stop and reach down. When she got there a large rattler had struck it twice on the hand. That was Friday. The funeral was Sunday afternoon. And last Tuesday Emil Klemann's eldest boy, a little lad of eight, was burried.[2] They did not deside what the trouble was. Emil's wife would not allow a post mortem.

Two weeks ago tonight—no—tomorrow[—]I drove into town to spend my pay check. I had so many things to see to and it got late and Mrs G[ordon] wanted me to stay over so I did. Then it turned in and rained all night and when I drove out Sunday evening the mud was fierce. One of the tugs broke and I got my feet so muddy I just told Nell to go on home and tell 'em I was coming. She sure came home all right. They didn't happen to see her and she was waiting patiently at the gate when I got here. Guess I didn't walk more than a mile but my feet were like tubs.[3]

Last Saturday I drove my team home. Hitched the single buggy on behind and drove Nell back single. Chall had the cast off and shoe on. We drove over to the claim Sunday. He said he would miss Goulds but it would seem kind of good to get home again.

I certainly enjoyed that portion of your letter marked "private" or "confidential" or something of the sort. Am having a lot of sewing done—a green riding suit, a silk dress, a couple of pretty serge waists, etc. Will speak to Yulius next time I go home. Mike Donahue says the only way for me to get along with him is to marry him any way.

Seriously, I'm rather like the Dutchman's son—"Hans she [*sic*] dont like the girls and one can not get married alone[.]" Of course if you say so I'll make arrangements at once[.] What would you advise? Which one? The Dutchman, The Swede, the Norwegian, the Scotch-Irish, or the Englishman? Financially I suppose it would be best to take the old cuss who adores me for he probably hasn't much longer to adore. Morally—The Norwegian[4] would be the best choice. He's got lots of religion. I could notice it on him befor I began to get acquainted with him. Personally I'd prefer a president of some sort.[5]

I haven't any thing against Iowa only there's never any room for me in it. I'm always stepping on someone or getting stepped on. If I want to go any where it seems always to inconvenience the whole tribe more or less and then perhaps I have to go alone and that isn't pleasant when I'm not acquainted—of course—out here where I know folks it wouldn't be so bad. I'd sure like to go back once more but shucks! Whats the use? I can't be my self when I am there. I feel as if it made no difference what I said or did I'd be misjudged any way. It makes me miserable and every one else too. I'm much better off out here where people haven't been studying me always to prove that I'm like certain of my relatives. I can't afford the trip any way.

I don't want that $35 back. Who says I regreted it? It meant a sacrifice at the time but thats past now. I'm getting along well enough. You dont need to consider returning the money. Unless you want to give the book to some one else. You're welcome to the money any way.

Am not sitting up late many nights—at least I haven't been but I suppose I'll have to now I'm filling my "Hope box"(?)

I was weighed two weeks ago while in town and weighed the least I have for several years. Still I don't have to stand twice in a place to make a good shadow.

Will certainly appreciate reading those letters and will try to get them back promptly.

Well I must close before my flat iron gets cold[.]

Love to all

Bachelor Bess

P.S. Snowed Wednesday. The thermometer in school room 27° above zero Thurs. morning[.]

* NOV. 11, 1916 / FT. PIERRE, SO. DAK.
TO MRS. M. M. COREY

Dear Mother,—Guess I'm equal to writing a few lines.

We had our social a week ago last evening. Had a fair crowd, took in close to thirty dollars and I've received many compliments on the program and the management.

I got home in the wee small hours and was up before seven the next morning and did up Mrs Moultons work while she made a ride and got my pay check. In the afternoon I got ready and went to town. Got there about six oclock in the evening. Mrs Gordon and I attended a political meeting that evening.

Ethel Corey and Arthur Erickson at the time of their wedding in 1916.
Photo courtesy Margaret Nelson.

I came back Sunday eve—and I guess I must have been napping for the first thing I knew I didn't know where I was at. It was quite late when I got to Moultons and I've never given them any explanation either.

Mrs Gordon said she received her barrel of apples a week ago Friday—that is two weeks ago yesterday[—]and thot you said you sent me a barrel at the same time. I told Mr Moulton and he went down Monday. He was to pay the freight and bring them out but he found that Chall had taken them out to the claim. So I still have no apples and will eventually have the freight bill to pay I presume.

I haven't been home since last time. I just couldn't go that last two Saturdays before the Social and last Saturday I was too near all in it seemed. Mrs Moulton, the two boys[1] and myself planned to drive down last evening and take my sewing machine home.—The sewing machine was given to me for my "hope box." It was so stormy I didn't go.

Was not very well pleased with the returns of the election—in the county. The Equal Suffrage Bill[2] went through so I can vote next time and help levy taxes as well as pay them.

This getting married—I don't like the notion a tall. I always wanted a Swede or a president. I didn't think about the president till after Wilson had married again and then Ethel married a Swede. Of course I couldn't marry a Swede now—Oh I *could* but it would be such a sameness. You wouldn't want *two* Swede "son's-o'-guns" as Don [Moulton] would say.

This gent here is a Scandihooligan but he isn't a Swede.[3] He's got lots of religion but it isn't hurting him any. He believes that women should *obey*—the bible says so. I think you'd admire him he has such an open countenance. He says it wouldn't be so bad only when he and his cousin were little kids they put their fingers in their mouths and stretched them from ear to ear to see who could have the biggest mouth. His folks found it out and beat him for it, but his mouth never went back in shape. He's kind of nice tho and has no stock or family in this country except a Ford that isn't paid for yet.

Hastily yours
Bachelor Bess

P.S. I expect to go to the State Teachers association Meeting at Watertown Thanksgiving week. The district pays my car fare.

Many many thanks for the apples.

And say, ma, if you'll pick out a husband for me I'll try my gol darnedest to land him[,] honest I will[.]

> Lovingly yours
> B.B.

✳ DEC. 5, 1916[1] / FT. PIERRE, SO. DAK.
TO MRS. M. M. COREY

Dear Ma and the rest,—Haven't heard from you for several hundred years and neither has Chall. I know I haven't written for most that long and I don't know where to begin.

Did I tell you about my birthday? I cam home from school that evening to find a beautiful birthday cake awaiting me. It was all pink and white with the full number of candles. Mr and Mrs Moulton and the boys were going to town that evening so Edith Young came down to spend the night with me. We had *some* time. This Scandihooligan that works here was very nice. He helped do up the work and then we had a concert that lasted till a late hour. The next morning he didn't come over and build the fire and call us till plumb seven o'clock but he helped get breakfast and we got to school by nine tho we broke the buggy getting there. That Friday evening I went home and the next day cleaned the attic. Chall finished picking the corn that day—there must be 85 bushel any way.

Well I worked at that bloomin house till five o'clock Sunday and got back up here rather late. That whole week was one grand rush. Friday eve Mr and Mrs Moulton were invited to some sort of a small party so "de Scan" and I staid home with the kids. We undressed the kids and put them to bed while I cleared the table then he wiped the dishes. Gee! such a stack of 'em, dinner and supper both, and bread to start. Then I had to mend some stockings. I just fetched 'em out and sat by the fire. Thot if he knew I was a good hand at mending I might win a happy home but thunder! He informed me that he didn't think he had ever been in love with a girl and he didn't believe in *short* engagements. I might just as well wait for a president!

The next day (Saturday) I packed my suitcase and went to town—attended the teachers meeting Saturday afternoon[2] and left Sunday forenoon, with the bunch, for Watertown. The meeting was fine. There were 2,247 teachers registered. I enjoyed it very much

Elizabeth Corey with fellow teachers from Stanley County at the meeting of the South Dakota Educational Association in Watertown, November 1916. Photo courtesy Paul Corey.

especially Congressman Teso of O[hio]. and Dr Strayer of the School Survey and [David] Bispham the noted baratone singer.[3]

When I got back Thanksgiving morning I found that Mrs Moulton hadn't taken Nell out on Sunday as she intended as the Barn was under quarentine for hoof and mouth disease and she couldn't get her out. Was very thankful that it proved to be only an epidemic of sore mouth and not hoof and mouth disease. Nell is all right and is being kept away from the infected portions of the place and stock.

Chall met me that forenoon. He looked like he'd lost his last or best friend at first. He brought a cow hide in, One of my Old Janes got indigestion or some thing and checked in. Was mighty glad it wasn't anthrax or some of those supposedly contagious diseases.

I had to get a new cook stove to take home that night as Chall had just discovered that a large portion of the bottom of the old one was gone entirely. Its a good thing it came so "sudden't' loik" for I hadn't time to think how it would hurt my pocket book. ($15.00) Then I was glad, too, that he discovered how the other stove was before it burned the house down.

Chall brought me up Sunday and the rest of the barrel of apples (My how I enjoy them) and took my sewing machine home with him. He said he'd have his sewing all done up when I came home again but I couldn't get him to offer to do any of mine. Chall has the prettiest little dog named "Scoop" and a dove,—one of the prettiest I've ever seen[—]has adopted our place for a home. Chall always refers to him as the "Dove 'o peace." The dove and dog play together, but Boss, the cat, seems to feel too dignified to join in the sport. I solomnly predict that some day Boss will forget his dignity and then instead of a "Dove 'o peace" Chall will have scarcely a piece of dove.

When I got here Sunday I found a letter from Frederick waiting for me. I guess he is coming down Christmas.

Have to ride to school now-a-days. Calvin [Moulton] rides Lassie and I ride Shorty. Today Lassie got loose and came home. We wanted to bring Lassie's saddle and bridle home so Calvin could ride her to-morrow and, kid fashion, we mapped out a way that auto work. We put the little saddle on behind the big one and fastened it on to the big one securely then I mounted and put Calvin on behind. He began to imagine all sorts of things. We had a little wild west show of our own. Shorty is blocky built and quite fat and he's no colt either. I never thot of his pitching but I had his head well up and managed to keep it up. Calvin was quite as amazed as I was. He said "Well what's he doin' " I spurred him for all I was worth and kept his head up—thot I could make him run and he did—what he could with out leaving off pitching. He couldn't do much but shake us up. I felt as if he jarred most all of my constitutional ammendments loose. At last I got Calvin off and as he wouldn't let us both ride him we both walked. Now if this letter is badly written and spelled you may lay it all to Shorty.

Say I've read those letters over several times but would like to read them several times more[;] is they any hurry about them(?)

Must close and hit the perch. Write some time if its only a card. Say that old cow that croaked would have been fresh in a week or so. Think she might have postponed that checking in for a few weeks.

Yours with love
Bachelor Bess

* DEC. 16, 1916 / FT. PIERRE, SO. DAK.
  TO MRS. M. M. COREY AND FAMILY

> The Dry Run School would be pleased
> to have you share their Christmas pie
> with them, Friday afternoon,
> December twenty-second, at one o'clock.[1]
>
> Fort Pierre
> December Fifteenth

Calvin Moulton ——————————————— Miss Corey

* JAN. 6, 1917 / FT. PIERRE, SO. DAK.
  TO MRS. M. M. COREY

Dear Mother,—I got home Christmas eve and as we were going over to Goulds for the day, Christmas, we thot there would be so many things to do in the morning we better open the box that evening. Many thanks for the sauce dishes. Have been needing some for a long time. Two or three were cracked a little about the edges but they'll hold just as much as the rest. The dried apples, too, will help out wonderfully this spring. They will make the jelly and such hold out longer. I had forgotten about the handkerchief and those of yours you left here— have waited to send them and your stockings at once but there is always one or tother some where else it seems[.] Guess I'll have to send them on the installment plan one at a time.

Chall has ordered his saddle a 14½ inch so there is no possible danger of my ever useing it.

I wouldn't be surprised if Chall wasn't back in Iowa yet before the year was up. He doesn't seem satisfied. Says he isn't making any thing out of it as it is and wants me to turn the whole place over to him for a term of years and let him have my half of things for the up keep of the place. I don't feel that I can do that. He hasn't gotten rich this year—neither have I unless debts make a fellow rich. He said he could make more money working out in Iowa and of course I could not expect him to stay if he feels that way about it. He has one colt, two heifer calves, his clothes, board and Dr. paid and I have about $750.00 debts ahead of me[.]

Of course the profits will increase each year but if he doesn't wish to chance it we'll have to call it off.

It will mean a great loss to me if he goes now. Will always rather regret that I went in debt instead of away to school[.]

That was some blizzard we had the day after Christmas. The loss of stock was quite some. Rathbuns lost fifty head of cattle and I've heard of other losses but I don't remember now.

I washed, ironed, churned, baked, scrubbed and mended while home. So you may know I was busy. My sewing machine helped me out on the mending beautifully.

You know I lost my yarn mittens last fall and started to knit some more. I finished the second one while I was home and a half hour later found the other pair so gave the new ones to Chall.

We've certainly had cold weather. One morning I had the school stove red hot for twenty minutes and the thermometer only said 10° above zero. They have it all rigged so if the weather is bad at any time we can just stay at the school house. I think that is why it turned warm New Years day and has been very comfortable since tho as Mildred used to say it isn't so "pison hot yet[.]"

Am going to write Rob and Paul. I wonder if I send their letters with this to save postage if they will be offended.

Must close. May you have many Happy New Years. Was certainly glad to get that card from [you] at Christmas.

Yours
Bachelor Bess.

* JAN. 6, 1917 / FT. PIERRE, SO. DAK.
  TO PAUL COREY

Dear Paul,—Many thanks for the pop corn. Had been hungry for some for quite a while. One evening I said that if you folks knew how hungry I was for some good popcorn I believed you'd send me some so Mrs Moulton asked why I didn't write and tell you and I said I didn't like to. The pop corn we get here isn't so very nice.

That was a cute collar you sent for Scoop but Ill wager you wont get any vote of thanks from him. Its too handy for Chall to grab ahold of when he goes to strap him. He is a mighty smart Scoop. One day during vacation I made some cookies. I went to the door and called "Hot cookies" at Chall. He and Scoop were finishing the calfshed.

Chall yelled, "Hot cookies Schoop, Come on." and how they did *come on*. I didn't approve of feeding cream cookies to a dog but Chall said he didn't like the "rinds" and so he broke off the edges for the dog.

Last fall Chall told me about the bees in the crib and I told Calvin about them. He asked me at least a dozen times afterward if they had taken the honey yet and how they did it. When he found that we got some honey for Christmas and I still knew nothing about how they got at it he was quite disappointed.

The kids here were going out coasting this morning and little Don said "I slide on my belly and Calvin slides on his pants." We never know what he will say next.

Chall's chickens sure look fine. He'll have two dozen hens this next year.

Well I must close. Write some time.

Lovingly your sister Bess

✳ FEB. 4, 1917 / FT. PIERRE, SO. DAK.
TO MRS. M. M. COREY

Dear Mother,—There was a lecture in Fort Pierre January 16th and Edith Young and I drove down that evening after school intending to drive out the next day. I had to get Nell shod and they were working over time at the shop and I couldn't get her shod till late in the evening (Wednesday). So we didn't come out till Thursday eve. So I lost two days of school. I made it count tho. I visited my County Superintendant and took my eighth grade pupil over to visit the legislature. We visited both the House and the Senate. We heard House Bill 54 pass the Senate. That was providing for the return of insane patients to the states they had been shipped in from. In the House we heard a Bill providing for the care of Old Soldiers Widows at the State Home debated. We met Mr Wheelon[1] and were invited up to the house but declined. We had supper. Mr Gillette was kind enough to ask us to the picture show[2] and we went, and after the picture show we went to the Theater and hear "The Little Lost Sister." We came back late and slept late the next morning. Chall was in town the next day. I let him read your letter which I had just received.

Was out of school two days the following week. They thot I was going to check in but I fooled them a trip. Last Monday was a pretty nice day but rather cold. Mr Lund[3] laid out a road for us—no it was the Monday before he made a road for us. Well any way we went to school Tuesday morning and it began to storm before we got there and oh! how it stormed. We didn't get home till Friday evening.

Mr Hueston was out yesterday and it was 40° below zero. It was pretty good yesterday. It must have been up to zero any way. But last night it began to storm and we are having another howling blizzard. If we get to school tomorrow we will stay all week.

You must have received that bunch of letters ere this. I didn't put in those booklets because they were a different size. I have your stockings and handkerchieves ready to mail but dont know how many stamps they will require.

About those two chickens Chall traded for oats—No, of course I don't have to pay for them. Chall said if I'd pay the $2 for the Xmas goose and the express on the pigs or something like that he'd call it square. Its very unjust for you to keep roasting me for my selfishness and injustice. You did give me a great deal to help me get a start. I appreciate that, but I didn't ask for it and if you gave me so much you have little left for the rest I'm sure I'm not to blame. If you think I've sacrificed nothing its because you don't know. I don't care how much you give Chall or Ethel or any of the rest and you certainly don't need to feel from any thing I write that I want any of you to give me anything. I should not have made the references I did in my letters for I might have known they would be misunderstood and incur censure. If you had been in my place I don't think you'd have seen the joke either at first. It was this way. I was not to get my pay check till the first week in January and I had bills from Dr Younge,[4] [and] Dr Walsh, and Chall had been getting some clothes at Fishers and their bill was up to something over $106.00 and they wanted me to make a payment and then there is a barn bill and of course the note at Rowes and the $500.00 mortgage and my board[.]

Chall had said he would pick up a second hand saddle for $5 or $10 that would do for a time and if you sent him his money we could let it go on that cow he wants and I could use the money to help where it was needed most. Which would keep down some of this 10% interest. Well you sent him the money on condition that he put it all into a saddle and of course he did. He has a saddle—that as one man says—"He has no more use for such a saddle than a cat has for seven tails["] and three years from now when he really has some riding to do that saddle will be useless to him, for it will be too small. As it is I don't see how he can ride much with out my investing in a saddle horse for he rode Nell the last time I was home and that saddle gall broke out again. Rowdy isn't fit to ride and the other two mares are to raise colts if they are cared for.

Then Rob sent the pigs. It was surely good of him to send them and I suppose it was all right his giving them all to Chall. He naturally would expect Chall to be more interested in them than I. But you see as I was so crowded and Chall says there is about $150.00 worth of machinery that he must have this spring and he wants to buy a grade bull—a short horn for $65[—]and that isn't what I want or what is needed at all and it just seemed at first that to have to feed three or four hogs and then buy one to butcher was almost too much. I can see the joke, tho, now. Of course I aught not expect you to appreciate how I feel about wanting a little more education so I can go a little higher. I've gotten along without it all these years and folks naturally feel that I dont need it if I've done with out it this long. You never have understood me but I thot when you took up Christian Science that some day you would come to understand me and know me as I am and not as you have always made yourself believe that I must me [sic] according to material law.

Say, this little Don is a great one. Often when some one expresses surprise at something one of the children do Mrs M[oulton] will say "Oh thats not to be surprised at! Look at their mother[.]" The other day Don said "Sometimes when we are out doors Calvin don't talk at all, he just goes ———" and he led off a lingo worse than pig latin. Mrs Moulton said "Well thats silly. I'm surprised at Calvin doing such a crazy thing[.]" Don said "Oh! it aint to be sprised at. Look at the mother he's got[.]"

The other night he almost hugged my neck in two and then jumped down and exclamed "There, thats real love." He is surely the limit.

Well I must close. We haven't had the mail for a week and no prospect of getting it as I can see. With Love

Bess

---

* FEB. 11, 1917 / FT. PIERRE, SO. DAK.
TO MRS. M. M. COREY

Dear Mother, We camped at the school house all last week. Mary Young stayed with us so I was plenty busy with the house work and school work and the two youngsters to look after. I regret it a little, too, as I had hoped to write the first grade exams the 22nd 23rd & 24th of this month.[1] I'd like to read up some but dont seem to get to it very fast. Last Friday afternoon the children made valentines. Am sending you one that apealed to me. You can set it up in front of the book case if you like.

Mr Moulton got word this morning that his horses were exposed to the Stomatitis the other day in town. He is much worried. We are going to stay at the schoolhouse again this week and he said if at any time Nell began to show signs of coming down to bring her home. They have it so bad in town, I hope Chall gets next[2] and doesn't put his team in the barn.

I've got Chall's doctor bills all paid now and sent him fifteen dollars toward a new suit. I hope he gets it right away.

Have been on speaking terms with this gol darned Norwegian[3] for most four weeks. Shall try to keep on speaking terms till spring comes. You see he goes to school with us and shovels out the bad places and then he comes over in the middle of the week to see if all is well and he doesn't look half so homely as he did. Mrs Moulton seems quite encouraged. She's planning a little too strong tho.

I should not have sent you that last letter. I auto know better than ever try to explain any thing but it seems like I don't.

Lovingly yours—Bess

❋ MARCH 15, 1917 / FT. PIERRE, SO. DAK.
TO MRS. M. M. COREY

Dear Mother,—Aunt Rate writes that she ordered carnations and violets. The thot of violets makes me home sick. I can't remember seeing real violets in South Dakota and like "Hed" with the bananas I was "so fond of them." I hope they will stay nice a long time. And may you have many happy birthdays[.][1]

Its great weather we're having. Some days like the good old summer time and some like Greenland's icy mountains. Most every one around here is "fighting a cold." A small lad of my acquaintance seems to be suffering with a cold in the head and as a matter of course his friends suffer with him. I asked him once if he hadn't a handkerchief. He felt in his pocket and replied "No, but I got a cork." He was so amazed at my amusement that I didn't even suggest his using the cork.

Did I tell you that the last time I was in town I had my picture taken with the Wendte crowd? I told them they just wanted me for "background" but they insisted that I belonged to them and put me between Mrs Corey and Mary Hall with Paul and Tass in front. There were ten or a dozen of us.

My first graders and I are still batching in the school house and I think from the way the storm is raging tonight that we will batch for some time to come. My "family," as little Don says, are a bed and asleep.

I looked out, one evening this week, just as it was getting dark and saw a bunch of stock at the northeast corner of the school yard. One at the edge of the bunch moved and I called to the children that I believed there was a buffalo with that bunch of horses. Mary [Young] looked and said "Why, Miss Corey, your dreaming! Those are *all* buffalo.["] I wasn't convinced and got my cap and overshoes on to go see. The children tried to persuade me not to go. I don't know what they expected the buffalo to take me for. They were buffalo all right—seven or eight of them. Before I got to the fence the leader came toward me sniffing. But like the Irishman he changed his mind and they were soon racing across the flat as if the bad man was after them. Calvin says if that old fellow had kept on coming my way much longer I'd have come back as fast as if my mamma called me.

I haven't heard from Ethel since Xmas or from you or Chall since January 18th so I suppose you are all well and busy. I suppose I shouldn't expect a letter from you oftener than eight or ten weeks now there are four of us for you to write to.

I made half a dozen pillow slips last Saturday. I shan't use my pillows without slips just to keep folks from thinking I'm going to get married. Must close—Lovingly—Bachelor Bess

❋ APRIL 8, 1917 / FT. PIERRE, SO. DAK.
TO MRS. M. M. COREY

Dear Mother,—Was so glad to hear from you and so sorry I sent you my "dawg."[1] I miss him so! He was the cheerfulest critter—he never failed to bring a smile no matter what happened. The only dog I ever really cared for too. I hope he gets plenty of light, he was used to lots of light. Wont you have some candy? Its swell—chocolate covered nuts. You see I quarreled with that gol darned Norwegian, [Mr. Lund,] after Chall left this morning, and he went off to town. He came back in time for supper with the mail, the war news,[2] and a very nice box of candy for me. He said I should be willing to argue religion with him now. Wait till he tries it again! I'll tell him to read Prov. 14:7[3]—then he can go to town and get me another box of candy. I have another box of candy coming any way. The other day Mr Moulton found a puzzle that he was sure couldn't be worked. I said I thot it could. He said he'd get me a box of candy if I did. I worked it, too, I did. I intended to go down home last Friday evening. The river was still high so I would have to go by way of town which makes it a mighty long trip. It was rainy and disagreeable so I "shanged me moind."

Yesterday morning I threw back the covers and jumped out of bed and kind of smashed my right foot. Chall came up last evening and took Nell back with him so I have to start in riding Shorty again. Suppose I'll make out all right.

Much ob[l]iged for the stamps had just sent for $1's worth so I'm well supplied.

Chall seemed to think you didn't know he sent the butter knife. He had a clerk send it because he was in a hurry or some-thing.

Don't blame the fountain pen for its inclination. Its because of the Germans you know.[4]

Wonder if you've changed those insurance policies yet.[5] Ethel will always be *Ethel* and Ethel will always be *honest* but a woman must obey her husband and if you are going to change the policies why dont you have them made out to the boys? That would keep the "Scan's" out of it. And for goodness sake *don't, don't* expect me to marry a he-angel for they don't produce 'em out here.

Did I tell you about the buffalo at the school-house? They've been gone for several days and I hope they don't come back.

Did you receive an announcement of Mary Lanigan's marriage?

Well I must close and hit the perch. Oh say this morning the kids were looking for Easter eggs and chicks. They each found one with a little rooster beside it then Don found another egg and after looking around for a minute he exclaimed "Why, where's the rooster(?)" At breakfast they were discussing as to whether or not the eggs were rabbits eggs and Don grabbed up his little rooster and exclamed "Sure they're rabbit's eggs! Do you think *this* could lay an egg like that?["]

Must close—Love to all
Bachelor Bess

✳ MAY 20, 1917 / FT. PIERRE, SO. DAK.
TO MRS. M. M. COREY

Dear Mother, Yes they always pass the plate in Pierre, I think they do every where. I think my school is to close the first of June.

Yes, I thought you'd be mad about my dawg. Better send him back. I know I miss him more than you would. I'll pay all the expenses. Poor cuss! I known how it feels to not be appreciated.

And you think the thoughts I entertained killed those poor little pigs? Shucks!! Just think of the thots you've held over me ever since I was born, most, in regard to my disposition and character and such! I seemed to thrive on it. And the Bible says something about the wind being tempered to the shorn lamb. Or don't you think its the same with pigs?

Am glad you have a scheme about that policy. If it doesn't work and you think you want it the other way I'll do my best. I just thot if some felt I'd had my share already it would be as well for some one else to have the responsibility, and the kicking, and the chance. As you say Fuller and Robert have other responsibilities—but then—Ethel's married and I *might* (?) marry and we might raise a dozen or thirteen little Scan's[1] apiece—and we'd have responsibilities also.

Had a nice letter from Ethel's a few weeks back. She didn't say then that any one was sick. She says if I come down we can attend institute together. I'd sure like to go. Gee!

Say, mamma, what's it like when you're in love? How would I know if I got it? Folks say I've got it and it scares me. I'm like the Dutchman "How should I know if it is vitch or vat or in or out or vat it is!" They say I'm getting thin but I don't feel thin. My bones aren't sticking through my clothes any way. My duds are getting so loose my bones don't touch 'em much. That black skirt I couldn't wear last summer because it was too tight—you auto see it now! And my riding suit—of course the middy [blouse] helps the looks of it but I can't pin the skirt up, to any advantage, and I have to hitch 'em up on one hip every time no one is looking. I got to thinking the other day how dreadful it would be if Shorty should dump me and my skirts should catch on the [saddle] horn. Then of course he'd come home and there I'd be in my middy only. Well I sent to town the very next day for elastic to put in those skirt bands. Haven't got it in yet tho.

My seventh and eighth grade pupils are reviewing for the final exams which come off the 24th and 25th inst. Some times they work as late as six or six thirty and then I have my other work so I'm putting in long days.

Am also trying to finish my reading circle work before school lets out. Don't know if I'll make it or not. Have finished one book and two chapters of the other.

Tell Robert I had a nice letter from Lydia yesterday and she and Dave [Bull] want us to come down to make them a visit while he is out here. If he comes.

I suppose Fuller is home ere this. Will try to send him a tax receipt soon.

How long has Paul been a scout? And isn't Cousin Mary[2] coming up before she goes east? Would try to show her a good time tho I couldn't promise to make her brides maid or any thing like that. We haven't a car but we have a good top buggy * * * * *

How is the servant problem? Id like to solve it for you.

Much Love
Bachelor Bess

＊ MAY 31, 1917 / FT. PIERRE, SO. DAK.
TO MRS. M. M. COREY

It's all right your blaming me for Chall losing the pigs. I did see them once. But, Thank the Lord! I never did see the fellow Ethel married.

＊ JUNE 11, 1917 / FT. PIERRE, SO. DAK.
TO MRS. M. M. COREY

Dear Mother, your letter came that last week of school when everything was rushed. I had to hustle early and late with the reading circle work, final exams, last day picnic, etc. I finished up June first.

Anyway, They Cant Blame Me For This

The humorous postcards of Bess's day often made it possible to convey a delicate message without giving undue offense. Photo courtesy Cultural Heritage Center, Pierre, S.D.

Chall met me in town the next day. The river was up so he had to go to town the long way so he just went out to Moultons that eve and started home in the rain Sunday morning.

When Chall was up to Moultons after Nell he was saying that I might have either of those schools near here[1] and some of the patrons in each district were anxious for me to take their school. I thot if I took one of those I'd be near enough home so I could help out some but Chall was just set against it. He said there was at least one family in each district that he knew *no one* could get along with and he wouldn't hear to my considering either of them. I thot there was no use trying it if he was so set against it. I got a letter from Lydia about then. She said they were talking of putting her on the school board[2] instead of Miss Peckham who was leaving for Florida. I thought right away there would be a good chance for me. Its a three room village school and they wanted me last year. I spoke of it on the way home but Chall had changed his mind and was just as determined that I take one of the schools near home. I told him it would be all right if we could get along with out squabbling and he didn't expect to much of me. For you know as well as I do that with more stock there is quite enough to keep me busy all day with out any school work.

When I spoke of solving the servant problem there was a girl here that I would like to have sent down. You'd have liked her I think and although she isn't quite sixteen she has gone ahead with the work at home for two or three years and I've been there and know her work is all right but thats all off now. I would have liked to come myself but Chall thot I was needed so badly at home here so I spent my last cent before I left town so there is no show of my getting there this summer.

Institute begins June 18th and lasts for two weeks. Mrs Gordon wants me to come down the 14th or 15th and take care of the place while she goes down to Huron to take care of Anna. My board wont cost me any thing if I do that. That will help some. You know I'm in pretty deep again $500 mortgage and more that $85 store bill. I have tried to deal on the square but I'm afraid now I haven't. When Chall would pull off some stunt or other he would insist that I should not write of it to you and I felt that so long as he didn't wish to write it there was no use for me to tattle[.] I'd only get roasted for it. I suppose perhaps I should have told you some things. I'll have to take the roasting some time any way.

You spoke once of my store bill. I've learned some reasons for its size just lately. When I came home there was dried apples enough to make six peanut butter glasses of apple butter and there wasn't a sign of any other fruit left. Chall was telling a short time ago how good Goulds were to him[.] He said they sure appreciated the fruit and jelly and dried apples he took over from time to time. I didn't say any thing but when I took some rubbish out to the heap there were cans with apple and berry labels on them and such things count up. Then, too, I sent him fifteen dollars to get him a suit last winter—he had said he wanted a twenty dollar suit but that was more than comparatively wealthy cattle men can afford and he had no *good* place to keep it and the last one you got him only cost seven so I thot fifteen was all I could afford—thats more than my best suit cost. Well he got a *twenty-five* dollar suit and charged the other ten to my account. He insisted that I get about $150 worth of machinery this spring and I told him that I just couldn't get it[.] I didn't have and couldn't get the money. He wanted machinery that men who have farmed here for years have never owned. He insisted that I get a bull. I just couldn't, thats all there was to it. Coming home Chall said I wouldn't get a bull as he told me to and he would not bother with borrowing so consequently there would be no crop of calves next year. I said "Well if that is the case I'd better sell the cows before winter and not risk loosing two or three more and no chance of gain." He didn't say any thing. The other morning (Friday) he was telling how much I owed him and told of some money which he said was mine but he just put it on his account and checked it out to pay my bills. I asked why he didn't have it placed to my account, if it was mine, and let me pay my own bills. He said it was more convenient for him the other way. He acted grouchy all day and that evening I happened to ask why he put that old fly trap out by the chicken house. (When it is laying at a little distance that round hole makes it look like a childs indoor toilet[.]) He said there wasn't any other place to put it. I said it could have been put down cellar or up in the attic or out to Sally's. He flew all to pieces and I said if he was going to fly into a temper over a thing like that I didn't see any hopes of getting along a whole year. He said if I wasn't going to be satisfied with the way he did things he could pack his suit case just as quick as any one or a little quicker. I asked if he had ever heard me express any unreasonable dissatisfaction. He said no but he knew I was dissatisfied from what Mrs Gould and Mrs Donahue said. I asked him what they had said and reminded him that I hadn't seen either of them to talk to them alone since last summer, neither had I corresponded with either of them—only to write a note to Mrs Gould in answer to hers and she give that to Chall to read. I told him that I had never expressed any dissatisfaction to them and if there was any misunderstanding I was willing to go right over there with him and see what could be done to straighten it out. He didn't seem to want to do that. The next morning he started out saying that he'd let me know by night—whether or not he'd take care of the stock any longer. When he came back in the evening he wanted to know what I was going to do. I told him that depended on him—he said when he left he'd let me know by night whether he was going to take care of the stock any longer and when he told me his dicision I'd know what to plan on. He said he had talked it over with Mr Gould and Mr Gould persuaded him to come back and talk it over. I told him to go ahead and he said well if I said that I needed him and couldn't get along with out him he'd stay of course. I told him he needn't expect me to make any such fool speech. He said "Then you want me to go—its no advantage to *you* to have me stay!" I told him that I didn't say *that* but it looked to me as if there would be *some* advantages either way.

Then he began to talk about dividing the stock and I told him he might divide them into two lots as evenly as possible—there are eight—an even number. He got sore about that—said I treated him just like a kid. I asked him how else he might wish to be treated—he said some thing about treating him as a stranger[.] I told him very well "I would be apt to tell a stranger that as he broke the contract with out reasonable cause he need not expect me to keep up to mine[.]" Yesterday morning he said he'd stay till I made arrangements for the stock. I said I'd make no arrangements for the stock so long as he was caring for them. He said he was through Monday morning.

As I have to leave so soon to be gone for more than two weeks will leave the stock at Donahue's till I hear from you and make some arrangements with the bank.

Chall said once "Well mother told me last summer what to look for so I've been expecting it[.]" I said "I thot as much." Then he began to hedge and said you only told I was dissatisfied with him or the way he did.

Now he isn't of age yet and I don't know that you have given him his time.[3] I'll describe the stock—the increase you know—and you can write what you think. I'll see the bank as soon as I hear from you and see what can be done.

Chall has been off some where with the Hanson boys today. He is in with them thick. He said the other day I hadn't given them a square deal and here last summer he made an awful fuss if I treated them civil. He has asked several people about work and had several offers.

I've most all his clothes washed but am afraid I'll not have time to get them all ironed and mended.

Will send you a copy of the contract. It is just the way he wanted it.

There are three last summer or fall heifers, one December heifer, and two spring calves, one heifer and one stear. Then Kates and Rox colts. That makes eight head.

I forgot to tell you that Chall said he'd pay for that suit. He has told some that he just broke even last year—he wasn't in debt any but he wasn't ahead any—he was going to stay because I'd be out so much if he quit. That was quite a while back he was telling that and he represented that he was only out his time. Now do you think if he'd worked any where else and paid his own doctor bills that he'd be any ahead of what he'll have when he disposes of his share of the stock?

Well I must go for the cows[.]

Hastily—Bess.

* JUNE 18, 1917 / FT. PIERRE, SO. DAK.
  TO MRS. M. M. COREY

Dear Mother,—I came down last Friday. Jennie Speer wanted to come to town so rode down with me and drove Nell back.

Jennie saw Chall leave town but I didn't get to see him. He has a job near Draiper,[1] I understand.

I thot as long as Chall is leaving the community and you kind of objected to his having money in cattle and so long as the cattle were mortgaged perhaps the most satisfactory thing for all concerned would be to put a value on the eight head and give you an interest bearing note for Challs half and you give me a receipt or paper showing what it was for etc. I wrote to Mr Moulton and asked him if he had a half interest in those eight head and was going to put a price on them and let the other fellow "give or take" what he'd put the price at. I haven't had time to hear from him yet. I put their value at $150.00. I asked Mr Donahue [about] what I did[.] Mr Moulton and he figured on it a few minutes then said he couldn't buy cattle now at any price and he wouldn't want to say what they were worth but if he were buying and had a chance at a bunch like that, he'd try to get them for $125.00.

Now when I hear from Mr Moulton I'll let you know and you can set your price. That looks to me like the best I can do.

I'm very much afraid that the time will come when Chall will feel that Mrs Gould has not been so much his friend as he has thought. I have been remembering lots of things of late that I didn't think so much of when they happened. You know last fall before Chall's foot was so he was fit to do a day's hard work Mrs Gould persuaded him that he would be much ahead if he let them keep the cows for the milk and so much beside and he got a job and worked out. He said he'd take the fruit and vegetables over and put them in Goulds cellar. I told him if he wanted to work out all right but I would dispose of the stock. He got to thinking it over and decided to stay with it. He said he could see where he'd come out far ahead by staying with it. He said the other day that Mrs Gould had asked him a good many times what he wanted to stick around over there for when he could make more for himself some where else. Mrs Gould knew what that contract was, and they've been wanting more cows to take care of, and it looks to me as if she had an ax to grind. She came to me that day at the club and spoke of Chall's going, of the stock, and said if there was any thing Horace could do about the stock or to help me get straightened around he'd be glad to.

They have had a good deal to do with his notion that the best clothes obtainable were none too good for him in spite of the fact that there was no place out there to wear such clothes or place suitable to keep them in proper condition. My salary looked big to them and they couldn't reckon expenses so I'm sure they were back of some of his most unreasonable demands.

Must close and go to bed. When is Paul coming? Mrs [C. M.] Corey has invited us down there [to Van Metre] for a visit[.]

Lovingly—Bess.

[Enclosure]

Contract[2]

State of South Dakota   Elizabeth F Corey

SS

Stanley County   Chall R Corey

This agreement entered into this 7th day of April 1917 between Elizabeth F Corey and Chall R Corey—

That the said Chall R. Corey agrees hereby to run land and stock of said Elizabeth F Corey for a term of twenty four months commencing February 12, 1917 and to expire February 12, 1919, for which service truly rendered and labor of up keep of place the said Elizabeth F Corey agrees to furnish board, pay half of all doctor and dental bills, give half of increase of stock and half increase of all poultry and half of surplus crops.

Elizabeth F Corey

_____   _____

_____

* JULY 22, 1917[1] / FT. PIERRE, SO. DAK.
  TO MRS. M. M. COREY

Dear Mother,—Yours of the 28th ult. received some time ago and yours of the 18th inst. received this morning. You said you couldn't write definitely on any thing till you heard Challs "particulars" and there was no use my writing til I heard from you.

Bankers here get money from the east which they loan on stock not to exceed $25 per head. Some times they chance it and loan more than that. It is customary to include the increase in such mortgages to offset their risk. I bought eight cows and mortgaged twelve head of stock and their increase. At the end of the year we had lost practically two cows and two claves [sic] leaving ten head beside the increas— one colt and four or five calves. Now Chall didn't wish to quit then and thot it as well not to divide the increase till he was through[.] It would look something like putting the property in my wife's name. So the young stock was included in the mortgage because it is customary and it was necessary in order to make their security as good as the year before.

The money Chall had in the place and stock was squared up. He disposed of his share of the chickens—sold the young ones to Mrs Hanson and took the old ones over to Mrs Gould.

No, I've never had my store account settled up since you were up here. I paid on it every time I could. Once as much as $50 and lesser amounts at other times. Once I had it down to something around $30 but now its over $90 and I haven't put any thing on it for weeks.

Mr Moulton wrote me the other day. He said he couldn't judge stock he'd never seen but the three yearlings might be worth $45 or $50[,] the three calves $35 to $40 and the colts $40. His figures are sky high—far more than the stock could possibly sell for. I thot my price the limit. So that leaves

Mr Donahues estimate	$225
Mr Gordons	240
My	250
Mr Moultons	335

Mr Gordons figures are just about what could have been realized out of the bunch July 1st. Now if you are going to settle for cash please deside on a reasonable price and let me know as soon as possible. If you went to law he wouldn't get a cent. I'm not even under a moral obligation to give him a half interest in more than one of the colts and five calves. If you are not going to settle for cash, or note rather, you can have the yearling colt, the two oldest heifers and the heifer calf. That will leave me one short yearling, one December calf and the little steer calf and the little colt. If you are going to take the stock please arrange to have them removed at once. One dam is dry and the other nearly so. Every one is short of water and I've enough to do with out taking care of the bunch till he[Chall]'s twenty-one and then have to give up the best of the bunch.

Am sorry Rob got spilt. Must be he doesn't stand in with the Ladies like he used to. I thot of him on his birthday, and of Paul on his, but as they never have time to answer my letters I thot it would be an imposition to write. Will send them each a book mark and wish them many happy returns.

When Institute began Mrs Gordon decided not to go to Huron. There was lots going on that first week. I made up my mind that if I did not go down to Van for that Saturday and Sunday I wouldn't get down there this summer so wrote Mrs Nordin a card and packed my suitcase. One of the girls were there while I was packing and I got a hunch. I said "My riding suit isn't ironed but I'm going to stick it in for it always rains when I go to Van Metre." And would you believe it! It rained so hard before I got there that Albin came to meet me horseback. Of course I only had Saturday and Sunday to stay and we had company and a great time. They kept me there till the last minute. We visited till eleven Sunday evening and got up at one to catch that crazy train. It was dark and the team wouldn't keep the trail and we fetched up in the south east corner of the pasture. We just caught the train and that was all. As I got off the train Mrs Gordon got on. She had been called to Huron by the death of the new baby. Mrs Burgette of Capa

Dry Run School

District No. 7,
Stanley County,

SOUTH DAKOTA.

"Goodbye."

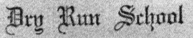

We've spent some busy happy
days,
In learning How and Why;
Now we must go our different
ways,—
It's time to say goodbye.

It's time to say goodbye, my
dears,
And don't forget it's true
We are saying "God be with
you," when
We say goodbye to you.

You'll enter soon on Life's
great school,
Where all must toil and try;
Your teacher's heart goes out
with you,—
Goodbye, my dears, goodbye.

Sincerely your teacher,

ELIZABETH F. COREY.

*End-of-school bookmark tokens presented to her students at Dry Run
School by Elizabeth Corey in 1917. Extras sent to Rob and Paul Corey.
Photo courtesy Cultural Heritage Center, Pierre, S.D.*

came down on the same train and I took her in to board. So with Mr Gordon and the dog that made four to keep house for. There was also tickets to sell at the show[2] two or three nights and the launch party and the Eighth Grade Commencement Exercises.[3] So it kept me busy. To cap the climax—a day or two after Mrs Gordon left, I took a handful of matches out of a box just as I've done dozens of times but that time they exploded in my hand. The muscles of that hand and arm contracted as if in a spasim then instantly relaxed and I threw the matches from me. Mrs B[urgette] helped put them out but they burned the linoleum in several places. Folks said the reason my hand didn't hurt me more was because it was burned so horribly. I didn't stop cooking or dish-washing or writing, or anything, and my hand is all right now. Only one scar about the size of a fifty cent piece and several smaller ones. It sure was a fierce looker for a few days. The day after Institute closed I came out with Mr Reese in the car and put in some mighty busy days between then and the fourth getting ready and helping drill the bunch for the Fourth.

MONDAY JULY 23

Last night I had to stop and go to Hansens on an errand.

By the day after the fourth my hand was so I could milk without difficulty and on Friday Mary D[onahue]. and I were going to take the cows over. Friday morning Donahues separator went to pieces and there they were milking twenty cows beside five of mine. If I took my cows home it wouldn't help them much so Mary and I came over and got my separator and took it over for them to use till they could get a part for theirs back from the factory. Am expecting the cows and separator home any day. My pond is mighty low and perhaps we'll have rain before its dry. I expect the black cow will be fresh by the time she gets home if she isn't all ready. Six to milk will seem quite a few till I get used to it. Its a mighty good thing I haven't had them here these last few days while I've been so busy with Nell. Mr Hanson says he'll have Mr Valentine[4] come out this afternoon or in the morning so I'll soon know, I hope, whether she'll have to be shot or not. I'm glad its Nell and not Chall or some of the rest of you.

Must close and go to work with Nell[.]

Lovingly yours
Bess.

Fuller and Teresa Corey at the time of their wedding in 1917. Photo courtesy Mildred Corey Adcock.

Bess's sister Ethel, married to Carl Arthur ("Art") Erickson and living in Winthrop, Minnesota, prevailed upon Bess to come live with her for a period of time toward the end of 1917. The event was the impending birth (on January 4, 1918) of Ethel's first child, Margaret Helen. It is perhaps indicative of the manner in which the sisters had overcome their youthful rivalries that Ethel should wish Bess, rather than their mother, to be with her at this important moment.

✳ DEC. 1, 1917[1] / WINTHROP, MINN.
TO MRS. M. M. COREY

Dear Mother, Many thanks for the popcorn. Mr Parker brought it out. The sack was broken but he put it into another sack and it didn't look as if much had spilled. Have enjoyed it greatly and so have some of the rest.

The past month has been reasonably nice weather but it is getting frightfully cold tonight.

I like Winthrop quite well. Ethel had a "Coffe[e] Cluster" for me this after noon. I have another note to write and want to help Ethel do the dishes before my soldier boy[2] gets here.

With regards to all I am

Sincerely yours,
Elizabeth—

✳ MARCH 3, 1918 / FT. PIERRE, SO. DAK.
TO MRS. M. M. COREY

Dear Mother, Yours rec'd. Was very glad to hear from you. Was going to write a long letter to you and Ethel both and send it by way of Ethel but only have a few minutes so will write you here in town.

Am inclosing a check for ($150.00) One hundred and fifty dollars. Will remit a check for interest on same if you say so.

Am glad you have the place in Atlantic.[1] I never liked the East side myself if I remember rightly. Am glad you sold the home place to Robert. I'd rather he had it than anyone else.

Margaret Morgan Corey and Paul Corey after their move to Atlantic, Iowa, in 1918. Photo courtesy Margaret Nelson.

Had a nice letter from Fuller. He said he had applied for a ten days furlough. I hope he gets it. Was telling a friend of mine about it and she told me a story which I'm going to tell you and you may take the hint if you like. She said she once wanted to go to Chicago to visit her brother Ed so she wrote her brother's wife and told her to manage it some how. She had Ed lay down on the floor and then wired my friend "Ed is very low. Come at once." She went.

Any message sent me in care of the Post Master will reach me in a very few hours.

Have registered for "Emergency Service" Subject to call any time after June 1st—to go *any where.*[2] May get to France as soon as Fuller does. The explanation says it may mean Canteen service back of trenches. I may not be called at all.

Hastily,
Bess

* APRIL 28, 1918 / FT. PIERRE, SO. DAK.
 TO MRS. M. M. COREY

Dear Mother, Those cards and things I sent and none of them cared for—if you will kindly send them back to me I'll refund the postage and see that it never happens again.

My school will be out the day before Decoration Day if nothing more happens but we are expecting some thing more to happen any time.

No, it will be impossible for me to go to Atlantic and be called from there. I promised Aunt Rate and Fuller that I'd come if he—Fuller—got a furlow but he isn't going to have a furlow and I'm *out* of funds and have orders to attend six weeks summer school. Will work my way. If I was there when called it might mean a trip back here and needless delay. Will have an opportunity to attend C[hristian] S[cience] services every Sunday during summer school this year.

Had a card from Anna Stewart, at Xmas time I think it was, but I never answered it. I seem to have lost interest in letter writing this past year. Don't think I'll ever get back to it again.

That home made handkerchief Margaret made you and a pair of stockings I sent you while I was at Moultons last year. Perhaps you've laid them away some where.

When Chall was here I told him if he wanted to save the feathers Id make him a pair of pillows. He left about enough for one pillow. I didn't have the price of the ticking last summer. Had a woman doing a little sewing for me a while back and she made the ticks, tick covers, and a pair of slips. I was going to put initials on the slips but seem to have lost the forms. Last evening when I came to put the feathers in, I found that part of them were live feathers and part just chicken feathers so did not mix them but put part in each tick. I put the negatives inside the package and have it all wrapped to send you next time I go to town. I haven't prints from many of them myself but I suppose there's no use wasting tears over such things. If there is any thing else around here you care for, let me know so I can send it to you or arrange for you to get it later.

Did you ever send me that package containing a skirt for the Indians? I never received it.

The means you say you suggested to Fuller I spoke of in reference to *myself* and no one else.

Last Friday it rained and yesterday morning it was a howling blizzard. This morning it turned to rain again and has rained all day. Great pools stand where the drifts were yesterday.

There was to have been a Red Cross Social[1] over east last eve. I was to escort or be escorted by a "fellow teacher." Gave it up on account of inclement weather.

Had company for supper Tuesday evening. Four of them but one was a lady. They had a great bragging about my corn-bread—that is all but one of them did. He said it didn't compare with the biscuits he made for dinner. They were just swell. Almost broke their teeth out eating them they were so hard but that was the fault of the oven.

My friend in Mitchell[2] is sending me the Christian Herald again. I'm forced to admire the presistence of the Germans at any rate.

Must close and hit the perch or I'll be late for school in the morning. We are using the *War* time which is an hour earlier than central time used to be.

Yours
Bachelor Bess.

Despite her protestations, Bess did return to Iowa for a visit during the spring of 1918, staying probably about two weeks and enjoying it thoroughly, as her letter of May 19 indicates.

✳ MAY 19, 1918 / FT. PIERRE, SO. DAK.
TO MRS. M. M. COREY

Dear Mother,—Anna [Stewart] and I had plenty of time to visit the shops as our train didn't leave till a quarter of four. I purchased a corset for $1.50 that would have cost me five here and it fits just fine.

Anna phoned and they held her train at Avoca. Just as she got off at Avoca I heard the band begin to play and opened the window. They stopped quite near. They seemed to be escorting about a dozen young men with suit cases, whom I learned later had been called to go into training at various camps. Anna was talking to me through the window and was called away. She came back just as the train pulled out to tell me that one young man out from Harlan shot himself to keep from going. I thot of Dewitt[1] and a sick feeling went over me. I can hardly wait to hear from some of you.

Made much better train connections coming back. Had breakfast at Sam K's[2] again and got into Pierre 1:35[.]

Went to the land office and they said I might make final proof on that other eighty any time and need not wait for next December.

Went up to Mrs Wheelons[3] for a while and Lena and Ourville took me and my suitcase to the boat landing. When I got across a gentleman carried my suitcase for me. Had some fun in Fort Pierre and came out the next day with Mr Speer.

Some of my patrons thot I'd been gone so long I auto just close school at once and not finish up. I didn't feel rich enough to let $130.00 slide that way.

Well I certainly enjoyed my visit and left Iowa with a desire to go back again some time.

Will enclose a piece of velvet[4] I misappropreiated and if you put that elastic I left in with that skirt when you send it and tell me what it cost I'll make it right.

Yours—Bess

✳ JUNE 30, 1918 / FT. PIERRE, SO. DAK.
TO MRS. M. M. COREY

Dear Mother,—Your card received the other day and I guess I had a letter from you some time before. I've kind of forgotten.

Am sorry for Maurine.[1] Hope she is better. She will be with you likely ere you receive this and you can pass what ever is interesting on to the rest.

My school closed June 6th[.] I went to see the Clerk that eve and didn't get home till the next forenoon. Haven't I written you since? Seems like I have. Had but a few hours at home before leaving for town to begin institute work in Pierre June 10th.

A bunch of us girls rented a furnished cottage and batched. We had *some time*.

Institute only lasted a week. I caught a ride out to a big picnic south of town and went home with R T Parkers. Mrs Parker took me over to Speers the next day and I caught up my team and Ruth[2] came home with me.

One of the neighbors was working here for a couple of days and then Ruth and I went to town and brought the little Hansen girls home with us. Roy's wife hasn't been expected to live for weeks and as I couldn't do any thing there I thot it might help some if I brought the youngsters out here for a spell. Little Fern is four years of age and badly spoiled. She was also having a swell time with the mumps and had never been away from her mother before. Dont ask me why I haven't been writing letters. I asure you my undertaking was a howling success. We had hardly crossed the river on the way home before she began to howl for her mother. I let her drive to change her mind. She almost put us into a big ditch and Myrtle grabbed for the lines. Fern jerked them away and said "Stop it! I just get so ding busted mad at you Myrtle!" I had to watch them so carefully on account of snakes. The boys killed an enormous rattler in this box outside the door the Saturday evening before. They think that is what took so many of my baby chicks.

The youngsters are gone now and for a few days I've been alone except for the bed bugs they left and the calls of some of my undesireable neighbors.

Did I tell you all that Elmer Ziggler, one of Stanley County's most *noted cattle men*, and his third wife, and Ben Thompson[,][3] who swiped my sweater, and Pat Hobro's wife, have leased this land south of me and the Sonnenschein place and are all living on the Sonnenschein place? Some of them go through here once or twice a day. The other day I sat here looking over a pan of lettuce with the door pushed partly shut to keep out the sun. I heard a sound and glanced out the window in time to see Mr Ziggle[r], with true Indian deftness remove the tub from the top of the water barrel. At the same time some one tried the screen door and exclamed "Door's hooked!" Some one said "Well *knock.*" So some one knocked and I went to the door. It was Ziggle[r], Thompson, and another guy. They wanted a drink and I brought in and strained a pitcher of water[4] and they drank glass after glass. If Ziggler didn't talk so freely you'd think he was a full blooded Indian. I like him very much. He dropped down Indian fashion, and talked for several minutes. All the time he talked to me he seemed like a great big half shy but very friendly school boy. I noticed that when either of the others spoke he shot a keen glance about the place and I'll venture to say that when he left he could have told some things about this place that *I* don't know.

They are too close to be dangerous as far as stock is concerned *I* think but intend to have my saddle horse and the colts branded as soon as convenient any how.

Folks say that Thompson and the Hobro woman are running a boot legging joint and all that goes with it.

Mrs. M. R. Donahue has been in Pierre for some time. Stub Gould[5] told at Parkers the other evening that the Donahues were the proud parents of twin soldiers but every one thinks its just one of his lies. I can hardly wait to hear the facts.

A storm[6] did considerable damage over a large territory last Tuesday evening. Every one around here who had a cave or cellar went into it I guess—except myself. I forgot to. Was looking out the south window here and it looked so funny to see things dancing and skipping about. I never noticed the clouds and so saw nothing to be afraid of. Was very fortunate—more so than any of my neighbors—tho it did leave my buggy the wrong side up for traveling. It required the help of a saddle horse to put it back on its wheels. Glen is going to help me take the top off in the morning.

Glen made me some new halter ropes with the snaps attached. They're fine.

George Hueston and John Johnson were here to supper the other evening. Mr Hueston was telling of a big snake he killed out to the claim. It was so large in the middle he cut it open and found it had swallowed a piece of an old dish rag in which was a mouce nest with several baby mice. Mr Johnson with his characteristic drollness remarked on the patriotism of the American snakes and their willingness to use substitutes. I wish Chall could have heard him.

Must close. Love to all

Bachelor Bess

✻ JULY 14, 1918[1] / FT. PIERRE, SO. DAK.
   TO ETHEL COREY ERICKSON

Dear Sis, Received this letter from Mother and she asked me to
send it on to you so will write a few lines to go with it. Guess I've been
oweing you a letter for ages. I don't think I'll ever get back to my old
letter writing habit. And the amount of work I've had on [my] hands
this year "must be seen to be appreciated" as they say in stories.

You spoke of having such a terrible headache. Am sure you've had
ample time to recover from it. Hope you do not have them frequently.

I surely was disapointed by your not getting to Iowa when I did. I
wanted to see you and little Margaret so. I just couldn't hardly give
you up. My! how I want to see that baby. Have thot of some thing to
make for both her and my other little niece when I get to it. There is
quite a similarity in their names isn't there? Margaret Helen Erickson
and Harriet Ellen Messix.

I hope Arthur's[2] health is better. What is he working at now?

Should like to see the new rug. Wish my hubby would get me one
for my birthday.[3]

What do I mean by going across the sea? Oh, nothing much. I
vollunteered for emergency service, to go any where at any time after
June 1st.

Your chickens were surely doing well when you wrote. Mine
would do well if they had a chance. I was gone over a week in Iowa
and a week at Institute and they were only fed once a day and the
owls, snakes, and hawks have made havoc among them. Have taken
of[f] eighty some chicks and have just forty-three left. Goulds still have
my shot gun. I suppose I better charge it up to profit and loss and get
a new one. They've been by here times enough and they know how
bad I need it. I believe the satisfaction Mrs Gould gets out of my loss
bothers me as much as the loss does. I'd have gained by borrowing
money at ten percent and buying a gun. My little rifle isn't heavy
enough. While I was at Institute the men killed a big rattle[r] in the
box by the door, which they said had been eating baby chicks. I killed
one in the chicken yard before that. This morning I heard a chicken
squall out by the barn. I ran out there in my bed room slippers and
there was a big rattler coiled and a few feet from it lay one of my nice
young chickens in convulsions seemingly. Believe me! That snake was
soon a deader. I suppose the chicken tried to pick his eyes out while
he was asleep. The hawks come right down in the yard. When I came

up with Win[4] the other day one sat out here eating a chicken. I tried my toy cannon but couldn't even jar a feather loose. I used to shoo 'em away with the dish towel but now I throw clods or a pipe wrench or just any thing.

Howard Speer was drafted and goes to Camp Dodge[5] a week from Monday I believe. And with him goes one of my most undesireable neighbors—the fellow who stole my sweater and has been living on the Sonnenschein place with Pat Hobro's wife.[6]

Some of us were to the river Friday for currants. I only got a few and want to go again. I put them up with white corn syrup. Some say you cant use corn syrup for jelly but I did and it jelled for me.

Say, some time try your corn gem recipe using half corn meal and half rolled oats and no white flour. Folks say my gems are fine. Some times I bake it in the dripping pan to save washing the other pans. They also make quite a fuss over a war cake I've worked out a receipe for. I use corn syrup and corn starch which makes it wheat-less and sugar-less. It *is* good if I do say it myself. I bake it in gem pans or layers. I've thot out a couple of sugar-less cake fillings I want to try out when I get time. By the way my recipes are "milkless" also. I used water in the gems and a tiny pinch of soda as well as baking powder.

The Tuesday before the Fourth one of the neighbors told me they'd be over in the morning to start the plow so I hurried home and moved the manure pile. Spread it where the plowing was to be done, you know[.] Had five big loads—all I could put on the wagon and some of it was pretty heavy. I started about four in the afternoon and had to finish the next morning. The first load made me tired, the second made me ache, and the third made me numb, then it went better. When I got through I left the harness in the wagon. It seemed as if I couldn't reach the pegs to hang it up.

One night last week a bunch of range cattle broke into the potato patch[7] and came up around the house. I ran out in my nightie three times and chased them away. Then the next day I built fence. Eight posts and two anchors with three wires and every post hole over two feet deep. The neighbors brag on it. It looks good and is solid.

You can send this on to ma. And write.

                                        With love—Yours—B.B.

* AUG. 4, 1918[1] / FT. PIERRE, SO. DAK.
TO MRS. M. M. COREY

Dear Folks,—Yours received. Am going to enclose a couple of stamps and then I'm square. Now I make a motion that if this endless letter continues that we each use our own stamps and envelopes as it doesn't cost a bit more and saves bulk in sending. Do I hear a second?

Had a card from Fuller right after he reached Camp Dix.[2] I answered right away with a letter and haven't heard from him since. That's the only word I've had from him since I left Iowa. Am wondering if something happened to my letter.

I tried baking bread the other day. I'd eaten so much corn bread that I got so I squealed like a pig under the gate at thot of eating it and squawked like a roupy old hen after eating it. Also seemed to be getting stiff as a foundered steer so thot it time to change.

I took 2 c[ups] oat meal & 2 c. corn meal and scalded well with lots of water. [W]hen cool enough added water to make a batter and 1 cake of yeast[.] The next morning I needed stiff with flour, led raise and put in pans. It made four big loaves of swell bread. Next time I'll use less water and part corn starch for stiffening. That will make a smaller batch and require less flour.

Did I give you that cake recipe?

$\frac{1}{3}$ c shortening $\Big\}$ beat
$\frac{2}{3}$ c white sirup

Add 3 egg yelks. beat.   salt and
and 1 c corn starch   flavoring
    & 1 t.s. baking powder. beat.   mystery

Add beaten whites one tbs at a time beat well and bake in gem tins or layers.

Makes about sixteen drop cakes.

Sugerless iceing
$\frac{3}{4}$ c white sirup boil until it hairs and beat into stiffly beaten white of an egg. Beat until cool enough to spread. If it hardens too soon set over boiling water. For layer cake use chopped fruit or nuts with it between layers.

Swell dope

No! I'm not sure I have that name correct. How do you pronounce it according to Webst[ers?][3] Is it M*a*rine or M*o*rine or M*ow*rin or M*aw*rine? I pronounce it every way by turns so's to hit it once in a while.

Howard Speer rather expects to be sent home soon, as he couldn't stand the test for soldier or taxi driver. They may give him a job as cook. Perhaps if he comes home he will come by way of Atlantic and stop off for a few days. I hope some of you can do some thing to show him a good time for he is a good lad and has always had all the hard knocks. I think he'd like to go through the canning factory[4] or see the Avoca Deer.[5] Will send his address tho he said there was talk of moving them[.]

Did I tell you that my neighbor, Ben Thompson, shot a finger off a few days before they entrained? They sent him and his record in charge of a man with a gun and we hear that he got twenty years at Fort Leavenworth.

This has surely been a great summer and if experience makes a person rich I'll soon be a xxxx Wouldn't you like to see me on the water wagon? Or riding a plow? Or a mowing machine? I can just make my little five foot mower hum.

Mike Donahue killed a big rattler and hung it on the fence and I nearly got a one trip ticket across the high divide in consequence. I started over to Speers on Win with a gallon pail of stuff in one hand and a hat without a fastening. Win smelled the snake and I didn't. When she began to misbehave I put up my hand with the pail in it to grab my hat. Of course she saw that and went crazy. If I'd let go the hat and pail and pulled a few tucks out of the saddle horn I'd have been all right but I didn't think of that till next day. When I found I was going I realized that a piece on the right stirrup had torn into my boot and I was fast by one foot[.] I slid my hand down the rein and jerked the stirrup at the same time knowing that error cannot harm God's child.[6] It seems almost un believeable but at the same instant she jerked the reins free, my foot cam loose and Win went across the lake bed as if she had a bunch of tin cans tied to her tail. I sat down the pail and went after her. Tried it again and after a few circus stunts she succeeded in whirling and giving me a swift ride for about a quarter of a mile. By the time I got back for the third try Glen Speer got there. He removed the snake from the fence and picked up my hat and pail. He offered to ride her for me but I thot I couldn't afford to give up to her so he added his persuasive powers and we got by. After another swift ride I came back and put on my hat and took the pail and I finished my trip as I started it with the exception of a shortage of hair pins and a hole in the side of one of my eleven dollar boots. The next day I found a scraped place about the side of my thumb nail and a small bruise on the inside of my left knee showed for a little while. I got a new pair of stirrups but I don't like them. Am going to take them back. Have to watch Win every minute now when I ride her and Kate is just as bad when I drive her. I've only driven her to town once. She pulled off three fancy stunts. Mr Speer says I should not drive her to town any more. He says if I'd meet a car on the "loop" there'd be no show for me. Guess I'll use Nell after this.

Had some company this summer who left me some bed bugs—the gol-durned blood thirsty German variety. Come help me get rid of 'em—wont you?

How's every body?—Love to all[.]

Elizabeth F Corey

---

* OCT. 22, 1918 / ROWE, SO. DAK.
TO MRS. M. M. COREY

Dear Mother,—Yours of September eleventh was received some three weeks later. I didn't get the mail for three weeks after school began.

So Chall was in Minnesota. Some of my neighbors said they heard he was to be in Fort Pierre for the fair. I didn't see him but thot he might be about any way.

No, It was after Fuller went to Camp *Dix* that he wrote me a card and I answered by letter. When I didn't hear from him I thot he had sailed and waited for you or his wife to send me his oversea address. I didn't even know his wife's[1] address—don't yet for that matter.

Its a pity they couldn't have sent me over instead of Fuller. Not even my wife would have cared a darn if I went and I'd have liked to go. That reminds me about the shoes. Did I tell you, I wonder? I got a new pair of shoes a while back—cost me twelve bucks. Mrs. R——. T——. and I were going down the street and met a guy[2] who wanted to know where we were bound for. I said some where to cash those shoes till time to start home. He wanted to see the shoes so I obligingly un-wrapped them. He admired them—told how much he paid for the last pair he purchased as if he thot six dollars an awful price. I said "That isn't bad. What do you suppose these cost?" He wouldn't guess so I told him. He gave a whistle of surprise. Now I've known that gentleman for years and tho he is well supplied with this world's goods I've always considered him like Barkis[3]—"a trifle near." So I thot he was voicing his opinion when he gave that long whistle. I exclamed "Gee! aren't you glad you don't have to by shoes for me!!["] He said "Oh, I don't know." The tone caused me to begin wrapping up the kicks very hastily. My panicy feeling increased when I discovered Mrs. R. T. had dropped off the map. He told me he'd buy me all the "danged shoes" I wanted if I'd only marry him. I finished that package in a manner that would cause a shoe clerk to loose his job even with the present shortage of help. I beat it, calling over my shoulder the [*sic*] he probably didn't know that it sometimes required four or five pair a year. I thot that would settle him, but he came to see me after that—one moon light evening—and proposed right. From the time I was a little kid I always declared I'd never marry a German and every man who has really made a full fledged proposal to me—and got it finished—has bee[n] a German. Seems to me the Lord doesn't give me much of a chance to choose.

Am about ten miles from home, twenty-five from Fort Pierre, fifteen from Draper and twenty six from Murdo.[4] My school house is about twenty by thirty feet and I live in the school house with fuel and water furnished. The Spanish Influenza[5] seems to have terrorized all South Dakota. The schools are all closed "till further notice." I am doing up my mending and drawing my eighty five dollars a month.

Was in Fort Pierre Friday on business. "Hank Monk" took me down. He drives an Elk, now instead of the old stage coach. He put the top down either to save it or my top piece. He hung on to the wheel and I sat close so I could grab for his coat tails if we hit a bump. Have been to Draper, Murdo, down to Bishards and over to Thorntons since then.

Am not surprised at their finding Ethel's ring. I've thot of it many times and have been knowing that "there is nothing lost in Mind."[6] Many of my belongings have come to light also. Haven't heard of that pin I lost on the way to Dakota several years ago tho.

Had my shoulder out of commission again a while back but it's O.K. now.

I have a lad of fourteen in school who looks so much like Olney did at that age that it quite startles me at times. He reads just exactly like Olney used to and he has the same dreamy ways at times then again he is very unlike him.

Have any of you heard from Glen Speer? He is still at Camp Dodge. He had the Influenza and was in the hospital twelve days.

Dr Youngs of Pierre, who was so kind when Chall was crippled up, passed on Friday noon. They say they have a funeral every other day in Fort Pierre and more than that in Pierre.

Well I guess I better close and hit the perch[.]

> Lovingly
> Elizabeth.
>
> Rowe or Fort Pierre or Draper[7]

P.S. Mr Bearry wishes to know what chance there is to buy apples by the barrel down there and have them shipped. They usually buy at least twenty bushels in the fall but he didn't get the chance to this fall and box apples are $3.75 per, or about four dollars a bushel.

Makes me think of the Sunday evenings long ago when we used to have popcorn, apples and nuts. Guess those evenings are among Walt Mason's[8] "Has wasers."

How much are apples per bu. and per bbl down there please?

> E.F.C.

✳ DEC. 10, 1918 / DRAPER, SO. DAK.
TO MRS. M. M. COREY

Dear Mother, To what "lost art" do you refer? I don't know much about art but I know better than to take up with any Art I know.

Aunt Cora[1] need not worry—or any one else for a while yet. The gentleman who professed such intrest in my foot gear is already a "has Wuzzer." I stepped on him. He still sends me the "Christian Herald" and I'm in hopes he will send me another of those Scripture Calendars for Xmas.

You ask what I live on. It's the neighbors mostly. At present I'm worried at the prospect of having to give up a Xmas dinner (Turkey) on account of a "previous engagement." When I'm home I batch. I've learned how to make gingerbread and tea and hobnobs. The neighbors give me buttermilk to make pancakes and the days are too short for more than two meals when I'm at home. I weigh 215 pounds, more or less.

Do you know Quakers? What do they call them that for? We've got one. A regular John G. He lives over east here about two miles. I've been there a couple of times. He's extremely quiet, extremely mild, extremely modest, and extremely dignified. When he smiles he looks as if it embarassed him worse than it would most men if you caught them kissing their neighbors wife. Well you know me. I let Mrs. Lier do most of the talking and watched my chance. I made him laugh twice till the tears started and then he looked so miserable for half an hour afterward I tried to feel sorry for him. Why he's worse than a preacher to be around.

Have had a letter from that crazy Daisy [Hamm] at last. She went off and got married with out saying a word to me about it and left me to most worry my head off when I wasn't too provoked. She got back to earth at last and wrote the same lonely kind of letter they all write. Guess I'll enclose it. I expect she makes more fuss over that man than a cow with a spotted calf. I don't think I shall ever marry.[2]

Sunday eve when I retired it was raining. When I awoke the next morning the world was white and it was still storming. Only had two pupils[.] They were all here today (the day ones) but it is storming again to-night. There were drifts this morning that hustled a team to get through. I fear this ends my joy rides for a while.

Must close, Love to all—

Yours,
Elizabeth F Corey.

* DEC. 25, 1918 / DRAPER, SO. DAK.
TO MRS. M. M. COREY

Dear Mother, I expect this will be the last time I'll write to you this year.

Victor brought the mail over the other morning and there wasn't a single letter. Had thot I'd get a Xmas card from you any way.

We are having fierce weather. I got a few Xmas cards several weeks ago but haven't them mailed yet. The roads are all but impassable. We had a community dinner here today and folks had great times getting here. The first crowd got here at twelve-thirty—almost. I made the coffee and furnished the sugar and mashed potatoes and string beans. Dinner was served "Cafeterria" style (I suppose that word is misspelled) mostly. They lined up, took napkins, plates, cups, knives and forks and passed along the serving table and filled their plates to suite themselves. I managed the rest of the serving with the help of one of the ladies. One fellow came back to fill his plate the third time remarking that he could still walk. That seemed to be the only limit. Once when I was working at the stove with my back to the crowd I heard the Quaker—the mild, the modest, the quiet, the dignified John G.—ask one of the ladies if she had ever seen the old school house look so well before. I also caught the quick answer "Oh, yes[,] I've been here several times this fall." The remarks that followed were quite gratifying.

Well I must close.

Lovingly—
Elizabeth

* JAN. 26, 1919 / DRAPER, SO. DAK.
  TO MRS. M. M. COREY

Dear Mother,—Yours of November 6th twice answered so just a few lines to thank you for the voile and lace. The lace is what Ethel was to have part of, isn't it? Guess Ill send it to her and let her take what she wants then I can use what is left with out being afraid of running her short. I certainly appreciat it all right. That makes two thin white waists I have to make up. Must get them made up soon as I haven't a single one at present. My last one got lost on the road down here—No, not *off* me but out of the rig when I rode, with "Hank Monk" once.

Had a swell time in the [Black] Hills. The enclosed card quite expresses my sentiments as I gazed up at "The Wall."[1]

School is still school and Johnnie is still Johnnie. A few days ago he came to a problem. "What must the marked price of goods be in order that the merchant may throw of[f] 20% and still gain 20%?" I knew what the problem was and kept an eye on Johnnie. The more he studied it the more bewildered he became. At last he looked up and said "Why, teacher, I can't work no such problem as this. It aint got no head on it."

It has been warm ever since I came back. The snow is most all gone except in, and around the school yard where it is still four or five feet deep in places.

Must close. Wonder why I dont hear from you. Thanking you again for the waist I am

Lovingly yours
Elizabeth Corey.

Should you wish to send word to me in a hurry wire in care of Peter Leir Draper S.D.

At this point, almost ten years to the day from its beginning, Bess Corey's long parade of homesteading letters comes to its end. Readers will have taken note already of the entropic nature of the sequence, initiated with such an enthusiastic gush of energy in 1909, that early vitality largely sustained through 1910, then gradually tapering off. A slower pace is evident during the middle years; then come the scattered letters of 1918, accompanied by Bess's confessions of personal weariness and failure of purpose. Her remark of April 28, 1918, echoed in almost the same words three months later, really says it all: "I seem to have lost interest in letter writing. . . . Don't think I'll ever get back to it again." And her words to her mother as the year closes, that she expects this may be her final letter for the year, is prophetic beyond her intent.

To explain this cessation is not difficult. Although one might wish sequences as lively as this to persevere endlessly, they seldom do, and the reason for the dropping off of Bess Corey's letters home can be discerned in their beginning. I have spoken of the serendipitous joining of ideal writer with ideal audience in 1909. But by 1918 the rush that had motivated Bess to relate everything in the commotion around her had wound down considerably; the vein was playing out. At the same time, her one-time audience, the expectant "Ma and the rest," was no longer intact. Olney was dead. Fuller was gone from home and married. Ethel the same. Rob was married and farming the home place. That left, but for a time only, Margaret and Paul, and when they moved into Atlantic there really was no more good reason to write. The round robin letters that circled from Bess to Ethel to Margaret represented an attempt of sorts to locate a new reason for continuing the story and a viable method. But nothing, eventually, worked.

In addition, the farm which Bess (in her mind's eye) recalled with such nostalgia and whose preservation as she had known it she proclaimed vital to any thought of her ever returning to Iowa, that farm was no more. It had no more escaped the metamorphosis than had the family itself. The Corey farm that represented her childhood could be preserved in amber only in Bess's memory; ultimately she saw the truth of that (probably had guessed it as early as her final extended visit to Marne in 1913, the summer Olney died). Her brief photographic surge had been an effort at saving certain memories, but these snapshots never could be more than feeble surrogates for the real thing; indeed, such photos usually mark the passing of the real, which is gone forever with the snap of the shutter. For life, Bess found, is fleeting, the poet quite right. The Great War in Europe finished, everyone around Bess seemed to be settling down to their own individual lives and personal affairs. And so must she.

In Stanley County, as well, time refused to stop, and nothing was as it had been. Not only had that gigantic tract of high plains grasslands been hacked into three parts, creating Jackson and Haakon counties and thereby reducing considerably the ample dimensions of Bess's precious western universe, Stanley County, but the land itself was, at long last, coming to be recognized as unfit for standard farming. Ever since the settlement era had gotten under way, there had been continued population leakage as dribs and drabs of homesteaders backtracked to more favorable climates. Such defections were hastened whenever a true drought hit, as it had in 1911. And the incentive to raise wheat west of the river was diminished when the war, with its highly inflated prices, ended in the armistice of 1918. A turnabout was coming, one which would not be completed until the land itself returned to a semblance of its former self and use.

In his novel *Marginal Land*, Horace Kramer presents an accurate portrait of those high plains beyond the Missouri during the ebb tide of settlement. There was a day when every quarter-section quickened with the stimulus of its own life-packed claim shack; Kramer's day is not that but the day after: "The land lay like the giant green swells of an ocean that had been frozen into immobility—as though God had stretched out his hand over the troubled world and given it peace. . . . The horses had not had a drop of water since morning. . . . out here in the grass he had not found the least trace of water, not even a puddle in the deeper crevices between the folded hills where clumps of reedy grass would seem to promise one."[1] Kramer's disconsolate traveler notes here and there a deserted shanty that has not yet been moved, torn down, or fallen in upon itself. But he sees no sign of "the vanished dwellers of these forlorn huts." What do meet his eye occasionally are desolate shacks "about ten feet square, battened with tattered black tarpaper, and with a rust-eaten stovepipe sticking up through the roof. Many were still furnished—a little cast-iron stove, a cot spring folded up against the wall, a table, and chairs of some sort. There were dishes and utensils, even remnants of food—ham butts, prunes, bread heels— all ravished by the little people that scurried to cover in the cracks of the floor and in the musty garments hanging like suicides on the walls."[2] It is clear that these claim shanties, most of them, had been intended as the beginnings of farms. But their owners are departed, gone, as if in a panic, and on the broad sweep of prairie they have left "not a furrow turned, a tree planted. No water—no gardens—nothing but the middens of rusted cans and the tall spears of needle grass leaning in at the doors to see what had become of the fainthearted pioneers who had briefly disturbed their immemorial solitude."[3]

That Bess Corey was no "fainthearted pioneer" is something that her letters establish beyond a shadow of a doubt. But there was precious little that even a dynamo like Bess could do to alter the basic climatic conditions of her corner of the world. And although we understand that Bess had presence of mind enough not to attempt standard eastern grain farming, what might have been a saving grace was wiped out by the advancing wave of technology. During the years of her letter writing, that decade stretching between 1909 and 1919, there had arrived in America a new family steed: the automobile. From this date a ranch devoted to the breeding of horses could only find itself on the slow road to obsolescence, along with the harness shop, livery stable, and buggy whip.

What Bess had left, as always, to sustain her was her chosen profession. Fortunately, as it turned out, since 1909 her achievement in the classroom had ever more fully overshadowed her original wish to work the land. There still existed rural schools aplenty, and even if homesteaders seemed to be consistently fewer, the towns remained (for the time being at least), as a good many of the original settlers sooner or later moved to be close to where the current action might be. Pierre flourished, as state capitals do, and eventually, after 1926, when a highway bridge spanned the Missouri, there came a steady flood of

Students at Lance Creek School, ca. 1921 (Annie Ahboltin at left front). Photo courtesy Ann Ahboltin Sheeley.

vacationers heading for the Hills, Yellowstone Park, and points west. Fort Pierre jelled, as it were, remaining pretty much as it had been when Bess first knew it and as it remains today: a stage set awaiting the return of its cast of homesteaders.

In Atlantic, Iowa, Paul Corey, the youngest of "our tribe," completed high school. Somewhere along the road (did the letters of Sister Bess have any influence here?) Paul decided to become a writer, and he made plans to attend the state university. His mother came, too, and together they established a new home in Iowa City. There, in 1925, with Bess beside her at the end, Margaret Morgan Corey died, age sixty-two. She was buried alongside her husband and her son Olney in Monroe Cemetery, close to the farm. Her estate, when settled and apportioned among her heirs, was put to some interesting uses. Paul used his inheritance to marry his campus love, poet Ruth Lechlitner, and carry her off to Europe for a year of young adventure. Bess did not travel quite so far. Ever since becoming a teacher, she had managed somehow to keep one step ahead of advancing laws which on a rather regular basis were raising the educational requirements for teachers. Gone was the day when one might teach forever with no

Paul Corey at the time of his graduation from Atlantic High School, 1922. Photo courtesy Margaret Nelson.

more than eighth- or ninth-grade schooling. Bess for years had been advised to obtain a high school diploma—had at one time made tentative plans to go into residence in Nebraska for just that purpose. Now the diploma was becoming a necessity if she were to renew the certificate by virtue of which she remained a schoolma'am and thereby put bread on her table.

Accordingly, as the summer of 1926 waned, Bess arranged to enroll in Fort Pierre High School, leaving her homestead claim (to which she was now referring as her "ranch") in the hands of a couple named Brumbaugh; they were to care for the homestead, it seems, in return for the use of the house and land. In Fort Pierre, when all things were considered—her formal schooling, her institute experience, her age (she was thirty-eight)—Bess was allowed to join the senior class providing that she enroll for an extremely heavy schedule of courses. One can only imagine the fortitude it must have demanded, at Bess's age, to be schooled with students of seventeen and eighteen (many of them younger than Bess's own rural pupils). But Bess's remark to her mother so long ago, that she would not give up till she dropped, had not been an idle boast.

The class of '27 at Fort Pierre High School was eighteen in number if one included Flora Bee Huston, who had been a babe in arms when Bess sought work from her parents at the Huston House before filing her claim in 1909 (but Flora would marry and drop out before the 1926–27 school year was over). The other students must have been a bit stunned at first to observe this much, much older woman sitting beside them in classes (she was, some seniors thought, the age of their parents, and they may not have been far off the mark). The students saw little of "Miss Corey," as she was invariably deferred to at FPHS. Understandably, her classmates enjoyed next to no social interchange with Bess; generally they realized that, other things being equal (which they were not), Miss Corey's bone-crushing class schedule left her no time at all for those extracurricular delights which attracted her classmates and where all the "fun" was being had. It seems that no study hall periods were included in Bess's daily schedule; all assigned homework was literally that. Across the years she is remembered, when remembered at all, as dressing plainly but neatly, as having blond hair (darkish or light, depending upon who is recalling it), as speaking in an attractively husky voice, as bearing herself with a special dignity belonging to the mature and self-proven. In a town

Fort Pierre High School, from which Elizabeth Corey took her diploma with the class of '27. Robert Kolbe Dakota Collection.

where everyone quite literally knew everyone else, the students soon became aware that Elizabeth Corey lived somewhere out along Bad River, had taught in Stanley County schools for some time, and was returning now to update her credentials. Aside from that she was the mysterious stranger in their midst.[4]

"Quiet" and "neat"—this pair of adjectives comes repeatedly to the minds of those recalling the Miss Corey of Fort Pierre High School. But a pair of more specific impressions stands out. The first is the red warning flag which a student was likely to get from parents terrified at the thought that Bess Corey, come into town from that disreputable Bad River country, would surely be likely to tell their sheltered daughters about all manner of shady items that they had no business knowing, terrible things like drunkenness and rape and, even worse, things like sex between animals and people. The other impression stems from parental concern as well but is quite different: the memory that a father who knew everyone and everything going on in the region had never once mentioned Miss Corey's name to his high school senior daughter. By his silence he had indicated quite positively—if passively—that nothing of a shameful nature existed in Bess's background; for if it had, his daughter knew that he would have voiced his disapproval.[5] Somewhere between these two poles, undoubtedly, stood the real Elizabeth Corey.

The school year passed and graduation time arrived, Bess taking her place on May 27 with the others in line for diplomas. It had been decided among the parents of the 1927 graduates that, rather than going for the traditional one-time use and somewhat wasteful expense of caps and gowns, the young women would be dressed in stylish apparel personally selected but with everyone garbed in the identical color: lavender purple.[6] And so Bess Corey followed their lead, even to sitting for her graduation portrait at the studio of photographer R. E. Miller in Pierre. At the appropriate moment, she was prepared to accept her diploma; it came bound elegantly in blue suede and signed with a flourish by the superintendent of schools, Charles E. Booth.[7]

Naturally, the course of events was not as smooth as it might appear; Bess's life seemed never to flow quietly. For one thing, the Missouri chose that time to go on one of the worst of its annual rampages: the great flood of 1927. As soon as she was able to leave Fort Pierre, Bess went to Spearfish, a favored vacation spot on the northern edge of the Black Hills but also the site of a state normal school where, it seems, she had made plans to enroll for college-level work. In a letter to Ethel, Bess recounts her most recent cliffhangers, demonstrating that though her letters might be fewer, they had lost none of their color:

Spearfish, S.D.[8]
June 7, 1927

Dear Sis:

Have worried some because I've not had a line from you for so long but presume you are very busy as usual so will procede to write another chapter of my autobiography for you to read when you have time.

The fourth week before school closed I came down with scarletina and was ordered to "go home and go to bed and stay there till next Monday morning." Then it started to rain. It rained and rained and rained some more. When Monday morning came I was so weak I couldn't get up one flight of stairs without hanging on to the banister like grim death to a sick monkey and it was still raining and both rivers rising.[9] By evening every one had moved out of the building but myself. The water was nearly four feet deep on the

Class of '27, Fort Pierre High School. Back row, left to right: Norman Pugh, Don McFarland, Edna Farrell, Clara Leap, Claudia Huckfeldt, William P. Hart, Edna Speer, Thelma Sorensen, Cecilia Callahan, Vernon Snyder, Charles Weirauch. Front row, left to right: Elizabeth Corey, Glen Whitney, Doris Duncan, School Superintendent Charles E. Booth, Marie La Valle, and Oscar Saffel. Not shown: Eustas Book. Photo courtesy William P. Hart.

ground floor. I thought myself perfectly safe on third floor till they told me the foundation could not be depended upon—then I caved in and they took me to Pierre. About the time I began to get myself pulled together I came down with "summer flu" and when I got back to school there was all that work to make up so had to let some of the entrance exams go.[10] So here I am lined up for twelve weeks heavy work with a heart that is mighty near busted, but still I grin. I finished with the class but my diploma is held till I get these credits in.

Commencement was May 27th and the next day or two were busy ones—just gathering up the pieces. Then that Sunday eve Mrs Gordon was taken very ill and I took care of her. Went over Thursday afternoon and packed up some of my stuff.

Mr Brumbaugh came for me Thurs. afternoon—It had been raining much of the time since commencement but we loaded up my stuff and started for the ranch in an open car in the rain.[11] We

Another terrible flood on Bad River. This one, in May 1927, jeopardized graduation plans at Fort Pierre High School. Photo courtesy Verendrye Museum.

made it by supper time. I tell you that man is the end of the limit to handle a car. I spent two strenuous days unpacking, sorting, storing, washing, ironing, packing, and planning work around the place. All the while it was raining by spells. Friday afternoon I came back to town. It rained the first fourteen miles. Sunday night I came up here.[12] Don't know if I'll get to draw a long breath this summer or not.

I surely wish I could see you all. It would take a good month to tell you all that has happened the past few months.

I wish you knew the Brumbaughs. They are surely great workers. The way they are cleaning and fixing up the place would do you good. It is a tremenduous relief to me. I wish you could see the little trees and the dam. We can have ice next summer.

Must close as I have more than thirty more letters to write and regular work begins tomorrow.

Would surely like to know if you and the rest were well and if you had the head stones fixed and paid Uncle Chall[enge D. Brown] yet. The last he wrote he said Paul and I were the only ones he'd heard from about it.

Must close.
Lovingly,
Elizabeth.

Rather than return at once to teaching rural school, Bess Corey took advantage of a new opportunity. On the eastern edge of Pierre stood an institution begun in 1887 when the Pierre Board of Trade donated 180 acres of land on which to establish the Indian Industrial School. On the reservations, school facilities for Indian students were sparse indeed, but young men and women could come to Pierre and be trained in various capacities, obtaining a decent grammar school education as well. The Industrial School grew. By 1919 a simpler name had evolved: the Pierre Indian School.

If parents of teenage children had felt uneasy about the prospect of an adult woman of experience from Bad River attending their local high school, the presence of the Indian school made them even more nervous. Fort Pierre parents were reluctant to have their daughters associating with (much less being attracted by) any of the young Indian men enrolled in the school just across the Missouri bridge (since their schools competed in athletics, it was impossible to keep the students from being aware of one another's existence). A classmate of Bess's affirms the exotic appeal of many of the handsome young men with their brown skins, glossy hair, and piercing black eyes.[13]

Because the Pierre Indian School was operated under federal aegis, Bess when she joined its staff became a government employee— not at first as a teacher but as matron of the dining room, supervising a group of Indian employees. At least by the 1928–29 school year, Bess had landed her new post. She visited during the summer of 1928 in Iowa, stopping in Harlan for a time with her aunt Jennie Dunlavy, at whose home she had boarded nearly a quarter of a century earlier during her first years as a country schoolma'am—and not with total satisfaction on either side. Now, however, Aunt Jennie had mellowed considerably with age, and so had Bess Corey. Bess did not see her brother Paul on this trip. He and his new wife, Ruth, were living in France and dreaming of careers as writers, he as novelist, she as poet. But Ethel was established now in a farm home just down the road toward Marne from the Corey place, which Rob had tilled since 1918. Bess wrote her there regarding the ill health of the elderly Dunlavys:

Harlan, Iowa[14]
Sept. 24, '28

Dear Sis:

Many thanks, I got the letters this morning. Was so glad to get them—the one from Rapid [City, S.D.] contained thirty bones which I did not beg, borrow or steal but represents a wee bit I had salted down. I think it was the brine perhaps which caused the envelope to crack. Thanks so much for sending them.

I phoned to Lilah yesterday but it was such an effort to converse I did not try to talk to you.[15] But I see, as you predicted, that the mail man began leaving my letters at your place as soon as I told him I was going up to Rob's.

Aunt Jennie got a nice long letter from Paul this morning. They have very pleasant apartments with meals at what would be ninety cents a day in our money. M'gosh! I'm goin' over!

Aunt Jennie said J.D. seemed better when I was here but I guess I've been here long enough to see what he's usually like. Only *one* meal she hasn't had to take him to the toilet once or twice before we finished. He is just as lovely, lovable, and considerate as ever. Some times he raves for hours. Today he talked again of taking his life—asked her to shoot him. Later he suggested my doing it. I became too interested, I fear—told him I had noticed the two guns—asked him which he preferred that I should use. He said the smaller was no good so I said I supposed I'd have to use the large one. He changed the subject and has not returned to it. Thats that![16]

Poor Aunt Jennie! She says that its her work that keeps her up and I believe it. When the work is done she knits while I read aloud and we have such good times.

I asked her if I secured some employment here if she would rent me a room so I could stay here nights. She said, "You bet I will and it wont cost you much either!" I've a notion to look around. It would give Aunt Jennie a *comparatively* sane person to talk to of an evening and that might help some.

> Must close and go down.
> Lovingly,
> Elizabeth F. Corey.

By November of 1928 Bess was on the job, and she wrote to her Aunt Rate in Atlantic, Iowa, telling of her duties at the Indian school in a letter which Aunt Rate forwarded to Ethel with the word that she "han't time to do much talking" but, since "Bessie" had requested that her letter be "passed around," she was complying, even if in great haste:

> Pierre, S. Dak.[17]
> Nov. 4, 1928

Dear Aunt Rate:

Your letter is on top so will write a few lines to you. Thanks ever so much for sending me the dolled up letters and hat and all. Think the 77 will even up for the 'phone calls and stamps.

I hope your house cleaning is done and you are back at your regular work. Some day those hours of potato digging will seem just a dream. They already seem like that to me. And here I am still fighting Indians—I suppose I shouldn't say that for most on my detail [in the dining hall] are very nice and twenty four are almost like clock work already. Will have more new ones tomorrow making thirty-four in all. Am glad to get to swap off a few for I overheard one vow today that she would kill me if I tried to stay the year through. Am always a bit curious about such things so decided at once to stay. They surely hate to have to clean up but I like my part of the work.

I can hardly realize I am on Uncle Sam's pay roll and have already received one check on the U.S. Treasurey. I wonder how in the world I got that hunch to rush back just in time to fall into a position that other people pray, fight, or fish for, and go through all sorts of red tape to get. They tell me I'm in line for some thing so very much better and have asked me to write the Civil Service exams in January. When I get my new detail trained in the way they should go will review up a little and try to answer my letters better also.

Please send this on to Sis or Lilah if you have opportunity. Want to write them soon.

Lovingly,
Little Bessie

Bess's apparent joy in her new work did not produce total happiness for her in family relationships (but she had always claimed to be the curse of the Corey clan), for a letter written by a cousin who spent time in South Dakota draws a rather different picture: [18]

. . . only once while I was in Dakota did I have any contacts with Elizabeth who was always referred to as Bess by the aunts [Hat and Rate] in Atlantic.

The dates escape me since there seems to be nothing to relate to my visit there. At the time I went to the Indian School where Bess was the dining room matron my visit was limited to a very short one. The aunts had told me that Bess had made some rather

The Indian school east of Pierre, S.D., where Elizabeth Corey was employed for five years after 1928. Robert Kolbe Dakota Collection.

caustic remarks about my *finally* getting to work [and] my efforts to contact her were very unrewarding as she remained seated as I was taken to her room. With such a frosty reception you may understand why any attempt to cultivate warm family relationships were not resumed. [I was told] that at one time when she was walking on the street in Fort Pierre she came upon an Indian boy who had on a sweater of hers that she kept in a trunk in the schoolhouse where she lived. She is purported to have walked up to him and demanded that he give it to her. Beyond the fact that he yielded to her demand no information was available.

Yet even this writer, so clearly put off by Bess, and for what specific reason we shall never know, stood in some awe of a young woman who would homestead on her own, as Bess had done some twenty years previously, adding: "I have always admired her pluck in proving the 400 [sic] acres of land there in the rattlesnake country. Though my trips to Pierre were infrequent and I never experienced the situation myself others have said that when the rattlesnakes emerged [in spring] to sun themselves on the river banks the stench was most foul." During the early fall of 1929 Ethel Corey Erickson sent Paul Corey "another piece of wonderful news about our family," this concerning Bess, who had secured "a position as teacher in the Indian school on a saleray of $1200 a year." [19] And if Ethel were not mistaken,

Bess was given her board in addition. To Ethel, this was confirming evidence of the genuine beauty of life—as it must have seemed to Bess herself.

Bess remained at the Pierre Indian School for five years. What she was doing to earn her daily bread immediately after terminating her service there is uncertain, but Paul Corey believes her to have been on relief, as the present-day welfare was then known. Certainly there is every reason to believe that this may have been so, for Stanley County had fallen upon even harder times than were afflicting the rest of the country. The stock-market crash of 1929 had plunged the nation into the Great Depression, and its effects were felt keenly in South Dakota, where a drastic plunge in farm prices was compounded by disastrous climatic problems. Bess Corey had lived through periods of drought before, but never in her lifetime had there been dry years to compare with those of the early and middle 1930s—the "dirty thirties" as they have come to be known on the plains, where they are recalled even today with a dread unmatched by any other threat.

By 1934 all hope had evaporated of making much of a living farming or ranching. By summer nothing green was left in the pastures to sustain grazing cattle, and they were shipped by the boxcar load to eastern fields. During that year the great dust storms began. Whistling winds picked up the loose topsoil and flung it eastward in immense, choking clouds. The black blizzards had afflicted Oklahoma and Kansas and the Texas Panhandle in previous years; now they hit the Dakotas in earnest. A new exodus from Stanley County was under way as family after family packed up what it could and took to the roads, heading toward eastern refuges or joining caravans from Nebraska and Kansas and every other western state affected by the Dust Bowl, trailing westward toward the sunset. Even those toughened homesteaders who had stuck it out through thick and thin until now were, many of them, discouraged by this latest hammerblow of nature.

Paul Corey, now in his early thirties, chose this time to make his first visit to his sister in Stanley County. He was appalled at conditions. Seen in retrospect, the year 1935 appears to have been a comparatively quiescent time in the history of the great drought, but any respite was temporary and deceptive, for 1936 saw the area plagued by dust storms of even greater severity. Paul found even in 1935 that Bess's prized quarter-section homestead, now joined with the land she had purchased from Fuller in 1917, was all but lost: "Dust from the previous year had drifted to the tops of fence posts in places."[20] Drifts like

A "black blizzard" dust storm raging at the time of Paul Corey's 1935 visit to South Dakota. Photo courtesy Library of Congress.

black snow rippled across many a field, and against some barns the wind had piled curiously twisted slopes up which one could walk directly onto the roof.

Never one to be undone by circumstance, Bess Corey took the requisite examinations and renewed her teaching certificate in 1935.[21] She appears to have located a teaching job in the desolated Sansarc area, near where she and Lida Smith in 1909 had searched for unclaimed homesteads. The Sansarc school closed forever at the end of the 1935–36 academic year, a victim of the Dust Bowl, which had decimated the rural population. Then Bess was fortunate in locating a school in the vicinity of Midland, where she had first touched her foot to Stanley County soil. But it was essential for her to obtain more advanced schooling in order to satisfy the forever changing and rising requirements for teacher certification. For her college, she chose NNIS in Aberdeen, where she had enjoyed the operatic concert given by Johanna Gadski during the SDEA convention of 1915. The college had been upgraded to four-year teachers college status, and there were many reasons that may have influenced her to select it, including her numerous contacts with college personnel beginning with the days when Vice-President Woodburn had led the Stanley County summer normal institute. A further impact had been made by professors such as A. H. Seymour, M. M. Guhin, and Keo King at SDEA conventions. At the Watertown SDEA in 1916 the NNIS college president, Willis

During the drought year of 1935, blowing dust drifted as high as the eaves of many South Dakota barns. Photo courtesy Library of Congress.

Johnson, had been elected to head the state teachers organization. The college had developed a specialty in one-room rural school education, led by some of these educators along with Professor Vernon Culp; every country teacher was aware of its reputation. The president of the college now was Carl G. Lawrence, familiar to Bess through his service in Pierre as state superintendent of instruction and also through the exploits of his physicist son, Ernest O. Lawrence, who by then had invented the atom-smashing cyclotron and in 1939 would be awarded the Nobel Prize for physics. But perhaps an even greater attraction in Aberdeen was the fact that Charles E. Booth, who had been superintendent of Fort Pierre schools at the time Bess received her high school diploma, was now a professor at NSTC. It would be pleasant to live in a relatively large place for a few weeks, for the city, although hit hard by the twin blows of depression and drought, boasted some 18,000 residents and was a center of railroad activity as well as the county seat of Brown County. Not least among her reasons for attending NSTC that summer was the assurance that her friend Mary Donahue, of the red-headed clan at Donahue School but now a grown woman, had become a rural teacher in Bess's footsteps and, having relatives established in Aberdeen, would be attending the same college.

Bess's summer school plans for 1936 were complicated by a family disaster of massive proportions: the death from cancer of her only sister, Ethel Corey Erickson, on May 22. Ethel left eight children, the eldest, Margaret (Nelson), just out of high school and hoping to be able to study journalism at the University of Minnesota, the youngest, Marie (Harmon), an infant of nine months. Upon her arrival at Midland at the end of August to begin her school year, Bess penned a fast letter to Margaret, who following her mother's death had mailed a letter to South Dakota which Bess had just belatedly received:

Midland, S. Dak.[22]
Aug. 27, 1936

Dear Margaret:

Yours of August third was more than three weeks reaching me but that need not happen again. Was so glad to hear from you.

When school closed last Spring I had just time to get my stuff moved into Pierre and get ready to leave for Aberdeen for Summer School. Finished S.S. on Friday July 10th and left for Pierre that afternoon with Mary Donahue—three of us in a coupe. The thermometer stood at 117° in the shade as we left. Could not drive fast and suffered with the heat till we got to Ipswich[23] where I persuaded the girls to put wet towels at the open windows—they also put one over knees—then we traveled in comparative comfort only we had to stop often to resoak the towels. We reached Pierre about eleven that evening to find a terrible fire raging at the Pierre Indian School where I spent nearly five years.[24] It took several of the larger buildings.

The following Tuesday I moved my belongings [from my homestead] to Fort Pierre. The school I taught last year [near Sansarc] I was to teach this year but the family with the most pupils decided to move so they could hardly keep the school going for what were left.

I had to borrow money to finish Summer School and the powers that be would not let me have employment because I was a teacher [and thereby had an income, which many did not] so I was in a bad row of stumps for awhile. Two weeks ago had a letter from a friend saying their teacher had resigned and if I wanted the school come and get it. And believe you me I did.

Am living in the school house on the oiled highway. Fifty miles out from Fort Pierre—ten miles beyond Hayes and fifteen miles from Midland.[25] The bus, the mail carrier, and the oil man pass my door regularly and there is a telephone in the school house. A telegram sent to me at Midland would be phoned right out to me and not be from two to four days on the road as last year.

As soon as my contracts were signed I went to Pierre and told
the best dentist I wanted some furniture on the instalment plan.
He xrayed my mouth and the next day pulled all my teeth but the
six lower front ones which I will try to keep as long as possible. My
mouth bled terribly for some eight hours but was healed the next
day so I could eat potatoes, eggs and sausage. Bread and butter
is the hardest thing to eat. Will have to pay the dentist $100.⁰⁰.
Have bills amounting to about $75.⁰⁰ to meet interest and taxes etc
$125.⁰⁰ My salary for the year is $450⁰⁰[.] The difference will have
to feed and clothe me.

You know I let my certificate lapse those seven years I was out of
the teaching game but did well enough at summer school to get
two A's and two B's—enough credits to fully re-instate my certificate. Am so thankful for that for I wont have to attend summer
school next summer.

Had hoped to get it settled about a school earlier. Had thot
Chall's had little Marie and as soon as I knew I had some thing to
live on I wanted to offer to take Jennie for the year.²⁶ Thot she was
old enough so I could keep her right with me at school and that
would make it easier for Betty and Beverly to keep the home up
and for you to go on to school. Please tell your father that if I can
help out that way at any time I'll be glad to do all my circumstances will allow.

Am very glad you are going to college and trust you will do well
in your chosen field for the world is sadly in need of good clean
journalism. Please write when you get settled. My address will be
Midland till next June if nothing happens.

Your mother's greatest joy was her family. She lived for their ad-
vancement and successes. I think the look of peace and content on
her face at the last only shows her confidence in her family's going
on to clean useful lives and I'm sure you will all live so as to never
break that confidence.

My school begins next Monday. Hope this reaches you before
you leave Van Wert.²⁷

> Lovingly,
> Aunt Elizabeth.

Margaret Erickson did manage to go off to Minneapolis and enter the
University of Minnesota. But it was the depth of the Depression, and
there was no money to be had and, desperate at the prospect of having

to abandon her plans in mid-year, she took a job as a maid during Christmas break in the hope of staving off what seemed the inevitable demise of her college career.[28] As Christmas break came to an end, she poured out her feelings to her Aunt Bess, and Bess responded in a manner that could only have cheered her and make her seem less alone and abandoned than she must have felt:

Midland, S. Dak.[29]
Jan. 5, 1937

Dear Margaret:

Was so happy to receive your letter yesterday and glad you made a start in the University of Minnesota. I sincerely hope you can stay with it to the finish.

You certainly did well in Latin. That is not an easy subject either. I wish I could have taken it in high school but they said it was too hard as I was carrying double work. Hope you do as well in other subjects. Last summer the Superintendent was looking over my re-cords and said, "It seems funny but you get your A's in the difficult subjects instead of the easy ones."

About that home you worked in—I think I know how you feel about it—you have my sympathy. I feel that way about postum—It looks like coffee but it isn't and I can hardly like it for what it *is* because of what it *isn't*.

I always wanted to "work out" when I was a kid but the folks wouldn't let me. After I came to Dakota I thot, "Now's my chance!" Thot if I were to continue to be a teacher I needed the dicipline of taking instructions and orders from others. I tried to make my face as expressionless as that of an Englishman's butler upon occasion. I also tried to treat the mistress as I would wish a servant to treat me. I could look quite calm when I was almost furious enough to fight a buzz saw. What I hated worst was to bathe the dog.!!! Did they ever ask you to bathe the dog?

If you are inclined to swear at any one you see I sure as tunket will try to stay out of sight. Did you ever hear of my experience with swearing? When things went hay wire, instead of saying "words" I used to set my teeth. Some times the fillings would just pop and snap. Chall said I should learn to cuss as a matter of economy—it would relieve my feelings and save dental bills. One day Ruth Speer was over and I was going to put the harness on Winnie and draw a barrel of water. When I came with the collar

she reached out and planked one of her feet down on one of mine
then just stood there and grinned—yes, honest, she grinned. Was
perfectly helpless, dropped the collar and began beating her with
my fist exclaiming, "You bloomin' homely, lop-eared, squint-eyed,
knock-kneed, old maid's nag! Don't you know the difference between my cornfield and the public hi-way? *Get off and walk*!!" She
winked and stepped off. There was Ruth all doubled up laughing
till the tears ran down her face—never did a thing to help me. And
me? My jaws ached. I'd said *all that* through set teeth. Made up
my mind swearing would never help me a bit

Will have to tell you about *my* kitchen some time—kitchenette
perhaps I should say. If it were much smaller I'd have to walk in
and back out.[30] It is really very handy and nice tho the modern con-
veniences are conspicuous by their absence.

Yes, I'm sure you'll have orchids some time.[31]

Who is Dewey?[32] Please make me acquainted with the family.

Am spending my vacation alone in the school house because I
am broke. Also had a lot of work to do.

Have paid back most of the money I had to borrow last summer
and am trying to sell the buildings off the ranch to meet other
obligations.[33]

Am well and happy and glad to hear from you.

> With love,
> Elizabeth F. Corey.[34]

Bess, as her letter suggests, had determined to concentrate upon
her career as a schoolma'am, renewing her teaching certificate in
1938, again in 1941, and every third year thereafter until 1950.[35]

By the end of the 1930s the Coreys had another writer in the
family, Paul in 1939 having begun to publish his Mantz Trilogy, based
upon his life at Corey farm. The trilogy was complete and the United
States had been involved in World War II for nearly eight months
when Bess wrote to Paul in Cold Spring, New York, where he and
Ruth were then living with their infant daughter, Anne Margaret:

> Pierre, S. Dak.[36]
> July 26, 1942

Dear Paul and all,

Ever since last January when I received the holiday greetings of
you all I've been going to write, but am in a country where all sorts
of things happen—Had you been following my tracks for the past

six months you'd have the "makin's" of a book and be too dizzy to write it.[37]

Anne Margaret must be quite a girl by now. I got a friend, Mrs Little Thunder, to make me a family of dolls to send for her birthday, then delayed sending them till I heard from you so as to be sure where to send them. Had a vague feeling that Uncle Sam might give you a job and the address of the whole family might be changed.

Had a part in the sugar ration registration—It was interesting—only had to have an interperter for one and that was Brave Big Head. The New Holy's, Little Thunder's, Little Cloud's and Weasel Bear's all understand English.

We have had rain and more rain this year.[38] School was supposed to close May 15 but it was June 10th before I got home. Bridges and roads washed out so badly. "Believe it or not"[39] my home seemed to be in a land of lakes and had to follow around the ridges among the lakes to get to my place.

Native wheat grass had taken possession of my house yard. I measured some that was $43\frac{1}{2}$ inches high. If I don't forget will inclose some of the heads.

I came to town the last Tuesday in June and haven't been home except for a few hours to pack up some of my stuff. Am living with Rose Solberg at *508 W. 3rd St.* You remember I staid here one winter when Rose was away and her father was poorly.

Had a chance to go back to the school I had last year with a 10% raise in salary. That wasn't enough as I lacked a hundred & fifty dollars of meeting my obligations last year.[40] Am offered a school sixteen miles out from Pierre with more than twenty dollars a month in advance of last year's salary. Think I shall sign on the dotted line soon.

Did you know that Aunt Rachel has not been well? Not since last April. Said she shut up her house as though she were going to Europe and went to a convalessent home. (That word isn't spelled correctly.) She has been having treatment for some heart difficulty and high blood pressure.[41]

Have had no word from Rob's in months. Have written at least four letters. Presume I have inadvertantly offended. Heard in a round about way that he is as bad off as ever.[42]

Do you remember A. M. Jackley the State Snake Eradicator? They have moved to the house next this one. Hope some day he

Bess Corey in Pierre, S.D., 1943. Photo courtesy Margaret Nelson.

will take me to the country and teach me the proper methods of locating and eradicating snakes.

Its almost dinner time so love to all.

Bess.

In 1945 Bess was teaching in the area of Draper, S.D., and, at age fifty-seven, preparing for the day when she might leave her profession and go into retirement. It had been some time since she had lived on her homestead, and the neighbors whose tarpapered shacks once might be sighted from her location along Bad River—the Stones, Speers, Carlisles, Reeses, Goulds—had long since grown up and married, moved away, retired into Fort Pierre, or died. During World War II the government had taken over a huge tract of that land once filled with homesteaders' shacks and used it as an aerial bombing range. Bess was eager now to get out from under her burden, and in May 1946 her tract was transferred to its new owner, Fred C. Demmon of Fort Pierre.[43] The $2,000 Bess received was used to purchase a tiny home from another single woman, Grace Heron, located on the very outskirts of Pierre. The address, appropriately enough: Elizabeth Street.[44]

Bess's niece Margaret Erickson was unable financially to sustain her college career. She followed in her Aunt Bess's footsteps by teaching in Iowa rural schools for a few years, then moved to Des Moines where in the spring of 1947 she married Frederick B. Herbert and settled on Lay Street. Bess was running into trouble with her eyes and, even though she now listed her religion officially as Christian Science, she did as she had always done, supplementing positive thinking with aid from the medical profession. Her problem, probably, was cataracts, and she had surgery in South Dakota but had gone back to work too soon afterward (as always she lived hand to mouth and needed the money). Driving to and from her school over bumpy roads disrupted the surgeon's handiwork. Even more drastic surgery was called for. Fred Herbert himself had undergone some complex surgery on his eyes, and he volunteered the name of his surgeon, Dr. Mathieson, in Des Moines. Bess took the train to Des Moines during the fall of 1947, underwent an evaluation, and scheduled an operation. For the interim, new glasses, which would improve her sight, were prescribed. Neither of Bess's eyes was in good condition and one, Fred was told by the surgeon, resembled the yolk of an egg, scrambled.[45]

Bess's brother Challenge and his wife, Emily, lived southwest of Des Moines in Creston, and Bess went to visit with them while she awaited the day for her surgery to take place. Creston lay on the way to Marne, and the Challenge Coreys accompanied Bess on her final visit to Corey farm to view the scenes of her childhood and renew her friendship with her sister-in-law Lilah. Rob Corey had died during World War II and Lilah had remarried, this time to Leonard A. Morris. At the farm, Bess met Leonard as well as all the clan who could manage to gather for the occasion, including a number of younger relatives with whom this was to be her first—and last—direct contact. It was a

Bess Corey during her final visit to Corey farm, with brother Challenge Corey and grandnieces Sharon (left) and Eileen Corey, 1947. Photo courtesy Lilah Corey Morris.

good time for her. From Chall Corey's home Bess wrote to thank Margaret and bring her up to date on her condition:

Creston, Ia[46]
December 7, 1947

Dear Margaret

I wondered a little whether to write to you or your husband. I certainly appreciated his interest and efforts in my behalf. Have had the new glasses a week and get along well on dark days or by artificial light but not so well during the bright part of the day.

I am so anxious to get the eye operation over with for it will be sixty days from then before I can have permanent glasses. I need so to get back to work.

I have my bonds here ready to cash.[47] With the acrued interest they will amount to more than $400.⁰⁰. If I could have the operation soon I think that would carry me through but that isn't the whole story. I need to raise $700 by the first of next May. If I can get back to work and earn part of it I think I can borrow the rest. It means the difference between my own income and "Old Age Subsistance" in the future, and May 15ᵗʰ is the dead line.

Dr Mathesons says that after leaving the hospital I must, for at least two week, not lift, push, stoop, or put on my shoes. I will need no nursing but to have drops put in my eye. I wondered if you could help me locate such a place in Des Moins as you have lived in Des Moins for several years. I wanted so much to see you but Emily explained that it was impossible because you were so far out that it took several hours to drive and and several to drive back down town again.

I hope you will write to me and write big so I can read it myself.[48]

> Love,
> Elizabeth C.

The operation was performed successfully. It was arranged that Bess would board with the widow of a Des Moines physician, a woman who could be trusted to put the prescribed drops in her patient's eyes properly and regularly and see also that she did not break doctor's orders by stooping or otherwise jeopardizing her surgical repair work.[49]

Even so, it was Margaret's feeling that Bess, in her perennial scramble to meet the payments on her loans, again returned to her teaching too rapidly. But something else gave Margaret even greater cause for alarm. While recuperating in the hospital, Bess had begun to pass blood and, interpreting it as a resumption of her monthly "celebration," elatedly spoke of a happy and somewhat miraculous return to youth. Margaret, with perhaps greater experience and knowledge of things medical, had reservations. Recalling her own mother's terrible death from cancer, she feared for Aunt Bess's welfare.[50]

Lilah Corey Morris and Bess had continued to be close friends, and in the spring of 1954, when Bess was desperately ill with the cancer her niece had suspected, requiring more care than could be provided by the woman tending her, Lilah and Leonard Morris traveled to

Monroe Township Methodist Church near Corey farm, where Elizabeth Corey is buried beside her parents. Photo courtesy Margaret Nelson.

Pierre to be with her. The end was coming. Her beloved (yes, beloved) brother Fuller had perished the year previously, and her own life span enclosed his now like protective parentheses. Toward the middle of April, Bess entered St. Mary's Hospital. Three weeks later, on the fourth of May, at 8:30 in the evening, Bess Corey died.[51] On May 7, a Friday, the Christian Science service was read over her body, after which the train carrying Bess's coffin began the final return to Marne.[52] In 1919, during the changes in Margaret Morgan Corey's life (turning the farm over to Rob and moving with Paul to Atlantic), Bess's mother had drawn up her last will and testament.[53] It bequeathed "to the youngest of my said children, remaining single at the time of my decease," a burial plot she owned in the Monroe Township Cemetery adjoining the little Methodist church where in years past the whole family had worshipped. Rather clearly, Margaret had in mind the only child in the family likely to be remaining single, her long-time sparring partner, Bess.

On Sunday, May 10, 1954, with the spring blossoms of Shelby County breaking out all around, her coffin borne by six of her nephews, Bachelor Bess came to the end of her journey, rejoining the Corey clan in the closest possible proximity to the farm where she had been born.[54]

✳ AFTERWORD *by Wayne Franklin*

This fascinating document of life on the land illuminates a glam-
orous but often misunderstood aspect of American history. The glamor
and the misunderstanding come down, at last, to a single word: *homesteading*. Few words evoke more quickly in the American mind so
much of the lore of the national past. But few half-truths are more
persistent in this land of self-aggrandizing myth than the belief that
great stretches of the American continent were given out free to needy
settlers who simply homesteaded their farms and ranches. Those who
read history know that the famous Homestead Act was, to the contrary,
a very late, very modest, and very unsuccessful effort at distributing
the government's land for free and in small amounts to ordinary
citizens.

Passed in 1862, that act was the means, over the next three decades, by which only 370,000 successful applicants acquired their
land. Even if we assume that each applicant represented a family unit
of six people, it is hard to see that any more than 2 million individuals
benefited from the Homestead Act in its first three decades; in the
same period, however, the population of the nation *increased* by some
32 million, so that most of those new citizens (and most of the 31
million already present in 1860) had no share in the benefits. In some
ways, the homestead movement seems like a sham intended to maintain the illusion that individual action mattered even though in the
nation as a whole power was more and more a matter of organization—
of corporate social and economic combinations. Henry Nash Smith is
right in reminding us that the law of 1862, rich with agrarian promise,
was cruelly out of place in a land where urbanization and industrial
economics were leaving the modest farmer very little but the shadow

of an old faith. And of course farming itself was more and more a matter of capitalization, industrial apparatus, and market production.

Because the total number of beneficiaries of the Homestead Act was so small and the limits on the amount of land available to any person were quite low, the whole quantity of land distributed for free was very small. A much larger amount was sold either directly by the government to individual landholders or in large tracts to speculators, who might derive large profits from the natural increase in land prices. In addition, within the nation as a whole, the federal government gave away for free to railroad corporations a total of 91 million acres of land, great quantities of which were in turn sold—often at handsome profits, again—to secondary speculators or small holders. One can easily calculate that those 91 million acres would have made, at 160 acres apiece, close to 600,000 additional homesteads, almost twice the number actually distributed between 1862 and 1890.

And the actual land homesteaded by small holders was often none of the best. Due to the late date of the Homestead Act, much of the homesteaded land lay west of the nation's richest regions; a great deal of it, as Elizabeth Corey's poignant letters from the dry lands of South Dakota demonstrate, was simply past the line where eastern agriculture could be more than intermittently possible. In Bess Corey's agriculturally rich home state of Iowa, where the paradigms of the East could be applied rather well, settlement came early enough that by 1862 (by which point Iowa had been a state for sixteen years) much of the public land already had been distributed. During that state's early development, almost 5 million acres (about one-seventh of its total area) were given by the federal government to railroad corporations. By contrast, eventually a total of only about 900,000 acres was distributed to settlers there under the Homestead Act. Contrast this with the enormous quantities of land which came into the possession of single men or small syndicates. In Illinois, Missouri, Kansas, and Nebraska, one Irish-American speculator, the legendary William Scully, purchased on his own some 220,000 acres, which he largely rented (rather than sold) to tenant farmers. Or, again in Bess's Iowa and its northern neighbor Minnesota, the Close Brothers of England were offering a full 500,000 acres of land for sale in the 1880s, the decade when Bess was born. In that same decade, it was estimated that within the past few years alone foreign investors had purchased more than 20 million acres in the nation. The traffic in public lands was one of the first great scandals of national history. The homesteading myth was one means by which that scandal was covered over.

It was a common observation, at the time of the American Revolution, that hundreds of years would be required before the new nation had spread its cultural dominion to the Pacific. The agrarian optimists who entertained that vision couldn't have been more wrong. Thomas Jefferson, one of those who foresaw a long, slow progress westward, hoped that American lands (which of course would have to be taken by hook or by crook from the natives first) would come into the hands of the upright yeoman farmer. But it was Jefferson, too, who made the biggest real estate speculation in American (perhaps in world) history by buying Louisiana, all 566 million acres of it, from France in 1803. Fueled by enormous population increases and industrial growth, by 1890 (or so Frederick Jackson Turner declared) the nation had converted much of this land to economic uses Jefferson hardly could have foreseen. And very little of it had come free and clear into the hands of the small farmer of Jefferson's imagination. As time passed, in fact, the percentage in the hands of small holders in some regions declined dramatically. In Nebraska in 1880, for instance, 18 percent of the farms were operated by tenants; by 1890 the figure had risen to 24 percent. By the start of the new century, more than a third of all American farmers were tenants, while a good many more were so encumbered by mortgages (as Bess was to be even before she got the deed for her 160 acres) that they were tenants in all but name. In Smith's view, again, the distance between Jeffersonian myth and the ideals of the Homestead Act, on the one hand, and the economic realities of America, on the other, was farther than the distance between Bess Corey's home in Marne, Iowa, and her claim in Stanley County, South Dakota.

Surely it was the quite different reality of landownership in the United States which made the mythology of the homestead so appealing. Perhaps it is the complexity of the present American economy which continues to make the bright, simple idea of homesteading so attractive today. Certainly some powerful forces must account for the fact that an institution which affected so few people has been enshrined at the center of national memory.

I do not mean to detract from Bachelor Bess's heroic insistence on proving up her claim in South Dakota. But note that she never really inhabited the farm into which she poured a good deal of money and a great deal of work. Perhaps if she had not taught school (as so many of the single women homesteading in Dakota did) but had thrown herself on the land's mercy, success might have come to her early and full. But the land she chose, even though it apparently was much better than the claims of most homesteaders, held little mercy for the kind of agriculture to which Bess had been bred, and no amount of labor could have made it good cropland of the sort that the wet-climate farming of the East demanded. A quarter-section in Iowa or even in eastern South Dakota might have made Bachelor Bess into Farmer Bess. She clearly recognized the limits on her land. Her dream of a horse ranch, for instance, was a shrewd counter to the slim chances for an agricultural fulfillment in Stanley County. But in Stanley County she could not even become the horse rancher she wished to be. And, as Philip Gerber points out in his excellent commentary on Bess's letters, even if she had, her horses would have been out of place in the surreal modern landscape of her West, a landscape that contained both cowboys and cars, mercilessly dry, glaring stretches of outdoor space, and plush hotels complete with atriums, telegraphs, and telephones.

It is a world, nevertheless, which in Bachelor Bess's letters comes to vivid life. If her "ranch" never was a success, the life she lived on it or all around it in the countryside nearby definitely was. With her wonderful sense of frontier humor, her ear for contemporary speech, her eye for the colorful detail, even her candor in working through the lingering anxieties of what must have been a difficult young adulthood, Bess gives us access to a time and place which were of our century but which are distant in so many ways from our end of it. We can be thankful to Bachelor Bess for having taken so much time to record what passed before (and within) her seventy-five years ago, thankful to her family (including her youngest brother, Paul) for saving the record she produced, and thankful to Philip Gerber for so painstakingly presenting her letters to readers for the first time. In these energetic letters sent home from the edge of modern America we all can stake a claim.

✳ NOTES

Introduction

1 *Sisseton, South Dakota,* promotional pamphlet of the Chicago, Milwaukee & St. Paul Railway, 1893, p. 1.

2 Ole Olson, Jr., *Information in Regard to the Opening of the Rosebud Indian Reservation, in Gregory County, South Dakota* (Sioux Falls: W. G. George, n.d. [1902]), pp. 2–3.

3 Mrs. A. N. Holm to Miss Grace H. Carpenter, June 24, 1905, TL (typed letter) (copy of ALS [autograph letter signed] in South Dakota Cultural Center, Pierre).

4 *Free Homesteads and Deeded Lands [in] Central South Dakota* (Pierre: West Land Company, n.d.), p. 1.

5 The family included Margaret Morgan Brown (1863–1925), James Olney (1886–1913), Henry Fuller (1889–1953), Robert Longfellow (1894–1943), Ethel Gertrude (1896–1936), Challenge Richard (1898–1975), and Paul Frederick (b. 1903).

6 Harold H. Schuler, *A Bridge Apart: History of Early Pierre and Fort Pierre* (Pierre: State Publisher Company, 1987), pp. 8–9. Schuler's book is the most recent and the most complete account of Stanley County and its environs.

7 Quoted in ibid., p. 28. Governor N. H. Ordway's remark was first printed in the *Signal,* August 18, 1880.

8 George P. Keiter, *Pierre City, Fort Pierre, Hughes and Sully Counties, South Dakota, Directory for 1910–1911* (St. Paul: Keiter Directory Company, 1910), p. 171.

9 Schuler, *A Bridge Apart,* pp. 30–31.

10 Ibid., pp. 20–28, contains a full account of the early history of freighting from Fort Pierre to the Black Hills.

11 Ibid., p. 31.

12 "Doors of Historic Locke Hotel Closed for Good," *Capital Journal*, June 2, 1978; "The End of an Era," *Pierre Times*, April 1, 1978; and Jan LaFurge, "Locke Hotel Closes Doors," *Huron Daily Plainsman*; in Clipping Files, South Dakota Historical Society, Pierre. All contain similar histories of the Locke Hotel. See also Schuler, *A Bridge Apart*, pp. 134–139.

13 Schuler, *A Bridge Apart*, p. 139.

14 *Hughes County History* (Pierre: Museum and State Historical Office, 1937), p. 115.

15 Doane Robinson, *South Dakota* (Chicago: American Historical Society, 1930), vol. 1, pp. 536–537. The schoolchildren actually contributed the sum of $4,656, considerably in excess of the sculptor's fee of $2,500.

16 "'Scotty' Philip, Buffalo King, Dies," *Dupree Leader*, July 27, 1911, and "Death of 'Scotty' Philip," *Bad River News*, July 27, 1911, in Clipping Files, South Dakota Historical Society, Pierre. Both contain summaries of Philip's efforts to preserve the buffalo as a species.

17 Laura Iversen Abrahamson's manuscript diary (1895–1903) in the archives of the South Dakota Historical Society, Pierre, contains a typical example. Laura's father filed a claim about twenty miles south of Bad River in 1895, built a home and barn, and then moved his family to the homestead, only to discover that water sources were inadequate. A year later he was forced to dismantle his house and move to a new claim along Medicine Creek, where the water supply was somewhat more dependable.

18 *Prairie Progress in West Central South Dakota* (Sioux Falls: Midwest Beach, 1968), and Irene Caldwell, ed., *Bad River (Wakpa Sica), Ripples, Rages, and Residents* (Pierre: State Publishing Company, 1983), are two of the many books that contain detailed accounts of early dwellings on Stanley County homesteads.

19 Data concerning Clarence E. Coyne (1881–1929) are contained in Clipping Files, South Dakota Historical Society, Pierre.

20 Grace Reed Porter, "Twenty Five Years in South Dakota," Manuscript Collections, South Dakota Historical Society, Pierre.

21 Edgar A. Edwards, "Teacher Certification Laws in South Dakota," *South Dakota Historical Collections* no. 18 (1936), p. 265.

22 *Prairie Progress* and Caldwell, ed., *Bad River* are replete with stories of these and other Stanley County families mentioned in the Corey letters.

23 Bess Corey saved her program from the Johanna Gadski recital and mailed it to Marne, writing beneath the prima donna's photograph: "She was simply grand."

Elizabeth Corey's Homesteading Letters

JUNE 1, 1909

1 Lida Smith, like Bess Corey, was a rural schoolteacher. Bess and Lida met through their schoolteaching activities, and Bess became friendly with the Smith family around 1905. They lived in Harlan, county seat of Shelby County and the largest town near the Tennant area, where Bess's school was located. The Smith residence was not far from the home of Bess's Aunt Jennie and her husband, James D. Dunlavy.
2 A tiny settlement in the former Indian lands south of the Cheyenne River and northwest of Fort Pierre.
3 Lindsay was a post office settlement beyond Sansarc in the sparsely settled ranching region northwest of Fort Pierre.
4 Mrs. T. N. Scarborough was Mrs. Smith's sister and Lida's Aunt Nora.
5 Bess probably means the observance of Memorial Day or Sunday *morning*.
6 Probably for high school graduation, a big event in 1909 Harlan.
7 George E. Stewart, a young man of Bess's and Lida's age in Harlan. The Stewarts were among Bess Corey's best friends in that city.

JUNE 3, 1909

1 For data concerning Midland, S.D., see the Introduction, and the Epilogue.
2 Midland in 1909 had a trio of hotels. Bess probably went up to the Dakota or the Bastion House.
3 A claim was one of the 160-acre tracts on which a homesteader was allowed to file a claim.
4 To "prove up" referred to the process of filing with the government land office all proof that regulations of the Homestead Act had been complied with. Upon proving up, one received a deed to the property.

JUNE 6, 1909

1 The then-booming town of Hayes was the site of a land office where claims might be filed.
2 Clarence E. Coyne, born in Illinois, came to Fort Pierre in 1906. He was twenty-five when he met Bess in Hayes and well on his way into an illustrious career. Eventually he became involved in the motion-picture business in Fort Pierre, where he also owned the weekly *Times* and served as a director in the Fort Pierre National Bank. He became mayor of Fort Pierre and sheriff of Stanley County. On the state level he was director of the Motor Vehicles Bureau, then secretary of state, then lieutenant gover-

nor, and when he died unexpectedly in 1929 at the age of forty-seven he was being touted as a gubernatorial candidate. Bess's judgment of Coyne was astute.

3 The post office nearest Scarborough Ranch in north-central South Dakota close to the Cheyenne River.

4 The T. N. Scarboroughs moved from Iowa to South Dakota in 1907. If Will were then Fuller Corey's age, he was twenty. Russell was twelve (a year older than Challenge Corey) and Ruth three.

5 Gumbo snatchers were so-called because of their taking homesteads in the sticky, claylike soil of the one-time open range.

6 Mary Lanigan was a member of a Catholic family living near Corey farm. She was near Bess in age, a schoolteacher, and one of Bess's dearest friends.

7 Valerie Harris was the eldest daughter of Ben Harris, who had a farm diagonally across the crossroads at Corey farm in Iowa.

JUNE 22, 1909

1 The state capital and chief city in the central portion of the state, on the Missouri River. See Introduction.

2 Fort Pierre is directly across the Missouri from Pierre. See Introduction.

3 For data concerning the Locke Hotel, see Introduction.

4 Mrs. Frank A. Twiss.

JUNE 23, 27, 29, 1909

1 Frank A. Twiss was manager of the Locke Hotel.

2 Huston House, a three-story frame hotel on the banks of the Missouri, was owned and operated by Mr. and Mrs. George S. Huston.

3 Another small Fort Pierre hotel.

4 The George A. Gordons ran a boardinghouse in Fort Pierre. Mr. Gordon was an entrepreneurial local businessman, and Mrs. Gordon became Bess's closest friend in town.

5 Avoca, a railroad junction about fifteen miles from Marne, Iowa, had a reputation for being a "tough town," according to Paul Corey, and the name of the town became a euphemism for "hell," a word the Corey children were not allowed to use as an expletive. The fact of this interdiction is borne out by the language of Bess's letters.

6 Apparently one of the motor launches used as ferryboats in plying the Missouri between Pierre and Fort Pierre and available for chartered excursions.

7 For data on "Scotty" Philip's Buffalo Pasture, see Introduction.

JULY 5, 1909

1 The "Carlson place" was a relinquishment. If Bess had been able to meet Carlson's price, he would have told her exactly when he planned to relinquish his claim at the Land Office so that she could be on hand there to file her own claim immediately.
2 Bess's coats had been left inadvertently at the Shannon House hotel, which on July 2, 1909, was gutted by fire.
3 The Majestic Theater was one of the enterprises of the George Gordons, and Bess's employment at their boardinghouse clearly includes free admission to the shows.
4 A famous Missouri River steamboat.
5 Bad River, as it empties into the Missouri, bisects Fort Pierre.
6 The Gordons' dog.
7 Twigs was the family dog at Corey farm and seven-year-old Paul Corey's most constant playmate.

JULY 18, 1909

1 James D. Dunlavy had married Bess's Aunt Jennie E. Corey (1859–1936) in 1899. They lived in Harlan, Iowa, where Bess, while attending summer normal institute, sometimes boarded with them. For personal reasons that stemmed from these times, Bess was not a wholehearted admirer of Uncle J. D., as she generally called him, and the present reference undoubtedly is edged with irony.
2 *Capsolin* was a patent medicine containing capsicin ($C_9H_{14}O_2$), a chemical taken from plants closely related to the cayenne pepper and used externally for medicinal purposes. It raises the temperature of the skin and causes it to flush—in Bess's case, to blister.
3 Synonymous with a deed of ownership.
4 A claim which is being given up by the original claimant and turned back to the government before the homesteader has "proved up" on it. See Bess's letter of August 14, 1909.
5 A country inn where travelers might refresh themselves and stay the night.

AUGUST 10, 1909

1 Probably M. B. Hastings. See Bess's letter of August 14, 1909.

AUGUST 14, 1909

1 Grace Haynes, daughter of a farm family living about two miles north of Corey farm. She was roughly Ethel Corey's age.

2 A land man, sometimes called a locater, helped homesteaders to find unclaimed quarter-sections of land on which they might file. This land man was M. B. Hastings.

3 Maurice B. Hastings was a single man aged twenty-seven in 1909. He was a real-estate dealer in Pierre and acted in land-man capacity.

4 For data concerning Grace Reed (Porter), see Introduction. See also Porter's manuscript report, "Twenty Five Years in South Dakota" at the South Dakota Historical Society, Pierre.

5 Bess's paternal grandmother, Anna Mariah Johnson Corey (1835–1912), married Jeremiah O. Corey (1814–1896) in 1855. In 1909 she was seventy-four years old and residing in Atlantic, Iowa, county seat of Cass County and seven miles from Marne.

6 Bess taught the local rural school two miles north of Corey farm during the 1908–9 school year.

7 James D. Dunlavy, usually called Uncle J. D.

AUGUST 18, 1909

1 Bess has filed upon a rather unorthodox tract. Instead of being a traditional quarter of a section, her claim is the east half of the southwest quarter-section and the west half of the southeast quarter-section. This exists within section two of township three north and thirty east of the Black Hills meridian. See sketch, p. lxiii.

2 A school director was a member of the district school board having responsibility for the rural schools (generally not more than one or two) lying within the district.

3 The Reeses, who came to Dakota from Missouri, homesteaded in Antelope School District near Bess's claim on Bad River. In 1909 Henry Reese was twenty-eight and Ella Reese twenty-five.

AUGUST 20, 1909

1 For data concerning Grant and Mae Stone, see Introduction.

2 Rose Gillette, sometime teacher of the rural school nearest Corey farm.

AUGUST 21, 1909

1 Grant and Mae Stone's four children; Bess liked to pun.

2 Fuller Corey (1889–1953) would turn twenty in September 1909.

3 To break sod was to open the prairie with a special breaking plow equipped to tear through the matted grass roots and lay a broad strip of turf on its back. One of the homesteading requirements was that a portion of a claimant's tract must be tilled.

4 Bess had left a trunk and other possessions at Corey farm to be freighted to South Dakota when she was settled there. The rolls of pieces she mentions may refer to bits of fabric used to mend clothing and/or bits of material that can be made into washrags and rag carpet.

5 The younger Corey children appear not to have comprehended that sister Bess was going to be away for a very long time.

AUGUST 29, 1909

1 Uncle James (Jim) Dunlavy.

2 Olney Corey (1886–1913) was taking examinations for teacher certification.

3 Byron Clow was a Fort Pierre politician.

4 Adolph Buchholz, a Bohemian neighbor in Bess's area.

5 Young women in the area of Corey farm. Hazel Groat, a farm wife, was considered to be "loose."

6 Bess is punning. The dams tended to dry up in late summer, allowing a crop of weeds to spring up.

7 The holograph letter carries the stain left by the squashed bedbug.

8 Teton was the westward railroad stop nearest to Fort Pierre. Established as the Northwestern Railroad laid track through the region, it never developed as a community.

9 This appears to be Bess's last contact with Lida Smith. The two young schoolma'ams had boarded at the same home when teaching school in Iowa about two miles from each other. It was not uncommon, Paul Corey recalls, for his sister to have problems with other women of her age, and apparently she came to consider Lida as something of a floozy.

SEPTEMBER 12 AND 13, 1909

1 In 1909 John Porter was eighteen years old.

2 Howard Speer was the oldest son of Bess's neighbors William Grant Speer and Mattie L. Store Speer. In 1909 Howard was sixteen years old.

3 Little Porcupine Creek, which flows into Bad River.

4 Oscar C. Walton came to South Dakota from Missouri in 1908 when he was twenty-one years of age. His claim on Bad River was near Bess's, and he was the most youthful member of the board which directed Speer School.

5 Perhaps ambiguous. Does Bess mean Ella Buchholz or Ella Van Hise?

6 A euphemism for menstruation; surely an offhanded form of reassurance for a worrying mother whose daughter has gone off to live in the wild, wild West. The remark is not unrelated to Bess's frequent quips about "bein' awful good."

7 To leave; a slang expression synonymous with "hit the road."

8 Momence, Ill., was the family home of Bess Corey's mother, Margaret Morgan Brown Corey (1863–1925). One of her brothers had married a Scramlin.

9 Slang meaning "Do you have something you want to ask?"

10 These appear to be teaching materials used by Bess in 1908–9 and which she is giving to Mary Lanigan for use in Mary's teaching.

11 Friejouff Erickson, a neighbor to Bess on Bad River.

SEPTEMBER 26, 1909

1 In predicting a clash between the Irish Oscar Walton and herself, Bess invokes the traditional Irish-English opposition.

2 Buchholzes.

3 Jhelmer Blumgreen (spelled in various ways by Bess as well as by others) was another homesteader in the Antelope District; Bess later purchased her team of black mares from him.

4 There appears to have been an Ella in the Erickson family also.

5 A part of the slang expression "23-skidoo," meaning "get out of here fast."

6 Tepid; lackluster; unenthusiastic.

7 These were 1908–9 pupils in Bess's school: she passed out rulers as end-of-year mementos, and these boys perhaps were absent.

8 The married name of Ida Wever, a good friend from the 1905 era when Bess taught school near Tennant, Iowa, south of Harlan.

9 Bess's good friend, Anna Stewart, of Harlan, Iowa.

10 As there is not yet a U.S. parcel post system, Bess must go (or send) into Fort Pierre for her package, which contains some of the items she had asked her family to ship to her. A storage charge is made for each day the package remains in the railroad depot.

OCTOBER 10 AND 13, 1909

1 The clerk of the school board issued the warrant for a teacher's salary; it must be endorsed by at least one other member of the three-member board before it became valid.

2 Mr. Brown, another homesteading neighbor, was on the school board and could endorse Bess's warrant.

3 Claimholders near Bess's homestead.

4 Tragedies of this sort were not uncommon among newcomers unaccustomed to South Dakota weather. In 1907 Florence Brown went out to her claim during good weather to establish some January residence days. A blizzard trapped her in her claim shanty and only the fact that her horse broke free and was able to make it to a neighboring homestead, thereby

giving the signal that something was amiss, saved her from death by freezing or starvation.

5 The Speers most likely to be sliding on the ice that day are: Howard and Glen, sixteen; Maggie, twelve; Fannie, ten; Herbert, eight; Clayton, six; and perhaps Ruth, three.

6 Jennie Noon and her mother were Iowa neighbors who lived on the farm directly north of Corey farm.

7 Orla Harris, an Iowa neighbor, younger brother of Valerie.

8 Oscar Walton and Ella Buchholz. Bess employed a question mark within parentheses when she wished to express doubts—in this case perhaps to speculate on whether Oscar would bring Ella or someone else with him.

9 Terrence and Johnnie Lanigan, brothers to Mary Lanigan, Iowa neighbors.

10 Walter Alexander Brown (1860–1950), an older brother of Margaret Corey.

OCTOBER 17, 1909

1 Glen Speer.

2 A reference to George Stewart of Harlan; the suggestion here is that George should have married Bess, keeping her close to her friends in the Harlan-Marne area.

3 Another neighbor and homesteader along Bad River. She and her son Mack (or Max?) each had a separate claim.

4 Irish expression for potatoes.

5 Postcards cost only a penny to mail. But perhaps Bess is referring here to the cost of the pictorial postcards then very popular—and to the considerable number of them that she was both receiving and sending.

NOVEMBER 6, 1909

1 Bess's euphemism for her outdoor toilet or privy.

2 For the box social, held as a part of the entertainment.

3 Trade name of a cast-iron stove used for heating.

4 A game where, for a fee, one threw a "fishline" over a wall or curtain behind which the persons running the game attach a "fish" (a trinket) to the line.

5 George W. Keyser and Abraham Bunker operated the Keyser and Bunker Lumber Yard in Fort Pierre.

NOVEMBER 16 AND 21, 1909

1 Fischer Brothers general store, established in 1889 by Frank, Anton, and Charles Fischer on Deadwood Street in Fort Pierre, was one of the largest

suppliers to the homesteaders, who often would purchase provisions sufficient to last the entire winter and transport them to their claims before
autumn rains made roads and trails impassable. Fischer Brothers moved
to a new location on Main Street in 1900; their slogan was "Everything to
Eat and Wear."

2 Rudolph Klemann, then twenty years of age, was the son of Henry Klemann (Bess would teach Klemann School in 1910–11).

3 Joseph and Julius Bahr homesteaded in War Creek Township about one-
half mile from Bess's claim, making them her closest neighbors. In 1909
Joseph was thirty-seven, Julius thirty-four. Being naturalized citizens, they
spoke with heavy German accents which amused Bess and which she
mimicked.

DECEMBER 7, 1909

1 Nickname for Fuller Corey.

DECEMBER 8 AND 11, 1909

1 The five-year-old daughter of Grant and Mae Stone.
2 Paul Corey recalls Nielsons as a jewelry store in Walnut, Iowa.
3 Probably Bess's neighbor, Ben Share.
4 John Jay Corey (1860–1928).

DECEMBER 21, 1909

1 The Alfred Long family farmed two miles east of the Coreys.
2 Paul Corey believes this reference to concern Jennie and "Grandma" Noon,
who lived north of Corey farm, rather than meaning Bess's Aunt Jennie
Dunlavy of Harlan and Grandma Corey of Atlantic, Iowa.
3 Both Fuller and Olney Corey possessed violins and played by ear. As a
young man, Fuller played for neighborhood dances in Iowa.

DECEMBER 28 AND 31, 1909

1 Ben Share and his mother homesteaded in Bess's neighborhood. Apparently they were Jewish.
2 The connection was suggested by the Speers' belief that a relative had
married a Scramlin of Momence, Ill. In 1884 Alice Theressa Scramlin
(1864–1956) married Margaret (Brown) Corey's brother Walter. Margaret
seems not to have responded positively to this suggested relationship, as it
is not insisted upon and is not mentioned in subsequent letters.

3 A way of referring to Oscar Walton, who is Irish.

4 Apparently slang for dollars.

5 Ten-year-old Fannie Stone.

6 Possibly an Anglicized version of Sonnenschein, a family with a ranch south of Bess's territory.

JANUARY 13, 1910

1 Bess probably is referring to either George or Clarence Rovang, settlers living south near the Sonnenschein Ranch.

2 Organized in Walnut, Iowa, in 1893, the German Bank was located in one of the oldest business buildings still standing in Walnut. Predictably, during World War I its name was altered to the American State Bank, one effect of the wartime intolerance of things German. The Corey family did some banking at the German Bank, and Paul Corey believes the bank held the mortgage on Corey farm.

3 One of Bess Corey's grammar school teachers.

4 While attending school in Walnut, Bess boarded with the Copleys.

5 Bess had been recruited into the Royal Neighbors, a women's lodge in Fort Pierre.

6 Clay Township, location of Corey farm in Shelby County, Iowa.

JANUARY 28, 1910

1 The Scripter family were neighbors of Bess's along Bad River. The parents probably were Seymour and Anna Scripter (listed in 1915 census records as being ranchers in Stanley County); the children are Florence and her two brothers, Erle and Art.

2 The brothers Bahr.

3 Hugh Armstrong, a neighbor living near Corey farm. The implication here seems to be that Hugh and Bess were one-time sweethearts and that Bess is still halfway in love with him.

4 Wife of Uncle Walter Brown. Thettie is the Alice Theressa Scramlin Brown thought by the Speer family to establish a kinship between them and the Coreys.

FEBRUARY 3, 1910

1 Slang for money.

2 Teachers institute concerned group meetings held throughout the school year at which teachers presented programs and attended lectures and demonstrations aimed at the improvement of instruction. The specific ref-

erence here is to the summer normal institutes, at which attendance was mandatory and which lasted up to two weeks. It was sometimes permissible for a teacher to attend an institute in her home state while visiting there during the summer.

3 The brothers Bahr.

4 Robert S. Vessey (1858–1929) was governor of South Dakota from 1909 to 1913. He presided over ceremonies inaugurating the newly built state capitol (see Introduction).

5 Ruth was three, Clayton six, and Herbert eight. There was not much room for them to play in a claim shack.

FEBRUARY 27, 1910

1 One day when Margaret Corey drove her buggy to Walnut, a rearing horse smashed the buggy top.

2 Bess is mixing her metaphors here; the usual expression is "tight as Dick's hatband."

3 A whistle- or flutelike instrument with six finger holes designed to produce varying tones. Bess Corey experienced an intense yearning for music on the plains.

4 A local expression meaning "to go crazy," as Yankton was the site of the state hospital for the insane. Bess is adapting rather rapidly.

5 Art Scripter.

MARCH 22 AND 25, 1910

1 Probably Joe Bahr.

2 Probably the daughters of Ben Wiseman, a neighbor of Bess's.

3 War Creek, just west of Bess's claim, is one of the larger tributaries of Bad River.

4 Shiner was a family dog on Corey farm. He had been told not to get into the milk and to keep the cats out of it as well. But when the cats did get into the milk, Shiner decided to get his share by joining in the feast.

5 Grace Reed. The county superintendent of schools was required to visit every school in the county every year. These visits usually were unannounced.

6 Fuller seemed to be leaning toward filing a claim of his own in South Dakota.

7 This is Fuller's horse Nell, which he will bring to South Dakota with him.

8 A local girl, of British Isles heritage, had married Pete Sorensen(?), a Dane. Such an intermarriage, says Paul Corey, was bound to raise eyebrows and cause talk in the rather insular world of Clay Township.

9 She led the choir at the Monroe Township Methodist Church, where the Coreys attended services rather regularly.

10 The common name for rhubarb. Roots could withstand the trip by freight and be planted in Bess's garden for a crop the next season.

11 In linear measurement, a rod equals 16 feet. Her plot of plowed ground will approximate 1,650 feet in length.

12 The sloping juncture of two hills, a natural drainage for water; a gully.

APRIL 10 AND 18, 1910

1 Fred Bertram.

2 Probably Maggie Speer, then thirteen and aspiring to become a teacher like Bess.

JULY 3, 1910

1 Presumably Fuller Corey drove his sister to the Dunlavys in Harlan, where she would catch her train back to South Dakota. Very likely Bess's visit to Iowa was used to persuade Fuller, soon to turn twenty-one, not to abandon his plans for coming west and filing claim on a tract of homestead land.

2 Lida Smith's mother. Apparently, Bess's falling out with Lida did not finish her friendship with the Smith family in Harlan, for Mrs. Smith also escorted Bess to her train.

3 The Range was a department store in Fort Pierre.

4 A town south of the Bad River area about thirty miles, in Jones County.

5 Later spelled Kempton.

6 Robert L. Yokum, a Fort Pierre businessman, owned a building at Deadwood Street and Second Avenue that housed his bar. The upper story was known as the Yokum Hotel. Yokum also owned a pair of buffalo which he had trained to pull a cart, a stunt which he displayed in various cities across the nation.

JULY 21, 1910

1 Mary Buchholz managed Bob Yokum's hotel in Fort Pierre.

2 Bess's aunt Mary Frances Corey (1857–1932), sometimes known as Aunt Moll.

3 For data concerning the new South Dakota state capitol, see Introduction.

4 The school was known as Klemann School because of its proximity to the homestead of the Klemann family—a local custom in naming schoolhouses. Henry Klemann and his wife, Sidwina, both came from Germany; in 1910 both were fifty years old. Their children were Emil, twenty-five;

Rudolph, twenty-one; Julius, ca. eighteen; Emma and Oscar, sixteen; and Margerete, fourteen. The Klemanns came to South Dakota in 1890.

5 Walton Porter, one of the school directors for Klemann School. He married Grace Reed, the county superintendent of schools.

6 J. A. Gillaspie.

7 George Jones.

8 Professor Thompson was one of the educational leaders brought into Fort Pierre to lead the summer normal institute for Stanley County teachers.

9 A rat is a tapering roll of crimped hair used to puff out a hairdo, which is turned over it, as in the pompadour style much used in Bess's youth (the last days of the Gibson Girl look). To make such a device was the reason for Bess's repeated requests that her family send the lock of her own hair she has kept in a drawer at the farm.

10 A daughter of Ben Wiseman who is close to Bess in age.

11 Probably the Coreys' neighbor, Ben Harris, father of Valerie and Orla.

12 During the summer of 1910 the roof was raised on the house at Corey farm and three rooms added, a move which Bess applauded and which, it appears, she had urged upon her mother.

13 Alta Brown, Bess's cousin, daughter of Challenge Dunn Brown (1854– 1948).

AUGUST 7, 1910

1 Ben Share, the "wandering Jew" of Bess's letters.

2 One of the great hobby crazes of the period was homemade photographic postcards, which obviated the need to write a letter and enclose a photograph.

3 Buffalo berries, also called buffalo-peas, are acidic, edible red berries which grow on a low shrub. They are used in jellies and the like.

4 Possibly this was for use as a rat. The natural hair would have an obvious advantage over a substitute made of fabric or other such material.

5 Daylilies, like many other rooted plants, could be transported in a ball of soil for replanting elsewhere.

SEPTEMBER 25, 1910

1 A cistern was rather essential in semiarid country. Eaves troughs and spouting from the shack roof could be used to pipe rainwater directly into an underground cistern, where it might be saved for washing or, if need arose, for drinking. Such water often would be cleaner than that taken from an open dam.

2 Outside the Corey kitchen door a cave-cellar had been dug where milk and butter would keep in warm weather.

3 A current joke about a woman's girth, which Bess good-naturedly turns upon herself. The joke concerns a woman so large that a man attempting to embrace her would need a piece of chalk to mark his place as he traveled her circumference.

4 *Passe-partout*—the process of creating a picture frame with a pasteboard back and a glass front. Between these is placed the picture, with an ornamented mat next to the glass. Strips of paper pasted over the edges seal the frame.

5 The "dodads" possibly are rats, used in place of the roll of Bess's own hair which Mrs. Corey seems unable to get around to sending, despite Bess's repeated requests.

OCTOBER 2 AND 3, 1910

1 Fuller has become aware of backtracking, especially of the habit of young people, for a variety of reasons, to homestead only until they are able to prove up, then sell out and return to their place of origin.

2 Baking-powder pancakes.

3 On Corey farm, Fuller had a horse named Fred and Rob Corey had a pony named Babe.

OCTOBER 6 AND 7, 1910

1 Bess's caution is rather ambiguous, but she seems to be alerting her mother to letters being read surreptitiously either by Fuller or by the Klemanns. Privacy of mail was a concern; elsewhere Bess speaks of the need to be certain that an envelope is sealed tightly. A postcard, of course, was notoriously fair game for anyone through whose hands it passed.

OCTOBER 27, 1910

1 The Reading Circle involved a group of schoolma'ams who were assigned books in common—pedagogical or cultural—to report on and discuss in group meetings held at times other than the more formal teachers meetings or institutes.

2 He was drunk.

3 "Sham" is a nickname for Oscar Walton, who is leaving his homestead for life in Fort Pierre.

4 Anna Stewart of Harlan, Iowa.

5 Jennie Noon.
6 An outhouse or privy. Bess appears to be amused by the children's lack of inhibitions.

NOVEMBER 1, 1910

1 This is Bess's first use of the "Bachelor Bess" signature in her letters to the family at Corey farm.

NOVEMBER 7, 1910

1 Paul Corey supposes this to mean only the two oldest Lanigan boys, Johnny and Terrence, and not to suggest a serious family breakup.
2 A garment of lace or cambric used to cover the neck, especially when worn with a low-cut waist.
3 The wax is the residue left from using the schoolhouse as a dancehall.
4 Maud Hemsted, the teacher at School #9, near Corey farm.
5 The Raleigh Company was one of the first to send agents peddling their wares house to house in rural districts. The salesmen traveled with well-stocked wagons, a kind of general store on wheels.

NOVEMBER 15, 1910

1 Bess Corey's birthday, ever a sentimental occasion for her.
2 Oscar C. Walton.
3 A fellow teacher and good friend in Stanley County.
4 Ben Share.
5 Before emigrating to South Dakota, the Carlisles had lived in Missouri Valley, Iowa, not far west of Bess's home near Marne. Frank Perry Carlisle filed on a homestead along Bad River in 1907 and the rest of his family arrived at about the same time as Bess, the spring of 1909. In 1910 Frank Carlisle, a director of Klemann School, was fifty-one, his wife, Katherine, forty-four. The boys who escorted Bess home would be Malcolm, fifteen (Bess's seventh-grade pupil), and Charles, ten.
6 Bess slept with Margerete Klemann, then fourteen years old.
7 Another use of "Avoca" as a euphemism for "hell."
8 Outhouse or privy.
9 Oscar Walton.

NOVEMBER 25, 1910

1 Henry Klemann.
2 The Royal Hotel was another business run by the entrepreneurial Gordons.

3 He is "young Porter," but not John Porter or Walton Porter, it appears. In any event, the Gordons are busily matchmaking for their good friend Bess.

DECEMBER 5, 6, 7, 1910

1 Without collateral.
2 Fred Bertram, a neighbor, also called Fritz.
3 Missouri-born Lyle Moulton, age thirty, was a rancher in the Dry Run District west of Bess's claim. In 1909 he had married a Danish-born wife, Margaret, twenty-four. In 1916, Bess would board with the Moulton family.
4 Stones' horse.
5 The "Christmas Tree" apparently refers to a party given for neighboring families at the schoolhouse as Christmas approached.

DECEMBER 12, 1910

1 The common name for tuberculosis, a "scare" word, the great killer at that time of people Bess's age.
2 A possible allusion to Margaret Corey's intention to return to teaching; connected also with a neighborhood dispute as to whether Rose Gillette or Maud Hemsted should be the teacher at the local school.
3 The corn crop has been picked and safely put into winter storage or sold.

DECEMBER 24 AND 26, 1910

1 This appears to be the Christmas Tree, in preparation for which Bess has been raising funds.
2 Flagg Carlisle (1889–1969), son of Bess Corey's neighbors Frank and Katherine Carlisle, was one of Bess's most consistent friends during her early years in Stanley County. He was a schoolteacher and also an attorney. Following the partition of Stanley County in 1914, Flagg established a law practice in Kadoka, county seat of newly created Jackson County, and spent the remainder of his life there.
3 A jabot is a frill of lace or other soft material used to decorate the front of a woman's bodice (what Bess calls a waist).
4 This could refer to Mrs. Frank Carlisle or to young Katherine, as both had the same name. Young Katherine was six and a pupil at Klemann School.
5 Young Frank Murphy was a clerk at the Range Mercantile Company in Fort Pierre. He is among the crowd driving to the pow-wow in automobiles.
6 A tongue-in-cheek remark wherein Bess plays upon a piece of folklore which says that Indians subsist primarily upon the flesh of their pet dogs. She is fully conscious of the effect this remark will have upon her dog-loving brothers at home.

JANUARY 16, 1911

1 Margaret Corey had two reasons to be "angry": Bess's extravagance in purchasing the Blumgren team of black mares, and Bess's apparent dismissal of any suggestion that Margaret might return to teaching.

2 This refers to Margaret's belief that she could step into a schoolroom and at once resume the career she had given up in 1885.

3 He means that the teeth are not yet ground down by use, which would be a tell-tale sign of age.

4 It was common practice to pick up a claim shack from an abandoned homestead, or to purchase one from a backtracker, and drag it with horses to its new location.

JANUARY 25 AND 26, 1911

1 Brother of Flagg, Malcolm, and Charles Carlisle.

2 Fuller's claim lay just north of Bess's and, in fact, the two tracts had an adjoining boundary. The legal description of Fuller's land was Lots 3 and 4 and the south half of the northwest quarter of Section 2 in Township 3 North of Range 30 East of the Black Hills Meridian. It comprised a fraction in excess of 160 acres. See sketch, p. lxiii.

FEBRUARY 6, 8, 9, 10, 1911

1 The Rovangs homesteaded in the territory south of Bess's claim.

2 A wiener sausage; Bess is still pursuing her tale of being offered dog sausage at the Indian pow-wow.

3 For her Reading Circle, presumably.

FEBRUARY 21, 1911

1 Harry Berg, a baker in Fort Pierre.

2 Harry Berg. In his unpublished recollections of life in Stanley County (p. 37), William P. Hart states that the fellow's "name was Harry Berg, but everyone called him Dago Harry."

MARCH 6 AND 9, 1911

1 Homesteading neighbors.

2 In order to encourage homesteading, the railroads offered "emigrant cars" in which a family could travel with their household possessions and stock. The car would have rather primitive kitchen facilities and bunks for sleeping.

3 A nonvenomous snake, fast-moving.

4 Charles J. Lavery, a Fort Pierre physician.

5 The year 1911 brought a very dry season and many Stanley County home-steaders lost their crops and backtracked. Bess, who liked to emphasize the positive, made almost no references to the disastrous consequences of the 1911 drought.

6 Will Speer, brother of W. G. Speer.

MARCH 13, 1911

1 Fuller brought his horse Nell with him to South Dakota; she is not to be confused with the Nell that is a part of Bess's team of black mares.

2 Paul Corey believes this to be a member of his mother's Eastern Star organization.

3 The Missouri River tributary south of Bad River; it flows through the Badlands.

4 Apparently, Mrs. Corey has not yet sent Bess's lock of hair, and Fuller did not bring it with him.

5 Fritz Bertram had given Bess a box of fancy stationery for a Christmas gift.

MARCH 19, 1911

1 Fuller is describing his trip on the emigrant car. His traveling companion is not identified. They took the alternative route of the Northwestern through Nebraska, crossing the state diagonally northwest to Bonesteel, Dallas, and Colome in the Rosebud territory of South Dakota. From Colome Fuller heads north to the town of Winner, some sixty miles south of Fort Pierre.

2 By the time he reaches Vivian, Fuller is roughly thirty-five miles from Bad River and his claim.

3 The Corey horse used for drawing the buggy in Marne.

4 In laying out the original quarter-sections of land for homesteaders, the government surveyors drove stakes to identify the corners of each tract. If these could not be located, then the tract would need to be surveyed again, at the homesteader's expense.

MARCH 29, 1911

1 Fred Bertram.

2 Grace Reed Porter.

3 County superintendent of schools in Shelby County, Iowa. Bess has in mind taking on a spring term at an Iowa school, which would end in time for her to meet her institute obligation in Fort Pierre in July.

APRIL 2, 1911

1 A literal translation of the German (probably used by Joe and Julius Bahr) which Bess found colorful.

APRIL 6, 1911

1 Paul Prairie Chicken (1867–1939) was actually Charles La Moore, an Indian whose size dwarfed Bess Corey. He stood over six feet in height and weighed nearly four hundred pounds. He had lived on Bad River since 1887 and was one of the most colorful characters in Bess's vicinity.
2 An expression for begging, probably the equivalent of "standing in line at a soup kitchen."
3 A red clay stone much used by the Sioux for making pipes; pipestone is the common name, *catlinite* the scientific (named after George Catlin, the painter-explorer who visited Fort Pierre in 1831). The stone comes from Pipestone County in southeastern Minnesota.
4 A stringed instrument much like a zither.

APRIL 27, 1911

1 Bess appears to have made a move toward economy, but her roof needs to be spouted (fitted with eaves and downspouts) in order to catch rainwater for her cistern and the drinking-water barrel which always stood just outside her door.

APRIL 28, 1911

1 F. S. Rowe and Company was run by Fred S. Rowe and William H. Frost. One of Fort Pierre's oldest and largest hardware and farm implement stores, it was located on the east side of Deadwood Street. The building is still in use today.

MAY 5, 1911

1 Enclosed with this letter is a newspaper clipping advertising for sale an oval panel on which sits a disgruntled bulldog who through his muzzle manages to complain: "All I Did Was Growl a Little!" The clipping was intended to make a point with Margaret Corey, of course, but apparently she chose to ignore it, because the notes for her reply, penciled on the verso of Bess's envelope containing this letter, include only these bits of news to be relayed to Stanley County:

> Maudes letter
> your writing paper

> School out June 23
> Picnic May 24
> Fish weighed 4 pounds
> Colt named Sally

2 Charles M. Corey was a stockman from the Wendte, S.D., area. In 1911 he was fifty-one years of age; his wife, Carrie (Reinhodt), Danish-born, was forty-six. Bess Corey felt a special affinity with these Coreys because, although they were not native Iowans, they had moved to Stanley County from Iowa, and because among their six children was a son named Paul.

3 M. B. Briggs was a Stanley County stockman who had been living in South Dakota since 1890.

4 This refers to the marriage of George Stewart of Harlan, Iowa. Bess's paragraph lends credence to her brother Paul's conjecture that his sister "had more than just a soft spot" for George (Paul Corey to author, July 5, 1988).

MAY 11, 1911

1 The dried manure of cows—and in earlier days of the buffalo—made a good, hot-burning fuel. In the present context, this is Bess's way of saying that she is running out of funds.

2 Paul Nagel and his brother Clemens were living with the Klemanns, but precisely why is never said. They may have been orphaned children of Wisconsin relatives or had a similar family connection.

3 Grace Reed Porter (now married to Walton Porter), the county superintendent, is working with Frank Carlisle, a member of Bess's school board at Klemann School.

MAY 14 AND 27, 1911

1 This appears to be the autoharp mentioned in Bess's letter of April 16, 1911.

2 Although the days of the open range were waning, there still were herds used to roaming free over Stanley County, and a fence was essential to homesteaders attempting to raise crops.

3 Beauty was Fuller's horse, which he probably raised from a colt. Clearly she was the pride and joy of Margaret Corey—the equivalent of a new car—and Bess is striking out where she knows she can make her point.

4 Bad River has a steeper drop than the average stream, increasing the danger of flash flooding.

5 An ambiguous reference. Bess's uncle Challenge Brown (1854–1948) had a son named Normal (1880–1966), but he was married in 1907 to Florence Burcham. Uncle Chall also had a daughter named Alta (1889–1973) (this is the Alta Brown to whom Bess writes), but she was married to Emil

Anderson. Normal and Florence Brown had a daughter named Alta, born in 1909, and this reference might represent a slip of the pen, being actually a belated congratulation to the Browns on the birth of Alta.

6 John A. Holmes, a lawyer and judge who had lived in South Dakota since 1882, resided at 900 Grand Avenue in Pierre.

7 Bess's friend from Harlan, Iowa, one of those she saw on the day before she and Lida Smith first set out for Stanley County in 1909.

JUNE 15, 1911

1 Apparently this is the inference which Margaret Corey took from Bess's mention of the horse Beauty on May 14, 1911.

2 Presumably this refers to Bess's loss of her beloved father, Edwin O. Corey, dead of pneumonia at the age of forty-eight during the winter of 1904–5.

3 Bess's acceptance of such a gift from Fred Bertram might signify the seriousness of their relationship, or it might represent no more than a neighborly act. Mention of the gift would give Margaret Corey pause, certainly, and might furnish "Mrs. Grundy" with fuel for gossip.

4 Patrick Holland was a Fort Pierre tailor. See Bess's letter of August 20, 1911.

AUGUST 18, 1911

1 Attendance at teachers summer normal institute was mandatory and non-attendance could mean the loss of certification.

2 Possibly Anastasia V. Hart, a dressmaker in Fort Pierre, who may have been working at the Hollands' just then.

3 Mark J. Walsh was a physician in Fort Pierre until 1917, when he moved to Rapid City to specialize in his eye, ear, nose, and throat practice.

4 This problem might indicate hernia or a spinal problem.

5 The Leslie School District west of Fort Pierre was a good deal further from Bess's claim than either Speer School or Klemann School. Mrs. McGuire appears to be a school-board member.

6 Thomas School was in the same district as Klemann School, hence much more convenient for Bess's purposes.

7 Bess's aunt Rachel Elizabeth Corey (1872–1943), who had settled in Atlantic, Iowa.

8 Bess was persistent in the attempt to obtain her lock of hair left at the farm more than two years previously.

9 Another of Bess's rare references to the drought of 1911, which decimated the rural population of Stanley County. She prefers always to accentuate the positive.

AUGUST 20, 1911

1 J. F. Thomas, later a grocer in Pierre, was then homesteading not far from Bess. At Thomas School, the directors were, besides Mr. Thomas, Henry Klemann and Frank Carlisle (Thomas School and Klemann School being in the same district).

2 Challenge Dunn Brown (1854–1948), brother of Margaret Corey. Alta May Brown (1889–1973) was Challenge Brown's sixth child and very close in age to her cousin Bess.

AUGUST 25 AND 26, 1911

1 An example of Bess Corey's positive thinking. 1911 was a horrible year for farmers and ranchers, a disastrous one for many homesteaders.

2 The words "tornado" and "cyclone" were, and perhaps still are, used interchangeably in the Midwest.

3 Another euphemism for the privy or outhouse.

4 In southeastern South Dakota, close to the Minnesota border; site of the state agricultural college, later South Dakota State University.

SEPTEMBER 4, 1911

1 Thomas School.

SEPTEMBER 5 AND 11, 1911

1 To the home of J. F. Thomas, where she will board while teaching Thomas School (1911–12).

2 The name Bess has given her colt. Typically, it is a play on words, on the one hand a cussing euphemism, on the other an Anglicized version of *billet doux* (a love letter from her Nell?).

3 Emmie Lou appears to be the 1910–11 teacher at Thomas School.

4 J. F. Thomas was then thirty-seven, his wife, M(ildred?) E., thirty-six, and their daughter Mildred nine.

SEPTEMBER 20, 1911

1 Paul Corey recalls that no male farmer in his school district wished to be school director and so the school did not open. Margaret Corey raised a fuss, as Paul would be required to walk two miles to another school. To solve the dilemma, she had herself appointed school director, but she made no friends in the neighborhood by doing so.

2 Pete Deidrickson, a neighbor farming about a mile south of the Coreys,

wanted Fuller to work for him (as he had in the past), but Fuller would not be free until he had proved up on his South Dakota claim.

SEPTEMBER 23, 1911

1 A way of referring to Fuller's Nell, a bay, to distinguish her from Bess's black mare.

OCTOBER 7, 1911

1 Fuller was born September 30, 1889.
2 The barn that was wrecked by the cyclone is now being sold for scrap lumber.
3 Bess is technically correct here, it would seem. And yet, without Bess's example and her urging, Fuller would probably have remained on the farm at Marne.
4 *Lorna Doone: A Romance of Exmoor* (1869) by Richard D. Blackmore (1825–1900) was an extremely popular nineteenth-century novel.

OCTOBER 14, 1911

1 A euphemism for drunk.
2 Mildred Thomas, age nine.
3 Frank E. Obele, a rancher in Antelope Township, was twenty-five in 1911, his wife, Emma, the same age.

OCTOBER 24, 1911

1 Alta Hoyle, Bess's pupil, and her parents were, like Bess, adherents of Christian Science. See Bess's letter of February 13, 1912.
2 Stanley County ranchers often accompanied their cattle on the seven hundred–mile trip to the Chicago stockyards, both to see that the cattle were well cared for and to enjoy a big-city holiday. Mr. Thomas is selling off his herd in anticipation of moving to Fort Pierre, where he will go into the grocery business.
3 A rural schoolma'am with whom Bess became good friends. Lydia was a Nebraskan who came to Stanley County about 1909. In 1912 she was thirty-one years of age.
4 President William Howard Taft visited Pierre on Sunday, October 23, 1911, attending services at the Methodist church, taking luncheon with Governor Robert S. Vessey at the new St. Charles Hotel (which far outshone the Locke and to this day, although now apartments, is a showplace of Pierre),

and delivering his "Great Peace Speech" to an estimated two thousand listeners in the city auditorium.

5 President Taft was not as large as Paul Prairie Chicken but probably ran him a close second; both weighed in excess of three hundred pounds.

NOVEMBER 2, 1911

1 A probable reference to Charles La Moore (Paul Prairie Chicken). Bess took a good deal of kidding about her "fondness for chicken," which was an oblique reference to her own solid two hundred pounds.
2 Stanton Stone, age seven.
3 To the Thomas residence.
4 Charles H. Leggett, then a homesteading neighbor, later operated a flour and feed store in Fort Pierre.

NOVEMBER 19, 1911

1 Brown's Livery Barn.
2 A popular magazine.
3 The state convention of SDEA (South Dakota Educational Association) was to be in Pierre. It would be the first such annual convention for Bess.
4 Probably Sonnenschein, a rancher to the south of Bess and Fuller.

DECEMBER 8, 1911

1 Emmie Lou was moving and so selling her household equipment.
2 For data concerning the capitol, see Introduction.
3 For data concerning Gen. William H. H. Beadle, see Introduction.
4 The local name for the interurban car that crossed the railroad bridge between Pierre and Fort Pierre on a regular schedule during the day.
5 To the Thomas residence, where Bess was boarding.

JANUARY 4, 1912

1 Manuel Sylva, a Stanley County rancher.
2 The family with whom Lydia Taylor boards.
3 The Rutterfords had three boys; Edgar Rutterford was Bess's pupil in 1912.
4 A euphemism for vomiting.
5 It appears that Bess tired of waiting for her lock of hair to be sent from the farm and purchased one in Fort Pierre which turned out not to be a good match to her own.

6 To the Thomas residence.

7 Often a slab of soapstone, sometimes brick-shaped, which was heated on the stove and carried in a buggy, wrapped in a blanket, for warming one's feet.

8 Bess's cousin Alta Brown had married Emil Anderson.

9 Probably from Grandma Corey, who lived in Atlantic, Iowa.

JANUARY 28, 1912

1 Margaret Corey used the verso of Bess's November 2, 1911, envelope to compose the message which then probably was telephoned in to the nearest telegraph office:

> ELIZABETH F. COREY   C. H. LEGGETT   FT. PIERRE S. DAK.
> JAN 26TH   GRANDMA DIED THIS MORNING.   FUNERAL ON
> MONDAY.

2 When a horse was hitched to a buggy, its reins were fastened to the ends of a swingletree (or singletree), a crossbar pivoted at its center. A pair of swingletrees, used when a team of horses were pulling together, was known as a doubletree. Where the swingletrees came together, the reins were inclined to become entangled. Fuller Corey had worked out a wire guard which served to bridge the gap between the swingletrees, eliminating much of the hazard. He received a patent on his invention. But in 1912 that was something akin to designing a new buggy whip, for people were about to trade their horses for Fords.

3 See the diagram of Bess and Fuller's claims, p. lxiii.

4 Edwin O. Corey's sister Hattie May (1863–1937). She never married. In 1912 she was forty-nine years old.

5 Edwin O. Corey's sister Rachel Elizabeth (1872–1943). She never married. In 1912 she was verging on forty. Bess's rather impractical suggestion indicates her great anxiety concerning settlement of the plots adjoining her claim that one day might be melded into a single ranch.

FEBRUARY 4 AND 6, 1912

1 Fuller's riding horse was ever on his mind. Eventually Beauty was struck by lightning and killed.

2 The ice was cut on Bess's dam and packed into her cistern, where it would melt slowly and provide fresh water during summer weather.

3 See note 2, Bess's letter of January 28, 1912.

4 The ice would be piled onto a stoneboat for hauling overland, as its weight could easily break a buggy or sleigh.

5 Fuller means *salts*, probably Epsom salts (magnesium sulphate), a cathartic.

FEBRUARY 13, 1912

1 Bess Corey became interested in Christian Science while a teenager, and she appears to have become an even more serious adherent as she matured. As her letters might suggest, Bess was chiefly responsible for making a Christian Scientist out of Margaret Corey, who began to take its teachings more seriously after the death of her son Olney.
2 A type of folding bed. One side folded up to form the back of a couch, while the opposite side folded downward to provide backing to the calves of the leg. In a tiny claim shack, folding beds were highly valued as space savers.
3 Fuller is on his claim, Bess fifteen miles away at the Thomases'.

FEBRUARY 20 AND 21, 1912

1 Fuller is referring to letters inquiring about his patent. He appears never to have found someone to finance its manufacture and put it on the market for him.
2 It was precisely such a remark that was guaranteed to keep alive the animosity between Bess and her mother.
3 Persons applying for patents were required to submit a working scale model of their apparatus. Apparently, someone had questioned a detail of Fuller's model.
4 The butter shipped from Corey farm had turned rancid en route to Stanley County even though sent in February.

FEBRUARY 27, 1912

1 It appears that Alta Hoyle may be staying overnight at the Thomases' and sleeping in the same bed as Bess.
2 The family with whom Lydia Taylor boards.
3 1912 was a leap year.

MARCH 8, 1912

1 Margaret Corey had begun a practice of sending Bess a detailed record of income and outgo on the farm.
2 This appears to refer to the summer of 1908, when Margaret Corey was in Council Bluffs, Iowa, for a hemorrhoid operation and left Bess in charge of the farm.

3 Apparently a reference to Bess's year of boarding at Grant Stone's. Young Stanton, then five years old, slept with Bess.

4 Bess's urging her mother to purchase the fur coat she has always coveted is symptomatic of Bess's own practice; for example, her haste in purchasing her team of black mares before prudence has a chance to take effect.

5 Friends of the family living in Walnut, Iowa. Walnut High School seems preferable to Bess because of its proximity to Corey farm. Also, Olney had boarded with the Crows.

6 Bess's lodge in Fort Pierre. She probably considers dropping it because she is able to attend meetings so seldom.

MARCH 17, 1912

1 Fuller means *selling.*

2 Slang for money.

MARCH 22, 1912

1 Eugene Field (1850–1895), the extremely popular American poet and journalist, author of "Little Boy Blue," "When the Frost Is on the Punkin," and "Little Orphant Annie."

2 The Thomas Grocery Co. in Pierre.

3 Very likely a reference to Joe Bahr, Bess's German neighbor and sometime beau.

4 Bess's mother, Margaret Corey.

APRIL 8, 1912

1 Bess has adopted the western expression for gully or draw: *cañon.*

2 The Gordons owned the picture show located in the Majestic Theater.

3 Another symptom of leap year.

4 Probably a joke. Bess had threatened to follow the mention of any male friend's name with the notation "he's married" in order to forestall curiosity about a potential marriage.

5 Joseph Schomer, a stockman, was thirty-seven in 1912, his Iowa-born wife, Hattie, thirty-six. Their children were Alice, nine; Clayton, eight; Harold, five; and Joseph, four.

6 Edgar Rutterford, Bess's pupil.

7 Not identified.

8 Homesteading neighbors.

9 Bess's uncle Sherman Andrew Brown (b. 1865) had just died. Sherman was a twin of Ulysses Grant Brown (1865–1947) and their names reflect their birthdates.

10 Twigs wandered from Corey farm one day and was shot in the head by a neighbor, William Noon. He recovered, but was blinded in the left eye.

1 Walton Porter.
2 A pun on the expression "The Good Die Young."
3 Enclosed with this letter are samples of a sky-blue cotton fabric in a linen weave and a blue and beige striped cotton fabric.

1 Mr. Ketchen possibly was Mrs. Thomas's brother.

1 This may be the mother of Frank Murphy, the clerk at the Range Mercantile Co. in Fort Pierre.
2 Mrs. Douglas was proprietress of a boarding house in Fort Pierre.
3 Fred Bertram, Bess's neighbor and erstwhile swain, is being married, probably in Fort Pierre, which would have the nearest Catholic church. Frances is not identified by last name, but it seems likely that "Fritz" has converted to Catholicism on her account.
4 To the Douglas boarding house.
5 Jay Robar, Fort Pierre jeweler and another former Iowan, was then twenty-three.
6 A music teacher who boards at the Douglases'.

1 Bess's black mare Nell has had a colt.
2 The veterinarian.
3 Whenever possible, Bess attended the county commencement exercises honoring those graduating from eighth grade as she was likely to have pupils or former pupils among the graduates.
4 Since Bess stood five feet seven inches, Mr. Robar would be five feet six.

1 The Black Hills of South Dakota, commonly called the Hills.
2 Until rather recently, silver dollars were commonly circulated in western states; the western reliance upon silver in contrast to eastern reliance upon

gold reached a climax in William Jennings Bryan's "Cross of Gold" oration delivered at the Democratic Convention of 1896.

3 The estate of Grandma Corey.

JULY 28, 1912

1 Because the county superintendent of schools was allowed to serve only two consecutive terms, Grace Reed Porter had left that office and had been succeeded by W. W. Warner.

2 A teacher of pedagogy and English at Fort Pierre High School.

3 A Fort Pierre oculist.

4 Chairman of the Fort Pierre school board and later the secretary of the Northern Trust Company, bonded abstractors; he also was a realtor and a partner with John D. Cannon in an insurance office. In 1912 McPherson was thirty-seven, his wife, Nina, thirty-three. Both were former Iowans.

5 Mrs. McPherson's mother.

6 Chauncey Mahutga, the McPhersons' hired man, had a homestead seventeen miles southeast of Fort Pierre which he left in 1917, selling his goods at auction.

7 If true, an example of the colorful details of Bess's life now lost to us.

AUGUST 11, 1912

1 Fuller could not sell because he did not prove up on his claim until 1913.

AUGUST 14, 1912

1 See Bess's remark (July 28, 1912) about not studying during institute.

2 Harlan High School.

AUGUST 25 AND 26, 1912

1 Margaret Hickey, a schoolteacher born in Illinois but a resident of South Dakota since 1885. In 1912 she was thirty-two years old.

2 Twenty-two-year-old Bernard Vessey, a cousin of Governor Vessey, was famous locally as a singer. When President Taft attended services at the Pierre Methodist church, Vessey sang the tenor solo in the anthem "Come, Holy Spirit," performing "beautifully, and with much feeling"; when he performed at the Wide Awake Revival in Lead, S.D., in 1919, the *Deadwood Telegram* called him "South Dakota's best tenor." Until Bess attended the SDEA convention in Aberdeen, S.D., in 1915, Vessey's may have been the finest singing voice she had heard.

SEPTEMBER 25, 1912

1 This appears to be Bess's newest label for her claim.
2 The present teacher at Speer School boards at the Stones'.
3 A homesteading family living near Bess's present school.
4 His full name was Henry Fuller Corey.

OCTOBER 13, 1912

1 Bess's friend Emy (or Emmie) Lou apparently had married Frank Obele.
2 Probably a reference to "Daddy" Krug.
3 Probably Bess's friend, Mrs. Gordon, in Fort Pierre, who seems to have been intent on making a match for her.

NOVEMBER 3, 1912

1 Bess was becoming increasingly devoted to the teachings of Mary Baker Eddy, founder of Christian Science. She quotes often from Mrs. Eddy's *Science and Health, with Key to the Scriptures* (1875).

NOVEMBER 10, 1912

1 Fuller has returned to Corey farm.
2 Jim was an old, black, "string-halted" horse on Corey farm.
3 Alta Brown's family, who live on War Creek west of Bess's "farmstead." Mr. Brown is caring for Bess's horses while she is away teaching, but she would like to lease her land as pasture unless Fuller has made an arrangement with Brown that would rule that out.
4 Nathaniel Hawthorne's didactic short story, standard grammar school reading.

JANUARY 6, 1913

1 A dentist in Walnut, Iowa.
2 Apparently "in town" here refers to Walnut. Bess's friend and neighbor Valerie Harris had married George Mutim, who farmed northwest of the Monroe Township Methodist Church.
3 Emma Schief was the wife of Henry "Hank" Schief, who lived one-half mile west of Corey farm, toward Walnut. Dave and Henry Lamers were about the same age as Bess and lived north of the Methodist church. Mrs. Cook was a local woman who had worked on an occasional basis for Margaret Corey. Marten (Martin?) Peterson was Bess's age, son of a local family.

4 Council Bluffs, Iowa, where Bess changed trains.
5 An attorney who handled the Coreys' farm business; he had lent money to Margaret Corey.
6 Regina Murphy, age nineteen.
7 The wife of Roy Norman, who ran a livery stable in Fort Pierre. Mrs. Norman may have run a boarding house.
8 At that time, Fort Pierre was unique in having a supply of natural gas. It came from the deep artesian wells that had been drilled in the area, was separated from the hot water at the gas plant, and was piped into homes for heating and cooking.
9 To Bess's claim, so that she can put in some of her required residence time.
10 She has attempted to get water from her dam.

JANUARY 13, 1913

1 A friend of Margaret Corey and the Brown family. She lived in Chicago. Although referred to as "Cousin Sue," she may not have been a true relative.
2 *Christian Science Journal.* Apparently Mrs. Singleton had been helped by Christian Science practices, and Bess is urging her mother to investigate and, perhaps, do likewise.
3 A most painful act for Bess, who valued her team of black mares highly. (Later she would buy them back.)
4 A trick of some sort played upon the Corey neighbor Bill Noon by another neighbor, Mr. Backsen.

JANUARY 19, 1913

1 The newspaper in Walnut, Iowa.
2 In a disastrous fire early in January 1913, the Walnut Public School, which Bess had attended, burned to the ground.

JANUARY 29, 1913

1 Bess was given to premonitions, and the nagging thought of having a camera of her own appears to anticipate the death of Olney Corey. See also Bess's similar remark in her letter of February 3, 1913.
2 The family of Lydia Taylor, where Bess often visited. Lydia's parents are W. H. Taylor, sixty-four, and Anna Taylor, fifty-seven. They live in the Bad River area.
3 Lydia Taylor's niece.

4 Probably Lydia's brother, a twenty-year-old rancher in Custer County, S.D.
5 Then and now a popular summer resort in northern Minnesota.

FEBRUARY 3, 1913

1 Fuller rode from his claim to Iowa on his horse Sandy, a sorrel gelding with a reputation as an outlaw.
2 Viola Deidrickson, only child and daughter of Pete Deidrickson, the Coreys' neighbor. Her father's affliction with tuberculosis of the hip caused the Coreys to feel particularly protective of Viola.

FEBRUARY 9, 1913

1 *Freckles*, the popular novel by Gene Stratton Porter, published in 1904, had sold more than half a million copies by 1913.
2 A search failed to identify the novel to which Bess alludes here.
3 Wessner was a character in Porter's *Freckles*.
4 A common name for an accumulation of pus in an infected area.

FEBRUARY 20, 1913

1 Probably Harry Berg of Fort Pierre.
2 Enclosed is a newspaper clipping: "Here's Chance for Rural Schoolboy to Get Medal." It announces a contest among country school pupils age ten to fifteen for the best eight hundred–word essay on the maintenance and repair of country roads. The contest is sponsored by the federal government "good roads division."

MARCH 4, 1913

1 William Bogus, postmaster.
2 In 1913 John Norman was sixteen.
3 John's sister, close to Bess's age.

MARCH 10, 1913

1 *Cudjo's Cave*, the abolitionist novel by John T. Trowbridge (1863).
2 Bess has retrieved her team of black mares, her pride and joy.
3 Fuller's land patent was issued on August 27, 1913, but he must have proved up at the Land Office prior to that. The arrangement here is that Bess will pay the taxes on Fuller's 160 acres in return for which she gains the right of using his land as she sees fit. She intends to combine Fuller's

quarter-section with her own (they have a common boundary line) and lease all 320 acres to Grant Stone. Grant cares for Bess's horses while she is away teaching; in return he is allowed to "work" them when the need arises.

APRIL 13, 1913

1 Maud Hemsted, the local schoolteacher, and her son, about nine years old.

APRIL 21, 1913

1 *A Girl of the Limberlost*, the popular novel by Gene Stratton Porter, was published in 1909 as a sequel to *Freckles*.
2 The Hoisingtons lived south of Fort Pierre and Bad River in the Dean District. Harold's sisters were Ada, then nineteen, and Bernice, then twenty. Both were teachers.
3 A horse-ranching neighbor, born in Indiana.

APRIL 26, 1913

1 The E. G. Ficks lived on a north-south road two miles east of Corey farm.
2 Will Speer, then fifty-one.
3 David Bull of Weta, S.D. Eventually he and Lydia Taylor married.

MAY 9, 1913

1 Apparently Bess has walked the ten miles or more into Fort Pierre, which she sometimes did in favorable weather. It is not clear just what "deed" is meant. It may concern her arrangement with Fuller regarding his land.
2 Business houses in Fort Pierre. J. A. Ferguson ran a confectionery.
3 Hoisingtons, brother and sister.
4 Ada Hoisington and Fuller Corey were seeing a good deal of each other, being in close proximity, as Ada had been teaching at Speer School in 1912–13. Bess is suggesting this friendship may lead to marriage.
5 Fuller's sorrel gelding.

MAY 10, 1913

1 This confrontation of her mother as adult to adult rather than daughter to mother marks an important step in Bess's maturation. Evidently she received satisfactory word from Margaret Corey, for she returned to Corey farm.

SEPTEMBER 3, 1913

1 Bess seems to have arranged to attend a summer normal institute in Harlan, Iowa.
2 Will Speer. Apparently Fuller had arranged that Will should pay the taxes on his claim rather than Bess.
3 If a homesteader did not conform to the rules for residence on a homestead, a "claim jumper" could notify the Land Office and possibly have the claim revoked. Then the land could be claimed by the informer and sold to another homesteader as a relinquishment.
4 Albert Gunderson, president of Gunderson Land Company in Pierre. He also was an attorney, wrote title insurance, and made farm loans.
5 The Grant Stones.
6 Probably Horace Dean and his family, who live not far from Bess south of Bad River in Dean District.
7 Parents of Mae Stone.
8 Cuttings of plants which could be shipped in a damp wrapping; the stems would develop roots (as with ivy and geraniums).
9 The claims of Howard Speer and his sister Jennie.
10 Bess now has Olney's box camera and is planning to develop snapshots she had taken in Iowa of the Methodist church near the farm, of Mrs. Corey, and of Fuller and Paul and the horse Beauty.

SEPTEMBER 11, 1913

1 George Robertson ran a lumber- and coalyard in Fort Pierre.
2 If the wood dried out, the buggy would become rickety and might even fall apart like the wonderful one-hoss shay.
3 Porcupine Creek.
4 A regular churchgoer at the Methodist church near Corey farm. Apparently he was in Bess's snapshot.
5 Possibly a reference to a "stop smoking" bet between Grant Stone and Fuller Corey.

SEPTEMBER 26, 1913

1 The patent to Fuller's land, issued August 27, 1913.
2 The federal parcel post system went into operation on January 1, 1913.

OCTOBER 8 AND 10, 1913

1 Wherever there was the prospect of water, a homesteader was sure to plant saplings of trees such as willows in an attempt to relieve the monotony of the landscape and provide shade.

2 Robert Jennings, then twenty-eight, was a rancher in Antelope Township near Bess.

3 Margaret Corey had written of a hearse which was an automobile rather than the usual horse-drawn conveyance. For whatever reason, the motorized hearse was used to carry a corpse from San Francisco to New York. Iowa was on the cross-country highway that it used, and young Paul Corey, whose school was near that highway, witnessed the hearse as it passed.

4 W. W. Warner.

5 Eighty acres were left in the section, east of Bess, just as eighty acres were left to her west, her own claim occupying the center portion of the south half of the total section of land. See diagram p. lxiii. Glen Speer was turning twenty-one and could file his own claim.

6 Margaret Corey was beginning to have difficulties with a neighborhood project for the straightening of Indian Creek which would mean the dredging of a ditch across a valuable portion of Corey farm.

OCTOBER 17, 1913

1 An insurance payment from Grandma Corey's estate.

2 Here Bess stops writing with ink and continues with pencil.

3 With its news of the insurance payment.

NOVEMBER 14, 1913

1 Valley Springs, S.D., is a town in the corner where Iowa, Minnesota, and South Dakota have common borders. Fuller's destination may have some connection with a relative of the Stone family, Stanton Delbert Stone, who was then living in Valley Springs.

2 Bess means Oacoma, on the western bank of the Missouri River, opposite Chamberlain, S.D.

3 Bess and the Stones are pushing the match between Fuller Corey and Ada Hoisington.

4 See Bess's remark of September 3, 1913, regarding the slips of plants.

5 November 16, 1909, an unhappy time, her first birthday away from Iowa when she was isolated by snow two feet deep and wondering whether any of her family knew or cared that it was her birthday.

DECEMBER 5, 1913

1 Probably a reference to "Daddy" Krug, Bess's persistent suitor. He seems to have inspired a variety of nicknames.

DECEMBER 14, 1913

1 Rorbeck was a tiny crossroads community in Shelby County—blacksmith shop, general store, a few homes—and the store had just burned down.
2 Apparently Margaret Corey was contemplating remarriage to a neighbor, Rasmus L. Torkleson.
3 The potential indemnity to Margaret Corey for allowing the drainage ditch to be dug across her land.
4 Bess's friend Roy Norman of Fort Pierre, who seems to have been a deputy sheriff in addition to running a livery barn.
5 John W. Stroup, a local rancher.
6 Bess had sent her mother a snapshot of Fuller and Ada Hoisington perched atop her small barn.
7 Fuller has headed for Iowa and the farm.

JANUARY 2, 1914

1 Lydia Taylor had to get back to her teaching post in the tiny railroad town of Weta; apparently the weather was favorable enough for Bess to drive her down in her buggy, drawn by her pair of black mares.
2 Bess used her new Christmas stationery for this letter.
3 Bess purchased an organ from her Aunt Jennie Dunlavy in Harlan, Iowa, as a birthday gift for her sister, Ethel. It was placed in the Corey living room, but no one ever learned to play it.

JANUARY 23, 1914

1 Enclosed with this letter is a sample of Bess's tatting, the black strips of tatting joined by white threads to create the effect of lace.
2 Probably Margaret and William Reese.

FEBRUARY 14, 1914

1 Enclosed is a newspaper clipping, "Pullin' off the Covers" by Tom P. Morgan, which reminisces about Morgan's boyhood when he and his brother Bill slept in the same bed. Each night one or the other would wake up freezing, the other having pulled all the covers onto himself. The piece ends in typical sentimental fashion, with Tom hoping that Bill, long since dead, "isn't cold tonight, 'way out there on the hill."
2 The young brother of Flagg Carlisle. From Bess's description, he appears to have perished from some disease such as rabies.

MARCH 8, 1914

1 The Coreys' neighbor Fern Armstrong.
2 Slang, meaning they have broken up.
3 A euphemism. Mrs. Donahue was in her final month of pregnancy.

MARCH 22, 1914

1 A good example of Bess's double messages, offering on the one hand to pay her mother's fare to South Dakota and on the other explaining that she will need to go further into debt to do it.

APRIL 5, 1914

1 John Norman, the Normans' son. Bess has gone on to Fort Pierre, then, apparently, to Pierre.
2 Francis M. Byrne, of Faulkton, was then governor of S.D.
3 Carl G. Lawrence, later president of Northern State Teachers College in Aberdeen. His son Ernest won the Nobel Prize for physics in 1939.
4 The Frank Carlisles had moved into Fort Pierre. In 1916 Frank ran for county commissioner.
5 The local midwife.

JUNE 8, 1914

1 Katheryn Donahue was seven years old.
2 Refers to railroad cars; an idiom equivalent to "beat the band": to hurry.
3 One of the Stones' horses.
4 The Sonnenschein Ranch lay south of the Bad River area.
5 The snake's rattles.
6 In Fort Pierre. The ice wagon made daily deliveries to homes, bringing ice cut from the river during the winter and packed in sawdust for summer use.

JULY 5 AND 6, 1914

1 Dr. Wallace Franklin Jones held degrees from Illinois State Normal, the University of Illinois, Teachers College, Columbia University, and New York University, where he took his doctorate in 1911. In that same year he came to the University of South Dakota as head of the Education Department. As the author of a recently published book, *Principles of Education*, he was a natural star to be imported for the edification of teachers attending summer normal institutes, a preeminence confirmed by his appointment in 1919 as dean of education at the University of Southern California.

2 David Bull.

3 George Coler, a bachelor age thirty-two from Kansas, operated a restaurant in Fort Pierre.

4 Flagg Carlisle, at this point still a schoolteacher, is on the verge of opening a law practice in the newly created Jackson County.

5 In the Dean District directly south of Fort Pierre and across Bad River.

JULY 26, 1914

1 David Bull of Weta, S.D.

2 Apparently a friend from Iowa who has come to visit.

3 On the verso of Bess's envelope Margaret Corey has written: "4th sheet I sent to Fuller." She has taken seriously Bess's comment at the end of the letter that "some of this" may be sent on to Fuller, who is visiting relatives in Illinois. The missing page concerned Ella Griffen, most likely a good friend of Fuller's.

4 Marcus Texley, then twenty-seven, by 1915 was a clerk in the newly created Haakon County, west of Bess's claim.

5 She will not be permitted to do so.

6 Uncle Ulysses Grant Brown lived near Momence, Ill.

SEPTEMBER 21, 1914

1 Margaret Corey and Paul went to visit her relatives in the Momence, Ill., area. Challenge Dunn Brown lived in Boswell, Ind., about sixty miles from Momence.

2 Bess is teaching Mathews School, about three miles out of Van Metre along the Northwestern Railroad.

3 Andrew Seieroe was the father of one of Bess's pupils and a member of the school board at Mathews School.

4 Roy Newlin, then twenty-two, and his wife Perle, then twenty-one.

5 Virgil Strunk, then seventeen, was Bess's ninth-grade pupil at Mathews School.

6 Frederick Nordin was fifteen. His mother, Betsie Erickson Nordin, forty-three, was the wife of C. W. Nordin, forty-five, a rancher in the Van Metre area.

7 Bess's euphemism for privy.

8 The privies at Mathews School.

NOVEMBER 15, 1914

1 By this time the war in Europe had been raging for three months, yet Bess has not commented on it, nor has her mother, apparently. A good example

of the isolated position of the United States at that time—and even more so, perhaps, of the isolation of Stanley County from the rest of the world.

2 Both families live in the school district. The Andersons have homesteaded on the opposite side of Bad River from Newlins, and perhaps the Parkers have also. A typical instance of a rural schoolma'am's extracurricular duties; also of the high esteem in which a teacher was held.

3 Bill Bogus of Fort Pierre.

4 No enclosures exist.

5 Wilbur Travers, thirty-two, a rancher from Nebraska, had lived in South Dakota since 1897.

6 Roy Newlin's brother, age twenty, of Van Metre.

7 Mr. and Mrs. Arthur Newlin operated the Pierre Hay and Feed Co.

DECEMBER 13, 1914

1 Bess's pupil, fourteen years old and in the seventh grade.

2 Lona Alice Brown (1885–1968), oldest child and daughter of William Ralph Brown.

3 Normal Claude Brown (1880–1966), oldest child of Challenge Dunn Brown. At that time he was farming in Indiana, as Bess thought.

4 Rob Corey's horse.

5 Fritz Bertram and his wife had moved to the Ozarks (see Bess's letter of March 8, 1914), owing Bess $16.

6 George Mutim, who married Valerie Harris in Marne.

7 Bess had been away from her claim too much to qualify under the strict residency requirements of the Homestead Act.

8 The second-grade certificate, earned by examination, was valid for one year in a district named by the county superintendent; it permitted the holder to teach in all grades below high school.

9 Bess did not prove up until 1916.

10 The collecting of felt pennants advertising various colleges, towns, etc., was the latest decorating craze for young folk. They covered their walls with them.

11 David Bull, Lydia Taylor's friend, appears to have been Bess's also.

12 The country school near Corey farm.

JANUARY 7, 1915

1 Margaret Corey has used the verso of Bess's envelope for the note: "Sent to Anna S[tewart]—to be returned."

FEBRUARY 22, 1915

1 The birthday of Abraham Lincoln, February 12, was always a day of special celebration and programs for schoolchildren.

2 The school districts held competitions in areas such as spelling, mathematics, handwriting, and funny storytelling, after which the winners advanced to a county-wide contest.

3 The birthday of George Washington, February 22, was another day of special programs and schoolroom decoration.

4 Henry Wadsworth Longfellow (1807–1882), author of "Evangeline," "The Song of Hiawatha," and "The Courtship of Miles Standish," was then probably the most widely read and admired of nineteenth-century American poets.

MARCH 6, 1915

1 Hannibal L. Putnam, a twenty-five-year-old rancher of the Van Metre area, was a native South Dakotan.

2 The full significance of the Newlins—and Bess—being without transportation is only hinted at.

3 The paragraph beginning "Mr Putnam" breaks off so abruptly that, with Bess's hasty "B B" signature, it suggests that she had a chance to have her letter mailed if it were ready immediately.

MARCH 22 AND 24, 1915

1 The window of the confectionery store in Fort Pierre.

2 The heroine of *Alice in Wonderland* facing the formidable Queen of Spades.

3 The son of Carl Mathews, then fifty, and his wife Alzada, forty-seven.

APRIL 17, 1915

1 Bess is using a poor-quality six-by-ten-inch stationery ripped into half-sheets.

2 The box is at the railroad depot in Van Metre, three or four miles distant, and people were not always as helpful as they might be.

3 One advantage of being a rural schoolteacher was that you could take time off when you wanted, or needed, it. The time had to be made up later, of course.

4 Railroad personnel were more accommodating in that day, it would appear—perhaps a special favor for a schoolma'am?

5 David Strunk, forty-six, his wife, Amanda, forty-two, and their children, Doris, twelve, and Virgil, eighteen.

6 Mary Frances Corey (1857–1932), Edwin Corey's oldest sister. Paul Corey suspects that Bess is doing "a bit of spoofing."

7 Fuller Corey stood six feet two inches.

8 Alfred Noren advertised himself as "The Shoe Man" in Pierre. His son Paul worked for him.

MAY 19, 1915

1 The laws governing the amount of homestead land that might be claimed were being altered to recognize the marginal quality of so much of the western territory soil. The 160-acre limitation is being doubled, a development that could alter Bess Corey's plans rather drastically, as she suggests here.

JUNE 1, 1915

1 Bess is quite correct. The last really big flood on Bad River had been in 1905; it had even wiped out the iron bridge across the river in Fort Pierre.

JUNE 5 AND 6, 1915

1 If Bess, under the new regulations, could file on the eighty acres lying west of hers, she would gain a common border with Fuller's land extending through most of her property.

2 Philip, S.D., named for James "Scotty" Philip, had beaten Midland in the struggle to be named county seat of the newly formed Haakon County.

3 Of Rowe and Co., the hardware and farm implement company of Fort Pierre. He may have been a member of the local school board.

4 Depression.

5 The drainage ditch being put through a part of Corey farm.

6 Margaret Corey was beginning to turn the farming over to her sons, the heavy work to Rob, the chicken raising to Challenge.

7 Robert Corey was renting land raising hay (or cutting it on shares), a first step in his eventual takeover of Corey farm.

8 Ethel was being courted by Arthur Erickson, the hired man of Ed Armstrong, the Coreys' neighbor to the northwest. The reference to "battles" may possibly refer to a perceived fondness of Mrs. Armstrong for the hired man.

9 The Charles M. Coreys of Wendte, S.D.

JULY 11, 1915

1 Ethel Corey was nineteen. This would be her last summer as a single woman, for she would be married in August 1916 to Arthur Erickson.

2 The Palmer Method of producing perfect handwriting was based upon the formation of correct attitudes and habits. It required "good, hygienic posture," the use of upper-arm muscles rather than the wrist, and proper equipment (paper, pens, penholders, blue-black ink), which could be purchased from the A. N. Palmer Company, one of whose chief offices was located in Cedar Rapids, Iowa. The regular, rhythmical practice of making pages full of push-pull and oval strokes was based on right-handedness, and those pupils who were left-handed were strongly encouraged to mend their ways. At its best, the Palmer Method produced an attractive, flowing writing, each letter perfectly formed.

JULY 16, 1915

1 Ethel is in Fort Pierre while Bess attends the summer normal institute.

2 Carl Arthur Erickson, whom Ethel will marry in 1916.

3 Marvel Mutim, one of Ethel's close friends from church.

4 Glee Lyons was the younger sister of Ed Armstrong's wife, Fern. Paul Corey conjectures that the "help" concerned a miscarriage, an event that would have been kept from his young ears.

5 The hired man, of course, was Art Erickson, who also was Ethel Corey's boyfriend. He quit his job at Armstrongs', possibly because of his relationship (real or imagined) with Fern Armstrong. In any case, Ethel recognizes the volatility of the situation.

6 Mable Ninnen was a friend of Ethel's who taught the school near Corey farm, but the "class" referred to is Sunday school class at Monroe Township Methodist Church, and the "League" is Epworth League, a Methodist organization.

JULY 21, 1915

1 Belle Brindly, another church friend of Ethel's.

2 See note 5, Ethel's letter of July 16, 1915.

AUGUST 24, 1915

1 Anna Scripter was seventy-four.

2 A euphemism for suicide.

3 Seymour Scripter was seventy-five.

4 A euphemism for vomiting.

5 They are joking about Ethel Corey's "Swede."
6 To exaggerate and "pull the wool over their eyes."

SEPTEMBER 3, 1915

1 Robert Corey has turned twenty-one on July 18; he can now file a home-stead claim if he wishes.
2 "Chinned"—talked.

DECEMBER 4, 1915

1 The envelope exists but the letter is gone.

DECEMBER 13, 1915

1 Bess has written "buisness," then altered it to "business."
2 L. F. Nickel, the Fort Pierre tailor, has a ranch at Wendte, S.D.
3 Bess has attended the statewide SDEA convention in Aberdeen. She saved and forwarded to Marne the program for the featured entertainer of the conventioneers, Mme. Johanna Gadski of the Metropolitan Opera.

JANUARY 17, 1916

1 Johanna Emilia Agnes Gadski (1872–1932), German soprano who made her debut at the Metropolitan Opera in New York in 1895. Overzealous patriotism ended her career in 1917 and she returned to Berlin, but she came back to the United States in 1921. She specialized in Wagnerian roles.

FEBRUARY 6, 1916

1 Mrs. Hill appears to be clerking at a Fort Pierre hardware store.
2 A leap year activity.
3 For certificate renewal.

FEBRUARY 29, 1916

1 Laura Ellen Brown (b. 1891), daughter of Challenge Dunn Brown, had married Louis Harold Johnson, an Indiana farmer.
2 A pun on Ethel Corey's siege of grippe (flu).
3 Bess became fond of citing *Science and Health*.

MARCH 12, 1916

1 Named after the heroine of stories by Eleanor Hodgman Porter (1868–1920); Pollyanna is a girl of irrepressible optimism who finds good in everything—sometimes known as the "glad girl." Such clubs were in keeping with the optimism (or the need for it) of frontier life.

APRIL 19, 1916

1 Challenge Corey, eighteen, had begun his extended visit to Bess's "ranch," and she put him in charge of running it.

APRIL 21, 1916

1 The "fight" reflects school board trouble. The rest of the letter indicates that Bess is attempting to work her difficulties out via Christian Science principles.

MAY 31, 1916

1 Synonymous with Memorial Day.

JUNE 25, 1916

1 Mrs. Shaw's connection with Bess's family seems to have been a spurious one.
2 Ada Hoisington married Allan Stirling and went to live west of Fort Pierre.
3 Ethel Corey would marry Art Erickson on August 31.
4 Elizabeth Myers, Stanley County superintendent of schools 1915–16.

JULY 29, 1916

1 Horace Henry "Stub" Gould (b. 1885) and his wife, Lulie (Louella, b. 1890), were very close in age to Bess. With their children, Prudence, Edith, Hortense, Georgia, Richard, and Gerald, they came to Stanley County from Sparta, Wis. They lived near Bess with the Henry Reeses until they moved into the Hjalmer Bloomgren house when the Bloomgrens left the territory.
2 This appears to be the date on which Bess was successful in proving up, for her patent was issued the following December.
3 A precept of Christian Science.
4 She is planning for Margaret Corey's visit to South Dakota.

SEPTEMBER 12, 1916

1 A happy ending (of sorts) to the Newlin tragedy: the birth of a child to replace their lost daughter.
2 A resident of the Dean District south of Fort Pierre.
3 Bess is boarding at the home of Lyle Moulton, age thirty-six, and his Danish-born wife, Margaret, thirty. Their children are Calvin, six, and Donald, three.

OCTOBER 3, 1916

1 Bess's "writing paper" is made for the purpose of recording checks and is printed with terms such as *Date, No., Drawn By, Favor Of, Last Endorser, Drawn On,* and *Amount.* She is using the versos of these ledger pages, of course.
2 Julius Bahr.

OCTOBER 20, 1916

1 Fuller Corey had worked for Bob Jennings. Stories of snake-bit children were fairly common newspaper fare in homesteading days. The Jennings child was Robert, Jr., not quite two years old.
2 The child, who was seven, had been named after his grandfather Henry Klemann.
3 Bess has been walking in gumbo.
4 Probably Mr. Lund. See Bess's letters of November 11, 1916, and February 4, 1917.
5 President Woodrow Wilson married Mrs. Edith Bolling Galt on December 18, 1915. Bess is being whimsical.

NOVEMBER 11, 1916

1 Calvin and Donald.
2 Bess was becoming more of a feminist, but she was overly optimistic, as the woman's suffrage bill had another two years to go before it would finally pass in the House of Representatives and be on its way toward being officially an amendment to the Constitution (in August 1920).
3 Mr. Lund.

DECEMBER 5, 1916

1 On the verso of the envelope Bess has written: "Mrs Gordon wrote you at Walnut. Get it?"
2 The statewide convention of SDEA in Watertown, S.D.
3 See Introduction.

DECEMBER 16, 1916

1 Written in ink on a page of six-by-eight-inch drawing paper, folded, to give the appearance of a formal invitation. The names of Calvin Moulton and Miss Corey appear on individual cards, one inch by two inches, enclosed with the invitation.

FEBRUARY 4, 1917

1 Albert Wheelon, who had registered claims at the U.S. Land Office, was now into real estate, loans, and insurance in Pierre.
2 The day of the movie theater was arriving. In 1916 F. H. Gillett purchased the moving picture equipment owned by Clarence E. Coyne, took a lease on the Gordons' Majestic Theater, and opened to the public on the first of December.
3 Bess's Norwegian swain.
4 Alfred H. Young, physician, with offices at 114 Capital Avenue in Pierre.

FEBRUARY 11, 1917

1 The examinations that might earn Bess a first-grade teaching certificate, one which would be valid for three years rather than for the two years allowed under the second-grade certificate.
2 An expression, probably adopted from local Germans, meaning "to understand" or "to get the information on."
3 Mr. Lund.

MARCH 15, 1917

1 Margaret Corey's birthday was March 11.

APRIL 8, 1917

1 Why and how Bess has sent Chall's dog Scoop to Iowa is not clear.
2 This is the first notice Bess appears to take of World War I.
3 "Leave the presence of a fool, for there you do not meet words of knowledge."
4 Bess was writing in ink and having difficulties. She appears to be mocking the widespread tendency to blame everything on the Germans, with whom the United States has just gone to war.
5 Margaret Corey was upset because Ethel had married against her wishes and she was threatening to cut her out of her insurance policies.

MAY 20, 1917

1 Bess appears to be throwing out a hint that she might marry Mr. Lund, despite their differences over religion and female subservience.
2 Probably Challenge Dunn Brown's daughter Mary Ruth (b. 1896).

JUNE 11, 1917

1 Bess is on her homestead. She is speaking of Speer School and Klemann School.
2 Lydia Taylor is in Weta.
3 Chall Corey is nineteen; traditionally a child "owed his time" to his parents until he reached the age of twenty-one.

JUNE 18, 1917

1 Draper, S.D., about forty miles south of Fort Pierre in Jones County.
2 The contract enclosed is a handwritten copy.

JULY 22 AND 23, 1917

1 Bess encloses samples of the silk bookmarks given as end-of-school favors to her pupils, blue for boys, pink for girls.
2 Bess helps out at the Majestic Theater where, apparently, Mrs. Gordon was in charge of selling tickets.
3 Bess encloses a copy of the Stanley County eighth-grade commencement exercises, at which the principal address was delivered by E. C. Woodburn, vice-president of NNIS in Aberdeen. Her former pupil Herbert Speer is among the graduates.
4 A local veterinarian, possibly Joseph Valentine.

DECEMBER 1, 1917

1 The date is approximately one month prior to the birth of Ethel's daughter Margaret Helen Erickson.
2 Possibly Fuller Corey? (But Fuller was married in August 1917 to Teresa I. Taylor, which might make such a visit unlikely.) One of Bess's various "beaus"?

MARCH 3, 1918

1 Margaret and Paul Corey were preparing to move to 1101 Birch Street, Atlantic, Iowa, partly in order to facilitate Paul's attendance at the high school there.

2 There had been a nationwide drive—including Stanley County, S.D.—to recruit women with skills of all types for volunteer service. Bess was among the first to sign up.

APRIL 28, 1918

1 Indicative of the manner in which life in Stanley County adapted to changing conditions: box- and rag-rug socials gave way to Red Cross socials.
2 "Daddy" Krug.

MAY 19, 1918

1 Dewitt Curtis, son of the choir leader at the Methodist church near Corey farm and Olney Corey's one-time competitor for first tenor.
2 "Daddy" Krug served Bess breakfast in Mitchell, S.D.
3 Mrs. Albert Wheelon, wife of the Pierre realtor.
4 The velvet sample is not with the letter.

JUNE 30, 1918

1 The wife of Robert Corey in a brief, unhappy marriage.
2 Ruth Speer was then twelve years old.
3 A rancher, twenty-five years old.
4 The water was kept in a barrel beside the front door; it was strained to remove the "squiglies" (organisms of various sorts) that developed in standing water.
5 The nickname of Bess's neighbor Horace H. Gould.
6 Bess means tornado.

JULY 14, 1918

1 The letter was sent in round-robin fashion from Bess to Ethel in Winthrop, Minn.; Ethel sent it on to Margaret Corey in Atlantic, Iowa.
2 Ethel's husband, Art Erickson.
3 Apparently Art has purchased a new rug for Ethel on her birthday in April.
4 A horse.
5 An induction camp in Iowa perhaps one hundred miles from Marne and Atlantic. Army draftees from Stanley County were sent here.
6 Ben Thompson.
7 An instance of the continuing problem with range cattle, who once had been accustomed to having all of Stanley County for their pasture.

AUGUST 4, 1918

1 This letter also went first to Ethel, then to Margaret.
2 Bess means Fort Dix, N.J., near Philadelphia, an important embarkation port for soldiers sailing to the war in France.
3 The corner of the letter with the last part of "Websters" is clipped off. Ethel Corey Erickson has noted in the margin: "Chall was talking and snipped this off no harm done." Chall Corey was visiting Ethel in Minnesota.
4 Beginning in August, the canning factory in Atlantic would be processing corn.
5 Near Avoca, along the west branch of the Nishnabotna River, a sizable herd of deer lived in the brush. These deer, along with the canning factory, apparently constituted the area's tourist sights.
6 More *Science and Health*.

OCTOBER 22, 1918

1 Teresa Taylor Corey.
2 This appears to be "Daddy" Krug, for he is the man who sends Bess the *Christian Herald*. See Bess's letter of December 10, 1918.
3 A character in Charles Dickens's *David Copperfield*.
4 A town in Jones County, South Dakota, directly west of Draper. Bess is located southwest of her homestead, at Bearry School in Rowe District.
5 The great flu epidemic of 1918 was nationwide.
6 Mary Baker Eddy's teachings again.
7 Bess seems to indicate that mail addressed to any of these post office locations will reach her.
8 Walt Mason (1862–1939), the most popular humorist-poet of the day. His "prose poems" appeared in more than two hundred newspapers. George Ade called him the "high priest of horse sense," William Allen White the "Homer of modern America, particularly the America of the country town." He published collections with titles such as *Rhymes of the Range* (1910), *Ripply Rhymes* (1913), *Horse Sense* (1915), and *Terse Verse* (1917). Mason is credited with originating the quip: "If you don't like Nebraska weather, wait a minute." His influence upon Bess Corey's prose style seems unquestionable.

DECEMBER 10, 1918

1 Cora Liptrap Brown (1876–1951), second wife of Challenge Dunn Brown, whose first wife died in 1897. She and Challenge were visiting Margaret Brown at this time.
2 She never did.

JANUARY 26, 1919

1 The Wall is the great cliff created by erosion at the edge of the Badlands. Over this precipice storm-driven cattle sometimes toppled to their deaths. The town of Wall, S.D., is not far away.

Epilogue: 1920–1954

1 Horace Kramer, *Marginal Land* (Philadelphia: J. B. Lippincott, 1939), pp. 1–4.
2 Ibid., p. 10.
3 Ibid.
4 ALS, Edna Brzica to Gerber, November 12, 1986; ALS, Celia M. Ellis to Gerber, November 12, 1986; ALS, Clara Leap Graham to Gerber, January 25, 1987; TLS (typed letter signed), William P. Hart to Pauline G. Davies, October 20, 1986; TLS, William P. Hart to Gerber, November 8, 1986; ALS, Vera C. Ritzo to Gerber, November 20, 1986.
5 Graham and Ellis.
6 Interview with Clara Leap Graham, Santa Cruz, Calif., March 23, 1987.
7 Bess's graduation photograph and her Fort Pierre diploma are in the possession of Margaret Erickson Nelson.
8 ALS, Elizabeth Corey to Ethel Corey Erickson. Bess appears to have taken some special summer work, perhaps normal courses, at the college in Spearfish, S.D., in 1927. Credits earned via these courses were to accrue toward completion of her diploma requirements at Fort Pierre High School.
9 During April and May 1927 the *Daily Capital Journal* (Pierre, S.D.) continued to tell of heavy rains causing floods on the Mississippi, Arkansas, and Yazoo rivers. In South Dakota the April rainfall of 1927 had been exceeded only three times in the past thirty-six years. On a single day, between noon and 2 P.M., Bad River rose eighteen inches. At Pierre the Missouri rose twenty inches in a single day, flooding the road leading to the highway bridge across the river, and all railroad operations west of Pierre came to a halt as several hundred feet of track were washed out at Midland along with railroad bridges across Bad River at Weta, Midland, and Wendte.
10 For entrance to the college at Spearfish.
11 Following the western custom, this is what Bess now called her homestead.
12 To Spearfish.
13 Graham to Gerber.
14 ALS, Elizabeth Corey to Ethel Corey Erickson.
15 Robert Corey married Lilah Elizabeth Flathers on June 14, 1921. Ethel and Lilah were neighbors in the Corey farm vicinity in 1928.

16 James D. Dunlavy died November 11, 1928.

17 ALS, Elizabeth Corey to Rachel Corey.

18 ALS, "Vivian" to Gilbert Lee Corey, received May 24, 1975. The writer is Vivian Dale Corey, daughter of Bess's uncle Franklin Brewer Corey (1867–1936), who settled in Atlantic, Iowa. Vivian was eleven years Bess's junior, and while she would have known Aunt Hattie and Aunt Rate rather well from their common residence in Atlantic, she was a child of ten when cousin Bess left for South Dakota. Her residence in Grand Island, Neb., puts Vivian in reasonable proximity of the Bad River country of South Dakota, but precisely what business took her to that state is not known.

19 ALS, Ethel Corey Erickson to Paul Corey, undated but early fall 1929.

20 Paul Corey, "Lurching toward Liberalism: Political and Literary Reminiscences," *Books at Iowa* 49 (November 1988): 61.

21 Records, State Office of Education, Pierre, S.D.

22 ALS, Elizabeth Corey to Margaret Erickson.

23 A town thirty miles directly west of Aberdeen, S.D., on U.S. Highway 12.

24 See also "Fire Destroys Indian School Dormitory," *Daily Capital Journal* (Pierre, S.D.), July 11, 1936, p. 1.

25 Bess is located fifteen miles north of Midland, S.D., on U.S. Highway 14. The school was known as Liberty School. Ervin Sheeley told Gerber, August 1989.

26 Margaret Erickson's sister Jennie (b. August 5, 1931) was five years old.

27 A small town between Leon and Osceola in southern Iowa (Decatur County), where the Erickson family then lived and where Margaret attended high school.

28 TLS, Margaret Nelson to Gerber, June 25, 1989.

29 ALS, Elizabeth Corey to Margaret Erickson.

30 The identical remark was made by Bess concerning the "chicken coop" shack she used temporarily in 1909 while boarding with the Stone family as she began her first South Dakota teaching job at Speer School. It probably is an oblique remark about her size as well. During the 1930s especially, a time of great financial constraints, it was not at all unusual for a rural schoolteacher to be given living space in the schoolhouse as a part of her salary.

31 A girl in Margaret's position could do little more than dream of having orchids, which became a highly popular flower for corsages during the 1930s.

32 While attending the University of Minnesota during the fall quarter of the 1936–37 academic year, Margaret lived at the home of her Aunt Ellen and Uncle Dewey Malmstedt.

33 This signals the approaching end of Bess's long-time ambition to establish a horse ranch in Stanley County.

34 Readers will note the considerable improvement in the "correctness" as-

pects of Bess's writing. Perhaps her year at Fort Pierre had served to clear up her problems in spelling and punctuation, or perhaps she is writing now under more ideal conditions of time and space. In these post-1919 letters, her handwriting has become more legible, controlled, and smooth-flowing.

35 Records, State Department of Education, Pierre, S.D.

36 ALS, Elizabeth F. Corey to Paul Corey.

37 Probably an oblique reference to Paul's rapid publication since 1939 of his three Mantz novels, as well as a final reference by Bess to her own letters as a form of autobiography.

38 South Dakota was undergoing another one of its cyclical changes of weather from dry to wet.

39 Ripley's "Believe It or Not" column was then at the peak of its popularity, running in hundreds of daily newspapers.

40 In more than thirty years, Bess seems never to have "caught up" in her struggle to get ahead financially.

41 Aunt Rachel Elizabeth Corey, for whom Bess had been named, would die in 1943.

42 The reason for the silence probably was Robert Corey's protracted death from cancer. His wife, Lilah, who was caring for him at home on Corey farm, had little time for correspondence. Rob died on June 5, 1943.

43 Records, Office of Register of Deeds for Stanley County, Fort Pierre, S.D.

44 Telephone directory for Pierre, S.D., 1950; also, Records, Office of Register of Deeds for Hughes County, Pierre, S.D.

45 TLS, Margaret Erickson Nelson to Gerber, October 1, 1986.

46 ALS, Elizabeth Corey to Margaret Erickson Herbert.

47 Probably wartime savings bonds, which teachers were encouraged to purchase via salary deduction during World War II.

48 The words "write big" are circled for emphasis.

49 Margaret Erickson Nelson to Gerber.

50 Ibid.

51 "Hospital List," *Daily Capital Journal* (Pierre, S.D.), May 6, 1954.

52 "Obituary," *Daily Capital Journal* (Pierre, S.D.), May 11, 1954.

53 Autograph copy of will of Margaret M. Corey, dated March 1919. Added notations include "Copy of will drawn in spring 1919[.] Will in strong Box Farmers Savings Bank[,] Atlantic" and "My Old Strong box—Bess[.]"

54 "Obituary."